Lecture Notes in Computer Science   4352

Commenced Publication in 1973
Founding and Former Series Editors:
Gerhard Goos, Juris Hartmanis, and Jan van Leeuwen

T0205283

Tat-Jen Cham   Jianfei Cai
Chitra Dorai   Deepu Rajan
Tat-Seng Chua   Liang-Tien Chia (Eds.)

Advances in Multimedia Modeling

13th International Multimedia Modeling Conference, MMM 2007
Singapore, January 9-12, 2007
Proceedings, Part II

 Springer

Volume Editors

Tat-Jen Cham
Jianfei Cai
Deepu Rajan
Liang-Tien Chia
Nanyang Technological University, School of Computer Engineering
Block N4, Nanyang Avenue, Singapore 639798
E-mail: {astjcham,asjfcai,asdrajan,asltchia}@ntu.edu.sg

Chitra Dorai
IBM T.J. Watson Research Center
Yorktown Heights, NY 10598, USA
E-mail: dorai@watson.ibm.com

Tat-Seng Chua
National University of Singapore
School of Computing, Department of Computer Science
Singapore
E-mail: chuats@comp.nus.edu.sg

Library of Congress Control Number: 2006939133

CR Subject Classification (1998): H.5.1, H.5, I.4, H.2.4, I.3, H.3-4, E.4

LNCS Sublibrary: SL 3 – Information Systems and Application, incl. Internet/Web
and HCI

ISSN   0302-9743
ISBN-10   3-540-69428-5 Springer Berlin Heidelberg New York
ISBN-13   978-3-540-69428-1 Springer Berlin Heidelberg New York

Springer is a part of Springer Science+Business Media

springer.com

© Springer-Verlag Berlin Heidelberg 2007
Printed in Germany

Typesetting: Camera-ready by author, data conversion by Scientific Publishing Services, Chennai, India
Printed on acid-free paper   SPIN: 11968153   06/3142   5 4 3 2 1 0

Preface

The 13th International Multimedia Modeling Conference (MMM) was held in Singapore on January 9–12, 2007, organized by the School of Computer Engineering, Nanyang Technological University (NTU). The conference venue was the Nanyang Executive Centre, located within NTU's 200 hectare Jurong campus in the west of Singapore, and it also served as the main conference accommodation.

The main technical sessions were held on January 10–12, 2007, comprising 2 keynote talks, 18 oral presentation sessions in 2 parallel tracks, and 2 poster sessions. A wide range of topics was covered in the conference, including multimedia content analysis (retrieval, annotation, learning semantic concepts), computer vision/graphics (tracking, registration, shape modeling), multimedia networking (coding, peer-to-peer systems, adaptation), multimedia access (databases, security) and human–computer interaction (user interfaces, augmented reality).

This year a bumper crop of 392 paper submissions were received for publication in the main conference. In order to achieve our goal of instantiating a high–quality review process for the conference, a large and motivated Technical Program Committee had to be formed. Thankfully, we were able to rely on the help of many committed senior researchers and eventually a review structure was created comprising 18 Area Chairs, 152 Program Committee members and 36 additional reviewers. The review process was rigorous and double blind, with each paper assigned to three to four reviewers, and further managed by an Area Chair who provided additional input and recommendations to the Program Chairs. In addition, there was collaboration with other conferences with overlapping review periods to avoid accepting papers which were submitted simultaneously to different conferences. Through the conscientious efforts of the reviewers, all submissions received at least two reviews, while over 97% of submissions received at least three to four reviews. Subsequently, all papers were considered carefully, with significant deliberation over borderline papers. Eventually, only 72 papers were accepted for oral presentation and 51 papers accepted for poster presentation, resulting in a competitive acceptance rate of 31.4%. The only distinguishing difference between the oral and poster papers was the mode of presentation – all accepted papers were considered full papers and allocated the same number of pages. Additionally, there were two paper awards given out at this conference: the Best Paper Award, and the Best Student Paper Award.

Outside of the main technical sessions, there were also four special sessions on Networked Graphics Applications (NGA), Services and the Assurance in Multimedia Mobile Information Systems (SAMM), Networked Multimedia Systems and Applications Focusing on Reliable and Flexible Delivery for Integrated Multimedia (NMS) and Ubiquitous Multimedia Service (UMS). The paper review for these special sessions was handled separately by different organizers and Program Committees, and accepted papers were presented on January 9, 2007.

There was also a conference banquet on January 11, 2007, which featured a dinner boat cruise along Singapore's harbor front on the Imperial Cheng Ho.

We are heavily indebted to many individuals for their significant contribution. In particular, Linda Ang was very helpful in maintaining the Web-based review management system and solving technical crises almost instantly. Su-Ming Koh was crucial in creating, maintaining and handling all registration-related matters effectively and efficiently. Poo-Hua Chua promptly handled all matters related to the main conference Web site. Hwee-May Oh consistently kept the Organizing Committee in tow by checking and monitoring the action plans before and after every meeting. We thank the MMM Steering Committee for their invaluable input and guidance in crucial decisions. We would like to express our deepest gratitude to the rest of the Organizing Committee: Industrial Track Chair Chang-Sheng Xu, Local Arrangements Chairs Wooi Boon Goh and Kin-Choong Yow, Publicity and Sponsorship Chairs Sabu Emmanuel and Kap-Luk Chan, and Workshop Chairs Chiew Tong Lau and Fang Li. We are also most sincerely appreciative of the hard work put in by the Area Chairs and members of the Technical Program Committee, whose detailed reviews under time pressure were instrumental in making this a high-quality conference.

We would like to thank the Lee Foundation and PREMIA for their generous sponsorship, as well as help from the School of Computing, National University of Singapore, ACM SIGMM, and the Singapore Tourism Board. Finally, this conference would not have been possible without strong and unwavering support from NTU's Centre for Multimedia & Network Technology (CeMNet).

January 2007

Tat-Jen Cham
Jianfei Cai
Chitra Dorai
Deepu Rajan
Tat-Seng Chua
Liang-Tien Chia

Organization

Organizing Committee

General Co-chairs:	Tat-Seng Chua (National University of Singapore, Singapore)
	Liang-Tien Chia (Nanyang Technological University, Singapore)
Program Co-chairs:	Tat-Jen Cham (Nanyang Technological University, Singapore)
	Jianfei Cai (Nanyang Technological University, Singapore)
	Chitra Dorai (IBM T.J. Watson Research Center, New York)
Industrial Track Chair:	Changsheng Xu (Institute for Infocomm Research, Singapore)
Workshop/Tutorials Co-chairs:	Chiew Tong Lau (Nanyang Technological University, Singapore)
	Fang Li (Nanyang Technological University, Singapore)
Publications Chair:	Deepu Rajan (Nanyang Technological University, Singapore)
Local Arrangements Co-Chairs:	Wooi Boon Goh (Nanyang Technological University, Singapore)
	Kin-Choong Yow (Nanyang Technological University, Singapore)
Publicity and Sponsorship Co-chairs:	Sabu Emmanuel (Nanyang Technological University, Singapore)
	Kap-Luk Chan (Nanyang Technological University, Singapore)
Registration:	Su-Ming Koh
Webmaster:	Linda Ang
	Poo-Hua Chua
Secretary:	Hwee-May Oh

Steering Committee

Yi-Ping Phoebe Chen (Deakin University , Australia)

Tat-Seng Chua(National University of Singapore, Singapore)

Tosiyasu L. Kunii (Kanazawa Institute of Technology, Japan)

Wei-Ying Ma (Microsoft Research Asia, China)

Nadia Magnenat-Thalmann (University of Geneva , Switzerland)

Patrick Senac (Ensica, France)

Program Committee

Area Chairs

Edward Chang
Lap-Pui Chau
Shu-Ching Chen
Ajay Divakaran
Alan Hanjalic
Mohan Kankanhalli
Zhengguo Li
Chiawen Lin
Wolfgang Mller-Wittig

Wei Tsang Ooi
Silvia Pfeiffer
Mei-Ling Shyu
Qibin Sun
Daniel Thalmann
Marcel Worring
Jiankang Wu
Changsheng Xu
Roger Zimmerman

Members

Lalitha Agnihotri
Terumasa Aoki
Pradeep Kumar Atrey
Noboru Babaguchi
Selim Balcisoy
Qiu Bo
Shen Bo
Ronan Boulic
Djeraba Chabane
Lekha Chaisorn
Ee-Chien Chang
Kai Chen
Lei Chen
Mei-Juan Chen
Shoupu Chen
Xilin Chen
Yi-Shin Chen
Shao-Yi Chien
Eng Siong Chng
Hao-hua Chu
Jen-Yao Chung
Pablo de Heras
    Ciechomski
Serhan Dagtas
Ravindra Dastikop
Michel Diaz
Zoran Dimitrijevic
LingYu Duan
Kun Fu

Sheng Gao
John M. Gauch
Yu Ge
Enrico Gobbetti
Romulus Grigoras
William I. Grosky
Junzhong Gu
Xiaohui Gu
Zhenghui Gu
Mario Gutierrez
Jiro Gyoba
Daniel Haffner
Xian-Sheng Hua
Haibin Huang
Qingming Huang
Weimin Huang
Zhiyong Huang
Benoit Huet
Andres Iglesias
Horace Ip
Xing Jin
Xuan Jing
James Joshi
Marcelo Kallmann
Li-Wei Kang
Ahmed Karmouch
Pavel Korshunov
Jose Lay
Clement Leung

Chung-Sheng Li
He Li
Huiqi Li
Liyuan Li
Mingjing Li
Qing Li
Te Li
Xuelong Li
Ying Li
Rainer Lienhart
Joo-Hwee Lim
Jian-Liang Lin
Weisi Lin
Karen Liu
Tiecheng Liu
Yang Liu
Ying Liu
Alexander Loui
Kok-Lim Low
Guojun Lu
Hanqing Lu
Zhongkang Lu
Hongli Luo
Jian-Guang Luo
Jiebo Luo
Jianhua Ma
Namunu Maddage
Nadia Magnenat-
    Thalmann

Enrico Magli
Stephane Marchand-
   Maillet
Bernard Merialdo
Kazunori Miyata
Soraia Raupp Musse
P.J. Narayanan
Luciana Nedel
Chong Wah Ngo
Noel O'Connor
Ee Ping Ong
Vincent Oria
Pietro Pala
Feng Pan
Nilesh Patel
Wen-Hsiao Peng
Julien Pettre
B. Prabhakaran
Regunathan
   Radhakrishnan
Kalpathi Ramakrishnan
Lloyd Rutledge
Shin'ichi Satoh
Dieter Schmalstieg

Guus Schreiber
Nicu Sebe
Ho Kim Seon
Ishwar Sethi
Timothy Shih
P. Shivakumara
Haiyan Shu
Alan Smeaton
Cees Snoek
Luiz Fernando Gomes
   Soares
Yuqing Song
Alexei Sourin
Yeping Su
Lifeng Sun
Hari Sundaram
Jo Yew Tham
Yu-Kuang Tu
Jean-Marc Valin
Svetha Venkatesh
Frederic Vexo
Kongwah Wan
Jinjun Wang
Xingwei Wang

Yu Wang
Jongwook Woo
Yi Wu
Yi-Leh Wu
Lexing Xie
Ruiqin Xiong
Ziyou Xiong
Xiangyang Xue
Xiaokang Yang
Susu Yao
Kim-Hui Yap
Chai Kiat Yeo
Rongshan Yu
Xinguo Yu
Chengcui Zhang
Haihong Zhang
Lei Zhang
Zhongfei Zhang
Jinghong Zheng
Xiaofang Zhou
Guangyu Zhu
Yongwei Zhu

Additional Reviewers

Marco Agus
Alia Amin
Michael Blighe
Rui Cai
Kuan-Ta Chen
Songqing Chen
Rodrigo Mendes Costa
Carlos Augusto Dietrich
JL Dugelay
Arjan Egges
Eric Galmar
Stephane Garchery
Zhen Guo

Michiel Hildebrand
Keith Jacoby
Minseok Jang
Xiaoxi Jiang
Saubhagya Ram Joshi
Mustafa Kasap
Andrew Kinane
Duy-Dinh Le
Bart Lehane
Dongyu Liu
Mentar Mahmudi
Joanna Marguier
Jean Martinet

Simon Moncrieff
Manuel Menezes de
   Oliveira Neto
Ciaran O'Conaire
Marcelo Soares Pimenta
Dimitris Protopsaltou
Tele Tan
Ba Tu Truong
Changhu Wang
Jian Yao
Ruofei Zhang

Table of Contents

Multimedia over P2P

Content II

Applications II

Computer Vision II

Image Processing II

Multimedia Signal Processing and Communications II

Image Classification and Recognition

Advanced Media Processing and Security

Ubiquitous Multimedia Service (UMS)

Services and the Assurance in Multimedia Mobile Information Systems (SAMM)

Networked Mulitmedia Systems and Its Applications Focusing on Reliable and Flexible Delivery for Integrated Multimedia (NMS)

Networked Graphics Appications (NGA)

Real-Time Streaming Audio Codecs for QoS Benchmarking Purposes

Luisa M. Regueras, María Jesús Verdú, and Rafael Mompó

University of Valladolid, ETSI Telecomunicación, Spain
{luireg,marver,rmompo}@tel.uva.es

Abstract. With the rising popularity of the real-time audio streaming applications, it is important, in order to support (and to charge) properly these new services, to understand and characterize the behaviour of these new applications. This paper studies the traffic associated with a specific audio streaming on-live service, the radio over the Internet, and presents some analyses and comparisons of different streaming media products. In addition, the user's viewpoint is also taken into account, since it is ultimately the users (and their degree of satisfaction) who will decide whether a service goes to be or not successful. Finally, the study estimates the real bandwidth used by the on-line radio and examines how a cable network based on DOCSIS, have to be planned in order to be able to support this new service.

Keywords: real-time applications, streaming audio, listeners' standpoint, streaming platforms, quality, traffic analysis, end-user QoS.

1 Introduction

The rising popularity of the Internet and increasing deployment of broadband technologies, like xDSL or cable modems, has increased the use of streaming media applications. Web sites are offering streaming videos and audios of news broadcasts, music and live sporting events. Users can access these streaming audio and video clips through a Web browser by simply clicking on a link and having the Web browser start up an associated streaming player.

Every time more users listen to the radio or watch the television over the Internet. One of the main reasons for broadcasting live across the Internet is to reach a wider and/or more dispersed audience. For example, according to [1], the global standard in Internet media and market research, in Spain, about 23% of the Internet users with more than 16 years old listened to Internet radio over the last three months of 2001 and the first three months of 2002. In addition, Nielsen/NetRatings also found that in Hong Kong, an astonishing 58% of those who responded and had Internet access used either a cable modem or high-speed telephone connection to access the Internet. So, not surprisingly, their rates for using Internet radio were among the highest worldwide, 38%. On the other hand, about 19 million Americans listen to Internet radio each week, according to research firms Arbitron Inc. and Edison Media Research. That is still tiny compared with the 277 million who listen to regular radio

T.-J. Cham et al. (Eds.): MMM 2007, LNCS 4352, Part II, pp. 1 – 10, 2007.

each week, but the number of Internet listeners has grown fast. Just three years ago, only 11 million listened to Internet radio each week. [2]

Streaming-media content presents a number of new challenges to systems designers and network operators. For example, compared to traditional Internet applications, real-time streaming audio has very strict and ambitious requirements, especially with respect to the end-to-end delay, jitter and reliability. Unfortunately, despite these new characteristics and the challenges of a rapidly growing traffic component, its performance and impact on the network is still largely unknown. Over the years, there have been several studies measuring the performance of Internet backbones and end-hosts [3] as well as detailed studies on the Web traffic [4]. However, there have only been some wide-scale empirical measurements of streaming media across the Internet [5]. While the existing empirical studies have been valuable in helping to understand some behaviour characteristics, they are not sufficient to neither characterize the streaming audio performance nor evaluate its impact on the network [6].

The aim of this paper is to study the traffic associated with an extremely popular specific real-time streaming audio service, such as the Internet radio. Starting from this study, we present an analysis of the characteristics of the main streaming media products: RealNetworks RealPlayer, Microsoft Windows MediaPlayer, Apple QuickTime Player and NullSoft WinAmp Player, according to parameters such as the inter-arrival time, the packet size, the traffic flow pattern, etc. Finally, using these results, we examine the impact of introducing this service into a particular data network, the DOCSIS cable network. This is very important when it comes to fairly allocating the network resources and defining charging schemes [7].

2 Methodology

The experiment was conducted through two PCs connected to the campus network, which was in turn connected to the Internet, through a Fast-Ethernet network (see Fig. 1). During the experiment, one client PC streamed audio sequences from a broad number of radio servers, connected to the Internet through access points in different places in the world, while the other PC captured the generated traffic. In pilot tests, we verified that at no time, during the playout of any of the radio clips, neither were the CPU or memory overly taxed nor was the maximum last-hop bandwidth the bottleneck.

We collected several traces of audio traffic. Some of them were obtained, and filtered, running WinDump on a separate host, and analyzed later with tcptrace and xplot, along with some original scripts written by us, whereas other were obtained and examined using Agilent Protocol Inspector, a very powerful commercial tool. So, the traffic originated or/and received by the end-users has been captured in order to have a view of the application behaviour from the client side instead of the server side (like it is done by [8]).

All the experiments were run Monday through Friday from 9:00 am to 6:00 pm, for six months. Before and after each run, ping and tracert were run to verify that the network status had not dramatically changed during the run.

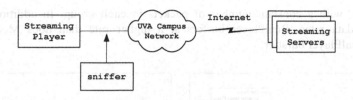

Fig. 1. Experimental Setup for Real-time Streaming audio Measurements

Moreover, in order to compare and analyze the on-line streaming audio and the different players we selected a large number of radio servers and clip sets with different encoding rates and served by different streaming platforms (like it is done by [9]). We also selected clips from several nets since media clips that appear on the same Web site may actually be served from different nets. In addition, we captured traffic in different sessions dispersed throughout the time.

3 Performance Analysis

From the audio traces received from several on-line radio channels, in this section we present and compare some structural properties of traffic generated by the on-line streaming audio applications in according to the use of different streaming platforms. So for example, we have seen that most of on-line radio broadcasts make use of the RealNetworks Real Player (52.6%), followed by Windows Media Player (37%), and finally by Nullsoft WinAmp and Apple QuickTime Player (9% and 1.5%, respectively). On the other hand, all the streaming platforms recommend the use of their respective proprietary streaming protocols running preferably over UDP; though there is also the option to stream the clip over TCP or using standard HTTP. However, and in spite of the conventional wisdom that the congestion-control and reliability mechanisms in TCP make it less suitable that UDP, we have observed widespread use of TCP. Firewall restrictions may be a key factor [10].

Moreover, we have observed that the predominant port numbers are 1755 y 554 (53% and 35%, respectively). The port number 1755 is related to Windows Media Player; while 554, together with 7070, are used by Real Player and QuickTime Player; since these ones are related to the use of RTSP. On the other hand, WinAmp Player gets connected to the SHOUTCast server, whose default access port is 8000, but there is the possibility of specifying any other. Finally, the presence of HTTP (nearly 5% analyzed cases) must not join the particular use of any streaming tool.

3.1 Network Analysis

The performance of currently available streaming media products plays an important role in the network impact of Internet radio, or in general in the streaming audio applications. First of all, RealPlayer packet sizes are distributed over a large range of values (the packet sizes are spread more widely over a range from 0.5 to 1.4 of the mean normalized packet size, as it is shown in Fig. 2.a) and the packet interarrival time is low and varies considerably. The analysis of the "activity" on the connection (that is, the packet arrival pattern) shows that Real Player generates bursts or groups of packets, with a constant number of packets in each group. In addition, for all encoding data rates, RealPlayer buffers at a higher rate than does MediaPlayer, making RealPlayer burstier.

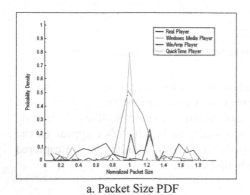
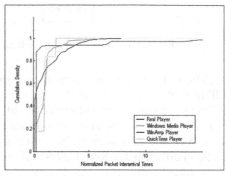

a. Packet Size PDF   b. Packet Interarrival Times CDF

Fig. 2. Network Analysis Normalized Results: **a**. Packet Size PDF (Probability Density Function). **b**. Packet Interarrival Times CDF (Cumulative Density Function).

In second place, the Windows MediaPlayer packet sizes show more regularity than RealPlayer packet sizes. MediaPlayer packets have a high density at one packet size. The sizes of MediaPlayer packets are concentrated around the mean packet size, normalized to 1. In a typical low data rate clip, over 80 per cent of MediaPlayer packets may have a size between 800 bytes and 1000 bytes. For high data rate clips, MediaPlayer has two high density distribution packet sizes, one at 1500 bytes contributed by the first IP fragments, and another at the size of the last IP fragment, the remaining part of the large application layer packets. In addition, the CDF of packet interarrival times is quite steep around a normalized interarrival time of 1 (see Fig. 2.b) and the packets have a very regular pattern, indicating that most MediaPlayer packets arrive at constant time intervals. Thus, the packet interarrival analysis combined with the packet size analysis suggests that MediaPlayer traffic has a more constant bit rate than RealPlayer traffic.

On the other hand, the WinAmp packet sizes are distributed over a large range of values (around 0.8 and 1.2 of the mean normalized packet size, see Fig. 2.a) and the packet interarrival time is low and varies considerably, showing a bursting behaviour, just like RealPlayer. However, in this case, the data flow is determined by the receive window advertised by the receiver.

And finally, with QuickTime, the packet sizes are distributed around the mean (following a Gaussian distribution), the CDF of packet interarrival times is quite gradual (see Fig. 2.b) and the interarrival time is quite variable, indicating the typical behaviour of a variable bit rate traffic.

Moreover, at the same size buffer, RealPlayer and WinAmp begin playback of the clip before MediaPlayer and QuickTime. If all begin clip playback at the same time, MediaPlayer and QuickTime have a smaller buffer and may suffer from more quality degradations due to jitter. So, from the network perspective, RealPlayer and WinAmp generate burstier traffic that is harder for the network to manage. Here, it is important to indicate the emergencies of real-time are different between the interactive mode, such as interactive talking, and the non-interactive mode, such as audio broadcasting. The latter usually allows a longer playout delay than the former. In fact, in according to [11], if the network is in large jitter and the system is also in non-interactive mode, the playout delay can be increased more than if it was in interactive mode.

In short, we are able to say the performance of audio streaming systems is highly dependent on the audio codecs and their reaction to packet loss and instantaneous delays. Understanding the interaction between audio encoding and the dynamic behaviour of the Internet is significant for designing adaptive audio transport mechanisms [12].

3.2 Quality Perceived by the User

Finally, in order to completely characterize an application, the user requirements and quality have to be determined and accounted. The network providers and application designers do not only need to know the optimal conditions to perform successfully the chosen task, but they also need to establish the minimum quality required for the media and the thresholds beyond which increasing objective quality (and hence bandwidth) does not imply an increase of user's satisfaction. The measurements of the network-level QoS parameters have to be translated into QoS parameters from the user's viewpoint. Since it is the end-user who will determine whether a service or application is a success, it is necessary to understand and measure the quality perceived and requested by the end-user. However, this subject has not been widely addressed by the network research community [13] and remains a hard problem.

In ITU-T recommendation P.861, an algorithm for Objective Test was described on the basis of objective quality measure called Perceptual Speech Quality Measure (PSQM). However, bearing in mind that transacting such a test requires some additional expensive test device which has not been field-proven, we opted for making subjective tests. As expected, subjective test is a time consuming process and mandates assistance of lots of people. Yet this is the traditional way of assessment of Voice Quality.

Thus, we made several quality tests. These tests were based on the responses of twenty listeners (not directly involved in the work) who participated in a blind comparison. Each participant once listened to each clip recorded in the formats being compared (different streaming platforms or different encoding rates). All clips were played through a computer speaker system.

In the first degradation test (with an assessing question similar to that one used in [14]), two separate recording systems (for a same streaming platform) were used simultaneously for two different, and close, encoding rates. The participants were asked which of the two clips sounded better. In this case, the results showed that most of listeners did not observe a distinction between both clips. In addition, it was interesting to know that, contrary to our early expectations, several listeners (30%) were more satisfied with the fragment encoded to the lesser bit rate.

Secondly, a similar degradation test was made in order to compare two different streaming systems (Windows Media and RealPlayer, for example). In this context, we saw as almost the 100% of listeners answered that the two fragments (recorded under stability conditions) were almost identical. However, under instability conditions (that is, when the network was congested), the listeners chose the fragment played by RealPlayer as the best one (this same result is obtained in [15]). This result is connected with the use of buffer made by the two streaming platforms. We did not accomplished comparisons with QuickTime and WinAmp because, at first, we were able to verify that, for a same encoding rate, both of them provide listenings of worse quality than those of the other two streaming systems.

Finally, the listeners also listened to the radio fragments encoded by different rates (8, 16, 20 and 32 kbps) and determined which their satisfaction degree was (see Fig. 4). The arithmetic mean of any collection of opinion scores is called Mean Opinion Score or MOS [16]. So, we verified that an increase in the encoding rate (and therefore an increase in the use of network resources) does not mean a "proportional" increase in the quality perceived by the users. In addition, according to [17], it is presumable to think this difference will be still minor when the users are involved in an engaging task instead of listening to the radio.

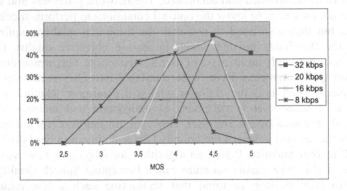

Fig. 3. Satisfaction test vs. Encoding rate

4 Evaluating the Impact of Internet Radio on Cable Networks

As soon as we have characterized the behaviour of Internet radio, it is important to analyze the impact of introducing this service into a particular data network, like the Euro-DOCSIS cable network. So, in this section, from an estimation of the real bandwidth used by the on-line radio, we make an analysis of how the cable networks have to be planned in order to be able to support this new service.

We have chosen DOCSIS since it is the de-fact standard in the cable industry and is now also issued as an ETSI specification. The RF interface specification was later widened to include a variant for the European standards (8 MHz wide channels), what it is known as Euro-DOCSIS. Thereby, Euro-DOCSIS is a specification derived from DOCSIS which follows the IP approach over Ethernet.

On the other hand, as well as the network characteristics we must also to take into account the specific characteristics of the Internet radio service:

- It goes accompanied of the data service.
- The users, who listen to the radio across the Internet, go on requesting Web pages at the same rate than before using the new service.

Thus, in order to evaluate the impact of the Internet radio on the cable network, we have subtracted the real bandwidth used by the radio to the channel bandwidth (equation 1); where N is the number of simultaneous users on the cable network, p_{radio} is the percentage of users who listen to the radio across the Internet among all Internet users, v_{radio} is the real bandwidth used by the on-line radio (which is different of the encoding rate), Rt is the total bandwidth of the channel and Rt_{data} is the rate available for the data transmission.

$$Rt_{data} = Rt - N \cdot p_{radio} \cdot v_{radio} \tag{1}$$

From the analysis of on-line radio traffic, we have already calculated the general overload for the different encoding rates and streaming systems, because of the control information sent together with the user data. Therefore, we obtained the mean Ethernet frame size and real throughput, v_{radio}, for the most important encoding rates.

Besides, it is important to indicate that Rt is the total bandwidth of the channel by subtracting the throughput used by the management messages and other protocols and applications. The cable-modem systems carry control and management information, which makes use of a variable bandwidth in the channel. According to the specification of the MCNS RF interface [18], where we can see the different factors that limit the real information rate flowing by the cable-modem systems, and we obtained that between 70% and 97% of the nominal binary rate is useful information (Ethernet frames).

On the other hand, from M/M/m queuing model, we have used the model described in [19], for the download of Web pages for any system according to its characteristics and the number of users. We have checked that this type of traffic follows the behaviour showed in the equation 2, where N is the number of simultaneous users on the network in stability conditions, Rt_{data} is the rate available for the data transmission, p_{web} is the mean Web page size and λ_u is the Web page request rate (around $1/8$, according to [20]).

$$N = 0.9 \frac{R_t}{pweb \cdot \lambda_u} \tag{2}$$

So finally, by joining all studies and data, we can see, for example, that when the 20% of active users listen to the radio across the Internet at an encoding rate of 16 kbps,

Table 1. Internet radio in the cable network (v_{radio} is the estimation of the average value obtained for the different streaming tools and codification schemes - 16, 20 and 32 kbps)

RADIO							
P_{radio}	N_{radio}	Rt_{data}	λ_u	p_{web}	v_{radio}	N_{data}	%N
0	0	26624	0.125	60	-	399	0.00%
10	40	25965	0.125	60	16.5	389	-2.48%
20	80	25306	0.125	60	16.5	380	-4.95%
10	40	25306	0.125	60	33	380	-4.95%
20	80	23988	0.125	60	33	360	-9.90%

the number of active users that can be simultaneously on the cable network is reduced by 4.95%. These same results are obtained when only the 10% users listen to the radio at an encoding rate of 32 kbps. Other data about the impact of Internet radio on the number of simultaneous users of the cable network are shown in the Table 1.

5 Conclusions

In this paper we have presented an analysis of an empirical study of the main streaming media products RealNetworks RealPlayer, Microsoft Windows Media Player, Apple QuickTime Player and Nullsoft WinAmp Player. For these systems, we have examined different behaviour characteristics, such as the interarrival time, the packet size and the flow pattern. Our analysis shows that each streaming product has distinctly different behaviour characteristics, which are summarized in the Table 2. So, we can emphasize the following conclusions:

- For the same streaming tool, the traffic characteristics are independent of the used port (the own streaming protocol port or the HTTP port). These results would have been different if the users had accomplished control actions, like rewind or pause.
- The tools, and not the encoding schemes, are those that mark the profile of the generated traffic. The audio transmission reproduced by two different streaming systems and with a same codification scheme has two different flow patterns. Moreover, different codification schemes (as it is the case of the use of CBR or VBR transmission techniques) hardly vary the results obtained for a same streaming system.

Thus, the difference in the network traffic is marked by the tools, although both of them use the same transport protocol. So, for example, Real Player and QuickTime have very different statistics though they both use RTSP. This fact allows identifying the traffic belonging to different applications when they share the same port number.

In addition to examine the behaviour of different network characteristics, we have also conducted quality assessment from the end user perspective. We argue that only by integrating users' requirements into service design the utility of the future Internet could be maximized. Regarding the QoS and pricing decisions, the providers and operators should know customers' opinions about the offered data services [21].

The definition of QoS from the perspective of users and systems-level network designers diverges. From the perspective of the ISP, QoS approaches that focus on optimizing objective QoS may inform resource allocation mechanisms at a systems level. However, it is not clear to what degree such improvements result in improvements perceived by a user. This problem is compounded by the observation that any definition of objective thresholds that might be established is subject to context-dependent behaviour. Subjective QoS thresholds are therefore not fixed throughout a user's interaction. [22] Thus, in order to offer properly this new service it is necessary a trade-off among the quality (from the end-user's point of view), the use of network resources and the number of simultaneous Internet users in the network. The number of users and the quality is influenced by the audio encoding rate (that is, the use of network resources); but there is not a direct relation between a bigger use of bandwidth and the quality perceived by the end-user. In fact, a lot of times a bigger encoding rate does not imply a better level of quality from the end-user's perspective; but only a bigger cost and use of network resources. However, the content providers broadcast and encode audio streams at bigger bit-rates every time.

Table 2. Streaming tools: Overview

Characteristic	Windows Media	RealPlayer	WinAmp	QuickTime
Packet Pattern	Fixed length	2/3 packets lengths	Fixed Pattern. Several sizes	Around the average
Packet Size	Variable	Variable	Close MSS	Variable
Arrival Rate	Constant	Burst	Burst	Variable
Inter-arrival Time	High	Low	Low	Medium
Buffering Rate	< playout	> playout	> playout	< playout
Buffer size (default)	5 seconds	30 seconds	24 seconds	10 seconds
TCP Ports	1755	7070, 544	8000	7070, 544
Quality	Very Good	Very Good	Fair	Good

Finally, it is interesting to emphasize that the use of multicast UDP would have big advantages. In this case, in equation 1 we could replace the number of users (N) by the number of radio channels (C), where N will usually be bigger than C and thus, the impact of radio service on the network will be lesser.

Moreover, on-line radio is a live streaming audio service where all the users who listen to a same on-line radio channel have to receive the same information and some operations, like pause and rewind, do not make sense. Thus, the cable operators can obtain great advantages by installing radio servers in their network header too.

References

1. Nielsen//NetRating: Nielsen/NetRatings First Quarter 2002 Global International Trends report. (2002)
2. McBride, S.: Where the Listeners Are. The Wall Street Journal On-Line, December 13, 2004. Page R4. URL: http://www.edisonresearch.com/home/archives/WSJ12-13-04.pdf
3. McCreary, S., Claffy, K.C.: Trends in Wide Area IP Traffic Patterns - A View from the Ames Internet Exchange. Proc. of the 13th ITC Specialist Seminar on IP Traffic Modeling, Measurement and Management, USA. (2000), 1–11.
4. Hernández–Campos, F., Donelson, F, Jeffay, K., Ott, D.: What TCP/IP Headers Can Tell Us About the Web. Proc. of the ACM SIGMETRICS/Performance, USA (2001), 245-256.
5. Li, M., Claypool, M., Kinicki, R.: MediaPlayer™ versus RealPlayer™ - A Comparison of Network Turbulence. Proc. of the 2nd ACM SIGCOMM Internet Measurement Workshop, ACM Press, New York, USA, (2002) 131-136.

6. Boyden, S., Mahanti, A., Williamson, C.: Characterizing the Behaviour of RealVideo Streams. Proc. of SCS SPECTS 2005, USA, (2005) 783-791.
7. Courcoubetis, C.: A study of simple usage-based charging schemes for broadband networks. Telecommunications Systems, (2000), 15(3), 323-343.
8. Wang, Y., Claypool, M., Zuo, Z.: An Empirical Study of RealVideo Performance Across the Internet. Proc. of the ACM SIGCOMM Internet Measurement Workshop, USA (2001).
9. Regueras, L.M., Verdú M.J., Mompó, R.: Impact of the live radio on the Internet, and the real-time streaming audio, in the ComUNITY cable system from Com21. Proc. of the Internetworking 2003 International Conference. USA (2003).
10. Merwe, J.v.d., Sen, S., Kalmanek, C.: Streaming Video Traffic: Characterization and Network Impact. Proc. of the 7th International Workshop on Web Content Caching and Distribution (WCW), USA (2002).
11. Tseng, K., Lai, Y-C., Lin, Y-D.: Perceptual Codec and Interaction Aware Playout Algorithms and Quality Measurement for VoIP Systems. IEEE Transactions on Consumer Electronics, (2004), 50(1), 297-305.
12. Roychoudhuri, L., Al-Shaer, E., Hamed, H., Brewster, G.B.: Audio Transmission over the Internet: Experiments and Observations, IEEE ICC Symposium on the Next Generation Internet, (2003).
13. Dalal, A.C., Perry, E.: A New Architecture for Measuring and Assessing Streaming Media Quality. Proc. of Workshop on Passive and Active Measurement (PAM 2003), USA (2003).
14. Qazzaz, I.: Verification of Voice over IP (In Network Integration Solution area). Master Thesis Report, Chalmers University of Technology, Gothenburg, Sweden (1999).
15. NSTL: Comparison Testing of RealAudio 8 and Windows Media Audio. Test Report (2000). URL: http://www.nstl.com/ Downloads/real-vs-windows-media.pdf
16. Pracht, S., Hardman, D.: Voice Quality in Converging Telephony and IP Networks. White Paper, Agilent Technologies (2001).
17. Anderson, A.H., Smallwood, L., MacDonald, R., Mullin, J., Fleming, A,: Video data and video links in mediated communication: What do users value?. International Journal of Human Computer Studies, (2000), 1(52), 165-187.
18. CableLabs: Data-Over-Cable Service Interface Specifications, Radio Frequency Interface Specification 2.0", Cable Television Laboratories, Inc, SP-RFIv2.0-I02-020617 (2002).
19. Parrilla, E.: Estudio de los sistemas de modems de cable como infraestructura para los servicios de la Sociedad de la Información en las nuevas redes de televisión por cable. Doctoral Thesis, University of Valladolid, Spain (1998).
20. Abdulla, G.: Analysis and Modeling of World Wide Web Traffic. Ph.D. Dissertation, Computer Science Department, Faculty of the Virginia Polytechnic Institute and State University, Virginia, USA (1998).
21. Pulakka, K.: Fuzzy Systems for Adaptive SLA Management in DiffServ Enabled IP Networks. ICEFIN Workshop 2004, Tampere, USA, (2004).
22. Bouch, A., Kuchinsky, A., Batí, N.: Quality is in the Eye of the Beholder: Meeting Users' Requirements for Internet Quality of Service. HP Labs Technical Report, HPL-2000-4, (2000).

Exploiting Video Stream Similarity for Energy-Efficient Decoding

Juan Hamers, Lieven Eeckhout, and Koen De Bosschere

ELIS, Ghent University, Belgium
{jmhamers,leeckhou,kdb}@elis.UGent.be

Abstract. Energy consumption is a key issue in modern microprocessor system design in general, and in the design of mobile computing devices more in particular. This paper introduces a novel approach to energy-efficient media stream decoding that is based on the notion of media stream similarity. The key idea is that platform-independent scenarios of similar decode complexity can be identified within and across media streams. A client decoding a media stream annotated with scenario information can then adjust its processor clock frequency and voltage level based on these scenarios for reduced energy consumption. Our evaluation done using the AVC decoder and 12 reference streams shows an average energy reduction of 46% while missing less than 0.2% of the frame deadlines on average.

1 Introduction

Energy consumption is a key design issue for many of today's systems. This is especially the case for battery-operated devices such as laptops, mobile phones, PDAs, digital cameras, audio/video players, *etc.* Multimedia applications, and video applications more in particular, are increasingly popular applications on most of these devices, which are very often battery-operated and resource-constrained. Energy-aware and resource-aware processing thus is a very important issue on these devices.

This paper proposes a novel approach to media decoding that substantially reduces energy consumption. Our approach is based on the notion of media stream similarities both within and across media streams. An offline platform-independent analysis, which is to be done at the content provider side, determines similarly encoded frames across the various media streams in the database. These frames are grouped in so called scenarios. The key point is that all the frames from a given scenario exhibit a similar decode complexity, *i.e.*, require similar compute power and energy consumption at decode time. Scenario information is then annotated to the media streams in the content provider's database. In order to exploit the scenario information for energy-efficient video decoding, the client needs to be profiled using a few scenario representatives. This profiling associates platform-specific tuning with the platform-independent scenarios. The client then uses the scenario information encoded in the media stream along with

T.-J. Cham et al. (Eds.): MMM 2007, LNCS 4352, Part II, pp. 11–22, 2007.

the client's scenario-aware tuning information for driving the energy-efficient decoding.

The mechanism proposed in this paper is applicable to a wide variety multimedia system environments where a content provider provides media streams as a service to its end users. The media stream decoding application that we specifically focus on in this paper is video decoding using the AVC decoder.

This paper makes the following contributions.

- We introduce and exploit the notion of intra and inter video stream similarity. To the best of our knowledge, there is no prior work that describes and exploits video stream similarity. We identify video stream similarity based on macroblock information of the encoded video stream. We show that the platform-independent intra and inter video stream scenarios correlate very well with decode complexity at the client side.
- We show that video stream similarity has an important application for energy-efficient video decoding. The platform-independent scenario information can be translated into platform-dependent tuning information in terms of client side optimal processor clock frequency and voltage level. This enables the client to decode a video with reduced energy consumption while meeting the soft real-time deadlines. Our experimental results show a 46% reduction in energy consumption while missing less than 0.2% of the frame deadlines on average.

2   Scenario Identification by the Content Provider

Figure 1 Illustrates how video streams are annotated with scenario information by the content provider. The content provider maintains a database of video streams; shown in the left top corner of Fig. 1. The content provider collects a macroblock profile for all of the video streams in the database. A *macroblock profile* counts the number of macroblocks of a given type per frame.

The purpose of a macroblock profile is to characterize the decode complexity in a platform-independent way, *i.e.*, a macroblock profile is independent of the decoder as well as the system on which the video stream is to be decoded. A macroblock profile thus is a large matrix in which the rows are the various frames in the video stream and in which the columns are the macroblock counts for each of the macroblock types.

Once a macroblock profile is collected for the video streams in the database, all the frames can be viewed as points in a multidimensional space, which we call the *frame space*, see Fig. 1. The various dimensions in the frame space are the macroblock types; this is a 22-dimensional space in our setup. We then apply cluster analysis in the frame space. Cluster analysis finds groups of frames, called *scenarios*, so that frames with similar macroblock characteristics belong to the same scenario, whereas frames from different scenarios show different macroblock characteristics. Note that cluster analysis is done on the collection of frames from all video streams in the database. As such, scenarios may be formed consisting of frames from different video streams. In other words, we identify similarities

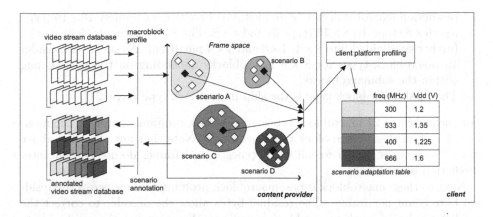

Fig. 1. Annotating video streams with scenario information by the content provider

at the frame level within a given video stream (intra video stream similarity) as well as across video streams (inter video stream similarity).

Once the scenarios are identified, we then annotate all the video streams in the content provider's database with scenario information. The annotation is done at the frame level by adding scenario identifiers. Note that annotating the video streams in the database is a one time cost, *i.e.*, profiling and annotating the video streams as well as identifying the scenarios in the frame space needs to be done only once. Whenever a new video stream is added to the database, a macroblock profile needs to be computed for the new video stream and the frames need to be annotated with scenario information.

We now discuss in more detail the following issues related to scenario identification by the content provider: (i) macroblock profiling, (ii) identifying the video stream scenarios using cluster analysis, and (iii) annotating the video stream with scenario information.

2.1 Macroblock Profiling

Macroblock profiling captures a platform-independent image of the decode complexity at the frame level. Although the discussion below on macroblock profiling is geared towards the H.264/AVC decoder [1] that we target in this work, similar profiles can be computed for other types of media streams. A macroblock consists of 16×16 picture elements. We identify the following macroblock types.

- An intra prediction macroblock only uses already transmitted macroblocks of the same image for predicting samples of the given macroblock. There are two flavors of intra prediction macroblocks, namely 16×16 (type 1) and 4×4 (type 2). The 4×4 macroblock consists of 16 4×4 subblocks which are encoded separately.
- An inter prediction or a motion compensated macroblock uses previously transmitted images for predicting samples of the given macroblock. An inter

prediction macroblock can be divided into 4 partitions, namely 16×16 (type 3), 16×8 (type 4), 8×16 (type 5) and 8×8. The 8×8 submacroblock can be further subdivided into 8×4, 4×8 and 4×4 partitions. As such, we consider 15 macroblock types for 8×8 macroblocks depending on the partitioning within the submacroblocks.
– The final macroblock type is the skip macroblock type (type 21).

For each of these 21 macroblock types, macroblock profiling computes the number of each of these macroblock types per frame. Note that not all of the above macroblock types appear for all frame types, *e.g.*, I frames do not contain inter prediction macroblocks.

Next to these macroblock types, macroblock profiling also measures the residual byte count per frame. (The residual bytes allow the decoder to correct the predictions based on the macroblock encoding.) We normalize the residual byte count in order to bring it in the range of the macroblock type counts — note that we will use the macroblock profile to build the frame space.

2.2   Video Stream Scenario Identification

We identify video stream scenarios through cluster analysis in the frame space.

Cluster analysis [2] is a data analysis technique that is aimed at clustering n cases, in our case frames, based on the measurements of p variables, in our case macroblock characteristics. The final goal is to obtain a number of groups, containing frames that are encoded similarly.

The cluster technique we use, called *linkage clustering*, starts with a matrix of distances between the n frames. As a starting point for the algorithm, each frame is considered as a group. In each iteration of the algorithm, the two groups that are most close to each other (with the smallest *linkage distance*) will be combined to form a new group. As such, close groups are gradually merged until finally all frames will be in a single group. This can be represented in a so called *dendrogram*, which graphically represents the linkage distance for each group merge at each iteration of the algorithm. Having obtained a dendrogram, it is up to the user to decide how many clusters to take. This decision can be made based on the linkage distance. Indeed, small linkage distances imply strong clustering whereas large linkage distances imply weak clustering. The distance metric that we use in the frame space is the Manhattan distance. There exist several methods for calculating the distance between groups of frames all potentially leading to different clustering results. In this paper, we consider the *furthest neighbor* strategy, also known as *complete linkage*. In complete linkage, the distance between two clusters is computed as the largest distance between any two frames from the clusters (or thus the furthest neighbor).

2.3   Video Stream Scenario Annotation

Annotating the video streams with scenario information can be done in two ways. One possibility is to embed scenario information in the video stream. This may break compatibility with existing decoders though. A better solution is to maintain the scenario information in a separate scenario stream. This stream can then be sent along with the video stream. The stream based solution is particularly interesting because it nicely fits within the container structure that is often used in multimedia streams, see for example the MP4 container format [3].

Note that the amount of scenario information that needs to be sent from the content provider to the client is very limited, no more than $\lceil log_2 N_s \rceil$ per frame with N_s the number of scenarios. This scenario information can be highly compressed by exploiting scenario locality. A video stream typically remains in the same scenario for a given amount of time, $i.e.$, the scenario IDs do not tend to change in subsequent frames of a video stream. As such, the scenario stream that needs to be sent from the content provider to the client can be compressed using a run-length encoding scheme (scenario-ID + number of occurrences).

3 Scenario-Driven Decoding at the Client Side

The client can exploit the scenarios annotated to the video streams for driving the energy-efficient decoding. Before actually decoding video streams on the client side, we first need to profile the client by building the *scenario adaptation table (SAT)*, see Fig. 1. The SAT contains the appropriate frequency and voltage for each of the scenarios. These frequencies and voltages are determined in such a way that a frame belonging to the scenario still meets its deadline while minimizing the decoder's energy consumption. Once the SAT is filled in, $i.e.$, the client is 'calibrated', video streams can be sent to the client and the client will adjust the frequency and voltage levels per frame according to the scenario the frame belongs to. The overall goal is to reduce the energy consumption while meeting the deadlines. Note that the calibration step needs to be done only once for a given client.

We now discuss how the client is to be profiled for filling in the scenario adaptation table. We subsequently detail on the scenario-driven decoding.

3.1 Client Profiling

In order to enable client profiling, the content provider needs to determine a *scenario representative* for each scenario, see Fig. 1. The scenario representatives can be determined as part of the cluster analysis for identifying the scenarios. We select the frame that is closest to the cluster's centroid as the scenario representative. As such, the scenario representatives are frames taken from various video streams.

The content provider sends these scenario representatives to the client for client profiling. The client then decodes these scenario representatives and monitors their decode time, $e.g.$, by using hardware performance counters that are available on all modern microprocessors. Once the decode time T_{decode} at frequency F is known for a given scenario, the scenario operating frequency is computed as

$$\theta \times F \times T_{decode}/T_{deadline} \tag{1}$$

with T_{deadline} being the time between two deadlines. The assumption that is being made in this formula is that the cycle count remains nearly constant when scaling the clock frequency. This may not be true in general because the memory access latency remains constant while scaling the processor clock frequency. However, for the video application that we target in this paper, this seems to be a good enough approximation. We conducted experiments changing the processor clock frequency while keeping the memory access latency fixed to 80ns and observed that the cycle count remains almost constant; the accumulated deviation over the entire 100MHz – 2GHz range is less than 3%.

The θ parameter in the above formula for computing the scenario operating frequency adds an additional scaling; the reason for this scaling parameter is twofold. First, the cycle count has the above mentioned small deviation when scaling the clock frequency. Second, some frames in a scenario may require a higher frequency than the scenario representative for meeting the deadline. However, given the fact that the variability within a scenario is rather small, this scaling parameter is fairly close to 1 in practice. In our experiments θ is set to 1.15.

The scenario operating voltage level is then determined based on the scenario operating frequency — this is dependent on the chip technology in which the processor is built (in most of today's processors frequency and voltage form readily known pairs, often called processor-modes). The end result of the client profiling process is a filled in SAT that summarizes the operating frequency and voltage level per scenario.

3.2   Scenario-Driven Voltage Scaling

Scenario-driven video decoding is fairly straightforward once the scenario adaptation table is available. Upon receiving a new frame, the corresponding scenario info is read and the operating frequency and voltage level are retrieved from the SAT and are established in the processor. The process of changing frequency and voltage level at run time, is a well known mechanism that is called dynamic voltage and frequency scaling (DVFS).

Frequency and voltage scaling are well understood mechanisms that are very powerful in reducing energy consumption [4]. In a region where clock frequency and voltage are linear to each other, the dynamic power consumption is cubic in the voltage or frequency. As such, reducing the frequency by a factor R results in a $\sim R^3$ reduction in power consumption, or a $\sim R^2$ reduction in energy consumption. Because of this cubic relationship to power and quadratic relationship to energy, DVFS is a very popular technique in energy-efficient design. In fact, several commercial processors employ DVFS, see for example the Intel XScale processor [5] and the Transmeta Crusoe processor [6].

4   Experimental Setup

Our experiments are done using version JM6.1 [7] of the reference implementation of the H.264 Advanced Video Coding (AVC) codec [1].

We use 12 video sequences, consisting of 297 frames, showing a wide variety in amount of spatial detail and movement. The results presented in this paper are obtained for these video streams in CIF resolution (352×288 pixels per frame). Further, we consider content-adaptive variable-length coding (CAVLC) and a IPPPP... GOP structure, *i.e.*, there is one I frame followed by 15 P frames.

The performance results presented in this paper are obtained using detailed cycle-level processor simulations using the SimpleScalar/Alpha v3.0 tool set [8]. Microprocessor energy consumption is estimated using Wattch v1.02 [9]. These simulation tools were extended to model combined frequency and voltage scaling. Following [10], we model the relation between clock frequency and supply voltage as:

$$f \sim \frac{(V - V_{\text{th}})^\alpha}{V} \qquad (2)$$

When applying frequency scaling we vary the frequency in steps of 10MHz. We also experimented with 100MHz frequency steps and the results were very similar to what we present in this paper. We also model the time cost for scaling the processor operating frequency and voltage.

The baseline processor model used in this paper is a contemporary 4-wide superscalar microarchitecture, *i.e.*, up to four instructions can be issued per cycle. We also evaluated 2 different processor configurations, one with shallower resources and one with wider resources. The results were similar to what is reported here.

5   Evaluation

5.1   Scenarios Correlate w/ Decode Complexity

Before evaluating the energy-efficiency of scenario-based video decoding, we first evaluate how well the scenarios track decode complexity. For this purpose we set the scenario operating frequency scaling factor θ to 1.0 for now, *i.e.*, deadlines will be missed frequently, and we plot the scenario operating frequency versus the minimal 'oracle' processor frequency that still meets the deadline, which is a measure for the decode complexity.

Figure 2 shows this plot for the table video stream. This graph clearly shows that the scenarios are capable of tracking the decode complexity very well. For example, the first part of the table video stream seems to be much more complex than the second part; the frame-level scenarios clearly track this change in decode complexity very well. The scenarios also discriminate I frames from P frames; the points around 1.7+ GHz are all I frames.

5.2   Scenario-Driven Video Decoding

We now evaluate scenario-based video decoding in terms of energy reduction and missed deadlines. In all of these experiments, we assume a leave-one-out methodology. This means that when evaluating the efficacy of scenario-based

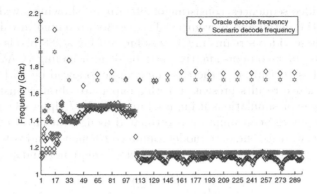

Fig. 2. Tracking decode complexity using 32 scenarios for the table video stream

video decoding for a given video stream we leave that video stream out of the content provider's database for building the scenarios. This reflects what is to expected in practice whenever a new video stream is added to the content provider's database.

In the following results we consider 32 scenarios. This results in no deadline misses for all of the video streams except for foreman; the foreman video stream misses 1.3% of its deadlines.

Figure 3 shows the normalized energy consumption for each of the video streams. The energy consumption is normalized to the energy consumption while decoding all the video streams at a single fixed clock frequency that guarantees that all frames in all video streams are decoded within the deadlines. In other words, the minimum clock frequency is determined by the most computationally demanding frame in all of the video streams. This is the 'reference' bar in Fig. 3. The 'oracle' bar shows the normalized energy consumption while decoding all the frames at the minimum clock frequency per frame; this cannot be achieved in practice unless an oracle mechanism is assumed. We observe that the maximum achievable energy reduction is high for most of the video streams; the most computation demanding video stream is mobile and the oracle video decoding mechanism cannot reduce the energy reduction consumption by more than 33%. Scenario-based video decoding is capable of achieving most of the potential energy reduction. On average, frame-level scenario-based decoding reduces energy consumption by as much as 46%, whereas the oracle mechanism achieves an average reduction of 53%.

5.3   Scenario Encoding Cost

Scenario-aware video streams need to be annotated with scenario IDs. Table 1 quantifies the number of bits for annotating video streams with frame-level scenarios. Video streams showing little scenario locality such as coast guard require more bits to encode scenario information than other video streams. The average

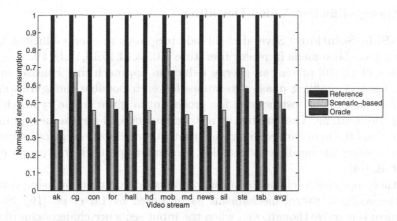

Fig. 3. Normalized energy reduction through scenario-based video decoding; there are 32 scenarios in total

Table 1. Cost of scenario annotation for entire video streams in number of bits for 32 scenarios

Video stream	ak	cg	con	for	hall	hd	mob	md	news	sil	ste	tab	avg
Bits needed	702	1476	621	981	945	630	972	639	1386	873	1242	756	**935.25**

cost per video stream assuming run-length encoding is less than 1K bits. This corresponds to less than 100 bits per second on average – this is an increase of less than 0.02 % to the encoded video stream. We thus conclude that the cost for encoding scenario information is very small.

6 Related Work

6.1 Video Decoder Complexity

Horowitz *et al.* [11] present a platform-independent characterization of the H.264/AVC video decoder in terms of macroblock types and the number of fundamental operations required to perform the key decoder subfunctions. This characterization is then linked with experimental results from 3 hardware platforms. Mattavelli and Brunetton [12] characterize video streams in a platform-independent manner by counting the number of inter prediction macroblocks, the number of intra prediction macroblocks, the number of skip macroblocks, *etc.* For predicting the decoder performance on a particular platform using these platform-independent metrics, they then employ linear regression. This approach requires profiling a large number of video stream segments which may be impractical on resource-constrained embedded devices. These two studies [11,12] do not exploit similarities within and across video streams.

6.2   Energy-Efficient Video Decoding

Client-Side Solutions. Several client-side proposals to energy-efficient video decoding have been made in recent literature [10,13,14,15,16,17,18,19].

Hughes *et al.* [10] present an energy reduction approach that consists of two phases. First, a profiling phase determines for each possible configuration the maximum 'budget' of instructions for processing a given frame type without missing the deadline. The number of instructions needed for the next frame is predicted and the hardware configuration that will minimize energy consumption without missing the deadline is installed. A similar approach was proposed by Choi *et al.* [14].

Another approach to client-side energy-efficient decoding is by using control-theoretic feedback-control mechanisms as proposed by Lu *et al.* [16]. Such a mechanism is reactive though, *i.e.*, when the input sequence changes complexity, the mechanism needs to learn how to deal with that.

Gheorghita *et al.* [15] propose a proactive scenario-based DVFS approach that is based on static analysis of the video decoder. This analysis identifies input variables with a large impact on execution time. Scenarios are then determined based on the possible values that can be taken by these variables. Their technique is unable to exploit the fine-grained scenarios as we do in this paper; Gheorghita *et al.* only identify two scenarios in a video decoder application, one for decoding I frames and another one for decoding P frames.

Offline and Content Provider Assisted Solutions. All of the previous approaches rely on the resource-constrained client for analyzing the input stream complexity. Offline and content provider assisted scenario annotation relieve the client from this task.

Huang *et al.* [20] propose an offline bitstream analysis methodology for energy-efficient video decoding. They assume a setup where the video stream is loaded from the desktop to the portable device using a device-specific program that predicts the device's processor cycle requirements at the macroblock level and adds frequency and voltage level information as metadata to the bitstream. An important downside to this approach is the need for a specialized program for each client platform.

The approach most related to our approach is the one proposed by Chung *et al.* [21]. Their key idea is to annotate the decoding cost to each frame in a video stream with its decoding time normalized to the decoding time of the first frame in the video stream. These decoding times are measured by the content provider. Chung *et al.* assume that the decoding cost at the content provider correlates very well with the decoding cost at client side. This however is not always the case because the platforms may be very different (both the decoders as well as the processor and system architectures).

7   Conclusion

This paper proposed an energy-efficient video decoding methodology based on video stream similarity. The key idea is to identify scenarios both within and across video streams in a platform-independent manner. Video streams in a content provider's database are then annotated with scenario information which is exploited by the client through dynamic voltage and frequency scaling. To the best of our knowledge, this paper is the first to identify and exploit video stream similarity. Our evaluation shows that scenario-based video decoding reduces overall energy consumption by 46% while meeting almost all frame deadlines.

As part of our future work, we will apply this methodology to other multimedia applications. In fact, we believe that the framework presented in this paper is a general methodology that can be applied to various applications in the embedded multimedia and signal processing domains.

Acknowledgements

Juan Hamers is supported by a BOF grant from Ghent University. Lieven Eeckhout is supported by the Fund for Scientific Research-Flanders (Belgium) (F.W.O.-Vlaanderen). This research is also supported by the Institute for the Promotion of Innovation by Science and Technology in Flanders (IWT), the HiPEAC Network of Excellence and the European SARC project No. 27648.

References

1. Ostermann, J., Bormans, J., List, P., Marpe, D., Narroschke, M., Pereira, F., Stockhammer, T., Wedi, T.: Video coding with H.264/AVC: Tools, performance and complexity. IEEE Circuits and Systems Magazine 4(1) (2004) 7–28
2. Johnson, R.A., Wichern, D.W.: Applied Multivariate Statistical Analysis. fifth edn. Prentice Hall (2002)
3. ISO/IEC: Information technology – coding of audio-visual objects – part 14: MP4 file format. (ISO/IEC 14496-14:2003)
4. Brooks, D., Bose, P., Schuster, S.E., Jacobson, H., Kudva, P.N., Buyuktosunoglu, A., Wellman, J.D., Zyuban, V., Gupta, M., Cook, P.W.: Power-aware microarchitecture: Design and modeling challenges for next-generation microprocessors. IEEE Micro 20(6) (2000) 26–44
5. Intel: Intel XScale Core Developer's Manual. (2004) 273473-002.
6. Transmeta Corporation: LongRun Power Management: Dynamic Power Management for Crusoe Processors. (2001)
7. ITU: H.264/AVC reference software. (http://iphome.hhi.de/suehring/tml/download/)
8. Burger, D.C., Austin, T.M.: The SimpleScalar Tool Set. Computer Architecture News (1997) See also http://www.simplescalar.com for more information.
9. Brooks, D., Tiwari, V., Martonosi, M.: Wattch: A framework for architectural-level power analysis and optimizations. In: Proceedings of the 27th Annual International Symposium on Computer Architecture (ISCA-27). (2000) 83–94
10. Hughes, C.J., Srinivasan, J., Adve, S.V.: Saving energy with architectural and frequency adaptations for multimedia applications. In: Proceedings of the 34th Annual International Symposium on Microarchitecture (MICRO-34). (2001) 250–261

11. Horowitz, M., Joch, A., Kossentini, F., Hallapuro, A.: H.264/AVC baseline profile decoder complexity analysis. IEEE Transactions on Circuits and Systems for Video Technology **13**(7) (2003) 704–716
12. Mattavelli, M., Brunetton, S.: Implementing real-time video decoding on multimedia processors by complexity prediction techniques. IEEE Transactions on Consumer Electronics **44**(3) (1998) 760–767
13. Acquaviva, A., Benini, L., Riccó, B.: An adaptive algorithm for low-power streaming multimedia processing. In: Proceedings of the Conference on Design Automation and Test in Europe (DATE). (2001) 273–279
14. Choi, K., Dantu, K., Cheng, W.C., Pedram, M.: Frame-based dynamic voltage and frequency scaling for a MPEG decoder. In: Proceedings of the 2002 International Conference on Computer-Aided Design (ICCAD). (2002) 732–737
15. Gheorghita, S.V., Basten, T., Corporaal, H.: Intra-task scenario-aware voltage scheduling. In: Proceedings of the 2005 International Conference on Compilers, Architectures and Synthesis for Embedded Systems (CASES). (2005) 177–184
16. Lu, Z., Hein, J., Humphrey, M., Stan, M., Lach, J., Skadron, K.: Control-theoretic dynamic frequency and voltage scaling for multimedia workloads. In: Proceedings of the 2002 International Conference on Compilers, Architectures and Synthesis for Embedded Systems (CASES). (2002) 156–163
17. Mohapatra, S., Cornea, R., Dutt, N., Nicolau, A., Vakatasubramanian, N.: Integrated power management for video streaming to mobile handheld devices. In: Proceedings of the 11th Annual ACM International Conference on Multimedia (MM). (2003) 582–591
18. Shin, D., Kim, J., Lee, S.: Intra-task voltage scheduling for low-energy, hard real-time applications. IEEE Design and Test of Computers **18**(2) (2001) 20–30
19. Yuan, W., Nahrstedt, K.: Practical voltage scaling for mobile multimedia devices. In: Proceedings of the 12th Annual ACM International Conference on Multimedia (MM). (2004) 924–931
20. Huang, Y., Chakraborty, S., Wang, Y.: Using offline bitstream analysis for power-aware video decoding in portable devices. In: Proceedings of the 13th Annual ACM International Conference on Multimedia (MM). (2005) 299–302
21. Chung, E.Y., Benini, L., De Micheli, G.: Contents provider-assisted dynamic voltage scaling for low energy multimedia applications. In: Proceedings of the 2002 International Symposium on Low Power Electronic Design (ISLPED). (2002) 42–47

Optimization of System Performance for DVC Applications with Energy Constraints over Ad Hoc Networks

Lifeng Sun[1], Ke Liang[2], Shiqiang Yang[1], and Yuzhuo Zhong[1]

[1] Department of Computer Science and Technology, Tsinghua University,
100084, Beijing, China
[2] School of Computing, National University of Singapore
sunlf@tsinghua.edu.cn, liangke@comp.nus.edu.sg

Abstract. We investigate optimization of system performance in the below scenario: capturing and transmitting videos by single or multiple video sensors using distributed video coding (DVC) over ad hoc networks. There is an intrinsic contradiction in this scenario that could affect the system performance: the contradiction between the decoding quality and network lifetime. In this paper, we propose a joint optimization between the decoding quality and network lifetime using a quantitative metric of system performance, which is defined as the amount of collected visual information during the operational time of the video sensor. Based on the proposed metric, an optimal encoding rate is determined, which results in an optimal system performance. The simulation results show that the optimal encoding rate can be determined to achieve the optimal system performance.

Keywords: Distributed video coding, ad hoc networks, energy, optimization.

1 Introduction

An ad hoc network is formed by wireless nodes without any established infrastructure. Each wireless node in an ad hoc network can act as a source, a receiver, or a relay for transmission. Ad hoc networks are unstable due to high packet loss probability, rate fluctuate, frequent route updates and node mobility. Recently, video streaming over ad-hoc networks becomes a young and hot topic in research and industry. In this application, video cameras are embedded into the sensors, which can capture, process, and transmit videos to receivers.

There are two challenges in transmitting video over ad hoc networks: First, since video cameras in ad hoc networks are usually powered by batteries and have limited computing capability and memory, it is necessary to design a new video codec to replace the conventional video encoder, which is complex and power-consuming. Second and more critically, since the resource is limited, a rate allocation strategy should be proposed to find the optimal encoding rate which results in the optimal performance of system, which means high decoding quality and long network lifetime.

T.-J. Cham et al. (Eds.): MMM 2007, LNCS 4352, Part II, pp. 23–31, 2007.

To cope with the first challenge, distributed video coding (DVC) [1,2,3,4] is proposed to lower down the computational burden of the encoder by shifting the motion compensation module from the encoder to the decoder. Further more, DVC has built-in error-resilient ability due to the channel coding techniques. Therefore, DVC encoder is lightweight and power-saving, and these features are propitious to wireless terminals.

It is more critical but more difficult to cope with the second challenge. In order to achieve higher decoding quality, higher encoding rate should be allocated to the video sensor. However, higher encoding rate brings higher power consumption which results in shorter network lifetime. The problem can be formulated as the mutual conditionality between the decoding quality and network lifetime. In other words, how to utilize the limited resource efficiently to achieve best system performance. In [5], the amount of collected visual information is defined as a quantitative metric of performance for single-source system. This metric is intuitionist to describe the properties of visual information function V(R): Non-decreasing, homogenous, concave and bounded, fast degradation around zero.

In this paper, we give a quantitative expression of visual information based on DVC rate distortion function of the video frame. Using this expression, we can find an optimal encoding rate for the video sensor of DVC application, and the optimal rate results in the optimal system performance.

The rest of the paper is organized as follows: In section 2, we will describe the fundamental models (include the ad-hoc network scenario model, the proposed rate-distortion model and the power model). In section 3, we will define the visual information and give the quantitative metric of system performance. In section 4, we will present the rate allocation scheme based on section 3 and analyze the simulation results. Finally, section 5 concludes the paper.

2 System Models

In this section, some system models are given to formulate the optimal problem. We first introduce the DVC rate distortion model based on Slepian-Wolf and Wyner-Ziv theorem [6,7]. And following, base on the DVC rate distortion model, the expression of visual information of a video frame is given.

2.1 DVC Rate Distortion Model

DVC originates from DSC (Distributed Source Coding), and the source is replaced by video sequences. Consider two successive video frames, X_{n-1} and X_n, in the video sequence, where the subscript n-1 and n denote the time indexes. $\hat{X}_{n-1}$ and $\hat{X}_n$ are reconstructed frames of X_{n-1} and X_n separately. In DVC scheme, X_{n-1} is encoded by a conventional intraframe encoder, unlike predictive coding scheme, X_n is encoded by a Wyner-Ziv encoder without the knowledge of X_{n-1}. At the decoder, with the help of $\hat{X}_{n-1}$, which is regard as *side information*, X_n is reconstructed as $\hat{X}_n$.

The information-theoretic rate-distortion bounds for Wyner-Ziv coding are first established in [8]:

$$R_{X|Y}(D) \le R_{WZ}(D) \le R_X(D) \tag{1}$$

Where X denotes the to-be-encoded source, Y denotes the side information. $R_{X|Y}(D)$ is the rate distortion function of inter-frame coding (predictive coding), and $R_X(D)$ denotes the rate distortion of intra-frame coding. $R_{X|Y}(D) = R_{WZ}(D)$ means that Wyner-Ziv coding is lossless in case of the source X and the side information Y are jointly Gaussian sequence, and MSE (Mean Squared Error) is used as the distortion measure. In [9], a generalization of the rate distortion function was given for Wyner-Ziv coding of noisy sources in the quadratic Gaussian case.

Notice that the distortion decays exponentially with rate, we give a more precise distortion function using exponential decay function, and the proposed rate distortion function can be represented as:

$$D = D_0 + \alpha \cdot e^{-R/\beta} \qquad (2)$$

Where D_0, α, and β (decay constant) can be estimated experimental data of the video sequence via regressive technologies. The main difference between the proposed rate distortion function and that in [9] is the decay constant β, which is fixed in [9] and does not change with video sequence.

We use *foreman* sequence for experiment, as is shown in Fig.1. The proposed rate distortion has good fitting property with (SSE, EMSE) = (71.24, 2.179).

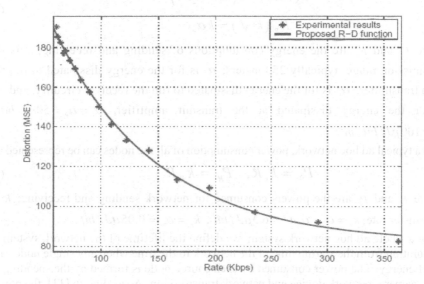

Fig. 1. Proposed R-D function

2.2 Network Scenario Model

We study the case where a number of nodes capturing and transmitting videos to a receiver in an ad hoc networks. As shown in Fig.2, $node_{1-6}$ is deployed in different place with different initial energy and transmits videos to the receiver $node_0$ using single hop or multiple hops.

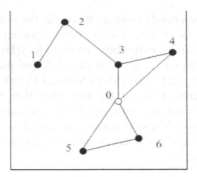

Fig. 2. Network scenario of ad hoc video sensor network

2.3 Power Consumption Model

We use the radio model presented in [10], which is an d^2 energy loss estimation for channel transmission. In order to transmit a k-bit message from node i to node j directly, the energy consumed of sending and receiving can be figured out by:

$$E_S(k,d) = k(\alpha_1 + \alpha_2 d^2)$$

$$E_R(k,d) = k\alpha_r$$

(3)

where E_S and E_R are the energy consumptions of sending and receiving; d is the transmission range, typically 250 meters; α_1 is for the energy dissipated to run the radio transmitter, α_r is for the energy dissipated to run the receiver circuitry, and α_2 is for the energy dissipated at the transmit amplifier, $\alpha_1 = \alpha_r = 50nJ / bit$, $\alpha_2 = 100 pJ / bit / m^2$.

In a typical ad hoc network, power consumption of all the nodes can be represented as:

$$P_S = k_s R, \quad P_R = k_R R$$

(4)

Where P_S and P_R are the powers consumed for network sending and receiving; R is the transfer rate; $k_s = \alpha_1 + \alpha_2 d^2 = 6.3 \mu J / bit$, $k_r = \alpha_r = 0.05 \mu J / bit$.

For a whole ad hoc network system, we define the lifetime of the network system as the duration from the startup time of the network to the time when any single node runs out of energy. The power consumed by each source node is formed by the spending of CPU, camera, network device and network transmission. According to [11], the power consumed by a node is relatively constant over time. The only variability comes from the network transmission. So the lifetime can be figured out by:

$$T = \min_i \{ E_i / (P_{Ti} + P_{Ci}) \}$$

(5)

Where E_i is the total energy of node i, P_{Ci} is the constant part of power consumed by it, which includes power of CPU, camera and other devices. P_{Ti} represents the average power for transmission. The receiver is not taken into account because it is very different from other source nodes. During the final time, nodes energies fall to a very low level and BER arises, so the theoretical lifetime is a little longer than in reality.

3 Visual Information and System Performance Model

In order to measure the system performance, visual information is introduced. For an image, visual information is determined by the encoding rate and the variance of the image. For a video sequence, motion activity is regard as an more important factor. When a uniform video coding technology is used, visual information is determined by the activity of the to-be-encoded video frame. Generally speaking, more motion (comparing with the previous video frame) the to-be-encoded video frame has, more visual information it contains.

The amount of collected visual information during the operational lifetime has been defined as the metric of system performance in [5]. It should be noted that when the rate is low, small increment of rate brings big increment of decoding quality. However, when the rate is relatively high, large increment of rate brings small increment of decoding quality. Therefore, there exists a contribution function $\phi(R)$, which denotes the contribution of encoding rate R to the decoding quality.

For an image, visual information is defined as the amount of information needed to communicate for the image. Undoubtedly, visual information is in direct proportion to bit-rate of the image, in another word, the visual information function is non-decreasing to bit-rate. Intuitively, the visual information is convex at high rate.

However, we have no idea of the feature of visual information function at low rate. There are two possibilities at low rate: concave or convex. If it is convex, the visual information function is similar with the PSNR curve, thus the visual information can be regarded as the information of the image.

In our opinion, visual information of a video sequence is determined by not only the variance of video frames in the video sequence, but also the similarity of successive video frames. Therefore, we define the visual information from R-D function: D(R):

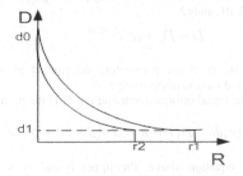

Fig. 3. R-D curve of video sequence

From Fig. 3, we can find some interesting facts in R-D curve:

1. d0 means the largest difference (MSE measured) between the two successive video frames. The curve will have a larger d0 if large motion is observed in the video

sequence. If the bit-rate is zero, it means the to-be-decoded frame is taken place by the previous frame.

2. Different R-D curve have different variance. Larger variance, the curve farther from the zero. And this is the feature of visual information in images.

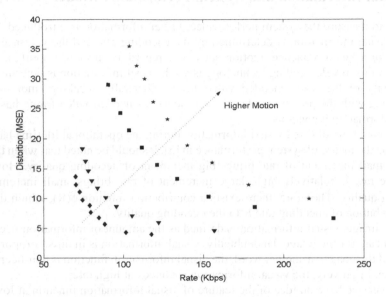

Fig. 4. Relationship of visual information with motion

For a video sequence, as shown in Fig. 4, larger motion, more visual information can be achieved. On the other hand, for an image, larger variance, more visual information can be achieved.

Therefore, we regard the area, which is formed by the two coordinate axes and the R-D function, as the visual information. For example in fig.3, the visual information is the area formed by d0, d1, and r2.

$$D = D_0 + \alpha \cdot e^{-R/\beta} \qquad (6)$$

In this equation, D_0, α, β are parameters determined by the video sequence (quantizes, variance, and motion respectively).

We can compute the visual information using this R-D function:

$$V(R) = \int_{r=0}^{R} D(r)dr - D(R) \cdot R = \alpha \cdot \left[\beta - (R + \beta) \cdot e^{-R/\beta} \right] \qquad (7)$$

As shown in the equation above, the upper bound of visual information is determined by the motion of the video sequence and the variance of the video frames.

We can also get the contribution of bit rate to the visual information:

$$\phi(R) = \frac{dV}{dR} = \frac{1}{\beta} \cdot R \cdot e^{-R/\beta} \qquad (8)$$

4 Rate Allocation and Validation

We first use the concept of visual information in single-source video applications, in this case, we joint optimize the decoding quality and the network lifetime.

We use the ratio of visual information achieved to the energy consumed to indicate the efficiency of the system.

If the fame-rate is fixed, the energy consumed is in proportion to the bit rate according to equation 3, and the efficiency can be formulated as equation 8.

$$\frac{V}{E} = \frac{\alpha \cdot \left[\beta - (R + \beta) \cdot e^{-R/\beta}\right]}{K \cdot R} \tag{9}$$

Where K is a constant, which means that the transmission energy consumed is determined by the bit-rate. To get the optimized rate allocation, let $\dfrac{d\dfrac{V}{E}}{dR} = 0$, we get the equation:

$$e^x = x^2 + x + 1, \qquad x = \frac{R}{\beta}$$

$$R \approx 1.8\beta \tag{10}$$

The variable β can be regarded as the effect fact of motion, which is in inverse proportion to the similarity of successive video frames. We just classify the motion of the video into three types: Low, Middle, and High.

And the simulation results of rate allocation for single source video (foreman sequence for experiment) are shown below:

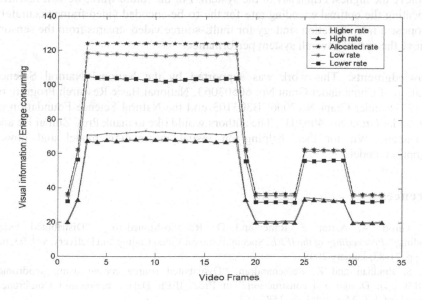

Fig. 5. Rate allocation simulations

As shown in the Figure5, the rate allocated by the proposed algorithm can achieve the highest efficiency of the system.

Since visual information of a video sequence is determined by the motion of the video sequence and the variance of the video frames. Therefore, the higher motion the video sequence has, the lower efficiency (which we defined as the ratio of visual information achieved to the energy consumed) achieved. We can see the simulation results shown in the figure above, in the low motion area (from the 3th frame to the 17th frame), high efficiency is achieved. On the other hand, in the high motion area (from the 20th frame to the 24th frame), efficiency is lowered down.

If a very low rate is allocated to encode the video frames, low visual information is achieved though the encoding rate is low, which results in low system efficiency. When the rate is increasing, the system efficiency is getting higher. As shown in the figure above, the optimal system efficiency is achieved when the rate is allocated using $R \approx 1.8\beta$.

5 Conclusions

We investigate optimization of system performance in the scenario of capturing and transmitting videos by single or multiple video sensors using distributed video coding (DVC) over ad hoc networks. We propose a joint optimization between the decoding quality and network lifetime using a quantitative metric of system performance, which is defined as the amount of collected visual information during the operational time of the video sensor. In the simulation, we classify the motion of the video into three types: Low, Middle, and High. Different types have different β, which is regarded as the effect fact of motion. The simulations show that the rate allocated by the proposed algorithm can achieve the highest efficiency of the system. For the future work, we will research on allocating the optimal encoding rate for the to-be-encoded video frame accurately and propose a rate allocation strategy for multi-source video streams from the sensors to achieve the optimal overall system performance.

Acknowledgments. This work was supported by the National Natural Science Foundation of China under Grant No. 60503063, National Basic Research Program of China (973) under Grant No.2006CB303103 and the Natural Science Foundation of Beijing under Grant No. 4063037. The authors would like to thank Prof. Zhihai He and Prof. Dapeng Wu for their helping on visual information model and power consumption model.

References

1. B. Girod, A. Aaron, S. Rane and D. Rebollo-Monedero , "Distributed video coding," *Proceedings of the IEEE*, Special Issue on Video Coding and Delivery, vol. 93, no. 1, pp. 71-83, January 2005.
2. S. S. Pradhan and K. Ramchandran, "Distributed source coding using syndromes (DISCUS): Design and construction," in Proc. IEEE Data Compression Conference, Snowbird, UT, Mar. 1999, pp. 158 –167.

3. A. Aaron, R. Zhang, and B. Girod, "Wyner-Ziv coding of motion video," in Proc. Asilomar Conference on Signals and Systems, Pacific Grove, CA, Nov. 2002.
4. A. Aaron, S. Rane, R. Zhang, and B. Girod, "Wyner-Ziv coding for video: Applications to compression and error resilience," in Proc. IEEE Data Compression Conference, Snowbird, UT, Mar. 2003, pp. 93–102.
5. Zhihai He; Dapeng Wu, Accumulative visual information in wireless video sensor network: definition and analysis, IEEE International Conference on Communications (ICC 2005), Seoul, Korea, May 16 - 20, 2005 Page(s):1205 - 1208 Vol. 2
6. J. D. Slepian and J. K. Wolf, "Noiseless coding of correlated information sources," IEEE Transactions on Information Theory, vol. IT-19, pp. 471– 480, July 1973.
7. A. D. Wyner, "Recent Results in the Shannon Theory," IEEE Transactions on Information Theory, vol. 20, no. 1, pp. 2–10, Jan. 1974.
8. A. D. Wyner and J. Ziv, "The rate-distortion function for source coding with side information at the decoder," IEEE Trans. Info. Theory, vol. IT-22, pp. 1 - 10, January 1976.
9. D. Rebollo-Monedero and B. Girod, "A generalization of the rate-distortion function for Wyner-Ziv coding of noisy sources in the quadratic-Gaussian case," in Proc. IEEE Data Compression Conferaence, DCC-2005, Snowbird, UT, Mar. 2005.
10. Wendi Rabiner Heinzelman, Anantha Chandrakasan, and Hari Balakrishnan, "Energy-Efficient Communication Protocol for Wireless Microsensor Networks," Proc. Hawaiian Int'l Conf. on Systems Science, January 2000.
11. Wu-chi Feng, Brian Code, Ed Kaiser, Mike Shea, Wu-chang Feng, Louis Bavoil, Panoptes: Scalable Low-Power Video Sensor Networking Technologies, ACM Transactions on Multimedia Computing, Communications and Applications, January 2005.
12. Zhihai He, Yongfang Liang, Lulin Chen, Ishfaq Ahmad, and Dapeng Wu, Power-rate-distortion analysis for wireless video communication under energy constraint, IEEE Trans. Circuits Syst. Video Technol., vol. 15, no. 5, pp. 645–658,. May. 2005.

Distributed Video Coding with Trellis Coded Quantization

Qiwei Liu[1], Houqiang Li[1], Yan Lu[2], and Feng Wu[2]

[1] University of Science and Technology of China, Hefei, 230027, P.R. China
liuqiwei@mail.ustc.edu.cn, lihq@ustc.edu.cn
[2] Microsoft Research Asia, Beijing, 100080, P.R. China
{yanlu, fengwu}@microsoft.com

Abstract. In conventional video coding systems, the encoder performs predictive coding (motion estimation) to exploit the temporal similarity, which make its complexity much higher than that of the decoder. The Wyner-Ziv theory or Lossy Distributed Coding theory suggests that when frames are separately encoded but jointly decoded, similar coding efficiency could be achieved. Trellis coded quantization (TCQ) is a powerful quantization method which has already shown its power in distributed source coding area. Recently, some applicable Wyner-Ziv video coding systems have been proposed. In this paper, based on the PRISM system, TCQ is employed to improve the performance. In order to minimize the complexity increase, only 4-state trellis is used, and no codebook is trained or stored, and we also propose a method to solve the refinement problem. Some other changes are also made to further improve the performance. Experimental results indicate that though the simplest TCQ is used, gain is also achieved over scalar quantization[1].

Keywords: Wyner-Ziv coding, Distributed Video Coding, Trellis Coded Quantization.

1 Introduction

In today's video coding standards, such as the MPEG and H.26x, the complexity of an encoder is much higher than that of a decoder, because it's the encoder's task to perform some computationally heavy operations such as motion estimation to achieve high compression efficiency. Such architecture is well suited for downlink transmission model of broadcasting, where video is compressed once and decoded many times. However, with the emergence of media-rich uplink wireless video transmission applications, for example, wireless video sensors, mobile camera phones and so on, low-complexity encoders are needed, because the processing power and memory of these devices are all limited.

Recently, some Distributed Video Coding (DVC) schemes have been proposed to provide the complexity reverse for encoder and decoder [1], [2]. These schemes are based on Distributed Source Coding theories: Slepian-Wolf theory [3] for lossless

---

[1] This work is done during Q.Liu's internship at MSRA.

T.-J. Cham et al. (Eds.): MMM 2007, LNCS 4352, Part II, pp. 32–40, 2007.

coding and Wyner-Ziv theory for lossy coding [4]. The Slepian-Wolf theory states that even if two statistically dependant discrete signals are losslessly encoded by two independent encoders but jointly decoded, the same rate can be achieved as they are encoded and decoded both jointly. The counterpart of this theorem for lossy source coding is Wyner-Ziv theory. Let X and Y be two dependent Gaussian random signals, and let Y be the side information for encoding X. Wyner-Ziv theory states that the conditional rate mean squared error distortion function for X is the same whether Y is known at decoder only or both at encoder and decoder.

The PRISM system proposed in [1] is a practical implementation of distributed video coding. The encoder divides each frame into non-overlapping blocks and then the blocks are classified into skip, intra, and several syndrome coding modes. For skip mode, the block is not coded at all. For intra mode, the block is intra-coded. For syndrome coding mode, a channel code is used to partition the quantized codewords (low frequency DCT coefficients) into cosets, and the syndrome (coset index) is transmitted along with a CRC check of the quantized codewords. In order to not exceed the correcting ability, the coefficients are coarsely quantized, and refine bits are needed. The other coefficients are entropy coded. The decoder performs motion estimation to generate various versions of side information for syndrome coded blocks, and the first decoded block that matches the CRC is chosen. The performance is better than intra coding, but there is still a large gap from conventional interframe coding.

TCQ [5] is a powerful quantization method as a source coding counterpart of trellis code modulation [6] in channel coding. The basic idea of TCQ is to use an expanded signal set and use coded modulation for set partitioning. For encoding a memoryless source at R bit/sample, a scalar codebook with 2^{R+1} codewords is designed and then partitioned into four subsets, each contains 2^{R-1} codewords. One bit is expanded by a well designed rate 1/2 convolutional code and used to select the subset and R-1 bits are used to specify a codeword from the chosen subset. Given a data sequence, the Viterbi algorithm is used to find the sequence of codewords that minimizes the mean square error between the input sequence and the output codewords. TCQ has been applied to distributed source coding schemes [7], [8], and shows good performance.

In this paper, we mainly focus on bringing TCQ into our distributed video coding system based on PRISM scheme. TCQ is used in a form that is suitable for DVC's features, and we proposed a method to solve the refinement problem. We also propose the idea of using side information to help the reconstruction of intra-coded high frequency DCT coefficients, which is shown to be of great use.

2 Proposed DVC Scheme with TCQ

The first frame in each picture group is called Key-frame, and is coded using a conventional intraframe codec. The other frames in a GOP are called Wyner-Ziv frames, and are intra coded but inter decoded. The block diagram of the codec is shown in Fig. 1. It illustrates the encoding and decoding process for syndrome coded blocks of Wyner-Ziv frames. Our contributions mainly focus on "TCQ & BaseQuan".

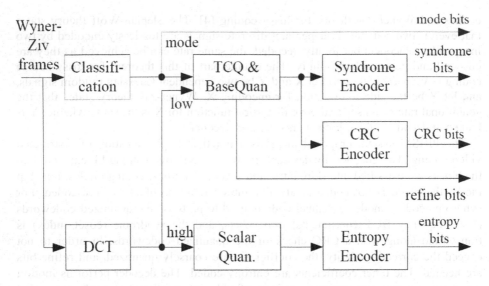

Fig. 1. Block diagram of the encoder for Wyner-Ziv frames

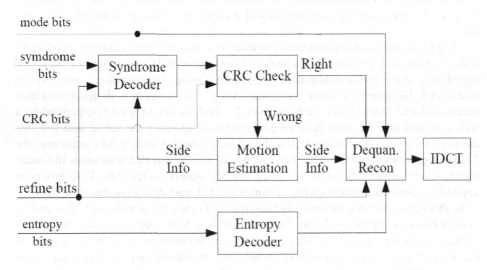

Fig. 2. Block diagram of the decoder for Wyner-Ziv frames

2.1 Encoder

Each Wyner-Ziv frame is first divided into non-overlapping 16x16 sized spatial blocks, and then each block is classified into different modes including skip, intra and several inter modes. Different blocks exhibit different correlation degrees with their temporal predictor, so this step is needed to facilitate the use of channel code. Actually, it is a tough task to estimate the correlation degrees without access to the previous frames in strict intra encoder, and we have not yet found a good way to get through, so here we assume the classification step is done near optimally (actually, coarse motion estimation is used in our experiment).

Then, 8x8 sized DCT is applied to each of the four subblocks in a 16x16 macroblock. For skip blocks, none of the coefficients are coded. For intra blocks, all the coefficients are scalar quantized and run-length Huffman coded. For inter blocks, 49 high frequency coefficients (in zigzag order) of each subblock are also scalar quantized and then run-length Huffman coded. The remaining 15 low frequency coefficients of each subblock are gathered to form a 60-length sequence, and then they are TCQ quantized and syndrome coded. This coding process is discussed in detail in the following paragraphs.

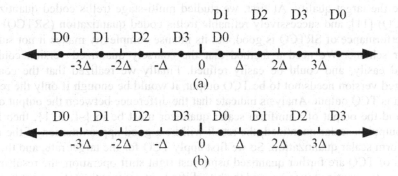

Fig. 3. Two kinds of subset partitioning

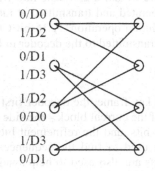

Fig. 4. 4-state trellis we used

TCQ is first introduced in [5], and then other forms of TCQ, such as ECTCQ [9] and UTCQ [10], are introduced to further improve its performance. ECTCQ has the best performance, but it requires stored codebooks, and the codebook design process uses an iterative, computationally intense algorithm which must be repeated for each desired rate and source distribution. The resultant codebooks lack structure and require a binary tree search for their use. All these features depart from the scenario of DVC scheme where a low complexity encoder is required. So we tend to UTCQ, which uses uniform thresholds and reconstruction levels at the encoder, and the quantization thresholds are simply the midpoints between the reconstruction levels within a subset. This allows for fast computation of codeword indices requiring only scaling and rounding. UTCQ uses a modified subset partitioning (see Fig. 2(a)) which result in a small performance penalty at rate above 2 bpp. In our scheme, TCQ is only applied to low frequency coefficients, so the rate is always higher than 2 bpp, and it is actually syndrome coded TCQ here, so we use normal subset partition as shown in Fig. 2(b). As Viterbi algorithm is used in TCQ quantizer, the complexity increases rapidly along with the increase of trellis states. In order to minimize the complexity increase caused by TCQ, we use the simplest 4-state trellis in our scheme, as shown in Fig. 3.

In order to not exceed the correcting ability, a coarsely quantized version (base quantization) of the coefficients is also needed as well as the refinement bits to achieve the target quality. At first, we studied multi-stage trellis coded quantization (MSTCQ) [11], and successively refinable trellis coded quantization (SRTCQ) [12]. The performance of SRTCQ is good, but its intense complexity makes it not suitable for our scheme. We need a method that the coarsely quantized version could be attained easily, and could be easily refined. Finally we realized that the coarsely quantized version needs not to be TCQ output, it would be enough if only the refined version is TCQ output. Analysis indicate that the difference between the output of our TCQ and the output of a uniform scalar quantizer must be in {-1, 0, 1}, then if the TCQ output is scalar quantized, the result will be a good approximation of the result of uniform scalar quantization. So we first apply TCQ for the target rate, and then the outputs of TCQ are further quantized using just right shift operation, the result is just the coarsely quantized version, and the bits shifted out are just the refinement bits.

Then the space of the base quantized codewords is partitioned using a Euclidean space trellis channel code. Here we use a 256-state rate 1/2 trellis code from [6]. The syndrome (coset index) is generated and transmitted at rate 1bit/sample. This can be done through a simple convolution operation. A 16-bit CRC check of the 60 (15x4) quantized coefficients is also transmitted to the decoder to help decoding.

2.2 Decoder

Using the previously decoded key frame, the decoder first performs motion search to generate candidate predictor of the current block – the side information. Then, the side information, mode, syndrome bits, and the refinement bits are sent to the syndrome decoder. Viterbi algorithm is used to find the sequence in the set indexed by the syndrome. Here refinement bits are also used to help syndrome decoding, while they are not used in [1]. And then the output of the syndrome decoder, that is the base quantized codeword, is used to generate the 16-bit CRC and compared with the CRC transmitted by the encoder. If the CRC matches, this block is declaimed to be successfully decoded. If they do not match, motion search is used to get the next candidate predictor, and the above procedure is repeated.

Actually, when TCQ is used, there is a problem with the syndrome decoding algorithm. When two paths enter the same state of the syndrome trellis, their states of the TCQ trellis are most likely to be different, so if we want to get the best result, no paths should be deleted, and the trellis structure will turn into a tree structure whose size grows exponentially with the length of the sequence, and this is of course not realistic. This defect will be diminished if the states of the syndrome trellis are much more than the states of the TCQ trellis, which is just the case in our scheme, 256 states for syndrome versus 4 states for TCQ.

When syndrome decoding is finished, the recovered base quantized coefficients are refined to target step size, and then they are used along with the predictor to obtain the best reconstruction of the source. Here we use the same linear estimator as in [7]. Not only the syndrome coded low frequency coefficients are reconstructed using estimator, the intra coded high frequency coefficients are also reconstructed using estimator. The high frequency coefficients are intra coded because their correlation with the corresponding predictor is weak. But weak doesn't mean none, so using an estimator can also increase the reconstruction precision.

Finally, all the coefficients are inverse zigzag scanned to form a 2-D block, and IDCT is applied to get the pixel values.

3 Experimental Results

Fig. 4 and Fig. 5 show the rate-distortion performance for the first 15 frames of Foreman (QCIF), and Mother and Daughter (CIF) video sequences. For curve "tcq" and "sq", the first frame is in intra mode, the remaining 14 frames are coded using all modes. For each sequence, the quantization step of the first frame is also changed to make its quality to be the same as the whole sequence. The running time of encoding is about 1.5 times of the time when all frames are intra mode encoded, and it is much shorter than H.264 I frame encoding with RDO, so we can know that the encoding is

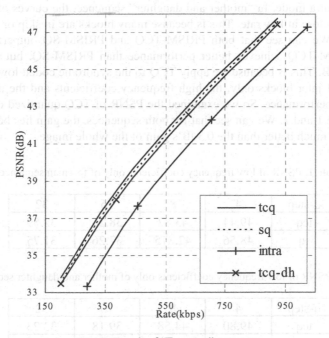

Fig. 5. Result of "Foreman" sequence

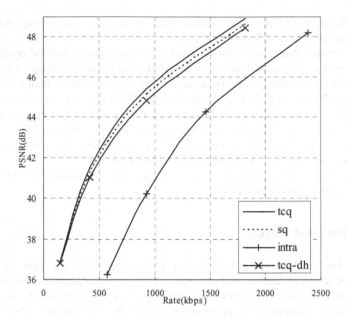

Fig. 6. Result of "Mother and Daughter" sequence

really simple. The curve labeled "intra" shows the result when all the blocks are forced to be intra mode. In "mother and daughter" sequence, the curves of "tcq" and "sq" are very close at low rate. This is because many blocks are in skip or intra mode in that case. We can see that both PRISM-TCQ and PRISM-SQ outperforms intra coding. PRISM-TCQ achieves better performance than PRISM-SQ, but the gain is less than 0.3dB. This is because we apply TCQ to the syndrome coded low frequency coefficients of inter blocks only, the high frequency coefficients and the intra blocks averaged the performance. So we examined the PSNR of TCQ quantized coefficients only, see table 1 and 2. We can see that for both sequences, the gain lies between 0.8-1dB, which is much better than the 0.3dB's gain of the whole image.

Table 1. PSNR of low frequency coefficients only of foreman sequence

q-step	4	8	16	32
tcq	49.44	43.82	38.25	32.59
sq	48.56	42.875	37.26	31.75

Table 2. PSNR of low frequency coefficients only of mother and daughter sequence

q-step	4	8	16	32
tcq	49.80	44.58	39.18	33.23
sq	48.76	43.66	38.22	32.65

The curve labeled "tcq-dh" shows the result when high coefficients are reconstructed without side information, the PSNR of high coefficients drops about 0.2-1.4 dB, and results in about 0.1-0.6dB drop of the whole image. We also observed that if refinement bits are not used to help syndrome decoding, much more error blocks appear.

4 Conclusions and Future Work

In this paper, we proposed a distributed video coding scheme where the powerful TCQ is used, and its refinement problem is solved. This improved the quality of TCQ quantized codewords about 0.9dB. Since TCQ is applied to low frequency coefficients in inter blocks only, and it's used in the simplest form, the gain of the whole image is not much. We also proposed the idea of using side information to reconstruct intra coded coefficients in inter blocks, experimental results show that this can greatly improve the performance especially for large quantization step situation.

It is our future work to apply TCQ to the other high coefficients and the intra blocks to fully utilize its power.

Acknowledgment

This work is supported by NSFC under contract No. 60572067, Open Fund of MOE-Microsoft Key Laboratory of Multimedia Computing and Communication under contract No. 05071803.

References

1. R. Puri and K. Ramchandran, "PRISM: A new robust video coding architecture based on distributed compression principles," *40th Allerton Conference on Communication, Control and Computing*, October, Allerton, IL, 2002.
2. A. Aaron and B. Girod, "Wyner-Ziv Video Coding with Low Encoder Complexity," *Proc. International Picture Coding Symposium, PCS'04,* San Francisco, CA, December 2004.
3. D. Slepian and J. K. Wolf, "Noiseless coding of correlated information sources," *IEEE Transaction on Information Theory*, vol. 19, pp. 471–490, July 1973.
4. A. D. Wyner and J. Ziv, "The rate-distortion function for source coding with side information at the decoder," *IEEE Trans. Inform. Theory*, vol. IT-22, pp. 1–10, Jan. 1976.
5. M. W. Marcellin and T. R. Fischer, "Trellis Coded Quantization of Memoryless and Gauss-Markov Sources," *IEEE Trans. Commun.*, vol. 38, pp. 82–93, Jan. 1990.
6. G. Ungerboeck, "Channel coding with multilevel/phase signals" *IEEE Trans. Inform. Theory*, vol. IT-28, pp. 55–67, Jan. 1982.
7. S. S. Pradhan and K. Ramchandran, "Distributed source coding using syndromes (DISCUS): design and construction," *Proceedings of the Data Compression Conference (DCC)*, March, Snowbird, UT, 1999.
8. Y. Yang, S. Cheng, Z. Xiong, and W. Zhao, "Wyner-Ziv coding based on TCQ and LDPC codes" *Proc. Of 37th Asilomar Conf. on Signals, Systems, and Computers*, Pacific Grove, CA, Nov. 2003.

9. M. W. Marcellin, "On entropy-constrained trellis coded quantization," *IEEE Trans. Commun.*, vol. 42, pp. 14–16, Jan. 1994.
10. J. H. Kasner, M.W. Marcellin and B.R. Hunt, "Universal trellis coded quantization" *IEEE Trans. Image Processing*, vol. 8, no. 12, pp. 1677–1687, Dec. 1999.
11. H. A. Aksu and M. Salehi, "Multi-stage trellis coded quantization (MSTCQ)," *Proc. Conf. Information Sciences and Systems* Baltimore, MD, Mar. 1995.
12. H. Jafarkhani and V. Tarokh, "Design of Successively Refinable Trellis-Coded Quantizers" *IEEE Trans. Inform. Theory*, vol. 45, no. 5, pp. 1490–1497, Jul. 1999.

An Efficient VLSI Architecture for Full-Search Variable Block Size Motion Estimation in H.264/AVC

Seung-Man Pyen, Kyeong-Yuk Min, and Jong-Wha Chong

Dept. of Electronic Engineering, Hanyang University, Seoul, Korea
himani815@hotmail.com

Abstract. In this paper, an efficient VLSI architecture of full-search variable block size motion estimation (VBSME) suitable for high quality video is proposed. Memory bandwidth in high-quality video is a mainly responsible for throughput limitations and power consumption in VBSME. The proposed architecture is designed for reducing the memory bandwidth by adopting "meander"-like scan for a high overlapped data of the search area and using on-chip memory to reuse the overlapped data. We can reuse the previous candidate block of 98% for the current one and save memory access cycles about 19% in a search range of [-32, +31]. The architecture has been prototyped in Verilog HDL and synthesized by Synopsys Design Compiler with Samsung 0.18um standard cell library. Under a clock frequency of 67MHz, The simulation result shows that the architecture can achieve the real-time processing of 720x576 picture size at 30fps with the search range of [-32~+31].

Keywords: block matching algorithm, motion estimation, VLSI, VBSME, H.264/AVC.

1 Introduction

A video sequence usually contains a significant amount of temporal redundancy. The block matching algorithm (BMA) based on the motion estimation and compensation is widely used in many video coding standards such as H.26x, MPEG-1, -2, and -4 to remove temporal redundancy. The fixed block size - block matching algorithm (FBS-BMA) is to divide the current frame into several macroblocks, and to search for a best matched block within a search range in a reference frame. In case of FBS-BMA, if a macroblock consists of two objects moving into different directions, the coding performance of the macroblock is worse than that of two objects moving into one direction. To compensate for the demerits of FBS-BMA, variable block size - block matching algorithm (VBS-BMA) is adopted in the advanced video coding standards.

In the H.264/advanced video coding (AVC), VBS-BMA consists in partitioning a macroblock into 7 kinds of blocks including 4x4, 4x8, 8x4, 8x8, 8x16, 16x8 and 16x16 as it is shown in Fig. 1.

In this way, the coding performance is improved, because BMA performs the function of making a macroblock segmented into 7 different sizes. Although VBS-BMA achieves higher coding performance than that of FBS-BMA, it requires a high

T.-J. Cham et al. (Eds.): MMM 2007, LNCS 4352, Part II, pp. 41–50, 2007.

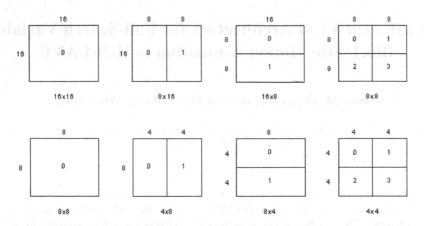

Fig. 1. The various block sizes in H.264/AVC

computation effort since 41 motion vectors of 7 different sizes should be computed for each macroblock. Therefore, many efficient hardware architectures such as systolic array [8], 1-D processing element (PE) array [6] and 2-D PE array [4] [7] [10] have been proposed for implementing VBS-BMA. The 1-D PE array is a simple structure, as it is easier to control and less gates than a 2-D PE array, but it is normal to search the sum of absolute difference (SAD) against only one row or a column of the macroblock at a time. On the other hand, the 2-D PE array is a complex structure as it is more difficult to control and has more gates than a 1-D PE array is and has, but it should compute the motion vector of a search point at a time. So 2-D array is suitable structure for high quality video. In the high-quality video with large frame size and search range, the memory bandwidth is a major bottleneck in the motion estimation architecture. To reduce memory bandwidth, the motion estimation architecture has to access each pixel just once and reuse the overlapped data. The architecture is designed for reducing the memory bandwidth by adopting "meander"-like scan in order to access to each pixel just once and by using on-chip memory to reuse the overlapped data. The proposed architecture can perform full-search VBS-BMA and it can achieve all 41 motion vectors of the macroblock.

The rest of this paper is organized as follows:

In section II, the proposed architecture is described in detail. The experimental result and the conclusion are given in section III and IV, respectively.

2   The Proposed Architecture

Fig. 2 shows the block diagram of the proposed architecture, which consists of an on-chip memory, a ME control unit, a 16x16 PE array, a SAD adder-tree and a comparator unit.

To reuse the overlapped data, the search area static random access memory (SRAM) is the SRAM to store the pixel data of the search area and the current block SRAM is the SRAM to store the pixel data of the current macroblock. The ME control unit generates

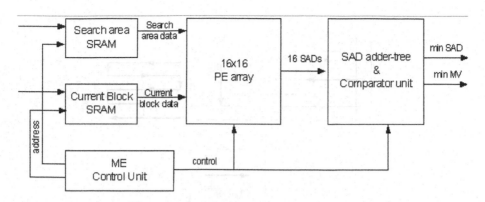

Fig. 2. Schematic overview of the proposed architecture

the address signals of the search area SRAM and the current macroblock SRAM, and generates the control signals to control other blocks. The 16x16 PE array computes sixteen 4x4 SADs of the 16x16 candidate block. The adder-tree is employed to compute the SADs of all the 41 subblocks from the SADs of the 4x4 subblocks. Comparator unit should find the best matched MV with the minimum SAD.

2.1 The Data Scheduling for Data-Reuse

In the full-search BMA, each current macroblock should be compared with all the candidate blocks in search area in order to find the best matched macroblock. So the full-search BMA require a high memory bandwidth. In order to reduce memory bandwidth, we adopted the "meander"-like scan (Fig.3) of the search area that obtains the high overlapped data of the search area. If the search point moves into the horizontal direction, the candidate blocks are many overlapped again and again in comparison with the previous candidate block. 16x1 8bit pixels data of the present candidate block can be only changed in comparison with the previous candidate block. In the case of Raster order scan, 16x16 pixels data of the candidate block can be changed when the search point is changed to the next line. As 16x16 pixels data of the candidate block is changed when the search point is changed to the next line, 16x16 PE array needs more 15 cycles than "meander"-like scan in order to load the pixel data of the candidate block. In order to reduce 15 cycles each of PE needs search data buffer to store the pixel data of the candidate block [5]. The proposed architecture adopted a "meander"-like scan of the search area that gives an actual support to simple control and efficient memory size.

The "meander"-like scan format has the three directions of the data-flows. In the odd line of the search area, the direction of the data-flow moves into the right. In the even line of the search area, the direction of the data-flow moves into the left. When the computations for the rows of search area are finished, the direction of the data-flow moves into the bottom.

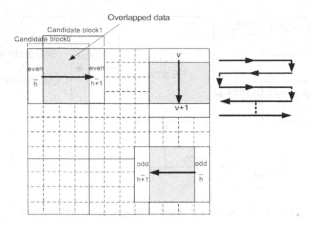

Fig. 3. The "meander"-like scan of the search area

2.2 The Whole Architecture

The proposed architecture is illustrated in Fig.4.

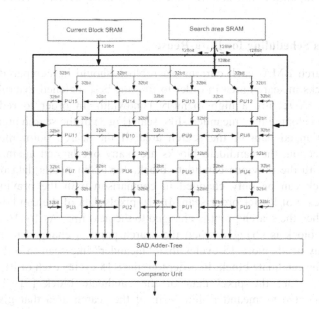

Fig. 4. The whole architecture

The architecture is composed of 16 processing units (PU), a SAD adder-tree and a comparator unit. Two SRAM modules are used to store the search area and the current macroblock. Each SRAM module is composed of 16 SRAMs in order to manipulate address generation. The 16x16 PE array computes sixteen 4x4 SADs of the 16x16 candidate block. It is composed of 16 PUs. Each PU is used to compute one of 4x4 SADs of a candidate macroblock. The sixteen 4x4 SADs of the candidate block can be computed cycle by cycle after the placement of the pixel data of the current macroblock and the pixel data of the candidate block. In the SAD adder-tree, the SADs of sixteen 4x4 subblocks are used to obtain the SADs of the 41 subblocks of 7 different sizes. The 41 motion vectors are obtained by the comparator unit that composed of the 41 comparing elements. The PUs are connected to each neighboring PU and are able to shift data to other PU on the left, on the right or on the bottom side.

2.3 The Process Unit (PU) Architecture

Fig.5 shows the architecture of the PU.

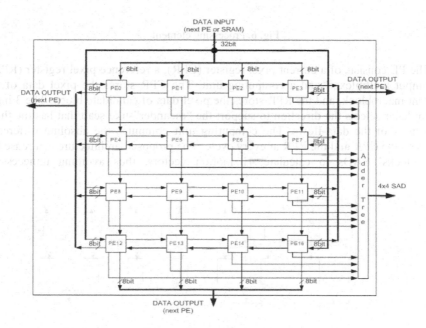

Fig. 5. Processing unit

The PU consists of a 4x4 PE array and adder-tree. The data width of input port and output port is 32bit. The PEs are connected to each neighboring PE and are able to shift data to the neighboring PEs. The PE0, PE4, PE8 and PE12 receive the reference pixels from the SRAM module or left PU, and other PE receives the reference pixels from left PEs when the data-flow moves into the right. The PE3, PE7, PE11 and PE15 receive the reference pixels from right PU when the data-flow moves into the left, and the PE0, PE1, PE2 and PE3 receive the reference pixels from the upper PU when the data-flow moves into the bottom. The SAD of the 4x4 block, which are the outputs of a 4x4 PE array, can be added to get 16 SADs by using the 5 adder-trees.

2.4 The PE Architecture

Fig.6 shows the architecture of the PE.

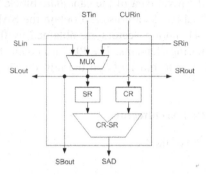

Fig. 6. Processing element

The PE consists of a current pixel register (CPR), a reference pixel register (RPR), a 3 input multiplexer, and a computing unit. The CPR stores the pixel data of the current macroblock, and the RPR stores the pixel data of candidate block. The 3 input multiplexer selects the direction to support the "meander"-like scan that has the three directions of the data-flows. The computing unit computes the absolute difference between the CPR and the RPR at every cycle. The proposed architecture can reuse the 4x4 blocks' SADs to calculate 41 motion vectors, thus avoiding unnecessary

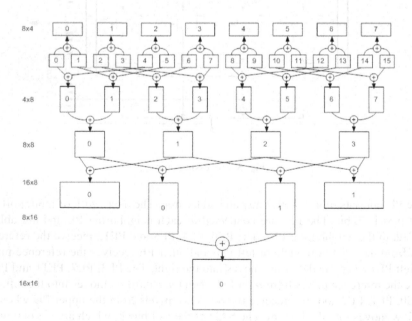

Fig. 7. The SAD adder-tree

computations. In the SAD adder-tree (Fig.7), the SADs of sixteen 4x4 subblocks are used to obtain the SADs of all the 41 subblocks of 7 different sizes.

The comparator unit that composed of 41 comparing elements (Fig.8) finds the minimum distortions as well as the corresponding motion vectors.

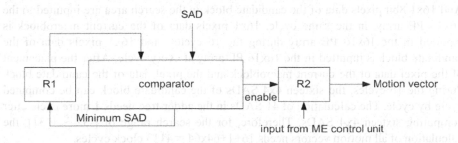

Fig. 8. The Comparing element

Table 1. Data-flow Schdules

CLK	1st column		--		--	15th column		--		16th column		--	
--	PE0	PE1	--	PE15	--	PE16	PE17	--	PE31	PE240	PE241	--	PE255
0					--				--	C(0,0) R(-32,-32)	C(0,1) R(-32,-31)	--	C(0,15) R(-32,-17)
1					--	C(0,0) R(-32,-32)	C(0,1) R(-32,-31)	--	C(0,15) R(-32,-17)	C(1,0) R(-31,-32)	C(1,1) R(-31,-31)	--	C(1,15) R(-31,-17)
63	C(0,0) R(16,-32)	C(0,1) R(16,-31)	--	C(0,15) R(16,-17)		C(14,0) R(30,-32)	C(14,1) R(30,-31)	--	C(14,15) R(30,-17)	C(15,0) R(31,-32)	C(15,1) R(31,-31)	--	C(15,15) R(31,-17)
64	C(0,0) R(16,-31)	C(0,1) R(16,-30)	--	C(0,15) R(16,-16)		C(14,0) R(30,-31)	C(14,1) R(30,-30)	--	C(14,15) R(30,-16)	C(15,0) R(31,-31)	C(15,1) R(31,-30)	--	C(15,15) R(31,-16)
65	C(0,0) R(15,-31)	C(0,1) R(15,-30)	--	C(0,15) R(15,-16)	--	C(14,0) R(29,-31)	C(14,1) R(29,-30)	--	C(14,15) R(29,-16)	C(15,0) R(30,-31)	C(15,1) R(30,-30)	--	C(15,15) R(30,-16)
--	--	--	--	--		--	--	--	--	--	--	--	--
127	C(0,0) R(-32,-31)	C(0,1) R(-32,-30)	--	C(0,15) R(-32,-16)	--	C(14,0) R(-18,-31)	C(14,1) R(-18,-30)	--	C(14,15) R(-18,-16)	C(15,0) R(-17,-31)	C(15,1) R(-17,-30)	--	C(15,15) R(-17,-16)
128	C(0,0) R(-32,-30)	C(0,1) R(-32,-29)	--	C(0,15) R(-32,-15)	--	C(14,0) R(-18,-30)	C(14,1) R(-18,-29)	--	C(14,15) R(-18,-15)	C(15,0) R(-17,-30)	C(15,1) R(-17,-29)	--	C(15,15) R(-17,-15)
129	C(0,0) R(-31,-30)	C(0,1) R(-31,-29)	--	C(0,15) R(-31,-15)		C(14,0) R(-17,-30)	C(14,1) R(-17,-29)	--	C(14,15) R(-17,-15)	C(15,0) R(-16,-30)	C(15,1) R(-16,-29)	--	C(15,15) R(-16,-15)
--	--	--	--	--		--	--	--	--	--	--	--	--
4111	C(0,0) R(16,16)	C(0,1) R(16,17)	--	C(0,15) R(16,31)	--	C(1,0) R(30,16)	C(1,1) R(30,17)	--	C(1,15) R(30,31)	C(15,0) R(31,16)	C(15,1) R(31,17)	--	C(15,15) R(31,31)

Comparing element consists of a comparator and two registers. R1 register stores the minimum SAD for comparison and R2 register stores the motion vector from the ME control unit when the current SAD is less than the SAD of R1 register.

Table.1 shows the data sequence in the PE array for the current macroblock and the search area. C(x, y) is the pixel data in the current macroblock and R(x, y) is the pixel data in the search area.

At the beginning of VBS-BMA, 16x1 8bit pixels data of the current macroblock in the current block SRAM are inputted to the 16x16 PE array during the first 16 cycles. And 16x1 8bit pixels data of the candidate block in the search area are inputted to the 16x16 PE array, in the same cycle. 16x1 pixels data of the current macroblock is inputted in the 16x16 PE array during the 16 cycles, and 16x1 pixels data of the candidate block is inputted in the 16x16 PE array at every cycle. After the placement of the pixel data of the current macroblock and the pixel data of the candidate block during the 16 cycles, the sixteen 4x4 SADs of the candidate block can be computed cycle by cycle. The calculation of 41 SADs in the adder-tree needs 1 more cycle after computing sixteen 4x4 SADs. Therefore, for the search range of [-32 ~ + 31], the calculation of all motion vectors needs 16+1+64x64 = 4113 clock cycles.

3 The Simulation and Synthesis Result

The architecture has been prototyped in Verilog HDL, simulated by ModelSim and synthesized by Synopsys Design Compiler with Samsung 0.18um standard cell library. The total gate count is about 109k. The gate of 16x16 PE array requires 79.1k and the rest gates are spent on the comparator unit to find the minimum SAD, the adder-tree to obtain the SAD of all the 41 subblocks, and the control unit. For the search range of [-32~ +31], the total 58kb on-chip memory is required to store the search area and the current macroblock. Table.2 shows the performance of the proposed architecture.

Table 2. The Performance of the proposed architecture

Algorithm	Full Search
Number of PE	256
Searching range	32x32, 64x64
Gate count	109k
On-chip memory	58kbits
Process	Samsung 0.18um standard cell library
Block size	4x4, 4x8, 8x4, 8x8, 8x16, 16x8, 16x16

Table.3 shows the comparison between the proposed architecture and other full-search VBSME architectures.

From the table.3 it can be observed that the architecture requires less gate count and on-chip memory.

Table 3. Comparison of four VLSI architecture for VBSME

	[6]	[7]	[5]	proposed
Number of PE	16	16x16	16x16	16x16
Searching range	32x32 16x16	64x64	64x64, 32x32	64x64 32x32
Gate count	108k	-	154k	109k
On-chip memory	-	96k bits	60k bits	58kbits
Process	0.13um	0.5um	0.28um	0.18um
Block size	7 kind of block sizes	16x16, 8x8, 4x4	7 kind of block sizes	7 kind of block sizes

4 Conclusion

We proposed an efficient VLSI architecture of VBSME suitable for high quality video compression. To compute the SADs of all the 41 subblocks from sixteen 4x4 subblocks and the minimum SADs against the 7 different blocks, the architecture consists of a 16x16PE array, an adder tree and comparator unit. The architecture can achieve high speed operation by combining simple processing element architecture with regular interconnection, and can reduce the memory bandwidth by adopting the "meander"-like scan for a high overlapped data of the search area and using on-chip memory to reuse the overlapped data. Compared with the raster-order scan of the search area, the "meander"-like scan can save memory access cycles about 19% in a search range of [-32, +31]. The architecture allows the real-time processing of 720x576 picture size at 30fps with a search range of [-32~+31], under a frequency of 67MHz.

References

1. De Vos, L., Schobinger, M.: VLSI Architecture for a Flexible Block Matching Processor, Vol. 5. NO. 5. IEEE Transactions on Circuits and Systems (1995)
2. Jen-Chieh, Tuan., Tian-Sheuan, Chang., Chein-Wei, Jen.: On the Data Reuse and Memory Bandwidth Analysis for Full-Search Block-Matching VLSI Architecture, Vol. 12. IEEE Transactions on Circuits and Systems for Video Technology (2002)
3. Komarek, T., Pirsch, P.: Array Architectures for Block Matching Algorithms, Vol. 36. IEEE Transactions on Circuits and Systems (1989)
4. Yu-Wen, Huang., Tu-Chih, Wang., Bing-Yu, Hsieh., Liang-Gee, Chen.: Hardware Architecture Design for Variable Block Size Motion Estimation in MPEG-4 AVC/JVT/ITU-T H.264, Vol. 2. Proc. IEEE International Symposium on Circuits and Systems (2003)
5. Min-ho, Kim., In-gu, Hwang., Soo-Ik, Chae.: A Fast VLSI Architecture for Full-Search Variable Block Size Motion Estimation in MPEG-4 AVC/H.264, Vol. 1. Asia and South Pacific (2005)

6. Yap, S.Y., McCanny, J.V.: A VLSI Architecture for Advanced Video Coding Motion Estimation, Proc. IEEE International Conference on Application-Specific Systems, Architectures, and Processors (2003)
7. Kuhn, P.M., Weisgerber, A., Poppenwimmer, R., Stechele, W.: A Flexible VLSI Architecture for Variable Block Size Segment Matching with Luminance Correction, IEEE International conference on Application-Specific Systems, Architectures, and Processors (1997)
8. Kittitornkun, S., Yu Hen Hu.: Frame-Level Pipelined Motion Estimation Array Processor, Vol. 11. IEEE Transactions on Circuits and Systems for Video Technology (2001)
9. De Vos, L., Stegherr, M.: Parameterizable VLSI Architectures for the Full-Search Block-Matching Algorithm, Vol. 36. IEEE Transactions on Circuits and Systems (1989)
10. Rahman, C.A., Badawy, W.: A Quarter Pel Full Search Block Motion Estimation Architecture for H.264/AVC, IEEE International Conference on Multimedia and Expo (2005)

A Secure and Robust Wavelet-Based Hashing Scheme for Image Authentication

Fawad Ahmed and M.Y. Siyal

School of Electrical and Electronic Engineering, Nanyang Technological University,
50 Nanyang Avenue, 639798, Singapore
{pka534086, eyakoob}@ntu.edu.sg

Abstract. The purpose of an image hash is to provide a compact representation of the whole image. Designing a good image hash function requires careful consideration of many issues such as robustness, security and tamper detection with precise localization. In this paper, we present a novel hashing scheme that addresses these issues in a unified framework. We analyze the security issues in image hashing and present new ideas to counter some of the attacks that we shall describe in this paper. Our proposed scheme is resilient to allow non-malicious manipulations like JPEG compression, high pass filtering and is sensitive enough to detect tampering with precise localization. Several experimental results are presented to demonstrate the effectiveness of the proposed scheme.

Keywords: Image hashing, image authentication, security, discrete wavelet transform.

1 Introduction

The widespread use of multimedia technology has made it relatively easy to tamper digital images. This poses a potential security problem, especially when digital images are transmitted over the Internet. A simple way to authenticate digital images is to calculate the image hash using standard cryptographic hash functions like MD5 or SHA1 and form a digital signature using some public key encryption algorithms like the RSA [1]. However, the direct use of cryptographic hash functions in multimedia applications, like image authentication is hampered by the fact that a single bit change in the image would produce a completely different hash. In practice, it is common that a digital image may undergo some content preserving manipulations such as JPEG compression. These operations, although may not change the visual appearance of the image, however, the cryptographic hash value will be completely different. From this discussion, we note that multimedia image authentication requires techniques which should be some what resilient to content preserving manipulations like JPEG compression, while at the same time be fragile enough to detect malicious manipulations. Several image authentication schemes have been proposed in recent years. These schemes can be broadly classified into two types: watermark-based and hash-based. Watermarking techniques embed an imperceptible signal into a cover work to form a watermarked image. At the

T.-J. Cham et al. (Eds.): MMM 2007, LNCS 4352, Part II, pp. 51 – 62, 2007.

receiver's end, the extracted watermark from the watermarked image is used for authenticating purpose [2]. In contrast to watermark-based techniques, hash-based (or digital signature-based) techniques extract a set of features from the image to form a compact representation that can be used for authentication [3]. The features used for generating the image hash should be *key-dependent* so that it becomes extremely difficult for an attacker to create a forgery. In addition, it should be extremely difficult to derive the secret key if the image hash is exposed.

As compared to cryptographic hash functions [1], the field of image hashing is passing through an evolution stage. Since cryptographic hash functions are matured and well studied for more than a decade, it is very natural to design image hash functions that besides meeting the requirements of multimedia applications follow the security features of a cryptographic hash function. It should be noted that the objective of a cryptographic hash function and an image hash function are not exactly the same. For example, there is no robustness or tamper localization requirement in case of a cryptographic hash function. In recent years, a number of researchers have proposed many interesting and novel ideas to formulate image hash functions. Lu and Liao [4] have proposed an image authentication scheme that uses the parent-child pairs located at the multiple scales in the wavelet domain to obtain an image hash. The signature obtained by this scheme however does not depend on any secret key and can be extracted/verified by anyone who has the knowledge of the algorithm. Lu [5] has shown that the scheme proposed in [4] is secure against counterfeit attacks. However, it not clear whether the scheme proposed in [4] is secure against the Defeat-the-Scheme Attack (DSA) shown in this paper. Lin and Chang [6] have proposed an image authentication technique that relies on the invariant relationship between any two selected DCT coefficients which are at the same position of two different 8 x 8 image blocks. They use secret keys to select the blocks and the DCT coefficients. Similarly, Sun and Chang [7] have proposed a robust and secure scheme for authenticating JPEG images. Their scheme relies on features extracted in the DCT domain.

In this paper, we first investigate some of the existing image hashing schemes proposed in the literature and show a few weaknesses that we have discovered. In most of the previous techniques, a secret key is used to select a subset of the image content for generating the hash. In this paper we adopt a different approach. We first modulate the content of the image using a secret key and then extract the hash in the modulated domain. We employ block-based approach for generating the image hash. Although block-based approaches are generally considered more vulnerable to several attacks [8], [9], [10], we shall show that with our proposed technique, it becomes difficult to launch these attacks. Specifically, we are more focused in this paper on the security aspect of the hashing scheme.

In Section 2, we highlight some problems associated with feature extraction and security of block-based hashing schemes for image authentication. In Section 3, we present a new wavelet-based hashing scheme for image authentication which addresses the problems highlighted in Sections 1 and 2. The security aspect of the proposed scheme is presented in Section 4. In Section 5, we present some experimental results to demonstrate the effectiveness of our proposed scheme. Section 6 concludes the paper with some future work.

2 Problems with Block-Based Image Hashing Schemes

In this Section, we present some problems that we have found in block-based schemes that uses DCT or Wavelet domain features to generate the image hash. To keep things simple, we focus on DCT domain features, however, the same argument also applies on the features extracted in the wavelet domain. The first problem is regarding the reliable extraction of DCT coefficients in an image block for hash generation. We will show in Section 2.1 that sometimes it is difficult to extract reliable DCT features in an image block. The second problem that we shall discuss is about the security of block-based DCT schemes against an attack which we call as *Defeat-the-Scheme Attack* (DSA). In DSA, the purpose of the attacker is to manipulate an image block in such a way that visually it gets distorted; however, the block may still be authenticated. Hence the purpose of the attacker is not to create a counterfeit, but to defeat the authentication scheme. The third problem that we would be discussing is how an attacker might take the advantage of weaknesses in the feature extraction stage to launch the well known collage attack [8], [9]. The collage attack is mostly described for watermarking techniques; hence it would be interesting to see the implications of this attack on image hashing schemes.

2.1 Weaknesses in the Feature Extraction Stage

The schemes proposed by Lin and Chang [6] and Sun and Chang [7] derive content-based features by dividing an image into non-overlapping blocks of size 8 x 8 pixels and then taking the DCT of each block. For example in [6], the feature vector is formed by selecting DCT coefficients from a vector indexed in a zigzag order. Likewise in [7], the DC coefficient and three AC coefficients are selected from the zigzag scan of the 8 x 8 DCT block. The selection of the AC coefficients is based on a random sequence that is kept secret. We argue that in areas of an image that has smooth texture; very few non-zero DCT AC coefficients are available for feature extraction. In some cases these features become zero after JPEG compression. Hence the scheme proposed in [6] and [7] or any other scheme that uses a similar approach may have problems in such cases. We now give an example to exemplify our point. Consider the Cameraman image shown in Fig. 1. The background area of this image has smooth texture. Table 1 shows the DCT coefficients for the 8 x 8 block marked in Fig. 1. It may be observed that besides the DC coefficient, there are only four non-zero AC coefficients. Out of these AC coefficients, two are -1 which are insignificant. Table 2 shows DCT coefficients of the same block when the image shown in Fig. 1 is

Fig. 1. Cameraman image

Table 1. DCT coefficients of the 8 x 8 block of Cameraman image shown in Fig. 1

1456	0	0	0	0	0	0	0
-5	0	0	0	0	0	0	0
6	0	0	0	0	0	0	0
-1	0	0	0	0	0	0	0
0	0	0	0	0	0	0	0
0	0	0	0	0	0	0	0
0	0	0	0	0	0	0	0
-1	0	0	0	0	0	0	0

Table 2. DCT coefficients of the 8 x 8 block of Cameraman image shown in Fig. 1 with JPEG quality factor of 50

1452	0	0	0	0	0	0	0
0	0	0	0	0	0	0	0
9	0	0	0	0	0	0	0
0	0	0	0	0	0	0	0
0	0	0	0	0	0	0	0
0	0	0	0	0	0	0	0
1	0	0	0	0	0	0	0
0	0	0	0	0	0	0	0

JPEG compressed with a quality factor of 50. We observe that only one non-zero AC coefficient is now left with its sign preserved. Hence in such a situation, it is difficult to realize the scheme proposed in [6] and [7] as there are hardly any non-zero DCT AC coefficients available to generate the feature vector. This type of situation is quite common in real life images. In Section 3 we show a method to counter such a problem.

2.2 Defeat-the-Scheme-Attack

The purpose of this attack is not to create a counterfeit image, but to defeat the authentication process. Using this attack, an attacker can modify all or part of an image and the modified image will still be correctly authenticated. Such type of attack is also mentioned by Radhakrishnan and Memon in [10]. For example, in case of block-based DCT hashing scheme, an attacker can manipulate an image block in such a way that the values of the low and middle frequency DCT coefficients of the image block in the zigzag order are very slightly perturbed; however, the visual appearance of the image block is changed. To illustrate this attack, we modified the DCT block shown in Table 1 by changing the coefficient at the location (5, 6) from 0 to -250. We then took inverse DCT of the tampered DCT block. The result of the inverse DCT is

Table 3. DCT coefficients of the 8 x 8 image block shown in Fig. 3

1456	0	0	0	0	0	0	0
-5	0	0	0	0	0	1	0
6	0	0	0	0	0	0	0
-1	0	1	0	0	0	0	0
1	0	0	0	0	0	0	0
0	0	0	0	0	0	-250	0
0	0	-1	0	0	0	0	0
-1	0	0	0	0	0	0	0

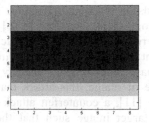 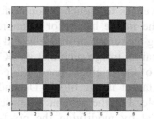

Fig. 2. 8 x 8 block of the Cameraman image marked in Fig. 1

Fig. 3. 8 x 8 block shown in Fig. 2 transformed after the DSA attack

shown in Fig. 3. What we observed was something quite interesting. Although the low and middle frequency DCT coefficients of the original and the tampered image blocks in the zigzag order remains the same as shown in Table 1 and Table 3 respectively. However, the spatial domain representations of these two blocks are completely different as illustrated in Fig. 2 and Fig. 3 respectively. In Fig. 2, we show the original image block while in Fig. 3 we show the image block after the DSA attack. Selecting DCT coefficients besides -250 to form the image hash will result in false acceptance since visually the two blocks are different. From this discussion we conclude that merely using a secret key to select a set of DCT coefficients is not sufficient to prevent an attacker from launching the attack described above. As a matter of fact, the attacker does not even need to know the secret key to launch this attack.

2.3 Counterfeit Attacks

In [8], Holliman and Memon proposed a counterfeit attack on certain block-based oblivious watermarking schemes. Through this attack, a forged image can be considered as authentic. Similarly Fridrich et al. [9] have proposed the well known collage attack which is a variation of the attack proposed in [8]. The collage attack makes the job of the attacker easier as it does not require the knowledge of the watermark logo. Unlike watermarking schemes, it will be interesting to see how counterfeit attacks can be performed in image hashing schemes. In case of image hashing, the DSA attack discussed in Section 2.2 is much easy to launch as compared to a counterfeit attack. In DSA attack, the objective of the attacker is to modify the whole or certain part of the image such that it gets authenticated no matter how the visual appearance of the image looks like. However, for a counterfeit or collage attack, the attacker has to modify the image blocks in such a way that not only the image gets authenticated, but the modified image should look visually similar to the attacker's target image. We believe that launching a counterfeit attack for block-based hashing scheme is difficult as compared to block-based watermarking schemes. The reason is because in watermarking schemes, each image block is watermarked with the same watermark logo and the secret key. So if an attacker can form a database of images watermarked with the same key and the watermark logo, he/she can pick the image blocks that resembles the most with the corresponding block of the target image. In case of image hashing, the scenario is a bit different. The complexity and effectiveness to launch a counterfeit attack depends on the type of features used to form the image hash. For example, if only DC coefficients are used in [6] or [7], creating a counterfeit image would then require altering the pixels value in each block of the target image such that its DCT DC coefficient becomes equal or close in values to that of the original image, while the modified image block remains visually similar to the target image block. Depending on the type of image, this attack may seem plausible. For the scheme proposed by Xie *et al.* [11], a counterfeit attack can be launched by modifying the pixels value of the target image such that the MSB obtained after taking the average of each 8 x 8 image block of the modified image is equal to that of the corresponding original image block. In addition, the modified image should be visually similar to the target image.

3 Proposed Scheme

In this Section, we propose a new wavelet-based image hashing scheme to address the problems that have been highlighted in Section 2. We form the image hash by using wavelet coefficients of the LL, LH and HL sub-bands. Our scheme uses a novel key-based intensity transformation that makes it extremely difficult to launch the attacks discussed in Section 2. In the following sub-sections, we explain the hash generation and image authentication processes.

3.1 Hash Generation

Following are the steps in the hash generation process:

1. The input image I of dimension N x N is partitioned into non-overlapping blocks, each of dimension P x P. This gives a total of N^2/P^2 blocks. We represent each block by B_i, where $i = 0,...,(N^2/P^2)$-1. Let $B_i(x, y)$ represent the gray value of a pixel at spatial location (x, y) in the block B_i. Let $K_0(w)$ be a secret key that has randomly placed unique integer entries, where $w = 0,...,P^2$-1. Let $C(\bullet)$ be a circular shift right function. From $K_0(w)$, we further obtain P^2-1 keys as follows:

$$K_i(w) = C(K_{i-1}(w)) \qquad i = 1,......,P^2 - 1. \tag{1}$$

2. Using P^2 different keys, a random intensity transformation is applied to each block by modulating each pixel of B_i with an integer from $K_i(w)$ to get intensity-transformed blocks, $\overline{B_i}$. If the number of blocks is greater than the number of keys, the key sequence is repeated. We shall call this transformation as Key-based Intensity (KI) transformation.

$$\overline{B_i}(x, y) = \big(B_i(x, y) + \alpha K_i(w)\big)\beta K_i(w), \quad 0 \le x, y \le P - 1, \; 0 \le w \le P^2 - 1. \tag{2}$$

3. By taking $\log_2(P)$ wavelet decomposition of each transformed block, scalar wavelet coefficients are obtained. Let the scalar wavelet coefficients of the sub-bands LL, LH and HL of the ith block be represented by $\omega_{iLL}, \omega_{iLH}$ and ω_{iHL} respectively. The hash of each block is calculated as follows:

$$Hx_i = \omega_{i_{LL}} + \omega_{i_{LH}}.$$

$$Hy_i = \omega_{i_{LL}} + \omega_{i_{HL}}.$$

(3)

4. Intermediate hash, $\overline{H}(I)$ is formed which is a set of vectors containing hashes of all the blocks of I.

$$\overline{H}(I) = \{(Hx_0, Hy_0), (Hx_1, Hy_1), \ldots, (Hx_Z, Hy_Z)\}, \ where \ Z = \frac{N^2}{P^2} - 1.$$

(4)

5. The final hash $H(I)$ is formed by permuting the entries of $\overline{H}(I)$ with another secret key, K_P. The reason for permuting the hash entries is to prevent an attacker from knowing the transformed hash values of each image block.

$$H(I) = permute_{Kp}\left(\overline{H}(I)\right).$$

(5)

6. The sender transmits the image I and the hash $H(I)$ to the receiver. The integrity of the hash can be protected by using a public key cryptosystem [1].

3.2 Image Authentication

Following are the steps in the image authentication process:

1. The received image $\hat{I}$ of dimension $N \times N$ pixels is processed through the same sequence as shown by Steps 1-4, Section 3.1 to get the hash, $\hat{H}(\hat{I})$.

$$\hat{H}(\hat{I}) = \{(\hat{H}x_0, \hat{H}y_0), (\hat{H}x_1, \hat{H}y_1), \ldots, (\hat{H}x_Z, \hat{H}y_Z)\}, \ where \ Z = \frac{N^2}{P^2} - 1.$$

(6)

2. Inverse permutation is applied to $H(I)$ to obtain the intermediate hash $\overline{H}(I)$

$$\overline{H}(I) = inverse\_permute_{Kp}\left(H(I)\right).$$

(7)

3. Define a difference vector between the calculated and the received hash:

$$Dx_i = \left|Hx_i - \hat{H}x_i\right|.$$

$$Dy_i = \left|Hy_i - \hat{H}y_i\right|.$$

(8)

4. The ith block of the received image $\hat{I}$ is considered as tampered if either $Dx_i > \tau$ or $Dy_i > \tau$. The image $\hat{I}$ shall be considered as unauthentic if any of the blocks is found to be tampered.

4 Security Analysis

In this Section, we shall show by a number of experimental results that after applying the transformation given by (2), it becomes extremely difficult to launch the attacks that we have discussed in Section 2. The first problem discussed in Section 2.1 was the extraction of reliable DCT features in image areas that have smooth textures. In Fig. 1 we have highlighted an 8 x 8 image block having a smooth texture whose DCT coefficients are displayed in Table 1. However, after applying the KI transformation given by (2), the situation is quite different. Figure 4 shows the Cameraman image after the KI transformation and Table 4 shows the DCT coefficients of the transformed image block at the same location that was marked in Fig. 1. It is worth noting that the transformation introduce a random noise like pattern throughout the image. As a matter of fact, the KI transformation changes the whole texture of the image. The interesting point to note is that this change in texture is a function of the image pixels and the secret key $K_i(w)$. Since for each image block, a shifted version of $K_0(w)$ is applied, therefore a different random pattern is used for modulating the pixels of each block. We next show that because of the KI transformation, the DSA attack becomes quite difficult.

Fig. 4. Cameraman image after applying the KI transformation

Table 4. DCT coefficients of the 8 x 8 image block marked in Fig. 1 after applying the KI transformation

25971	3966	143	-1853	2293	-746	-598	2241
307	-2254	372	-526	-2224	2905	2003	2715
2637	3873	-136	-283	-2793	-960	-100	3755
-4086	-3320	1682	-54	-3457	4506	151	-409
527	-849	-2550	-669	-5966	-2899	-74	-465
33645	672	2520	771	1558	-5420	1273	716
179	711	-1207	-2786	4249	1663	2967	-513
-1266	-2325	3932	2957	2721	158	1365	2412

Table 5. DCT coefficients of the 8 x 8 image block shown in Fig. 3 after applying the KI transformation

24174	-306	-910	2824	-2928	1469	120	-2479
-5823	840	1645	-474	1498	1856	-732	420
-3081	-5785	-1610	-3172	-2360	-1946	6062	-3034
-499	3700	-5687	-2203	1055	1900	-2902	1092
200	2868	1090	-2015	3820	2440	-1592	1837
-1381	2606	423	-63	-1064	2565	674	1404
148	-2911	1405	1274	-1671	-1698	-6020	290
1691	5235	-3747	-2792	2723	-351	2502	-1228

To illustrate this fact, we modified the Cameraman image by replacing the 8 x 8 block shown in Fig. 1 with the DSA attacked block shown in Fig. 3. Without KI transformation, the DCT coefficients of the DSA attacked block are displayed in Table 3. As discussed earlier, the low and middle frequency DCT coefficients of the original image block and the DSA attacked block are almost similar (see Table 1 and Table 3) despite the fact that both the blocks have different visual appearance. We then applied the KI transformation to this image. Table 5 shows the DCT coefficients of the 8 x 8 DSA attacked block. Looking at Table 5, we see that after the KI transformation, there is a huge difference between the DCT coefficients of the original 8 x 8 block (Table 4) and the DSA attacked block (Table 5). Hence, we conclude that the proposed KI transformation thwarts the DSA attack. In addition, it also helps to generate non-zero DCT AC coefficients for image blocks that otherwise have only few non-zero DCT AC coefficients because the corresponding blocks have smooth texture.

Though our above discussion is concerned with DCT coefficients, the same argument also applies for wavelet domain features as proposed in this paper. For example, Table 6 shows the LH and HL wavelet feature of the 8 x 8 image block shown in Fig. 1 after performing its first level wavelet decomposition. Due to smoothness in the image block, most of the wavelet coefficients are zero. Table 7 shows the LH and HL coefficients of the same block after applying the KI transformation. We can see that due to the KI transformation, we get all non-zero wavelet coefficients which can be used for generating the hash. In addition, since the KI transformation is a function of both the pixels and the secret key, therefore it is extremely difficult for an attacker to predict the wavelet coefficients of an arbitrary image block.

We next illustrate that the proposed KI transformation also makes it extremely difficult to launch a counterfeit attack. Table 8 shows the HL wavelet coefficients for the block shown in Fig. 1 and its preceding block. Both the blocks visually appear very much similar. As shown in Table 8, the wavelet coefficients of these two blocks are also quite similar. We then applied the KI transformation with the same key $K_o(w)$ to all the blocks. The purpose of using the same key is to suppress the effect of the change in the key for each block and observe how the multiplication of the pixels

Table 6. LH and HL wavelet coefficients of the 8 x 8 image block shown in Fig. 1

0	0	0	0
0	0	0	0
-1	-1	-1	-1
-1	-1	-1	-1

0	0	0	0
0	0	0	0
0	0	0	0
0	0	0	0

Table 7. LH and HL wavelet coefficients of the 8 x 8 image block shown in Fig. 1 after applying the KI transformation

-78	-376	1125	1079
-180	-364	-1635	997
-1279	-3868	1438	1233
1023	-4955	-438	2717

222	4409	642	3935
920	-578	3392	-5027
1698	-3021	-1000	638
-1592	1174	4532	-1889

Table 8. HL wavelet coefficients of the 8 x 8 image block shown in Fig. 1 and its preceding block

0	0	0	0
0	0	0	0
0	0	0	0
0	0	0	0

0	-0.5	-0.5	0
-0.5	-0.5	-0.5	-0.5
0	0	-0.5	0
0	0	-1	0

Table 9. HL wavelet coefficients of the 8 x 8 image block shown in Fig. 1 and its preceding block after applying the KI transformation

252	383	762	4565	5111	30	-2183	-682
760	-650	3897	-5825	-2609	521	1359	-1919
2033	-3459	-1173	703	-311	619	5107	-4153
2869	-1377	5127	-2226	-1823	-629	-6068	1713

values with the key produce changes in the wavelet coefficients. It can be seen in Table 9 that the HL wavelet coefficients obtained are quite different. This explains the fact that even for similar looking blocks; it is difficult to predict the values of wavelet coefficients. Counterfeit attacks in such a situation becomes extremely difficult because an attacker cannot predict the values of the wavelet coefficients of an image block after the KI transformation. Secondly, because the KI transformation involves both pixels values and a different key for each block, therefore the attacker can never be sure whether the original image blocks and the target image blocks will map to the same value, as shown by Table 8 and Table 9.

5 Experimental Results

In this Section, we present some further experimental results to demonstrate the robustness of our proposed scheme against JPEG compression, high pass filtering and its fragility to catch malicious tampering. In our experiments, we have used images of size 256 x 256 pixels and have divided them into non-overlapping blocks of size 16 x 16 pixels. This gives a total of 256 blocks. For each block, a random gray-level transformation is applied as given by (2). After performing experiments on a number of images, we have observed that the values of τ =280, α =2 and β =0.05 gives good results. The size of the hash is 1024 bytes. Figure 5 shows the Cameraman image with tampering indicated by the circles. Figure 6 shows the detection result. All the tampered areas were successfully detected. Figure 7 shows the detection result when the Cameraman image was JPEG compressed with a Quality Factor (QF) of 40. There was no tampering detected. Figure 8 shows the detection result when the Cameraman image was high pass filtered. Again no tampering was detected. From these results we observe that our proposed scheme is quite sensitive to detect malicious tampering and at the same time is resilient against JPEG compression and high pass filtering.

Fig. 5. Cameraman image with tampering indicated by the circles

Fig. 6. Detection result for Fig. 5

Fig. 7. Detection result (JPEG QF: 40. No tampering detected)

Fig. 8. Detection result (High pass filtering. No tampering detected)

6 Conclusion

In this paper, we have proposed a wavelet-based hashing scheme for image authentication that is resilient to allow JPEG compression, high pass filtering and is sensitive to catch malicious tampering with precise localization. We have shown that weaknesses in the feature extraction stage can be exploited to launch a number of attacks. To counter these attacks, we have proposed a new transformation method that uses a secret key to directly modulate the image pixels in the spatial domain. Our experimental results show that the proposed transformation besides enforcing security also makes the system quite sensitive to changes in the pixels. This helps to catch malicious manipulation with a good degree of accuracy as shown by the results presented in Section 5. A disadvantage of this transformation is that the system is not very highly robust against non-malicious manipulations. The robustness of the system can be increased by increasing the threshold; however this will make the system less sensitive against malicious manipulations. Our scheme is more suitable for applications that demands high security and sensitiveness against tampering with a moderate degree of resilience against non-malicious tampering like JPEG compression. We are currently working to explore new ideas that can allow more degree of resilience against non-malicious tampering with more powerful and comprehensive security mechanisms.

References

1. Schneier B.: Applied Cryptography. John Wiley & Sons Inc. USA (1996)
2. Wong P. W., Memon N.: Secret and Public Key Image Watermarking Schemes for Image Authentication and Ownership Verification. IEEE Trans. on Image Processing, Vol. 10, No. 10 (2001) 1593-1601
3. Fridrich J., Goljan M.: Robust Hash Functions for Digital Watermarking. Proc. Int. Conf. on Information Technology: Coding and Computing (2000) 178-183
4. Lu C. S., Liao H.-Y. M.: Structural Digital Signature for Image Authentication: An Incidental Distortion Resistant Scheme. IEEE Trans. on Multimedia, Vol. 5, No. 2 (2003) 161-173
5. Lu C. S.: On the Security of Structural Information Extraction/Embedding for Images. Proc. IEEE Int. Symposium on Circuits and Systems. Vancouver. Canada (2004)
6. Lin C.Y., Chang S.-F.: A Robust Image Authentication Method Distinguishing JPEG Compression from Malicious Manipulation. IEEE Trans. on Circuits and Systems for Video Technology, Vol. 11, No. 2 (2001) 153-168
7. Sun Q., Chang S.-F.: A Robust and Secure Media Signature Scheme for JPEG Images. Journal of VLSI Signal Processing, 41 (2005) 305-317
8. Holliman M., Memon N.: Counterfeiting Attacks on Oblivious Block-Wise Independent Invisible Watermarking Schemes. IEEE Trans. on Image Processing, Vol. 9, No. 3 (2000) 432-441
9. Fridrich J., Goljan M., Memon N.: Further Attacks on Yeung-Mintzer Fragile Watermarking Scheme. Security and Watermarking of Multimedia Contents II. In Wong P. W., Deip E. J. (eds.): Proc. of SPIE, Vol. 3971 (2000)
10. Radhakrishnan R., Memon N.: On the Security of the Digest Function in the SARI Image Authentication System. IEEE Trans. on Circuits and Systems for Video Technology, Vol. 12, No. 11 (2002) 1030-1033
11. Xie L., Arce G. R., Graverman R. F.: Approximate Message Authentication Codes. IEEE Trans. on Multimedia Vol 3, No. 2, (2001) 242-252

Automatic TV Logo Detection, Tracking and Removal in Broadcast Video

Jinqiao Wang[1], Qingshan Liu[1], Lingyu Duan[2], Hanqing Lu[1],
and Changsheng Xu[2]

[1] National Lab of Pattern Recognition,
Institute of Automation, Chinese Academy of Sciences, Beijing 100080, China
{jqwang, qsliu, luhq}@nlpr.ia.ac.cn
[2] Institute for Infocomm Research, 21 Heng Mui Keng Terrace, Singapore 119613
{lingyu, xucs}@i2r.a-star.edu.sg

Abstract. TV logo detection, tracking and removal play an important
role in the applications of claiming video content ownership, logo-based
broadcasting surveillance, commercial skipping, and program rebroadcasting with new logos. In this paper, we present a novel and robust
framework using tensor method for these three tasks. First, we use tensor based generalized gradient and the OTSU binarization algorithm to
logo detection, and propose a two level framework from coarse to fine
to tracking the TV logos. Finally, we extend the regularization PDEs by
incorporation of temporal information to inpaint the logo region. Due to
the introduction of the structure tensor, the generalized gradient based
method can detect the logo region by tracking the change rate of pixels in
spatio-temporal domain, and the region of logo removal is well filled in a
structure-preserving way. Since temporal correlation of multiple consecutive frames is considered, the proposed method can deal with opaque,
semi-transparent, and animated logos. The experiments and comparison
with previous methods are conducted on the part of TRECVID 2005
news corpus and several Chinese TV channels with challenging TV logos, and the experimental results are promising.

1 Introduction

TV stations often use a special logo (i.e., TV logo) to distinguish their broadcast video from others, so TV logo plays an important role in claiming video
content ownership. Besides this, TV logo detection, tracking and removal can
also be used to detect commercial video, monitor the TV signal status, and rebroadcast the programs with a new logo. Several works have been developed
for logo detection and removal. Meisinger et al. [1] used the difference image
between consecutive frames to extract the logo mask with an assumption that
the video content changes over time except the logo, and the frequency selective extrapolation technique was employed for logo in-painting. But such an
assumption implied that this method could only handle the opaque logo. Yan
et al. [2] utilized a learning approach (i.e., neural network) to classify candidate

T.-J. Cham et al. (Eds.): MMM 2007, LNCS 4352, Part II, pp. 63–72, 2007.

logo regions as True or False by using local color and texture features. Overlapping and inpainting methods were used to logo removal, separately. Similar to [1] difference images were used to determine the candidate logo regions. This learning-based approach relies on large amounts of manually labeled samples for training. Albiol *et al.* [3] used the time-averaged gradients of a series of successive images plus morphological operations to extract the coarse mask of a TV logo and only one frame (the last one) is selected from a shot to perform the gradients-based matching within the coarse logo mask. In [4], we proposed a robust logo tracking approach based on generalized gradient, but only the opaque and semi-transparent TV station logos are considered.

In this paper, a framework incorporating logo detection, logo tracking and logo removal using tensor method is proposed, and it can deal with opaque, semi-transparent, and animated TV logos. We first calculate the generalized gradients over a sequence of images to alleviate the noisy edges from the cluttered background and enhance the incomplete contour (i.e., remove partial occlusion from blending) by temporal accumulation. Then the OTSU algorithm [5] is used to locate and extract the mask of a logo from the generalized gradient image, for it is robust to low contrast, variable background intensity and noise. The template matching is utilized to logo detection and a two-level framework is used to logo tracking from coarse to fine. Finally, the regularization PDEs [6] are employed to fill the TV logo regions of video frames with a structure tensor to preserve the edge information and local geometric properties. The proposed algorithm for logo detection, logo tracking and logo removal is analyzed in detail and compared with previous methods.

2   TV Logo Detection and Tracking

Most previous work only focused on the logo detection in static images, which often failed for semi-transparent and animated logos. In this paper, the temporal context is incorporated to enhance logo template modeling and matching for tracking the existence or absence of TV logos in broadcast video. The generalized gradient [4] is referred to the temporal extension of traditional gradient detection from a single image to a sequence of images. Different from simply averaging the gradients of multiple frames over time [3], we employ the technique of tensor gradient of a multi-image [7]. Explicit formulas for the direction along which the rate of change is maximum, and for the maximum rate of change itself, over multiple images in a video, can be derived.

2.1   Generalized Gradient

We treat a video segment as a multi-valued image by modeling as an array of ordinary color image. The gradient calculation in a multi-valued image is as follows. Let $I(x_1, x_2) : R^2 \to R^m$ be a multi-valued image with components $I_i(x_1, x_2) : R^2 \to R, i = 1, 2, ..., m$. For a color image, there are R,G,B components, namely $(m = 3)$. Assuming a video segment consisting of n frames, each frame having 3 color components. Through integrating temporal information from the time axis, a video segment is expressed as: $I(x_1, x_2) : R^2 \rightarrow R^{3n}$. The image value at a given spatial point (x_1^1, x_2^1) is a vector in R^{3n}. The difference between two image values at the points $M = (x_1^1, x_2^1)$ and $N = (x_1^2, x_2^2)$ is denoted by $\Delta I = I(M) - I(N)$. By dealing with $M - N$ as an infinitesimal displacement, the image value difference becomes the differential $dI = \sum_{i=1}^{2}(\partial I / \partial x_i) dx_i$. For each point $X = (x_1, x_2)^T$, the squared norm dI^2 is called the first fundamental form and is given by:

$$dI^2 = X^T G X \quad where \quad G = \sum_{j=1}^{3n} \nabla I_j \nabla I_j^T \qquad (1)$$

where G is a structure tensor, and ∇I_j corresponds to the spatial gradient of the jth color component. dI^2 is a measure of the rate of change in the multi-value image. For a spatial point (x_1, x_2), the orthogonal eigenvectors $\phi_\pm$ of tensor G provide the direction of maximal and minimal change in the spatio-temporal domain, and the eigenvalues $\lambda_\pm$ of tensor G are the corresponding rates of change in the temporal and spatial domain. For a sequence of images, the resulting edge is not simply given by the rate of maximal change λ_+, but by comparing λ_+ with λ_- in the form $f = f(\lambda_+ - \lambda_-)$ [8]. Since $f(\lambda_+ - \lambda_-)$ is the analog multi-spectral extension of $f = f(\|\nabla I\|^2)$ for single gray images($i.e., m = 1$), it reduces to the gradient-based edge detector.

By jointly considering R, G, B color components and employing temporal accumulation, the generalized gradients enhance the persistent edges belonging to a TV logo. It helps remove or weaken the noisy edges from changing background video content, as those edges are instable over time. As illustrated in Fig. 1, the energy distribution of enhanced edges at the CCTV-4 channel logo is stronger than that at the background area in the generalized gradient image.

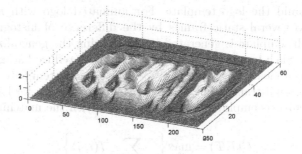

Fig. 1. Energy distribution of edges for CCTV-4 logo using generalized gradients

2.2 Logo Mask Extraction

TV logos are often fixed and composed of very few image pixels, such as several hundred pixels for CIF image size in MPEG-1 video streams. In order to make

full use of the mask information, we consider the logo in sub-pixel space. We first enlarge the generalized gradient image by triple using bilinear interpolation. and then the OTSU algorithm [5] is used to automatically binarize the image with an optimal threshold. Given an image represented by L gray levels $[1, 2, 3, ...L]$. The number of pixels at level i is n_i and the total number of pixels is N. The gray-level histogram is normalized and regard as a probability distribution $p_i = \frac{n_i}{N}$. The OTSU algorithm aims to maximize discriminant measure variable of the gray image. By utilizing the zeroth cumulative moment $\omega(k) = \sum_{i=1}^{k} p_i$ and the first cumulative moment $\mu(k) = \sum_{i=1}^{k} i p_i$ of the histogram, the optimal threshold k^* can be obtained by the discriminative criterion:
$\sigma^2(k^*) = \max_{1 \leq k \leq L} \left(\frac{(\mu(L)\omega(k) - \mu(k))^2}{\omega(k)(1 - \omega(k))} \right)$.

The OTSU algorithm is originally used in the binarization of document images. Like document images, TV logo regions show similar visual characteristics and pose similar challenges such as low contrast, variable background and noise. Moreover, the OTSU method is nonparametric and unsupervised, so it is very efficient and effective for automatic extracting the logo mask. Fig. 2 illustrates the mask extraction of a semi-transparent CCTV logo.

Fig. 2. TV logo mask extraction (Left to right: a frame from the original sequence, the generalized gradient image, and the logo's binary mask by OTSU algorithm)

2.3 TV Logo Detection

In consideration of the constant position of a TV logo, we calculate the generalized gradients over a sequence of images and apply the OTSU binarization algorithm to build the logo template. For animated logo with n frames, we separate it into several static frames by the difference of histogram to build templates. Each template is generated by calculating the generalized gradients every n frames. Such temporal accumulation helps to reduce background noises and to produce a clear contour of the TV logo. A logo template database including opaque, semi-transparent and animated logo is built for logo detection. Template matching is employed to logo detection with the matching criteria as below. Eq. 2.

$$C(I, T) = \max_k \left\{ \sum_{T_k(i,j)=1} I(i, j) \right\} \qquad (2)$$

where $I(i, j)$ is the binary image derived from the generalized gradients of consequent frames, and $T_k(i, j)$ is the matching template. k is the number of templates in the database. For opaque and semi-transparent logo, we compute the generalized gradients from 40 frames with the sampling rate of one frame out of five consecutive frames. As for animated logo with different periods $p_1, \ldots, p_n$, we compute the generalized gradients from 40 frames with the sampling rate of one frame out of $p_i(i = 1, \ldots, n)$ frames separately, then the gradient image is binalized with OSTU method and matched with the templates. If $C(I, T) \geq Threshold$, the TV logo is existent; otherwise, the TV logo is absent.

2.4   TV Logo Tracking

TV logo tracking is to compensate false logo detections in the broadcast and refine the true position of logo appearance, disappearance or change. Accordingly, a two-level logo tracking scheme is proposed. At both levels, for a detected TV logo with template T (for animated logo, there are several templates $T_1, \ldots, T_n$), the existence or absence of the TV logo is decided by Eq. 2. At the first level, a coarse resolution (i.e., more adjacent frames, say 20 frames) is used to roughly determine the boundaries of segments in the absence or the existence of a logo. At the second level, a fine resolution (say 1 frame) is used to precisely locate the transition points by shifting windows backwards and forwards around current time stamp. Twin thresholds are consequently applied.

When a new logo appears in the video streams, the logo detection algorithm is first used to extract the logo mask. If no matching template is find in the logo database, we use the logo mask as a new template and tracking the logo in the following frames. If the duration of the new logo is longer than 200 minutes, we consider we detect a new logo and add it to the database. For animated logo is few used and the detection of unknown animated logo is very time-consuming for searching the period of the logo. in this paper, we mainly consider the opaque and semi-transparent logos for the new logo detection.

3   TV Logo Removal

In TV program rebroadcasting or other applications, the TV logo needs to be removed from the video after detection. Since TV logo as an indicator is usually small and appears in the corner of the images without occluding the content of TV programs, we consider image inpainting technique in multi-value image for logo removal, i.e., filling the logo region with its neighbor data. Here, we present a multi-valued image regularization with PDEs (partial differential equation) [6] for inpainting the logo regions, and the structure tensor G in Eq. 1 is employed to preserve the local geometry of the multi-value image discontinuities. Different from computing the tensor G in logo tracking in video segment in which the position of TV logos is fixed, the inpainting of the logo region with the neighborhood requires calculating the tensor G around the logo region using 5 frames. We extend the image inpainting method in [6] to video inpainting by computing the structure tensor in spatio-temporal domain. a multi-valued regularization PDE that respects the local geometric properties is defined as, $\frac{\partial I_i}{\partial t} = trace(TH_i)$, $(i = 1, \ldots, n)$ where H_i designates the Hessian matrices of I_i and T is the tensor field defined as, $T = f_-(\sqrt{\lambda_+^* + \lambda_-^*})\phi_-^* \phi_-^{*T} + f_+(\sqrt{\lambda_+^* + \lambda_-^*})\phi_+^* \phi_+^{*T}$. $\lambda_\pm^*$ and $\phi_\pm^*$ are the spectral elements of the Gaussian smoothed structure tensor G in Eq. 1. f_+ and f_- are given as, $f_+(x) = \frac{1}{1+x^2}$, $f_-(x) = \frac{1}{\sqrt{1+x^2}}$.

The numerical implementation of the PDE is based on the local filtering interpretation. For each point (x_1, x_2), a spatially varying gaussian smoothing mask $G^{(T,t)}$ is applied, $trace(TH_i) = \sum_{k,l=-1}^{1} G^{(T,dt)}(k,l)I_i(x - k, y - l)$. In our experiments, 5×5 convolution kernels are selected. The masks of opaque, semi-transparent, and animated TV logos are obtained from the logo detection template after morphology operation . Examples of TV logo removal are shown in Fig. 3, in which the CCTV logo in (a) is semi-transparent. We can see that the edge information and local geometric properties are better preserved in Fig. 3.

(a)   (b)   (c)   (d)

Fig. 3. Examples of TV logo removal based on the regularization PDE. (a) and (c) are original frames with TV logos. (b) and (d) are frames with removed TV logos.

4   Experiment

Our experimental video data is extensively collected from TRECVID'05 news video corpus and several challenging Chinese TV channels. The video is in MPEG-1 format with the frame rate of 29.97 fps and the frame size of 352×240.

Referring to Fig. 4, our approach is compared with two previous algorithms: edge-based matching and pixel-wise difference computing. For each approach, the results by using different number of neighbouring frames are also compared. For edge-based matching, Canny edge detector is applied and the resulting edge images are time-averaged. In order to reduce false alarms, the OTSU method is employed to derive the final edge mask instead of morphology operators [3]. For pixel-wise difference computing, the gray-level difference images are temporally accumulated. The OTSU method is also applied to get the final mask. As illustrated in Fig. 4, our approach produces a solider and clearer contour with 40 frames to calculate generalized gradient than the other approaches. When the neighbouring frames are 150, all the three approaches get a clear contour. For relatively fewer neighbouring frames, our approach generally delivers better results. The number of neighbouring frames is decided by an application as it affects the temporal resolution.

Table 1 lists the tracking results of different channels including opaque, semi-transparent, and animated logos with the proposed two level tracking framework. The duration of each channel is around 30 mins.

In order to evaluate the performance of the proposed PDE based TV logo removal method, we compare it with the image inpainting method proposed by Oliveira in [9]. Fig. 5 shows some experimental results. We can see that the proposed method preserves the edge information and the homogenerity of

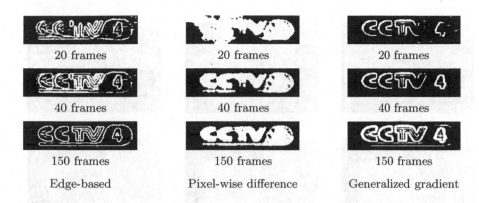

20 frames	20 frames	20 frames
40 frames	40 frames	40 frames
150 frames	150 frames	150 frames
Edge-based	Pixel-wise difference	Generalized gradient

Fig. 4. Comparison of three TV logo detection algorithms

Table 1. Experiment results of logo tracking. TV channels including opaque (MSNBC, NTDTV, LBC, CNN and NBC), semi-transparent (CCTV-4), and animated logos (CQTV, GZTV, HEBTV) are analyzed. The false alarm rate(FAR), the false reject rate(FRR) and F1 are used to evaluate the results.

Logo types	Tne name of TV channels	FAR(%)	FRR(%)	F1(%)
Station logo	MSNBC	0.4	0	99.80
	NTDTV	2.2	0.61	98.59
	LBC	1.74	0.24	99.00
	CNN	1.03	0.24	99.36
	NBC	2.42	0.2	98.68
	CCTV-4	3.9	0.52	97.76
Program logo	CQTV	2.4	0.32	98.63
	GZTV	2.11	0.84	98.52
	HEBTV	1.8	0.62	98.79

regions better than the Oliveira's method with the same iteration $iter = 30$. An example of logo removal with the regularization PDEs based method is given in Fig. 6, in which four templates are used to model the animated logo. The local geometric properties are better preserved in the frames with the animated logo removed. As shown in Fig. 3, the TV station logo "CNN" and the TV program logo "ELECTORAL VOTES" appear in the same video segment. Although the logo "ELECTORAL VOTES" is a little bigger TV logo, the proposed method also can give a satisfied performance.

All the experiments are run in P4 3.0 GHz desktop PC with 1 GB memory. The initial TV logo detection with 40 frames with the sampling rate of one frame out of five consecutive frames takes 105 milliseconds. The average time of logo tracking is 55 milliseconds for a coming frame. Since the frame rate in the broadcast video is 29.97 fps with the frame size of 352×240, the proposed logo detection and tracking algorithm is fast enough to catch up with the real time broadcast for processing one every three frames. The average time of the

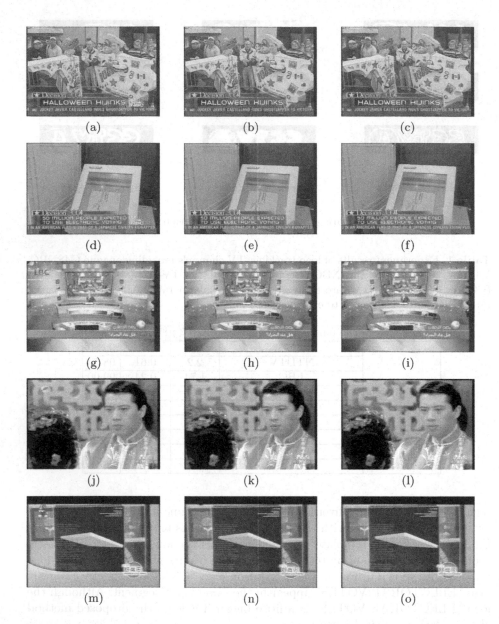

Fig. 5. Comparison between the regularization PDEs based approach and the Oliveira's approach. (a), (d), (g), (j), (m), (p), (s) and (v) are original frames with TV logos from different TV channels. (b), (e), (h), (k), (n), (q), (t) and (w) are frames with removed TV logo using the Oliveira's approach. (c), (f), (i), (l), (o), (r), (u) and (x) are frames with removed TV logo using the regularization PDEs based approach. From the comparison, we can see that logo removal with the tensor based regularization PDEs can better preserve the edge information and local geometric properties than using Oliveira's approach.

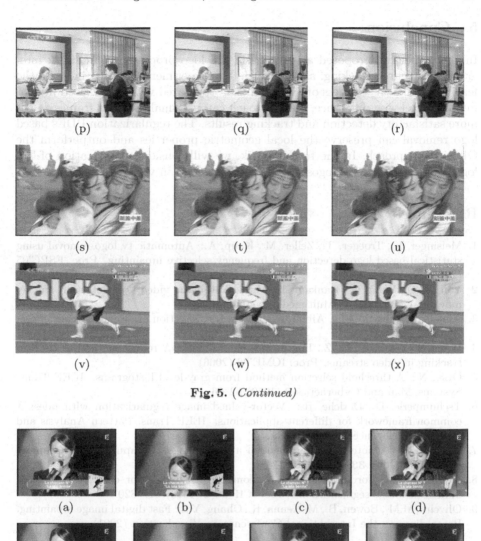

Fig. 5. (*Continued*)

Fig. 6. Examples of TV logo removal for animated logos. Four logo templates that are obtained by difference of logo images are used to model the animated logo. (a), (b), (c) and (d) are frames with the animated logo. (e), (f), (g) and (h) are frames with removed logos with the regularization PDEs based approach.

proposed logo removal with the regularization PDEs is 760 milliseconds with 20 iterations for one frame, which can not reach a realtime requirement. Next step, we will improve the speed of the algorithm.

5   Conclusion

In this paper, we proposed an automatic TV logo processing framework integrating detection, tracking, and removal. The experimental results indicate the feasibility and effectiveness of our approach. Compared with edge-based matching and pixel-wise difference, our approach can use small number frames to get more satisfactory detection and tracking results. The regularization PDEs based logo removal can preserve the local geometric properties and outperform the Oliveira's approach. In the further work, we will consider classification of TV logos, and insert virtual logos in the proper position in video streams.

References

1. Meisinger, K., Troeger, T., Zeller, M., Kaup, A.: Automatic tv logo removal using statistical based logo detection and frequency selective inpainting. Proc. ESPC'05 (2005)
2. Yan, W.Q., Wang, J., Kankanhalli, M.S.: Automatic video logo detection and removal. ACM Trans. on Multimedia System (2005)
3. Albial, A., Fullà, M.J.C., Albial, A., Torres, L.: Detection of tv commercials. Proc. ICASSP'04 (2004)
4. Wang, J., Duan, L., Li, Z., Liu, J., Lu, H., Jin, J.S.: A robust method for tv logo tracking in video streams. Proc. ICME'06 (2006)
5. Otsu, N.: A threshold selection method from gray-level histograms. IEEE Trans. Systems, Man and Cybernetics **9** (1979) 62–66
6. Tschumperlè, D., Deriche, R.: Vector-valued image regularization with pdes: A common framework for different applications. IEEE Trans. Pattern Analysis and Machine Intelligence **27** (2005)
7. Zenzo, S.D.: A note on the gradient of a multi-image. Comput. Vision Graphics Image Processing **33** (1986) 116–125
8. Sapiro, G.: Vector (self) snakes: a geometric framework for color, texture, and multiscale image segmentation. Proc. ICIP'96 **1** (1996) 817–820
9. Oliveira, M.M., Bowen, B., McKenna, R., Chang, Y.S.: Fast digital image inpainting. Proceedings on the International Conference on Visualization (2001)

Automatic Detection and Recognition of Athlete Actions in Diving Video

Haojie Li[1], Si Wu[2], Shan Ba[3], Shouxun Lin[1], and Yongdong Zhang[1]

[1] Institute of Computing Technology, Chinese Academy of Sciences,
100080, Beijing, China
[2] SAMI Lab, France Telecom R&D Beijing,
100080, Beijing, China
[3] School of Science, Beijing Institute of Technology,
100081, Beijing, China
{hjli,zhyd,sxlin}@ict.ac.cn, si.wu@orange-ft.com

Abstract. This paper presents a system for automatic detecting and recognizing complex individual actions in sports video to facilitate high-level content-based video indexing and retrieval. This is challenging due to the cluttered and dynamic background in sports video which makes object segmentation formidable. Another difficulty is to fully automatically and accurately detect desired actions from long video sequence. We propose three techniques to handle these challenges. Firstly, an efficient approach exploiting dominant motion and semantic color analysis is developed to detecting the highlight clips which contain athlete's action from video sequences. Secondly, a robust object segmentation algorithm based on adaptive dynamic background construction is proposed to segment the athlete's body from the clip. Finally, to recognize the segmented body shape sequences, the hidden markov models are slightly modified to make them suitable for noisy data processing. The proposed system for broadcast diving video analysis has achieved 96.6% detection precision; and 85% recognition accuracy for 13 kinds of diving actions.

Keywords: video analysis, action recognition, video object segmentation.

1 Introduction

In recent years, the analysis of sports video has attracted great attention due to its mass appeal and inherent structures which are suitable for automatic processing [1-3]. Most of these works focus on structure analysis [1], highlights detection [2] and video summarization [3] of TV broadcasting sports video. However, for sports professionals such as coachers and athletes, these analysis are not enough. It is desired for finer granularity analysis to provide detailed information such as action names or match tactics for coaching assistant and performance improvements. The aim of the proposed system is to automatically detect and classify athlete's actions for action-based sports video indexing and retrieval, which is extremely useful when coaches or athletes want to compare the performed actions with the same ones in video database.

T.-J. Cham et al. (Eds.): MMM 2007, LNCS 4352, Part II, pp. 73–82, 2007.
© Springer-Verlag Berlin Heidelberg 2007

Recognizing human actions in videos is a well-studied topic in computer vision community and various approaches have been proposed [4]. But in the field of sports video, due to the complex and dynamic background, there exist few works and most of them focus on tennis or soccer actions recognition. These works either take not much pains to segment players body [5-6] or need not accurate tracking and segmentation of the players [7-9].

One of the early work for sports action recognition was provided by Yamato *et al.* in [5]. They proposed using HHM to recognize six tennis stroke classes in a constrained test environment, where the feature, i.e., body shapes were extracted from a pre-known background. J. Sullivan *et al.* [6] presented a method for detecting tennis player strokes based on similarity computed by point to point correspondence between shapes. Although impressive results are given, the extraction of edge needs a clean background. In the work [7-9], the authors used statistical feature of optical flow or oriented gradient to recognize basic player's actions such as skate left/skate right, running/walking or skate left/skate right in a "medium field" or low resolution video sequence. However, these two works only present results with relative simple actions in simple background such as soccer field, tennis court or hockey field.

In this paper, we propose a system to automatic detect and classify complex actions in changeling dynamic background, more specifically, to detect and classify diving actions for broadcasting or training diving video sequences. To fulfill such task, the accurate segmentation of body shape plays important role. The system comprises three components: a highlight detection algorithm based on dominant motion and semantic color analysis; a video object segmentation algorithm based on adaptive dynamic background construction and the recognition component using slightly modified HMMs. The system performs automatically and achieves promising results.

2   Highlight Detection

Highlight is commonly referred to excited events in video sequence. In our case, it is defined as the clip containing the entire diving action, to say, from the diver's takeoff to entry into the water. It is agreed that successful highlights detection algorithms are domain-specific knowledge depended [1, 3]. Based on the observations of all kinds of diving actions, we develop a simple but effective approach to extracting the highlight clips from diving video. The approach exploits two facts of diving action:

1) At the end of action, i.e., when athlete is entering the water, a large area of swimming pool will appear in the bottom of image which color is mainly blue;
2) During the in-flight period, to focus the athlete in the center of image, the camera should tilt up/down which leading to distinct dominant motion mode in vertical direction. Fig. 1 illuminates two types of diving: platform diving and springboard diving and their respective distinct motion mode.

So, our highlight detection approach combines dominant motion and semantic color analysis as follows:

1) Highlight end point detection

step 1. Detect swimming pool for input frames, if the pool is appearing from the bottom of image gradually and the pool area exceeds 1/4 of the image then goto step 2; else goto step1;(this time instant is denoted as t1, which is usually corresponding to the deep valley of the bottom figures in Fig. 1).

step2. Check the vertical motion of the several frames after t1, if the mean value is above a given threshold Th, then goto step 3; else goto step1;

step3. Check the vertical motion and the pool area of the following frames. If the motion value becomes to near zero or the image is full of pool in about 30 frames, then goto step4; else goto step1;

step4. If the bottom of the image is the connected pool area and its size is above 1/4 of the image, then a highlight end point is declared to be detected and this time instant is denoted as t2; else goto step 1;

Step5. Skip a temporal gap of 600 frames and goto step 1 to repeat the next detection.

2) Highlight start point detection

A typical diving action lasts about 35~60 frames. So we test the vertical motion of the frame at time t0=t2-60, if it is near zero then t0 is deemed as the start point; otherwise, we repeat testing the frames before t0 until the motion value is near zero.

It is noted that the detection of swimming pool is not an easy task since pool color may vary due to different stadiums and lighting conditions. To overcome this problem, we build an adaptive pool color model which is learned for specific video sequence. A relaxed range for pool color in HSV space is first decided offline. Then for an input video, we detect pool in successive frames and select the frames whose pool area are gradually becoming larger from the bottom of image, which is the case when the athlete is flying to the water. The pixels which color fall in the initial range from such frames are sampled and refined to be represented with Gaussian Mixture Model (GMM) for the video.

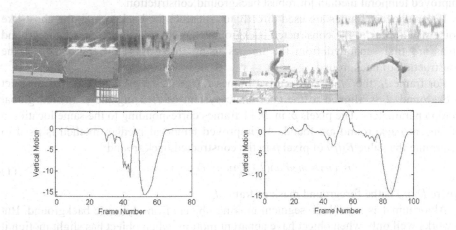

Fig. 1. Platform diving and springboard diving (top row) and their respective distinct motion mode (bottom row)

In TV broadcast diving game video, several replayed slow motion shots of the same action with same vertical camera motion pattern will follow the live shot. For later action recognition, we care only the "side-view" normal action. Since the slow motion views are replayed to enhance the normal view, the temporal gaps between them (5s to 20s) are smaller than the gap between two athletes' action (lager than 30s). Therefore, in step 5 we skip 600 frames for the next detection when detecting a highlight clip at current instant to filter out the slow motion shots.

3   Athlete Body Segmentation

For diving video sequences, the non-rigid deformation of athlete body, the obvious camera motion and cluttered background caused by the existence of referees or audience bring great difficulty for athlete body segmentation. We have proposed an object segmentation algorithm which can deal with such problems [10]. However, like other motion segmentation methods, it works poorly when the athlete has little motion in successive frames, which is the often case in diving videos at the early stage of a diving action. To overcome the limitation, we propose an improved version of the algorithm. To be self-contained, we first introduce the algorithm in [10] (called algorithm 1 hereafter) and then present the improved version (called algorithm 2 hereafter).

3.1   Algorithm 1

The core of algorithm 1 is to construct a background image for each frame of dynamic scene by registering multiple neighboring frames of current frame. The main steps of algorithm 1 are summarized as: 1) global motion estimation; 2) foreground separation; 3) background construction and 4) background subtraction.

The merit of algorithm 1 is that it adopted foreground separation technique and improved temporal median for robust background construction.

If the adjacent frames are used directly to construct the background, the ghost-like noise will appear in the constructed background. To eliminate such noise, foreground areas are first separated from the images using three-frame-difference before the construction of background.

For frame I_k, the $2L+1$ consecutive frames I_i $(i=k-L,...,k+L)$ are used to construct background. I_i is aligned to the coordinate system of I_k using the estimated global motion parameters. The pixels p_i in $2L+1$ frames corresponding to the same location p of current background are found. An improved temporal median method is used to determine the value $B_k(p)$ of pixel p in the constructed background:

$$B_k(p) = \underset{i}{median}(I_i(p_i)), \quad D_i(p_i) \neq 1 \tag{1}$$

where $D_i(p_i)$ is the foreground mask of frame I_i.

Algorithm 1 is suitable to segment moving objects from dynamic background. But it works well only when object have apparent motion, when object has slight motion it will fail (see Fig. 2)

Fig. 2. Segmentation results of Algorithm 1. Top row: original frames; Bottom row: segmented foreground objects.

3.2   Algorithm 2

The limitation of Algorithm 1 is that it takes no account of the object motion between frames when selecting frames to construct the background. This will lead to two problems: 1) Firstly, it uses consecutive neighboring frames. When object has little motion, many of the consecutive frames are similar and have no new contribution to background construction, but to degrade the performance of median filter since some of the background areas are occluded by object for most of the frames. 2) Secondly, it uses constant number of frames. When the object motion is large enough, fewer frames will suffice to the background construction thus extra computation is cost.

In Algorithm 2 the object motion between frames is considered. The principle is that we only select the frames with apparent object motion to construct the background image. There are many ways to estimate the magnitude of object motion such as the difference of two aligned frames. In this paper, we take the global motion between frames as the measurement of object motion based on the observation that the camera is always following the diver's motion when capturing the diver's movements. When the diver is moving, the camera also moves. So we can select the frames having salient global motion (larger than *Th1*), to say, *key-frames* instead of consecutive neighboring frames to build the background. Also, when the cumulative global motion exceeds a given threshold *Th2*, no more frames are needed.

Algorithm 2 first decides all the key-frames of a clip as follows:

1)   Neighboring frames with global motion larger than *Th1* are selected as key-frames.

2)   For the rest frames, if a frame's cumulative motion to the nearest key-frame exceeds *Th1*, it is selected as key-frame.

Then for the current frame I_k, we select L_1 and L_2 consecutive neighboring key-frames from the left and right of I_k respectively to build current background, where

$$L_i = \min(L, \arg\min_J CM_i(k, J) >= Th2) \tag{2}$$

and $CM_i(k,J)$ is the cumulative global motion from I_k to the Jth key-frame on the left/right of I_k.

Hence, in Algorithm 2 the frames and the number of frames used to construct the background image for each frame are adaptive to the object motion. The segmentation results of Algorithm 2 will be reported in Section 5.

4   Action Recognition with HMMs

The segmented body shapes of the athlete and shape transitions represent different diving actions. The *Hu* moments of shape are used as shape descriptors. For robust, we select the low-order, i.e. the first two *Hu* moments (denoted by *Hu1* and *Hu2*). However, *Hu* moments are rotation-invariant, for such sports as gymnastics or diving, the same posture at different direction are considered as different actions. To make rotation-sensitive, the body shape is divided into four sub-shape at the mass center (Fig. 3) and the *Hu1* of each sub-shape is computed. Finally, a 7-dimensional shape descriptor including the *Hu1* and *Hu2* of the body shape, the aspect ration of the bounding box of body and 4 *Hu1*s of sub-shape is obtained. This compact descriptor is robust to segmentation noise and discriminative enough to distinguish different postures.

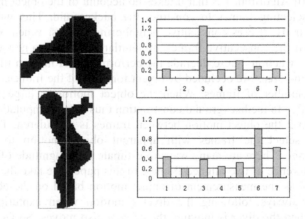

Fig. 3. Two body shapes and their shape descriptors' distribution

HMM is adopted as classifier since it has been shown a powerful tool for sequential data processing [4]. We use Continuous Hidden Markov Model (CHMM) with left-right topology. Each CHMM is trained based on Baum-Welch algorithm. Given an observation sequence, viterbi algorithm is used to calculate each model's output probability and the model with maximum probability is the recognition result.

However, as shown in Section 5.2, though the improved segmentation algorithm in Section 3 can achieve satisfying results for most of the clips, there are still some fails. These noisy shapes may affect the performance of the classifiers since that the correct model's observation probabilities for them may be smaller than the incorrect model's probabilities. To handle these noises, we employ a filtering technique to the original segmented shape sequence and modify the viterbi algorithm slightly when decoding.

The filtering algorithm considers the pose validity and size validity. For pose validity, we first cluster the training shapes using K-means method and then compute the distances between the shapes to their corresponding cluster. The largest distance of each cluster is used as the cluster-specific threshold. A test shape S is classified pose invalid if for all cluster Ci,

$$Dist(S, C_i) > Th_i \qquad (3)$$

Where $Dist(S,Ci)$ is the distance between S and cluster Ci, and Th_i is the threshold of cluster Ci.

For size validity, the mean shape size of the test sequence is computed and a test shape is considered invalid if its size is lager than two times of mean size or smaller than half of the mean size.

At the classifying stage, unlike the traditional HMMs, when compute the observation probability during viterbi process, the filter-out shapes are not counted in. This is implemented by assigning a small enough value to the observation probability for the shapes that have been filtered out. This method can efficiently prevent the adverse influence of these noisy shapes on the classifiers.

5 Experimental Results

This section reports our experimental results on the analysis of 6 diving videos, digitized in MPEG 1 format. The videos are about 6 hours and include 4 platform videos and 2 springboard videos. They come from 27th Olympic Games (Sydney, 2000), 9th World Tournament (2001, Fukuoka). The ground truth is labeled manually.

5.1 Highlights(Action Clips) Detection

To detect swimming pool area, the pool color is initially set as ($150 < H < 200$, $0.3 < S < 0.9$, $0.6 < V < 1.0$) and is further refined to a GMM with 2 components for each video. The action detection results for 6 videos are listed in Table 1.

Table 1. The highlights detection results

Videos	Count of action clip	Recall	Precision
3m Springboard	120	92.5%	94.8%
10m Platform	264	97.7%	97.3%
Total	384	96.1%	96.6%

As discussed in section 2, we only care the normal action for TV broadcasting videos. So a highlight or action clip is deemed as correctly detected only if it contains the normal action. The missed detections are mainly caused by the errors of camera motion estimation when checking the motion mode. The false detections are attributed to the confusing of replay shots when the live shots ahead are missed and some scenes when the camera showing action-like motion.

5.2 Athlete Body Segmentation

The improved algorithm, i.e., Algorithm 2 is applied to segment athlete body from action clips detected in 5.1. Compared with Algorithm 1(see Fig. 2), it achieves satisfying results for the entire clip. Fig. 4 and Fig. 5 show Algorithm 2's segmentation results for two types of diving: platform diving and springboard diving. However, the algorithm also fails to segment finely for some frames of some clips due to the errors in camera motion estimation, the blurring caused by fast motion and the dramatic reflecting of human body. Fig. 6 illuminates some failing examples. The values for *Th1* and *Th2* are set to 4 and 50 for image with 352*288 resolutions.

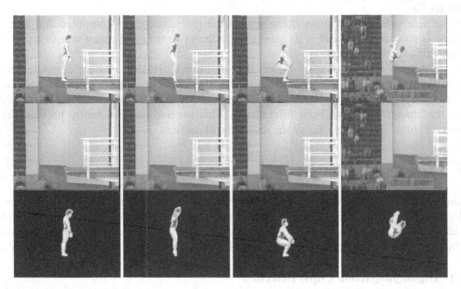

Fig. 4. Segmentation results for platform diving. Top row: original frames; Middle row: constructed backgrounds; Bottom row: segmented athlete bodies.

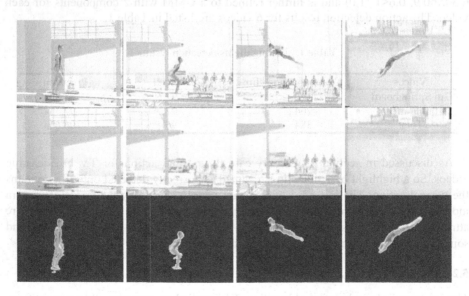

Fig. 5. Segmentation results for springboard diving

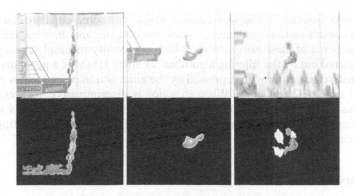

Fig. 6. Some failing examples of algorithm 2

5.3 Action Recognition

According to the diver's facing direction before takeoff and the body moving direction after takeoff, the diving actions are classified into six groups: forward dive, backward dive, reverse dive, inward dive, twist dive and arm stand dive with group id 1-6. The platform diving includes all the 6 groups dive while springboard diving includes group 1-5. In our preliminary work, we take platform diving as test data for action recognition. For all the 20 actions from the 4 platform videos, 13 actions are selected for experiments since the rest 7 actions have too few samples for training. The 13 actions occupy about 90% of the 4 videos. We randomly select 2/3 of these action clips for training and the rest 1/3 for testing and run 3 times.

For shape descriptors, the automatic segmented shapes by Algorithm 2 are used to compute testing descriptors and manually refined ones are used to compute training descriptors. The filtering algorithm and modified viterbi decoding method are employed when classifying these noisy shape sequences. We also test HMMs without the filtering process. The recognition results are summarized in Table 2.

The total accuracy of action recognition is about 85%, with about 4% improvement compared to the traditional HMMs. The results are encouraging. The errors mainly

Table 2. The action recognition results

No.	Action Code	Action Count	Recognized	Recognition Rate
1	107B	35	33	94.2%
2	205B	17	14	82.3%
3	207B	14	12	85.7%
4	207C	28	24	85.7%
5	305C	19	14	73.7%
6	307C	18	13	72.2%
7	405B	11	9	81.8%
8	407C	20	16	80.0%
9	5251B	12	12	100%
10	5253B	14	13	92.9%
11	6241B	18	16	88.9%
12	626B	15	13	86.7%
13	626C	16	13	81.2%
Total		237	202	85.2%

come from two aspects: 1) The segmentation results for some clips are noisy due to the errors in camera motion estimation, fast motion blurring and dramatic reflecting of human body. Some of these noisy shapes, which are usually incompletely segmented, cannot be filtered out by the filtering algorithm. 2) Since HMM is a generative model, its discriminative power may be depressed by the alike action pairs such as 305C and 307C, 207B and 207C and so on. When an action is discriminative, its accuracy will be high. This is the case for 107B, 5251B and 5253B, where 107B has a distinct pattern of running in the platform, 5251B and 5253B have distinct twisting pattern while different number of twist.

6 Conclusion and Future Work

We have presented a system for automatic action detection and recognition for high-level content-based video indexing and retrieval. In the three components of the system, the object segmentation and action recognition algorithms are general and can be applied to other kinds of sports videos analysis, such as gymnastics, trampoline, and so on. In the future, we need test the system on larger datasets and more complicate classifying methods should be adopted to improve the performance and to recognize the actions with small training samples.

Acknowledgements

This work is supported by the Key Project of Beijing Natural Science Foundation (4051004), and Beijing Science and Technology Planning Program of China (D0106008040291, Z0004024040231).

References

1. F. Wang, J.T. Li, Y.D. Zhang, and S.X. Lin, Semantic and Structural Analysis of TV Diving Programs, Journal of Computer Science and Technology, 19, 6, (Nov. 2004), 928-935
2. J. Assfalg, M. Bertini, C. Colombo, et al., Semantic annotation of soccer videos: automatic highlights identification, CVIU, 92, 2-3, (Nov.2003), 285-305
3. B. Li and M.I. Sezan, Event Detection and Summarization in Sports Video, Proc. IEEE Workshop on Content-Based Access to Video and Image Libraries, 2001
4. L. Wang, W. Hu and T. Tan, Recent developments in human motion analysis, Pattern Recognition, 36, 585-601, 2003
5. J.Yamato, J.Ohya, and K.Ishii. Recognizing Human Action in Time-Sequential Images using Hidden Markov Model. In CVPR,1992
6. J. Sullivan and S. Carlsson, Recognizing and tracking human action. In ECCV, 2002
7. Efros, A.A., Berg, A.C., Mori, G., Malik, J., Recognizing action at a distance. In ICCV, 2003
8. G.Y. Zhu, C.S. Xu, et al., Action Recognition in Broadcast Tennis Video Using Optical Flow and Support Vector Machine, In ECCV Workshop on HCI'06
9. W.L. Lu and J.J. Little, Tracking and recognizing actions at a distance, In CVBASE '06
10. S. Wu, S.X. Lin and Y.D. Zhang, Automatic Segmentation of Moving Objects in Video Sequences Based on Dynamic Background Construction. Chinese Journal of Computer, 28, 8, (Aug. 2005), 1386-1392

Event Detection Models Using 2d-BN and CRFs

Tao Wang, Jianguo Li, Wei Hu, Xiaofeng Tong, Yimin Zhang, and Carole Dulong

Intel China Research Center
8/F Raycom Infotech Park A, Beijing, P.R. China 100080
{tao.wang,jianguo.li,wei.hu,xiaofeng.tong,yimin.zhang,
carole.dulong}@intel.com

Abstract. In this paper, we propose two novel semantic event detection models, i.e., Two-dependence Bayesian Network (2d-BN) and Conditional Random Fields (CRFs). 2d-BN is a simplified Bayesian Network classifier which can characterize the feature relationships well and be trained more efficiently than traditional complex Bayesian Networks. CRFs are undirected probabilistic graphical models which offer several particular advantages including the abilities to relax strong independence assumptions in the state transition and avoid a fundamental limitation of directed probability graphical models. Based on multi-modality fusion and mid-level keywords representation, we use a three-level framework to detect semantic events. The first level extracts audiovisual features, the mid-level detects semantic keywords, and the high-level infers events using 2d-BN and CRFs models. Compared with state of the art, extensive experimental results demonstrate the effectiveness of the proposed two models.

Keywords: Semantic event detection, Three-level framework, Soccer highlights detection, SVM, HMMs, 2d-BNs, CRFs.

1 Introduction

As digital video data becomes more and more pervasive, semantic event detection becomes an active research field, such as video surveillance, sports highlights detection, TV/Movie abstraction and home video retrieval etc. The goal of event detection is to find meaningful events (*event type*) and their starting and ending time (*event boundary*). Through event detection, consumers can retrieve specific video segments quickly from the long videos and save much time in browsing. There is much literature on semantic event detection. However, semantic event detection is still a challenging problem due to the large semantic gap and the difficulty of modeling temporal and multimodality characteristics of video.

Existing works can be categorized into two kinds of models, i.e., segment classification and sequence labeling. Segments Classification Approach (SCA) treats event detection as a classification problem. The approach first selects possible event segments by a sliding data window or domain rules, and then predicts the semantic event type of each segment by classifiers. Duan et al [9] used game-specific rules to classify events. Although the rule system is intuitive to yield adequate results, it lacks

T.-J. Cham et al. (Eds.): MMM 2007, LNCS 4352, Part II, pp. 83–93, 2007.

scalability and robustness. Wang et al used SVM to detect events [8]. SVM is a good classifier particularly for small training set. However, it may not sufficiently characterize the relationships and temporal layout of features. Since traditional Bayesian networks are generally too complex to learn the graph structure and probability distribution accurately on limited training set, some researchers have to utilize Naive Bayesian classifier to detect specific events[3]. Naive Bayesian assumes that features are independent of each other, and consequently neglects the important relationships among features, too. In summary, SCA are simple and effective but have two main shortcomings. Firstly, they can not characterize long-term dependence within video streams, and thus may be myopic about the impact of their current decision on later decisions [7]. Secondly, it is difficult for them to determine accurate event boundaries, i.e., the starting and ending time of the detected events.

Compared with SCA, Sequence Labeling Approach (SLA) deals with event detection as a labeling sequence problem, i.e., decoding the most probable hidden state (semantic event label) sequence from the observed video sequence. The most popular model is Hidden Markov Models (HMMs) which provide well-understood training and decoding algorithms for labeling sequence [10,16]. While enjoying much historical successes to characterize the temporal dependence of sequence data, they suffer from one principal drawback: The structure of the HMM is often a poor model to characterize the true process producing the data. Part of the problem stems from the directed Markov property. Any relationship between two separated y values (e.g., y_0 and y_3) must be communicated via the intervening y's (e.g., y_1 and y_2). A first-order HMMs model where the $p(y_t)$ only depends on y_{t-1} can not capture this kind of non-local interactions.

Corresponding to SCA and SLA mentioned above, this paper proposes two novel models for semantic event detection, i.e., *Two-dependence Bayesian Network* (2d-BN) and *Conditional random fields* (CRFs). 2d-BN is a simplified Bayesian network which assumes that each variable depends on at most two variables. Under this assumption, 2d-BN can characterize feature relationships well and is easier for training and inference than traditional complex Bayesian networks. CRFs is an undirected probabilistic graph model which specifies the joint probability of possible label sequences by state and transition feature functions. Although it encompasses HMM-like models, CRFs offer several particular advantages including the abilities to relax strong independence assumptions in the state transition, and to avoid a fundamental limitation of directed graphical models[7,15].

2   System Framework

In general, events take place with particular patterns. Similar to the idea from content (word) to context (sentence) in text mining, the events in video are characterized by certain multimedia content elements and their temporal layout. For example, music and camera motion are two kinds of important content elements that often appears in movies; Video segments in movies with high tempo, extreme emotion and tense music usually indicate highlight scenes. By semantic keyword/concept detection, the content elements can be extracted as keywords. Furthermore, their temporal layout consists of the keywords sequence. Based on mid-level keywords representation, event detection can be intuitively looked upon as a segment classification or sequence labeling problem, i.e., infer event labels y according to observed keyword sequences $\mathbf{x}_k = [x_{k1}, x_{k2}, .., x_{kN}]$ with $k=1,..,K$ keywords, and N time slices.

Due to large semantic gap and curse of dimension, high-level semantic events can hardly be inferred from high-dimensional low-level features. Therefore it is essential to employ *mid-level semantic keywords* and *multi-modality fusion* to bridge the large semantic gap. Fig.1 illustrates our event detection framework. The framework consists of three level architectures, i.e., low-level feature extraction, mid-level keyword detection and high-level event detection modules. In processing, the low-level module first extracts multimodal audiovisual features from the video stream. Then the mid-level module detects semantic keywords from low-level features. Finally, the high-level module infers events from the multiple keyword sequences.

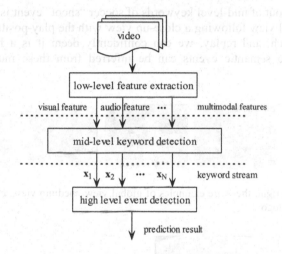

Fig. 1. A three-level framework of semantic event detection

In the mid-level module, keywords denote "basic" semantic concepts in a sampling frame or a shot, such as subject (face, car, building, water, grass), place (indoor, outdoor), audio type (silence, speech, music, explosion), camera motion (pan, tilt, zoom), and view type (global view, medium view and close-up view) etc. Generally, keywords depend on detailed applications and domain knowledge. In the case of soccer highlights detection, we detect following multimodal keywords for high-level event inference:

- $\mathbf{x}_1$ View type: View type plays a critical role in broadcasting videos. By accumulating HSV color histogram, we get the dominant color to segment the playing field region [12]. According to the area of playfield and the size of player, we then classify each sampling frame into global view, medium view, close-up view and out of view [3]. Fig. 2 shows examples of these view types.

86   T. Wang et al.

- x_2 Play-position: We classify the play-position of global-views into five regions as shown in fig. 3. Hough transform detects field boundary lines and the penalty box lines. Then a decision tree based classifier determines the play position according to lines' slope and position [3,8].

- x_3 Replay: It is an important cue for highlights, since a replay usually follows a highlight. At the beginning and ending of each replay, there is generally a logo flying in high speed. We detect logos to identify replay by dynamic programming [5].

- $x_{4,5}$ Audio keywords: There are two types of audio keywords: commentator's excited speech, and referee's whistle which have strong relations to soccer highlights such as goal, shot, and foul etc. Gauss mixture model (GMM) is used to detect above two keywords from low-level audio features including Mel frequency Cepstral coefficients (MFCC), Energy and pitch [9,13].

A temporal layout of mid-level keywords of soccer "shoot" event is shown in fig.4. If there is a global view following a close-up view with the play-position from ML to LL, excited speech, and replay, we can confidently deem it is a highlight event. Consequently, the semantic events can be inferred from these multiple keyword sequences.

Fig. 2. From left to right, these are examples of global view, medium view, close-up view, out of view, and replay logo

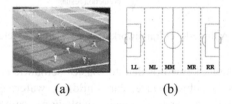

(a)   (b)

Fig. 3. (a) Hough line detection on a segmented playfield (b) Five detected regions in the playfield: left(LL), mid-left(ML), middle(MM), mid-right(MR) and right(RR)

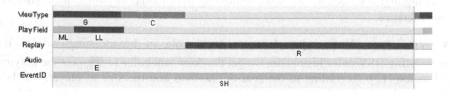

Fig. 4. Temporal layout of mid-level keywords for a shoot event. G: global view; C: close-up view; ML: middle left region; LL: left region; R: replay; E: excited speech, SH: shoot.

3 2d-BN and CRFs Models for Event Detection

To overcome the shortcomings of SVM and HMMs mentioned in section 1, this section proposes two novel models for event detection, i.e., *Two-dependent Bayesian Network* (2d-BN) and *Conditional Random Fields* (CRFs). They belong to segments classification approach (SCA) and sequence labeling approach (SLA) respectively.

3.1 Two-Dependence Bayesian Network

Given a N-dimensional keyword feature vector $\mathbf{x} = [x_1, x_2, ...x_N]$ and its event label y, the proposed 2d-BN assumes that each variable x_j depends on at most two variables, i.e. x_i and y. Supposing that x_i is given to be the parent of variables $\mathbf{x}_{\setminus i}$ where $\mathbf{x}_{\setminus i}$ indicates all elements in $\mathbf{x}$ except x_i as shown in fig.5, the joint probability of Bayesian networks are:

$$p(\mathbf{x}, y) = p(x_i, y) p(\mathbf{x}_{\setminus i} \mid x_i, y)$$

$$\cong p(x_i, y) \prod_{j=1, j\neq i}^{N} p(x_j \mid x_i, y) \underline{\Delta P_i}(\mathbf{x}, y) \tag{1}$$

Since $p(x_j \mid x_i, y) = p(x_i, x_j \mid y) p(y) / p(x_i, y)$, we further have:

$$P_i(\mathbf{x}, y) = p(x_i, y) \prod_{j=1, j\neq i}^{N} p(x_i, x_j \mid y) p(y) / p(x_i, y)$$

$$= p(y) p(x_i \mid y)^{2-N} \prod_{j=1, j\neq i}^{N} p(x_i, x_j \mid y) \tag{2}$$

In the training phase of 2d-BN, we estimate both the probability distribution and graph structure of 2d-BNs. For the probability estimation, the $p(y)$ is estimated using Laplace estimation[1]: $p(y=c) = \dfrac{\#(y=c)+1}{M+C}$, where $\#(y=c)$ is the number of instances satisfying $y = c$, M is the total number of training instances, and C is the number of event types. $p(x_i \mid y)$ is estimated using M-estimation [1]: $p(x_i = a \mid y = c) = \dfrac{\#(x_i = a, y = c) + k \times l}{\#(y=c)+k}$, where $l = p(x_i = a)$ and $k = C$ for C-class event detection problem. Similarly, $p(x_i, x_j \mid y)$ is estimated using M-estimation like $p(x_i \mid y)$.

Now we deal with the structure learning problem of 2d-BN, i.e. determining which feature x_i should be the parent node of $\mathbf{x}_{\setminus i}$. In literature, many score functions have been proposed for learning Bayesian network structure [14]. In 2d-BN, we use the mutual information $I(x_i, y)$ as the criterion:

$$I(x_i, y) = \sum_{x_i, y} p(x_i, y) \log \frac{p(x_i, y)}{p(x_i) p(y)} \tag{3}$$

Generally, the larger the value $I(x_i, y)$ is, the stronger the dependence between x_i and y. Hence the variable x_i with the largest mutual information score is selected as the parent node besides y.

Since 2d-BN is just an approximation to the exact Bayesian Network structure, $P_i(\mathbf{x}, y)$ selecting out only one variable x_i as the parent node of $\mathbf{x}_{\setminus i}$ may yield large variance and bias for the joint probability estimation of $p(\mathbf{x}, y)$. To solve the problem, we select those nodes $\{x_i\}$ whose mutual information satisfies $I(x_i, y) > \varepsilon$, as the parent nodes. Consequently, we obtain several joint probability estimates $P_i(\mathbf{x}, y)$. Then the final joint probability and event label y^* are robustly estimated by the geometric average as:

$$p(\mathbf{x}, y) = [\prod_{I(x_i, y) > \varepsilon} P_i(\mathbf{x}, y)]^{1/K}, \qquad y^* = \arg\max_y p(\mathbf{x}, y) \tag{4}$$

where K is the number of variables x_i satisfying the constraint $I(x_i, y) > \varepsilon$. The geometric average is analytically tractable, and yields much more robust probability estimation.

By the two-dependence assumption, 2d-BN is much easier to train than complex Bayesian Networks and achieves more robust model for small training set. Given M training samples, it is easy to find out that 2d-BN's training complexity is $O(N^2 M)$ for a keyword feature $\mathbf{x} = [x_1, x_2, ..x_N]$ with N time slices. In the event detection phase, we just look up those trained probability tables and infer the most possible event type y^* via Eq(2) and Eq(4). Hence 2d-BN can run very efficiently for event detection.

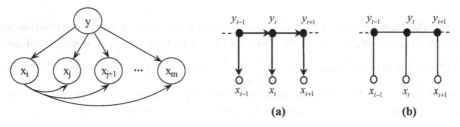

Fig. 5. One 2d-BN structure when assuming x_i to be the parent of variables $\mathbf{x}_{\setminus i}$

Fig. 6. (a)HMM models and (b)CRFs models

3.2 Conditional Random Fields

Contrary to directed HMMs, CRFs is an undirected probabilistic graphical model[15] as shown in fig.6. Let $\mathbf{x} = [x_1, x_2, ..., x_T]$ be the input *observation sequence* and $\mathbf{y} = [y_1, y_2, ..., y_T]$ be the corresponding *labeling sequence*, e.g., the sequence of event labels ($y_t = 1$ represents event and $y_t = 0$ for nonevent, $t = 1, 2, ..., T$). Conditioned on the observation sequence $\mathbf{x}$ and the surrounding labels $y_{\setminus t}$, the random variable y_t obeys the Markov property $p(y_t | y_{\setminus t}, \mathbf{x}) = p(y_t | y_w, \mathbf{x}, w \sim t)$, where $w \sim t$ means that y_w are neighbors of the node y_t in the graphical model, i.e. *Markov blanket*.

The conditional probability $p_\theta(\mathbf{y} | \mathbf{x})$ of CRFs is defined as follows:

$$p_\theta(\mathbf{y} | \mathbf{x}) = \frac{1}{Z(\mathbf{x})} \exp(\sum_{t=1}^{T} F(\mathbf{y}, \mathbf{x}, t)) \tag{6}$$

where $Z(\mathbf{x}) = \sum_y \exp(\sum_{t=1}^{T} F(\mathbf{y}, \mathbf{x}, t)$ is the normalization constant, $F(\mathbf{y}, \mathbf{x}, t)$ is the *feature function* at the time position t. For the first-order CRFs, the feature function $F(\mathbf{y}, \mathbf{x}, t)$ is given by:

$$F(\mathbf{y}, \mathbf{x}, t) = \sum_i \lambda_i f_i(y_{t-1}, y_t) + \sum_j u_j g_j(\mathbf{x}, y_t) \tag{7}$$

In which $f_i(.)$ and $g_j(.)$ are the *transition* and *state feature functions* respectively. $\theta = [\lambda_1, \lambda_2, ...; u_1, u_2 ...]$ is the learned weights associated with $f_i(.)$ and $g_j(.)$. Compared with the observation probability $p(x_t | y_t)$ of HMMs, the state feature functions $g_j(\mathbf{x}, y_t)$ of CRFs depend not only on the current observation x_t, but also on past and future observations $\mathbf{x} = [x_1, x_2, .., x_T]$. This permits CRFs to use more features of $\mathbf{x}$, especially long-term dependence features to describe non-local interactions. On the other hand, although SCA approach, e.g. SVM, is able to make the decision based on the local observation segments $[x_{t-d}, x_{t-d+1}, ..., x_{t+d}]$, its object function doesn't consider the transition feature functions $f_i(y_{t-1}, y_t)$ and long-term interactions outside the observed segment $\mathbf{x}$. So CRFs are better to model the event detection problem than HMMs and SVM.

The parameters $\theta = [\lambda_1, \lambda_2, ...]$ of CRFs are trained by maximum likelihood estimation (MLE) approach. Given M training sequences, the log likelihood L is written as:

$$L = \sum_{j=1}^{M} \log(p_\theta(\mathbf{y}^j | \mathbf{x}^j)) = \sum_{j=1}^{M} (\sum_{t=1}^{T} F(\mathbf{y}^j, \mathbf{x}^j, t)) - \log Z(\mathbf{x}^j) \tag{8}$$

It has been proved that the L-BFGS quasi-Newton method converges much faster to learn the parameters θ than traditional iterative scaling learning algorithms, such as GIS and IIS [15]. After the training of CRFs, the most probable labeling sequence $\mathbf{y}^*$ given an observation sequence $\mathbf{x}$ is inferred by:

$$\mathbf{y}^* = \arg \max_y p_\theta(\mathbf{y} | \mathbf{x}) = \arg \max_y \exp(\sum_{t=1}^{T} F(\mathbf{y}, \mathbf{x}, t)) \tag{9}$$

The most possible event label $\mathbf{y}^* = [y_1^*, y_2^*, ..., y_T^*]$ can be efficiently calculated by the Viterbi algorithm, which calculates the marginal probability of states at each position of the sequence using a dynamic-programming procedure like HMMs [4].

To detect event, CRFs can automatically decode the semantic event label and output both the event type and event boundary according to the whole observed keyword sequences. The *transition feature functions* $f_i(y_{t-1}, y_t)$ are predefined by CRFs model. Users only need to define the *state feature functions* $g_j(\mathbf{x}, y_t)$. At each time slice t of a given sequence $\mathbf{x}$, we usually assume a Markov blanket, and extract combined state features in the Markov blanket domain. In the case of soccer highlight detection, we empirically set the size of Markov blanket to be 5 slices, view type $\mathbf{x}_1$ to be one keyword sequence $\mathbf{v}$, and encode all the other mid-level keywords $[\mathbf{x}_2, \mathbf{x}_3, \mathbf{x}_4, \mathbf{x}_5]$ as another keyword sequence $\mathbf{w}$. The context combination based state features at time slice t are illustrated in fig. 7 and table 1. It is obvious that CRFs are more expressive to model temporal sequence than HMMs by allowing more dependencies on the observation sequence. In addition, the chosen state features may be at different granularity of the observation sequence.

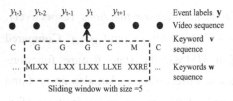

Event labels **y**
Video sequence
Keyword **v** sequence
Keywords **w** sequence

Sliding window with size =5

Fig. 7. Markov blanket of CRFs at time position t with size=5. In the case of soccer highlights detection, G: global view; M: medium view; C: close-up view; LL: left region; ML: middle left region; R: replay; E: excited speech.

Table 1. CRFs feature templates at time position t

Template for transition features
y_{t-1}, y_t

Template for state features
y_t $w_{t-2}, w_{t-1}, w_t, w_{t+1}, w_{t+2}, w_{t-1}w_t, w_tw_{t+1}$
y_t $v_{t-2}, v_{t-1}, v_t, v_{t+1}, v_{t+2}, v_{t-2}v_{t-1}, v_{t-1}v_t, v_tv_{t+1}, v_{t+1}v_{t+2}$
y_t $v_{t-2}v_{t-1}v_t, v_{t-1}v_tv_{t+1}, v_tv_{t+1}v_{t+2}$
y_t $v_{t-1}v_tv_{t+1}w_t$
y_t $v_{t-1}w_{t-1}, v_tw_t, v_{t-1}v_tw_{t-1}, v_{t-1}v_tw_t, v_{t-1}w_{t-1}w_t, v_tw_{t-1}w_t$

4 Experiments

In our experiments, we used libSVM[11], Intel OpenPNL [6] and FlexCRF[4] toolkits for the training/inference of RBF kernel SVM, first-order HMMs and first-order CRFs respectively. For the 2d-BN, we developed it by ourselves. To evaluate the performance of the proposed approaches, experiments of soccer highlights detection were conducted on eight soccer matches totaling up to 12.6 hours of videos. We define semantic events "goal", "shoot", "foul", "free kick" and "corner kick" as highlight events, and all others as non highlights. Five matches are used as training data, and the others as testing data. The ground truth is labeled manually.

To fairly compare the performance of RBF SVM, 2d-BN, first-order HMM, and first-order CRFs, we input same video segments for highlights detection. Since broadcasting soccer video generally uses a close-up view or a replay as a break to emphasize the highlights event, we first filter multiple keyword sequences to find candidate event segments, i.e. play-break units, using the algorithm described in [3]. Then each keyword stream of the play-break unit is time sampled and represented by a N-dimensional feature vector $\mathbf{x}_k = [x_{k1}, x_{k2}, ... x_{kN}]$ with $k = 1, 2, .., K=5$ keywords, and

N=40 time slices. To fuse multimodal cues, we adopt the flat fusion strategy [2] to concatenate the multiple keyword features x_k into one single feature for event detection.

4.1 Performance Comparison

The most widely used performance measures for information retrieval are *precision* (*Pr*) and *recall* (*Re*). Based on *Pr* and *Re*, the *F-score* = $2Pr\,Re/(Pr+Re)$ evaluates the comprehensive performance. Furthermore we define the *segment level measure* and *slice level measure* to evaluate event detection performance. For a predicted video segment, the segment level measure is true if there is at least 80% overlap with the real event region. Similarly, for a predicted video slice, the slice level measure is true if the predicted slice is in the real event region. Then the performance for a whole video is the average of all predicted segments/slices. Segment level measure is suitable to evaluate the recall because it is not dependent on accurate event boundaries. On the other hand, slice level measure can better evaluate how accurate the predicted event boundaries are. From table 2 and table 3, following observations can be made:

- For segment level measure, 2d-BN performs the best since it characterizes the relationships well among features. The CRFs achieves a little better performance than Segments Classifier approaches (SVM and 2d-BN) and better performance than HMM since it relaxes the strong first-order Markov dependence assumptions and avoids a fundamental limitation of directed graphical models.
- For slice level measure, CRFs outperform all other approaches particularly in precision performance since sequence learning approaches can automatically predict the event boundary better than rough SCA approaches (SVM and 2d-BNs). The lower precision of first-order HMMs further demonstrates its deficiency to model semantic event detection problem.

Table 2. Comparison on soccer highlight detection in *segment level measure*

Method	Pr	Re	F
SVM	86.9%	87.3%	87.10%
2d-BN	88.8%	89.3%	89.05%
HMM	79.5%	85.4%	82.34%
CRFs	89.8%	86.3%	88.02%

Table 3. Comparison on soccer highlights detection in *slice level measure*

Method	Pr	Re	F
SVM	73.4%	60.4%	66.3%
2d-BN	73.0%	70.8%	71.9%
HMM	70.0%	60.7%	65.3%
CRFs	78.5%	71.6%	74.9%

4.2 Performance of Multi-modality Fusion

Since 2d-BN and CRFs are probabilistic model on multimodal keywords, they can fuse multiple cues well by inferring the joint probability $p(x_1,x_2,..,x_k, y)$. Here, we use 2d-BN approach to demonstrate the fusion effect on different keyword combinations. From the table 4, it can be observed that:

- By fusing multimodal cues, 2d-BN achieves better performance than any single cues. For example, the best single feature R has the F-score 80.9%. But multi-modality fusion of (V+P+R+E+W) performs much better with F-score 89.0%.

- The number of selected features and their combination, i.e. feature selection, are very important for multi-modality fusion. For instance, fusion of (V+P+R) outperforms better than (V+P+E) and (V+P+E+W).

Table 4. Multimodal fusion on different features of soccer highlight detection in segment level measure. V:view type; P:play position; R: replay; E: excited speech; W:whistle.

Keyword	Pr	Re	F	Keyword	Pr	Re	F
V	32.8%	91.1%	48.1%	R+E	82.6%	75.9%	78.7%
P	43.9%	98.1%	60.6%	R+E+W	82.5%	78.4%	79.9%
R	84.8%	78.1%	80.9%	V+P+E	40.5%	96.4%	57.0%
W	60.4%	70.5%	64.4%	V+P+R	78.2%	83.1%	80.6%
E	64.5%	75.1%	68.8%	V+P+E+W	43.8%	96.6%	60.2%
E+W	63.1%	73.3%	67.2%	V+P+R+E	83.3%	89.3%	86.2%
V+P	37.1%	95.2%	53.2%	V+P+R+E+W	88.8%	89.3%	89.0%

5 Conclusion

In this paper, we propose two novel semantic event detection models using *Two-dependence Bayesian Network* (2d-BN) and *Conditional Random Fields* (CRFs) and systematically compared them with the traditional approaches of SVM and HMMs. Promising experimental results on soccer highlights detection demonstrate the effectiveness of the proposed two methods.

It is worth pointing out that both SCA (SVM and 2d-BN) and SLA (HMMs and CRFs) have their advantages and disadvantages, and can be applied for different applications. For example, if we just care about the rough position of each event or prior knowledge can filter possible event segments accurately, SCA is enough, e.g. 2d-BN. Otherwise, if we require the precise event boundaries without prior knowledge to segment videos, we have to use SLA, .e.g. CRFs.

Acknowledgments. The authors are thankful to YangBo, WangFei, Sun Yi, Prof. Sun Lifeng, and Prof. Ou Zhijian of Dept. CS. and EE. of Tsinghua university for the research on the mid-level audiovisual keywords detection.

References

1. Cestnik. Estimating probabilities: A crucial task in machine learning. In Proc. 9th European Conf. on Artificial Intelligence, pp. 147–149, 1990.
2. C. G. Snoek, M.Worring, and A. Smeulders. Early versus late fusion in sematic video analysis. In ACM Multimedia Conference, pages 399–402, 2005.
3. Ekin, A. M. Tekalp, and R. Mehrotr. Automatic soccer video analysis and summarization. IEEE Trans. on Image processing, 12(7):796–807, 2003.
4. FlexCRFs: Flexible Conditional Random Fields http://www.jaist.ac.jp/~hieuxuan/flexcrfs/flexcrfs.html
5. H.L. Bai, W. Hu, T. Wang, X.F. Tong, Y.M. Zhang, A Novel Sports Video Logo Detector Based on Motion Analysis, International Conference on Neural Information Processing (ICONIP), 2006.

6. Intel Open Source Probabilistic Network Library (OpenPNL) http://www.intel.com/research/mrl/pnl
7. J. Lafferty, A. McCallum, and F. Pereira. Conditional random fields: probabilistic models for segmenting and labeling sequence data. In Proc. of ICML, pp.282-289, 2001.
8. J. Wang, C. Xu, E.Chng, K. Wan, and Q. Tian. Automatic replay generation for soccer video broadcasting. In ACM Multimedia Conference, 2004.
9. L. Duan, M. Xu, T.-S. Chua, Q. Tian, and C. Xu. A mid-level representation framework for semantic sports video analysis. In ACM Multimedia Conference, 2003.
10. L. Xie, S.-F. Chang, A. Divakaran, and H. Sun. Structure analysis of soccer video with hidden markov models. Proc. ICASSP, 4:4096–4099, 2002.
11. LIBSVM: A Library for Support Vector Machines, http://www.csie.ntu.edu.tw/~cjlin/libsvm/
12. M. Luo, Y. Ma, and H.J.Zhang. Pyramidwise structuring for soccer highlight extraction. In ICICS-PCM, pp. 1–5, 2003.
13. M. Xu, N. Maddage, C.Xu, M. Kankanhalli, and Q.Tian. Creating audio keywords for event detection in soccer video. In IEEE ICME 2003, volume 2, pp. 281–284, 2003.
14. N. Friedman, D. Geiger, and M. Goldszmidt. Bayesian network classifiers. Machine Learning, 29(2):131–163, 1997.
15. Sha and F. Pereira. Shallow parsing with conditional random fields. In Proc. of HLT/NAACL, 2003.
16. X.K. Li, F.M., A hidden Markov model framework for traffic event detection using video features, In IEEE Proc. of ICIP 2004, pp.2901-2904.

Video Histogram: A Novel Video Signature for Efficient Web Video Duplicate Detection*

Lu Liu[1], Wei Lai[2], Xian-Sheng Hua[2], and Shi-Qiang Yang[1]

[1] Dept. of Comp. Sci. & Tech., Tsinghua University
[2] Microsoft Research Asia
lu-liu@mails.tsinghua.edu.cn, {weilai, xshua}@microsoft.com,
yangsq@tsnghua.edu.cn

Abstract. The explosive growth of information technology and digital content industry stimulates various video applications over the Internet. Since it is quite easy to copy, reformat, modify and republish video files on the websites, similarity/duplicate detection and measurement is essential to identify the excessive content duplication, so as to facilitate effective video search and intelligence propriety protection as well. In this paper, we propose a novel signature-based approach for duplicate video comparison. The so-called *video histogram* scheme counts the numbers of video's frames that are closest to a set of representative seed vectors chosen from the feature space of the training data set in advance. Then all the numbers are normalized to generate the signature of the video for further comparison. As our signature is a compact fixed-size vector with low dimension for each video, it requires less storage and computation cost than previous methods. The experiments show that our approach is both efficient and effective for web video duplicate detection.

1 Introduction

During past years, Internet continues to grow in its size, economic importance and interplay with human society since its emergence in the 1990s. As evidenced, there are at least 11.5 billion web pages by the end of Jan. 2005 [5]. The explosive growth of information technology and digital content industry also facilitates various multimedia applications over the Internet, especially in the format of video. Intrinsic to the prevalence of videos over the Internet, kinds of video search engines have been developed and even available for common users in recent years. For instance, Yahoo disclosed that it indexed more than 50 million audio and video files [1]. However, what makes this searching problem particularly inefficient is the unique challenge in this arena. Duplicate contents self-spread over the Internet in absence of central management or monitor on the web. Since it is quite easy to copy, reformat, modify and republish a "new" video file, there are potentially numerous similar and even duplicate contents in the initial searching results. It has been demonstrated that each video from the web has around five similar copies on average in Cheung's collection [3].

---

* This work was performed when the first author was visiting Microsoft Research Asia.

T.-J. Cham et al. (Eds.): MMM 2007, LNCS 4352, Part II, pp. 94 – 103, 2007.

We also give some queries to Yahoo video search engine, such as earthquake, Zinedine Zidane, Connie Chung, etc. There are almost about two or three duplicate videos among the ten results on the first web page. With the consideration that users generally care more about the first screen of the search results, the similar results obviously downgrade the users' perceptibility and experience. From this stand of view, identifying the similar video contents can facilitate efficient video search engines. Besides, providing an alternative copy in case of expired links and presenting the best version based on users' need could also benefit from the detection of similar contents [3].

Finding visually similar content is the central theme in the area of content-based image retrieval (CBIR) [2-4] [6] [7] [9]. A rich literature of previous works on video content comparison typically employ the temporal trace of the video, which is represented as a time series of feature vectors, and then search through part of or the entire video. For example, some schemes segment the videos into shots and identify each shot as a high dimensional feature vector, which is usually the attributes such as color, texture, shape, motion of one or more key frames [2] [4] [9]. Some other works re-sample the videos with high sampling rate and use the sequence of sampled frames' feature vectors to represent the entire video [6] [7]. The essential drawback of these works comes from the inevitable computation complexity of comparison. Since the video is represented as a sequence of high dimensional feature vectors, the comparison requires a lot of computation, which is at least linear with the length of the video. Although some special features are employed to degrade the dimension of frames' feature vector [6] [7], the sampling rate is still too high, e.g. 12fps in [6], to further decrease the computation of the entire videos' comparison. Besides, in order to compare, the long sequence of key frames or feature vectors should be stored first, so that it leads to large storage cost. The schemes are also sensitive to temporal changes and the performances degrade greatly if the sampling rate becomes lower or some temporal editing such as frame dropping exists. Therefore applying such algorithms in finding similar contents within a database of millions of videos may be not practical. Different with the schemes mentioned above, the method in [3] summarizes each video into a compact fixed-size signature and it is said to be applied in large scale databases. However the signature proposed in [3] is several feature vectors of frames whose dimension is up to 712, still too big to store and to meet the need of real-time comparison for search engines. More progress is still required before applying the comparison of videos to large scale, widely-sourced video databases.

In this paper, based on the investigation of the principal problem of similarity detection, we propose a novel signature-based approach to detect web video duplicate. In our scheme, several seed vectors are selected from the feature space of training data set by using heuristic methods as the first step. Then each video is re-sampled uniformly and the distances between all the sampled frames and the selected seed vectors are calculated. Based on the distances, the numbers of video's frames which are closest to each selected seed vector are recorded and normalized to generate the signature of the video at last. In this way, each video is summarized into a compact fixed-size signature, whose dimension is the same with the number of seed vectors (no more than 60 in our experiments), resulting in less storage and computation cost than others, e.g. the dimension of the signature proposed in [3] is more than 200 times of ours. In addition, our scheme is robust to temporal changes due to its low sampling rate and can be applied in all kinds of videos, especially the widely-sourced web videos since it doesn't use any domain-specific premise. The experiments demonstrate that the proposed method is both efficient and effective for web video duplicate detection.

The rest of the paper is organized as follows. Section 2 discusses how to generate video signature. The relationship between the signature's uniqueness and dimension is analyzed in Section 3, followed by the algorithms of seed vectors' selection in Section 4. Section 5 presents experimental results and we conclude this paper in Section 6.

2 Video Similarity Measurement

In this section, based on the survey and analysis of real web videos, we clarify the concept of similar/duplicate videos in the scope of this paper in the first subsection. Then our approach is introduced in the second subsection.

2.1 Definition of Similar/Duplicate Videos

Duplicate videos on the web are with roughly the same content, but may have three prevalent differences as below:

- Format: there are many video formats on the web nowadays such as MPG, AVI and WMV.
- Bit-rates, frame-rates, frame size: in order to facilitate storage, downloading, streaming or to meet other needs of users, the same video may be compressed at different qualities, reformatted to different frame-rates and sizes.
- Editing in either spatial or temporal domain: spatial and temporal editing are ubiquitous on web videos, e.g. logo appears on the top or bottom corner for different sources, the borders of frames are cut, a few frames are dropped due to network congestions, or a short clip is inserted into the original stream.

2.2 Signature Generation Scheme

Based on the definition of duplicate videos above, it's easy to find out that most frames of one video have a similar frame in the duplicate copy. So the feature vectors of duplicate videos' frames distribute similarly in the feature space, which is exemplified in Fig.1. In order to facilitate observation, the dimension of the feature vector is reduced to two by PCA (Principle Component Analysis). As a result each point in the figure stands for a frame, and Fig.1 shows the distribution of four videos' feature vectors, among which the first two are similar videos while the other two are totally different. It's evident that distributions of similar videos are with much likeness, while the dissimilar ones are completely different. In our approach, the signature called *video histogram* is proposed to represent the distributions of videos' feature vectors in the feature space.

In our scheme, videos are uniformly re-sampled first. Let $SV = (sv_1, sv_2 \ldots sv_m)$ be a set of feature vectors called seed vectors. Define an m-dimensional vector VS called *video histogram* as the signature of video with respect to SV as below:

$$
VS = (vs_1, vs_2, \ldots, vs_m) \quad where \quad vs_i = \frac{\sum_{j=1}^{N} I(sv_i = \arg\min_{1 \le k \le m} d(v_j, sv_k))}{N} \tag{1}
$$

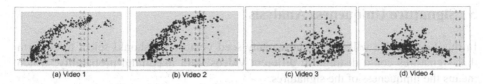

(a) Video 1   (b) Video 2   (c) Video 3   (d) Video 4

Fig. 1. Distribution of feature vectors, where video 1 and 2 are similar videos, while video 3 and 4 are totally different

$I(A)$ equals to 1 if A is true and zero otherwise. $d(*)$ is the Euclid distance. Each dimension's value of the signature means the percent of the videos frames which are closest to the corresponding seed vector with the same order in the SV. Thus the signature is a normalized vector that satisfy $\sum vs_i = 1$. Fig. 2 gives a simple example of a signature's generation process. There are three seed vectors. After counting the distances between N frames of the video and the three seed vectors, we get the numbers of frames closest to each seed vector ($n1, n2, n3$), and normalize them to generate the signature, which is (0.3, 0.3, 0.4) in this example.

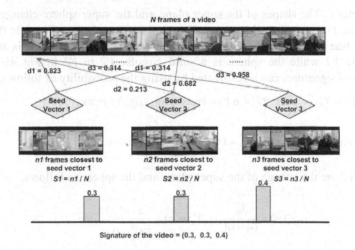

Signature of the video = (0.3, 0.3, 0.4)

Fig. 2. Signature Generation Process

Given signatures RS and QS of two videos, we can now define their similarity:

$$T(RS,QS) = 1 - \frac{1}{\sqrt{2}} d(RS,QS) \quad where \quad d(RS,QS) = \sqrt{\sum_{i=1}^{m} (rs_i - qs_i)^2} \qquad (2)$$

As duplicate videos have a majority of similar frames shown in Fig. 1 and similar frames would be closest to the same seed vector [3], the signatures of duplicate videos would be approximately the same.

Since our signature is a normalized low-dimensional float-point value vector, it requires not only smaller storage, but also less computation when compared. Furthermore, the sampling rate isn't required to be high so that the signature would not be sensitive to the changes of frame-rates and frame droppings as well.

3 Signature Uniqueness Analysis

In this Section, we will discuss how many seed vectors we should select to confirm that signatures could distinguish different videos with maximum probability, which means the uniqueness of the signatures.

In order to roughly estimate the uniqueness of the video signature, the probability of two random signatures that will be determined as similar is estimated. According to the definition, the signatures are on the super plane U as follows,

$$U = \{(u_1, u_2, ..., u_m) : \quad \sum_{i=1}^{m} u_i = 1, \quad u_i \geq 0, \quad 1 \leq i \leq m\} \tag{3}$$

Suppose the signatures of different videos distribute uniformly on the super plane, which is also the goal of our algorithms of generating suitable seed vectors described in Section 4. Assume the similarity threshold more than which the videos are determined to be similar is η. Based on similarity definition in Equation (2), the distance should be less than $r = \sqrt{2} * (1-\eta)$, which means the signatures are in a super sphere with diameter r. The shapes of the super plane and the super sphere change with the dimension m. For instance, when m equals to 2, the plane is a line $V1$ while the sphere is a shorter line $V2$ on $V1$ in Fig.3(a). And when m equals to 3, the plane is an equilateral triangle $V1$ while the sphere is a solid circular $V2$ in $V1$ in Fig.3(b). So the uniqueness of signatures can be estimated by using the probability as follows,

$$\text{Prob}(T(v_i, v_j) > \eta : \forall v_i, v_j \in V) = \text{Prob}(d(sig_{v_i}, sig_{v_j}) < r : \forall v_i, v_j \in V)$$

$$= \text{Prob}(d(x_i, x_j) < r : \forall x_i, x_j \in U) = \frac{V_2(m-1, \frac{r}{2})}{V_1(m)} \tag{4}$$

where $V1$, $V2$ are the cubage of the super plane and the sphere as follows,

$$V_1(m) = \frac{\sqrt{m}}{(m-1)!} \qquad V_2(m, r) = \frac{\pi^{\frac{m}{2}} r^m}{\Gamma(\frac{m}{2}+1)} \tag{5}$$

The probability curve by changing the dimension m is shown in Fig.4. Given a threshold $\eta = 0.9$, which means the videos are determined to be similar when the similarity of signatures is more than 0.9, the lowest probability is 2.9941e-008, small enough to ensure the uniqueness of the signature. As the super plane U would be multiangular in a high dimension m, the real probability is even lower than the value calculated by Equation (4).

Fig. 4 also shows that if the optimal set of seed vectors is selected, which means it makes the signatures of different videos distribute uniformly on the super plane U as is assumed, the number of seed vectors would be about 35 if the threshold η equals to 0.9. The algorithm of selecting seed vectors will be discussed in Section 4.

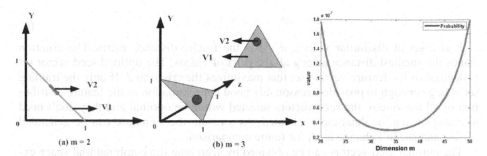

Fig. 3. (a) When $m = 2$, the super plane is a line $V1$ while the sphere is a shorter line $V2$ on $V1$ (b) When $m = 3$, the super plane is an equilateral triangle $V1$ while the sphere is a solid circular $V2$ in $V1$

Fig. 4. Given a similarity threshold 0.9, the probability with which different videos would be determined as duplicate changes with signature's dimension m

4 The Selection of Seed Vectors

The signatures change with different seed vectors sets. Optimal seed vectors set should make the signatures of different videos distribute uniformly on the super plane U, because if this is satisfied, the distance of random signatures is big enough to distinguish different videos with large probability as we analysis in Section 3. In this paper, two approaches to generate seed vectors – clustering method and searching method are proposed to get the optimal seed vectors set.

4.1 Clustering Method

Clustering method could be developed by intuition. Let's consider the simplest situation – two different videos and two seed vectors. The optimal seed vectors set would maximize the distance between the two videos. Generally, the frames of the same video are conglobated together as shown in Fig.1. If the centers of the two clustering are selected as seed vectors, the signatures of the two videos would be (1, 0) and (0, 1), whose distance is the largest between all effective signatures. Based on the observation, clustering all the frames in the training set to m sets, and selecting the centers of them as seed vectors is a practical approach.

4.2 Searching Method

As the signature's dimension m is much smaller than the number of videos in database, the clustering method, which selects the centers of m clusters, works not so well in large scale database. To overcome the limitation of clustering method, a heuristic searching method is proposed in our scheme.

Since all the signatures' distribution is not easy to obtain, we identify the smallest distance among all pairs as the criterion to judge the effectiveness of the seed vectors set. If the smallest distance is maximized, all the distances should be big enough to distinguish dissimilar videos with large probability as is supposed to. Therefore the criterion is given as follows,

$$J = \min\{d(sig_{v_i}, sig_{v_j}) : v_i, v_j \in V\} \tag{6}$$

V is a set of dissimilar videos. d (*) is the Euclid distance metric. The criterion stands the smallest distance among all the pairs of videos. The optimal seed vector set is deemed as the feature vectors set that maximizes the criterion J. If only the training set is huge enough to provide a reasonably good approximation to the feature distribution of all the videos, the seed vectors selected would be optimal and they don't need to change when the database is updated. As a result, the signature can be generated offline and needn't change at all for future comparison.

The optimal seed vectors can be obtained by searching the combinatorial space exhaustively based on the criterion, but it's too complex. So in our scheme, a heuristic search method SFFS [8] to get an approximate optimal set is employed.

5 Experiments Results

In this section, we present the experiments results on the videos crawled from the Internet to demonstrate the performance of our approach. All experiments use block-based color histograms as video frame features, which means each frame is divided to 2 by 2 blocks, and then the 64 dimension color histograms are extracted from each block. So the dimension of these feature vectors is 256. The Euclid distance is applied as the metric of feature vectors' distance.

We randomly choose about 600 web videos (more than 3G in file size in total) as training set. Then both the clustering method – k-means and searching method are employed to select the seed vectors among the feature space of training set. Suppose the similarity threshold is 0.9. As discussed in Section 3, the probability of any two videos would be identified to be duplicate achieves at the lowest point when the signature's dimension is 34. So in our experiments, we test three values of m 20, 40, 60.

Our survey shows that each video on the web has about zero to five duplicate versions. The differences among these versions have been described as the definition of duplicate videos in Section 2. However the numbers of web videos' real duplicate copies, which would cost a lot of labor to check, are not easy to obtain. So we conduct two experiments as follows. First, in order to overcome the limitation of absence of ground-truth, we simulate circumstances of web videos to produce their duplicate copies, so as to get ground-truth to evaluate the performance of our approach. Then, we do the experiments on real web videos and check the results by human.

In the first experiment, we randomly choose another 600 web videos as testing data, which don't overlap with the training data. We simulate these web video duplicate cases and randomly produce zero to five duplicate copies of each video. These changes include the random combination of converting format (e.g. from WMV to AVI or MPEG), changing bit-rate, reducing frame-rate (e.g. from 30fps to 10fps or 15fps), decreasing frame size (e.g. 2/3 or 1/2 times of original size), cropping (e.g. 15 or 20 pixels of borders are cut), adding logo on the top or bottom corner, etc. In this way, more than 1000 videos are generated and all the 2000 videos are used as ground-truth set to test the precision and recall of our approach. Let A denote the number of video pairs which are found to be similar using our approach on the ground-truth set. If among these A pairs, B pairs are in fact truly similar, then the precision ratio of the video signature algorithm is defined as B/A. The recall is defined as B/C where C is the total number of truly similar pairs in the ground-truth set. We set the similarity threshold 0.9. Table 1 shows the results of the experiments.

The experiments results demonstrate that the searching method performs much better than the clustering method. When employing the searching method, the result of $m = 40$ is almost the best, which is consistent with the analysis in Section 3.

Table 1. Searching and Clustering Method Results

Dimension	Searching Method: $m=$			Clustering Method: $m=$		
	20	40	60	20	40	60
Precision	73.36%	86.5%	87.59%	38.51%	69.05%	81.47%
Recall	63.02%	63.61%	58.65%	63.25%	61.04%	57.74%

Table 2. Intersection Results

Dimension	Searching Method: $m=$			Clustering Method: $m=$		
	20&40	20&60	40&60	20&40	20&60	40&60
Precision	97.07%	97.17%	95.76%	75.88%	82.7%	84.95%
Recall	47.9%	46.46%	46.86%	49.84%	46.82%	47.9%

In video search systems, the duplicate videos would be grouped to upgrade the users' perceptibility and experience as one of the most important purposes of duplicate detection. The correct groups give users good experience, while a wrong group will upset users GREATLY. It implies that high precision should be ensured with high priority. Furthermore, the database of search systems is so huge that precision is much more important than recall nowadays. In addition, our scheme focuses on less time and storage consuming so that the trade-off between high-recall and computation\storage cost should be achieved. Therefore we select a "high-precision" strategy and use the intersection of two results with different seed vector numbers to further improve the precision. The results in Table 2 show that the precision is improved greatly and able to achieve at 97% with combination strategy. When the searching method is employed, the precision by combining the dimension 20 and 40 is much better than the one by employing the dimension 60 alone with approximate computation complexity.

In the second experiment, we test our approach in about 5000 real web videos. In this experiment, we employ the combination strategy above and only use the sets of 20 and 40 seed vectors generated by searching method, based on which all the videos' signatures are obtained. Then we randomly select about 50 videos among the test data as query samples, and get their possible duplicate copies which have a similarity above the threshold 0.9 with the query sample. Because we don't have the ground-truth, all the possible duplicate copies are checked by human to determine whether they are real duplicate or not.

The number of each query video's duplicate copies is recorded. Table 3 shows the proportion of videos which have zero, one, two to five and above five duplicate copies in our query sample set. It is shown that most videos have more than one duplicate. On average, every video in query sample set has around 1.46 duplicate copies.

Table 3. The proportion of videos have N duplicate copies

N	0	1	2~5	>5
Proportion	6.25%	75%	16.67%	2.08%

Table 4. The Average Similarity of Real Duplicate Videos

Table 5. Average Precision of Real-life Web Video Duplicate Detection

Signature Dimension	40	20
Average Similarity	0.9841	0.9814

Similarity Threshold	0.9	0.95
Average Precision	90%	96%

As the test data is too huge and we can't get the real number of each video's duplicate copies, we can only get precision based on human's check. The average precision is about 90% when the similarity threshold is 0.9. During the check, we find that all the real duplicate videos' similarities are above 0.95. We calculate the average similarity of real duplicate videos, and find that it is 0.9841 when the dimension is 40 and 0.9814 when the dimension is 20 as shown in Table 4. So if we increase the similarity threshold to 0.95, the precision is improved up to 96% as is shown in Table 5.

All the test data sets above have none intersection with training data set from which the seed vectors are generated. This demonstrates that seed vectors selection is unrelated with testing data. If only we use a huge enough training data set, which can provide a reasonably good approximation of feature distribution, and employ a proper method to select the optimal seed vectors, they would be suitable for all the videos and the signatures needn't be regenerated when the database is constantly updated.

6 Conclusion and Future Work

In this paper, a novel signature-based approach named as *video histogram* is proposed to detect similar/duplicate videos on the Internet. And the uniqueness of the signature is also investigated. In our scheme, seed vectors are firstly selected based on clustering and searching. Then the signature of videos is generated by counting and normalizing the numbers of frames closest to each seed vector. The similarity of videos is measured by comparing their signatures. As our approach employs a compact fixsized signature with much lower dimension than the works before, it requires much smaller storage and cost less computation as well. Furthermore, our scheme doesn't use the domain-specific knowledge so that it can be applied in widely-sourced web videos. The experiments results demonstrate that our approach is robust to various temporal and spatial changes that duplicate videos may have and show that the precision can be up to 96% in real web videos.

In future work, better algorithms of seed vectors selection would be employed to improve the performance and make our signature-based approach more robust for web video search engines. Some novel methods would be also used to further reduce the storage and comparison complexity of signatures for web-scale applications.

References

[1] http://www.searchenginejournal.com/index.php?p=2036

[2] Aoki, H., Shimotsuji, S., Hori, O.: A Shot Classification Method of Selecting Effective Key-frames for Video Browsing. In Proceedings of the 6th ACM international conference on Multimedia, 1996, pp 1-10.

[3] Cheung, SC., Zakhor, A.: Estimation of Web Video Multiplicity. In Proceedings of the SPIE -- Internet Imaging, pages 34-36, San Jose, California. January 2000.

[4] Dimitrova, N., Abdel-Mottaleb, M.,: Content-Based Video Retrieval by Example Video Clip. In: Proceedings of IS&T and SPIE Storage and Retrieval of Image and Video Databases VI, Vol.3022. 1998. 184~196.

[5] Gulli, A., Signorini, A.: The indexable Web is more than 11.5 billion pages. In Poster proceedings of the 14th international conference on World Wide Web, pages 902--903, Chiba, Japan, 2005. ACM Press.

[6] Hua Xian-Sheng, Chen Xian, Zhang Hong-Jiang, Robust Video Signature Based on Ordinal Measure. International Conference on Image Processing (ICIP 2004), October 24-27, Singapore, 2004.

[7] Li, Z., Katsaggelos, AK., Gandhi, B.: Fast video shot retrieval based on trace geometry matching. Vision, Image and Signal Processing, IEE Proceedings- Volume 152, Issue 3, 3 June 2005 Page(s):367 – 373.

[8] Pudil, P., Ferri, F.J., Novovicova, J., Kittler, J.: Floating search methods for feature selection with nonmonotoniccriterion functions. Pattern Recognition, 1994. Vol. 2 - Conference B: Computer Vision & Image Processing., Proceedings of the 12th IAPR International. Conference on.

[9] Tan, Y.P., Saur, D. D., Kulkarni, S. R., Ramadge, P. J,,: A Framework for Measuring Video Similarity and its Application to Video Query by Example. IEEE Int. Conf. on Image Processing, 1999.

VOD Multicast Using CIWP and P2P Partial Stream Transfer

Kwang-Sik Shin, Wan-Oh Yoon, Jin-Ha Jung, and Sang-Bang Choi

Inha University, Dept. of Electronic Engineering, 253 Yonghyun-Dong, Nam-Gu,
Incheon, Korea
kwangsik@inha.ac.kr

Abstract. Providing VOD in the internet is one of the challenging technologies. When a new client joins an ongoing multicast session for VOD service, the servers using CIWP scheme for the VOD multicast creates an additional unicast channel to serve the partial stream. And, the unicast channel consumes a certain amount of the I/O bandwidth of the server, as well as some of the network resources between the server and clients. This problem can be solved by using p2p local transfer between the clients to deliver the partial stream. In this paper, we propose a new VOD multicast scheme that is based on the CIWP scheme and the p2p transfer of the partial multimedia stream. In the p2p approach, unexpected dropout of a client, due to the failure of the connection or departure from the current session, can disrupt the partial stream transfer for the other clients. Thus, we also propose a procedure to recover from this kind of unexpected dropout. Our simulation results show that the proposed scheme reduces the network bandwidth on the server side dramatically, reduces the average waiting time of the client, and improves the service quality.

Keywords: multimedia stream, multicast, CIWP, p2p communication.

1 Introduction

The number of users making use of VOD (video on demand) services has increased with the improvement of the network environment on the client side. However, the network resources on the server side have not been able to keep pace with the increased expectations of the users. In streaming multicast services, the network resources on the server side include the I/O bandwidth of the server and the communication links of the paths from the server to the client's ISP (Internet Service Provider). In order to guarantee the client continuous playback, the video server has to reserve a sufficient amount of server bandwidth for video streams before serving requests from clients. However, the available server bandwidth is limited, and the quality of a multimedia service depends on the efficient utilization of the network resources.

By focusing on multicast trees [1-6], many researchers have explored to utilize the server resources efficiently. In the multicast tree approach, the network resources are dedicated to video objects rather than to users. This approach allows many users to share a single video stream.

T.-J. Cham et al. (Eds.): MMM 2007, LNCS 4352, Part II, pp. 104–114, 2007.

In this paper, we present a new VOD multicast scheme that is based on the CIWP (client-initiated-with-prefetching) [5-6] scheme and the p2p (peer-to-peer) transfer of the partial multimedia stream. In the proposed scheme, all clients receive multimedia data mainly from the multicast stream in the CIWP. However, a client who arrives later receives the part of the video that has already been played from one of the clients who arrived earlier by means of the p2p transfer algorithm. Also, to reduce excessive data traffic among clients, we use a threshold based algorithm, in which the server initiates a new complete multicast stream, in order to satisfy a client request after a predefined threshold time [7]. Moreover, we prevent an earlier client from serving a later arriving client after receiving one half of the whole stream from the server by limiting T_i to $L/2$, where T_i represents a threshold value, which is used to start a new complete multicast stream for video i, and L_i denotes the length of video i.

We perform simulation studies using a set of videos and compare the proposed scheme with the FCFS (first-come, first-served) batching, basic CIWP and threshold based multicast schemes. Simulation results show that the proposed scheme reduces the network bandwidth on the server side dramatically, reduces the average waiting time of the client, and improves the service quality.

In the p2p network environment, the unexpected dropout of a client, due to the failure of the connection or departure from the current session, can affect the partial stream service to other clients sharing the same session. The high-level multicast scheme with p2p patching makes a tree using a unicast between clients [8-10]. The high-level multicast scheme employs p2p transfer both for the base stream and patching. Due to the use of unicasting based on the tree structure, all of the clients belonging to a subtree rooted at the failed client are affected. Thus, the high-level multicast requires a time needed for recovery procedure, and, consequently, the failure of the client seriously affects the overall performance. However, since the proposed algorithm is based on multicasting, the procedure used to recover from the dropout of a client is very simple. We implement a procedure for recovering from the failure of a client in the partial stream receiver thread. Then we perform simulations to estimate the influence of unexpected client dropouts.

2 P2P Model for Partial Multimedia Stream

2.1 Overview

As described in section 1, the proposed p2p transfer scheme for partial multimedia streams employs the threshold based algorithm for multicast stream delivery and p2p transfer among clients for the partial stream. Fig. 1 depicts the interactive operations required for channel initialization and the stream service process with its control messages and data flow. To describe the relationship among the clients, we represent each client as a node. Each node has a parent or child relation with successive nodes depending on the order of arrival. In Fig. 1, node 1 is a parent of node 2, and node 3 is a child of node 2. Nodes 1 and 2 are ancestors of node 3, and nodes 2 and 3 are descendants of node 1.

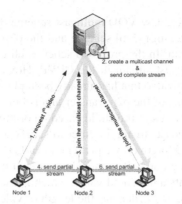

Fig. 1. Multicast channel initialization and stream service process for clients

When the server receives a request from node 1, it creates a multicast channel and starts sending the multicast stream to node 1. If the server receives another request for the same video i from node 2, while transmitting video i to node 1, it sends control information to node 2 about ongoing multicast session of video i and node 1 for the partial stream. Node 1 is the parent node of node 2 and becomes a local server for the partial stream. Then node 2 joins the session and prefetches the ongoing multicast stream for video i. At the same time, node 1 transmits the partial stream that has already been multicasted by the server to node 2. After a while, when node 3 requests the same video, the server sends control information to node 3, in order to inform it about the ongoing multicast stream, node 2, and the master node. Now, node 3 joins the multicast session too. If node 2 does not have enough a partial stream needed by node 3, node 3 has to retrieve the missing part from node 1. In this case, node 1 becomes the master node of the session. We give a detailed the master node and description about this particular case using an example in the following.

2.2 P2P Transfer of the Partial Stream

Fig. 2 shows a multicast stream transferred by the server through the multicast channel, partial streams transferred by nodes through a p2p channel (it is a unicast channel), and data segments stored in each node's buffer as a function of the elapsed time, when node k arrives at time t_{k-1}. To give a brief explanation, it is assumed that the data stream of video i is divided into several segments of equal size. We sequentially enumerate each segment and logically divide the client's disk buffer into two parts, i.e., *pBuffer* and *cBuffer*. *cBuffer* is the buffer used to save the ongoing multicast stream received from the server, while *pBuffer* is used to save the partial stream received from the parent node and master node. Because the server continuously multicasts the complete stream until all of the segments of video i have been transferred, *cBuffer* is required to save them and it operates in a wrap-around fashion, because of its limited size. If one node needs to provide a partial stream to another node, it has to read the partial stream contained in *pBuffer*, in order to send it. When the node in question needs to transfer a partial stream contained in *cBuffer* in addition to that contained in *pBuffer*, the corresponding data segments are moved from *cBuffer* to *pBuffer* before

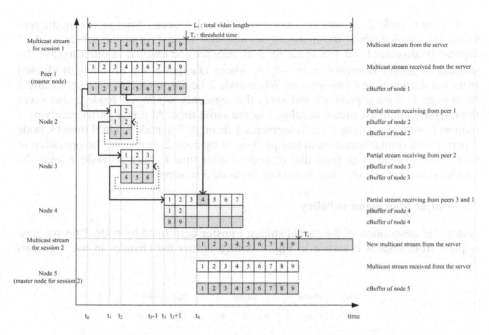

Fig. 2. Description of the proposed p2p transfer of the partial stream

they are transferred to another node. Note that the movement of the data from *cBuffer* to *pBuffer* is merely a logical operation. The amount of space used for *pBuffer* and *cBuffer* dynamically changes, and a part of *cBuffer* can be used for *pBuffer* in the implementation. In this paper, we assume that both of these buffers are fixed in size and segments are moved from *cBuffer* to *pBuffer* to simply the explanation. This process is managed by the buffer management policy of the proposed algorithm, which is explained below. When allocating buffers in each node, the disk manager first assigns *cBuffer*, and then *pBuffer* is assigned. When the server receives a request for video i from node 1 at time t_0, it initiates a multicast session of length L_i. Node 1 becomes the master node in this session and saves the multicast stream of length T_i in *cBuffer*, if it can allocate enough disk space, where T_i is the threshold time of video i.

The first node in the session is referred to as the master node, since it provides a partial stream that is not offered by the other nodes in the same session. If the available disk space of the first node is less than bT_i, where b is the playback rate, the node only stores segments until a second node arrives in the session. When the second node that has extra disk space that is equal to bT_i arrives in the session, it becomes the master node. If the second node does not have sufficient disk space either, the procedure continues until a node with enough disk space can be found. If each node saves all the segments required to provide service for nodes that arrive later, more disk space than necessary will be used to receive the multimedia service. Each node has a different amount of available disk space, and the request from each node arrives at arbitrary times. Therefore, each session needs a master node to supplement the partial stream that cannot be provided by other nodes.

At time t_1, node 2 requests the same video from the server. After receiving the requisite information about the multicast session and node 1 from the server, node 2 separately allocates local disk space for both *pBuffer* and *cBuffer*, in order to save the streams of length $vLength·b = (t_1 - t_0)·b$, where *vLength* is the time length elapsed from the starting time of the session. When node 2 begins to receive segments 1 and 2 from node 1, it starts playback and saves the segments in *pBuffer*. Node 2 also saves the ongoing multicast stream in *cBuffer* at the same time. At time t_2, after receiving a request from node 3, node 2 sends segments 1 through 3 to node 3. Until time t3, node 3 performs a similar operation to that performed by node 2. However, the operation of node 3 is quite different from that of node 2 after time t_3, because node 4 joins the multicast session at a time that is too late for node 3 to support.

2.3 Buffer Management Policy

A detailed description of the partial stream transfer performed by node 3 for the new request from node 4 is shown in Fig. 3, which shows the changes in the segments

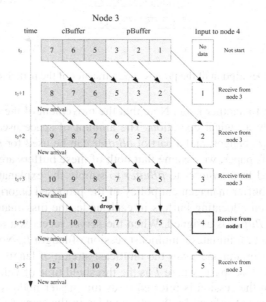

Fig. 3. Changes of partial stream segments stored in node 3's two buffers and segments delivered to node 4

stored in node 3's two buffers and the segments delivered to node 4 as a function of the elapsed time after time t_3. To describe the operation that occurs when *pBuffer* or *cBuffer* is full, we will now explain the buffer management policy used in this paper.

(1) All segments in *cBuffer* must be preserved until playback.
(2) If *pBuffer* has extra space when a node begins to play a segment contained in *cBuffer*, those segments that have been already been played back are moved to *pBuffer* in order of segment sequence number. Otherwise, they are removed from *cBuffer* in first-in first-out order.

(3) Those segments contained in *pBuffer* that have already been transferred to another node can be removed, except in the case of the segments stored in master nodes.

At time t_3-1, *pBuffer* and *cBuffer* of node 3 contain segments 1 through 3 and segments 4 through 6, respectively, as shown in Fig. 2, and node 3 starts to play back segment 4 at this time. At this time, node 3 receives segment 7 from the multicast channel. Then, it transfers segment 4 to *cBuffer* according to policy 2. Segments 5 and 6 are preserved until playback in accordance with the buffer management policy 1, and node 3 starts to deliver segment 1 to node 4, since node 4's request arrives at time t_3. At time t_3+1, node 3 finishes the delivery of segment 1 to node 4, removes segment 1 from *pBuffer* in accordance with policy 3, moves segment 5 from *cBuffer* to *pBuffer* in accordance with policy 2, and saves the newly arriving segment (segment 8) in *cBuffer*, and the same operations are repeated until t_3+4.

However, at time t_3+4, node 3 discards segment 8 from *cBuffer*, instead of moving it to *pBuffer*, in accordance with policy 2. Note that *pBuffer* contains segments 5 through 7 now. Because node 3 has already removed segment 4 at time t3, the master node takes the place of node 3 and sends segment 4 to node 4. After this time, node 3 can continuously transfer segments 5 through 7 to node 4. Thus, most of the partial stream is relayed by parent nodes, and only the portion of the partial stream that the parent nodes do not have is provided by the master node.

From Fig. 4, we can determine the portion of the partial stream that node 4 has to receive from the master node. If $t_4 - 2t_3 > 0$, node 4 can receive the partial stream between t_3 and $t_4 - t_3$ from the master node. Thus, if node 4 arrives earlier than $2t_3$, node 3 can provide node 4 with all the required partial stream.

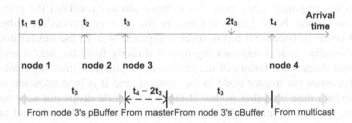

Fig. 4. Node 4 receives streams from node 3, master, and multicast channel

During the complete multicast session of video i, node 1 delivers two segments (1,2) to node 2 and one segment (4) to node 4, node 2 delivers three segments (1-3) to node 3, and node 3 delivers six segments (1-3, 5-7) to node 4. If all of the nodes allocated a *pBuffer* of length T_i, node 1 would deliver two segments (1,2), node 2 would deliver three segments(1-3), and node 3 would deliver seven segments (1-7).

The above example shows that, if each node allocates a disk space larger than *vLength·b*, which is the buffer size required by the proposed buffer management mechanism, the size of the partial stream delivered by each node to the client that arrives next becomes larger and larger. Thus, the proposed buffer management policy reduces the disk usage of the clients. This example shows why all of the codes, except for the master, allocate a *pBuffer* of size *vLength·b*, even though most of the nodes may have enough disk space to allocate a larger buffer.

2.4 Recovery from Client Dropout

In the p2p approach, if a client's connection fails or the client departs from the current multicast session, the partial stream transfer for the other clients can be disrupted. These kinds of node dropouts can be handled by a two-step failure recovery procedure: Detecting failure and recovering from the failure. In the partial stream transfer, clients can detect the dropout of the parent or master node by constantly monitoring the incoming traffic. If the rate of arrival of the partial stream is below a certain level or there is no response, the recovery procedure is performed. Therefore, node dropouts are detected by the receiving node, and, most of the time, the recovery procedure is performed locally without the involvement of the server.

If a node fails or departs from the current multicast session, the relevant master node provides the child of the failed node with the remainder of the partial stream. However, when the master node fails or departs from the current session, the following recovery procedure is performed. In the proposed algorithm, the failure or departure of the master node does not always affect partial stream channels. In the example shown in Fig. 2, such a failure affects the partial stream service when the master node (node 1) fails or departs before the second node (node 2) has received whole partial stream from the master.

The time required for node 1 to finish its delivery is twice the time difference between the arrival of node 1 and that of node 2 in the same session. In other words, if t_d (node 1)$\geq 2* t_a$(node 2) $- t_0$, where t_0, t_d(node k) and t_a (node k) represent the session start time, and the arrival and departure times of node k, respectively, the recovery procedure is not required, since node 2 will have already received the partial stream from the master node. Node 3 does not require the recovery procedure either. In fact, only node 4 needs it, because it has to receive segment 4 from the master node. In this case, exceptionally, node 4 requests segment 4 directly from the server and, as a result, the server detects the failure of the master node and transmits segment 4 to node 4. Node 4 becomes the master node in the session, and it is in possession of more of the partial stream than the other nodes. If the master node drops out very early in the transmission, the server selects the second node as the master node and provides it with the part of the partial stream that it does not already have. Then, the second node becomes the new master node. However, in this case, the extra partial stream is very small. Since the probability that the above conditions are satisfied is relatively small, the chance for the server to be involved in the partial stream transfer is very small.

3   Simulations

Numerous videos having widely varying popularities are likely to be stored on a real video server. In this section, we show the performance of the VOD multicast using CIWP and P2P partial stream transfer by means of simulations. We also perform a simulation for the FCFS batching, the basic CIWP, and the threshold based multicast schemes, in order to compare their performances with that of the proposed scheme. In the simulations, we obtain the average waiting time for the client requests as a function of the server bandwidth.

In our simulation models, it is assumed that the client requests arrive at the server according to a Poisson process with an average arrival rate of λ. It is interesting to note that the access frequencies to various movies can be characterized by the generalized Zipf distribution [11]. If movies are sorted according to the access frequency, then the probability of requesting the ith most popular movie is given by $p_i = f_i / \sum_{j=1}^{N} f_i$, where $f_i = 1/i^{1-\theta}$, $i = 1, \cdots, N$, N is the total number of videos on the server, and θ is a parameter used for the distribution. The access skew changes with the parameter θ. A value of $\theta = 0.271$ is known to closely match the popularities generally observed for video store rentals [4]. Then, the request rate for video i is $\lambda_i = p_i \lambda$. Moreover, we assume that all clients have enough disk space for *pBuffer* and *cBuffer*, and the network does not cause a performance bottleneck, in order to be able to focus on the operations of the algorithms in the simulations.

The workload and system parameters chosen for the simulations are listed in Table 1 Each simulation run generates 10,000 requests. The server has a total of 50 videos, the request arrival rate is 100 requests per minute, and the video runtimes follow a uniform distribution from 70 to 110 minutes. We assume that the whole network is composed of 90 ISPs. This is the number of ISPs currently registered in South Korea, as provided by the National Internet Develop Agent of Korea in May 2006. We assume that the popularity of requests in the same group follow Zipf's law with skew factor $\theta = 0$, and the popularity of video i among the groups also follows the generalized Zipf's law with skew factor $\theta = 0.271$ [11]. In the threshold based multicast and the proposed multicast scheme, $Li/2$ is used for the value of T_i.

Table 1. Parameters chosen for the simulations

Parameter	Average	Range
Number of videos	50	N/A
Request rate (requests/min)	100	80-120
Video length (minutes)	90	70-110
Skew factor (movie selection)	0.271	N/A
Number of groups	75	N/A
Skew factor (group selection)	0	N/A

3.1 Server Bandwidth Versus Number of Requests

Fig. 5 shows the average server bandwidth required by each multicast method over time in the stable state. In this figure, we can see that the number of channels created by the proposed multicast scheme is much less than that of the other three schemes, because a server channel is created only to serve the main multicast session. In the existing scheme, the server has to create unicast channels for partial stream delivery as well as for the multicast session. This figure shows the excellent performance of the proposed multicast scheme compared to that of the other three methods. The proposed VOD multicast scheme reduces the consumption of the server bandwidth by 35 %.

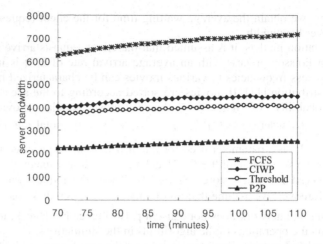

Fig. 5. Server bandwidth over time in stable state

Since the run lengths of videos are between 70 and 110 minutes, the bandwidth required by each scheme is stabilized after 70 minutes, as shown in this figure.

3.2 Unexpected Client Dropouts

If a client's connection fails or the client departs from the current multicast session, the relevant master node provides the child of the failed node with the remainder of the partial stream. When the master fails or departs from the current session, the server will provide the corresponding node with the portion of the partial stream that it does not have, if the given condition of Section 2.4 is satisfied. Note that the failure or departure of the master node does not affect the partial stream channels if the given condition is not satisfied. As a result, if the client that dropped out is the master and satisfies the condition, the server has to provide the new master node with some portion of the partial stream.

Table 2. Extra server channels versus dropout rate

Dropout rate	Number of extra server channels	Sum of extra server channel lengths (min.)
5%	6	38
10%	9	63
20%	16	98

In the following simulation, we limit the number of available server channels to 1800, and the number of requests for each minute is 90. For the number of available server channels of 1800, all of the server channels are used for the most part during the simulation run, due to the high request rate. Table 2 shows the number of extra server channels required to transmit the partial streams that are required by new master nodes. The table also shows the sum of the extra server channel lengths for a given dropout rate. In the table, the dropout rate is the number of dropped nodes divided by the number of generated nodes. From the table, we know that the probability of the server having to be involved in the partial stream transfer is very small when clients fail or depart from the current session. Note that the average length of the extra channel is between 6 and 7 minutes.

Fig. 6 shows the variation of the client's average waiting time as the dropout rate of the clients is increased. If a client that dropped out is a master node and satisfies the given condition, an extra server channel has to be used to provide the new master node with some portion of the partial stream. When all the server channels are used for multicast and partial stream services, new client requests have to be delayed until a channel becomes available. In other words, newly arriving clients have to wait for the server channel to become available when the server bandwidth usage is saturated. The expected waiting time of a new request increases slowly with increasing dropout rate, as would be expected, since the dropout of a client may require an additional server channel. Note that the expected waiting time of the CIWP and threshold schemes is decreased even though the waiting time is very long.

The reason for this is that the chance for the server to be involved in the partial stream transfer is very small since the probability that the condition of Section 2.4 are satisfied is relatively small. Moreover, required partial stream is not a lot when the condition is met.

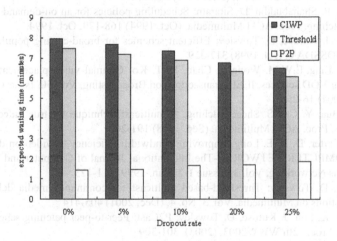

Fig. 6. Expected waiting time versus unexpected dropout rate of clients

4 Conclusion

The proposed method reduces the server bandwidth by using surplus disk resources on the client side and the transfer of the partial stream between clients to minimize the load of the server. Also, to reduce the excessive data traffic caused by partial stream transfers between clients, we modify the threshold used to initiate a new multicast session. That is, we limit the value of T_i to less than $L_i/2$. We group clients according to their ISP, in order to be able to transfer partial streams among clients.

Various simulations were performed to demonstrate the performance improvement in terms of the server bandwidth usage and the client's expected waiting time. As compared with threshold based multicast, we obtain the following results from the simulations. The proposed multicast scheme reduces the consumption of the server bandwidth by 35 % when the network is composed of 90 ISPs, the request rates are in the range of 80 through 120, and 10,000 client requests are generated. Moreover, it also significantly reduces the client's waiting time, because the server provides only the multicast stream, while the partial streams are provided by clients using the same local ISP. In the proposed multicast scheme, the influence of unexpected drops on the client's waiting time is negligible.

Acknowledgements

This work was supported by INHA UNIVERSITY Research Grant.

References

[1] P. J. Shenoy, P. Goyal, H. M. Vin: Issues in multimedia server design. ACM Computing Surveys, Vol. 27, No. 4. (Dec. 1995) 636-639

[2] A. Dan, P. Shahabuddin, D. Sitaram: Scheduling policies for an on-demand video server with batching. Proc. ACM Multimedia. (Oct. 1994) 168-179, Oct. 1994.

[3] L. Gao, J. Kurose, D. Towsley: Efficient schemes for broad-casting popular videos. in Proc. NOSSDAV. (Jul. 1998) 317-329

[4] W.K.S. Tang, E.W.M. Wong, S. Chan, K. T. Ko: Optimal video placement scheme for batching VOD services. IEEE Transactions on Broadcasting, Vol. 50, Issue 1. (Mar 2004) (Mar 2004) 16-25

[5] K. A. Hua, Y. Cai, S. Sheu: Patching: A multicast technique for true video-on-demand services. Proc. ACM Multimedia. (Sep. 1998) 191-200

[6] S. W. Carter. D. D. E. Long: Improving bandwidth efficiency of video-on-demand servers. COMPUTER NETWORKS-The International Journal of Computer and Telecommunications Networking, Vol. 31, Issue 1-2. (Jan. 1999) 111-123

[7] L. Gao, D. Towsley: Threshold-based multicast for continuous media delivery. IEEE Transactions on Multimedia, Vol. 3, No. 4. (Dec. 2001) 405-414

[8] Y. Guo, K. Suh, J. Kurose, D. Towsley: P2Cast: Peer-to-peer patching scheme for VoD service. Proc. 12th WWW2003. (2003). 301-309

[9] M. Castro, P. Druschel, A.-M. Kermarrec, A. Nandi, A. Rowstron, A. Singh: SplitStream: High-bandwidth content distribution in a cooperative environments. Proc. IPTPS'03. (Feb. 2003) 292-303.

[10] T. Do, K. Hua, M. Tantaoui: P2VoD: Providing fault tolerant video-on-demand streaming in peer-to-peer environment. Proc. ICC 2004 (Jun. 2004). 20-24

[11] G. Zipf: Human Behavior and the Principle of Least Effort. Addison-Wesley (1949).

Multimedia Service Composition for Context-Aware Mobile Computing*

Eunjeong Park and Heonshik Shin

School of Computer Science and Engineering,
Seoul National University,
Sinlim-dong, Gwanak-gu, Seoul 151-742, Korea
{ejpark,shinhs}@cslab.snu.ac.kr

Abstract. Various computing environments and user contexts require customized
applications including composite services. We propose a middleware called SON-
CMC (Service Overlay Network for Context-aware Mobile Computing) which
supports multimedia service composition on overlay network for mobile computing. Our approach provides customized applications to mobile users by composing
services such as web services based on user requirement and the contexts of mobile
devices. Utilizing the large variation in quality of service between media servers
and mobile devices, SON-CMC reconfigures the service composition graph to reduce the total data traffic and the response time of applications. It also aims to
achieve load balancing by applying a service routing algorithm to the overlay network, which is modeled as a common peer-to-peer network. Experimental results
demonstrate that our context-based scheme enhances service composition in terms
of response time and preservation of network resources.

1 Introduction

Mobile computing requires multimedia applications to adapt dynamically to the user's
role, capability, and current environment, even though the source content remains unchanged. These changing service patterns lead to a service composition in which previously dispersed services are aggregated into a customized application. For example,
service composition could be initiated by virtually connecting five service nodes to
provide annotation, speech-to-text conversion, translation, sliding bar-attaching, and
transcoding services to a mobile user. In addition to being a way of achieving customiza-
tion, recent research has asserted that service composition is more fault-tolerant, flexible
and scalable than conventional centralized approaches to service provision [1,2,3]. Thus
service composition has received a lot of research attention. The *eflow* system [1] includes a composite service description language (CSDL) for designing process schemes
for composite processes. The *sflow* approach [2] addresses the resource efficiency and
agility of service federation in a service model which allows parallel and interleaved services. *SpiderNet* [3] supports a quality-aware service composition, which can automatically compose services. However, most existing solutions cannot be applied directly

---

* This work is a part of a research project supported by Korea Ministry of Construction & Transportation (MOCT) through Korea Construction Engineering Development Collaboratory Program Management Center (KOCED PMC) at Seoul National University.

T.-J. Cham et al. (Eds.): MMM 2007, LNCS 4352, Part II, pp. 115–124, 2007.

to mobile computing, since they have been developed for users on wired networks and take no account of the characteristics of mobile environment. Although the processing power of mobile devices has improved greatly, short battery life is still critical to multimedia applications on mobile devices. In this paper, we introduce a middleware called SON-CMC (Service Overlay Network for Context-aware Mobile Computing) which composes multimedia services in the context of mobile computing.

The quality of service (QoS) of multimedia content is commonly degraded to an acceptable level in mobile devices, to cope with the scarcity of resources, including narrow network bandwidth, short battery life, limited memory, and relatively slow CPUs. If services subject to QoS degradation are composed in later part, large amounts of data which will be pruned by QoS control, flow through the service composition process. To minimize any increase in network traffic, it is essential to reduce the overhead of service composition on the overlay network. The belated pruning of data traffic in a service composition increases processing time of each service and communication time between services. Therefore, the sequence of services should be scheduled to reduce total data traffic so long as the result is consistent with the user's intention. SpiderNet[3] includes commutable service components capable of swapping the execution order of adjacent services. However, only two adjacent services can be swapped, and the process involves constructing two service composition graphs for the two services. As the number of services that may be swapped increases, this approach becomes ineffective because of the exponentially increasing number of composition graphs. We introduce the precedence index (PI) of a service which formalizes the reordering of services. The precedence index represents the profitability of executing the corresponding service in advance which achieving the same results. We aim to reduce data traffic and make composite services faster in automatic service composition.

To support the composition process, SON-CMC monitors the current network status, residual energy, and other system resources of the mobile device. This context supports the dynamic adjustment of QoS of applications and the service composition graphs which reflect users' requirements. For example, low residual energy of a mobile device causes the degradation of multimedia data and affects the precedence index of specific services. SON-CMC also supports load-balanced service routing on an overlay network while maintaining the fast response time of applications. We use the well-known P2P protocol, *gnutella*, to integrate service discovery and routing. Hence, our system is easily applicable to P2P networks with a few modifications.

The rest of this paper is organized as follows: Section 2 describes the system model of mobile devices, applications, and the service composition. Section 3 introduces SON-CMC middleware and service composition process. Section 4 evaluates the performance of the proposed approach and in Section 5 we come to some conclusions.

2 System Model

Our system model is designed for the service overlay network illustrated in Fig. 1. A service overlay network consists of service nodes (SN_j) that provide various services (S_i), which can be replicated on many service nodes. A service link may be composed of

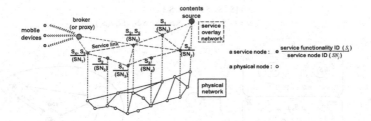

Fig. 1. The SON-CMC environment

Table 1. Notations

Symbol	Description	Symbol	Description
A_i	An application	$ER_{batt}(A_i)$	Average energy consumption rate of A_i
Q_i	QoS of A_i	t_i	Remaining execution time of A_i
CR_{batt}	Residual energy	λ	Disconnection rate of wireless network
CR_{CPU}	Available computing power	DR_{tx}, DR_{rx}	Network bandwidth
CR_{mem}	Available memory capacity		

multiple links in the physical network, and the topology of the service overlay network can be of various types, such as a mesh, spanning tree, or adjacent connections [4].

In this section, we detail the system model of mobile devices, multimedia applications, and QoS, followed by a formal description of context-aware service composition.

2.1 Mobile Devices Running Multimedia Applications

The QoS of all applications running in a mobile device should be controlled, so that they do not exhaust the resources of the device, including residual battery energy, memory and CPU capacity. A mobile device M has an application set $A = \{A_1, A_2, \ldots, \}$ and a resource set $R = \{R_{batt}, R_{CPU}, \ldots\}$, where CR_i is the available capacity of the resource R_i. Other profiled information and the monitored context are summarized in Table 1.

Our system aims at providing adaptive composite applications with appropriate QoS in accordance with the residual resource of the mobile devices, exploiting the fact that lower-quality multimedia content requires less traffic, power consumption, and computation. For example, a video service with the parameters {SIF, 30fps, 650Kbps} consumes 4.42W in a mobile device, whereas a service with the profile {QSIF, 20fps, 100Kbps} consumes 3.88W [5]. The relation between QoS and the average resource consumption is profiled and can then be utilized to set dynamic QoS parameters. A mobile device estimates its resource consumption rate $E(R) = \{ER_{batt}, ER_{mem}, \ldots, ER_{|R|}\}$ for executing the application set $A = \{A_1, A_2, \ldots, A_{|A|}\}$, and it has the consumption constraint $CReq(R)$. For instance, the energy limitation of a mobile device impose a constraint as follows:

$$CReq(R_{batt}) : \sum_{i=1}^{|A|} ER_{batt}(A_i) \cdot t_i \leq CR_{batt}. \tag{1}$$

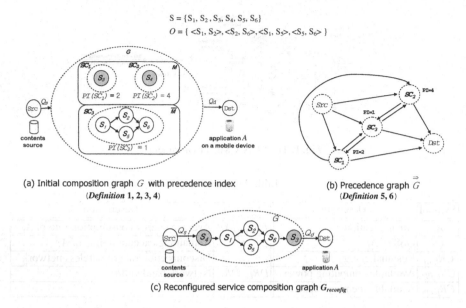

$$S = \{S_1, S_2, S_3, S_4, S_5, S_6\}$$
$$O = \{ <S_1, S_2>, <S_2, S_6>, <S_1, S_5>, <S_5, S_6> \}$$

(a) Initial composition graph G with precedence index
(*Definition* 1, 2, 3, 4)

(b) Precedence graph $\overset{\Rightarrow}{G}$
(*Definition* 5, 6)

(c) Reconfigured service composition graph $G_{reconfig}$

Fig. 2. Reconfiguration of service composition graph with precedence index

If this resource constraint is not satisfied, QoS control is performed to degrade the QoS of the application which will yield the largest energy saving [6]. The process of QoS control is described in Section 3.1.

Suppose that application A_i consists of a user's composite service request, presented as a composition graph G_i, with the service set $S_i = \{S_i^1, S_i^2, \ldots\}$ and the dependency relation O_i, which describes the dependency of G_i. This means that media content with a QoS level of Q_s is delivered to a mobile application A_i, at a QoS level of Q_i through composite service G_i.

2.2   Reconfiguration of Service Composition for Mobile Computing

In this section, we model the reconfiguration of a service composition graph. As shown in the previous section, our service composition is reconfigured through automatically reordering the sequence of services to reduce total data traffic on overlay network. For simplicity, we will model a specific application A on a mobile device. As shown in Fig. 2, the QoS of the media content (Q_s) and of the mobile application (Q_d) can be specified with the service composition graph $G = \{S, O\}$ in which S represents the service set and O represents the dependency relation of strictly connected services. G represents some services connected by the adjacency relation O with strict dependency, and others with unspecified connections. Each service $S_i \in S$ has an allowable input and output format sets and a QoS boundary. We categorize the service set S using the notion of reconfigurability of the order of execution.

Definition 1. Multi-positional service. A service S_i is *multi-positional* if and only if the dependency between S_i and the precedent (or following) service is not strictly specified.

Definition 2. Reconfigurable composition graph. A service composition graph G is *reconfigurable* if and only if the whole graph is not connected and the corresponding service set is composed as $S = \{M, \overline{M}\}$ where M is a set of multi-positional services and $\overline{M}$ is its complement.

Multi-positional services can float in G so long as the result is consistent with the user's intention. S_3 and S_4 in Fig. 2 (a) are multi-positional services which can be located anywhere in G if and only if the input and output formats, including the QoS boundary, are consistent with adjacent services. If G is reconfigurable, the system can adapt the order in which services are executed so as to more efficiently with changing environmental conditions. G can be transformed to a connected graph by moving the services in M and the components (maximal connected subgraphs) in $\overline{M}$ with respect to the precedence index. The notions of sub-composition and the precedence index are defined as follows:

Definition 3. Sub-composition. A sub-composition SC_i is the connected maximal subgraph of G.

A composition graph G can be reconfigured using the precedence index (PI) of each sub-composition and the relation between sub-compositions.

Definition 4. Precedence index. $PI(SC_i) = \alpha \cdot ITO(SC_i) + \beta \cdot IPR(SC_i)$,
where $ITO(SC_i) = input(SC_i)/output(SC_i)$ and $IPR(SC_i)$ is the processing rate for $input(SC_i)$. A large value of $ITO(SC_i)$ means that the sub-composition creates a small amount of output that incurs a small workload for the adjacent services, and little data traffic. The weighting factor α and β compensate for the scale of the composition metrics. $ITO(SC_i)$ and $IPR(SC_i)$ are determined by the types of the services and by the environmental conditions, including the resource capacity. Semantically, the precedence index of SC_i indicates how profitable if it is to perform this sub-composition in advance. If $PI(SC_i)$ is higher than the indices of other sub-compositions, prior execution of SC_i will be preferred. However, if the preceding and succeeding sub-compositions are inconsistent with each other in terms of formats and QoS boundaries, the consistency relation overrides their precedence indices.

The acceptable input, output formats and QoS boundaries of a service S_i are $In(S_i)$, $Out(S_i) = \{Type_1, Type_2, \dots\}$ and $QB\_In(S_i), QB\_Out(S_i) = \{QB\_Scope_1, QB\_Scope_2, \dots\}$ and the consistency between sub-compositions can then be expressed as:

Definition 5. Precedence relation $SC_i \Rightarrow SC_j$. A sub-composition SC_i is able to precede SC_j, if $(Out(S_i) \cap In(S_j) \neq \emptyset)$ and $(QB\_Out(S_i) \cap QB\_In(S_j) \neq \emptyset)$.

The precedence index and precedence relation are implicated in the precedence graph of G as follows:

Definition 6. Precedence graph $\vec{G}$. $\vec{G} = \{SC, \mathcal{PR}\}$, where SC is the set of sub-compositions in which the node SC_i is labeled with $PI(SC_i)$, and $\mathcal{PR}$ is the set of precedence relations based on the formats and quality boundaries of these sub-compositions.

Fig. 2 (b) shows an example of a precedence graph.

After a precedence graph $\overset{\Rightarrow}{G}$ has been obtained, a reconfiguration process traverses $\overset{\Rightarrow}{G}$ in order to obtain the maximum gain in terms of aggregated precedence indices while meeting the precedence relations. It builds the reconfigured composition graph G_{reconf}, which is deterministic. The process of reconfiguration is described in Section 3.2 and an example of such a graph is shown in Fig. 2 (c).

2.3   Service Routing on Overlay Network

Having constructed the reconfigured service composition graph G_{reconf}, the system needs to support service routing by selecting appropriate service nodes and connecting them. A service S_i can be replicated on many service nodes and a service node SN_j can support many services. Service routing chooses the service node SN_j to provide service S_i, and repeats this process for all $S_i \in G_{reconf}$, while considering the residual resource, load balancing of the overlay network, and the response time of the application. To achieve this goal, the service routing algorithm finds a set of candidate service routings $\widetilde{G} = \{\widetilde{G}_1, \widetilde{G}_2, \ldots, \}$ for the service composition G_{reconf}.

The service routing algorithm explores the overlay network to find an approximately optimal service routing $\widetilde{G}_{opt}$ while fulfilling the following requirements:

***Requirement 1.* Admission control considering the residual resource of SN_j**
To select SN_j as the service node for S_i, the resource consumption of S_i should be less than the available resources of SN_j. The services concurrently executing in SN_j made up the active service set AS_j and its list of allowable resource capacities, $CR(SN_j) = \{CR_1(SN_j), CR_2(SN_j), \ldots CR_{|R|}(SN_j)\}$, correspond to resource set $R(SN_j) = \{R_1, R_2, \ldots, R_{|R|}\}$. Thus the following resource consumption constraint needs to be satisfied:

$$\sum_{\forall S_k \in AS_j} ER_\gamma(S_k) \cdot t_k + ER_\gamma(S_i) \cdot t_i < CR_\gamma(SN_j),$$

$$\text{for all } R_\gamma \text{ with time-based } ER_\gamma(S_k) \text{ and } ER_\gamma(S_i),$$

and

$$\sum_{\forall S_k \in AS_j} ER_\gamma(S_k) \cdot input(S_k) + ER_\gamma(S_i) \cdot input(S_i) < CR_\gamma(SN_j),$$

$$\text{for all } R_\gamma \text{ with quantity-based } ER_\gamma(S_k) \text{ and } ER_\gamma(S_i),$$

$$(2)$$

where $ER_\gamma(S_i)$ is the rate of consumption of the resource R_γ for service S_i and t_i is the remaining execution time of S_i. If the rate of consumption of resource R_γ is proportional to service time, as is the case with battery energy, the upper equation applies; but if resource consumption is determined mainly by the amount of input data, which is what happens with memory, the lower equation is used.

***Requirement 2.* Load balancing for reduced service time**
Severe contention at a specific service node tends to increase the response time of applications. To prevent contention at specific service nodes, the service routing process should minimize the contention rate by means of service composition. Each service

node SN_j in the candidate routing $\widetilde{G}_k$ calculates its contention rate, as a measure of the overload on the service node incurred by servicing S_i. Using these contention rates, we can express $LBF(\widetilde{G}_k)$, which is the load balancing factor of $\widetilde{G}_k$, as follows:

$$LBF(\widetilde{G}_k) = \sum_{\forall SN_j \in \widetilde{G}_k} \max_{R_\gamma \in R(SN_j)} \left\{ \frac{\sum_{\forall S_k \in AS_j} ER_\gamma(S_k) \cdot t_k + ER_\gamma(S_i) \cdot t_i}{CR_\gamma(SN_j)} \right\},$$

for all R_γ which have a time-based $ER_\gamma(S_k)$ and $ER_\gamma(S_i)$,

or

$$LBF(\widetilde{G}_k) = \sum_{\forall SN_j \in \widetilde{G}_k} \max_{R_\gamma \in R(SN_j)} \left\{ \frac{\sum_{\forall S_k \in AS_j} ER_\gamma(S_k) \cdot input(S_k) + ER_\gamma(S_i) \cdot input(S_i)}{CR_\gamma(SN_j)} \right\},$$

for all R_γ which have a quantity-based $ER_\gamma(S_k)$ and $ER_\gamma(S_i)$.

(3)

In addition to balancing the service overlay network, we also need to ensure that the composite services are responsive. The estimated response time of $\widetilde{G}_k$ is calculated as follows:

$$TST(\widetilde{G}_k) = \sum_{S_i \in \widetilde{G}_k} processing\_time(S_i) + \sum_{L_j \in \widetilde{G}_k} communication\_time(L_j), \quad (4)$$

where L_j is a service link in $\widetilde{G}_k$ and $processing\_time(S_i)$ is the computing time incurred in the service node $SN_j \in \widetilde{G}_k$ for executing S_i. Our service routing algorithm selects the most smallest value of a weighted sum of $LBF(\widetilde{G}_k)$ and $TST(\widetilde{G}_k)$. Hence, the goal of our service routing can be expressed as follows:

$$\widetilde{G}_{opt} = \widetilde{G}_k : \min_{\forall \widetilde{G}_k \in \widetilde{G}} \{\lambda \cdot LBF(\widetilde{G}_k) + \mu \cdot TST(\widetilde{G}_k)\}. \quad (5)$$

Readers are referred to [7] for the details of service routing algorithm.

3 Design of the Service Composition System

In this section, we describe the details of the SON-CMC process of service composition.First, the environment of a mobile device is parameterized by monitoring components in SON-CMC middleware. Knowing the monitored context, the QoS of the multimedia application is dynamically controlled so that it neither exhausts the system resource nor disappoints the user. The target QoS consecutively affects the precedence index of the service composition graph and the order in which services are executed. Based on the reconfigured composition graph, the service routing algorithm explores the service overlay network with the aim of finding the best composition. We will now detail each part of the service composition process. Service composition is performed by middleware on the proxy server (broker), service nodes, and mobile devices [7].The middleware structure consists of components that are essential to enable mobile computing to adapt to contextual changes. SON-CMC middleware is composed of two layers: basic middleware and service middleware. Basic middleware includes the components which monitor aspects of the network, the power situation, and the device location, gathering information which is needed to support appropriate adaptive behavior. Service networking manages data monitoring and communication between components in the upper layers. In the service middleware, service composition and QoS managers cooperate to run the service composition and service routing algorithms on the basis of profiles of the applications and the filtered context. The composition manager also sends the location of the mobile device to the handoff manager, which is part of the middleware on the proxy server, and seamlessly transfers relevant information to a new proxy server.

3.1   Dynamic QoS Control of Mobile Applications

If the constraint on resource consumption of a mobile device represented by Equation (1) is not satisfied, QoS control is performed, reducing the QoS level of the application which yields the largest resource saving [7]. We assume that the relation between QoS and resource consumption is predefined by profiling, using the results such as data shown in Table [5]. Until the resourcecapacity CR_i becomes sufficient to run the applications, algorithm selects a series of victim applications A_{victim} to have their QoS degraded, where A_{victim} yields the largest resource saving at each selection.

3.2   Reconfiguration of the Service Composition Graph

We assume that parallel execution of services in a sub-composition SC_i is allowed, but SON-CMC does not permit parallel execution of sub-compositions. Multicasting and the aggregation of sub-compositions are beyond the scope of this paper. Reconfiguration process first collects sub-compositions (SC_i) by extracting maximally connected subgraphs which are obtained by the depth-first search. Next, the algorithm sets up the precedence index of each SC_i based on the amount of input to and output from SC_i, and $IPR(SC_i)$. The precedence graph is composed of precedence indices and precedence relations which are created from the formats and QoS boundaries of sub-compositions. Finally, a modified traveling salesman algorithm is used to find a near-shortest path through the precedence graph. Because the cost of visiting SC_i should be be determined from the precedence index and the execution order, the gain achieved by a precedence index, $GPI(SC_i)$, is used as the cost value, and is determined as: $GPI(SC_i) = PI(SC_i)/execution\_order$. Traversing $\overrightarrow{G}$ to maximize $AGPI(\overrightarrow{G})$, which the aggregated of all values of $GPI(SC_i)$, the algorithm achieves the reconfigured composition graph G_{reconf}.

Algorithms for reconfiguration of service composition and service routing are detailed in [7].

4   Performance Evaluation

We evaluate a performance of our approach by simulating SON-CMC on *ns-2* [8] using the *gnutella* [9] protocol. The architecture of simulator includes P2P overlay network, socket adaptation components and trace-based mpeg-4 streaming. Our test application is a multimedia application for mobile devices which are supplied by our service composition using trace data from real movies. The underlying physical topology was generated by GT-ITM using 18-node, 50-node, and 100-node transit-stub models [10]. To construct the overlay network, we utilized the well-knwon P2P network, *gnutella*, which connects service nodes. The number of connections that can be accepted by a node is set to *connection_degree*. We modified the gnutella protocol to search composite services and to manage probing agents. We modeled the services using various precedence indices, which are uniformly distributed over the gnutella network. Each node has a monitoring facility for detecting current system information, including the number of jobs, residual energy, and memory capacities.

Our simulator models the whole processes of service composition which are described in Section 3. We initially evaluated our approach by measuring the average response time

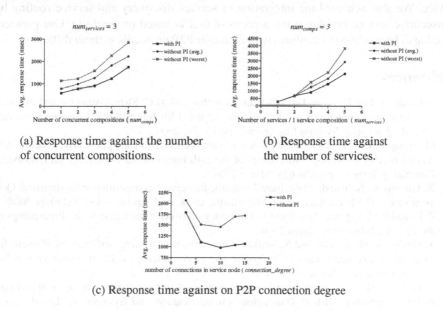

(a) Response time against the number
of concurrent compositions.

(b) Response time against
the number of services.

(c) Response time against on P2P connection degree

Fig. 3. Performance of SON-CMC

of all video frames. Fig. 3 (a) shows the result of composition with precedence index (PI) while increasing the number of concurrent service compositions from 1 to 5. Each service composition is made up of 3 services. As shown in the Fig. 3 (a), the average arrival time is 25% shorter with a PI-based approach than with a non-PI-based approach, in the average case, and the gap widens as the number of service compositions grows.

PI-based composition outperforms the conventional approach when the number of services in a composition is large. We measured the average response time of frames while varying the number of services in a composition (Fig. 3 (b)). Although there is little benefit for 2 composite services, when there are 5 services, PI-based composition is 22% faster than non-PI-based composition, in the worst case.

We also investigated the effect of P2P network parameters on service composition by varying *connection_degree* of the gnutella protocol, as shown in Fig. 3 (c). The response time declines until the *connection_degree* rises to 10; but more than 10 connections increase the response time, because of the overhead of the probing agents and discovery time.

5 Conclusions

We have designed an entire process of multimedia service composition for mobile computing. Our approach adapts the composition graph and the use of service routing for the context of mobile devices with the support of monitoring components. By reconfiguring service composition graph, we improve the response time of mobile applications by reducing the traffic on the service overlay network. Consequently, our system increases the number of services that can be supplied during the battery life of a mobile device. We also achieved the integration of service discovery and service routing by consecutive service probing using a protocol that is based on *gnutella*. Our protocol could also be modified to conform with common P2P protocols without difficulty.

References

1. F. Casati, S. Ilnicki, L. jie Jin, V. Krishnamoorthy, and M.C. Shan, "Adaptive and dynamic service composition in eflow," Proceedings of the 12th International Conference on Advanced Information Systems Engineering, pp.13–31, 2000.
2. M. Wang, B. Li, and Z. Li, "sflow: Towards resource-efficient and agile service federation in service overlay networks," Proceedings of the 24th International Conference on Distributed Computing Systems, pp.628–635, March 2004.
3. X. Gu and K. Nahrstedt, "Distributed multimedia service composition with statistical QoS assurances," IEEE Transactions on Multimedia, vol.8, no.1, pp.141 – 151, February 2006.
4. Z. Li and P. Mohapatra, "The impact of topology on overlay routing service," Proceedings of the 23th IEEE Infocom, March 2004.
5. Y. Huang, S. Mohapatra, and N. Venkatasubramanian, "An energy-efficient middleware for supporting multimedia services in mobile grid environments," IEEE International Conference on Information Technology, 2005.
6. E. Park and H. Shin, "Cooperative reconfiguration of softwre components for power-aware mobile computing," IEICE Transactions on Information and Systems, vol.E89–D, no.2, pp.498–507, February 2006.
7. E. Park, "Service overlay network for context-aware mobile computing," Technical report TK-06-01, 2006. http://cslab.snu.ac.kr/~ejpark/tk-06-01.pdf.
8. VINT Project, Network Simulator-2. http://www.isi.edu/nsnam/ns/.
9. Q. He, M. Ammar, G. Riley, H. Raj, and R. Fujimoto, "Mapping peer behavior to packet-level details: A framework for packet-level simulation of peer-to-peer systems," Proceedings of IEEE/ACM International Symposium on Modeling, Analysis and Simulation of Computer and Telecommunication Systems, 2003.
10. K. Calvert, M. Doar, and E. Zegura, "Modeling internet topology," IEEE Communications Magazine, 1997.

Characterizing User Behavior Model to Evaluate Hard Cache in Peer-to-Peer Based Video-on-Demand Service*

Jian-Guang Luo, Yun Tang, Meng Zhang, and Shi-Qiang Yang

Tsinghua University, Beijing 100084, China
{luojg03,tangyun98,zhangmeng00}@mails.tsinghua.edu.cn,
yangshq@mail.tsinghua.edu.cn

Abstract. Peer-to-peer (P2P) based video-on-demand (VoD) systems rely on the cooperation among peers to reduce the server workload. Recently, hard cache is used to further improve the system scalability, because the contents will not be immediately cleaned up when the users get offline. However, how many practical benefits hard cache will bring to the P2P based VoD service has not been well studied and still remains far from clear. In this paper, we first characterize user behavior model with the benefit of millions of real VoD traces and identify several practical factors which potentially impact the system performance. Then we further conduct extensive trace-driven simulations to evaluate the scalability of P2P based VoD system with hard cache enabled and some interesting results are found.

1 Introduction

In recent years, the great success of peer-to-peer (P2P) in file sharing [1][2] and live streaming [3][4][5] applications stimulated many research efforts in the area of scalable P2P based video-on-demand (VoD) streaming service [6][7][8][9]. However, it is not a trivial task to take full advantage of P2P concept in practical VoD service. First of all, quite different from live streaming service, users in VoD systems can request various contents at any time. This so-called asynchronous characteristic of VoD severely reduces the cooperation opportunity between peers, and thus is believed as running counter to the design philosophy of P2P networks. Second, in a typical VoD system, there are generally thousands of or even more video files sharing on the server, resulting in various popularities among those "on-demand" objects. It is clear that if the requests for one file are fairly few, the benefit gained from P2P network will not be considerable. Third, dynamic join and leave in peer community lead to high churn rate for VoD service, which would potentially deteriorate the performance of P2P networks.

* This work is supported by the National Natural Science Foundation of China under Grant No.60432030 and National Basic Research Program of China (973) under Grant No.2006CB303103.

T.-J. Cham et al. (Eds.): MMM 2007, LNCS 4352, Part II, pp. 125–134, 2007.
© Springer-Verlag Berlin Heidelberg 2007

As evidenced, simulation results in [10] have showed that traditional cache-and-relay (CR) scheme in P2P VoD is less optimistic when request asynchronism, file popularity, and user dynamics are considered.

Aiming to explore more cooperation between peers in CR scheme, some previous works, [11] for instance, advocated *hard cache*, i.e. using hard disk to cache the video contents, to further improve the system scalability. Apparently, peers with hard cache enabled are capable to cache more contents than those who only use the temporary memory, so-called *soft cache*. Furthermore, the cached content in hard cache will not be cleaned up immediately when the users get offline. The benefits of hard cache over soft cache intuitively come in two aspects: On one hand, if the users request contents watched previously, it is no need for him to fetch the contents again from server or other peers. On the other hand, when the users login again, the content cached in the hard disk could be used to favor others.

While the advantage of hard cache is widely recognized, how many practical benefits hard cache will indeed bring to the P2P based VoD service has not been well studied and still remains far from clear. In this paper, we are hence motivated to investigate the problem of evaluating the scalability of hard cache in P2P based VoD service. To do so, we first characterize user behavior model, with the benefit of millions real VoD workload traces, in terms of file popularities and user and request dynamics, which are regarded to play key roles in system performance. Although the traces are collected from client/server (C/S) streaming service, we claim that they substantially reflect the real users' behaviors since users care nothing about underlying techniques. Then we further conduct extensive trace-driven simulations to evaluate the scalability of hard cache in P2P based VoD systems with two different cache replacement schemes. The results show that hard cache indeed improves performance properties in terms of higher cache hit ratio, while the overall benefits should be carefully considered due to the popularity differences among video objects and low recurrence of end users. To the best of our knowledge, this is the first work to examine the scalability of hard cache with the consideration of practical user behavior model.

The remainder of the paper is organized as follows: In section 2, we analyze the real workload traces and identify the key aspects of user behavior model. In section 3, we first introduce a general P2P based VoD system model and then evaluate hard cache through trace-driven simulations. Finally, we conclude the paper in Section 4.

2   User Behavior Model in VoD Service

Since P2P networks benefit from mutual cooperation between participating peers, users' behaviors, including join, leave and request, will definitely impact the system performance. Therefore it is important to characterize practical user behavior model in VoD service before the evaluation could be done. In this section, we mainly analyze millions of real workload traces, achieving an insightful understanding to the key aspects which will be retrieved to conduct simulations in next section.

2.1   Trace Statistical Analysis Methodology

In this subsection, we first briefly introduce the methodology to collect and statistically analyze the workload traces and then we will retrieve the user behavior model in next subsection.

Information of Traces. The workload traces used in this study were collected from CCTV.com, the website of the Chinese largest television station. In the 100-day period of our study, there are in total more than 20,000,000 traces. In this VoD system, more than 8,000 video clips are encoded at about 300kbps for on-demand service. The lengths of those files range from tens to thousands of seconds.

Information of User Identification. For each request, the server records 44 fields in the trace file, in which we use the Player ID instead of the Client IP Address to distinguish users. Please note that in the traces the player ID is unique unless the player has been configured for anonymity. The anonymous IDs have a well-specified prefix, and can be easily removed from our analysis. This eliminates nearly two-thirds of the requests from our traces, and *7,400,473* traces with unique player ID left. However, we believe that participation behavior is independent of whether or not a user configures his/her player for anonymity, and thus we can still reveal the representative user behavior model of VoD system from the remaining traces.

Service Session Model. We define a session as the duration between the time when a user joins and leaves the VoD system. Since the server only records the traces at the granularity of requests, we further define a session as a sequence of requests from a single user while each interval between two sequential requests is no greater than 20 minutes. The relationship between requests and sessions is schematically depicted in Figure 1. It should be stressed that the user can request multiple video files in one session, which we believe can represent the user behavior as joining and leaving the system better than that used in [10][12]. Generally, when a user stops watching a video clip, he/she may leave the VoD system, or request another video file or another position in the same video file after a short thinking time. The 20 minutes used in our session model is an estimated threshold of the thinking time between two sequential requests in one session.

2.2   User Behavior Model in VoD Service

With the above methodology, we make statistical analysis to the service traces and present insightful understanding to key aspects of user behavior model which play important roles in determining the system performance of P2P based VoD service.

File Popularity Variance Model. As mentioned previously, a typical VoD service usually comprises a number of video files on the streaming server. The popularity variances among video files are potentially of great influence on the

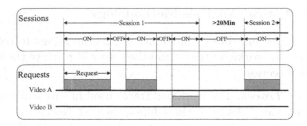

Fig. 1. Relationship between requests and sessions

performance of P2P networks. Herein we analyze the file popularity in following two aspects:

(1) Popularity evolution. After a video file is available on the streaming server, its popularity, that is, the request rate will evolve over time. This so-called popularity evolution substantially determines how many requests there are for this file and how these requests change. Figure 2 hence depicts a 30-day popularity evolution over a sample set of news video and music video clips. We can see that: (i) For news video (red solid lines), most requests arrive in only several days after their initial launch on the server; (ii) For music video (blue dotted lines), the daily request rate roughly keeps stable during this period. Clearly, the request rate of news video clips exhibit higher "time-efficacy" characteristic, so we can conjecture that the cached content of news video should be updated faster than music video to achieve a better cache hit ratio in practical P2P based VoD systems.

(2) Popularity skewness. As similar to most existing works, e.g. [12], we also investigate the popularity skewness, that is, the popularity distribution for each file, among various video files on the server. Figure 3 depicts the statistical distribution of requests for the 8,000 files. Observe that more than 90% requests stick to the most popular 1000 files. Since the fundamental design philosophy of P2P networks expects the aggregation of requests from users so that the benefits of mutual cooperation accrue, we believe the popularity convergence within a small set of video file is helpful in P2P VoD system design.

User and Request Dynamics Model. In addition to file popularity, the dynamics of user and request is also of significance for the overall performance of P2P networks in VoD service. Here we present our statistical results as following two aspects:

(1) User recurrence. User recurrence here is defined as the occurrence frequency of service subscribers, which will greatly impact the performance of hard cache. We can image that if the users only enter the systems once, the content cached in its hard cache will not be meaningful again. On the contrary, a higher user recurrence is potentially favorable for hard cache scheme in P2P VoD service. In the statistical analysis, the 7.4 million requests are from more than 1.2 million different users, showing a low user recurrence characteristic. Figure 4 then depicts the CDF curve of the number of users with session number.

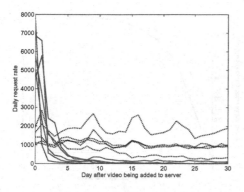

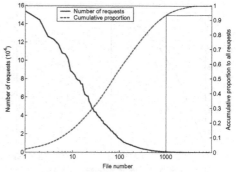

Fig. 2. Popularity evolution   **Fig. 3.** Popularity skewness

Observe that more than 65% of the users enter only once, while more than 95% of users subscribe less then 10 times in 100 days. In next section, we will further discuss the impact of user recurrence to the performance of hard cache in P2P based VoD systems.

(2) Request recurrence. Besides the user recurrence, we also have a look at the metric so called request recurrence, which means the frequency of segments of video files being requested by the same client. Since the timestamps in the traces all are in the granularity of seconds, we reasonably define a second of video content as a segment. Figure 5 depicts the CDF curve of frequency of requests for video segments. The blue solid line denotes the times of segments being requested from one end user. We can see that more than 86% of the segments are requested only once, while only 5% of the segments are requested more than twice. Furthermore, In order to testify the hard cache scheme, we also depict the number of requests for each segment over sessions, shown as the red dotted line in Figure 5. It is easy to find out that nearly 10% of the segments will be requested again from user in latter sessions, which might be helpful to increase the local cache hit ratio for these segments when hard cache is enabled.

Towards this end, we have analyzed the real service traces for the purpose of understanding the user behavior model in VoD service. Although file popularity, user and request dynamics are not capable to describe the whole profile of user behaviors, they definitely play key roles in the performance of P2P VoD service. In the next section, we will focus on examining the practical scalability of hard cache with aid of the user behavior model.

3 Scalability Evaluation of Hard Cache in P2P VoD

In section 2, we have presented the user behavior model in terms of file popularity and user, request dynamics. In this section, we mainly evaluate the scalability of hard cache in P2P VoD with the aid of practical user behavior model. In the next two subsections, we first provide a brief introduction to main components

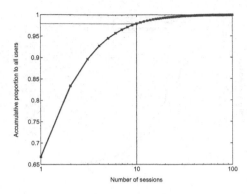

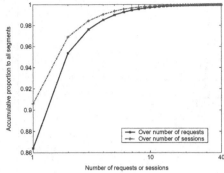

Fig. 4. CDF of users over number of sessions

Fig. 5. CDF of video segments over request number and session number

in general P2P based VoD systems, and then conduct trace-driven simulations to discuss the performance of hard cache.

3.1 General Architecture of P2P Based VoD Service

In general, there are mainly three components in a typical P2P VoD system, as shown in Figure 6: (1) Video server: The server offers on-demand streaming service and sometimes need multiple centralized or distributed video servers to balance the workload. The server publishes video files, responds to the requests from end user and streams video contents to the peer community; (2) Client: The clients request available video files on the server. In P2P based VoD systems, clients (also called peers) also acts as a light-weighted server to benefit others with the contents it cached; (3) Tracker: The tracker takes the responsibility to record cache information of end clients in P2P community. This registry service can be implemented in either centralized way or distributed manner, for example DHT services [13].

Before we proceed to the simulations, let's identify a representative service cycle for an end client in this P2P VoD system. When a user logins, it first checks the contents in the hard disk and reports the cache information to the tracker for registry. As known, if the client accesses the service for the first time or with hard cache disabled, the cache of the client should be empty and thus the user only need to send an empty-of-cache message to the tracker. When the client wants to play a video clip, it first check whether the video segments are stored in its local cache. If so, it begins the playback immediately. Otherwise, the client needs to query the tracker to find where it could download the absent segments. After getting the query results from the tracker, it will try to fetch the segment from other peers or video server before the playback can be started. During the lifetime, the client periodically updates its cache information to the tracker. When the client leaves, it will remove the corresponding cache information from the tracker.

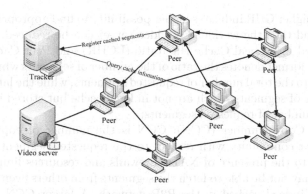

Fig. 6. A general architecture of P2P VoD systems

In this paper, our main target is to study the scalability of P2P VoD systems. Although the streaming mechanism used by clients to fetch the segments from P2P networks, the size of video segments, and the frequency for the clients to update their cache information will impact the system performance, in our following simulations, we make following assumptions for simplicity: (1) Clients receive the video segments at the playback rate so that the playback can be sustained. (2) A segment is designed as a second of video content. If the bit rate of video stream is 512Kbps, then the size of a segment is 64K bytes. (3) Clients update the cache information to the tracker every second, so that the tracker is able to record the updated cache information of every peer at the granularity of video segments.

3.2   Performance Evaluation of Hard Cache

With the general P2P VoD system discussed above, we begin to conduct trace-driven simulations to evaluate the performance of hard cache.

Cache Replacement Schemes. In P2P based VoD systems, the cache capacity at end client side is limited. Accordingly a cache replacement scheme is indispensable to refresh the cached contents. In the following simulations, we mainly use two representative cache replacement schemes as below:

(1) First-In First-Out (FIFO): the client will replace the segment which is first put into the cache;

(2) Most Copy Cached (MCC): the client will substitute the segment which has the most cached copies in the whole service community. For simplicity of performance evaluation, we reasonably assume that the client can get the number of cached copies of each segment from the tracker.

Evaluation Metrics. Besides, we adopt two categories of performance evaluation metrics as below:

(1) Cache Hit Ratio (CHR): CHR is defined as the ratio of the number of segments which could be located in at least one peer to the total number of requested

segments. A higher CHR indicates higher possibility to find appropriate upstream relay peers and thus the workload of video server can be reduced. CHR can be further divided into Local Cache Hit Ratio (LCHR) and Peer Cache Hit Ratio (PCHR). The former denotes the ratio of the number of segments which are cached in local cache to the total number of requested segments, while the later is the ratio of the number of segments which are not in local cache but stored in other peers to the total number of requested segments;

(2) Cache Copy Number (CCN): CCN is the number of copies cached in the whole peer community with respect to the requested segment. In real P2P systems, due to the presence of NATs, firewalls and resources limitation of end users, peers may not be able to fetch the segments from others even though those segments are indeed cached in the P2P network. A larger CCN of a segment implies higher probability for peers to successfully access the segments from other peers, and thus the workload of video server in practical systems will be further reduced.

Scalability Evaluation. We developed a trace-driven simulation tool to measure the CHR and CCN of P2P based VoD system based on the real workload traces. In the following simulations, we only compare the hard cache with soft cache in terms of identical cache capacity to catch the vital differences between them. To make the question clear, we assume that all the clients are homogeneous in cache capacity.

Figure 7(a) depicts the average CHR with two cache replacement schemes as the cache sizes of peers increase. Obviously, either in hard cache (HC) or soft cache (SC), the CHR increases along with the cache size in both FIFO and MCC schemes. However, in soft cache, even though the cache size at end clients is without any limitation, which will be the upper bound of system scalability in ideal case, the CHR is smaller than 80%.[1] While with hard cache enabled, the CHR is much higher, say more than 90%, but it is still smaller than 95% as the cache size is unlimited. Actually, it is not surprising if we recognize the fact that the contents cached in peers are available only when they are online. Since the statistical results in section 2 has shown low user recurrence in practical VoD system, the improvement of hard cache is carefully considerable. As shown, we can also observe that in all cases, the CHR of MCC scheme is always higher than that of FIFO. It is because the MCC scheme takes the global cache information into account for cache replacement.

We further divide the benefits of hard cache into LCHR and PCHR separately. Figure 7(b) and (c) depicts the average LCHR and PCHR as cache size increases respectively. As shown in Figure 7(b), FIFO achieves better performance than MCC in LCHR, which could be explained as: when replacing segments in hard cache, MCC will erase the segments with the most copies in the system and be likely to miss this popular segment. In Figure 7(c), observe that FIFO shows worse than MCC in PCHR. This is because MCC tends to keep the segments which are not in other peers. Comparing the curves of LCHR and PCHR, we can

---

[1] The evaluation results of soft cache are not equal to that of [10] because they adopt different session model.

find out a surprising but interesting result: the increase of LCHR benefited from hard cache is comparable, if not higher, to that of PCHR. In original motivation, the hard cache is to improve the cooperation between peers; however, from the simulation results we can see that hard cache benefits the peer itself as well.

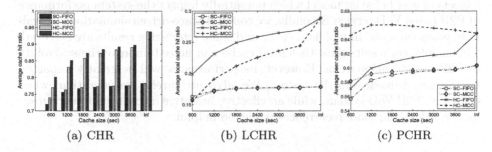

| (a) CHR | (b) LCHR | (c) PCHR |

Fig. 7. Average cache hit ratio vs. cache size

Figure 8 further graphs the distribution of segments over cache copy number (CCN). It is clear that more segments tend to have larger CCN in the system when the hard cache is enabled, which implies that hard cache will indeed achieve better system scalability in P2P based VoD services than soft cache.

Figure 9 shows the CHR in hours within the 100 days over the number of requested segments when the cache size is unlimited. Observe that the CHR increases along with the number of requests in the system in both case of soft cache and hard cache. It is an attractive feature since P2P networks benefit with the growth of the system scale. An interesting question arises here: *Is there any milestone where the system can accommodate to more users without more consumption of server bandwidth?* In this paper, we leave it as an open question because the scalability of real VoD system is rather complex and we believe only the measurement of widely deployed systems can make a clear answer.

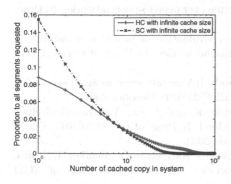

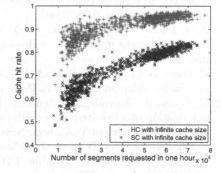

Fig. 8. Distribution of segments over number of cached copies

Fig. 9. Cache hit ratio vs. number of segments requested

4 Conclusion

In this paper, we are motivated to evaluate the scalability of hard cache in P2P based VoD streaming service. Our original contributions come in two-fold: Firstly, we analyze millions of real VoD workload traces to identify several key aspects of user behavior model which potentially impact the system performance of P2P based VoD service. Secondly, we conduct trace-driven simulations to evaluate practical scalability of hard cache and some interesting results are achieved. The simulation results show that hard cache can indeed improve the scalability of P2P based VoD systems. However, its performance will be greatly impacted by the user behaviors in the system. We advocate careful considerations when designing P2P VoD systems while an effective incentive mechanism to encourage longer online and more recurrences might be helpful.

References

1. BitTorrent. http://www.bittorrent.com.
2. KaZaA. http://www.kazaa.com.
3. X. Zhang, J. Liu, B. Li, and T.-SP Yum. CoolStreaming/DONet: a data- driven overlay network for live media streaming. In Proc. of IEEE INFOCOM, March 2005.
4. M. Zhang, J.-G. Luo, L. Zhao, S.-Q. Yang. A peer-to-peer network for live media streaming using a push-pull approach. In Proc. of ACM Multimedia, November 2005.
5. PPLive. http://www.pplive.com.
6. T. T. Do, K. A. Hua, and M. A. Tantaoui. P2VoD: providing fault tolerant video-on-demand streaming in peer-to-peer environment. In Proc. of IEEE ICC, June 2004.
7. Y. Guo, K. Suh, J. Kurose, and D. Towsley. P2Cast: peer-to-peer patching scheme for VoD service. In Proc. of WWW, May 2003.
8. Y. Cui, B.C. Li, and K. Nahrstedt. oStream: asynchronous streaming multicast in application-layer overlay networks. IEEE JSAC, vol. 22, pp. 91-106, January 2004.
9. J.-G. Luo, Y. Tang, S.-Q. Yang. Chasing: an efficient streaming mechanism for scalable and resilient video-on-demand service over peer-to-peer networks. In Proc. of IFIP Networking, May 2006.
10. J.-G. Luo, Y. Tang, J. Zhang, S.-Q. Yang. Evaluation of practical scalability of overlay networks in providing video-on-demand service. In Proc. of IEEE ICME, July 2006.
11. C. Dana, D. Li, D. Harrison, and C.-N. Chuah. BASS: bittorrent assisted streaming system for video-on-demand. In Proc. of IEEE MMSP, October 2005.
12. E. Veloso, V. Almeida, W. Meira, A. Bestavros, and S. Jin. A hierarchical characterization of a live streaming media workload. In Proc. of the ACM SIGCOMM Internet Measurement Workshop, November 2002.
13. S. Rhea, B. Godfrey, B. Karp, J. Kubiatowicz, S. Ratnasamy, S. Shenker, I. Stoica, and H. Yu. OpenDHT: A public DHT service and its uses. In Proc. of ACM SIGCOMM, August 2005.

Cooperative Caching for Peer-Assisted Video Distribution

Pan-Hong Guo[1], Yang Yang[1], and Hui Guo[2]

[1] Dept. of Computer Science and Technology, University of Science and Technology Beijing, Beijing, 100083, China
[2] Dept. of Electronic and Information Engineering, The Hong Kong Polytechnic University, Hung Hom, Kowloon, Hong Kong
phguo@cs.ustb.edu.cn

Abstract. In this paper, we described a framework for peer-assisted multi-path video distribution combined with cooperative caching. The target of this framework is to aggregate peers' storage and bandwidths to facilitate video-on-demand streaming. To achieve this goal, we employ segment-based video caching and the segments are distributed in respective peers. Specifically, the source bit stream is based on layered scalable video coding for cost-effective video distribution. For achieving low -cost collaboration, a utility-based partial caching scheme is proposed and detailed discussed. Extensive simulations on large, Internet-like topologies were performed to demonstrate the effectiveness of this proposed framework.

Keywords: Cooperative caching, peer-to-peer networks, segment-base caching, distributed caching.

1 Introduction

To tackle the scalability issue of the unicast-based media streaming architectures, hierarchy-based (tree-based) solutions were proposed in the literature, such as IP-multicast [1], application-level multicast (ALM) [2, 3, 4, 5] and proxy-based structure [6, 7]. In the hierarchy of IP-multicast, the server acts as root-node and the clients act as the leave-nodes. The intermediate nodes are routers that provide point to multipoint transmission through packet replication. The ALM tree purely consists of the server and the clients. In ALM, data are delivered over hierarchical multicast delivery tree out of a set of unicast-based connections among ordinary clients. The proxy-based hierarchy consists of the original server, multiple proxy servers and the clients. The proxy servers are dedicated devices that are usually powerful (e.g., huge disk volume, huge memory size, large I/O bandwidth, etc.) and stable, as compared with ordinary clients.

The IP-multicast has seen a very slow deployment because of its high demand on router capability [8]. The ALM has also seen a very slow deployment because the tree is usually very unstable. In proxy-based hierarchy, the proxy servers are usually deployed on the edge of the Internet, it does not need the router support and much more stable than ALM. Several works [9, 10, 11] have constructed content delivery networks (CDNs) by

T.-J. Cham et al. (Eds.): MMM 2007, LNCS 4352, Part II, pp. 135–144, 2007.

introducing a dedicated set of proxy servers [12] so as to provide high performance media distribution services over the Internet. Despite that proxy-based hierarchy has proven to be effective, it does not solve the scalability problem completely. The reason is simply that the deployment of proxy servers, which must be powerful and stable online servers, is still an expensive cost. Presently, some research has been conducted to study the effectiveness data sharing of P2P-based [13, 14, 15] or BitTorrent-like overlay systems [16, 17].

2   Cooperative Distribution Architecture

In this paper, we proposed a peer-based cooperative streaming architecture with distributed caching for delivering media content effectively over the Internet. The basic idea there is to ask the concurrent peers to cooperate to improve the streaming quality mutually. The proposed architecture combines the strengths of many techniques such as multi-source/multi-path streaming, P2P overlay networks and distributed proxy caching. Specifically, we try to improve the streaming quality of a later client through the help of one or more earlier client(s) in the same neighborhood, given that there is no dedicated powerful proxy server. The proposed system is based on the layered scalable video coding source bit-stream. Assume an earlier client, Client A, watched and stored the title at a specific quality (via distributed caching), a later client, Client B, collects the data cached by *peer server* -- Client A and, at the same time, requests more data from the original server (via multi-source streaming). As a result, Client B will enjoy better quality than Client A did. Client B, in turn, also caches its data (partially or entirely) so as to serve others later on. With the same logic, an even later client, Client C, will enjoy even better quality by the multi-path streaming from original server, client A and client B. The procedure is illustrated in Fig.1. Clearly, the quality of a certain title will improve progressively as more clients viewed it, because of more chances for cooperation. Note that the later client could be Client A/B if they want to watch the same title again. This is very useful for Video-on-Demand (VOD) those hottest titles.

In this paper, we focus on the following two problems. The first problem is on the distributed multi-source based video streaming. In our architecture, except the original server, all the other sources are peers which are heterogeneous in many aspects including contents cached, bandwidth, and availability, etc. We solve this problem through a receiver-driven protocol that is based on a sliding-window mechanism. The second problem is about the distributed cache replacement scheme for each peer. In general, ordinary clients can hardly provide sufficient disk space to cache all media data they viewed. Therefore, contents must be selectively cached/replaced according to a certain replacement policy. However, existing replacement schemes for traditional proxies tend to make clients cache similar low quality contents. This is ill-suited to our multi-source streaming model. To address this problem, we proposed a novel utility-based cache replacement scheme to help clients cache content that has the potential of providing better performance in the future cooperation, taking into account both the characteristics of clients and their peers.

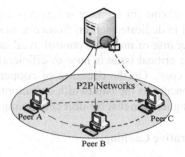

Fig. 1. Illustration of peer-assisted quality enhancement

3 Segments Distribution and Caching

3.1 Segment-Based Caching

Segment-based caching has been proved as an effective way for multimedia caching. So in our proposed system, we still use segment-based cooperative caching scheme. In centralized P2P system, there should need an Index server for coordination of distributed cache. The Index server should be a reliable and always-on entity in the network. Definitely, the original server can act as an Index Server that maintains a subset of indices of media segments in the system for content location. A media segment index should contain a location list of peers, each of which caches a copy of the media segment, and the access information of this segment, which is used for replacement operations. We assume that each media object is expressed as a segment-link. The segment link is illustrated in Fig. 2.

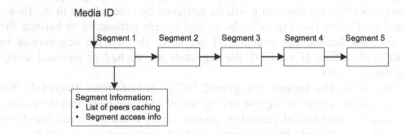

Fig. 2. Segment link maintained in Index Server

The segment locating is conducted in two steps: the first step is to route the request to index server; and the second step is to select a peer that caches a copy of the segment via the info of segment link which maintained in Index Server. The selection of serving peer can be optimized according to the capacities and workloads of pees caching the demanded segments. Once the demanded segment is successfully located, the media streaming between the serving peer/proxy server and the requesting peer is established.

Note that our proposed scheme for segment location is a centralized policy that all segment indexes are stored in dedicated server. Someone maybe wonder that whether it would be a bottleneck because of intensive control overhead. As a matter of fact, in cooperative web caching, a critical issue is how to efficiently locate web pages with minimum communication costs. On the occasion of cooperative streaming caching, however, is not a major concern as the bandwidth consumption for streaming objects is of orders of magnitude higher than that for object indexing and discovering.

3.2 Utility-Based Cooperative Caching

In this section, we propose a distributed utility-based fine-grain cooperative cache replacement scheme. We evaluate each segment and assign a utility index for it. The utility index is essentially a measurement of the potential value that the segment, if cached, would help other peers. The objective of our replacement policy is then to maximize the utility indices of all the segments cached subject to the cache size constraint. Evidently, when the cache is full, the segments with smallest utility indices should be replaced by newer segments with higher utility indices. Moreover, the utility index of a segment needs to be evaluated dynamically instead of assigning a constant value. When a new segment arrives, an initial utility index is assigned, and then the index will be updated periodically until it is flushed out. In this way, the cache management can effectively handle the emergences of new hot titles.

The key of our cache replacement scheme is to measure the utility index for each segment. The calculation of utility index should take into consideration not only the properties of local cache but also the status of those potentially cooperative caches. We define the utility index for a client, C, to cache a certain segment, g, as follows:

$$I(C,g) = W(C,g)^{k_1} + F(C,g)^{k_2} \qquad (1)$$

where $W(C,g)$ indicates the cost for C to obtain the segment g, $F(C,g)$ represents the estimated frequency that the segment g will be retrieved by other clients in the future if it is cached by C. The two exponentials, k_1 and k_2, are introduced to balance the impacts of the two factors. For example, if set $k_1=0$, the scheme degenerates to traditional LFU algorithm. If set $k_2=0$, the segments are cached or replaced solely according to retrieval cost.

The rationale of the two factors, $W(C,g)$ and $F(C,g)$, is as follows. Intuitively, the utility index should be a function of cost savings of other future peers that the current peer will service. Without loss of generality, assume X is a client in the neighborhood of C and X will be requesting the segment g. If C doesn't cache g, X will have to obtain g from the original server directly or from other peer servers from P_g, which represents the set of potential peer servers that have cached g. In this case, the cost for X to obtain g will be $W(X,g)$, which is close to $W(C,g)$ because the distance between X and C is much smaller than that between X and any other peer server or the original server. However, if C caches g, X will retrieve g from C because they are closest. The cost associated is $W(X,C,g)$. The cost savings is then $W(X,g)$ minus $W(X,C,g)$. Since $W(X,C,g)$ is usually much smaller than $W(X,g)$ and $W(X,g)$ is close to $W(C,g)$, the cost savings is approximately equal to $W(C,g)$, which is readily collectible. On the other hand, if the title is hot, many clients in the neighborhood of C may also view it in future. That is, $F(C,g)$ is large. Obviously, caching g in C may lead to more cost savings because of g's potential high retrieval frequency. Therefore, the utility index of a segment is directly related to the above two factors and is empirically defined as the product of them in our scheme.

To calculate the cost function, $W(C,g)$, two observations need to be considered. Firstly, the number of peers having cached the segment g, i.e., $|P_g|$, has a direct impact on the cost. For instance, if there are already many cached copies of the segment, the cost savings for client C to cache g should be much smaller, as compared with the case where only few copies have been cached. Secondly, as stated above, the heterogeneities of peers have direct impact on the system performance of our architecture. Specifically, three heterogeneities that influence the service capacity of a peer server are considered. These heterogeneities include (i) available bandwidth between the peer server and C; (ii) availability of the peer server; (iii) load of the peer server. A peer server with little available bandwidth, or frequently offline, or heavy loaded can hardly provide useful (reliable) service. In our work, we consider all the abovementioned factors and define the cost function $W(C,g)$ as follows.

$$W(C,g) = \frac{1}{\max\{V(P_g,C,g),V_0\}} \tag{2}$$

and

$$V(P_g,C,g) = \sum_{p \in P_g}\{P_a(p) \times (1 - P_L(p)) \times B(C,p)\} \tag{3}$$

where $P_a(p)$ is the probability that the peer will be online, $P_L(p)$ is the probability that the peer is overloaded and can not serve as a peer server, and $B(C,p)$ is the available bandwidth estimated and discretized . $P_a(p)$ is estimated by the peer itself as the ratio of average online time to total time elapsed. $P_L(p)$ is estimated similarly as the ratio of average load to the peer's maximum affordable load. Moreover, we set an empirical value, $1/V_0$, as the default value of $W(C,g)$ in case that P_g empty or all the peers in P_g fail to service the desired segment g. Note that, $W(C,g)$ of each segment is calculated only once when it first arrives the client C. We do not update its value periodically because $W(C,g)$ is a measurement on an average sense. Moreover, frequent update of $W(C,g)$ will cause much protocol overhead since the calculation consumes much network resources to collect necessary relative information.

$$F(C,g) = \begin{cases} \frac{1}{P_g} \cdot \sum_{p \in P_g} F(p,g) & P_g \neq \emptyset \\ F_0 & otherwise \end{cases} \tag{4}$$

To calculate $F(C,g)$, an initial value is first assigned using Equation (4) when a new segment comes in. Equation indicates that, if the client discovers some peers have cached g, it will use the mean value of those peers' current frequency as the initial value. Otherwise, it takes a default value, F_0.

If a segment is already cached, its frequency will be updated periodically using Equation (13) so as to match the popularity of the title. Specifically, we update the frequency in a smooth manner.

$$F'(C,g) = w_1 \times F(C,g) + w_2 \times \Delta_F(g) \quad s.t. \ w_1 + w_2 = 1 \tag{5}$$

where $\Delta_F(g)$ represents the frequency the segment has been used to serve other peers during the update period Δ, and the w_1 and w_2 are the relative weights of frequency of the two difference circumstances.

4 Performance Evaluation

In this section, we present the simulation results to demonstrate the performance of the proposed framework.

4.1 Simulation Setup

In all of the simulations, we use large hierarchical, Internet-like topologies. All of the topologies have three levels. The top level consists of several Transit domains, which represent large Internet Service Providers (ISPs). The middle level contains several Stub domains, which represent small ISPs, campus networks, moderately sized enterprise networks, etc. (Each Stub domain is connected to one of the Transit domains). At the bottom level, end hosts (peers) are connected to Stub domains. The first two levels (router-level) contain transit routers and stub routers, which are generated using the GT-ITM tool [18]. We then randomly attach end hosts (peers) to stub routers with uniformed probability. The network topology for the presented results consists of 5 transit domains, each with 10 transit nodes, and a transit node is then connected to 8 stub domains, each with 4 stub nodes. The total number of nodes is thus 1650 nodes.

During the simulation, there are totally 500 videos published in the network, each with 512 kbps constant playback bit rate and 1 hour length and is divided into 8 logical layers. Each *LL* is roughly 64kbps. In our simulations, a *LL* is further divided into a number of segments each with an interval for 10 seconds, while the length of the cooperation window is set to 2 minutes. That is, $t = 10s$ and $WT = 120s$. In our simulations, we randomly select 500 to 1500 nodes to build an overlay network. In default, the number of participated clients is 700. Each client reserves a fix sized disk space (the default value is 500MB) as its local cache. The maximum load (the maximum number of peers a client can support concurrently) is set to four. To simulate the probability that a peer is online, we utilized a two state Markov model. A client can be in two states: *Inactive* and *Active*. The transition of one client is independent on the states of other clients. The transition probability from Active to Inactive is randomly distributed in the range from once per 80 minutes to once per 160 minutes. The transition probability from Inactive to Active is also randomly distributed in the range from once per 40 minutes to once per 80 minutes.

For VOD service, client requests are generated as a Poisson process with arrive rate 15 requests/min. These requests are then uniformly distributed to those Active clients that are not viewing any title. This is reasonable because, in general, a client will not play more than one titles simultaneously. The popularity of video titles follows a *Zipf* like distribution with a default skew factor 0.271.

4.2 Simulation Results

One target of our simulations is to test the performance improvement of our multi-path cooperative streaming models in presented Section 2. The other target is to demonstrate the effect of our distributed utility-based fine-grained cooperative cache replacement (*DUFC*) policy. We compare *DUFC* with the LRU-based fine-grain cache replacement scheme (*LRUF*). *LRUF* replaces the least recently used segments firstly and adopts the fine-grain replacement pattern introduced in [19].

Note that, were it not for the proposed peer-assisted cooperative streaming architecture, all the clients would receive at most a quality of 200 kbps, which already reaches the bottleneck bandwidth of its connection to the server. With the proposed architecture, no matter what cache replacement schemes are adopted, the overall performances are improved drastically. For example, the average quality of all the titles is at least doubled, as shown in Fig.3. For the hottest titles, the quality improved for several times, see Fig.4.

We simulated our proposed system using *DUFC* and *LRUF* respectively. The results are shown in Fig.3, where the *x*-axis represents the simulation time and the *y*-axis is the average quality of all requests generated with the metric of bit rate experienced.

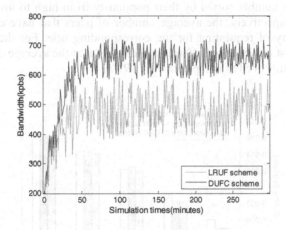

Fig. 3. Average quality for all requests

As shown in Fig.3, although the average quality in the initial period of simulations is low, it keeps on improving with time and converges into a high and steady value finally (After about 50 minutes for *LRUF* and 75 minutes for *DUFC*). The reason is that the caches of most peers were not filled in full in the early time of simulations. During this period, it was hard for a client to find peers for cooperation. As time went on, more and more data got cached in the cluster of peers, which increased the opportunities for peers' cooperation. However, because of the limit of the cache size, the quality will not increase infinitely but fluctuate around a steady value. Another obvious observation is that *DUFC* results in a higher quality enhancement (over 25%) than *LRUF*. This is because *DUFC* can make more efficient use of limited disk space,

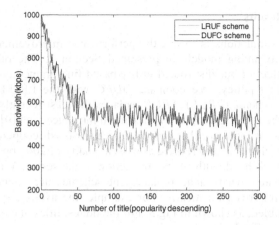

Fig. 4. Average quality of different titles

by caching more useful segments that improve the efficiency of cooperation among peers in return.

We further explain the conclusions above using Fig.4. In the figures, the *x*-axis represents the title number sorted by their popularity from high to low, while the *y*-axis represents, respectively, the average number of peers that have cached the title and average quality of requesting for the corresponding title. For the sake of clear presentation, we list only the top 300 titles. We found that the average quality of those titles still greatly improved as compared with *LRUF*.

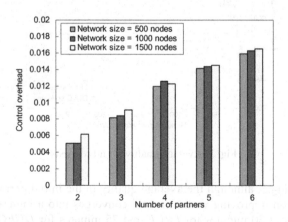

Fig. 5. The control overhead as a function of number of partners

The main concerning issue of the proposed mechanism is the network overhead because there are frequent information exchanges between peers. In our proposed system, the video stream is partitioned to many segments, each node periodically exchange segment's availability information with partners, and then schedules which segment is to be fetched from which partner accordingly. Usually, the number of partners is a key factor to the control overhead. Fig.5 depicts the normalized control overhead as a function of the average number of partners in a stable environment, i.e., the lifetime of each node equals to the playback duration of streaming, typically as 60 min. In this experiment, we define the control overhead as the ratio of control traffic volume over video traffic volume at each node. The source bit stream is composed of 3 logical layers, which has mean value of 64kpbs bandwidth for each layer. The figure shows that the overhead in the system is trivial which compared with video content traffic (1.62% with MAX value). Definitely, the control overhead increases with a larger number of partners, but with the increasing of overlay network size, the control overhead keeps invariability on the whole.

5 Conclusions and Future Work

In this paper, we propose a low-cost peer-assisted streaming framework for hetero-geneous peer-to-peer networks with cooperative caching. In this framework, published videos are encoded into multi-layered source bit stream and split into many of segments, which are distribute to overlay peers. The main design philosophy is that outbound bandwidths from multiple peers who have viewed and cached the same title before can be aggregated to serve a single video streaming request. We propose the protocol for the multi-source cooperative streaming and the distributed utility-based fine-grain cooperative cache replacement scheme. We conducted extensive simulation experiments on large, Internet-like topologies by GT-ITM topology generator. Simulation results demonstrate that the proposed architecture bring in significant quality enhancement. The average quality of all the titles is more than doubled. For the hottest titles, the quality improved for several times. In our future work, we plan to implement our prototype and deploy it over PlanetLab[20], which can evaluate its performance in the real Internet environment.

References

1. S. E. Deering. Multicast Routing in a Datagram Internetwork. PhD thesis, Stanford University, December 1991.
2. K. Lee, S. Ha, et al, "An Application-level Multicast Architecture for Multimedia Communications," In Proceedings of ACM Multimedia, Los Angeles, USA, 2001. 398~400
3. Cui Y, Li BC, Nahrstedt K. "oStream: Asynchronous streaming multicast in application-layer overlay networks," IEEE Journal on Selected Areas in Communications, 2004, 22(1):91-106.
4. S. Banerjee, B. Bhattacharjee, and Christopher Kommareddy. "Scalable application layer multicast," In Proceedings of ACM SIGCOMM, August 2002.
5. Duc A. Tran, Kien A. Hua and Tai Do. "ZIGZAG: An efficient peer-to-peer scheme for media streaming," In Proceedings of IEEE INFOCOM, April 2003.
6. J. Liu, J. Xu, "Proxy caching for media streaming over the internet", IEEE Communications Magazine, special issue on proxy support for streaming Internet, 2004, 42(8): 88~94
7. J. Liu, X. Chu, and J. Xu, "Proxy cache management of fine-grained scalable video strea-ming," In Proceedings of IEEE INFOCOM, 2004.

8. C. Diot, B. Levine, B. Lyles, et al, "Deployment Issues for the IP Multicast Service and Architecture", IEEE Network, 2000, 14(1):78~88
9. B. Krishnamurthy, C. E. Wills, and Y. Zhang. "On the Use and Performance of Content Distribution Networks," In Proceedings of SIGCOMM IMW 2001, Nov. 2001
10. Akamai Technologies, Inc. FreeFlow overview. http://www.cs.washington.edu/homes/ratul/akamai/freeflow.pdf
11. A. Vakali, G. Pallis, "Content Delivery Networks: Current Status and. Trends", IEEE Internet Computing, 2003, 7(6): 68-74
12. Hui Guo, Jacky Shen, Zhiguang Wang, Shipeng Li, "Optimized Streaming Media Proxy and its Applications", to appear in Elsevier Journal of Network and Computer Applications, Elsevier Science Publishers.
13. Alan T.S. Ip, J.C. Liu, John C.S. Lui, "COPACC: An Architecture of Cooperative Proxy-Client Caching System for On-Demand Media Streaming," to appear in the IEEE Transaction on Parallel and Distributed Systems.
14. V. Gopalakrishnan, B. Silaghi, B. Bhattacharjee, and P. Keleher, "Adaptive replication in peer-to-peer systems," In Proceedings of 24th International Conference on Distributed Computing Systems (ICDCS'04), March 2004.
15. Jungohn Yim, Gil Yong Kim, Young-Sung Son, "Cooperative caching framework of VOD using P2P technology," In Proceedings of 11th International packet video workshop, 2001.
16. J. Pouwelse, P. Garbacki, D. Epema, and H. Sips. The BitTorrent P2P file-sharing system: Measurements and analysis. In Proceedings of International Workshop on Peer-to-Peer Systems, Feb. 2005.
17. D. Qiu and R. Srikant. Modeling and performance analysis of BitTorrent-like peer-to-peer networks. In Proceedings of ACM SIGCOMM, Aug. 2004.
18. Zegura, E. W., Calvert, K., Bhattacharjee, S.: How to Model an Internetwork. In Proc. of IEEE INFOCOM'96, SF, CA, Mar. 1996.
19. R. Rejaie, M. Handley, H. Yu et al, "Proxy Caching Mechanisms for Multimedia Playback Streams in the Internet", In Proceedings of the 4th International Web Caching Workshop, San Diego, CA. March 1999.
20. PlanetLab website: http://www.planet-lab.org/

Metadata Management, Reuse, Inference and Propagation in a Collection-Oriented Metadata Framework for Digital Images

William Ku[1], Mohan S. Kankanhalli[1], and Joo-Hwee Lim[2]

[1] National University of Singapore, 3 Science 2, Singapore 117543
[2] Institute of Infocomm Research, 21 Heng Mui Keng Terrace, Singapore 119613
{kucheech,mohan}@comp.nus.edu.sg, joohwee@i2r.a-star.edu.sg

Abstract. Digital photography generates a lot more "shoeboxes" of photos than its conventional counterpart, resulting in image search and retrieval being more applicable. We briefly discuss some research challenges faced with the use of metadata in image search and retrieval. We then propose the structural use of metadata regularity of photos within collections (the *Group Effect*), in metadata management, reuse, inference and propagation. This application of the *Group Effect* is complemented by the *Social Networking Effect* whereby user interactions with image collections provide collaborative metadata. This is followed by our presentation of a set-theoretic approach to our framework (proposed in previous work [5,6]) and we then outline its application and utility.

Keywords: Image Metadata Management, Reuse, Inference, Propagation, Collection-Oriented Framework, Group Effect, Social Networking Effect.

1 Introduction

The high ease and low cost of digital photography empower people to take as many photos as they like. The "trigger-happy" user will find herself with tons of photos and while storage may not be an issue in terms of availability and costs, the user may have difficulties browsing, searching and retrieving from her massive collection, the exact photos that she may want to show to her family and friends. Image search and retrieval has become a needle-in-a-haystack issue. Nevertheless, digital photos have the capability to encode the "thousand words (and more) that they tell" in the form of metadata, which can be used in general to assist in search and retrieval. However, the key here is that the correct metadata and a proper search mechanism must be present in order for the search and retrieval in a digital photo collection to be workable. Unfortunately, the ideal type of annotation namely manual annotation is a tedious, inconsistent and erroneous process.

There has been significant research on automatic annotation. It is sufficient to state that at this point of time, there remain significant issues [1,10] that are yet to be fully addressed for efficient and accurate automatic annotation. Thus with large image collection, image search and retrieval has become an important research challenge. At a panel in ACM Multimedia 2005, the importance of image search and retrieval was

T.-J. Cham et al. (Eds.): MMM 2007, LNCS 4352, Part II, pp. 145–154, 2007.

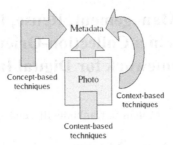

Fig. 1. The three main approaches to automatic metadata generation

emphasised by a panelist who said that *"Image retrieval may not be a killer app but not having it is an app killer"*.

An alternative approach to enhance existing image search and retrieval techniques is to generate more metadata from the context of the image. The simultaneous use of content-based, concept-based and context-based techniques (Figure 1) should result in better image search and retrieval. We observe that digital images are usually part of a collection and that this association could provide some context on the nature of the photos themselves. For example, one would expect that a photo album with the title "My birthday party" would only contain photos pertaining to a birthday party. This will give rise to some interesting observations. Thus, photos belonging to this particular collection should have some identical information such as the location and date. More importantly, one should be able to obtain more contextual information from a group of photos than from the photos individually, such as the event-type. This group contextual information could be used for inference.

A second observation is that when users share their photos, the user interaction could provide collaborative annotations. Using the above example, one could group together the various photos (taken by different users) at the birthday party and examine their respective annotations to infer new contextual information such as the names of the participants.

Our contribution in this paper would be to incorporate the above two observations namely the *Group Effect* and the *Social Networking Effect* into our collection-oriented approach which would make use of metadata regularity at the collection level to extract contextual metadata for reuse, inference and propagation. The injection of collaborative metadata would further fuel reuse, inference and propagation.

The rest of this paper is organised as follows. We shall first touch on some related work on context-based techniques. This is followed by a discussion of our collection-oriented approach which is based on the *Group* and *Social Networking Effects*. We then present our set-theoretic approach to our collection-oriented framework. We concluded by applying our approach to a set of photos taken at ACM Multimedia 2005.

2   Related Work

In the domain of digital photos, there are some work on metadata sharing and reuse on a group basis. LOCALE [8] tags unlabeled photographs using shared information based on other photos taken in the same area. The social-temporal-social context of a group of cameraphone users would influence the metadata values of their images [3]. Snap2Tell [2, 7] matches a photo taken with cameraphone with a database, using content-based features and metadata. Event and location groupings can be used to suggest name labels [9]. *MyPhotos* [11] describes a prototype system for home photo management processing that replaces traditional folders with photo groups.

In summary, present work do not make structured use of photo metadata regularity in conjunction with collaborative metadata for personal photo collections while at the same time, provides for metadata conflict resolution, reuse, inference and propagation at the collection level. This is what our collection-oriented framework would attempt to achieve.

3 Collection-Oriented Approach

Our collection-oriented approach of handling digital images is based on two effects namely the Group Effect and the Social Networking Effect. The Group Effect is essentially the establishment of metadata regularity from the observation that images are usually part of a collection. The Social Networking Effect refers to the observation that one could share digital photos with his family and friends through the Internet and which provides a channel for collaborative annotation. A detailed discussion on the Group and Social Networking Effects can be found in [6].

4 Metadata Reuse, Propagation and Inference

In this section, we shall briefly discuss the relationship of metadata reuse, inference and propagation. Figure 2 gives an overview picture of this relationship. Initially, the metadata of the photos in a collection are in a state of *equilibrium*. That is to say, no further inference could be achieved on the existing set of metadata. However, when there is an interaction, the equilibrium would be disturbed and new metadata would be detected, inferred and propagated. Here, an interaction is an action defined by one

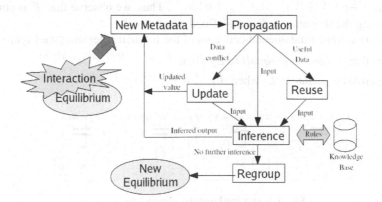

Fig. 2. Overview of the relationship between reuse, inference and propagation

of the following (but not limited to): Insert annotation(s), Create collection(s), Insert/Delete photo(s) into collection(s) and Merge/Partition collection(s).

Thus an interaction would trigger the propagation of new metadata within a photo itself and to other photos in the same collection. The new metadata could be an update to existing metadata or new useful information to be reused or as an input to an inference process. The updated or reused metadata could become an input to an inference process as well. The inference process may generate new metadata that would get propagated and this propagation cycle would go on until no further inference could take place. At this point of time, the existing metadata are examined to see if common metadata could be extracted and reused at the group level. When this is done and there is no further action, the photos are said to reach a new state of equilibrium. A further discussion on this issue together with the modeling of the relationship of metadata management, reuse, inference and propagation in some form of finite-state automata can be found in [6].

5 Collection-Oriented Framework for Digital Images

We had presented a collection-oriented framework for digital images in [5] and here we followed up with a set-theoretic approach to this framework.

5.1 Basic Definitions

Metadata Element definitions. The *(basic) metadata element E* is an *ordered pair (A,V)* consisting two members namely the *metadata attribute A* and the *metadata value V*. *E* can also be denoted as *<A,V>*. In set theory, a common definition of an ordered pair can be defined in the following manner: $(a,v)=\{\{a\},\{a,v\}\}$. *E* is *uninstantiated* when it does not have a metadata value. This is by defining *V* to be the empty set ($\emptyset$). In this case, we define *E* to be the *base metadata element* $\hat{E}$. This can be expressed as $E=\hat{E}$ *iff* $V=\emptyset$.

All metadata elements are *similar* to their base metadata elements : $E \sim \hat{E}$.

E can always be reduced to $\hat{E}$: $E \to \hat{E} \Rightarrow V = \emptyset$.

Given that $E=(A,V)=\{\{a\},\{a,v\}\}$, $\hat{E}=\{\{a\}\}$. Thus, we observe that $\hat{E}$ is simply a set containing the singleton *A*. *E* is undefined when $A=\emptyset$.

We next define some fundamental concepts of the metadata element (see Figure 3).

E_1 is defined to be *identical (equal)* to E_2 when $E_1 = E_2$, *iff* $A_1 = A_2 \wedge V_1 = V_2$.

E_1 is defined to be *similar* to E_2 when $E_1 \sim E_2$, *iff* $A_1 = A_2 \wedge V_1 \neq V_2$.

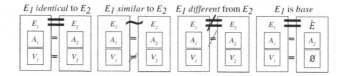

Fig. 3. Some fundamental element concepts

E_1 is defined to be *different* from E_2 when $E_1 \perp E_2$, *iff* $A_1 \neq A_2$.

E_1 is defined to be *not equal (unique)* to E_2 when $E_1 \neq E_2$, *iff* $E_1 \sim E_2 \vee E_1 \perp E_2$.

Metadata Schema definitions. The *metadata schema S* is a *set* of *(basic) metadata elements*. Hence, all elements in *S* are *unique*. Thus, $S = \{E_1, E_2, ..., E_{NE}\}$ where $NE = |S|$.

S is defined to be a *base schema (or schema template)* $\hat{S}$ when every of its elements is a *base element* (see Figure 4), that is $S = \hat{S}$, *iff* $\forall E \in S$, $E = \hat{E}$. Thus, $\hat{S}$ is essentially a *set* of *base metadata elements*.

S can be reduced to $\hat{S}$ by reducing every of its members to its base form.
$S \rightarrow \hat{S} \Rightarrow \forall E \in S \rightarrow \hat{E}$
We define some fundamental concepts of the metadata schema (see Figure 4).

S_1 is defined to be identical (equal) to S_2 when $S_1 = S_2$, *iff* $S_1 \setminus S_2 = S_2 \setminus S_1 = \varnothing$.

S_1 is defined to be similar to S_2 when $S_1 \sim S_2$, *iff* $S_1 \setminus S_2 \neq \varnothing \wedge \hat{S}_1 = \hat{S}_2$. S is always similar to $\hat{S}$.

S_1 is defined to be different from S_2 when $S_1 \perp S_2$, *iff* $\hat{S}_1 \cap \hat{S}_2 \neq \varnothing$.

S_1 is defined to be not equal (unique) to S_2 when
$S_1 \neq S_2$, *iff* $S_1 \setminus S_2 \neq \varnothing \vee S_2 \setminus S_1 \neq \varnothing \vee S_1 \sim S_2 \vee S_1 \perp S_2$.

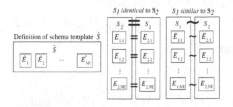

Fig. 4. Some fundamental schema concepts

Image Metadata Structure definitions. The *image metadata structure IM* of an image *I* is a *set* of *metadata schemas*. All elements in *IM* are *unique*. Thus, $IM = \{S_1, S_2, ..., S_{NS}\}$ where $NS = |IM|$.

IM_1 is defined to be identical (equal) to IM_2 when
$IM_1 = IM_2$, *iff* $IM_1 \setminus IM_2 = IM_2 \setminus IM_1 = \varnothing$.

IM is defined to be a *base image metadata structure (or image metadata template)* $\hat{IM}$ when every of its elements is a *base metadata schema*.
$IM = \hat{IM}$, *iff* $\forall S \in IM$, $S = \hat{S}$

IM can be reduced to $\hat{IM}$ by reducing every of its members to its base form.
$IM \rightarrow \hat{IM} \Rightarrow \forall S \in IM \rightarrow \hat{S}$

IM_1 is defined to be similar to IM_2 when $IM_1 \sim IM_2$, *iff* $IM_1 \setminus IM_2 \neq \varnothing \wedge \hat{IM}_1 = \hat{IM}_2$. IM is always similar to $\hat{IM}$.

IM_1 is defined to be different from IM_2 when $IM_1 \perp IM_2$, iff $I\hat{M}_1 \cap I\hat{M}_2 \neq \emptyset$.
IM_1 is defined to be not equal (unique) to IM_2 when

$$IM_1 \neq IM_2, \text{ iff } IM_1 \setminus IM_2 \neq \emptyset \vee IM_2 \setminus IM_1 \neq \emptyset \vee IM_1 \sim IM_2 \vee IM_1 \perp IM_2$$

Image Collection definitions. An *image group G* is defined to be a *subset of a powerset of a set of unique images*. Its corresponding *group metadata structure GM* is defined to be a *subset of a powerset of a set of image metadata structures*. Thus, the definitions and operations defined for image metadata structures are applicable here.

5.2 Operations

In this section, we shall show some operations that the framework can provide. We would look at operations involving the metadata element and the metadata schema.

Element operations

1. Determining if an element E is a base element $\hat{E}$.

$|E|=1 \Rightarrow E=\hat{E}$, otherwise $|E|=2 \wedge E \neq \hat{E}$

Given $E=(a,v)=\{\{a\},\{a,v\}\}$, $\hat{E}=\{\{a\}\}$

$E=\hat{E} \Rightarrow E=\{\{a\}\} \Rightarrow |E|=1$, otherwise $|E|=2 \wedge E \neq \hat{E}$

2. Determining the attribute a and the value v

For an ordered pair (a,v), $(a,v)=\{\{a\},\{a,v\}\}$

Let $(a,v)=\{\{a\},\{a,v\}\}=\{X_1, X_2\}$ such that $|X_1|=1 \wedge |X_2|=2$

Then $a=X_1 \cap X_2$ and $v=X_2 \setminus X_1$

3. Given that

$E=(a,v)=\{\{a\},\{a,v\}\}$, $E_1=(a_1,v_1)=\{\{a_1\},\{a_1,v_1\}\}$ and

$E_2=(a_2,v_2)=\{\{a_2\},\{a_2,v_2\}\}$

A. $E_1 \cap E_2$

A1. $E_1 \cap E_2=E=E_1=E_2$ iff $E_1=E_2$

$E_1 \cap E_2=\{\{a_1\},\{a_1,v_1\}\} \cap \{\{a_2\},\{a_2,v_2\}\}$

$E_1=E_2 \Rightarrow a=a_1=a_2 \wedge v=v_1=v_2$

$E_1 \cap E_2=\{\{a\},\{a,v\}\} \cap \{\{a\},\{a,v\}\}$

$E_1 \cap E_2=\{\{a\},\{a,v\}\}=(a,v)=E$

A2. $E_1 \cap E_2=\hat{E}$, iff $E_1 \sim E_2$ (This operation may be used to derive $\hat{E}$)

$E_1 \cap E_2=\{\{a_1\},\{a_1,v_1\}\} \cap \{\{a_2\},\{a_2,v_2\}\}$

$E_1 \sim E_2 \Rightarrow a=a_1=a_2 \wedge v_1 \neq v_2$

$E_1 \cap E_2=\{\{a\},\{a,v_1\}\} \cap \{\{a\},\{a,v_2\}\}$

$E_1 \cap E_2=\{\{a\}\}=\hat{E}$

A3. $E_1 \cap E_2 = \emptyset$, iff $E_1 \perp E_2$

$$E_1 \cap E_2 = \{\{a_1\}, \{a_{1,} v_1\}\} \cap \{\{a_2\}, \{a_2 v_2\}\}$$

$$E_1 \perp E_2 \Rightarrow a_1 \neq a_2$$

$$E_1 \cap E_2 = \{\{a_1\}, \{a_{1,} v_1\}\} \cap \{\{a_2\}, \{a_2 v_2\}\}$$

$$E_1 \cap E_2 = \emptyset$$

B. $E_1 \cup E_2$

B1. $E_1 \cup E_2 = E = E_1 = E_2$ iff $E_1 = E_2$

$$E_1 \cup E_2 = \{\{a_1\}, \{a_{1,} v_1\}\} \cup \{\{a_2\}, \{a_2 v_2\}\}$$

$$E_1 = E_2 \Rightarrow a = a_1 = a_2 \wedge v = v_1 = v_2$$

$$E_1 \cup E_2 = \{\{a\}, \{a, v\}\} \cup \{\{a\}, \{a, v\}\}$$

$$E_1 \cup E_2 = \{\{a\}, \{a, v\}\} = (a, v) = E$$

B2. $E_1 \cup E_2 = ?$, iff $E_1 \sim E_2$

$$E_1 \cup E_2 = \{\{a_1\}, \{a_{1,} v_1\}\} \cup \{\{a_2\}, \{a_2 v_2\}\}$$

$$E_1 \sim E_2 \Rightarrow a = a_1 = a_2 \wedge v_1 \neq v_2$$

$$E_1 \cup E_2 = \{\{a\}, \{a, v_1\}\} \cap \{\{a\}, \{a, v_2\}\}$$

$$E_1 \cup E_2 = \{\{a\}, \{a, v_1\}, \{a, v_2\}\} = ? \Rightarrow \text{conflict resolution}$$

B3. $E_1 \cup E_2 = \{E_1, E_2\}$, iff $E_1 \perp E_2$

$$E_1 \cup E_2 = \{\{a_1\}, \{a_{1,} v_1\}\} \cup \{\{a_2\}, \{a_2 v_2\}\}$$

$$E_1 \perp E_2 \Rightarrow a_1 \neq a_2$$

$$E_1 \cup E_2 = \{\{a_1\}, \{a_{1,} v_1\}\} \cup \{\{a_2\}, \{a_2 v_2\}\}$$

$$E_1 \cup E_2 = \{\{a_1\}, \{a_{1,} v_1\}, \{\{a_2\}, \{a_2 v_2\}\} = ? \Rightarrow \text{conflict resolution}$$

Schema operations. The following are some example operations at the metadata schema level.

A. $S_1 \cap S_2$

A1. $S_1 \cap S_2 = S = S_1 = S_2$ iff $S_1 = S_2$

A2. $S_1 \cap S_2 = \emptyset$ iff $S_1 \perp S_2$

A3. $S_1 \cap S_2 = S *$, iff $S_1 \sim S_2$

$$S_1 \sim S_2 \Rightarrow \hat{S}_1 = \hat{S}_2 = \hat{S}$$

Let $CS = S_1 \cap S_2$, $DS_1 = S_1 - CS$ and $DS_2 = S_2 - CS$

Then there exists $x_1 \in DS_1$ and $x_2 \in DS_2$ such that

$x_1 \sim x_2 \Rightarrow \text{conflict resolution}$

B. $S_1 \cup S_2$

B1. $S_1 \cup S_2 = S = S_1 = S_2$ iff $S_1 = S_2$

B2. $S_1 \cup S_2 = \{ S_1, S_2 \}$ iff $S_1 \perp S_2$

B3. $S_1 \cup S_2 = S *$, iff $S_1 \sim S_2$ => conflict resolution

$S*$ refers to an updated S.

6 Experiments

In this section, we would like to demonstrate the utility of the Group and Social Networking Effects. Suppose we want to build a personal photo collection of photos taken at ACM Multimedia 2005. One way to do so is to search Flickr with the tag "multimedia2005" that the conference organisers have provided [12], which rendered a total of 70 photos taken by four users, all labeled with the "multimedia2005" tag.

Table 1 shows the breakdown of the number of photos taken by these four users and the least and most recent dates the photos were taken on. Thus, we have four collections and our role here is to merge these four collections into one and to make use of metadata regularity for metadata management, reuse, propagation and reuse.

We want to first select the collection with high metadata regularity. This would allow for high reuse. We do so by using a simple metric here.

$$metadata\ regularity = number\ of\ photos \times average\ tag\ frequency$$

where $average\ tag\ frequency = \dfrac{\sum tag\ frequency}{number\ of\ tags}$

Table 1. Breakdown of Flickr search results

User	Number of photos	Least recent date	Most recent date
A	26	07 Nov 05	09 Nov 05
B	28	07 Nov 05	11 Nov 05
C	13	07 Nov 05	10 Nov 05
D	3	08 Nov 05	09 Nov 05

Tag Frequency refers to the percentage of the photos in which a particular tag appears. Table 2 shows the breakdown of tag frequency while Table 3 tabulates the computation of this simple metric and we would want to choose the collection with the highest value for the metadata regularity metric, which is the collection by User C. We would reuse tags which have a tag frequency of 100% and exported it to the group level metadata, which also includes the number of photos and the least and most recent dates. At this time of point, our group metadata is as follows:

GM_c = {number_photo=13[number], least_recent_date="07 Nov 05"[date], most_recent_date="10 Nov 05"[date], common_tag="singapore"[text], common_tag="2005"[text]}.

Table 2. Breakdown of tag frequency

User	Number of Tags	Tag Frequency (%)
A	12	Singapore (100%), ACM (100%), Multimedia (100%), others (4% - 8%)
B	30	3.5% - 7%
C	2	Singapore (100%), 2005 (100%)
D	1	YRB (33%)

Table 3. Tabulation of metadata regularity

User	Average Tag Frequency (%)	Metadata Regularity(no unit)
A	29%	754
B	4%	111
C	100%	1300
D	33%	33

We would now merge collections in decreasing order of the metadata regularity metric, i.e. A followed by B and finally D. In combining collections, we would reuse tags with tag frequency of 100% provided that the metadata regularity is above 100, i.e. not tags of a collection containing just one photo.

Combining the collections by users C and A, we have

GM_{CA} = {number_photo=39[number], least_recent_date="07 Nov 05"[date], most_recent_date="10 Nov 05"[date],common_tag="singapore"[text], common_tag="2005"[text], common_tag="acm"[text], common_tag="multimedia"[text]}

Here, the metadata values of the group metadata would be adjusted and updated accordingly, subject to conflict resolution. For instance, there would not be a duplicate tag "singapore". The final collection group metadata would be

GM_{CABD} = {number_photo=70[number], least_recent_date="07 Nov 05"[date], most_recent_date="11 Nov 05"[date],common_tag="singapore"[text], common_tag="2005"[text], common_tag="acm"[text], common_tag="multimedia"[text]}

Thus any new photo that is inserted into this collection but does not have any metadata would be able to reuse the group metadata.

7 Conclusion and Future Work

We briefly covered some problems faced in digital image search and retrieval and discussed how we could make use of metadata regularity (the Group Effect) and collaborative annotations (the Social Networking Effect). We next presented our set-theoretic approach to our framework (proposed in a previous work [6]) and outlined its application and utility in an example image collection that made use of both the Group and Social Networking Effects.

In our experiments, we showed that it is possible to generate more metadata from the application of the Group Effect from the collaborative metadata made available from the Social Networking Effect. This generated metadata may be further applicable for reuse, inference and propagation.

In future work, we would be working on the EXIF metadata of the photos used in our experiments as well as that of the official ACM Multimedia photo collection [20] and to similarly apply our set-theoretic framework to determine the metadata reuse, inference and propagation.

References

1. Dick C.A. Bulterman. Is it Time for a Moratorium on Metadata? IEEE Multimedia, Vol. 11 Issue 4, pp. 11 – 17, 2004.
2. Jun Li, Joo-Hwee Lim and Qi Tian. Automatic Summarization for Personal Digital Photos, PCM 2003, vol. 3, pp. 1536-1540, 2003.
3. Marc Davis, Simon King, Nathan Good and Risto Sarvas. From context to content: leveraging context to infer media metadata, ACM Multimedia 2004, pp. 188 – 195.
4. Exchangeable Image File Format (EXIF), Version 2.2, JEITA.
5. William Ku, Mohan S. Kankanhalli and Joo-Hwee Lim. A Collection-Oriented Metadata Framework for Digital Images, ICME 2006, pp. 761 – 764.
6. William Ku. Exploiting "The World is Flat" syndrome in digital photo collections for contextual metadata, accepted for IEEE ISM 2006.
7. Joo-Hwee Lim, Jean-Pierre Chevallet and Sihem Nouarah Merah. SnapToTell: ubiquitous information access from camera. A picture-driven tourist information directory service, MobileHCI 2004, pp. 21-27.
8. Mor Naaman, Andreas Paepcke and Hector Garcia-Molina. From Where to What: Metadata Sharing for Digital Photographs with Geographic Coordinates, CoopIS 2003, pp. 196-217.
9. Mor Naaman, Ron B. Yeh, Hector Garcia-Molina and Andreas Paepcke. Leveraging Context to Resolve Identity in Photo Albums, JCDL 2005, pp. 178 – 187.
10. Frank Nack. All Content Counts: The Future in Digital Media Computing is Meta, IEEE MultiMedia, vol. 7, no 3, pp. 10-13, 2000.
11. Yanfeng Sun, Hongjiang Zhang, Lei Zhang and Mingjing Li. *MyPhotos*: a system for home photo management and processing, ACM Multimedia 2002, pp. 81 – 82 .
12. http://www.flickr.com/photos/tags/multimedia2005/
13. http://av.comp.nus.edu.sg/gallery/ACM-Multimedia-2005

Confidence Building Among Correlated Streams in Multimedia Surveillance Systems

Pradeep K. Atrey[1], Mohan S. Kankanhalli[2],
and Abdulmotaleb El Saddik[1]

[1] School of Information Technology and Engineering,
University of Ottawa, Canada
{patrey, abed}@mcrlab.uottawa.ca
[2] Department of Computer Science, School of Computing,
National University of Singapore, Republic of Singapore
mohan@comp.nus.edu.sg

Abstract. Multimedia surveillance systems utilize multiple correlated media streams, each of which has a different confidence level in accomplishing various surveillance tasks. For example, the system designer may have a higher confidence in the video stream compared to the audio stream for detecting humans running events. The confidence level of streams is usually precomputed based on their past accuracy. This traditional approach is cumbersome especially when we add a new stream in the system without the knowledge of its past history. This paper proposes a novel method which dynamically computes the confidence level of new streams based on their agreement/disagreement with the already trusted streams. The preliminary experimental results show the utility of our method.

1 Introduction

Current surveillance systems often utilize multiple types of sensors like microphones [1], motion detectors [2] and RFIDs [3] etc in addition to the video cameras. As different sensors have different capabilities of performing various surveillance tasks, the designer of a multimedia surveillance system usually has different confidence levels in the evidences obtained based on the data of dissimilar sensors (we call sensor's data to be the "media streams" from now onwards) for accomplishing various tasks. For instance, the system designer may have higher confidence in a video stream compared to an audio stream for detecting faces, and may also have high confidence in an audio stream for detecting talking/shouting events.

In order to accomplish any surveillance task, the system assimilates relevant media streams. As the different streams have different confidence levels associated for accomplishing different tasks, it is important to utilize the confidence information of streams in their assimilation by appropriately assigning the weights to them [4]. The confidence in a stream is related to its accuracy. The higher

T.-J. Cham et al. (Eds.): MMM 2007, LNCS 4352, Part II, pp. 155–164, 2007.

the accuracy of a stream, higher the confidence we would have in it. In the assimilation process, it makes sense to give more weight to a stream which has a higher confidence factor.

However, the computation of confidence information for each stream is cumbersome especially when we dynamically add the new streams to a multimedia surveillance system. The usual approach for determining the confidence in a stream is to first compute, in advance, its accuracy and then assign the confidence level to it based on its accuracy. This is often difficult because the system may provide different accuracies for different events when detected based on different media streams. Precomputation of accuracies of all the streams, that too for all events under different contexts, requires significant amount of training and testing, which is often tedious and time consuming. Moreover, for the streams which are added later in the system, there is no way to find their past accuracy. Therefore, it is important to devise a method to dynamically determine the confidence levels of streams without precomputing it.

In this paper, we propose a novel method for dynamically computing the confidences in a newly deployed stream based on the knowledge of the existing "trusted" stream(s) and the agreement coefficient among the newly deployed stream and the existing trusted streams. We call a stream to be "trusted" if its confidence level is greater than a threshold. The agreement coefficient between the streams is computed based on how agreeing or disagreeing the evidences obtained based on them have been in the past.

To illustrate our core idea, we provide the example of TV news channels. Let we follow a trusted CNN news channel. We also start watching an arbitrary XYZ news channel and compare the news content provided on both the channels. Over a period of time, our confidence in the XYZ channel will grow if the news content of both channels are found to be similar, and vice versa.

Rest of this paper is organized as follows. In section 2, we describe the related work. We formulate the problem of determining confidence in a stream in section 3. Section 4 presents our proposed method. We present the experimental results in section 5. Finally, section 6 concludes the paper with a discussion on the future work.

2   Related Work

In the past, the confidence has been used in the context of data management in sensor networks. Tatbul et al. [5] compute the confidence in a stream based on how it has helped in making the accurate decisions in the past. Tavakoli et al. [6] proposed a method for event detection that uses historical and spatial information in clusters in order to determine a confidence level that warrants a detection report with high confidence. Ioannou et al. [7] also employed a confidence-based fusion strategy to combine multiple feature cues for facial expression recognition. However, the works at [5], [6] and [7] did not elaborate on how the confidence value is used in the integration of information.

Siegel and Wu [8] has pointed out the importance of considering the confidence in sensor fusion. The authors have used the Dempster-Shafer (D-S) theory of evidence to fuse the confidences. In contrast, we propose a model for confidence fusion by using a Bayesian formulation because it is both simple and computationally efficient[4].

In all the past works, the confidence in streams has been computed based on their past accuracy. This work is different from the past works in that, our method computes the confidence level of streams based their agreement/ disagreement with the trusted streams. Agreement coefficient among streams is computed based on how concurring or contradictory evidences they provide. Agreement coefficient between any two streams is different from mutual information [9] between them in that the former connotes the measure of mutual consistency or contradiction between the two streams while the latter implies how much information does one stream convey about another one.

3 Problem Formulation

We formulate below the problem of determining the confidence level of a media stream:

$\mathcal{M}1$. **S**is a multimedia surveillance system designed for detecting a set E of events, and it consists of $n \geq 1$ heterogeneous sensors that capture data from the environment. Let $\mathbf{M}^n = \{M_1, M_2, \ldots, M_n\}$ be the media streams obtained from n sensors.

$\mathcal{M}2$. For $1 \leq i \leq n$, let $0 < p_i(t) < 1$ be the *probability* of occurrence of an event based on individual i^{th} media stream at time instant t. The $p_i(t)$ is determined by first extracting the features from media stream i and then by employing an event detector (e.g. a trained classifier) on them. Also, let $P_\Phi(t)$ be the 'fused probability' of occurrence of the event at time t based on a subset $\Phi \in \mathcal{P}(\mathbf{M}^n)$ of media streams. The 'fused probability' is the overall probability of occurrence of the event based on a group of media streams [4].

$\mathcal{M}3$. For $1 \leq i \leq n$, let $0 < f_i(t) < 1$ be the system designer's *confidence* in the ith stream at time instant t. The confidence in at least one media stream is learned by experimentally determining its accuracy. More the accurate results we obtain based on a stream, more the confidence we would have in it. Also, there exists a subset $T \subseteq \mathbf{M}^n$ (with $|T| \geq 1$) of streams in which the confidence level of streams is greater than or equal to a threshold (say F_{spec}). We call them to be the "trusted" media streams.

We make the following assumptions:

$\mathcal{A}1$. All sensing devices capture the same environment (but optionally, the different aspects of the environment) and provide correlated observations.

$\mathcal{A}2$. The system designer's confidence level in each of the media streams is at least 0.5. This assumption is reasonable since it is not useful to employ a media device which is found to be inaccurate more than half of the time.

A3. The fused probability of the occurrence of event and the overall confidence increase monotonically as the more concurring evidences are obtained based on the streams.

The objective is to determine the confidence level $f_i(t+1)$ of a new non-trusted stream M_i at time instant $t+1$ given that its confidence level at time instant t is $f_i(t)$. In absence of any prior information, $f_i(0) = \epsilon$ (a positive infinitesimal).

4   Proposed Method

The proposed method determines the confidence in a new non-trusted stream using its "Agreement Coefficient" with the trusted stream(s). The agreement coefficient between the two streams is computed based on whether the evidence obtained by the system using them are concurring or contradictory.

4.1   Modelling of the Agreement Coefficient

Let the measure of agreement among the media streams at time t be represented by a set $\Gamma(t)$ which is expressed as:

$$\Gamma(t) = \{\gamma_{ik}(t)\} \tag{1}$$

where, the term $-1 \le \gamma_{ik}(t) \le 1$ is the *agreement coefficient* between the media streams M_i and M_k at time instant t.

The system computes the agreement coefficient $\gamma_{ik}(t)$ between the media streams M_i and M_k at time instant t by iteratively averaging the past agreement coefficients with the current observation. Precisely, $\gamma_{ik}(t)$ is computed as:

$$\gamma_{ik}(t) = \frac{1}{2}\left[(1 - 2 \times abs(p_i(t) - p_k(t))) + \gamma_{ik}(t-1)\right] \tag{2}$$

where, $p_i(t) = P(E_t|M_i)$ and $p_k(t) = P(E_t|M_k)$ are the individual probabilities of occurrence of event E based on media streams M_i and M_k, respectively, at time $t \ge 1$; and $\gamma_{ij}(0) = 1 - 2 \times abs(p_i(0) - p_k(0))$. These probabilities represent decisions about the events. Exactly same probabilities would imply full agreement ($\gamma_{ik} = 1$) whereas totally dissimilar probabilities would mean that the two streams fully contradict each other ($\gamma_{ik} = -1$) [4].

The agreement coefficient between two sources $\mathbf{M}^{i-1}$ and M_i is modelled as:

$$\gamma_{M_i,\mathbf{M}^{i-1}} = \frac{1}{i-1}\sum_{s=1}^{i-1}\gamma_{si} \tag{3}$$

where, γ_{si} for $1 \le s \le i-1$, $1 < i \le n$ is the agreement coefficients between the sth and i^{th} media streams. The agreement fusion model given in equation (3) is based on *average-link clustering*. In average-link clustering, we consider the distance between one cluster and another cluster to be equal to the average distance from any member of one cluster to any member of the other cluster [10]. In our case, a group $\mathbf{M}^{i-1}$ of $i-1$ media streams is one cluster and we find the average distance of new i^{th} media stream with this cluster.

4.2   Confidence Fusion

The *confidence fusion* refers to the process of finding the overall confidence in a group of media streams where the individual media streams have their own confidence level. Given that the two streams M_i and M_k have their confidence levels f_i and f_k, respectively, the system uses a Bayesian method to fuse the confidence levels in individual streams. The overall confidence f_{ik} in a group of two media streams M_i and M_k is computed as follows:

$$f_{ik} = \frac{f_i \times f_k}{f_i \times f_k + (1 - f_i) \times (1 - f_k)} \tag{4}$$

In the above formulation, we make two assumptions. First, we assume that the system designer's confidence level in each of the media streams is more than 0.5 (Refer to assumption $\mathcal{A}2$, in section 3). Second, although the media streams are correlated in their decisions; we assume that they are mutually independent in terms of their confidence levels [4].

For n number of media streams, the overall confidence is iteratively computed. Let F_{i-1} be the overall confidence in a group of $i - 1$ streams. By fusing the confidence f_i of ith stream with F_{i-1}, the overall confidence F_i in a group of i streams is computed as:

$$F_i = \frac{F_{i-1} \times f_i}{F_{i-1} \times f_i + (1 - F_{i-1}) \times (1 - f_i)} \tag{5}$$

4.3   Confidence Building Method

Given a set T of trusted media streams, the confidence level of the media stream M_i is computed as follows:

- Using a voting strategy, we divide the set T of trusted media streams into two subsets T_1 and T_2 (as shown in figure 1). This division is performed based on whether, at the current instant, the evidence obtained by the system using these two subsets are concurring or contradictory. Precisely, the subset, based on which, the system concludes in favor of the occurrence of event E with more than 0.50 probability are put in set T_1 and the rest in set T_2.
- The agreement coefficients γ_{i,T_1} (between the stream M_i and the subsets T_1) and γ_{i,T_2} (between the stream M_i and the subset T_2) are computed as described in section 4.1 (equation 3).
- Next, the system computes the overall confidence F_{T_1} and F_{T_2} in the subsets T_1 and T_2, respectively, (using equation 5).
- Finally, the system computes the confidence $f_i(t + 1)$ in the ith stream at time instant $t + 1$ as follows:

$$f_i(t+1) = \begin{cases} F_{T_1} \times \dfrac{f_i(t).e^{\alpha \cdot \gamma_{i,T_1}(t)}}{f_i(t).e^{\alpha \cdot \gamma_{i,T_1}(t)} + (1 - f_i(t)).e^{-\alpha \cdot \gamma_{i,T_1}(t)}} & \text{if } F_{T_1} \times \gamma_{i,T_1}(t) \geq \\ & \quad F_{T_2} \times \gamma_{i,T_2} \\ F_{T_2} \times \dfrac{f_i(t).e^{\alpha \cdot \gamma_{i,T_2}(t)}}{f_i(t).e^{\alpha \cdot \gamma_{i,T_2}(t)} + (1 - f_i(t)).e^{-\alpha \cdot \gamma_{i,T_2}(t)}} & \text{otherwise} \end{cases}$$

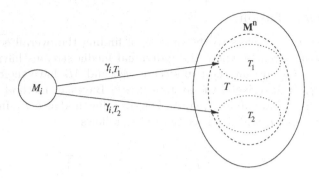

Fig. 1. The agreement coefficient between stream M_i and the subsets T_1 and T_2

The exponential terms $e^{\alpha \cdot \gamma_{i,T_1}(t)}$ and $e^{\alpha \cdot \gamma_{i,T_2}(t)}$ represent the growth in the confidence level at time t. $\alpha \in [0, \infty]$ is used as a growth rate with respect to overall confidence levels F_{T_1} and F_{T_2} of groups T_1 and T_2, respectively. The terms $\gamma_{i,T_1}(t)$ and $\gamma_{i,T_2}(t)$ denote the agreement coefficient at time t between the ith stream and the groups T_1 and T_2, respectively. In the above formulation, the denominator term acts as normalization factor to limit the confidence value within [0,1]. Note that if either T_1 or T_2 is found empty, their fused confidence levels (F_{T_1} and F_{T_2}, respectively) are considered to be of zero value.

5   Experimental Results

We show the utility of our method in a surveillance scenario. The surveillance environment is the corridor of our school building with a system goal to detect events such as humans running, walking and standing in the corridor. We use two video sensors (Canon VC-C50i cameras denoted by V_1 and V_2) to record the video from the two opposite ends of corridor as shown in figure 2. The two cameras are connected to a central PC (Pentium-IV 3.6 GHz). A Picolo-Pro video capture card is used to capture the image data.

For our experiments, we have used data of more than twelve hours which has been recorded using the system consisting of two video cameras. Over the period of more than twelve hours, the noticeable events occurred over for a period

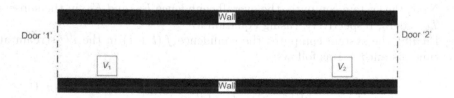

Fig. 2. The layout of the corridor under surveillance

of 1079 seconds. The details of various events and their total durations are as follows - humans standing events for 139 seconds, walking events for 798 seconds and running events for 142 seconds.

The system detects these events by processing the video frames. The video processing involves background modeling and blob detection. The background modeling is performed using an adaptive Gaussian method [11]. For blob detection, the system first segments the foreground from the background using simple 'matching' on the three RGB color channels, and then uses the morphological operations (erode and dilation) to obtain connected components (i.e. blobs). The matching is defined as a pixel value being within 2.5 standard deviations of the distribution. We assume that the blob of an area greater than a threshold corresponds to a human. An example of blob detection (with its bounding rectangle) in a humans "running" event is shown in figure 3. Once the bounding rectangle for each blob is computed, the middle point of the bottom edge of the bounding rectangle is mapped to the actual ground location using the caliberation information of the video cameras. This provides the exact ground location of human in the corridor at a particular time instant.

The system identifies the start and end of an event in video streams as follows. If a person moves towards the camera, the start of event is marked when the blob's area becomes greater than a threshold and the event ends when the blob intersects the image plane. However, if the person walks away from the camera, the start and end of the event is inverted. Based on the average distance travelled by human on the ground, a Bayes classifier is first trained and then used to classify an atomic-event to be one of the classes - standing, walking and running.

We present our preliminary results as follows. First, the system performed event detection and classification using only one stream i.e. video stream V_1. By comparing with the ground truth, we found overall accuracy of the video stream V_1 to be 68%. Based on the accuracy, we assigned a confidence level 0.68 to the stream V_1, and designated it to be the "trusted" stream. Note that, in our experiments, the threshold value used for trusted stream is 0.65. Determining the ideal value of this threshold is an issue which we will examine in the future

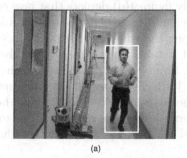 

(a)   (b)

Fig. 3. An example: Bounding rectangles along the detected blobs in the video frames of (a) Camera 1 and (b) Camera 2, corresponding to a hummas "running" event

work. Based on the agreement coefficient between the trusted stream V_1 and the other video stream V_2, the system uses our proposed method to compute the confidence in stream V_2.

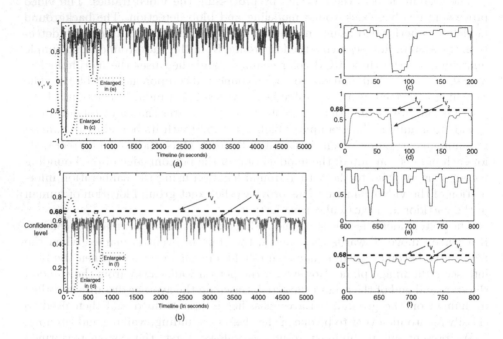

Fig. 4. Confidence building in V_2 stream

Timeline-based confidence building in the stream V_2 is shown in figure 4. Figure 4(a) shows how the agreement coefficient between V_1 and V_2 varies along the timeline, and figure 4(b) depicts how the confidence f_{V_2} in V_2 evolves along the timeline. Figures 4(c)-4(f) show the enlarged portions of some parts of figures 4(a)-4(b). For example, figure 4(c) shows how the agreement coefficient γ_{V_1,V_2} drops down below zero and then consequently figure 4(d) depicts that how confidence also decreases as the agreement coefficient decreases. Once the confidence level drops down at around 75th second along the timeline, the confidence f_{V_2} in stream V_2 also drops to almost zero and it takes approximately another 90 seconds to regain the same confidence level. Similarly, as can be seen in figures 4(e)-4(f), the confidence level f_{V_2} in stream V_2 decreases to 0.25 at time instant 642 and to 0.30 at time instant 740 as the agreement coefficient goes below 0.5, however, in these two cases, the confidence level picks up early close to the confidence level of trusted stream compared to when the agreement coefficient becomes negative.

Note that we have set the value of the growth rate α to be 1. With $\alpha = 1$, the system could gain the confidence level in V_2 upto 0.63. However, with higher growth rate ($\alpha \approx 5$), this maximum achieved confidence can go up to the level of confidence in the trusted stream. Again, determining the ideal value of growth factor α is an issue which is out of scope of this paper and will be investigated in the future.

To verify the utility of our method, we compared the average confidence level of stream V_2 determined using our method with the confidence level which is computed based on its past accuracy. It is observed that both are comparable (0.58 vs 0.60) as shown in Table 1.

Table 1. Comparison of the proposed method with the traditional approach

Method of computing confidence	Confidence level of V_2
Pre-computed confidence	0.60
Our method	0.58 (Average value)

6   Conclusions

This paper proposes a novel method to dynamically compute the confidence levels of new media streams in a multimedia surveillance system. The confidence in a new stream is computed based on the fact whether it provides evidence which concurs or contradicts with the already trusted streams. Though the preliminary results have shown that the confidence level computed using our method is comparable with the confidence level determined based on the traditional approach (past accuracy), we need to investigate in detail how the dynamically varying confidence level can contribute towards more accurate overall results for event detection in multimedia surveillance systems. It will also be interesting to examine the utility of the proposed method for dissimilar sensors such as microphones and motion detectors, and also for the different kinds of events such as audio events - talking, shouting, door knocking and footsteps.

Acknowledgements

We thank Prof Ramesh Jain for suggesting this research problem.

References

1. Atrey, P.K., Maddage, N.C., Kankanhalli, M.S.: Audio based event detection for multimedia surveillance. In: IEEE International Conference on Acoustics, Speech, and Signal Processing. (2006) V813–816
2. Rama, K.G.S., Atrey, P.K., Singh, V.K., Ramakrishnan, K., Kankanhalli, M.S.: A design methodology for selection and placement of sensors in multimedia surveillance systems. In: The 4th ACM International Workshop on Video Surveillance and Sensor Networks, Santa Barbara, CA, USA (2006)
3. Prati, A., Vezzani, R., Benini, L., Farella, E., Zappi, P.: An integrated multi-modal sensor network for video surveillance. In: The ACM International Workshop on Video Surveillance and Sensor Networks, Singapore (2005) 95–102

4. Atrey, P.K., Kankanhalli, M.S., Jain, R.: A framework for information assimilation in multimedia surveillance systems. ACM Multimedia Systems Journal (2006)
5. Tatbul, N., Buller, M., Hoyt, R., Mullen, S., Zdonik, S.: Confidence-based data management for personal area sensor networks. In: The Workshop on Data Management for Sensor Networks. (2004) 24–31
6. Tavakoli, A., Zhang, J., Son, S.H.: Group-based event detection in undersea sensor networks. In: Second International Workshop on Networked Sensing Systems, San Diego, California, USA (2005)
7. Ioannou, S., Wallace, M., Karpouzis, K., Raouzaiou, A., Kollias, S.: Confidence-based fusion of multiple feature cues for facial expresssion recognition. In: The 14th IEEE International Conference on Fuzzy Systems, Reno, Nevada, USA (2005) 207–212
8. Siegel, M., Wu, H.: Confidence fusion. In: IEEE International Workshop on Robot Sensing. (2004) 96–99
9. Conaire, C.O., Connor, N.O., Cooke, E., Smeaton, A.: Detection thresholding using mutual information. In: International Conference on Computer Vision Theory and Applications, Setubal, Portugal (2006)
10. Jain, A.K., Murty, M.N., Flynn, P.J.: Data clustering: A review. ACM Computing Surveys 31(3) (1999) 264–323
11. Stauffer, C., Grimson, W.E.L.: Adaptive background mixture models for real-time tracking. In: IEEE Computer Society Conference on Computer Vision and Pattern Recognition. Volume 2., Ft. Collins, CO, USA (1999) 252–258

Boosting Cross-Media Retrieval by Learning with Positive and Negative Examples*

Yueting Zhuang and Yi Yang

College of Computer Science and Technology, Zhejiang University
yzhuang@cs.zju.edu.cn, yangyi_zju@yahoo.com.cn

Abstract. Content-based cross-media retrieval is a new category of retrieval methods by which the modality of query examples and the returned results need not to be the same, for example, users may query images by an example of audio and vice versa. Multimedia Document (MMD) is a set of media objects that are of different modalities but carry the same semantics. In this paper, a graph based approach is proposed to achieve the content-based cross-media retrieval and MMD retrieval. Positive and negative examples of relevance feedback are used differently to boost the retrieval performance and experiments show that the proposed methods are very effective.

Keywords: Content-based Cross-media Retrieval, Multimedia Document, Relevance Feedback.

1 Introduction and Related Work

The traditional content-based retrieval includes content-based image retrieval [1], [2], [3], [4], content-based audio retrieval [5], [6], [7], content-based motion retrieval [8], [9] and content-based video retrieval [10], [11] and cross-media retrieval [12] is a new kind of content based retrieval. Compared with the traditional content-based retrieval systems, content-based cross-media retrieval is more powerful because the modality of query example and return results can be different. For example, users can query images by submitting either an example of audio clip or an example of image.

Multimedia Document (MMD), such as slide, WebPages and multimedia cyclopedias, is a collection of media objects that are of different modalities but of the same semantics. Since most of the existing query-by-example systems are designed to retrieve media objects of single modality, the performances are always weak to retrieve MMDs. As the MMD amount grows rapidly, there is an increasing need for an effective mechanism to manage them efficiently.

Relevance feedback has been shown to provide dramatic performance boost in many tasks. The learn-from-user technology consists of positive learning which makes use of positive examples and negative learning which learns from negative

* This work is supported by National Natural Science Foundation of China (No.60533090, No.60525108), Science and Technology Project of Zhejiang Province (2005C 13032, 2005C11001-05), and China-US Million Book Digital Library Project (www.cadal.zju.edu.cn).

T.-J. Cham et al. (Eds.): MMM 2007, LNCS 4352, Part II, pp. 165–174, 2007.

examples and it can be divided into short term learning in which the systems only focus on the current feedback and long term learning in which the systems take the past user interactions into account.

In this paper, we consider the problem of cross-media retrieval and the rest of this paper is organized as follows. In section 2, we construct a Uniform Cross-media Relationship Graph (UCRG). Section 3 illustrates the cross-media retrieval methods via the UCRG. In section 4, relevance feedback algorithms of positive and negative learning are proposed. Experiments and comparisons are presented in section 5 and section 6 gives the conclusions.

2   The Uniform Cross-Media Relationship Graph Construction

In this paper, we assume that there are no more than three kinds of media objects in an MMD, namely image, audio and text, and there are at least one media object in each MMD. However, the proposed methods can be easily extended to more kinds of media objects. If a media object obj_k belongs to an MMD MMD_i, MMD_i is the host MMD of obj_k and obj_k is the affiliated media object of MMD_i. To perform the cross-media retrieval, we first construct a Uniform Cross-media Relationship Graph (UCRG) in which media objects are vertices and the relationships among them are weighted edges. Let I, A, T and M represent the image, audio, text and MMD dataset, the proposed approaches are as the flowing 3 steps.

Step 1. The Weighted Intra-media Adjacency Graph construction. The Weighted Intra-media Adjacency Graph is actually three independent weighted adjacency graphs of image, audio and text. Here we give the approaches of weighted image adjacency graph construction and the weighted audio and text adjacency graphs can be built in the same way. To build the image adjacency graph, for each image $Img_i \in I$, there is a node and between any two nodes there is an edge. The weight of the edge W_{ij} between the two images $img_i, img_j \in I$ is defined as $W_{ij} = \|img_i - img_j\|$. The weights of all edges in the graph are then normalized.

Step 2. The Weighted Inter-media Adjacency Graph construction. The weighted inter-media adjacency graph is constructed by connecting the three intra-media graphs of image, text and audio. Considering media objects in the same MMD share the same semantics, for each $MMD_m \in M$ whose affiliated media objects are $obj_{m1}, obj_{m2}, ..., obj_{mk} \in I \cup A \cup T$, we put edges between each pair of the media objects $obj_{m1}, obj_{m2}, ..., obj_{mk} \in I \cup A \cup T$ with the weights of a very small constant.

Step 3. The UCRG construction. We define the length of a path as the sum of the weights along the path. To model the UCRG, we reconstruct the Weighted Inter-media Adjacency Graph by finding the shortest paths for all pairs of vertices in it, and then replace the weights W_{ij} by the length of shortest paths between each pairs of vertices V_i and V_j.

3 The UCRG Based Cross-Media Retrieval

The algorithm in [13] was initially proposed for predicting the label of the unlabeled data and it has been introduced into data ranking [14], multimodality learning [15] and image retrieval [4]. The main idea can be interpreted as intuitively in term of spreading activation networks [16] from experimental psychology, and in this paper, it is adoped to achieve the cross-media retrieval. Let Ω be the media object dataset. $\mathbf{W}$ represents the UCRG and W_{ij} is the weight of the edge in the UCRG between the two media objects $obj_i, obj_j \in \Omega$. $\chi = [x_1, x_2, ..., x_n]$ is the media object set and we define $\mathbf{Y}(0) = [y_1, y_2, ..., y_n]^T$ in which $y_i = 1$ if x_i is the query example or x_i is the affiliated media object of the query MMD and $y_i = 0$ otherwise. If the query examples are out of dataset, k nearest neighbors of the query examples in feature space are selected as query examples to set $\mathbf{Y}(0)$. The correlation matrix $\mathbf{C}$ of media objects is given by:

$$c_{ij} = \begin{cases} \exp(-W_{ij}^2 / 2\sigma^2) & if \quad i \neq j \\ 0 & if \quad i = j \end{cases} . \tag{1}$$

In order to avoid the self-reinforcement, the diagonal elements are set to zeros and after that, the correlation matrix of $\mathbf{C}$ is symmetrically normalized which is necessary for the convergence of the following iterations and we get:

$$\mathbf{C} = \mathbf{D}^{-1/2} \mathbf{C} \mathbf{D}^{-1/2} . \tag{2}$$

where $\mathbf{D}$ is a diagonal matrix with its (i,i)-element equal to the sum of the i-th row of $\mathbf{C}$. The score of $\mathbf{Y} = [y_1, y_2, ..., y_n]^T$ spreads along $\mathbf{C}$ and this propagating progress can be formulated as iterate:

$$\mathbf{Y}(t+1) = \alpha \mathbf{C} \mathbf{Y}(t) + (1-\alpha) \mathbf{Y}(0) . \tag{3}$$

until convergence. In equation 3, α is a constant smaller than 1 that specifies the relative amount of the information from its neighbors in UCRG and from its initial information. By the iteration equation $\mathbf{Y}(t+1) = \alpha \mathbf{C} \mathbf{Y}(t) + (1-\alpha) \mathbf{Y}(0)$, we have

$$\mathbf{Y}(t) = (\alpha \mathbf{C})^t \mathbf{Y}(0) + (1-\alpha) \sum_{i=0}^{t-1} (\alpha \mathbf{C})^i \mathbf{Y}(0) . \tag{4}$$

Since $0 < \alpha < 1$ and the eigenvalues of $\mathbf{C}$ in $[-1,1]$, $\lim_{t \to \infty} \sum_{i=0}^{t-1} (\alpha \mathbf{C})^i = (\mathbf{I} - \alpha \mathbf{C})^{-1}$ and $\lim_{t \to \infty} (\alpha \mathbf{C})^t = 0$. Let y_i^* denote the limit of the sequence $\{y_i(t)\}$, and we get:`

$$\mathbf{Y}^* = (1-\alpha)(\mathbf{I} - \alpha \mathbf{C})^{-1} \mathbf{Y}(0) . \tag{5}$$

For the sake of cross-media retrieval, after the propagation process reaching a global stable state, rank each media object obj_i of target modality according to its score y_i^* and top k with highest scores are returned. Considering the heuristic rules in [12], the score of the MMD consisting of media objects $x_1, x_2, ..., x_m \in \Omega$ whose corresponding scores are $y_1^*, y_2^*, ..., y_m^*$ is defined as equation 6 and the top k MMDs with the highest cores are returned.

$$MMDscore_i = \alpha \times \max(y_1^*, y_2^*, ... y_m^*) -$$
$$\ln(1 + \beta \times (\max(y_1^*, y_2^*, ... y_m^*) - \min(y_1^*, y_2^*, ... y_m^*))) \tag{6}$$

Clearly, the proposed approaches not only avoid the curse of dimensionality but also take all of the component media objects into consideration. Moreover, by the proposed approaches, users can query whatever they want by submitting whatever they have, without any constraint of media object modality and, consequently, the content-based cross-media retrieval can be achieved.

4 Learning with Positive and Negative Examples

Relevance feedback (RF) uses the terms contained in relevant and irrelevant results to supplement and enrich the user's initial query, allowing greater retrieval performance and it have been proved effective in many tasks [2], [3], [4]. Due to the asymmetry between relevant and irrelevant examples, they should be processed differently [4] and in this section, we give the different approaches of learning with positive and negative examples.

4.1 Learning with Positive Examples

In the long-term learning with positive examples, the UCRG is gradually refined as users interact with the system. Let $\mathbf{W}$ denote the UCRG and W_{ij} is the weight of the edge between the two media objects obj_i, obj_j in dataset. $P = \{p_1, p_2, ..., p_m\}$ denotes the positive example set and $Q = \{q_1, q_2, ..., q_l\}$ is the query example set. Considering the positive examples are semantically similar to each other and similar to the query example from user's perspective, we can refine the UCRG as:

$$W_{ij} \leftarrow \alpha W_{ij} \quad (obj_i, obj_j \in P \cup Q) . \tag{7}$$

where α is a suitable constant smaller than 1.

In the short-term leaning scheme, the positive examples are used to enrich the user's initial query. $\chi = [x_1, x_2, ..., x_n]$ is the media object set and $\mathbf{Ps}(0) = [ps_1, ps_2, ..., ps_n]^T$ is the initial positive score in which $ps_i = 1$ if x_i is the affiliated media object of the MMD which is the host MMD of a positive example, and $ps_i = 0$ otherwise. The positive scores spread along the UCRG until convergence. As stated previously, $\mathbf{Ps}^* = (1-\alpha)(\mathbf{I} - \alpha\mathbf{C})^{-1}\mathbf{Ps}(0)$ is the limit of the propagation where $\mathbf{C}$ is defined in equation 2. $\mathbf{Y}^*$ is then reset by $\mathbf{Y}^* \leftarrow \alpha\mathbf{Y}^* + (1-\alpha)\mathbf{Ps}^*$ and all the media objects and MMDs are re-ranked according to the updated $\mathbf{Y}^*$.

4.2 Learning with Negative Examples

In the long-term learning by negative examples, the proposed methods are almost the same as learning by positive examples. Let $\mathbf{W}$ denote the UCRG and W_{ij} is the weight of the edge between the two media objects obj_i, obj_j. $P = \{p_1, p_2, ..., p_m\}$ is the positive example set, $N = \{n_1, n_2, ..., n_m\}$ denotes the negative example set and $Q = \{q_1, q_2, ..., q_l\}$ is the query set. The UCRG is refined by:

$$W_{ij} \leftarrow \beta W_{ij} \quad (obj_i \in N, obj_j \in P \cup Q) . \tag{8}$$

where β is a suitable constant greater than 1.

A straightforward way of short-term learning by negative examples is to use a vector of negative score $\mathbf{Ns}(0) = [ns_1, ns_2, ..., ns_n]^T$ and initially for each media object $obj_i \in N$ set $ns_i = 1$. The negative scores spread along the UCRG and converges at $\mathbf{Ns}^* = (1 - \alpha)(\mathbf{I} - \alpha\mathbf{C})^{-1}\mathbf{Ns}(0)$. Reset $\mathbf{Y}^*$ by $\mathbf{Y}^* \leftarrow \alpha\mathbf{Y}^* + \beta\mathbf{Ps}^* - \gamma\mathbf{Ns}^*$ and re-rank the results. However it is not considerate for the following problems.

The first problem is that the returned results are always close to each other and they are close to the query examples in the UCRG. Hence, the negative examples are always close to the query examples and the positive results in the UCRG. Consequently, those nearby positive results will suffer big negative scores and the improper negative scores will spread further during the spreading iterations. Taking this fact into consideration, the following two actions of UCRG reconstruction are taken to overcome the problem.

Potentially, for a given media object, the more media objects which are very close to it, the higher negative score it may receive. However, if a media object is very close to many other media objects, the misunderstanding of it may causes heavy penalty during the propagation iterations. On the other hand, if a media object is very close to a lot of other media objects, it demonstrates the media object are likely ambiguous semantically. As a result, the first UCRG reconstruction method is as follows. Let ε be a suitable constant that is small enough and $\mathbf{W}$ is the UCRG, we define the transition matrix $\mathbf{T}$ as:

$$T_{ij} = \begin{cases} 1 & if \quad W_{ij} < \varepsilon \\ 0 & otherwise \end{cases} . \tag{9}$$

$\mathbf{F} = [f_1, f_2, ... f_n]$ is a vector reflecting how many media object are close enough to each media object in dataset and it is defined as:

$$f_i = \sum_{j=1}^{n} T_{ij} . \tag{10}$$

$\mathbf{RS} = [rs_1(0), rs_2(0), ..., rs_n(0)]$ is initially set to ones. Iterate

$$\forall rs_i(k+1) = \sum_{T_{ij} \neq 0} rs_j(k) / f_j + rs_i(k) . \tag{11}$$

until convergence, and the convergence issue has been proved in PageRank [17].

Let rs_i^* be the normalized limit of the sequence $\{rs_i(k)\}$ and we define the modified UCRG $\mathbf{W}^-$ for spreading negative scores as:

$$W^-_{ij} = W_{ij} \times \max(\exp(\alpha + \beta \times rs_i^*), \exp(\alpha + \beta \times rs_j^*)) \ . \tag{12}$$

After that, we can get the corresponding correlation matrix $\mathbf{C}^-$ in the same way of section 3.

The second method of the UCRG reconstruction before negative score propagation is to lengthen the distances between negative and positive examples and this approach is almost the same as the long-term learning. Practically, it is more efficient to modify the correlation matrix $\mathbf{C}^-$ directly. We omit the discussion due to the lack of space.

Another problem is that for a media object, the farther it lies from positive examples in the UCRG, the less possible it is also a positive one, however, if a media object lies far from negative examples, the possibility that it is a positive one is not necessary enhanced, since it may not get closer to positive examples either. As a result, the positive examples should make more contribution to the final ranking score than negative examples. Using Taylor expansion, equation 5 can be rewritten as:

$$\mathbf{Y}^* = (1-\alpha)\mathbf{Y}(0) + (1-\alpha)\alpha\mathbf{CY}(0) + (1-\alpha)\alpha\mathbf{C}(\alpha\mathbf{CY}(0)) + (1-\alpha)\mathbf{K} \ . \tag{13}$$

In equation 13, $\mathbf{Y}^*$ can be interpreted as the sum of a series of infinite terms. The first term is simply the initial input, the second term is to spread the scores of the query points to their nearby points, the third term is to further spread the scores, etc. Based on the discussion, the negative scores should use only the first k terms and we get:

$$\mathbf{Ns}^* = (1-\alpha)\sum_{i=0}^{k} \alpha^i (\mathbf{C}^-)^i \mathbf{Ns}(0) \ . \tag{14}$$

where $\mathbf{Ns}(0)$ is set in the same way of $\mathbf{PS}(0)$ according to the negative examples. $\mathbf{Y}^*$ is then updated by:

$$\mathbf{Y}^* \leftarrow \eta\mathbf{Y}^* + \beta\mathbf{Ps}^* - \gamma\mathbf{Ns}^* \ . \tag{15}$$

where η, β and γ are suitable smooth factors. Because the positive examples are semantically the same to the query examples, η equals to β practically. Because positive examples should make more contribution than negative examples, γ should be smaller than η and β. Finally, the media objects and MMDs are re-ranked according to the modified $\mathbf{Y}^*$.

5   Experiments

We experiment with 1000 Multimedia Documents consisting of 1000 images, 300 audios and 720 texts. The 1000 MMDs are divided into 10 semantic categories and each semantic category contains 100. Another 30 images and 20 audios as new media objects are used to test the performance when the query example is out of training set. For images, three types of color features (color histogram, color moment, color coherence) and three types of texture features (tamura coarseness histogram, tamura directionality, MSRSAR texture) are used and for audios, features of RMS energy, Spectral Flux, Rolloff and Centroid are used. We use the DTW distance and TF/IDF distance for audio and text objects. In our experiments, if the returned result and the query example are in the same semantic category, it is regarded as a correct result.

5.1 MMD Retrieval Performance

Table 1 shows the average MMD retrieval precision. The Users can query MMDs by submitting an example of image, audio or text as they wish. No more than 2 positive and negative examples as feedback are provided during each round of interaction in our experiments. As can be seen in table 1, the proposed approaches work finely and the precision can be significantly boosted by RF.

Table 1. The Average MMD retrieval precision

Scope \ RF Rounds	Without RF	1 Round RF	2 Rounds RF	3 Rounds RF
10	0.78	0.89	0.95	0.96
20	0.59	0.88	0.95	0.96
30	0.44	0.78	0.86	0.95
40	0.40	0.75	0.83	0.92
50	0.35	0.70	0.80	0.86
60	0.32	0.67	0.77	0.85

Figure 1 is a comparison of different retrieval methods after 1 round RF. To retrieve MMDs by media object in low feature space, the host MMDs of the media objects which are the k nearest neighbours of the query example are returned. It can be seen from figure 1 that because our method takes all kinds of media objects into consideration, the performance is higher than those which use only one type of media objects. Moreover, because the proposed MMD retrieval method is a kind

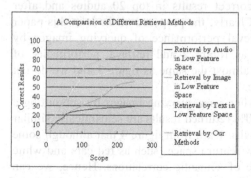

Fig. 1. A comparison of different retrieval methods after 1 round RF

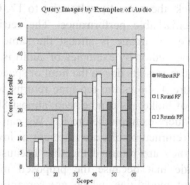

Fig. 2. Querying images by audio

of cross-media retrieval, user can either submit an example of image, text, audio or MMD to query MMDs by our method whereas the traditional retrieval methods can only deal with query examples of single modality.

5.2   Cross-Media Retrieval of Media Object

In this section, we mainly evaluate the cross-media retrieval performance of media object. Figure 2 shows average experimental results of querying images by an example of audio, figure 3 shows that of querying audios by an example of image and figure 4 is an example of cross-media retrieval.

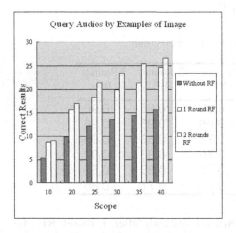

Fig. 3. Querying audios by image

Fig. 4. Top nine returns of querying images by submitting a sound of brake before RF

In our experiments, when user is querying images by audio objects existing in dataset, there are almost 15 correct results in top 30 returned images on average and the number reaches 26.5 after two rounds of feedback. When user is retrieving audios by image objects, there are nearly 10 correct results in top 20 audios and after feedback, the correct results raise to 17. Clearly, the proposed methods in this paper gain remarkable performance. The retrieval performance of querying images by examples of image is almost the same as figure 2 and retrieval performance of querying audios by examples of audio is almost the same as figure 3 and we do not present the results due to the limit of space.

Figure 4 shows the top nine returns when user querying images by submitting a sound of brake. As can be seen, almost 80% returned results are semantically similar to the query example before RF. We can also learn from figure 4 that although some of the returned results are different in low feature space (such as red cars and white cars), they are returned together because of semantic correlations. Hence, we can conclude that because the proposed method nonlinearly fuses media objects of different modalities, which are semantically complementary of each other, it can understand multimedia semantics precisely.

5.3 Query Examples Out of Dataset

If the query example is not in the training dataset, we call it new media object or new points and in this section, we do some experiments to evaluate the performance of cross-media retrieval when the query examples are new media objects. Figure 5 is the average retrieval performance of querying images by examples of new audios and figure 6 is the average retrieval performance of querying audios by examples of new images. As can be seen in the two figures, the proposed approaches are fairly robust when dealing with new points. Another observation is that RF can significantly boost the retrieval performance as before and we can conclude that the cross-media retrieval performance of the proposed methods is remarkable.

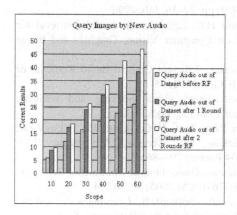

Fig. 5. Querying images by new audios   **Fig. 6.** Querying audios by new images

6 Conclusions

In this paper, a cross-media retrieval method is proposed. First, a UCRG is constructed, in which media objects of different modalities are uniformly represented, to reflect the pairwise correlation of every two media objects. The score of query example propagates along the graph until a global stable state is reached and media objects (MMDs) with the highest score are returned as results. Considering the difference between positive and negative examples, different learning algorithms with positive and negative example are proposed. Both long-term and short-term relevance feedbacks of positive and negative learning are investigated and cross-media retrieval performance is remarkably boosted.

References

1. H.J. Zhang, D. Zhong.: Schema for visual feature based image retrieval. In: Proceedings of Storage and Retrieval for Image and Video Database. USA, 1995. 36-46
2. Feng, H., Shi, R., and Chua, T.S.: A bootstrapping framework for annotating and retrieving WWW images. Proc. of the ACM Int. Conf. on Multimedia, pp. 960-967, 2004

3. X. He, W.Y Ma, and H.J. Zhang: Learning an Image Manifold for Retrieval, ACM Multimedia Conference, New York, 2004
4. Jingrui He, Mingjing Li, Hong-Jiang Zhang, Hanghang Tong, Changshui Zhang.: Manifold-Ranking Based Image Retrieval, ACM Multimedia Conference, New York, 2004
5. Namunu C Maddage, Changsheng Xu., Mohan S Kankanhalli, Xi Shao.: Content-based Music Structure Analysis with Applications to Music Semantics Understanding, ACM Multimedia Conference, New York, 2004
6. Guodong Guo; Li, S.Z.: Content-based audio classification and retrieval by support vector machines, IEEE Transactions on Neural Networks, Volume 14, Issue 1, Jan. 2003 Page(s): 209 – 215
7. E. Wold, T. Blum, D. Keislar, and J. Wheaton.: Content-based classification,search and retrieval of audio, IEEE Multimedia Mag., vol. 3, pp. 27–36, July 1996
8. M.Y. Wu, C.Y. Chiu, S.P. Chao,S.N. Y, and H.C. Lin.: Content-Based Retrieval for Human Motion Data,16th IPPR Conference on Computer Vision, Graphics and Image Processing (CVGIP 2003)
9. Meinard M¨uller, Tido R¨oder, Michael Clausen.: Efficient Content-Based Retrieval of Motion Capture Data, Proceedings of ACM SIGGRAPH 2005
10. Smoliar, S.W.; HongJiang Zhang.: Content based video indexing and retrieval, Multimedia, IEEE,Volume 1, Issue 2, Summer 1994 Page(s):62 - 72
11. Jianping Fan; Elmagarmid, A.K.; Xingquan Zhu; Aref, W.G.; Lide Wu.: ClassView: hierarchical video shot classification, indexing, and accessing, Multimedia, IEEE Transactions on, Volume 6, Issue 1, Feb. 2004 Page(s):70 – 86
12. Fei Wu, Yi Yang, Yueting Zhuang, and Yunhe Pan, Understanding Multimedia Document Semantics for Cross-Media Retrieval, LNCS 3767(PCM 2005), 993-1004
13. Zhou, D., Bousquet, O., Lal, T.N., Weston, J., and Schölkopf, B.: Learning with local and global consistency. 18th Annual Conf. on Neural Information Processing Systems, pp. 237-244, 2003
14. Zhou, D., Bousquet, O., Lal, T.N., Weston, J., and Schölkopf, B.: Ranking on data manifolds, 18th Annual Conf. on Neural Information Processing System, pp. 169-176, 2003
15. Hanghang Tong, Jingrui He, Mingjing Li, Changshui Zhang, Wei-Ying Ma.: Graph based multi-modality learning in Proc. ACM Multimedia Conference, Singapore, 2005.
16. J. Shrager, T. Hogg, and B. A. Huberman.: Observation of phase transitions in spreading activation networks." Science, 236:1092–1094, 1987
17. Amy N. Langville and Carl D. Meyer.: Deeper Inside PageRank

Searching the Video: An Efficient Indexing Method for Video Retrieval in Peer to Peer Network

Ming-Ho Hsiao, Wen-Jiin Tsai, and Suh-Yin Lee

Department of Computer Science, National Chiao Tung University
1001 Ta Hsueh Road, Hsinchu, Taiwan 300, ROC
{mhhsiao, wjtsai, sylee}@csie.nctu.edu.tw

Abstract. More and more applications require peer-to-peer (P2P) systems to support complex queries over multi-dimensional data. The retrieval facilities of most P2P systems are limited to queries based on a unique identifier or a small set of keywords. The techniques used for this purpose are hardly applicable for content-based video retrieval in a P2P network (CBP2PVR). In this paper, we present the design of a distributed P2P video sharing system that supports content-based video retrieval. First we will propose the compact signature generation of video shot which can be distributed in a P2P network and used as the basis for a source selection. Second, a Global Indexing structure based on proposed novel PVR-tree index schema allows communicating only with a small fraction of all peers during query processing without deteriorating the result quality significantly. We will also present experimental results confirming our approach.

Keywords: Content Based Video Retrieval, Multi-Dimensional Indexing, Peer to Peer Network.

1 Introduction

Peer-to-peer (P2P) has become a pervasive paradigm of data exchange. As more applications and users share or access data through P2P networks, many current systems seem inadequate due to the inability to support multi-dimensional queries efficiently. In such networks, such as Gnutella or Chord, users can search for items using a number of keywords, or simply by searching for a file name pattern, and then download them from the P2P network. However, those systems can only support exact match queries.

In this paper, we will address the problem of content based search in the context of video retrieval. The challenge in this problem is to implement an efficient content based video retrieval (CBVR) functionality. Suppose there are a large number of peers in the network, and each peer contains a large number of videos. When given a video shot, we want to find the most similar videos as quickly as possible. The super P2P network [1] which is more efficient for contents look-up is selected as the underlying architecture. Build on the above framework, the system first needs to consider how video shots can be effectively described, and then how descriptions can be efficiently maintained by indexing techniques.

T.-J. Cham et al. (Eds.): MMM 2007, LNCS 4352, Part II, pp. 175–184, 2007.
© Springer-Verlag Berlin Heidelberg 2007

Due to the limit on the network bandwidth and peer store, it is hard to transmit the feature vectors of each shot own by the peers to the super-peer. Clearly, compact signatures used to describe peer shots are a necessary step for efficient video indexing and searching in P2P network, especially when the amount of information is very large. Of course, searching performance largely depends on how to generate the signatures of video shots and how an index is implemented, especially in dynamic peer to peer network. If the signatures of video shots contain too much information, the super–peers will waste storage space and increase process power when building the index. However, less information will lead high communication overhead and decrease the retrieval performance. With this urgent need, we aim at developing a new indexing method for content based video retrieval in peer to peer network.

We propose a general and extensible framework for content-based video retrieval in P2P network. The super-peer P2P architecture [1] which is more efficient for video contents search is employed as the underlying architecture. To facilitate CBVR in such a setting, a novel developments of shot signature presenting and a new indexing method called the Peer Vector R*-Tree (PVR-Tree). The paper is a contribution to the new field of content based video retrieval in peer-to-peer network (P2PCBVR).

The rest of paper is organized as follows: In Section 2, we review related work. We present the Peer Vector R*-Tree indexing scheme in Section 3. In Section 4, a novel P2PCBVR search system is presented. An extensive performance study is reported in Section 5 and, finally, we conclude our paper in Section 6.

2   Related Work

Obviously, CBP2PVR is related work accomplished in two areas, namely Multi-dimensional index (MI) and information retrieval in P2P network.

2.1 Multi-dimensional Index

CBVR is about indexing videos by their visual content including spatio-temporal statistics. The basis unit of a video that holds semantics is the shot, which is a collection of successive video frames, and can be described simply as a continuous action in time or space [2].For achieving this task, all shot boundaries needs to be detected. Then, one needs to extract a multi-dimensional feature vector for each shot, and maintains a multi-dimensional index structure on these features. While issues of useful feature sets are clearly out of scope for this publication, in this paper we are concerned with how to index multidimensional data in a super-peer network.

MI works by partitioning the data space, clustering data according to partitions and using the partitions to prune the search space for queries. MI becomes difficulty in the context of CBVR, because in contrast to text retrieval, both videos and queries are represented by high-dimensional feature vectors. Indexing of such vectors is very hard, due to the *curse of dimensionality*[3]. A survey can be found in [3]. This fact results a search with sub-linear complexity a goal that is hard to attain. In order to overcome by the drawbacks of MI for high-dimensional data spaces, several approaches have been investigated to overcome the dimensionality curse.

The (DR) approach first condenses most of information in a data set to a few dimensions by applying singular value decomposition (SVD) [4]. To support fast retrieval, the data in the few condensed dimensions are then indexed. While the methods based on the DR approach provide a solution to the dimensionality curse, they have several drawbacks. Firstly, they are not readily applicable to dynamic databases because SVD has to be computed *a priori* on the entire data set and the computation is expensive. They work well only when the data is strongly correlated. Recently, although Kanth *et al.* [5] developed the technique for performing SVD-based DR in dynamic databases, it is not suitable for peer to peer network. Because peer content often update frequently, the re-computation cost will be very high.

The filter-based approach overcomes the dimensionality curse by filtering the vectors so that only a small fraction of them must be visited during a search. VA-file is the one classified into this category and has been show to be superior in nearly uniform data set. The LPC-file takes a filter-based approach in common with the VA-file [6]. The method is similar to that of the VA-file. However, unlike the VA-file which simply uses more bits to each dimension to increase the discriminatory power of the approximation, the LPC-file enhances it by adding polar coordinate information of the vector to the approximation. In this paper, we extend LPC-file and combine it with R*-tree to support efficient CBVR in P2P network.

2.2 Information Retrieval (IR) in P2P Network

Due to the popularity of peer-to-peer file sharing applications, many research communities have put significant effort on building new P2P systems to support more complex search. More progress has been made towards supporting complex multi-dimensional queries. A P2PR-tree is an extension of the R*-tree in P2P settings [7]. However, the maintenance of a dynamic R-tree in unstructured P2P networks is left unaddressed. The maintenance cost is expected to be considerably high, since every maintenance operation has to be communicated among peers with messages in order to finish. A quad-tree-based technique is proposed by Tanin and Harwood [8] capable of supporting range queries, which, however, builds on Chord and makes it only suitable for structured P2P networks.

Recently, NR-tree proposed in [9] is built in super-peers by indexing minimum bounding rectangles (MBRs) *summarizing* peer data in the same cluster at a coarse level. Not all data in peers are inserted into NR-trees and migrated to super-peers. Instead, only a small number of MBRs summarizing peer data are inserted. However, the importance issue is that the MBRs are not compact descriptions of peer information. Not only it is hardly to maintain by super-peer and it will lead high communication overhead during query processing, which will decrease the retrieval performance.

Tang *et al.* [10] present text retrieval in P2P systems and suggest that it can be extended to image retrieval as well. One of them (pVSM, peer vector space model) stores *(term, document id)* pairs in a structured P2P network, and then retrieves such pairs to perform text information retrieval. Those approach seems to be hard to translate to image data, since [11] reports the need for a large number of features when using text information retrieval methods on image data.

Hierarchical Summary Indexing (HSI) proposed in [12], is a general and extensible framework for searching similar documents in P2P network. The framework is based on the novel concept of Hierarchial Summary Structure. Second, based on the framework, it develops an efficient document searching system by effectively summarizing and maintaining all documents within the network with different granularity. HIS motivated our research in that it is a viable solution for P2P CBVR if a suitable peer data representation similar to the summary used for the text scenario in HIS can be found for peers containing multimedia data.

3   Representing and Indexing Video Shots

Let $\vec{v} = [v_1, v_2, ..v_m]$ be an m-features shot, and as a result of the approximation, the feature vector $\vec{v}$ is represented by the triplet $v' = (c, r, \theta)$, where c is the cell ID in which $\vec{v}$ lies, r is the length of feature vector $\vec{v}$ and θ is the angle between $\vec{v}$ and the diagonal from the local origin O of the cell to the opposite corner $\vec{d} = [d_1, d_2, ..d_m]$. The design goal of the triplet is to maximize the filtering power by using minimal information. However, unlike the VA-file which simply uses more bits to each dimension to increase the discriminatory power of the approximation, the PVR-tree enhances it by adding polar coordinate information of the vector to the approximation. The polar coordinate information is independent of the dimensionality and thus we need not use more bits to represent it as the dimensionality increases.

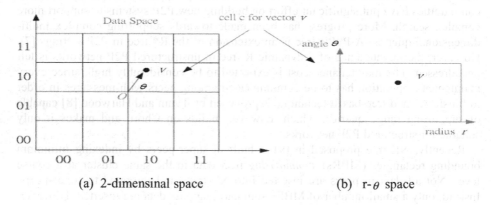

(a) 2-dimensinal space   (b) r-θ space

Fig. 1. Vector v and its approximation

The first component, c, is obtained by geometric approximations to feature vectors based on VA-file which divides the i-th dimension in to 2^d stripes. In other words, at each dimension, it choose 2^d -1 points to divide the dimension and the same bit b to each dimension.. Hence, the feature vector space is partitioned into cells and these cells are used to generate bit-encoded approximations for each vector. The cell is simply represented by the concatenation of the binary bit patterns for each dimension in turn. Fig. 1 (a) shows an example in two dimensions: the cell is represented by the sequence of bits (01, 01) where d=2, b=2.The method used for this stage is similar to that of the VA-file. Typically d is a small integer depending on the dimensionality and the data distribution.

The second step is to represent the vector $\vec{v} = [v_1, v_2, ..v_m]$ using the polar coordinates (r, θ) within the cell in which v lies. Give a feature vector $v, \vec{v} = [v_1, v_2, ..v_m]$, in an m-dimension space M, the θ is calculated as

$$\theta = \cos^{-1}\left(\frac{\vec{v} \cdot \vec{d}}{\|\vec{v}\| \|\vec{d}\|}\right) \tag{1}$$

Where $\|\vec{v}\| = r = \sqrt{\sum_{i=i}^{m} v_i^2}$ and $\|\vec{d}\| = d = \sqrt{\sum_{i=i}^{m} d_i^2}$.

It logically transforms the vector v to 2-dimensional r-θ space, as shown in Fig. 1 (b). In higher dimensions, the approximation of the $\vec{v}$ is a set of points on a hypersphere.

As a result, each feature vector can be represented as a signature composing of $v' = (c, r, \theta)$.

The drawback of LPC-file and VA-file is that they need sequential scan the index file. When the amount data is large, the computation cost is high. To Overcome it, we use R*-tree to index the triplet $v' = (c, r, \theta)$. The three vector component of the feature vector representation lends itself very nicely to indexing. Among various multi-dimensional access methods [6], the R*-tree [3], a variation of the original R-tree [7], has been widely accepted by industry and research community. The first component **c** can be used to prune away points based on the cell locality: cells close in space are clustered in the same leaf node represented as a minimum bounding rectangle (MBR).. . As we can see, we can generate a novel indexing structure Peer Vector R*-tree (PVR-tree) as shown in Fig. 2. The PVR-tree can divide into three: the leaf nodes contain corresponding feature vector, middle levels contain corresponding signature, and upper levels contain corresponding MBR.

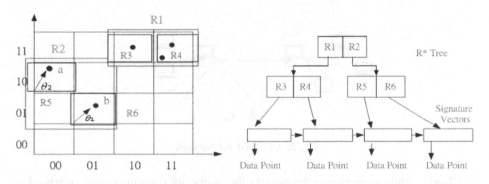

Fig. 2. Structure of PVR-tree

Dynamic maintenance operations arising from insertions and deletions on the indexing structure can be easily performed. When a new point is added in the data set, its (c, r, θ) component are first computed, followed by the standard insertion operation in R*-tree. Correspondingly, the data are inserted into the correct position in the signatures level and data level of the structure, respectively. Deletion operations are done in a similar way.

4 P2P CBVR

Our system facilitates video searching in distributed P2P network. In this section, we shall first discuss the super-peer P2P architecture, and then look at how such PVR-tree can facilitate the design of the proposed framework.

4.1 Super-Peer Network

Applications based on super-peer network are consuming a large portion of internet traffic. For example, KaZaA consumed approximately 37 percent of all TCP traffic, which are more than twice the Web traffic on the University of Washington campus network in June, 2002 [12]. Sandvide also estimates that 76 percent of P2P file shareing traffic belongs to KaZaA traffic and only 8 percent comes from Gnutella in the US [12]. Hence, in our framework, we have adopted a super-peer network model as shown in Fig.3. In this model, among a group of nearby peers (e.g., P1 and P2), some super-peers (e.g., S1 and S2) act both as a server to a set of clients. We assume that peers have reasonable computational capabilities. Peers should be capable of building feature vectors indexes and processing queries on their own data. A straightforward query processing mechanism works as follows: peers submit their query to the super peer of its group. The super peer will then broadcast the queries to other peers within the group. At the same time, the super peer will also broadcast the query to its neighboring super peers. This process is repeated until some criterion is satisfied, for example, a system specified TTL value that is decremented each time the query is broadcast, and the query is dropped when TTL =0.

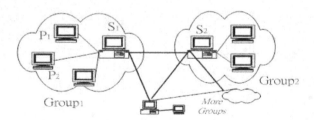

Fig. 3. A Super-Peer Network

Clearly, while a super-peer broadcasts the query, its communication overhead is high. We sought to minimize this overhead using an efficient indexing structure.

4.2 Global Indexing Structure

Built on the above framework, the system first needs to consider after generating signature of video shots, how signatures can be efficiently maintained by indexing techniques. After that, the real content-based search can begin.

4.2.1 Global Indexing Structure

Broadcast-based query will fragment in nature – a search does not reach all nodes in the network. Clearly, in order to deliver high quality telephony with the lowest possible costs, a multi-level index of P2P network, or Global Index (GI) was a necessary development and represents yet another paradigm shift in the notion of scaleable networks. The Global Index technology is a three-level network where super-peers communicate in such a way that every peer in the network has full knowledge of all available users and resources with minimal latency.

In our framework, we adopt the interesting concept, Global Indexing Structure proposed, which is closely related to the super peer P2P architecture we employed. Our scheme essentially indexes peer contents at different levels. The lowest level, named as Peer level, signature, a compact description of each shot is indexed. In the second level, named as group level, all shot signatures owned by a peer group are indexed. Finally, in the third level, named as global level, all shot signatures contained by all peers groups are indexed. Each level covers a wider video information scope than its former level, while performing coarser searching. With the signature information, queries only need to be forwarded to peers that potentially contain the answers. Each super peer maintains two indexes: the global level index of its group and its neighboring groups, and group level index of its group. By examining global level index, a super peer can determine which peer group is relevant. Similarly, by examining group level index, a super peer can determine which of its peers have the answers.

4.2.2 Build and Indexing Signature

How to build the signature representation—high-dimensional point for peer level, group level, and global level, respectively. Each peer may contain hundreds of videos. Similarly, each group may have a large number of peers and the whole super-peer network may contain a large number of groups. As the network size grows, efficient content-based video searching becomes prevalently important.

To be consistent with the framework, the video shot signatures is also done in levels—peer level, group level, and group level. For each peer, each of its video shots is first represented by a feature vector (fv) after feature extraction processing, Then, all fvs are used to generate compact signature composed of (c, r, θ) component. So far, video shots' processing has been built. Each peer use the PVR-tree structure to index it own video shots. Next, each signature is passed to its super-peer. Each super-peer will combine its group's signature by performing a union operation on its signatures. So far, each group's signature has been generated. Each super- peer use the PVR-tree structure to index its group's video shots. After a super-peer receives other super peers' signature information, it repeats the same step as generating global index.

4.3 Query Processing

Query processing is coordinated by super-peers, and part of the processing is pushed to peers as well. When a peer intends to issue a query, it sends the query to its super-peer. A super-peer, upon receiving a query from its passive-peer, followed by the hierarchical indexing search in order of global index, group index, and peer index, which is the reverse order of the signature construction. Then super-peer forwards the query to the corresponding groups and peers within the same group. The procedure is as the following steps:

1. Global index: When a query reaches the super peer, it is first mapped into its PVR-tree followed by KNN searching in. The query is then transmitted to the K most relevant groups.
2. Group index: At each group, the query is first mapped into its group corresponding PVR-tree, followed by KNN searching in. The query is then transmitted to the K most relevant peers.
3. Peer index: At each peer, similarly, the query is first transformed into the peer level's PVR-tree, followed by KNN searching in the local index to select the K most relevant video shots for final video shot similarity measure.

Finally, each peer returns K most relevant similar documents to the peer requesting the query.

5 Evaluation

In this section, we demonstrate the effectiveness of the proposed techniques with extensive experiments.

5.1 Simulation Setup

Experiments on CBP2PIR are hard: as there are no systems shipped to a wide public yet, there is no experience nor a snapshot about the data distribution over a whole P2P network. We tried to make the experiments as hard as possible for the system to obtain results. In order to show the effectiveness of the proposed method, we simulated the color video sequence matching algorithm by MPEG-7 test dataset, which includes various programs such as documentaries, news, sports, entertainment, education, scenery, interview, etc and consists of 1173 shots, which are randomly distributed to peers.

Initially there is only one peer in the network, and new peers keep joining until the network reaches a certain size (500). Each peer hosts data randomly drawn from real video shot signature preprocessed offline. To collect statistics, we randomly (based on certain ratios) inject a mixture of operations (peer join, departure, and search) into thenetwork. The proportion of peer join and departure is kept roughly the same to maintain a stable size of the network. On average, each peer issues 100 queries during the time it is online. For kNN queries, query points are uniformly distributed in space and k is 20.

The feature extraction module is responsible for generation a set of feature and their value from video clips. The features are all extracted in the compressed domain to reducing computation cost. Without losing the generality, the motion activity and color feature are selected as the descriptors of video clips for similarity matching. The Motion Activity of a video shot is represented by16 feature dimension and color is represented by 24 feature dimension.

In the experiments, we used four shot classes to test the performance of our algorithms. Among these test videos, the shots of the Close-Up Tracking (CUT) and the Walking Person (WP) were with high degree of motion. The shots covered in the Bicycle Racing (BR) and the Anchor Person (API) were with medium degree of motion and low degree of motion, respectively. Figs. 4(a) - 5(d) show the examples of these four shot types, with key-frames sampled per 40 frames.

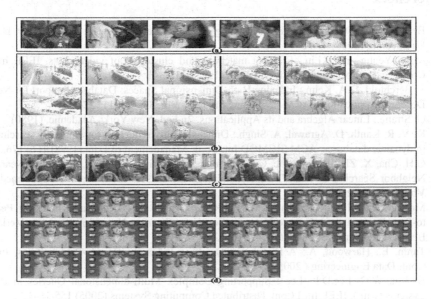

Fig. 4. Examples of the Close-Up (CUT), Bicycle Racing (BR), Walking Person (WP) and Anchorperson and Interview (API) shots

5.2 Evaluation of Retrieval Performance

In the experiment, each shot in these four classes was used as a query shot. The top 20 similar shots were returned as a query result for evaluating retrieval performance. Finally, the respective average recall and precision for each class were computed. The recall of these four kinds of shots exceeded 80% in which the recall of API, CUT and API were higher than 80%. The worst result was obtained by testing the BR shots, with the precision of 74%. The overall average recall and average precision were 81% and 78%, respectively.

6 Conclusion

Doing efficient query routing for CBVR applications in P2P networks requires knowledge about the data in each peer. This problem becomes hard because of the high dimensionality of the data represented. Within this paper, we have examined the issues of supporting CBVR in a distributed peer-to-peer information sharing system. We proposed a PVR-tree to index video shots. Based on this framework, we have presented a compact signature of video shots. Our experiments showed that CBVR in P2P an be easily adopted and our prototype system achieves remarkable achievements.

Acknowledgments. S.-Y. Lee's research is sponsored by NSC under grant number 95-2221-E-009-076-MY3.

References

1. B. Yang, H. Garcia-Molina.: Designing a Super-Peer Network. Int'l Conf. Data Engineering (2003) 49-60
2. M.M. Yeung and B.Liu.: Efficient matching and clustering of video shots. IEEE Int'l Conf. Image Processing, Vol.1. DC, USA (1995) 338-341
3. S. Berchtold, D.A. Keim.: Indexing High-Dimensional Spaces: Database Support for Next Decade's Applications, ACM Computing Surveys, Vol. 33. (2001) 322-373
4. G. Strang.: Linear Algebra and its Applications, 2nd ed. New York: Academic, (1980)
5. K. V. R. Kanth, D. Agrawal, A. Singh.: Dimensionality reduction for similarity searching in dynamic databases. ACM SIGMOD Int. Conf. Management of Data (1998) 166–176.
6. G.H. Cha, X. Zhu, D. Petkovic, C.W. Chung.: An Efficient Indexing Method for Nearest Neighbor Searches in High-Dimensional Image Databases. IEEE Tran. On Multimedia, Vol .4, No. 1. (2002) 76-87
7. Mondal, A., Yilifu, Kitsuregawa, M.: P2PR-tree: An R-tree-based Spatial Index for Peer-to-Peer Environments Lecture Notes in Computer Science, Vol. 3268. Springer-Verlag, Berlin Heidelberg New York (2004) 516–525
8. Tanin, E., Harwood, A.: A Distributed Quadtree Index for Peer-to-Peer Settings. Int'l Conf. Data Engineering (2005) 254-255
9. B. Liu, W.C. Lee,D.L. Lee : Supporting Complex Multi-dimensional Queries in P2P Systems (with), IEEE Int'l Conf. Distributed Computing Systems (2005) 155-164
10. C. Tang, Z. Xu, M. Mahalingam : pSearch: Information retrieval in structured overlays. First Workshop on Hot Topics in Networks. Princeton, NJ (2002)
11. D. M. Squire, W. M¨uller, H. M¨uller, J. Raki.: Content-based query of image databases, inspirations from text retrieval: inverted files, frequency-based weights and relevance feedback. 11th Scandinavian Conf. on Image Analysis. Kangerlussuaq, Greenland. (1999)
12. H. T. Shen, Y. Shu, B. Yu.: Efficient Semantic-Based Content Search in P2P Network. .IEEE Tran. On Knowledge and Data Engineering, Vol. 16, No. 7. (2004) 813-826

Integrating Semantic Templates with Decision Tree for Image Semantic Learning

Ying Liu[1], Dengsheng Zhang[2], Guojun Lu[2], and Ah-Hwee Tan[1]

[1] Emerging Research Lab, School of Computer Engineering,
Nanyang Technological University, Singapore, 639798
{liuying, asahtan}@ntu.edu.sg
[2] Gippsland School of Computing and Information Technology,
Monash University, Vic, 3842, Australia
{dengsheng.zhang, guojun.lu}@infotech.monash.edu.au

Abstract. Decision tree (DT) has great potential in image semantic learning due to its simplicity in implementation and its robustness to incomplete and noisy data. Decision tree learning naturally requires the input attributes to be nominal (discrete). However, proper discretization of continuous-valued image features is a difficult task. In this paper, we present a decision tree based image semantic learning method, which avoids the difficult image feature discretization problem by making use of semantic template (ST) defined for each concept in our database. A ST is the representative feature of a concept, generated from the low-level features of a collection of sample regions. Experimental results on real-world images confirm the promising performance of the proposed method in image semantic learning.

Keywords: Decision tree, Image semantic learning, Semantic template, Image feature discretization.

1 Introduction

In order to reduce the 'semantic gap', many algorithms have been proposed to associate low-level image features with high-level semantics. Machine learning tools such as SVM, Neural Networks and Bayesian classification are often used for image semantic learning [1,2,3]. On the other hand, some other researchers have found in their experiments that decision tree learning such as ID3, C4.5 and CART are mathematically much simpler and perform well in concept learning for image retrieval purposes. Decision tree learning is an extensively researched solution to classification tasks and has great potential in image semantic learning. Compared with other learning methods, decision tree learning is not only simpler but also robust to incomplete and noisy input features [4,5].

The difficulty in applying decision tree induction to image semantic learning lies in the difficulty in image feature discretization which is a challenging task [6]. To benefit image learning process, discrete image feature values should correspond to meaningful conceptual names. Algorithms like ID3 [4] require the value of the input attributes to be discrete. Some algorithms have been designed to handle continuous-valued attributes [7,8]. For example, C4.5 [7] uses a minimal entropy heuristic to find

T.-J. Cham et al. (Eds.): MMM 2007, LNCS 4352, Part II, pp. 185–195, 2007.
© Springer-Verlag Berlin Heidelberg 2007

binary-cuts for each attribute in order to discretize continuous attributes. Based on the understanding that multi-interval discretization could be better than only binary discretization and that it can lead to more compact decision trees, entropy-based multi-interval discretization method is introduced to find multi-level cuts for each attribute [8]. However, these generally designed algorithms usually do not provide meaningful quantization of image feature space. It has been reported that although C4.5 can handle continuous attributes, it does not work as well in domains with continuous attribute values as in domains with discrete attribute values [9].

To avoid the difficult image feature discretization problem in decision tree learning, we propose to convert low-level color (texture) features into color (texture) labels by making use of the semantic templates defined for each concept in the database. These semantic templates (STs) are integrated with decision tree (DT) learning to form the proposed algorithm, which is applied to an RBIR system to implement image retrieval with high-level semantics.

The remaining of the paper is organized as follows. In Section 2, we explain semantic template generation and low-level image feature discretization. Section 3 provides the details of the proposed algorithm. The experimental results are given in section 4. Finally, Section 5 concludes this paper.

2 Semantic Templates and Image Feature Discretization

Our purpose in building a decision tree is to associate the low-level features of image regions with high-level concepts. For our natural scenery image database, the following 19 concepts (classes) are selected: grass, forest, blue sky, sea, flower, sunset, beach, firework, tiger, ape fur, eagle, building, snow, rock, bear, night sky, crowd, butterfly and mountain. Each of these 19 concepts is given a concept label from 0,1,…, to 18 in sequence. The input attributes of the decision tree are the low-level region features and the output is one of the 19 concepts.

This section first describes the input attributes used in our algorithm, which are the low-level region features including color and texture. Then, we explain how to construct semantic template (ST) for each concept and how to make use of ST for image feature discretization.

2.1 Low-Level Image Features

In our system, each database image is segmented into different regions using JSEG [10]. For each region in the database, color feature and texture feature are extracted as its low-level features. The color feature we use is the HSV space dominant color as described in [11]. Gabor texture feature of each region is obtained using the POCS-ER algorithm proposed in [12]. Each dimension of the color and texture features is normalized to the range [0,1].

2.2 Semantic Templates Construction and Image Feature Discretization

The low-level color and texture features have to be discretized to be useful in decision tree learning, as they have continuous values. As explained before, proper discretization of continuous image features is still an open challenge. To avoid this problem, we propose to convert continuous color (texture) features into color (texture) labels by introducing semantic templates (STs),.

In order to construct STs, firstly, we collect a set of 40 sample regions from the database for each of the 19 concepts defined and form a training data set of 760 regions in total. For every concept, a semantic template (ST) is defined as the centroid of the low-level features of all the 40 sample regions. For the j_{th} sample region in class i, where $(j = 0,...,39)$ and $(i = 0,...,18)$, its color and texture features are given by: $\{h_j^i, s_j^i, v_j^i\}$ (dominant color in HSV space) and $\{\mu_{00_j}^i, \sigma_{00_j}^i, ..., \mu_{35_j}^i, \sigma_{35_j}^i\}$ (Gabor feature with 4 scales and 6 orientations) respectively.

Taking the first dimension of color feature and the first dimension of texture feature as examples, the centroid of the color and texture features can be calculated as:

$$\overline{h}^i = \frac{1}{40} \sum_{j=0}^{39} h_j^i \tag{1}$$

$$\overline{\mu}_{00}^i = \frac{1}{40} \sum_{j=0}^{39} \mu_{00_j}^i$$

Thus, we obtain a set of 19 STs, denoted as $ST_i = \{C_i, T_i\}$ with $i=0,...,18$. where $C_i = \{\overline{h}^i, \overline{s}^i, \overline{v}^i\}$ and $T_i = \{\overline{\mu}_{00}^i, \overline{\sigma}_{00}^i, ..., \overline{\mu}_{35}^i, \overline{\sigma}_{35}^i\}$ are the 'representative' color and texture features of concept i. We refer to these representative color and texture features as *color-template* and *texture-template* respectively.

By calculating the Euclidean distance between the color (texture) feature of a region and the color (texture) template of each concept, the color (texture) label of the region can be obtained, which is the label of the concept corresponding to the minimum distance. Taking color feature as example, the following algorithm explains how to obtain the color label for the j_{th} sample region in class i.

1) Calculate the distance between the color feature of this region and the color-template of each concept m $(m=0,...,18)$ as

$$d_{c(j,i)}^m = \sqrt{(h_j^i - \overline{h}^m)^2 + (s_j^i - \overline{s}^m)^2 + (v_j^i - \overline{v}^m)^2} \tag{2}$$

2) Find the minimum distance, $d_{c(j,i)}^{m_{min}} = \min d_{c(j,i)}^m$;

3) The color label of this region is: m_{min}

As a result, each region is represented by its color label, texture label. Both color and texture labels have 19 possible values each $(0,...,18)$. In this way, by making use of semantic templates, the continuous low-level image features are converted to discrete values. This discretization process is different from conventional methods which try to quantize each dimension of the image feature into different intervals. Unlike other methods which are designed for general purpose applications, our method is custom built for discretizing image features. In addition, the proposed method is computationally simple and easy to implement. To discretize an attribute, the proposed method needs only to compute the Euclidean distance between a region feature and each of the 19 semantic templates, in order to get the concept label that corresponds to the minimum of all the distances. The method used in C4.5 requires the computation of the entropies introduced by all possible partition boundaries to find the binary discretization boundary which corresponds to the minimum entropy.

Then, for each of the two partitions, the above process is repeated until the stop condition is achieved. Moreover, the above process has to be applied to each dimension of the image feature! Thus, in order to be used in our database, this algorithm has to be performed on each dimension of the 3D color feature and 48D texture feature. The multi-interval discretization method is even more computationally expensive [8].

3 The Proposed Algorithm

A decision tree can be obtained by splitting the training data into different subsets based on all the possible values of an attribute. The root node contains all the instances in the training set. Then, an input attribute is selected to split the training set into different subsets corresponding to different possible values of the attribute. This process is recursively applied to each derived subset up to the leaves of the tree. There are different ways to split the data resulting in different trees. To obtain small tree, a key issue is to select the most significant attribute at each level of the tree from those attributes which are not yet used for decision making [13]. Information gain is the most commonly used measure to decide which attribute to test at each non-leaf node of the tree [13].

In this section, we first explain how to select the most significant attribute for decision making, and then provide the details of the learning method.

3.1 Most Significant Attribute

Decision tree learning algorithms such as ID3 and C4.5 select the attribute with greatest information gain, based on the concept of entropy. Entropy, in information theory, characterizes the (un)certainty of an arbitrary collection of examples. The higher the entropy, the more information is needed to describe the data. Given a set S, containing m possible outcomes, the entropy of set S is defined as:

$$H(S) = \sum_{i=1}^{m} -P_i * \log_2 P_i \qquad (3)$$

where P_i is the proportion of instances in S that takes the i_{th} value of outcome. Information gain measures the reduction in entropy (gain in information) induced by splitting the dataset on a certain attribute E.

$$Gain(S, E) = H(S) - \sum_{v \in E} \frac{|S_v|}{|S|} H(S_v) \qquad (4)$$

where v is a value of E, $|S_v|$ is the subset of instances of S with E having value v, $|S|$ is the number of instances in S. The second term in equation (5) is the average entropy of attribute E over all possible values of E. We refer to this simply as 'entropy' of E. From equation (5), the attribute with greatest information gain is equivalent to the attribute with least entropy [13].

In our case, among the three input attributes: dominant color, Gabor texture feature, and spatial location; spatial location is obviously less significant for natural scenery images than color and texture features. We need to decide between color and texture which is more significant and should be used at the first level of the decision tree. In our experiments, the average entropy of color feature and texture feature are 2.06 and 1.69 respectively. It means that color feature provides more information in describing the images and should be used at the first level of the decision tree for decision making.

Now that we know color feature should be used first for decision making, the question is how to make decision? Given a region with color label i, should it be classified as class i? Or we need texture feature to make the decision which class it belongs to? To answer these questions, we propose to calculate the classification accuracy for each class using color feature and texture feature. The algorithm below explains the process of calculating the classification accuracy of color feature for each class.

1) For each class (concept), calculate the centroid of the color features of all the 40 regions as its *color-template*, $C_i = \{\bar{h}^i, \bar{s}^i, \bar{v}^i\}$ for $(i = 0,...,18)$.

2) Initialize an array as Correct_Num[i] = 0, to count the number of correct classifications.

3) For the j_{th} sample region in class i, calculate its Euclidean distance $d_{c(j,i)}^{m}$ to the *color-template* of each class, where $(m = 0,...,18)$.

4) Find the minimum distance $d_{c(j,i)}^{m_{\min}}$. If $m_{\min} = i$, then we consider this region correctly classified based on color feature, and

$$\text{Correct\_Num}[i] = \text{Correct\_Num}[i] + 1.$$

5) Repeat steps 2-4 for all the sample data.

6) Obtain the probability of correct classification for each class i, as:

$$P_c[i] = \text{Correct\_Num }[i] / 40, \quad \text{for } i=0,...,18. \tag{5}$$

This algorithm provides the classification accuracy for each class as the probability of correct classification $P_c[i]$ using color feature. The classification accuracy $P_t[i]$ for texture feature can be calculated in the similar way. The results are given in Table 1. This table also provides the classification accuracy $P_{ct}[i]$ using both color and texture features. The results in Table 1 are obtained for the training data of 760 regions and are used to identify which feature (color, texture or the combination of both) gives the best classification accuracy for each concept and hence which template (color template, texture template, or both) should be used as the ST of a concept.

It is found that some concepts can be well represented by their color features and the use of texture feature does not increase the classification performance. Similarly, for some concepts, texture feature alone is sufficient to represent the concept with significant accuracy, while for others, the classification accuracy is higher when both color and texture features are combined. For example, for sunset, the classification accuracy is 0.925, 0.65, 0.90 using color feature, texture feature and the combination of both, respectively. In this case, color feature alone represents the sunset region with highest accuracy. On the other hand, some concepts such as *firework* are well characterized by their texture features and including color feature in this case degrades the classification performance. This is because of the fact that different firework regions have different colors but their texture patterns are similar. For some other concepts like *tiger*, both color and texture features are needed for their representation.

Table 1. Classification Accuracy Using Color, Texture and Color combined with Texture

Concept Label	Concept	Color Feature	Texture Feature	Color & Texture
0	Grass	0.65	0.7	**0.875**
1	Forest	0.475	0.775	**0.925**
2	Blue sky	0.375	0.25	**0.8**
3	Sea	0.525	0.35	**0.725**
4	Flower	0.475	**0.7**	0.55
5	Sunset	**0.925**	0.65	0.9
6	Beach	0.6	0.35	**0.85**
7	Firework	0.0	**0.65**	0.45
8	Tiger	0.4	0.55	**0.675**
9	Ape fur	**0.775**	0.125	0.775
10	Eagle	**0.875**	0.325	0.675
11	Building	0.45	0.55	**0.675**
12	Snow	**0.9**	0.45	0.9
13	Rock	**0.725**	0.325	0.575
14	Bear	0.4	0.475	**0.85**
15	Night sky	0.875	0.675	**0.95**
16	Crowd	0.45	**0.75**	0.6
17	Butterfly	**0.45**	0.075	0.4
18	Mountain	0.275	0.35	**0.45**
Average		0.558	0.478	0.716

In conclusion, which template to use to represent a concept, we should choose the one that provides the highest classification accuracy. This selection has been shown in Table 5.1 by making bold-face the highest classification accuracy for every concept.

3.2 Deriving the Decision Rules

Once the semantic template for each concept has been constructed, we generate a set of decision rules to map the low-level features of a region to a high-level concept. The input attributes to the decision tree include: color feature, texture feature. The following algorithm details the process of decision tree induction.

1) At the first level of the tree, the color feature of a region is compared with each of the 19 *color-templates*, to obtain its color label.
2) For concepts such as *sunset, ape fur, eagle, snow, rock* and *butterfly*, decisions can be made at the first level of the tree, as indicated by results in Table 1. That means, if the color label of a region is 5 (or 9, 10, 12, 13, 17), it is classified as *sunset* (or *ape fur, eagle, snow, rock, butterfly*).
3) Otherwise, texture feature is required for further decision making. There are two cases at the second level of the decision tree: if the texture label of a region is 4(7,16), then it is classified as *flower (firework, crowd)*; for rest of the regions, both color feature and texture features have to be used in decision making. For instance, if both the color label and texture label of a region is 6, then it is classified as *beach*.

Hence, we derive a set of decision rules described in terms of color and texture labels as follows:

> ***If** the **Color label** of a region is '5(or 9,10,12,13,17)', **then** it is classified as *'sunset'*(or ape fur, eagle, snow, rock, butterfly).
> ***If** the **Color label** of a region is **NOT** {5,9,10,12,13,17} **AND** its **Texture label** is 4 (or 7,16), **then** it is classified as *'flower'*(or firework, crowd).
> ***If** both the **Color label and Texture label** of a region are 0 (or 1,2,3,6,8,11,14,15,18)', **then** it is classified as *'grass'*(or forest, blue sky, sea, beach, tiger, building, bear, dark sky, mountain).

For regions which do not belong to any of the 19 classes, we classify them as 'unknown'. To test the decision rules, a number of regions for each of the 19 concepts are collected from the database as test data. The test data consists of three testing sets of sizes 19*20, 19*25 and 19*30 that contain 20, 25 and 30 regions for each of the 19 concepts respectively. Given a test region with its color feature and texture feature, we first obtain its color label and texture label. Then, the above decision rules are applied to find out the concept of this region. Tested on the three test datasets, the average classification accuracy for the 19 classes are 0.784, 0.758 and 0.748 respectively. The overall average for the three test tests is 0.763.

In the proposed algorithm, the order in which features are selected to make decision is important to the classification outcome. The impact on classification accuracy can be seen in case of a conflict. For example, a region has color label as 9(ape fur) and texture label as 4 (flower). In this conflict, we are unable to classify this region without an ordering mechanism to specify the feature that should be given priority for decision making. Due to the limitation of low-level image feature in describing images, such conflict is unavoidable. Entropy (information gain) measures the capability of an attribute in describing the database images. In the case of such conflict, by selecting the attribute with smaller entropy (greater information gain), we intend to choose the feature which is more reliable for decision making.

3.3   Analysis

The proposed algorithm employs semantic templates to convert continuous valued image feature into discrete values. In this section, we compare the performance of the proposed method with ID3 and C4.5. The testing data are as described in Section 3.2, that is, three datasets with 19*20, 19*25 and 19*30 regions respectively.

ID3 and C4.5 are implemented using WEKA machine learning package [14]. Since ID3 does not accept continuous input values, we use color label, texture label as its input attributes. For C4.5, we use low-level color and texture features directly as input attributes, and let C4.5 discretize image features by itself. Fig. 1 provides the average of the classification accuracies for all the 19 concepts using different learning methods. The results show that the proposed method outperforms the other two. This proves that the image feature discretization method we proposed is more effective than the binary discretization method used in C4.5 for natural scenery image semantic learning.

These results provide evidence from our database to confirm the promising performance of the proposed method. However, extensive comparison of different learning methods is beyond the scope of this paper.

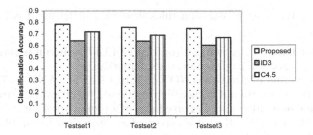

Fig. 1. Average classification accuracies for 19 concepts using different learning methods

4   Results and Analysis

4.1   Retrieval with Concepts

With the decision rules generated as in Section 3, we implement an RBIR system with high-level semantics. It is assumed that each image has at least one dominant region expressing its semantics. For most categories in our database, there is one dominant region in the relevant images. The images under a few categories contain two dominant images. For instance, all the 'firework' images in the database include regions of concepts 'firework' and 'night sky', 'bear' region always comes with 'snow' in category 'North pole bears'.

Our system supports users with query by keyword and query by specified region. That is, users can either submit a keyword as query, or specify the dominant region in the query image. In our experiments, we specify the dominant region of a query image. Using the proposed method, the concept of the specified region can be obtained. The system first finds a subset of images from the database containing region(s) of same concept as that of the query. Then, based on their low-level color and texture features, these images are ranked according to their EMD [15] distances to the query image. We refer to this process as '*retrieval by concepts*'.

4.2   Database and Performance Evaluation

We use 5,000 Corel images as our test set. These images are of 50 categories which are semantically different. 'JSEG' segmentation produces 29187 regions, an average of 5.84 regions per image. To measure the retrieval performance, we calculate the average Precision (Pr) and Recall (Re) of 40 queries with different total number of images retrieved (K=10,20,...100) and obtain the Pr~Re curve. The query images are selected from most of the 50 categories except those with very abstract labels. Example queries and the corresponding dominant regions are given in Fig. 2.

4.3   Experimental Results

The performance of our RBIR system using the proposed method for concept learning (*retrieval with concepts*) is compared with that of the RBIR system with only low-level image features (*retrieval without concepts*). The results in Fig.3 show clearly that using high-level concepts, the retrieval performance measured by Pr~Re is improved. As examples, the retrieval results for a few queries are given in

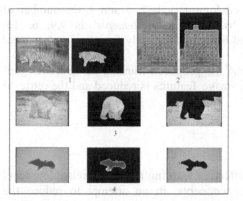

Fig. 2. Examples of query image and dominant regions

Fig. 3. Retrieval with/without concepts

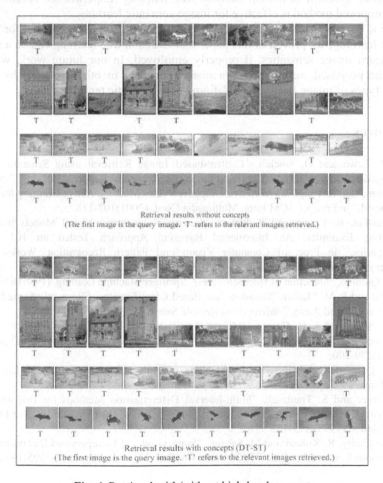

Retrieval results without concepts
(The first image is the query image. 'T' refers to the relevant images retrieved.)

Retrieval results with concepts (DT-ST)
(The first image is the query image. 'T' refers to the relevant images retrieved.)

Fig. 4. Retrieval with/without high-level concepts

Fig. 4. Among the top 10 images retrieved for query 1, 2, 3 and 4, the number of relevant images found by performing '*retrieval with concepts*' is 9,9, 6, 10, respectively, whereas there are 4, 5, 5 and 6 images correctly found using '*retrieval without concepts*'.

Our experimental results prove that using the proposed learning method, the 'gap' between the user semantics and low-level image features is reduced and the retrieval accuracy is improved

5 Conclusions

In this paper, we proposed a simple and effective learning method to relate low-level image features with high-level semantic concepts, in an attempt to reduce the 'semantic gap' in content-based image retrieval. By integrating semantic templates with decision tree learning, this method avoids the difficult image feature discretization problem in normal decision tree learning. Experimental results prove that the proposed method is effective for image semantic learning.

While it is yet an open research question that which learning tool is best for image semantic learning, we proved in this paper that decision tree learning can be a strong tool to learn image semantics, if properly employed. In our future work, we will extend the proposed method to learn image concepts in other domains by using different types of image features and defining new semantic templates.

References

1. C. P. Town and D. Sinclair, "Content-based Image Retrieval using Semantic Visual Categories," Society for Manufacturing Engineers, Technical Report MV01-211, 2001.
2. E. Chang and S. Tong. "SVM Active - Support Vector Machine Active Learning for Image Retrieval," in Proc. of ACM Inter. Multimedia Conf. (2001)107-118.
3. L. Fei-Fei, R. Fergus and P. Perona. "Learning Generative Visual Models from few Training Examples: An Incremental Bayesian Approach Tested on 101 Object Categories," in Proc. of Computer Vision and Pattern Recognition, Workshop on Generative-Model Based Vision. (2004) 178-185.
4. J. R. Quinlan, "Induction of Decision Trees," Springer Machine Leaning, (1986) 81-106.
5. M. Pal and P. M. Mather. "Decision Tree Based Classification of Remotely Sensed Data," in Proc. of 22nd Asian Conference on Remote Sensing (ACRS). (2001)245-248.
6. I. K. Sethi and I. L. Coman, "Mining Association Rules Between Low-Level Image Features and High-Level Concepts," SPIE Data Mining and Knowledge Discovery, (2001)279-290.
7. J. R. Quinlan, "C4.5, Program for Machine Learning." Morgan Kaufmann, Los Altos, Califonia, 1993.
8. P. Perner and S. Trautzsch, "Multi-Interval Discretization Methods for Decision Tree Learning," in Advances in Pattern Recognition, A. Amin, Dori D., Pudil P. and Freeman H., Editors. (1998) 475-482.
9. J. Dougherty, R. Kohavi and M. Sahami. "Supervised and Unsupervised Discretization of Continous Features," in Proc. of 12th Inter. Conf. on Machine Learning. (1995)194-202.

10. Y.Deng, B.S.Manjunath and H.Shin: Color Image Segmentation, in Proc. IEEE Computer Society Conf. on Comp. Vision and Pattern Recognition, CVPR '99, vol.2, (1999)446-451.
11. Y.Liu, D.S.Zhang, G.Lu, W.Y. Ma: Region-Based Image Retrieval with Perceptual Colors, Pacific-Rim Multimedia Conference (PCM2004), Tokyo, (2004)931-938.
12. Y.Liu, D.S.Zhang, G.Lu, W.Y. Ma: Study on Texture Feature Extraction from Arbitrary-Shaped Regions for Image Retrieval, Inter. Multimedia Modeling Conf. (MMM2006), Beijing, (2006)264-271.
13. T. Mitchell: Decision Tree Learning, in *Machine Learning*, T. Mitchell, Editor. The McGraw-Hill Companies, Inc. (1997)52-78.
14. http://www.cs.waikato.ac.nz/ml/weka/.
15. Rubner, Y., Tomasi, C., and Guibas, L.: A Metric for Distributions with Applications to Image Databases, in Proc. of IEEE Inter. Conf. on Computer Vision(ICCV), (1998)59-67.

Neural Network Combining Classifier Based on Dempster-Shafer Theory for Semantic Indexing in Video Content

Rachid Benmokhtar and Benoit Huet

Institut Eurécom - Département Multimédias
2229, route des crêtes
06904 Sophia-Antipolis - France
(Rachid.Benmokhtar, Benoit.Huet)@eurecom.fr

Abstract. Classification is a major task in many applications and in particular for automatic semantic-based video content indexing and retrieval. In this paper, we focus on the challenging task of classifier output fusion[1]. It is a necessary step to efficiently estimate the semantic content of video shots from multiple cues. We propose to fuse the numeric information provided by multiple classifiers in the framework of evidence logic. For this purpose, an improved version of RBF network based on Evidence Theory (NN-ET) is proposed. Experiments are conducted in the framework of TrecVid high level feature extraction task that consists of ordering shots with respect to their relevance to a given semantic class.

1 Introduction

Classifier fusion is a promising way for improving the performance of pattern recognition algorithms. Many authors proposed different ways of fusing classifiers [1,2,3]. In [4], a state of the art is presented, along with a dichotomy and an evaluation of differents classifeurs fusion methods used in the literature. Neural Network approaches seem to be able to give the better performances than GMM and Decision Template [3,4]. In the aim of the neural network study, this paper gives a novel fusion method inspired by RBF neural network and evidence theory, called Neural Network based on Evidence Theory (NN-ET). These methods are implemented for this purpose and evaluated in the context of content-based retrieval of video data.

This paper presents a novel fusion scheme based on neural network which is build within our semantic video content indexing and retrieval system. First, an overview of the architecture is given. A description of RBF neural network is then provided along with an explanation of how evidence theory can be used for classification and fusion. The experimental results presented in this paper are performed in the framework of TrecVid'05. This study reports the efficiency of different combination methods and shows the improvement provided by our proposed scheme. Finally, we conclude with a

---

[1] The work presented here is funded by France Télécom R&D under CRE 46134752.

T.-J. Cham et al. (Eds.): MMM 2007, LNCS 4352, Part II, pp. 196–205, 2007.

summary of the most important results provided by this study along with some possible extension of work.

2   System Architecture

This section describes the workflow of the semantic feature extraction process that aims to detect the presence of semantic classes in video shots, such as building, car, U.S. flag, water, map, etc ... First, key-frames of video shots, provided by TrecVid'05, are segmented into homogeneous regions thanks to the algorithm described in [5]. The algorithm is fast and provides visually acceptable segmentation. Its low computational requirement is an important criterion when one needs to process a huge amount of data like the TrecVid'05 database. An illustration of the segmentation result is provided on figure 1. Secondly, color and texture are extracted for each segmented region. Thirdly, vectors obtained over the complete database are clustered using K-Means to find the N most representative elements.

Fig. 1. Example of segmentation outputs

Representative elements are then used as visual keywords to describe video shot content. To do so, features computed from a single video shot are matched to their closest visual keyword with respect to Euclidean distance (or another distance measures). The occurrence vector of the visual keywords in the shot, called Image Vector Space Model (IVSM) is then build. Image Latent Semantic Analysis (ILSA) is applied on these features to obtain an efficient and compact representation of video shot content. Finally, support vector machines (SVM) are used to obtain the initial classification which will then be used by the fusion mechanism [6]. The overall chain is presented in figure 2.

For the study presented in this paper we distinguish two types of modalities : visual and motion features. The two visual features are selected for this purpose: Hue-Saturation-Value color histograms and energies of Gabor's filters [7]. In order to capture the local information in a way that reflects the human perception of the content, visual features are extracted on regions of segmented key-frames [8]. For some concepts like people walking/running, sport, it is useful to have an information about the motion activity present in the shot. Two features are selected for this purpose: the camera motion and the motion histogram of the shot.

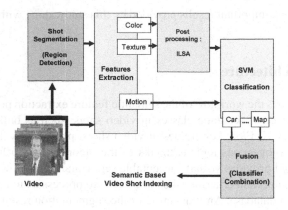

Fig. 2. General framework of the application

3 Classifier Fusion

3.1 Radial Neural Network (RBF)

RBF is a popular supervised neural network learning algorithm, which consists in a spacialization of the MLP network [9]. The RBF network is constitued by only the following three layer, as shown in (figure 3).

- *Input Layer :* Broadcast the inputs without distortion to hidden layer;
- *RBF Layer :* Hidden layer that contain the RBF function;
- *Output Layer :* Simple layer that contain a lineaire function.

Basis functions normally take the form $\phi = \| \vec{x} - \vec{\mu_i} \|$. The function depends on the distance (usually taken to be Euclidean) between the input vector $\vec{x}$ and a vector $\vec{\mu_i}$. The most common form of basis function used is the Gaussian function $\phi = \exp \frac{\| \vec{x} - \vec{\mu_i} \|^2}{2\sigma_j^2}$. where $\vec{\mu_i}$ determines the center of the basis function and σ_i is a width parameter that controls how is spread the curve. Generally, these centers are selected by using some

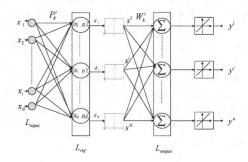

Fig. 3. RBF Classifier Structure

fuzzy or non-fuzzy clustering algorithms. In this work, we have used the k-means algorithm to select the initial cluster centers in the first stage and then these centers are further fine tuned by using point symmetry distance measure. The number of neurons in the output layer is equal to the possible classes of the given problem. Each output layer neuron computes a linear weighted sum of the outputs of the hidden layer neurons as follows:

$$y_i(x) = \sum_{i=1}^{N} \phi_i(x) W_i \tag{1}$$

The weight vectors are determined by minimizing the mean squared differences between the classifier outputs $y_k = \sum_{j=0}^{M} w_{k,j} s_i$ and target values t_k as following :

$$E = \frac{1}{2} \sum_{k=1}^{M} (y_k - t_k)^2 \tag{2}$$

The parameters (ΔW, $\Delta \mu$, $\Delta \sigma$) are given by (more detailed explanation can be found in [9]) :

$$\frac{\partial E}{\partial w_{k,i}} = \frac{\partial E}{\partial y_k} \frac{\partial y_k}{\partial w_{k,i}} \tag{3}$$

or $\frac{\partial E}{\partial y_k} = -(t_k - y_k)$, thus,

$$\frac{\partial E}{\partial w_{k,i}} = -(t_k - y_k) s_i \tag{4}$$

after computation, we obtain :

$$\frac{\partial E}{\partial \mu_{j,i}} = \sum_{k} \frac{\partial E}{\partial y_k} \frac{\partial y_k}{\partial s_j} \frac{\partial s_j}{\partial \mu_{j,i}} = \frac{s_j}{\sigma_j^2} (x_i - \mu_{j,i}) \sum_{k} (t_k - y_k) w_{k,j} \tag{5}$$

$$\frac{\partial E}{\partial \sigma_j} = \sum_{k} \frac{\partial E}{\partial y_k} \frac{\partial y_k}{\partial s_j} \frac{\partial s_j}{\partial \sigma_{j,i}} = \frac{2 s_j}{\sigma_j} \log s_j \sum_{k} (t_k - y_k) w_{k,j} \tag{6}$$

3.2 Evidence Theory

As we have seen in [4], solutions in combining multiple classifiers are numerous but each of them has weaknesses. Most treat imprecision, but uncertainty and reliability are ignored. Evidence theory allows to use uncertain data [10].

Let Ω be a finite set of mutually exclusive and exhausive hypotheses, called the *frame of dicernement*. A basic belief assignment (BBA) is a function m from 2^{Ω} to $[0, 1]$ verifying :

$$\begin{cases} m(\emptyset) = 0 \\ \sum_{A \subseteq \Omega} m(A) = 1 \end{cases} \tag{7}$$

For any $A \subseteq \Omega$, $m(A)$ represents the belief that one is willing to commit exactly to A, given a certain piece of evidence. The subsets A of Ω such that $m(A) > 0$ are called the *focal elements* of m. Associated with m are a *belief* or *credibility* function bel and a *plausibility* function pl, defined, respectively, for all $A \in \Omega$ as :

$$bel(A) = \sum_{B \subseteq A} m(B) \qquad (8)$$

$$pl(A) = \sum_{A \cap B \neq \emptyset} m(B) \qquad (9)$$

The quantity $bel(A)$ can be interpreted as a global measure of one's belief that hypothesis is true, while $pl(A)$ may be viewed as the amount of belief that could potentially be placed in A, if further information became available [11].

The decision rule can be given by different approches as following :

- Choose the maximum plausibilty hypothesis (pl);
- Choose the maximum pignistique probability hypothesis $(BetP)$.

$$BetP(w) = \sum_{w \in A} \frac{m(A)}{|A|} \qquad (10)$$

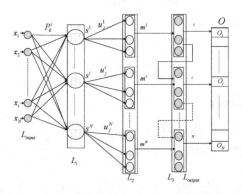

Fig. 4. Neural Network implementation of the evidence theoritic Classifier Structure

Application to Pattern Classification. The response of hidden unit i to an input vector x is defined as a decreasing function of the distance between x and a weight vector p^i. The output signal y^j from the jth output unit with weight vector w_i^j is obtained as a weighted sum of the activations in the n hidden layer:

$$y^j = \sum_{i=1}^{n} w_i^j s^i \qquad (11)$$

The evidence-theoretic classifier introduced in this paper can also be represented in the connectionist formalism as a neural network with an input layer L_{input}, two hidden layers L_1 and L_2, and an output layer $L_3 = L_{output}$ (Fig. 3). Each layer L_1 to L_3 corresponds to one step of the procedure described in following:

1. Layer L_1 contains n units (prototypes). It is identical to the hidden layer of an RBF network with exponential activation function ϕ and d is a distance computed using data. $\alpha \in [0, 1]$ is a weakning parameter associated to prototype i, where $\epsilon = 0$ at the initialization [12].

$$\begin{cases} s^i = \alpha^i \phi(d^i) \\ \phi(d^i) = \exp\left(-\gamma^i (d^i)^2\right) \\ \alpha^i = \frac{1}{1+\exp(-\epsilon^i)} \end{cases} \quad (12)$$

where $(\gamma^i = (\eta^i)^2)$ is a positive parameter defining the receptive field size of prototype $i = \{1, ..., n\}$.

2. Layer L_2 computes the BBA associated to each prototype. It is composed of n modules of $M + 1$ units each. The units of module i are connected to neuron i of the previous layer. The vector of activations $m^i = (m_1^i, m_2^i, ..., m_{M+1}^i)$ of module corresponds to the belief masses assigned by m^i.

$$\begin{cases} m^i(\{w_q\}) = \alpha^i u_q^i \phi(d^i) \\ m^i(\{\Omega\}) = 1 - \alpha^i \phi(d^i) \end{cases} \quad (13)$$

so,

$$m^i = (m^i(\{w_1\}), m^i(\{w_2\}), ..., m^i(\{w_{M+1}\})) = (u_1^i s^i, ..., u_M^i s^i, 1 - s^i) \quad (14)$$

where u_q^i represents the degree membership to each class w_q, by introducing a new parameter β [12] as $u_j^i = \frac{(\beta_j^i)^2}{\sum_{k=1}^{M}(\beta_k^i)^2}$.

3. The Dempster Shafer combination rule combine n different mass function in one single mass. It's given by :

$$m(A) = (m_1 \oplus m_2 \oplus ... \oplus m_N) = \sum_{B_1 \cap ... \cap B_n = A} \prod_{j=1}^{n} m_j(B_j) \quad (15)$$

This mass function has a particular structure, indeed, the mass restarted only on singleton and γ hypothesis. This particular structure is going to play an important role during the implementation of decision rule.

The n BBA's m^i are combined in L_3, composed of n modules of $M+1$ units. The activations vector of modules i is defined $\overrightarrow{\mu^i} = (\mu^i(\{w_1\}), ..., \mu^i(\{w_M\}), \mu^i(\Omega))$. where μ^i is the conjunctive combination of the BBA's $m^1, ..., m^i$

$$\begin{cases} \mu^i = \bigcap_{k=1}^{i} m^k = \mu^{i-1} \cap m^i \\ \mu^1 = m^1 \end{cases} \quad (16)$$

The activation vectors for $i = \{2, ..., M\}$ can be recursively computed using the following formula :

$$\begin{cases} \mu_j^i = \mu_j^{i-1} m_j^i + \mu_j^{i-1} m_{M+1}^i + \mu_{M+1}^{i-1} m_j^i \\ \mu_{M+1}^i = \mu_{M+1}^{i-1} m_{M+1}^i \end{cases} \quad (17)$$

4. Layer L_{output} gives vector O defined as:

$$\begin{cases} O = \frac{\mu}{K} \\ \\ K = \sum_{k=1}^{M+1} m_k \end{cases} \tag{18}$$

The different parameters ($\Delta\beta, \Delta u, \Delta\gamma, \Delta\alpha, \Delta P, \Delta s$) can be determined by gradient descent of output error for a given ν and input pattern x.

$$E_v(x) = \frac{1}{2}\|P_v - t\|^2 = \frac{1}{2}\sum_{q=1}^{M}(P_{v,q} - t_q)^2 \tag{19}$$

where $P_{v,q} = O_q + \nu O_{M+1}$ is the output vector with $q = 1, ..., M$ and $0 \leq \nu \leq 1$.

$P_{0,q}, P_{1,q}, P_{\frac{1}{M},q}$ represent the credibility, the plausibility and the pignistique probability rescpectively of each class w_q.

The derivate of $E_v(x)$ w.r.t β_j^i id given by :

$$\frac{\partial E_v(x)}{\partial \beta_j^i} = \sum_{k=1}^{M} \frac{\partial E_v(x)}{\partial u_j^k} \frac{\partial u_k^i(x)}{\partial \beta_j^i} \tag{20}$$

Let us now compute $\frac{\partial E_\nu(x)}{\partial u_j^i}$

$$\frac{\partial E_\nu(x)}{\partial u_j^i} = \frac{\partial E_v(x)}{\partial m_k} \frac{\partial m_k}{\partial u_j^i} = (P_{v,j} - t_j)\frac{\partial m_k}{\partial u_j^i} \tag{21}$$

In order to express $\frac{\partial m_k}{\partial u_j^i}$, we use the commutativity and associativity of the $\bigcap$ operator to rewrite the output BBA m as the conjunctive combination of two terms.

$$m = m^i \bigcap \bar{m}^i \text{with } \bar{m}^i = \bigcap_{k \neq i} \bar{m}^k \tag{22}$$

The vector can be computed by [13]:

$$\begin{cases} \bar{m}_j^i = \frac{m_j - \frac{m_{M+1} m_j^i}{m_{M+1}^i}}{m_j^i + m_{M+1}^i} \\ \\ \bar{m}_{M+1}^i = \frac{m_{M+1}}{m_{M+1}^i} \end{cases} \tag{23}$$

so,

$$\frac{\partial m_k}{\partial u_j^i} = s^i(\bar{m}_j^i + \bar{m}_{M+1}^i) \tag{24}$$

and,

$$\frac{\partial E_\nu(x)}{\partial u_j^i} = (P_{\nu,j} - t_j)s^i(\bar{m}_j^i + \bar{m}_{M+1}^i) \tag{25}$$

$$\frac{\partial E_\nu(x)}{\partial \eta^i} = \frac{\partial E_\nu(x)}{\partial s^i}\frac{\partial s^i}{\partial \epsilon^j} = \frac{\partial E_\nu(x)}{\partial s^i}(-2\eta^i(d^i)^2 s^i) \tag{26}$$

$$\frac{\partial E_\nu(x)}{\partial \epsilon^i} = \frac{\partial E_\nu(x)}{\partial s^i} \exp\left(-(\eta^i d^i)^2\right)(1 - \alpha^i)\alpha^i \tag{27}$$

$$\frac{\partial E_\nu(x)}{\partial p_j^i} = \frac{\partial E_\nu(x)}{\partial s^i}\frac{\partial s^i}{\partial p_j^j} = \frac{\partial E_\nu(x)}{\partial s^i}(2(\eta^i)^2 s^i(x_j - p_j^i)) \tag{28}$$

we need to compute $\frac{\partial E_\nu(x)}{\partial s^i}$:

$$\frac{\partial E_\nu(x)}{\partial s^i} = \sum_{k=1}^{M} \frac{\partial E_\nu(x)}{\partial P_{v,k}}\frac{\partial P_{v,k}}{\partial s^i} = \sum_{j=1}^{M}(P_{v,j} - t_j)(\frac{\partial m_j}{\partial s^i} + \nu\frac{\partial m_{M+1}}{\partial s^i})$$

$$= \sum_{j=1}^{M}(P_{v,j} - t_j)(u_j^i(\bar{m}_j^i + \bar{m}_{M+1}^i) - \bar{m}_j^i - \nu\bar{m}_{M+1}^i)$$

4   Experiments

Experiments are conducted on the TrecVid'05 databases [14]. It represents a total of over 85 hours of broadcast news videos from US, Chinese, and Arabic sources. About 60 hours are used to train the feature extraction system and the remaining for the evaluation purpose. The training set is divided into two subsets in order to train classifiers and subsequently the fusion parameters. The evaluation is realized in the context of TrecVid'05 and we use the common evaluation measure from the information retrieval community: the Average Precision.

The feature extraction task consists in retrieving shots expressing one of the following semantic concepts: *1:Building, 2:Car, 3:Explosion or Fire, 4:US flag, 5:Map, 6:Mountain, 7:Prisoner, 8:Sports, 9:People walking/running, 10:Waterscape, 11:Mean Average Precision (MAP).*

The RBF and NN-ET were trained with the same optimization algorithm (gradient descent). The number n of prototypes was varied between 2 and 10. For each value of n, the average training error rates are computed. Our proposed approach yields better results for small values of n and similar performance for higher values of n. The best number is $n = 5$, where we obtain the lower training error.

Figure 5 shows Mean Precision results of the two classifiers fusion methods compared in this work: the standard RBF and the evidence theory neural networks (NN-ET). The improvement in mean precision is clearly visible for all semantic concepts using NN-ET. It is a foreseen result since in the decision rule RBF takes just the *a posterior* probability. NN-ET, in contrast, convert this probability in the form of BBA's, which are then combined using Dempster Shafer rule combination. The fusion output can be presented as a belief function defining for each class a posterior probability interval. The width of this interval can be used as a mesure of the uncertainty attached to a fusion. This approach has been shown to allow decision making with reject options, and to have good classifier fusion performance as compared to other methods.

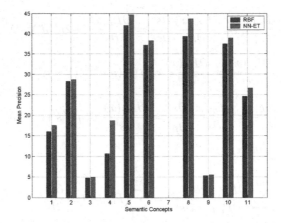

Fig. 5. Comparaison of RBF neural network and Neural Network based on Evidence Theory (NN-ET) fusion method

Besides, NN-ET presents more improvement for the concepts $(4, 5, 8)$ that on the rest, it can be explained, by the high number of false decision in classification using only the *posterior* probability, Evidence theory resolve this issue, introducing the degree of belief in our probability and the ignorance of our system.

We also notice a precision equal to zero for the concept (7), it can be explained by the fact that there is no video shot that represents this concept in the Trecvid'05 test data.

5   Conclusion

In this paper, we have presented an automatic semantic video content indexing and retrieval system. The reported system first employs visual features (HSV Histogram, Gabor filters) in order to obtain a compact and effective representation, followed by SVM based classification to solve the challenging task of video shot content detection. Two methods for combining classifiers are investigated in details. The RBF and Neural network based on Evidence Theory approach that it managed all the features most effectively and appears therefore to be particularly well suited for the task of classifier fusion.

This approach is based on a feeling of uncertainty to the classification model, considering complete or partial knowledge of the class. Inferior and superior expectations as well as of pignistique probability, propose several strategies of decision with arbitrary costs. We think that this methodology can be useful in the situations where the available informations are very incomplete and soiled by uncertainty.

We have started to investigate the effect of the addition of many other visual features (Dominant Color, RGB, Canny edges features,...) as well as audio features (MFCC, PLP, FFT), to see their influence on the final result. The addition of other modalities will allows us to evaluate how the different approaches are able to deal with potentially irrelevant data. In parallel, we have initiated a program of work about descriptor fusion. We believe such an approach, which may be seen as normalization and dimensionality reduction, will have considerable effect on the overall performance of multimedia content analysis algorithms.

References

1. L. Xu, A. Krzyzak, and C. Suen, "Methods of combining multiple classifiers and their application to hardwriting recognition," *IEEE Trans. Systems Man Cybernet*, vol. 22, pp. 418–435, 1992.
2. R. Duin and D. Tax, "Experiements with classifier combining rules," *Proc. First Int. Workshop MCS 2000*, vol. 1857, pp. 16–29, 2000.
3. L. Kuncheva, J.C.Bezdek, and R. Duin, "Decision templates for multiple classifier fusion : an experiemental comparaison," *Pattern Recognition*, vol. 34, pp. 299–314, 2001.
4. R. Benmokhtar and B. Huet, "Classifier fusion : Combination methods for semantic indexing in video content," *Proceedings of ICANN*, vol. 2, pp. 65–74, 2006.
5. P. Felzenszwalb and D. Huttenlocher, "Efficiently computing a good segmentation," *Proceedings of IEEE CVPR*, pp. 98–104, 1998.
6. F. Souvannavong, "Indexation et recherche de plans video par contenu semantique," Ph.D. dissertation, Phd thesis of Eurecom Institute, France, 2005.
7. W. Ma and H. Zhang, "Benchmarking of image features for content-based image retrieval," *Thirtysecond Asilomar Conference on Signals, System and Computers*, pp. 253–257, 1998.
8. C. Carson, M. Thomas, and S. Belongie, "Blobworld: A system for region-based image indexing and retrieval," *Third international conference on visual information systems*, 1999.
9. C. Bishop, "Neural networks for pattern recognition," *Oxford University Press, ch. Radial Basis Functions*, 1995.
10. G. Shafer, "A mathematical theory of evidence," *Princeton University Press*, 1976.
11. P. Smets and R. Kennes, "The transferable belief model," *Artificial Intelligence*, vol. 66, pp. 191–243, 1994.
12. T. Denoeux, "An evidence theoretic neural network classifier," *IEEE. International Conference on Systems, Man and Cybernetics*, vol. 3, pp. 712–717, 1995.
13. ——, "A neural network classifier based on dempster-shafer theory," *IEEE transactions on Systems, Man and Cybernetics*, vol. 2, pp. 131–150, 2000.
14. TRECVID, "Digital video retrieval at NIST," *http://www-nlpir.nist.gov/projects/trecvid/*.

Efficient Search with Changing Similarity Measures on Large Multimedia Datasets

Nataraj Jammalamadaka, Vikram Pudi, and C.V. Jawahar

Center for Visual Information Technology
International Institute of Information Technology
Hyderabad 500032, India
natraj@students.@iiit.ac.in, {vikram,jawahar}@iiit.ac.in

Abstract. In this paper, we consider the problem of finding the k most similar objects given a query object, in large multimedia datasets. We focus on scenarios where the similarity measure itself is not fixed, but is continuously being refined with user feedback. Conventional database techniques for efficient similarity search are not effective in this environment as they take a specific similarity/distance measure as input and build index structures tuned for that measure. Our approach works effectively in this environment as validated by the experimental study where we evaluate it over a wide range of datasets. The experiments show it to be efficient and scalable. In fact, on all our datasets, the response times were within a few seconds, making our approach suitable for interactive applications.

1 Introduction

Information retrieval schemes from multimedia collection often need to compare two multimedia objects and effectively measure their similarity [1,2,3]. A large class of such algorithms represent the multimedia content using an appropriate feature vector and refine the similarity measure using relevance feedback techniques. In this paper, we consider the problem of similarity search when the query object is matched against a large database. In the context of similarity search on large datasets, we specially focus on scenarios where the similarity measure itself is not fixed, but is continuously being refined. User gives direct or indirect feedback regarding whether each retrieved object is indeed similar to the query object or not.

In order to handle large datasets, we employ an index structure that helps narrow down the multimedia objects that actually need to be verified for similarity. The problem of exactly finding the k most similar objects from a large dataset is known to be time consuming. Our algorithm therefore, only attempts to retrieve the k most similar objects, approximately. Our experiments show that most of the objects retrieved are among the true k nearest neighbors.

Existing approaches [4,5,6] for efficient similarity search take a specific similarity measure as input and build index structures tuned for that measure. A few approaches were designed for changing similarity measures [7,8,9,10]. Even they do not perform satisfactorily for multimedia data and associated similarity measures. Realistic multimedia data is characterized by clusters in the data rather than random uniformly distributed data. Associated similarity measures are characterized by a large number

T.-J. Cham et al. (Eds.): MMM 2007, LNCS 4352, Part II, pp. 206–215, 2007.
© Springer-Verlag Berlin Heidelberg 2007

of dimensions where a few are actually dominant – *i.e.*, there is high variance in the weights/relevance of dimensions.

In contrast, our approach works effectively in this environment as validated by our experimental study where we evaluate it over a wide range of situations. The experiments show it to be accurate, efficient and scalable. While existing techniques degrade in the presence of clustered data and widely varying relevances of dimensions, our algorithm actually thrives in their presence. On all our datasets, the response times were within a few seconds, making our approach suitable for interactive applications related to multimedia retrieval.

1.1 Problem Statement

In many multimedia object retrieval systems, user presents the system with a query object (say an image or a video clip) and the system retrieves the k most *similar* objects from a database. Multimedia objects are typically represented by a vector of numeric features $X_1, X_2, \ldots, X_D$ which form a multidimensional space. Several approaches exist to measure similarity between multimedia objects [11,12]. Most of these approaches popularly utilize a weighted Euclidean distance to measure the (dis)similarity between points.

Formally, given a point $X = [X_1, X_2, \ldots, X_D]^T$ in a D-dimensional space and a query point $X' = [X'_1, X'_2, \ldots, X'_D]$, the weighted Euclidean distance between X and X' is given by:

$$distance^2(X, X') = \sum_{i=1}^{D} w_i(X_i - X'_i)^2, \tag{1}$$

where the vector $w_1, w_2, \ldots, w_D$ constitutes the weights along each dimension.

As the multimedia data set grow, scalability is becoming an important issue. When similarity function becomes dynamic, standard data structures become insufficient for the efficient search. We propose a scalable, efficient solution to this problem. We describe our simple and effective solution in Section 2. Performance of the algorithm is comprehensively analyzed in Section 3.

2 Our Approach

The natural approach to design systems for multimedia object retrieval from large databases is to build an *index* for similarity search. Index structures for similarity search is a well-studied field. Unfortunately, most of the available index structures in the literature require a *full* specification of the similarity measure as input. In our context, this is not possible because the similarity measure is continuously being refined by the user during the retrieval session.

Our approach is to build a simple and flexible index structure that can be used for similarity search based on the weighted Euclidean distance measure. It does not require a full specification of the similarity measure as input. Note that the proposed scheme is also applicable to many other distance measures directly or with minimal modifications.

2.1   Index Structure

The index structure is simple: For each of the D dimensions, a list is maintained that contains all the data points sorted along that dimension. In actual implementation, to prevent redundancy, these lists could contain only the pointers or ids of points and the actual points could be stored elsewhere. The lists can be stored on disk and be implemented as $B+$ *trees*.

Insertion and deletion of points from the index structure is simple: it only involves inserting and deleting the projections of those points from the lists of each dimension. These operations can therefore be accomplished in $O(DlogN)$ time for each point, where D is the number of dimensions.

2.2   Retrieval

The retrieval operation is designed to efficiently (but approximately) retrieve the k nearest neighbors of a query point. The pseudo-code of this operation is shown in Figure 1 and is explained below.

> **Retrieve(k, t, X', M):**
> 1 $neighbors = \{\}$
> 2 for each dimension d (in non-increasing order of weights):
> 3 $C = t$ nearest neighbors in dimension d
> 4 $neighbors = k$ nearest neighbors of X' among $(neighbors \cup C)$
> 5 return $neighbors$

Fig. 1. Approximate k-Nearest Neighbor based Retrieval

The algorithm takes as input k: the number of desired nearest neighbors, t: the number of candidate neighbors to consider along each dimension, X': the query point and M: the index structure. The output consists of the k nearest neighbors (approximately).

The neighbors of the query point is initialized to the empty set (in line 1 of Figure 1). Next, the dimensions are enumerated in decreasing order of their weights (line 2) and the nearest t neighbors along each dimension d are retrieved (line 3). This is done by searching for the query point in the list for dimension d in the index structure. This search will retrieve the point closest to the query point. Then, a linear traversal along the list from that point in both directions will retrieve the closest t points.

The t points obtained along each dimension are *candidate* points to be considered for being among the k nearest neighbors of X'. These points are compared with the nearest neighbors so far obtained to determine whether they are to be retained in the k nearest neighbor set, or to be discarded (line 4). Finally, the nearest neighbors obtained after enumerating points along all dimensions are output (in line 5).

2.3   Complexity Analysis

Consider N points in the database. Each point is D dimensional. As mentioned earlier, insertion is an offline process and can be done efficiently.

In the search operation Step 3 takes order complexity of $O(log(N) + D)$ and Step 4 takes $O(D)$. Thus the search operation takes $O(D*logN+k*D^2)$. Since $log(N) >> D$ we have the complexity of the search operation to be $O(D * logN)$. For the methods [7,10] order complexity cannot be arrived at and as the weight vectors improve the performance degrades resulting in looking at most of the disk blocks. We experimentally compare the performance in the next section.

2.4 Rationale Behind Design

Our approach has been to build a simple and flexible index structure that can be used for similarity search based on the weighted Euclidean distance measure. Rather than attempting to modify the index structure as the similarity measure is refined during a user-session, we use the same index structure for any combination of weights.

The key operation at the time of retrieval is to obtain the neighbors of the query point along each dimension. This is easily achieved in our approach since the index structure can access the nearest point in $O(logN)$ time and then merely traverse a linked list to enumerate its neighbors. Our approach works effectively because the neighbors along a particular dimension *do not change* when the weights of dimensions are modified.

The retrieve operation enumerates dimensions in non-increasing order of their weights. This means that the most important dimensions are enumerated first. This makes it likely that most of the true nearest neighbors are retrieved very early during the execution of the algorithm. This can be advantageous in situations where the user is interested in any neighbors that are within a specified threshold distance from the query point.

Finally, it should be noted that the retrieval algorithm only retrieves *approximately*, the k nearest neighbors. This is due to the fact that there may be nearest neighbors that are not among the nearest neighbors along any dimension. To compensate for this, the algorithm actually retrieves t nearest neighbors along each dimension, where $t \geq k$. Our experiments show that good accuracy is obtained for reasonable values of t.

2.5 Shortcomings

Consider the situation in Fig. 2(a). Here, Q is the query point and the circles marked around it are its true nearest neighbors. Let this region be R. Let R_1 be the region of points which are nearer to the query point along the dimension D_1. And let R_2 be the region of points which are nearer to the query point along the dimension $D2$. When the nearest neighbors to the point Q are desired then the points in regions $R1$ and $R2$ may interfere, because they are the closest points along their corresponding dimensions. Thus the algorithm may fail to retrieve the nearest neighbors. On further analysis we can classify this situation into three cases.

1. Consider the case when region R is a dense region. When the dimension D_1 is considered, along with the points in the region R, points in the region R_1 are also likely to be among the nearest neighbors. When computing the nearest neighbors along the dimension D_2, the points in the region R are preferred over those selected from R_1. Likewise, points from R_2 will also get eventually rejected leaving points only from R. Our algorithm is designed to take care of this.

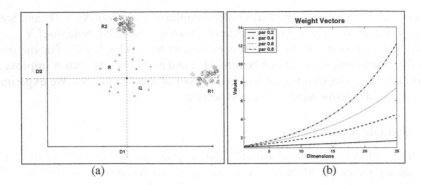

(a)   (b)

Fig. 2. (a) Suspected case of failure (b) Skew of the weight vector is increasing with the value of parameter

2. In the case when region R is sparsely populated, the nearest neighbors along each dimension are not necessarily from region R. Subsequently, many false positives are output by the algorithm. However this situation can be identified by seeing the actual number of intersections during the merge operation. This is then overcome by increasing the t/k ratio.
3. When the query point falls in a region which is extremely sparse, any point retrieved will be irrelevant. If there are no relevant objects in the database, errors in the retrieval process will not affect the overall performance.

3   Performance Study

In this section we evaluate the performance of our approach on both synthetic datasets and real datasets. The synthetic datasets consisted of uniformly distributed, clustered and mixed datasets. The real data set that we employed is from the Corel image collection. All the experiments are performed on a 3 GHz Intel Xeon PC with 4 Gigabytes of main memory, running RedHat Linux 2.6.5-1.

3.1   Accuracy

Since our algorithm only retrieves the k nearest neighbors *approximately*, we have performed detailed experiments to measure its accuracy. We measure accuracy in terms of the number of points retrieved by our algorithm that are actually among the k nearest neighbors. For comparison purposes, the actual k nearest neighbors were found using an exhaustive search algorithm. Accuracy could depend on different factors like the weight distribution and number of points retrieved.

Number of Points Retrieved. Our algorithm takes a parameter t that represents the number of neighboring points to be retrieved. Obviously, accuracy will improve as t is increased. We have therefore experimented with various values of the ratio t/k to determine suitable values for different datasets.

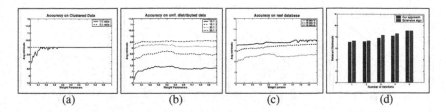

Fig. 3. Performance on various types of data sets. (a) Clustered data (b) Uniform data (c) Real data (Corel dataset) (d) Results of user testing. Our algorithm prefers data sets with concepts. With variances of relevance scores increasing, accuracy increases. Also for most of the weight vectors, our algorithm provides acceptable approximation.

The two curves in the graph of Figure 3 (a) show the accuracy when the values of the t/k ratio is equal to 1 and 5, respectively. The x-axis in this graph represents a parameter that is used to modify the weight vectors (described in Section 3.1) and the y-axis represents the accuracy. The value of k is set to 10. We observed in this graph that as the t/k ratio was increased, the accuracy also increased and reached 100% at 5:1 for all values along the x-axis.

Figure 3 (b) shows the results for the same experiment on the uniform dataset. Here also we observe that with increase in t/k ratio the accuracy goes high. Our algorithm performs better on data sets with one or more clusters (strong concepts). We note that most real-world datasets are likely to contain clusters, rather than being uniformly distributed and hence our approach suits them. This is especially true when the extracted features are relevant to the problem.

Weight Vectors. In order to study the effect of weight vectors on accuracy, we tried various weight vectors for the weighted Euclidean distance metric. Weight vectors denote the importance given to each component (dimension) of the feature vector.

The graph shown in Figure 2(b) shows the weight vectors used. Increase in the values of the component across weight vectors denote the user feedback. A similar plot from the previous experiment given in Figures 3(a) and 3(b) also show the variation of accuracy for different weight vectors. We observe that when the variance of weights is high (i.e, when some dimensions are much more relevant than other dimensions), accuracy is high. The reason for this is that the algorithm takes advantage of dimensions with high weights by enumerating them first. We note that in most multimedia applications, there would be some dimensions that dominate in importance.

Results on Real Database. We have tested the algorithm on the two real world scenarios. In the first scenario we have used a real image database and evaluated our algorithm against it. This experimental results indicate that our algorithm can efficiently perform on real world databases. In the second scenario we subjected our algorithm to user testing. We implemented our algorithm on a standard statistical relevance feedback based image retrieval system.

Figure 3 (c) presents the results of the experiment. We notice that the graph is in accordance the above mentioned results. As the weight vector gets more skewed along the x-axis the accuracy improves. Similarly, as the t/k ratio is increased the accuracy

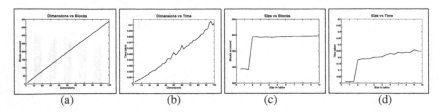

Fig. 4. (a) and (b) suggests that the algorithm has a linear complexity in dimensions and (c) and (d) suggests that the algorithm is logarithmic in size which is desired

improves. Figure 3 (d) gives the total number of relevant retrievals obtained by using our algorithm and the extensive search algorithm as validated by the users . In this experiment the number of desired images are 10 and the result is averaged over 10 users. Note that the accuracy reported in Figure 3 (c) is benchmarked against extensive search procedure. Though the accuracy reported is not 100% Figure 3(c) suggests that the images retrieved by our approach are relevant as validated by the user.

Response Time. We evaluated the response time of our algorithm for different datasets and parameters. We see that flat-files perform better than SQL and R-trees because the overhead of system calls in order to scan all the points is smaller for flat files. For the same reason, SQL performs better than R-trees. Our algorithm performs significantly better than any of these approaches because it does not need to scan through all points of the database – its index can help narrow down the search to only a few points. It may be argued that the R-tree index also could be used to narrow down the search for the k nearest neighbors. Unfortunately, this is not possible because the weight vector indicated in the user-session may be different from what was used in the R-tree construction.

3.2 Scalability

We studied the scalability of the approach in terms of the variation in response time and number of disk block accesses with respect to the database size (number of points) and the dimensionality. These studies were made on the clustered dataset.

Number of Dimensions. Figure 4(a) shows the effect of increasing number of dimensions on the response time of the algorithm. It is seen that the relation is linear. This is expected as per the complexity analysis done in Section 2.3, when $N >> D$. Figure 4(b) shows the effect of increasing the number of dimensions on the number of disk block accesses made by the algorithm. It is again seen that the relation is linear, further explaining the linear nature of the response times. In these graphs, each point is the average over all the 10 weight vectors used in earlier experiments and also over 10 different queries.

Database Size. Figure 4(c) shows the effect of increasing number of database points on the response time of the algorithm. It was seen that the relation is logarithmic. This is expected as per the complexity analysis done in Section 2.3. Figure 4(d) shows the effect of increasing number of database points on the number of disk block accesses made by the algorithm. It was again seen that the relation is logarithmic, further explaining the nature of the response times. Again, note that in these graphs, each point is the average over all the 10 weight vectors used in earlier experiments and also over 10 different queries.

The relationship between the number of blocks accessed and the dimension is given by $Blocks = (Height) * (D) + D * \sum_{i=1}^{D}(LNS(i))$ where Height is the present height of the tree, and $LNS(i)$ is the total leaf nodes accessed in the dimension i. This relationship explains the sudden transition in the Figure 4(d). We have used B+ trees to maintain all the points along each dimensions. Increase in the height of the tree as a result of increase in the size is responsible for the sudden transition. However, it is important to note that after the transition, the number of blocks accessed remained constant in-spite of huge increase in the size of the database (from 0.2 million to 1 million), thus indicating that the approach is efficiently handling *large* databases.

3.3 Comparison with Existing Approaches

Table 1 shows the blocks accessed of our algorithm as compared against the approach in Kurniawati *et al.* [10]. In this table, we show for datasets with varying number of dimensions, the following statistics: (1) LFO: the leaf fan out (2) IFO: inner node fan out (3) ltouch: the number of leaf nodes of the index structures that have been visited by the two approaches, (4) lused: the number of leaf nodes that actually contained some of the k nearest neighbors, and (5) the number of internal nodes accessed (inode). On observing the total number of block accesses($ltouch + lused + inode$) it is clear that our approach is almost consistently better than the approach in Kurniawati *et al.* [10]. In fact, it performs an order of magnitude better for high dimensions, which is often the case in multimedia datasets.

3.4 Heuristics for Performance Enhancement

Different distance functions. We have experimented with two variants of the distance functions with various weight vectors and t/k ratios to choose a better performing distance function both in-terms of accuracy and speed.

The first one is given by the $distance = \sum_{i=1}^{D} weight(i) * (query(i) - db(i))^2$ where D is the number of dimensions of the data. The second is $distance = \sum_{i=1}^{d}(weight(i) * (query(i) - db(i))^2)$ where d is the dimension that the algorithm is looking at. We observed that the second formulation is doing as good as the first function Figure 5(b) in terms of accuracy but in terms of time Figure 5(c) , it outperforms the traditional distance measures.

Stop criteria. Many of the applications have an acceptable accuracy and provides a scope for improvement in speed. At the end of each iteration we have a total number of t candidates(k being desired). Of these few of them(lets say $t1$) will match with result of exhaustive search algorithm. We call these $t1$ entries as correct additions. Observing the correct additions in Figure 5(a), we find that initially there are large number of correct additions, and later this rate decreases. We can safely conclude that at any given time

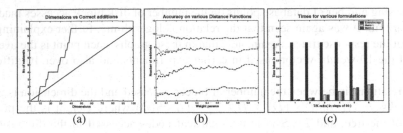

(a)   (b)   (c)

Fig. 5. (a) suggests a possible scenario of how accuracy increases with dimensions. (b) and (c) compare the accuracy and time taken for different distance metrics.

Table 1. Comparison of our approach with an existing one. Ours is an order times better than this, particularly for high dimensions.

Dimension	Our Approach					Kurniawati et al				
	LFO	IFO	ltouch	lused	inode	LFO	IFO	ltouch	lused	inode
2	682	1024	2.1	2.1	4	682	225	1.4	1.4	1
4	409	1024	4.3	4.3	8	409	146	4.5	2.7	2.2
8	227	1024	8.5	8.5	16	227	78	89.5	8.9	4.8
16	120	1024	18.5	18.5	32	120	40	740.6	25.9	20.4
32	62	1024	40.9	40.9	64	62	20	1613.0	41.0	87.0

s ($< T$), the accuracy of the algorithm is approximately $\frac{s}{T}\%$ of the total accuracy of the algorithm. Thus the above observation could be used as stopping criteria, given the acceptable accuracy.

Comments on Implementation. The optimal t/k for a given session may depend on the query scenario. This could be done by estimating the t/k ratio dynamically. The dynamic estimation could be done based on the following observations: (a) With the increase in dimensions the rate of correct additions is going down. (b) With each dimension, the distance(dis) of the ith nearest neighbor decreases. (c) As the t/k ratio increases, the distance of the ith nearest neighbor is decreasing. (d) The amount at which such distance would fall decreases with the t/k ratio.

4 Related Work

Content-based multimedia retrieval has been an active area of research [1,2,3]. Scalability of these approaches for large datasets of images has not received the due attention. A large body of work exists on the study of index structures for similarity search. These algorithms involve building a spatial access tree, such as an R-tree [5], k-d tree [4], SS-tree [6] or their variants. The index structures presented in these papers were novel, elegant, and useful. However they are not applicable in our study as they take a specific similarity measure as input and build index structures tuned for that measure. Recent attempts [7,8,9,10] on this problem focused on scenarios where the similarity measure itself is not fixed, but continuously being refined. These algorithms have taken a branch and bound approach, which may degrade to searching most of the tree structure. In this work, we focus on efficiently retrieving the data, with bounds on the time taken, when similarity measure is varying continuously.

5   Conclusion

In this paper, we addressed the problem of finding the k most similar objects in large datasets given a query object, when similarity measure is continuously being refined with user feedback. Our approach builds a simple index structure that can short-list the points to be considered for nearest neighbor search effectively even without a complete specification of the similarity measure. Experimental study over a wide range of datasets showed our approach to be accurate, efficient and scalable. In fact, on all our datasets, the response times were well within a few seconds, making our approach suitable for interactive applications.

References

1. Huang, T., Zhou, X.: Image retrieval with relevance feedback: From heuristic weight adjustment to optimal learning methods. In: International Conference on Image Processing. (2001) III: 2–5
2. Rui, Y., Thomas, S.H., Chang, S.F.: Image retrieval: Past, present, and future. In: International Symposium on Multimedia Information Processing. (1997)
3. Yang, J., Li, Q., Zhuang, Y.: Towards data-adaptive and user-adaptive image retrieval by peer indexing. International Journal of Computer Vision **56** (2004) 47–63
4. Bentley, J.L.: Multidimensional binary search trees used for associative searcing. Communications of the ACM **18** (1975) 509–517
5. Guttman, A.: R-trees: A dynamic index structure for spatial searching. ACM SIGMOD International Conference on Management of Data (1984) 47–57
6. White, D.A., Jain, R.: Similarity indexing with ss-tree. In Proc 12th International conference on Data Engineering, New Orleans, Louisiana (1996)
7. Faloutsos, C.: Searching multimedia databases by content. Advances in Database Systems. Kluwer Academic Publishers, Boston (1996)
8. Faloutsos, C., Equitz, W., Flickner, M., Niblack, W., Petkovic, D., Barber, R.: Efficient and effective querying in image content. J of Intelligent Information Systems (1994a) 231–262
9. Faloutsos, C., Ranganathan, M., Manolopoulos, Y.: Fast subsequence matching in time-series databases. ACM SIGMOD International Conference on Management of Data (1994b) 419–429
10. Kurniawati, R., Jin, J., Shepherd, J.A.: Efficient nearest-neighbor searches using weighted euclidean metrics. Technical report, Information Engineering Department, School of Computer science and Engineering, University of New South Wales (1998)
11. Rui, Y., Huang, T.S., Mehrotra, S.: Relevance feedback techniques in interactive content-based image retrieval. IS&T and SPIE Storage and Retrieval of Image and Video Databases VI, San Jose, CA, USA, Jan. (1998)
12. Tian, Q., Hong, P., Huang, T.: Update relevant image weights for content-based image retrieval using support vector machines. IEEE Inter. Conf. on Multimedia & Expo **18** (2000) 1199–1202

MuSQL: A Music Structured Query Language*

Chaokun Wang[1], Jianmin Wang[1], Jianzhong Li[2], Jia-Guang Sun[1], and Shengfei Shi[2]

[1] School of Software, Tsinghua University, 100084, Beijing, China
[2] School of Computer Science & Technology, Harbin Institute of Technology, 150001, China
{chaokun,jimwang,sunjg}@tsinghua.edu.cn
{lijzh,shengfei}@hit.edu.cn

Abstract. A music structured query language, called MuSQL, is presented in this paper. MuSQL consists of a schema definition sub-language and a data manipulation sub-language. The former is composed of schema-setup statements, schema-alter statements, and schema-drop statements. The latter is composed of selection, retrieval, extraction, insertion, update, deletion, commission, rollback, and other statements. MuSQL can be used to cut, delete and merge content of music, insert, delete and extract features of music, and exactly or approximately search music pieces, especially in the processing of music based on content. Also, it makes some music processing operations easier due to its built-in semantics. MuSQL has been implemented in a music data management system.

Keywords: Music query languages, structured query languages, music semantics, Backus-Naur Form.

1 Motivation

Query language is a basic aspect in the research field of multimedia data management. However, there is little work on music query languages, though music data become more and more important in the world.

In this paper, a music structured query language, called MuSQL, is proposed, which has been implemented in a music data management system [1]. MuSQL consists of a schema definition sub-language and a data manipulation sub-language. The former is composed of schema-setup statements, schema-alter statements, and schema-drop statements. The latter is composed of selection, retrieval, extraction, insertion, update, deletion, commission, rollback, and other statements. MuSQL can be used to cut, delete and merge content of music, insert, delete and extract features of music, and exactly or approximately search music pieces, especially in the processing of music based on content. Also, it makes some music processing operations easier due to its built-in semantics. To the best of our knowledge, this paper is the first one about structured query languages dedicated to music data.

The remainder of the paper is organized as follows. The related work is reviewed in Section 2. The schema definition sub-language of MuSQL is presented in Section 3. The data manipulation sub-language of MuSQL is proposed in Section 4. Conclusion and future work are given in Section 5.

---

* This work was supported by the NSF of China under Grant No. 60473077 and Program for New Century Excellent Talents in University.

T.-J. Cham et al. (Eds.): MMM 2007, LNCS 4352, Part II, pp. 216–225, 2007.

2   Related Work

The work on query languages is an important part of data management research. The music query language is also a key in a music data management system. Unfortunately, as far as we know, there is little work on this topic. MusicXML was presented as a symbolic music interchange format [2]; however, it needed XML Query to retrieve music data.

There are some general multimedia query languages. Li *et al.* proposed MOQL [3], which was based on ODMG's Object Query Language. Henrich and Robbert presented POQL^{MM} for object-oriented databases [4]. Amato proposed MMQL that was an extension of a traditional object-oriented query language [5]. Chang *et al.* presented QBOE, in which either data definition language or data manipulation language was through an object example [6]. Hirzalla and Karmouch proposed another data model and query language for multimedia data [7]. Zhang *et al.* proposed WebSSQL for querying multimedia data on the web [8]. However some of them are too general to express musical data and operations, while others cannot utilize inherent characteristics of music. A more detailed design is prerequisite to dealing with music data by these languages.

Aside from the preceding multimedia languages, there are some more general query languages. Dionisio and Cárdenas described a visual query language that could express questions over multimedia, timeline, and simulation data using a single set of related query constructs [9]. Arnold-Moore *et al.* presented a data model and query language for accessing structured documents expressed in SGML [10]. Abiteboul *et al.* presented the Lorel language, designed for querying semi-structured data [11]. Unfortunately, they still have the above pitfalls.

Different from music, there are some query languages for image and video. For instance, an ontological query language was proposed for content-based image retrieval [12]. Also, a content-based video query language CVQL was presented for video databases [13]. It is time to have a special query language for music data!

In this paper, the structured query language MuSQL is proposed for this purpose, which is based on the data model presented in [14]. MuSQL consists of many statements that will be described at length in the rest of the paper.

3   The Schema Definition Sub-language

The schema definition sub-language of MuSQL is presented in this section. It includes several statements related to schemas, e.g. schema setup, alter, drop, and so forth.

Backus-Naur Form, abbreviated as BNF, is a symbol set used to describe grammars of computer languages, which is given by John Backus and Peter Naur [15]. Almost every designer of a new programming language uses it to define the syntax rules of his language. In this paper, MuSQL is also described in BNF. The specification of BNF can be found in [15].

3.1   Schema Setup Statements

At first, schema setup statements are considered. They are all initiated by the keyword "CREATE", and are used to determine how to define music bases, music sets, and music views.

Music Base Setup Statements. The syntax of music base setup statements is

$$\langle music\_base\_def \rangle \longrightarrow \texttt{CREATE MUSIC BASE} \ \langle music\_base\_name \rangle$$
$$\langle opt\_base\_element\_list \rangle$$
$$\langle music\_base\_name \rangle \longrightarrow \langle identifier \rangle$$
$$\langle opt\_base\_element\_list \rangle \longrightarrow \epsilon$$
$$| \ \langle opt\_base\_element\_list \rangle \ \langle music\_set\_def \rangle$$
$$| \ \langle opt\_base\_element\_list \rangle \ \langle music\_view\_def \rangle$$

Let's create a music base called music_base_1 that includes no music set. The statement should be

$$\texttt{CREATE MUSIC BASE} \ \texttt{music\_base\_1} ;$$

A more general music base setup statement will be given later.

Music Set Setup Statements. In music set up statements, the definition of $\langle data\_type \rangle$ is

$$\langle data\_type \rangle \longrightarrow \texttt{CHARACTER}$$
$$| \ \texttt{CHARACTER (} \langle int \rangle \ \texttt{)}$$
$$| \ \texttt{INT}$$
$$| \ \texttt{NUMBER (} \langle int \rangle \ \texttt{)}$$
$$| \ \texttt{NUMBER (} \langle int \rangle \ \texttt{, } \langle int \rangle \ \texttt{)}$$
$$| \ \langle lob \rangle \ \langle opt\_lob\_semantic \rangle$$
$$\langle lob \rangle \longrightarrow \texttt{LOBI} \ | \ \texttt{LOBII}$$
$$\langle opt\_lob\_semantic \rangle \longrightarrow \epsilon \ | \ \texttt{(} \langle lob\_semantic \rangle \ \texttt{)}$$
$$\langle lob\_semantic \rangle \longrightarrow \texttt{TIME SECOND} \ \langle starting\_time \rangle \ \langle ending\_time \rangle$$
$$| \ \texttt{TRACK} \ \langle int \rangle$$
$$| \ \texttt{TIME SECOND} \ \langle starting\_time \rangle \ \langle ending\_time \rangle$$
$$\texttt{TRACK} \ \langle int \rangle$$
$$| \ \texttt{TRACK} \ \langle int \rangle$$
$$\texttt{TIME SECOND} \ \langle starting\_time \rangle \ \langle ending\_time \rangle$$
$$\langle starting\_time \rangle \longrightarrow \langle int \rangle$$
$$\langle ending\_time \rangle \longrightarrow \langle int \rangle \ | \ \texttt{INF}$$

Both LOBI and LOBII in the above forms are logical data structures, which are used to respectively store content data and feature data of music pieces. According to the actual requirements and situations, users can design appropriate physical storage structures to implement them. Of course, they can also be made as one same structure.

For convenience, in the implementation of LOBI and LOBII, large objects can be adopted because many existing sophisticated database manage systems support this kind of objects. For instance, in PostgreSQL, the function "lo_create( )" can be used to create large objects, and "lo_read( )"/"lo_write( )" read/write large objects.

Also, the necessary information is incorporated with these two logical types to express correlative semantics of music data. For example, the pattern "TIME SECOND 0

60" means that the corresponding field is relative to time. The time unit is second; the starting time is 0 second; and the ending time is 60 second. The symbol "INF" usually denotes the end time point of a piece of music. In addition, the pattern "TRACK n" is used to represent the n-th music track, where n is a natural number. For instance, the first track of a piece of music is denoted as "TRACK 1".

Example 1. Create a music set that has one meta attribute representing titles of music pieces, three segments of content respectively storing the content from the beginning to 10 seconds, from 10 seconds to 40 seconds and from 40 seconds to the ending, and two feature fields respectively storing the melody from the beginning to 30 seconds and the theme of the whole piece of music. The music set setup statement may be as follows.

```
CREATE MUSIC SET music_set_1
(title CHARACTER(20),
 s0p10 LOBI(TIME SECOND 0 10),
 s10p40 LOBI(TIME SECOND 10 40),
 s40p LOBI(TIME SECOND 40 INF),
 fs0p30 LOBII(TIME SECOND 0 30),
 theme LOBII(TIME SECOND 0 INF));
```

Obviously, the size of "title" can be another number instead of 20 decided by the user.

After such processing, the "lob" type has clearer semantics. And then, MuSQL statements, such as extract statements and retrieve statements introduced later, can deal with music data effectively.

Suppose that a user wants data of the first 30 seconds of pieces of a music set. Based on the semantics bound with ⟨lob_semantic⟩, the retrieval routine can only process data in the fields s0p10 and s10p40 automatically without considering the field s40p. Similarly, suppose that a user wants the melody of the first 20 seconds. Based on the semantics with the field fs0p30, the music data management system can directly intercept the preceding two thirds of this field. If he or she wants the melody of the first 40 seconds, the system will call the extraction routine to get the needed melody from the fields s0p10 and s10p40. It is perhaps requisite to combine the contents of the two fields at first.

Example 2. Create a music base music_base_2 that has two music sets. One called music_set_2 includes titles and melodies of music pieces, and the other called music_set_3 includes the content of the second track in the first 1 minute. Also, the title field in the first music set is not null, and a dependence exists between the two music sets. Without generality, let a field called *id* exist in the two music sets. The *id* field in the second music set is the foreign key of the first music set. And then, the statement may be written as follows.

```
CREATE MUSIC BASE music_base_2
CREATE MUSIC SET music_set_2
(id NUMBER(10) REFERENCE music_set_3(id),
 title CHARACTER(20) NOT NULL,
 theme LOBII(TIME SECOND 0 INF))
CREATE MUSIC SET music_set_3
(id NUMBER(10),
 t2s0p60 LOBI(TRACK 2 TIME SECOND 0 60),
 CONSTRAINT music_set_3_pk PRIMARY KEY(id));
```

Music View Setup Statements. An example of music view setup statement is as follows.

Example 3. Create a music view called music_view_1 from the fields *id* and *title* of the music set music_set_2 of the music base music_base_2. The statement may be

```
CREATE MUSIC VIEW music_view_1
AS SELECT id, title
FROM music_base_2.music_set_2;
```

3.2 Schema Alter Statements

In schema alter statements, "RENAME TO" predicate is used to change the name of a music set. "RENAME COLUMN" predicate only changes the name of a certain given field. "MODIFY" predicate changes types and constraints of given fields. "ARRANGE" predicate is used to arrange the content of music pieces. It alters some content fields to the expected types and implements the cutting operation of the music data model [14]. Obviously the implementation of these predicates needs the compiler to judge the correctness in the semantic analysis phase.

Arrange predicate is a feature of the music_set_alter statement. It is also a speciality of MuSQL. For instance, the following statement splits the field t2s0p60 of the music set music_set_3 into two fields. One stores the first 20 second content of the second track, and the other stores the next 40 second content of that track.

```
ALTER MUSIC SET music_base_3.music_set_1
ARRANGE FROM (t2s0p60)
TO (t2s0p20  LOBI(TRACK 2 TIME SECOND 0   20),
    t2s20p60  LOBI(TRACK 2 TIME SECOND 21  40));
```

The statement

```
ALTER MUSIC BASE music_base_2
RENAME TO music_base_5;
```

renames the music base from music_base_2 to music_base_5.

3.3 Schema Drop Statements

The schema drop statements are initiated with "DROP". For instance, the statement "**DROP MUSIC SET** music_set_1;" drops the music set music_set_1.

4 The Data Manipulation Sub-language

In this section, data manipulation sub-language of MuSQL is presented, which includes select, insert and other statements.

4.1 Select Statements

The select statement is the core of the data manipulation sub-language. Its definition is similar to that in the standard structured query language, such as SQL-2003. The non-terminal symbol ⟨selection⟩ is the content selected, and ⟨music_set_exp⟩ is the source of selection.

⟨select_statement⟩ ⟶ SELECT ⟨opt_all_distinct⟩ ⟨selection⟩
⟨music_set_exp⟩

⟨opt_all_distinct⟩ ⟶ ϵ | ALL | DISTINCT
⟨selection⟩ ⟶ ⟨scalar_exp_commalist⟩ | *
... ...

⟨music_set_exp⟩ ⟶ ⟨from_clause⟩ ⟨opt_where_clause⟩
⟨opt_group_by_clause⟩ ⟨opt_having_clause⟩
⟨opt_set_clause⟩
... ...

The following are some examples about selection statements.

Example 4. List titles of music pieces stored in both music_set_1 and music_set_3.

SELECT title
FROM music_set_1
UNION
(**SELECT** title
FROM music_set_3);

List all composers each of whom has more than 3 music pieces in music_set_3;

SELECT composer
FROM music_set_3
GROUP BY composer
HAVING COUNT (∗) >= 3;

4.2 Retrieve Statements

Both LOBI and LOBII are not considered in the previous selection statements. In MuSQL, retrieval statements are designed to deal with these tasks, whose BNF is as follows.

⟨retrieve_statement⟩ ⟶ RETRIEVE ⟨retrieve_commalist⟩ ⟨from_clause⟩
⟨similar_predicate⟩

⟨retrieve_commalist⟩ ⟶ ϵ | * | ⟨retrieve_column⟩
| ⟨retrieve_commalist⟩ , ⟨retrieve_column⟩

⟨retrieve_column⟩ ⟶ ⟨column_ref⟩ ⟨opt_lob_semantic⟩

⟨similar_predicate⟩ ⟶ SIMILAR ⟨similar_condition⟩ ⟨similar_degree⟩
⟨opt_similar_method⟩

⟨similar_condition⟩ ⟶ NOTE ⟨note_exp⟩ ⟨opt_in_similar_condition⟩
| INTERVAL ⟨interval_exp⟩ ⟨opt_in_similar_condition⟩

⟨opt_in_similar_condition⟩ ⟶ ϵ | IN (⟨similar_commalist⟩)

⟨similar_commalist⟩ ⟶ ⟨similar_column⟩
| ⟨similar_commlist⟩ , ⟨similar_column⟩

⟨similar_column⟩ ⟶ ⟨column_ref⟩ ⟨opt_lob_semantic⟩

There are two methods to represent a segment of music. One method is based on music notes, and the other is based on relations between the consecutive music notes. "NOTE" in the previous BNF represents that the first method is used. For convenience, each of the 128 music notes, through C_3 to g^6, is denoted by a number between 0 and 127. The duration of a music note is not considered in current MuSQL, however it can be added without difficulty.

$$\langle note\_exp \rangle \longrightarrow \langle note\_exp\_num \rangle \mid \langle note\_exp\_char \rangle$$

$$\langle note\_exp\_char \rangle \longrightarrow \langle note\_char \rangle \mid \langle note\_exp\_char \rangle - \langle note\_char \rangle$$

$$\langle note\_exp\_num \rangle \longrightarrow \langle note\_num \rangle \mid \langle note\_exp\_num \rangle - \langle note\_num \rangle$$

$$\langle note\_char \rangle \longrightarrow [\langle music\_level \rangle] \langle note\_element \rangle$$

$$\langle music\_level \rangle \longrightarrow \texttt{HIGH} \mid \texttt{MEDIUM} \mid \texttt{LOW}$$

$$\langle note\_element \rangle \longrightarrow \texttt{DOH} \mid \texttt{RAY} \mid \texttt{MI} \mid \texttt{FA} \mid \texttt{SOL} \mid \texttt{LAH} \mid \texttt{TI}$$

$$\langle note\_num \rangle \longrightarrow \langle int \rangle$$

Convenient for general users, MuSQL provides a simple music input method shown in the above definitions, i.e., a user can just use basic music notes (from DOH to TI) with optional music scales (HIGH, MEDIUM, and LOW). Please notice that the notes and scales used here are only approximate, and then they do not cover all music elements in the whole range from C_3 to g^6.

MuSQL also permits a user to query music pieces based on relations of notes. For example, the current MuSQL uses a character set $\{W, U, R, D, B\}$ to represent this kind of relations. R means the latter note is same to the former note. U means the latter is higher than the former by at most 3 semi-tones. W means the latter is higher than the former by at least 4 semi-tones. D means the latter is lower than the former by at most 3 semi-tones. B means the latter is lower than the former by at least 4 semi-tones. Therewithal, a string consisting of the characters can be used to denote a segment of melody. A user can also utilize another exacter method, i.e., he can use a sequence of signed integers to represent the segment.

$$\langle interval\_exp \rangle \longrightarrow \langle interval\_exp\_num \rangle \mid \langle interval\_exp\_char \rangle$$

$$\langle interval\_exp\_char \rangle \longrightarrow \langle interval\_char \rangle$$
$$\mid \langle interval\_exp\_char \rangle - \langle interval\_char \rangle$$

$$\langle interval\_exp\_num \rangle \longrightarrow \langle interval\_num \rangle$$
$$\mid \langle interval\_exp\_num \rangle \langle interval\_num \rangle$$

$$\langle interval\_char \rangle \longrightarrow \texttt{W} \mid \texttt{U} \mid \texttt{R} \mid \texttt{D} \mid \texttt{B}$$

$$\langle interval\_num \rangle \longrightarrow + \langle int \rangle \mid - \langle int \rangle$$

Furthermore, similarity qualification should be considered. The $m\%$ or n most similar music objects will be selected.

$$\langle similar\_degree \rangle \longrightarrow \texttt{TOP} \langle int \rangle [\texttt{PERCENT}]$$

$$\langle opt\_similar\_method \rangle \longrightarrow \epsilon \mid \langle similar\_method \rangle$$

⟨similar_method⟩ ⟶ UNDER ⟨similar_measure_name⟩

⟨similar_measure_name⟩ ⟶ ⟨identifier⟩

Differing from select statements, retrieve statements focus on music contents and features. The key of retrieval is the "similar" predicate. Firstly, some examples on similar predicate are given, and then several retrieve statements will be presented.

Example 5. Retrieve the top 10 most similar pieces of music, in whose first tracks a segment is similar to "DOH-RAY-MI" under the distance function similar_measure_1.

SIMILAR NOTE DO–RE–MI
IN (t1_1)
TOP 10
UNDER similar_measure_1

Retrieve the top 20% most similar music pieces, in whose beginning 60 seconds content of the second track a segment is similar to "DOH-RAY-MI" under the distance function similar_measure_1.

SIMILAR NOTE DO–RE–MI
IN (t2s0p60)
TOP 20 **PERCENT**
UNDER similar_measure_1

If the default distance measure is used, the "UNDER" clause may be omitted. For example, the default distance measure is used in the following statement.

RETRIEVE id , theme_2 (**TRACK** 3 **TIME SECOND** 0 **INF**)
FROM midi_ds_2
SIMILAR INTERVAL D–B–W–D–B **IN** (melody_1)
TOP 10;

If the ⟨retrieve_commalist⟩ includes lob types, the similar predicate can be used without the "IN" clause. In such situation, based on the ⟨lob_semantic⟩ in the retrieve statement, the retrieval routine should decide whether or not to find the content the user wanted, and how to execute the task efficiently. In other words, the combination of all lob types in ⟨retrieve_commalist⟩ consists of ⟨similar_commalist⟩. It is also one of the advantages derived from the semantics binding of lob types. And then, the statement

RETRIEVE melody_3 (**TRACK** 3 **TIME SECOND** 0 50)
FROM midi_ds_2
SIMILAR INTERVAL +3+5−1+4−5
TOP 10;

is equal to

RETRIEVE melody_3 (**TRACK** 3 **TIME SECOND** 0 50)
FROM midi_ds_2
SIMILAR INTERVAL +3+5−1+4−5
IN melody_3 (**TRACK** 3 **TIME SECOND** 0 50)
TOP 10;

4.3   Extract Statements

The BNF syntax of extract statements is as follows.

$$\langle \text{extract\_statement} \rangle \longrightarrow \text{EXTRACT INTO} \ \langle \text{music\_set\_name} \rangle$$
$$(\ \langle \text{column\_ref\_commalist} \rangle \ )$$
$$\text{FROM} \ \langle \text{music\_set\_name} \rangle$$
$$(\ \langle \text{column\_ref\_commalist} \rangle \ )$$
$$\text{USING} \ \langle \text{extraction\_method\_name} \rangle$$
$$\langle \text{extraction\_method\_name} \rangle \longrightarrow \langle \text{identifier} \rangle$$

Example 6. The statement

EXTRACT INTO music_set_1 (melody_1)
FROM music_set_1 (s0p)
USING extraction_method_1

means extracting melodies from the content field s0p of music set music_set_1 and storing it in the feature field melody_1. The extracting method is extraction_method_1.

Please note that the semantics of melody_1 is also (TIME SECOND 0 INF) if that of s0p is (TIME SECOND 0 INF). That is, the semantics of lob data type is transitive.

Example 7. The following two statements mean that the system extracts the melody of the third track from content fields t3s20p60 and t3s60p of the music set music_set_3 by the method extraction_method_2, and stores it into the field melody_3 of the music set music_set_3. And then it extracts the theme of the third track from that field by method extraction_method_3, and stores it into the field theme_t3 of the music set music_set_4.

EXTRACT INTO music_set_3 (melody_t3)
FROM music_set_2 (t3s20p60 , t3s60p)
USING extraction_method_2;
EXTRACT INTO music_set_4 (theme_t3)
FROM music_set_3 (melody_t3)
USING extraction_method_3;

If the semantics of t3s20t60 and t3s60t are respectively (TRACK 3 TIME SECOND 20 60) and (TRACK 3 TIME SECOND 60 INF), the semantics of the resulting melody_3 is (TRACK 3 TIME SECOND 20 INF).

For the limitation of space, many other statements, such as insert statements, delete statements, update statements, transaction processing statements, and index related statements, cannot be included in the paper.

5   Conclusion and Future Work

A music schema definition sub-language and a music data manipulation sub-language are proposed in this paper. They make up the structured query language MuSQL, which is dedicated to music query processing. MuSQL supports a lot of music operations, and is, so far as we know, the first structured query language focusing on music data. MuSQL is going to be continuously refined in the future.

References

1. Wang, C., Li, J., Shi, S.: The Design and Implementation of a Digital Music Library. International Journal on Digital Libraries **6**(1) (2006) 82–97
2. Good, M.: MusicXML in Practice: Issues in Translation and Analysis. In: Proceedings of the First International Conference MAX 2002: Musical Application Using XML, Milan, Italy (2002) 47–54
3. Li, J.Z., Özsu, M.T., Szafron, D., Oria, V.: MOQL: A Multimedia Object Query Language. In: Proceedings of the Third International Workshop on Multimedia Information Systems, Como, Italy (1997) 19–28
4. Henrich, A., Robbert, G.: POQL^{MM}: A Query Language for Structured Multimedia Documents. In: Proceedings of the First International Workshop on Multimedia Data and Document Engineering, Lyon, Frankreich (2001) 17–26
5. Amato, G., Mainetto, G., Savino, P.: A Query Language for Similarity-Based Retrieval of Multimedia Data. In: Proceedings of the First East-European Symposium on Advances in Databases and Information Systems, St. Petersburg (1997) 196–203
6. Chang, Y.I., Jair, S.H., Chen, H.N.: Design and Implementation of the QBOE Query Language for Multimedia Database Systems. Proceedings of the NSC – Part A: Physical Science and Engineering **21**(3) (1997) 205–221
7. Hirzalla, N., Karmouch, A.: A Data Model and a Query Language for Multimedia Documents Databases. Multimedia Systems **7**(4) (1999) 338–348
8. Zhang, C., Meng, W., Zhang, Z., Wu, Z.: WebSSQL — A Query Language for Multimedia Web Documents. In: Proceedings of the IEEE Advances in Digital Libraries, Washington, DC, USA, IEEE Computer Society (2000) 58–67
9. Dionisio, J.D.N., Cárdenas, A.F.: MQuery: A Visual Query Language for Multimedia, Timeline and Simulation Data. Journal of Visual Languages and Computing **7**(4) (1996) 377–401
10. Arnold-Moore, T., Fuller, M., Lowe, B., Thom, J., Wilkinson, R.: The ELF data model and SGQL query language for structured document databases. In: Proceedings of the Australasian Database Conference, Adelaide, Australia (1995) 17–26
11. Abiteboul, S., Quass, D., McHugh, J., Widom, J., Wiener, J.: The Lorel Query Language for Semistructured Data. International Journal on Digital Libraries **1**(1) (1997) 68–88
12. Town, C., Sinclair, D.: Ontological Query Language for Content Based Image Retrieval. In: Proceedings of IEEE Workshop on Content-based Access of Image and Video Libraries. (2001) 75–81
13. Kuo, T.C., Chen, A.L.: A Content-Based Query Language for Video Databases. In: Proceedings of IEEE International Conference on Multimedia Computing and Systems. (1996) 209–214
14. Wang, C., Li, J., Shi, S.: A Music Data Model and its Application. In: Proceedings of the 10th International Conference on MultiMedia Modeling, Brisbane, Australia, IEEE Computer Society Press (2004) 79–84
15. Peter Naur (ed.): Revised Report on the Algorithmic Language ALGOL 60. Communications of the ACM **3**(5) (1960) 299–314

Hardware Accelerated Skin Deformation
for Animated Crowds

Golam Ashraf[1] and Zhou Junyu[2]

[1] School of Computing, National University of Singapore
gashraf@nus.edu.sg
[2] Electronic Arts, Singapore
zhny@ea.com

Abstract. Real time rendering of animated crowds has many practical multimedia applications. The Graphics Processor Unit (GPU) is being increasingly employed to accelerate associated rendering and deformation calculations. This paper explores skeletal deformation calculations on the GPU for crowds of articulated figures. It compares a few strategies for efficient reuse of such calculations on clones. We further propose ideas that will reduce chances of detecting such duplication. The system has been implemented for modern PCs with Graphics Accelerator cards that support GPU Shader Model 3.0, and come with accelerated bi-directional PCI express bus communication. We have achieved a realistic crowd population of 1000 animated humans at interactive rates.

Keywords: skeletal deformation, skinning, crowd animation, GPGPU.

1 Introduction

The convergence of high quality audio, video, images and computer graphics has made current multimedia applications exciting and immersive. Recent advances in dedicated programmable hardware technologies open up a realm of possibilities for "faster, better and more". In the computer graphics domain, high quality rendering and animation are fast approaching real time performance.

These trends serve as principal motivation for this work. We have chosen articulated crowd rendering as a case study because of its wide application and compute intensive requirements. Smooth skin deformation for 3D avatars is expensive because every skin mesh vertex is affected by a few nearby skeletal joints and needs several matrix multiplications before weighted blending of each of the contributing deformations. A crowd of skinned 3D avatars has wide application in movies, games and interactive virtual environments (e.g. virtual shopping malls, discos, battlefields, insect colonies, etc.).

The main contributions of this paper can be summarized as follows: 1) Novel usage of graphics acceleration hardware for PCs to compute articulated skeletal deformation. 2) Comparison of different hardware accelerated skeletal deformation strategies for crowds. 3) Ideas for spatio-temporally distributing reused animation to clones without hampering visual aesthetics.

T.-J. Cham et al. (Eds.): MMM 2007, LNCS 4352, Part II, pp. 226–237, 2007.
© Springer-Verlag Berlin Heidelberg 2007

Fig. 1. Cached hardware skinning with geometry instancing for real time rendering of 1000 animated 3D humanoids. Judicious placement and cycle-time offsets of clones minimizes perceivable repetition. Character model and animation cycles sourced from [12].

A full fledged crowd animation system is beyond the scope of this paper. Thus we do not delve into essentials of crowd behavior like flocking, collision avoidance and navigation. The techniques proposed here can be easily integrated into the low level motor control and render modules of crowd animation systems. We also limit our discussion to CPU-GPU combinations in modern PCs, as these systems are more accessible to third party development than consoles.

This paper briefly introduces the GPU programmable pipeline and explains different ways in which the skeletal deformation model can be mapped on CPU-GPU systems. More specifically, we compare skinning calculations for the following cases: 1) Entirely on the CPU (*brute force software skinning*; serves as control case); 2) Per-individual skinning on the GPU (*brute force hardware skinning*); 3) Object space skinning computed for all current animated sets, and subsequently reusing them via: a) Intra GPU caching (*Vertex Texture Fetch*); b) GPU-CPU alternation (*texture read-back*). The last two methods employ a technique known as *hardware instancing* during the render pass. The idea is to reuse the same object space mesh data resident on the hardware buffer by repeatedly multiplying it with every member in another global transformation matrix list. This way, the amount of data transfer between the CPU and GPU is drastically reduced.

This paper is organized as follows: 2) Related work; 3) Brief introduction of GPU programmable pipeline; 4) Mapping of skeletal deformation on GPU; 5) Reduction of cloning artifacts; 6) Comparison of different skinning methods; 7) Summary.

2 Related Work

Accelerated crowd rendering has received a fair amount of interest. We examine some of these object and image based techniques employed recently. Skeletal deformation by itself is not without artifacts and may require pose-space refinements [8]. Such refinements via subspace deformation [7] and statistical estimation of skeletal motion from moving meshes [6] have been mapped to hardware. While these techniques have been used to render crowds with LOD and collisions, optimized hardware implementation issues have not been adequately addressed.

Tecchia et al. [14,15] present an image based rendering technique to achieve real-time rendering of hundreds of virtual humans. They replaced expensive geometric meshes with pre-rendered image impostors. A set of images of the human model are rendered offline from different viewing angles. During real-time simulation, the candidate image is chosen based on the angle between the camera and the imposter plane's forward vector, and the current pose for that sprite animation. This method is ideal for simple articulated figures like insects, but proves impractical for more complex creatures like humanoids. Apart from consuming a lot of texture memory, the visual quality for imposters near the camera is poor. The lack of depth and the fixed lighting conditions are easily discernable.

Aubel et al [1] proposed dynamically generated imposters to represent the virtual humans. Since unused poses are not stored, this method is much more memory efficient. They further economize the imposter representation by not storing every pose in the sprite animation. They perform a distance threshold between various parts of the skeleton to measure significant change in posture, and only the significant postures are cached.

In order to alleviate poor visual quality without sacrificing speed, different representations have been used for the same crowd avatar under different situations. Luebke D. et al [9] implement a level of detail (LOD) representation based on camera distance. Dobbyn et al [4] presents a novel hybrid combination of image-based and detailed geometric rendering system for crowds. By switching between the two representations, based on a "pixel to texel" ratio, their system can balance well between visual quality and performance, with low popping artifacts.

Coic et al [2] proposed a realistic real-time crowd rendering system based on three levels of detail (LOD). For close-up objects, they use a polygonal representation. At the intermediate level, they adapt a layered impostor technique to animated objects. As the object gets further, the number of layers is gradually reduced to finally reach the third-level, a one-polygon impostor. Pettré et al [13] recently adapted this technique for automatic terrain navigation using cylindrical connectivity graphs.

The game development community enjoys active support from software and hardware companies like Microsoft and NIVIDA. Periodic releases of SDK code samples provide a wealth of insight into current GPU technology [10,12]. Among these samples, we find NVIDIA's Vertex Texture Fetch (verlet integration in pixel shader and subsequent caching from vertex shader) and Microsoft's Geometry Instancing (one shot rendering of thousands of meshes using separate attribute and geometry buffers) very useful. These examples provide the basis of our exploration into efficient ways of exploiting the GPU for crowd rendering.

Almost all the crowd rendering systems described above [1,2,4,9,14,15] have been implemented to maximize CPU resources. As the GPU evolves and becomes more powerful, more operations can be offloaded to it from the CPU. Furthermore the GPU supports deep pipelined parallel (4-16 units) computation. So a well formulated problem can be computed much faster on the GPU [5]. However there are associated limitations to data structures and dependencies typical to such Single Instruction Multiple Data (SIMD) architectures. It is this area which our paper focuses on, comparing known GPU computation techniques and proposing faster ways of implementing high quality crowds of 3D avatars.

3 Background

3.1 GPU Pipeline

We briefly explain the portions relevant to our implementation here and refer the reader to [4] for more detailed information. The GPU has three main stages: primitive, vertex and pixel operations. Standard graphics operations have been implemented in hardware, commonly known as the Fixed Function Pipeline. Thus a mesh can be rendered with the default hardware encoded algorithms without writing a single line of GPU code. This fixed function pipeline can be overridden in modern GPUs at the vertex and pixel processing stages. GPU code, commonly referred to as *shaders*, can be written to manipulate vertex (positions, colors and normals) and pixel (colors, texture UVs, etc.) attributes.

The onboard graphics RAM (*VRAM*) is divided into 3 main parts: input data buffer, texture memory and output frame buffer. Typical sizes on consumer grade graphics cards range from 128MB to 256MB. Given the modest size of VRAMs, cached texture and model data need to be allocated with great care. The convention for developing shaders and hardware standards is usually defined by Shader Model X. We use Shader Model 3.0, as it supports access to texture memory from the vertex pipeline. Such access was unsupported earlier, since textures were meant to be manipulated just by the pixel pipeline.

The programmable vertex and pixel sections comprise of parallel logic units that accept individual data units from the input stream and run individual copies of the shader program instructions. The number of programmable pixel units is usually 4-6 times that of vertex units with faster access to texture memory. Thus the pixel pipeline is the preferred workhorse for multi-pass GPU simulations, where the simulation is computed into a texture by the first-pass pixel shader, to be subsequently processed by the second-pass vertex and pixel shaders.

3.2 Skinning

Skinning is a popular deformation technique for articulated figures. The mesh surface deforms according to the underlying bone hierarchy. Each mesh vertex is associated with normalized weights to one or more joints from the skeletal hierarchy. The skin deformation weights are used to interpolate the final position based upon the world space transformation of the bones, as shown in Eqn. 1.

$$\mathbf{v}'' = \sum w_i \mathbf{v}' \cdot \mathbf{B}_i^{-1} \cdot \mathbf{W}_i \tag{1}$$

where:

$\mathbf{v}''$: final vertex position in world space
w_i: weight of $joint_i$ and $\sum w_i = 1$
$\mathbf{v}'$: untransformed vertex position
$\mathbf{B}_i$: binding matrix (world matrix of $joint_i$ during initial skin attachment)
$\mathbf{W}_i$: current world matrix of $joint_i$ after computing forward kinematics.

Since **B** remains constant, $\mathbf{v}' . \mathbf{B}^{-1}$ can be pre-computed in order to optimize the skinning calculations. Having introduced the GPU pipeline and basic skeletal deformation theory, we now summarize some popular hardware and software skinning implementations.

Fixed Function Non-Indexed Skinning: The GPU can load up to four world matrices at a time and transform the vertices influenced by those four matrices. This process continues until all faces of the mesh are rendered.

Fixed Function Indexed Skinning: The GPU maintains a matrix palette. The maximum palette size varies between different devices. Each vertex in the mesh has up to four indices to identify the matrices in the palette that influence the vertex.

Shader-based skinning: Instead of using the hardware-supported matrix palette, the application loads the matrices into shader constant registers. Each mesh vertex loaded into the vertex buffer must have the following attributes: position, normal, bone indices and bone weights. The vertex shader operates on an individual vertex at a time, using the bone indices to read in the matrix values from the constant palette, and performs the blended skinning transformation shown in Eqn. (1).

Software Skinning: The deformation calculations are done completely by the CPU. The process takes an input mesh and the bone matrices, carries out the transformation and blending, then writes the result into another mesh. The resulting geometry represents the animation pose desired and can be sent to the GPU for rendering. Though CPU skinning is slower it is still popular as it easily supports post-skinning animation/geometry computations like collision, fur tracking, etc.

3.3 Hardware Instancing

Modern GPUs support hardware instancing by allowing separate attribute and geometry buffers. This way, for N instances of a given object, $N-1$ instances of the mesh need not be transmitted to the GPU, but simply reconstructed repetitively from the attribute set and the geometry set. This is much faster than software instancing and other verbose constructions of the display list.

Having introduced the basics of GPU pipeline, skinning theory and hardware implementations, we are now ready to cohesively explain our comparisons and findings for the optimal skeletal deformation technique for crowds. We heavily utilize Pixel Shader programming [5], Hardware Instancing [12] and Vertex Texture Fetch [10] in our implementations so the reader is advised to get more information on these topics.

4   Deformation Strategies for Crowds

The default way to render an avatar is to calculate its skin deformation once every frame. This may be alright for a crowd of up to 20-30 individuals. When implementing large crowds, per-avatar skin deformation and rendering becomes impractical. We clearly need to reuse animation, and hence the associated skin deformation calculations. We know that the GPU can calculate this faster than the CPU. However, the limited support for data structures and several additional programming steps prove as deterrents to crowd animation.

We exploit GPU skinning and prove that it is worth the extra trouble when calculating skinning for a significant number of poses every frame. The idea is to first calculate these poses in object space, and then apply an additional transformation matrix to place the clones in the virtual world. The best way to calculate reusable information on the GPU is to employ pixel-shaded simulation textures. Thus our core skinning algorithm is implemented in the pixel shader. Note that pixel shaders cannot directly access the attributes of every vertex in their original geometry form as they only receive a rasterized image of the geometry after camera projection and visibility culling. In order to ensure that every mesh vertex is correctly deformed in the pixel shader, we need to employ the simulation texture approach popular to General Purpose GPU computing [11].

4.1 Implementation Overview

Fig. 2 illustrates the main stages of our reusable hardware skinning implementation.

Step1. All necessary input attributes (position, normal, bone indices and skin weights) need to be packed into 2D textures (on the VRAM) that can be accessed by the *simulation* pixel shader.

Step2. A quad is then "rendered" with a dummy vertex shader, and the intended simulation pixel shader, such that every rasterized pixel on the quad corresponds to an associated vertex on the original skin mesh. The four corner vertices of the quad contain extreme texture coordinates (0,0), (1,0), (0,1) and (1,1), so that the interpolated texture coordinates for every rasterized pixel correctly reference the associated mesh vertex values in the input attribute textures.

Step3. The simulation pixel shader stores the deformation results in an output texture. This output texture can either be copied back to the system RAM (for subsequent construction of the geometry buffer by the CPU) or simply read back from the second-pass vertex shader (using Vertex Texture Fetch [10] technology).

We will discuss the performance of both methods later. Both methods use efficient hardware instancing introduced in Sec. 3.3, where all clone instances are rendered out with one primitive draw call. Let us now explain the details of each stage.

4.2 Texture Packing

Since a color texel can store only a maximum of 4 fields (*RGBA*), we need four textures to store all the necessary skinning information. This texture packing is done only once after loading the base mesh and before running the skinning simulation. In Fig. 2, each input texel stores the following information:

a. *TA* stores four bone weights
b. *TB* stores four blending indices
c. *TC* stores object space vertex positions and *u* color texture coordinate
d. *TD* stores object space normals and *v* texture coordinate

Textures *T1* and *T2* are the simulation textures containing the skinned positions and normals respectively. In modern GPUS, multiple render targets of 4-16 textures are possible for each pixel shader pass. So the values of *T1* and *T2* are calculated together and simply written out to different textures.

We now describe some important DirectX and HLSL level implementation details. For reasons of efficiency all our textures are squares, of dimension to the power of 2. All input textures are created with the flag *D3DPOOL_MANAGED*. This flag ensures that the Direct3D API maintains the texture in system RAM and makes a copy into VRAM whenever needed. Thus input texture resources do not need to be freed and recreated when the device is lost. The two output textures *T1* and *T2* are created with *D3DPOOL_DEFAULT* flag reserved for render target usage.

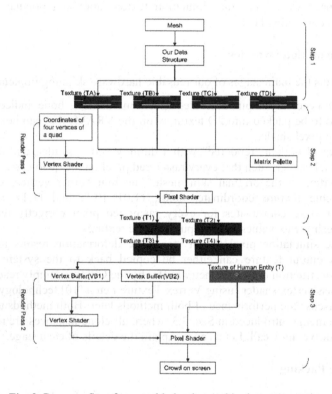

Fig. 2. Program flow for reusable hardware skinning computation

4.3 Hardware Skinning

As explained earlier in Step 2 in Sec. 4.1, a flat quad (the same size as the 2D skin mesh array) is rendered out to a texture in the simulation pass. The vertex shader does nothing except copying extra parameters onto the output structure, as the quad is already drawn in 2D screen coordinates. The subsequent pixel shader fetches the information from *TA, TB, TC* and *TD*, calculates the skinning information, and stores it into *T1* (positions) and *T2* (normals). An HLSL code fragment from the smooth skinning pixel shader is shown below.

```
struct MRTOUTPUT f
{
    half4 a : COLOR0 ;
    half4 b : COLOR1 ;
}

MRTOUTPUT SmoothSkin ( float4 input : POSITION,
                       uniform int iNumBones )
{
    half4 vPos = 0.0f ;
    half3 vNor = 0.0f ;
    float4 value1        = tex2D(textureA, input.Tex0);
    float4 aiIndices     = tex2D(textureB, input.Tex0);
    float4 position      = tex2D(textureC, input.Tex0);
    float4 normal        = tex2D(textureD, input.Tex0);
    float3 afBlendWeights = value1.xyz ;
    float fWeight, fLastWeight = 1.0 ;

    for (iBone = 0 ; iBone<3 && iBone < iNumBones; ++iBone )
    {
        fWeight = afBlendWeights [ iBone ] ;
        fLastWeight -= fWeight;
        vPos.xyz += mul(position, amPalette[aiIndices[iBone]])
                        * fWeight;
        vNor.xyz += mul(normal, amPalette[aiIndices[iBone]])
                        * fWeight;
    }
    vPos.xyz += mul(position, amPalette[aiIndices[iNumBones]])
                    * fLastWeight;
    vNor.xyz += mul( normal , amPalette[aiIndices[iNumBones]])
                    * fLastWeight;
    vNor = normalize (vNor) ;
    vPos.w = value1.z;

    MRTOUTPUT output;
    output . a = vPos;
    output . b = half4 (vNor , value1 .w) ;
    return output ;
}
```

4.4 Geometry Creation

Having explained the details of the packing and skinning stages, let us now describe the geometry creation stage (Step 3 in Sec. 4.1) in more detail. As mentioned earlier, there are two ways of accessing the object space skinning calculations for a posed avatar. 1) Read back these textures to system RAM. 2) Employ Vertex Texture Fetch from the GPU's vertex pipeline.

For the read back method, we incur a penalty for having to lock the render targets and copy the values from *T1* and *T2* to two new textures in system memory (*T3* and *T4* respectively). The skinned information is then transferred to a geometry data buffer (*VB1* in Fig. 2) in the VRAM. The per-instance attribute data, namely the individual global affine transformations, is saved in another VRAM buffer (*VB2* in

Fig. 2). During each hardware instancing cycle, all the elements in *VB1* are multiplied with the current element in *VB2*, to create the cloned instance.

For the Vertex Texture Fetch method, none of the simulation textures need to be read back to the system RAM. The CPU merely writes out a one time dummy geometry buffer that just contains the look up indices to the simulation textures. The abovementioned attribute buffer (*VB2*) still needs to be updated by the CPU. In the vertex shader, the corresponding object space position and normal information will be fetched from the simulation textures (*T1* and *T2*), before multiplying with the affine transformation provided in *VB2*. In the current range of GPUs, fetching texture data from the vertex pipeline is expensive. When done repeatedly (as in our application), this could give rise to severe performance drops. We realized through our experiments, that the same technique that yields superior performance for one-time vertex texture fetch methods like wave simulation [10], fails for repetitive accesses. Thus, the seemingly expensive CPU read-back and re-transfer of skinned information from GPU texture memory back to GPU buffer memory via the system RAM, outperforms Vertex Texture Fetch *when a large number of instances are involved.*

After the geometry is recreated for each instance, lighting calculations based on the skinned normal enhance the existing surface color texture. In the second render pass, apart from the geometry creation, the lighting is usually done in the vertex shader, and the final skin texturing is usually done in the pixel shader.

4.5 Texture Optimizations

Since the locking of GPU textures is expensive, and it is a necessary evil for the better performing read-back method (Sec. 4.4), we attempt to reduce the number of locks by combining the two simulation textures (*T1* and *T2*) to one larger texture. We simply store contents of *T2* at a fixed offset in *T1*. When retrieving values we just add an offset for the second lookup (normal). This entails significant performance gains as shown in Sec. 6.

5 Reducing Cloning Artifacts

Size, orientation and placement: The attribute buffer currently has four float components. The first two components store horizontal offsets (floor height can be determined from terrain height map), the third component specifies the scale, and the fourth component defines an angle to a common forward vector. By ensuring that the clones are suitably separated from each other, and move in different directions, a large part of the repetition perception problem is solved. For enhanced realism, the instance attribute buffer can be further enriched with color, material and slight geometric offset variations. We are continuing to work on the last aspect and hope to achieve an expressive parameter driven local deformation function that can. easily disguise two clones with slightly different overlaid geometry offsets.

Temporal Offsets: Though not as effective as judicious mixing of different sets of clones (acting out different motions), as outlined above, this idea can further introduce subtle variations among clones, especially for acyclic motions (e.g. waving, kicking, etc.).

Combining the ideas above, we implemented the following steps for satisfactorily reducing cloning artifacts. Assuming we need to render a crowd of N individuals, who are capable of M actions, and an average unit length of L frames per action, in order to get maximum variation:

a.   We divide the crowd into M *groups* of N/M clones. Every group acts on a particular motion, and may transit into another related motion cycle after some time.

b.   Every clone from a given group is placed as far as possible from other clones within the field of motion, with slightly randomized directions and sizes.

c.   Within a given group, we cache X skinned poses, (where $X <= L$), and distribute the X poses to sets of maximally separated $N/(M*X)$ clone sub groups. The cached skin deformation textures can be maintained in a queue. We can eventually cache all the skin poses if there is enough storage space in the system RAM. Otherwise, we can simply pop the oldest texture and push in new textures in the queue.

d.   Each sub group of clones is batch rendered.

These ideas allow us to create more variation in our animated crowds, and can be easily incorporated in the behavior and motor control modules of crowd AI. Though recent works on crowd navigation [13] address the variation problem more comprehensively with terrain analysis, path planning, and hierarchical billboards, the methods proposed here are simple and yield reasonable results as well. Fig. 1 shows the result of rendering 1000 instances after we integrate all the above ideas. The example uses 3 actions and each action sub-group uses one of 15 cached skin poses.

6   Results

We ran our experiments on a 3.2GHz CPU with 1GB RAM, PCI express bus, GeForce 6600 GPU and 128MB DDR2 VRAM. For brevity, we number our test cases here and refer to them with these numbers for the rest of this section. We had to unfortunately omit the "Render to Vertex Buffer" option as DirectX 9.0 (our current implantation platform) does not yet support that option. We subjected these methods to different instance loads, ranging from 100 to 1000 avatars. Sample clips can be found in [16].

1. Brute force hardware skinning (*h/w skin* in Fig. 3)
2. Brute force software skinning (*s/w skin* in Fig. 3)
3. Vertex Texture Fetch in our modified model (*vtx fetch* in Fig. 3)
4. One Combined Texture Read Back in our modified model (*readback* in Fig. 3)

In order to achieve a fair comparison, we applied the same animation (with identical clone attribute variation) to the instances for all the cases. We also disabled collision detection as we wanted to minimize additional work done by the CPU, as this would unfairly favor the GPU intensive skinning methods. For methods 1 and 2, in the original model, each instance randomly fetches an animation track from the animation set (*walk, idle, run*) and randomly selects a position to move to if it is

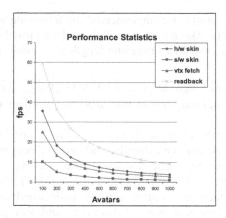

Fig. 3. Performance statistics

currently in the *walk* or *run* tracks. For methods 3 and 4, only one skinning calculation is done per frame, and then this skinning information is used to render the whole group (no caching and no mixing of groups).

From Fig. 3, we can see that method 4 performs significantly better than the rest for larger crowds. It produces the best results as we minimize the number of texture locks and successfully beat current crowd deformation techniques (methods 1 and 2). Though the performance dropped exponentially with the number of instances, we achieved a reasonably interactive rate of 10fps for a 1000 strong crowd without using any LODs or texture imposters, and it is 3-5 times better than existing hardware skinning methods. We also noticed a jump in performance when we removed conditional statements from our simulation pixel shader. Method 3 performs better than method 2, but loses out to methods 1 and 4 because of the expensive cumulative vertex texture fetch latency. Perhaps this will cease to be a problem in future hardware implementations, so we cannot rule out its potential yet.

7 Conclusion

The main contributions of this project can be summarized as follows:

1. We have proposed a novel pixel shader and hardware instancing approach to reusable hardware skinning for crowds.
2. We have compared different skin deformation computation strategies for PCs with graphics hardware acceleration and have identified a CPU-GPU approach as the most optimal method.
3. We have achieved realistic crowds with a small number of motions by carefully mixing up the cloned instances and employing temporal offsets to cached skin textures.

Acknowledgments. This research is supported by School of Computing, National University of Singapore Faculty Research Grant (R252000215112). We appreciate the insightful comments from our reviewers.

References

1. Aubel A., Boulic R., Thalmann D., *Real-time display of virtual humans: Levels of details and impostors.* IEEE Transactions on Circuits and Systems for Video Technology 10:2, pp 207-217, 2000.
2. Coic J., Loscos C., Meyer A.: Three LOD for the realistic and real-time rendering of crowds with dynamic lighting.(2005)
3. Daniel Jeppsson, *Real-time Character Animation Blending Using Weighted Skeleton Hierarchies*, 2000
4. Dobbyn S., Hamill J., Conor K. O., Sullivan C. O, *Geopstors: A real-time geometry/impostor crowd rendering system*, Symposium on Interactive 3D 2005
5. GPU Gems 2: Programming Techniques for High-Performance Graphics and General-Purpose Computation, Chapter 30, 33.(2005)
6. James D. L. and Twigg Christopher D., *Skinning mesh animations*. ACM Trans. Graph., 24(3):399-407
7. Kry P. G., James D. L., and Pai D. K. *Eigenskin: Real time large deformation character skinning in hardware*, ACM SIGGRAPH 2002
8. Lewis J.P., Cordner M., and Fong N., *Pose Space Deformation: A Unified Approach to Shape Interpolation and Skeleton Driven Deformation*, SIGGRAPH 2000
9. Luebke D., Watson B. Cohen J. Reddy M. Varshney, *Level of detail for 3D Computer Graphics*. Elsevier Science,. 2002
10. NVidia Samples: www.nvidia.com
11. GPGPU: General-Purpose computation on GPUs, http://www.gpgpu.org/
12. Microsoft DirectX SDK 9.0 - DirectX sample browser: *MultiAnimation*
13. Pettré, J., Ciechomski, P. d., Maïm, J., Yersin, B., Laumond, J., and Thalmann, D.: Real-time navigating crowds: scalable simulation and rendering: Computer Animation and Virtual Worlds 17, 3-4 (Jul. 2006), 445-455.
14. Tecchia F.,Chrysanthou Y., *Real-time rendering of densely populated urban environments*, Eurographics Rendering Workshop, 2000
15. Tecchia F., Loscos C., Chrysanthou Y, *Image-based crowd rendering*, IEEE Computer Graphics and Applications, 2002
16. Zhou J., and G. Ashraf, Hardware Accelerated Crowd skinning Demonstration: Video clips, http://www.comp.nus.edu.sg/~ashraf/papers/hwSkinning

Multimedia Web Services for an Object Tracking and Highlighting Application

Feng Lu and Liang-Tien Chia

Center for Multimedia and Network Technology, School of Computer Enginnering,
Nanyang Technological University, Singapore 639798
{lufeng, asltchia}@ntu.edu.sg

Abstract. Over the years, multimedia applications are getting increasingly more complex and large in scale. Multimedia Web Service is identified as one of the possible solutions to meet the challenges. The advantages of using Web Services are ease of application development, adaptive to changes, fault tolerance and etc. In the paper, a sample tracking application will be discussed and developed using multimedia Web Services (multimediaWS) approach. Throughout the paper, we will suggest some general rules on designing the multimediaWS as well as evaluate the pros and cons of using multimediaWS for multimedia application.

Keywords: Web Service, Multimedia service composition, Object tracking.

1 Introduction

The recent advances in distributed computing have made platform-independent software components, called Web Service, a growing trend in software architecture design. The process of dynamically compositing existing services to provide new functionalities has emerged as a cost effective way to deploy new network based distributed services. Coupled with the ease of Web Service composition not only enables the reuse of existing services, but also provides an attractive way for adaptive and customized multimedia applications.

1.1 Web Service Composition

There are two ways to describe the functionality of a Web Services, namely *semantic annotation* of what it does and *functional annotation* of how it behaves. In this paper, only the *functional annotation* approach will be presented. Web Service Description Language (WSDL) [1] is used to describe the Web Services, which specifies the syntax of messages that enter or leave a Web Service. WSDL, on the other hand does not handle the order of how the Web Services should be invoked. Web Service composition is defined as the problem of composing autonomous services to achieve new functionality [2]. Over the last few years, many Web Services flow specification language like WSCI [3] and BPEL4WS [4] are proposed for business domain application. However, most of the service compositions are still manually obtained.

T.-J. Cham et al. (Eds.): MMM 2007, LNCS 4352, Part II, pp. 238–247, 2007.
© Springer-Verlag Berlin Heidelberg 2007

1.2 Multimedia Web Services

Even up to today, most multimedia systems still rely heavily on building monolithic systems that need to be reengineered for every change in the application and little of which can be reused in subsequent developments even for similar applications [5]. Due to its service-oriented nature, Web Service composition has recently received increasing interests from the multimedia community to be the solution to build complex, large scale, flexible and adaptive multimedia applications. K. Nahrstedt and W. T. Balke summarized the challenges and status in building large scale multimedia systems and discussed the possibility of using Web Service composition as a solution [5]. S.Kalasapur, M. Kumar and B. Shirazi have researched the seamless integration of Web Services, with particular reference to a pervasive environment [6]. J.Liang and K. Nahrstedt further investigated service composition in advanced multimedia systems which consist of multiple content sources and destinations with different receiver requirements [7].

   To the best of our knowledge, most of the papers are concerned with the higher level issues of Web Service usage in multimedia application, such as service discovery and QoS. Most of these discussions are based on simulation and little work has been done to build up any actual multimedia system by using multimediaWS composition. Moreover, few people have investigated how web services should be systematically designed. In this regard, we realize that there is a need to develop a real application based on multimediaWS composition and propose general guidelines for multimediaWS design. In this paper, tracking application based on multimediaWS is elaborated, including its design principles, problems encountered during implementation, and evaluation of using multimediaWS. Tracking application is chosen because it's a representative and typical multimedia application.

1.3 Organization of Paper

The remainder of the paper is organized as follows. Section 2 presents the background and system architecture. Section 3 describes detailed design of the tracking application while section 4 discusses the experimental evaluation and pros/cons of using multimediaWS. In the end, conclusions are drawn in section 5.

2 Background and System Architecture

In this section, we will first introduce our tracking application, followed by a detailed study of various tasks involved. After that, necessary details regarding the hardware used in this application is presented.

2.1 Introduction to a Tracking Application

The goal of this application is not to improve on the various tracking applications in the literature [8], but to demonstrate the process of building up multimedia application based on multimediaWS. More importantly, to illustrate the consideration and issues identified during the project development.

The object tracking and highlighting application consists of two types of cameras and a 3M projector. At any time instance, only one camera will be used. Whenever a moving object (e.g. human) is detected, the projector will shine a beam on it and the light will follow the movement of that particular object.

Following assumptions are made at the beginning of the application: The location transformation matrix for the cameras and projectors are available. The network and multimediaWS provider are always accessible to the end users.

2.2 Object Tracking and Highlighting Tasks

An object tracking and highlighting application needs to carry out several processing tasks in order to accomplish its goals. Following are the key tasks involved:

Image capturing: First, the application needs to continuously obtain images from the camera. Due to the distributed nature of multimediaWS composition, it is important to minimize the latency in acquiring the image sources.

Object localization: Once a new image frame arrives, the application needs to perform motion detection and subsequently determine the location of the object.

Location transformation: Due to the different orientation of cameras and projectors, the location information obtained with reference to the camera system needs to be transformed into projector coordinate system.

Project lighting: Once exact object location is known, the projector will project a spotlight at the center of the moving object.

2.3 Hardware Architecture

Our tracking application uses two types of cameras and a single projector – a Sony SNC-RZ25P networked PTZ camera, a Logitech Quickcam Pro WebCam and a 3M X55i projector. Table 1 summarizes the critical features for these hardware devices.

Table 1. Characteristics of various devices used

Device Name	Important features
Sony SNC-RZ25P Networked PTZ camera	Remote network monitoring
	Direct panning/tilting
	High magnification auto-focus zoom lens
Logitech Quickcam Pro WebCam	High-quality webcam with built-in microphone
	Snap pictures and video instantly
	Zoom/focus adjustable
3M X55i projector	Brightness 2000 Ansi Lumens,
	Resolution XGA (1024 x 768)

3 System Design

The tracking application is developed based on a decentralized component-based approach, which in this case is equivalent to the composition of multimediaWS. Throughout this part, we will present the key design principles governing our work first. Followed by the detailed elaboration on how the multimediaWS are designed and how the actual system is implemented.

3.1 Design Principles

In Zhang and Chung's work [9], multimediaWS are defined as multimedia-oriented web services which generally involve transportation of multimedia contents over the web, and management of composite device for multimedia contents. Further more, most of the multimedia applications can be decomposed into one or more multimedia content source, a processing framework and output services. Based on the above understanding, following design principles are identified for multimediaWS construction:

1. MultimediaWS should not be defined for a particular device or processing element, instead, they should be defined for a whole category. Category is defined to be a group of software or hardware pieces which provide similar functionalities. For example, a Sony camera and a Logitech camera belong to the camera category, they both provide an image capture or a video sequence as the output, but one may have an auto-focus function which may be missing from the other.
2. Due to the heterogeneity existing among pieces in the same category, it is impossible to have a single set of multimediaWS suitable for all pieces in the same category. As a result, basic, medium and premium classes of multimediaWS are defined for each category. The multimediaWS are expected to be the same even for different applications.
3. It is entirely up to the designer what services should be defined as basic, medium or premium. In terms of hardware, the rule adopted in our application is "10-5-2", which means, all hardware devices used in this lab belonging to the same category are capable of providing basic multimediaWS, while 50% of the devices implement medium, and 20% for premium.
4. In terms of software, classes are defined based on the complexity of the scenarios. Simple scenarios can be dealt with by basic class, while more complex ones have to be handled by medium and even premium class. Take motion detection library as an example: in application where background is kept static, basic class is good enough to detect the moving object. But if the background is changing, we may need to use medium multimediaWS class.
5. Composite multimediaWS, which cut cross multiple categories, should be carefully defined as they may violate the generality property of multimediaWS.

3.2 MultimediaWS

With an understanding of the application, the next step is to define the multimediaWS used. From the description in section 2, the following categories can be identified, namely camera, projector and motion detection library.

Due to the existing heterogeneity, three classes of multimediaWS (basic, medium, and premium) are defined separately for the same category. Taking camera for example, at its basic multimediaWS, it is only capable of capturing images. Some other cameras also have functionalities of auto-focus or automatic gain. More advanced cameras may allow pan, tilt and zoom as well. The most recent cameras may even have streaming and simple motion detection built in. Based on the 10-5-2 rule suggested in section 2.1, the three classes of camera multimediaWS are defined as follows. Basic multimediaWS for camera only has means to get device information and capture an image. Medium multimediaWS class may contain service calls to enable auto-focus, auto-balance function of the camera. While the premium class allows the user to control the movement of the cameras, which include pan, tilt and zoom. The same concept is applied to define multimediaWS for projector and the motion detection library. For the motion detection library, the classification is done based on the precision provided. Basic multimediaWS assumes static background in motion detection, while medium class uses adaptive background generation algorithm to cater for the lighting variation. The sole purpose of defining different classes is to ensure the multimediaWS are as generic as possible while still being useful.

3.3 MultimediaWS for Camera

In this part, we will show a WSDL fragment for all three classes of multimediaWS for camera. The fine details are omitted for presentation purpose.

Basic multimediaWS for camera:

> <wsdl: operation name = "getCameraInfo" /wsdl>
> <wsdl: operation name = "getImage" /wsdl>

Medium multimediaWS for camera:

> <wsdl: operation name = "enableAutoFocus" /wsdl>
> <wsdl: operation name = "enableAutoBalance" /wsdl>
> <wsdl: operation name = "enableAutoGain" /wsdl>

Premium multimediaWS for camera:

> <wsdl: operation name = "moveCamear" /wsdl>
> <wsdl: operation name = "zoomCamera" /wsdl>
> <wsdl: operation name = "resetPosition" /wsdl>

Please note that the multimedaiWS from the lower class are not repeated in the higher class. In additional, only the "enable" methods are show here, and the corresponding "disable" methods are omitted for simplicity. All cameras used in a multimedia application should at least implement the basic multimediaWS to be useful. The Sony camera in this application implements the premium set of multimediaWS while the Logitech only implements the basic class of multimediaWS.

3.4 MultimediaWS for Projector

The same approach used for camera is imported here to define multimediaWS for projector. Since a basic multimediaWS for projector is sufficient for the tracking application, the medium and premium classes are not shown here.

Basic multimedia for projector:

> <wsdl: operation name = "spotLight" /wsdl>
> <wsdl: operation name = "rectangleLight" /wsdl>
> <wsdl: operation name = "displayPicture" /wsdl>

```
<wsdl: operation name = "showText" /wsdl>
<wsdl: operation name = "ellipseLight" /wsdl>
<wsdl: operation name = "setColor" /wsdl>
<wsdl: operation name = "getProInfo" /wsdl>
<wsdl: operation name = "showArrow" /wsdl>
<wsdl: operation name = "offProjector" /wsdl>
```

3.5 MultimediaWS for Motion Detection Library

The background scene in this application is static, thus a basic class for motion detection library is good enough. The basic multimediaWS for this processing element are defined as follows:

```
<wsdl: operation name = "setBackgorund" /wsdl.
<wsdl: operation name = "backgroundExists" /wsdl>
<wsdl: operation name = "getObjectCenter"/wsdl>
<wsdl: operation name = "getBoundingBox"/wsdl>
<wsdl: operation name = "locationCali" /wsdl>
```

4 System Implementation and Evaluation

4.1 Object Tracking System

After the multimediaWS for different multimedia elements are deployed[1], the application can be quickly built up. Both the Sony camera and 3M projector are directly connected to the Local Area Netowrk (LAN) while the Logitech webcam is connected to the multimediaWS provider host machine through Universal Serial Bus (USB) interface. The code for the tracking application is shown below:

C# code for the tracking application

```
/* myCamera, myProjector and mdl are the local proxies
for camera, projector and motion detection library web
services */
  byte[] tmp = myCamera.getImage();
  mdl.setBackground(tmp);
  while(true) {
      myProjector.offProjector();
      byte[] image = myCamera.getImage();
      result = mdl.getObjectCenter(image);
      //function to do calibration
      result = mdl.locationCali(result,camInfo,
proInfo);
      //highlight with fixed spotlight radius
      myProjector.spotLight(result[0], result[1], 100);
  }
//end of program code
```

---

[1] The multimediaWS for camera has already been implemented from other projects in this research center.

The above code is all the coding effort that is needed to develop a typical tracking application as mentioned in section 2 when the desired multimediaWS are available. In order to help the reader to have a better understanding, the underlying details of a Web Service invocation is depicted in figure 1 while a comprehensive demo on this object tracking application is shown in figure 2.

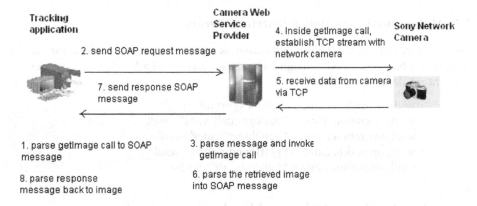

Fig. 1. Invocation details of getImage multimediaWS

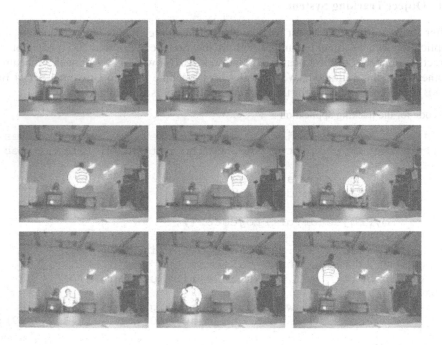

Fig. 2. Spotlight tracking on moving object. The images should be viewed from left to right, top to bottom.

4.2 Tour Guide System

With the accomplishment of the Object Tracking system, it is realized that the MultimediaWS developed for this particular system can potentially serve in other similar applications without any changes. In order to assess the reusability of the MultimediaWS developed, another application, Tour Guide System, which uses the same set of MultimediaWS, is designed and implemented.

Tour Guide System serves as a virtual tour guide. As soon as a stranger arrives and activates the system, the stranger's initial location is detected and the destination is to be specified by the user. After that, the camera starts to take pictures at a certain frequency to track user locations, while the projectors output instructive signs to guide the user to next step towards his destination, such as turn left, turn right, go straight, etc.

To develop a tour guide system which can be used in real life scenarios, it is possible that tens or even hundreds of cameras and projectors are needed depending on the architectures of the covered area. This would involve a lot of challenging issues such as handling over tasks between cameras, intensive cooperation between cameras and projectors, cost, etc. Since the main goal of developing a tour guide system in this project is to test whether the same set of MultimediaWS can be reused, a simplified tour guide system is designed and implemented instead. In the simplified system, only one camera and one projector are employed to guide the user from one point of a room to another point. It is assumed that the whole room is within the coverage area of the camera and the projector. Following code shows how the guide system is implemented and the demonstration is presented in figure 3.

C# code for the user guide application

```
/* myCamera, myProjector and mdl are the local proxies
for camera, projector and motion detection library web
services */
   byte[] bgd = myCamera.getImage();
   mdl.setBackground(bgd);
   while(true) {
        myProjector.offProjector();
        byte[] image = myCamera.getImage();
        result = mdl.getObjectCenter(image);
        //function to do calibration
        result = mdl.locationCali(result,camInfo,
proInfo);
        //display arrow sign to destination
        myProjector.showArrow(result[0], result[1],
destination[0], destination[1]);
   }
//end of program code
```

4.3 Evaluation of Using MultimediaWS

After both applications are successfully implemented, the whole development cycle is evaluated against the following aspects: simplicity in understanding and deployment, reusability and adaptability.

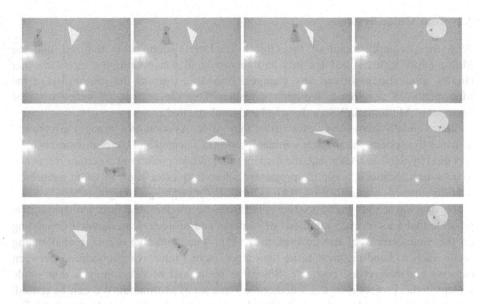

Fig. 3. Objects are placed at different start point but eventually get to the same destination point (the circle in the picture). The pictures should be viewed from left to right, top to bottom.

Simplicity in Understanding and Deployment. Based on the design principles described in section 3.1, the multimediaWS are not defined with reference to a particular device or processing element, but instead they are designed to be as general as possible. For example, after the initial learning process, end users can apply basic and medium multimediaWS for camera many times whenever a camera (which implements only up to medium class) is used in an application. This will save the end users a lot of effort to learn a brand new Web Service whenever a new camera joins the application. Meanwhile, users only need to learn the lower set of multimedaiWS whenever higher class is not a compulsory.

Reusability. The multimediaWS are carefully designed to avoid losing generality, meanwhile most components of a multimedia application can be categorized easily. All of these ensure that the multimediaWS can be plugged into new applications with little or no changes. For instance, new application like user navigation system as mentioned above, which uses projector light to direct user to his/her destination, can make use of the existing multimediaWS without changes.

Adaptability. Due to the generality enforced during design, the back-end implementation of the multimediaWS can be changed on the fly. Suppose a better algorithm for motion detection is available, we can simple implement the new algorithm at the multimediaWS provider side without end users' awareness. As multimediaWS are the same across the whole category, when one element fails, a new proxy for another element under the same category can be quickly generated and replace the existing one. There will be virtually no changes in the application. In this tracking application, the Logitech webcam and Sony PTZ camera can be used interchangeable while the application code remains the same except every time a new proxy needs to be created.

5 Conclusion

In this paper, we try to build up a multimedia application by using simple multimediaWS composition. During the development cycle, some general design principles are adopted and elaborated, classification for different classes of multimediaWS for the same category is illustrated using real examples, simplicity of using multimediaWS in application development is shown, as well as other aspects are evaluated. We hope with the introduction of this paper, users of multimedia service composition would have better insights to what need to be observed and taken care of. In this application, most of the multimediaWS used are related to the management of multimedia content. In future, the design principles and application related to transportation/synchronization of multimedia content will be explored.

References

1. Christensen, E. et al. The Web Service description language WSDL. http://www4.ibm.com/software/solutions/webservices/resource.html
2. Shankar, P. and Fox, A. SWORD: A Developer Toolkit for Web Service Composition. *In Proceeding of the Eleventh International World Wide Web Conference*, Honolulu, HI (2002)
3. A.Arkin, et al. Web Service Choreography Interface 1.0, http://wwws.sun.com/software/xml/developers/wsci
4. Curbera, F., et al. Business process execution language for web services. http://www-106.ibm.com/dveloperworks/webservices/library/wsbpel (2002)
5. K. Nahrstedt, W. Balke, A Taxonomy for multimedia service composition, *12th annual ACM international conference on Multimedia*, New York, NY, USA (2004)
6. S. Kalasapur, M. Kumar, B. Shirazi, Seamless Service Composition (SecCo) in pervasive environment, in *Proceeding of the first international workshop on Multimedia Service composition*, Singapore (2005)
7. Jin Liang, and Klara Nahrstedt, Service Composition for Advance Multimedia Applications, *12th Annual Multimedia Computing and Networking* (MMCN2005).
8. D. M. Garvila, The Visual Analysis of Human Movement: A Survey, *Computer Vision and Image Understanding*, Vol. 73, No.1, January, pp. 82-98 (1999)
9. Jia Zhang, Jen-Yao Chung, A SOAP-oriented Component-based Framework Supporting Device-independent Multimedia Web Services, in Procedding of Fourth International Symposium on Multimedia Software Engineering (2002).

A Novel Melody Line Identification Algorithm for Polyphonic MIDI Music

Sudha Velusamy*, Balaji Thoshkahna, and K.R. Ramakrishnan

Music and Audio Group(MAG),
Learning systems and Multimedia Labs,
Department of Electrical Engineering,
Indian Institute of Science, Bangalore 560012, India
sudha_v@satyam.com, {balajitn, krr}@ee.iisc.ernet.in

Abstract. The problem of automatic melody line identification in a MIDI file plays an important role towards taking QBH systems to the next level. We present here, a novel algorithm to identify the melody line in a polyphonic MIDI file. A note pruning and track / channel ranking method is used to identify the melody line. We use results from musicology to derive certain simple heuristics for the note pruning stage. This helps in the robustness of the algorithm, by way of discarding "spurious" notes. A ranking based on the melodic information in each track / channel enables us to choose the melody line accurately. Our algorithm makes no assumption about MIDI performer specific parameters, is simple and achieves an accuracy of 97% in identifying the melody line correctly. This algorithm is currently being used by us in a QBH system built in our lab.

1 Introduction

With the enormous growth in digital technologies, Music Information Retrieval (MIR) has become an interesting area of investigation. The goal of research in MIR is to develop new techniques and algorithms for analysis, indexing and efficient retrieval of musical information. One of the main branch of MIR is content based music retrieval (CBMR), where, music is retrieved by using it's content like melody, rhythm and tempo of the song. A special type of MIR system that retrieves music by the similarity of melody is the Query by Humming (QBH) system. In this system, a user hums a song and the system retrieves songs from the database that match the melody contour of the hum.

In the QBH context, the pitch (the perceived fundamental frequency) of a song plays an important role, as it carries primary information regarding the melody of the song. One of the most crucial problems of such a system is to track the pitch of the music data for the retrieval of melodically similar songs.

Generally, a sequence of non-overlapping note events, called the monophonic note sequence, constitutes the melody of a song. In case of polyphonic music, extracting such a single non-overlapping melody contour is an important issue.

---

* Currently with Satyam Applied Research Group, Bangalore, India.

T.-J. Cham et al. (Eds.): MMM 2007, LNCS 4352, Part II, pp. 248–257, 2007.

Most of the existing QBH systems work on monophonic / polyphonic symbolic music data like MIDI[1] and many techniques have been proposed for retrieving symbolic music using melodic similarity.

Monophonic MIDI files usually have a single track, which explicitly carries the melody information. But, in case of polyphonic MIDI files, it usually consists of multiple tracks and channels. Each of these tracks represent a separate instrument, which can play more than one note simultaneously. The melody of the song is interspersed among these instruments. Given a MIDI file, it is not immediately obvious as how to identify the sequence of notes, which corresponds to the melody of the song. Previous systems, which work on MIDI files, have databases containing monophonic melodic contours (such as folk melodies that consist of single non-chordal instruments[1]). But the perceived melody of the song, however, is rarely played by a single instrument. This may originate from different instruments at different instants of time. In this case, we need to identify a practical way of locating melody from the given song. In this work, we have proposed a novel method of melody line identification from polyphonic MIDI music.

This paper is organised as follows: Section 2 gives a short note about the MIDI format. We present a study on existing melody identification techniques in section 3. Section 4 discusses the proposed melody line identification algorithm. The the experimental results are presented in sections 5. Section 6 concludes the paper and gives our view of the proposed algorithm compared to other existing techniques.

2   Music Instrument Digital Interface (MIDI)

MIDI is a standardized protocol that allows electronic musical instruments to communicate with each other and with other storage devices. The musical data is encoded as symbols of events in MIDI. MIDI event contains the information about the note number, time duration of the note to be played, pressure level of the key pressed and information about the instrument that played the music.

MIDI data can be classified as monophonic and polyphonic music data. The monophonic music data of MIDI format codes the sequence of notes played by a single instrument and that note sequence directly represents the melody of the song.

The polyphonic MIDI songs contain maximum of 16 channels and each channel can carry notes of 8 instruments playing simultaneously. So, totally 128 instruments can be played. Each MIDI file contains one or more tracks of note events with information regarding the channel number, velocity of note transitions, the different instrument names, composer details etc. Each track can have multiple instruments. Although, there are many tracks, channels and instruments playing multiple notes simultaneously, only some of the notes are perceived as part of the melody of the song. So, the notes which are part of the melody, need to be automatically identified.

---

[1] Music Instrument Digital Interface.

3   Study on Existing Melody Identification Systems

Several methods for extracting melody from polyphonic MIDI files are reported in the literature. Blackburn et al [2] propose a method of splitting polyphonic music into parts using note proximity rules. But this method is designed for music with fairly uniform style. The system by Ghias et al [3] assumes that notes played by instruments beyond the 10th channel do not contain melody and simply discards those channels and derives melodic line using simple heuristics from lower channels.

Uitdenbogerd and Zobel [4] have proposed four different melody extraction methods. The first method, called the Skyline algorithm, collects all the notes in a MIDI file into a single channel and outputs the highest pitch line among the note sequence, as melody. But, the algorithm modifies the original duration of the notes for melody line extraction. This may lead to loss of original melody of the song. The other three methods calculate a channel entropy for selecting the best melody contributing MIDI channel. Chai [5] proposes a revision on skyline algorithm, which keeps original note durations unchanged. Another approach by Charnasse [6] uses the smallest among the simultaneous notes, for building the pitch contour.

The above three methods [4][5][6] give poor performance when, a single track contains multiple channels and when melody is located on the lowest pitch notes.

Tang's work [7] uses 5 different parameters like average velocity, polyphonic to monophonic (PM) time ratio, silence ratio, range name and track name. But, this method has the following drawbacks. It uses attributes which are performer specific. When the background, percussion instrumental music dominates the melody instrumental music, this algorithm works poorly. The PM ratio, silence ratio and note ranges require accurate threshold settings. For identification of melody lines from a MIDI file, string matching of track names is not an effective way.

In Ozcan's method [8] of melody extraction, the MIDI channels are clustered depending upon the pitch histogram, and the best k channels which are most similar to entire MIDI are selected as melody channel using the top rank approach. Finally, skyline algorithm is used to get the monophonic melody line.

David [9] built a melody line identification system which uses WEKA toolkit, and a random forest classifier for learning the track information. This method derives 12 descriptors from the MIDI songs and uses them for classification and identification of the melody track. The drawback of this method is the high number of attributes and the pre-requisite training required to identify the melody line.

In summary, the above mentioned methods of melody extraction or melody line selection use either songs of uniform style, performer specific MIDI attributes like channel number, track name, note volume and range etc, complex methods for classification or trial and error method varying the threshold. Most of these methods make assumptions about the percussion channels and volume of the melody channel which are highly dependent on the MIDI performer.

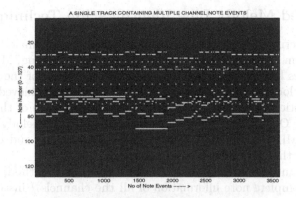

Fig. 1. Single Track of MIDI file containing multiple(all) Channel Note Events

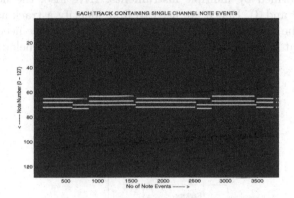

Fig. 2. A Track of MIDI file containing longer notes

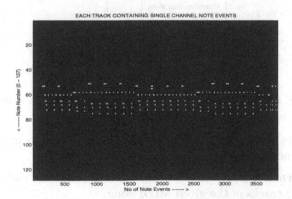

Fig. 3. A Track of MIDI file containing shorter notes

4   Proposed Melody Line Identification Technique

The main objective of our work is to develop an automatic melody line identification algorithm which is independent of the style of the song, MIDI performer specific features like track name, channel number, volume of the notes and the way melody is located throughout the MIDI file. This is achieved by analyzing the characteristics of the tracks, channels and the sequence of the notes coded in a MIDI file. Our goal is not to extract a monophonic melody contour from a polyphonic MIDI file, but to identify the melody track and channel which corresponds to the main melody.

MIDI files can be organized in two ways. In the first method, a single track contains the complete note information of all the channels / instruments. Each channel/instrument contains simultaneous notes, representing a chord (Fig 1). In the second method, multiple tracks have note events for multiple channels which are performed by multiple instruments. Here also, the note events are chordal (Figs 2 and 3). Hence, we need to first identify a track as the "melody track" out of the multiple tracks. In this "melody track", we need to search for the channel that holds the melody of the song, called the "melody channel".

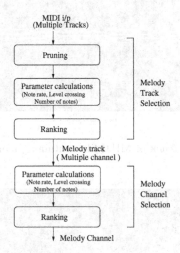

Fig. 4. Block diagram the melody line identification system

Figure 4 gives a clear picture of the algorithm. The two main steps of the melody line identification is,

- **Melody Track Selection:** Selecting a track, called the melody track, from the multiple tracks of the given MIDI song.
- **Melody Channel Selection:** Selecting the melody channel which contains the main melody of the given MIDI song from the selected melody track.

Now, selection of the melody track and melody channel are carried out in three steps.

1. Pruning of the tracks / channels
2. Calculation of track / channel parameters
3. Ranking of the tracks/Channels

A track / channel with the highest rank is selected as a melody track / melody channel. The stepwise explanation of the proposed algorithms is given in the following section.

4.1   Step1: Pruning of the Tracks/Channels

Notes coded in the MIDI files can be broadly classified into two types, namely the notes corresponding to the melody of the song and notes corresponding to the accompanying instruments. The following observations made on MIDI files help us to identify them separately

– Although, the melody line transits from instrument to instrument, it remains in a particular instrument for a minimum duration of 10 sec. This channel's/instrument's notes become part of the melody line during that time. So, it is enough to identify the channel which contains the melody line (melody channel).
– Instruments, which play background music, often produce accompanying notes of duration of less than 0.2 seconds or greater than 2 seconds. (Fig 2, 3). Too short or too long notes, present in the note sequence, do not contribute to the melody perception. According to Bello [10], a note should have at least 0.05 sec to be perceived as a part of the note sequence. Notes below 0.05 sec are considered to be spurious notes.
– The sequence of notes of the accompanying instruments do not have a large number of distinct notes. i.e., those sequences are played with 5 distinct notes at the maximum.

The above observations facilitates the pruning process. In the pruning phase, from each track, notes having duration less than 0.2 sec or greater than 2 sec are eliminated. The notes remaining after pruning, called the genuine notes, are the candidates for forming the melody line.

4.2   Step2: Parameter Calculation

For a given polyphonic MIDI file, various parameters are calculated for each track / channel. These parameters are: Note Rate, Level Crossing Rate and Note count.

Note Rate: This is the number of notes per unit time and denotes the amount of information in the tracks / channels.

Note rate = No.of non zero notes in the entire track(or channel) / Total time

Since, the note rate calculation is done on the pruned tracks / channels, a track / channel having a large number of notes is more likely to be the melody track / channel.

Level Crossing Rate (LCR): This is a parameter which measures the "waviness" of a note sequence. For a note sequence to be a melody line, it's rich note information and it's structure are both important. Sometimes, the genuine notes may simply move up and down (at a high frequency), but may not contribute to melody perception.For melody perception, the note sequence must be slow in pitch variation. LCR tells about the rate of variation of a sequence.

$$LCR = No. \ of \ times \ the \ note \ sequence \ crosses \ it's \ mean \ value \ / \ Total \ time$$

Distinct Note Count: It is a parameter which helps in fine tuning the algorithm. Tracks / channels containing less than 5 distinct notes in 10 sec duration are discarded.

4.3 Step3: Ranking

All the above mentioned parameters are calculated for each track. We normalize each of the parameters to a maximum value of 1 by dividing the respective parameters by the maximum values found across the tracks. This helps in ranking the tracks / channels based on their likelihood to form part of the melody track / channel.The best ranked track / channel is declared as the melody track / melody channel (melody line). Rank of the kth track/channel, $R(k)$, is calculated as

$$R(k) = \{(0.4 * NoteRate(k)) + (0.4 * LCR(k)) + (0.2 * DistinctNoteCount(k))\} \tag{1}$$

The fact that the above said parameters are found only on pruned tracks and channels, makes the algorithm simple and efficient.

4.4 Step4: Melody Track Selection

For selecting a melody track from the tracks of a given MIDI file, the above mentioned 3 steps are performed on each of the tracks. After calculating the rank, the track having highest rank is declared as a MELODY TRACK (T_M).

$$T_M = argmax_k\{R_T(k)\} \tag{2}$$

where $R_T(k)$ is rank of the kth track.

4.5 Step5: Melody Channel Selection

Melody channel selection process is same as the melody track selection, but is performed on the multiple channels of the selected melody track. After extracting the same set of parameters for each of the channel /instrument in the melody track, the rank of each channel is found as in 4.4. The channel which has the highest rank is declared as a MELODY CHANNEL (C_M).

$$C_M = argmax_k\{R_C(k)\} \tag{3}$$

where $R_C(k)$ is rank of the Kth channel. Note that the processes on the MIDI tracks and channels are done only for identifying the melody track / channel. But, the final melody line contains all the original notes of selected channel. We do not use the pruned version of the note sequence as the final melody line. If the melody channel happens to have chords, the non-overlapping monophonic melody line is obtained by using Kosugi's [11] method of chord deletion. In this method, the highest note of a chord is retained for the melody line if there is no new note sounded after the start of the chord. Else, the new note sounded after the start of the chord is taken for the melody line.

5 Experiments and Results

In this section, we present the details of experiments carried out and the results of our melody line identification algorithm. Since our main aim of developing a melody line identification system is to derive the melody features from MIDI format of Hindi songs of our QBH database, the same is used for testing the algorithm.

5.1 Database Information

The database contains a collection of 125 Hindi MIDI songs obtained from the various Internet sources. These files belong to various music categories like slow melodies, fast beats, movie theme music and pop album songs. The database is independent of music style, note range and volume. The database is split to have 20 % files for training and remaining 80 % of the files for testing.

5.2 Parameter Threshold Estimation

To learn about the charactersistics of tracks, channels and MIDI notes, we chose 25 files from the database as training files. These files are selected to have the music belonging to all the above mentioned categories. Since the training files are manually labeled with the melody track and melody channel number, they help us to learn about the note and track characteristics of melody track / channel like, minimum and maximum note duration to perceive as part of the melody, minimum number of notes required for each track to get declared as a genuinely useful track etc.

5.3 Experiments

Experiments are done on 100 test files to evaluate the melody line selection algorithm. Given a 10 sec clip of a MIDI file, all the tracks in that clip are pruned (as described in section 4.1) for selecting only the genuine tracks. Then the parameters (Note rate, LCR and Distinct Note Count) are calculated for each selected track and ranking done for each of them. The track with the highest rank is selected as the melody track.

Once the melody track is selected, the melody channel selection process is done on that track as explained in section4.5.

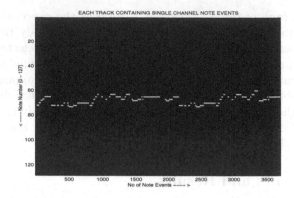

Fig. 5. A melody line extracted from a polyphonic MIDI file

5.4   Results

Figure 5 shows an example of an extracted melody line from a polyphonic MIDI file. The results of the melody line identifiation algorithm is given in the Table 1. As can be seen, the algorithm identifies the melody channel perfectly 97% of the time. For files where the MIDI transcription was way off from the original song, the algorithm seemed to fail. This was because these files did not satisfy the pruning constraints put by us on the MIDI files. The correctness of our melody line was ascertained with the help of an amateur musician.

Table 1. Performance of Melody Line Selection Algorithm

Test Results			
		No.of Correct Selection	
Music Type	No.of Songs	Tracks	Channels	Total Percentage
Slow Melodies	55	54	54	98.2
Fast Beats	30	29	28	93.4
Album Songs	15	15	15	100
Total	100	98	97	97

6   Conclusions

Melody line identification of music is a crucial issue of QBH systems. In case of polyphonic music, it is non-trivial to extract the melody line. In this paper, we have proposed a simple, computationally fast and efficient algorithm to identify the melody line from the symbolic music data. With the simple pruning and ranking technique proposed by us, we have obtained an accuracy of 97 %. Unlike other techniques, our algorithm does not make any assumptions on the performer specific MIDI attributes. Also the accuracy of our algorithm is high enough to compete with any of the existing techniques for automatic melody line identification.

Acknowledgements

The authors would like to acknowledge the support of Satyam Applied Research Group, Bangalore, India for partial funding of this work.

References

1. R.J.McNab, L.A.Smith,I.H.Witten and C.L.Henderson: Tune Retrieval in the Multimedia Library, Multimedia Tools and Applications, 2000.
2. S.Blackburn and D.DeRoure: A Tool For Content Based Navigation Of Music, Proc.of ACM Multimedia98, September 11, England 1998.
3. A.Ghias, J.Logan, D.Chamberlin, and B.Smith: Query By Humming Musical Information Retrieval in An Audio Database, Proc.of ACM Multimedia95, 1995.
4. A.Uitdenbogerd and J.Zobel: Melodic Matching Techniques For Large Music Databases, Proc.of ACM International Multimedia Conference, 1999.
5. W. Chai: Melody Retrieval On The Web, MS Thesis, Massachusetts Institute of Technology, Boston, 2000.
6. H.Charnasse and B.Stepien: Automatic Transcription of German Lute Tablatures An Articial Intelligence Application, In Computer Representations and Models in Music, Academic Press 1992.
7. Michael Tang, Chi-Lap Yip and Ben Kao: Selection of Melody Lines for Music Databases, In IEEE Proc.of the 24th Annual International Computer Software and Applications Conference, 2000.
8. Ozcan, Isikhan and Alpkocak: Melody Extraction On MIDI Music Files, Proc.of the Seventh IEEE International Symposium on Multimedia (ISM05), 2005.
9. David Rizo, Pedro J. Ponse de leon, Antonio and Jose: Melody Track Identification In MIDI Files, American Association for Artificial Intelligence, 2006.
10. J.P.Bello, G.Monti, and M.Sandler: Techniques For Automatic Music Transcription, Proc.of International Symposium on Music Information Retrieval, Plymouth MA, October 2000.
11. Naoko Kosugi, Yuichi Nishihara, Tetsuo Sakata, Masashi Yamamuro and Kazuhiko Kushima: A Practical Query By Humming System for A Large Music Database, Proc.of ACM Conference, 2000

Markerless Augmented Reality Using a Robust Point Transferring Method

S.K. Ong, M.L. Yuan, and A.Y.C. Nee

Mechanical Engineering Department, National University of Singapore,
9 Engineering Drive 1, Singapore 117576
{mpeongsk,mpeyml,mpeneeyc}@nus.edu.sg

Abstract. This paper proposes a robust point transferring method for markerless AR applications. Using this method, any points specified at the initialization stage can be stably transferred during the augmentation process. These transferred points can be used for registration, annotation and video augmentation in markerless AR applications. This proposed point transferring method is based on a simple nonlinear optimization model. The proposed method has several advantages. Firstly, it is robust and stable as it remains effective when the camera is moved about quickly or when the scenes are largely occluded or filled with moving objects. Second, it is simple as the points that will be used for registration, annotation and video augmentation are only required to be specified in one image. Lastly, it is fast as the proposed simple optimization model can be solved quickly. Several experiments have been conducted to validate the performance of this proposed method.

Keywords: Augmented reality, point transferring, nonlinear optimization.

1 Introduction

Vision-based methods offer a flexible and accurate tracking method for AR systems without any special cumbersome sensors. Current vision-based trackers used in AR systems mostly rely on markers [1]. However, if the markers are partially occluded or outside the field of view, the virtual contents cannot be augmented. In addition, the use of markers can be inconvenient as they require regular maintenance.

Markerless AR systems use natural features as an alternative to markers to robustly estimate the camera poses for augmentation based on their correspondences. The KLT tracker [2] has been applied in some AR systems [3, 4]. However, the KLT tracker depends heavily on the lighting conditions. In addition, the camera cannot be moved about quickly and the scene cannot be largely occluded, otherwise the natural features will be lost quite easily. These disadvantages limit the application of the KLT tracker in most of the markerless AR applications.

Most current markerless AR systems are based on the robust point matching approach [5, 6, 7]. The solution method must be able to deal with the problem of robustness due to outliers, large occlusion, and other factors. Gordon and Lowe proposed a markerless AR method based on Scale Invariant Feature Transform (SIFT) features [8]. SIFT features extraction is too slow to meet the real-time requirement in

T.-J. Cham et al. (Eds.): MMM 2007, LNCS 4352, Part II, pp. 258–268, 2007.

AR systems. Vacchetti *et al.* [6] proposed a 2D-3D registration method based on offline information using the TUKEY estimator. However, a 3D model is required in their method that might not be available. Comport *et al.* [7] proposed a model-based tracking algorithm based on visual servoing and robust M-Estimator to estimate the camera pose for markerless AR systems. However, the camera cannot be moved quickly and a lack of contrast around contours and large occlusions will lead to failure. Chia *et al.* [9] used two or more reference views to compute the current camera pose using an approximate homograph. However, their system would fail as the errors are accumulated. In some applications, the users may wish to place the virtual objects at a position that may lie in a region that has no distinct natural features. For example, the users would like to augment a virtual chair onto a smooth floor that has no distinct features. Hence, the issue is whether any virtual information can be augmented at any place. The problem is the transfer of any specified point in the live video. Li *et al.* [3] proposed a point transferring method based on the estimation of the trifocal tensors for augmenting live video. Yuan *et al.* previously proposed a point transferring method based on the projective reconstruction technique and the KLT tracker for markerless AR applications [4]. However, these two methods were based on the KLT tracker that limits their applications in most AR systems.

In this paper, a robust point transferring method based on a new simple nonlinear optimization model is proposed to transfer any points for registration, annotation, video augmentation in markerless AR systems. The following two major technical innovations have made the method more robust and accurate.

(1) A simple new nonlinear optimization method is used to estimate the projective matrices for point transferring, thus achieving faster results;
(2) A robust estimation method is used where outliers will be discarded twice during the point transferring process, making the results more accurate and robust.

The remaining of this paper is organized as follows. Section 2 describes a new nonlinear optimization model. Section 3 presents in details the proposed new point transferring method. Section 4 shows the experimental results. Section 5 discusses the related issues. Finally, conclusions are given in the last section.

2 Point Transferring

2.1 Notation

An image point m and a 3D point M are denoted as homogeneous vectors $m = (u, v, 1)^T$ and $M = (X, Y, Z, 1)^T$ respectively. For the kth image, the relationship between a 3D point M_i and its projection m_{ki} in the image plane is given by:

$$\rho m_{ki} = P_k M_i \tag{1}$$

where ρ is a non-zero scale factor. In general, $P_k = A[R_k, t_k]$, where A is the camera intrinsic matrix and (R_k, t_k) is the rotation and translation that relate the world coordinate system to the camera coordinate system.

Given two images I_0 and I_1, the only constraint arising from these two images is the epipolar geometry [13]. The fundamental matrix F encapsulates the epipolar geometry that can be robustly estimated from the point correspondences. Their corresponding projective matrices are often given as follows:

$$P_0 = [I \mid 0] \tag{2}$$

$$P_1 = [[e']_\times F \mid e'] \tag{3}$$

where e' is the epipole that satisfies $F^T e' = 0$.

2.2 Optimization Model for Point Transferring

Normally, given two reference images, the general model-based point transferring procedure for the kth image includes two major stages:

(1) The projective matrices P_0 and P_1 of the two reference images are obtained from the fundamental matrix. The 3D structures are reconstructed.
(2) For the kth image, general 2D-3D model-based pose estimation methods based on robust estimators are used to estimate the projective matrix P_k.

The major disadvantage of the general model-based method is that the results often lack accuracy and are prone to jitter. Without loss of generality, P_0 and P_k are re-formatted as follows:

$$s_0 m_{0i} = P_0 M_i \tag{4}$$

$$s_k m_{ki} = P_k M_i \tag{5}$$

Based on the mathematical analysis [10], s_0 can be assumed to be a constant. Hence, from Equation (4), M_i can be uniquely determined and denoted as follows:

$$M_i = \phi(P_0, s_0, m_{0i}) \tag{6}$$

Next, using Equation (6), $m_{ki} = (u_k, v_k)$ can be uniquely computed and denoted as follows:

$$\tilde{u}_k = \Omega_x(P_k, \phi(P_0, s_0, m_{0i})) \tag{7}$$

$$\tilde{v}_k = \Omega_y(P_k, \phi(P_0, s_0, m_{0i})) \tag{8}$$

Based on the minimization of the actual residual errors, the projective matrix P_k and the corresponding s_0 can be solved using the following optimization model:

$$\min \sum \left((u_k - \tilde{u}_k)^2 + (v_k - \tilde{v}_k)^2 \right) \tag{9}$$

Equation (9) is the new optimization model proposed to estimate the projective matrix P_k and the corresponding s_0. This model is simple as only 12 parameters need to be estimated in which the 3D structures are not involved. This allows the method to be executed quickly. Equation (9) can be solved using the Levenberg-Marquardt (LM) algorithm. In this paper, the general model-based method based on the least-median-of-squares (LMedS) estimation is used to estimate the starting point that will be used for the LM method. After P_k and the corresponding s_0 are estimated, the positions of the points that have been specified during the initialization stage can be computed using Equations (7) and (8). The transferred points can then be used for registration, annotation and video augmentation in markerless AR systems.

3 Robust Point Transferring Algorithm

The architecture of the entire algorithm is shown in Figure 1. It includes two major stages. The first stage is the initialization stage where two reference images are selected. Next, natural features are extracted and point correspondences are established. The projective matrices P_0 and P_1 of the two reference images are determined from which the 3D structures are reconstructed. Finally, any point that will be used for the AR applications, such as registration and annotation, is required to be specified in one image.

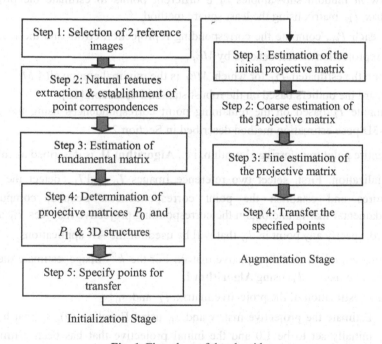

Fig. 1. Flowchart of the algorithm

During the augmentation stage, natural features in the current video frame are first detected and matched to one of the two reference images. The point transferring procedure consists of four steps, as shown in Figure 1. In the first step, the initial projective matrix for the current video frame is estimated using the model-based method based on the LMedS technique. Outliers will be discarded in this stage. In the second step, i.e., the coarse estimation stage, the initial projective matrix estimated in the first step is used as a starting point in Equation (9). Outliers will be further discarded according to the reprojection errors. In the third step, i.e., the fine estimation stage, based on the remaining point correspondences, the results that have been estimated in the second step are used as a new starting point in Equation (9) to estimate the final projective matrix and s_0. Finally, the points specified during the initialization stage will be transferred using Equations (7) and (8).

There are two main algorithms, namely, the estimation of the initial projective matrix and the point transferring method. The algorithm, denoted as **Algorithm I**, for estimating the initial projective matrix is based on the general model-based method and the LMedS estimation technique. This estimated initial projective matrix will be used as a starting point for the proposed point transferring method in this paper, denoted as **Algorithm II**, to obtain the final projective matrix that will be used to transfer any specified point.

Algorithm I for estimating the initial projective matrix is described as follows:

1. Draw m random sub-samples of 8 different points to estimate the projective matrix P_{ki} matrix using the least square method.
2. For each P_{ki}, compute the corresponding reprojection errors and the median of the reprojection errors, denoted by ME_i.
3. Retain the estimated P_{ki} for which ME_i is the minimal among all $\{ ME_i \}$.
4. Discard the outliers based on the robust standard deviation [13].
5. Compute P_k based on the remaining point correspondences using the general 2D-3D pose estimation method described in Section 2.2.

The entire point transferring algorithm, i.e., **Algorithm II**, is described as follows:

1. Initialization: First, select two reference images I_0 and I_1, detect the natural features and establish the point correspondences. Second, compute the fundamental matrix and obtain the corresponding projective matrices P_0 and P_1. Third, specify any point in I_0 that will be used for the AR applications.

2. Estimation of the initial projective matrix: For the kth image, estimate the initial projective matrix P_k using **Algorithm I**.

3. Coarse estimation of the projective matrix P_k and s_0:
   3.1 Estimate the projective matrix and s_0 using Equation (9). s_0 that has been initially set to be 1.0 and the initial projective that has been estimated in Step 2 are used as a starting point in Equation (9).
   3.2 Discard the outliers if the corresponding reprojection errors are larger than a given threshold. This threshold value is set based on experience. Normally, the value of this threshold can be set to be 2.0.

4. Fine estimation of the projective matrix P_k and s_0:

Estimate the final projective matrix using Equation (9) based on the remaining point correspondences. The projective matrix and s_0 that have been estimated in Step 3 are used as a new starting point in this step to estimate the final P_k and s_0.

5. Transfer the specified points:

Finally, based on the estimated P_k and s_0, estimate the positions of the specified points using Equations (7) and (8).

In this algorithm, the outliers will be discarded twice, which makes the results robust even when the scene is largely occluded or if there are moving objects in the scene. The proposed method can be used for registration, annotation and video augmentation in markerless AR systems. It should be noted that four planar points are required to be specified in one reference image to build the world coordinate system on which a virtual object or a video can be superimposed. Figure 2 shows an example where seven points have been specified during the initialization stage (labeled with the "+"). Four of the points that lie on the four corners of a sheet of white paper are used to augment the virtual teapot. The remaining three points were specified on a book, a teacup, and a teddy bear, respectively. The annotations "Book", "Tea Cup" and "Teddy Bear" were then linked respectively, to label these objects. During the augmentation process, the white paper was removed and some new objects, for example, the tripod box, were added into the scene. Using the proposed point transferring method, the virtual teapot and the annotations were stably augmented at their corresponding positions.

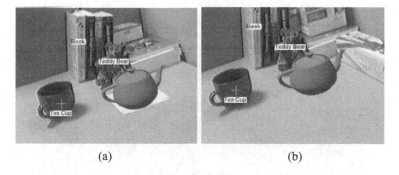

(a)   (b)

Fig. 2. Two examples illustrating point transferring for registration and annotation

4 Experiments

The methodology was implemented using Visual C++ under Microsoft Windows on a 3.0 GHz Intel Pentium R (4) CPU with 1 GB RAM. The video sequences were captured using an IEEE 1394 FireFly camera at 15 frame rates. The image size is 640×480. The system can perform the key operations of the proposed method at a speed of about 12.05 fps.

4.1 Registration and Annotation Experiments

Two experiments were conducted for registration and annotation in outdoor and indoor environments, respectively. In the outdoor experiment, seven points were specified during the initialization stage. Four of these points that lied on a smooth floor were used to augment a virtual chair. The remaining three points were used to label a few buildings in the scene. In this experiment, several persons were asked to

Fig. 3. Outdoor experiment

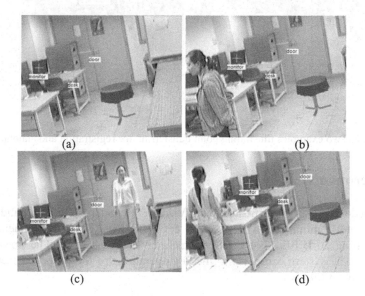

Fig. 4. Indoor experiment

walk about in the scene. Figure 3 shows the results of the outdoor experiment. When there were persons moving about in the scene, the seven points could still be successfully transferred. Note that in Figure 3(c), the annotation "Corridor" was not displayed because its corresponding point is outside of the field of view.

In the indoor experiment shown in Figure 4, a virtual table was superimposed on a specified region labeled by the four "+" on a smooth floor. The other three points were used to label a few objects in the laboratory. When several persons were walking about in the room, the virtual table and the annotations were still stably augmented at their corresponding positions.

4.2 Video Augmentation Experiment

In this video augmentation experiment, four planar points were first specified on a whiteboard, as shown in Figure 5(a). During the augmentation process, these four planar points were stably transferred using the proposed method and a movie could be played in this specified region on the whiteboard, as shown in Figures 5(b)-(d).

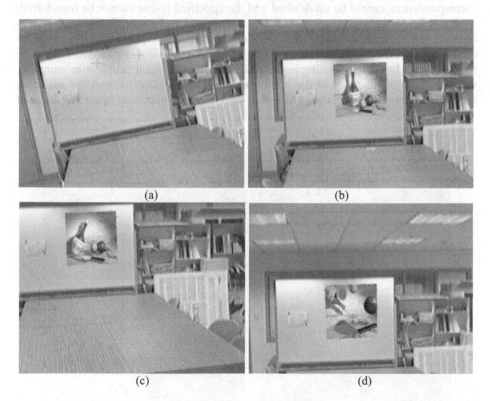

(a)   (b)

(c)   (d)

Fig. 5. Video augmentation experiment

4.3 Comparisons with the Authors' Previous Method

An experiment was conducted to compare the results obtained using the proposed method with the author's previous method which is based on the KLT tracker [4].

Four points that lied on the four corners of a sheet of white paper were specified on which the virtual bicycle will be superimposed using these two methods. Figures 6(a1) and 6(a2) were the results of the authors' previous method using the KLT tracker to transfer these four points while Figures 6(b1) and 6(b2) were the results using the method proposed in this paper. This result shows that when an object, such as a hand, was waved in the scene, the virtual bicycle was wrongly superimposed or could not be superimposed because of the limitations of the KLT tracker. However, using the method proposed in this research, the bicycle could be stably superimposed onto the paper during the entire process, as shown in Figures 6(b1) and 6(b2).

5   Discussion

In this paper, a robust and stable point transferring method is proposed for markerless AR applications. It should be noted that this method has a major limitation. The camera cannot be moved through large translation and rotation, otherwise the point correspondences cannot be established and the specified points cannot be transferred, such that the virtual information cannot be augmented at the specified places. This is because the traditional normalized cross-correlation score [13], which is used to establish the point correspondences, is not invariant to scale and rotation. This is, in fact, the wide baseline matching issue, which is still a difficult problem in computer vision [12, 14]. The speed of the current methods is too slow to meet the real-time requirement for AR applications. Although wide baseline matching is not the scope of

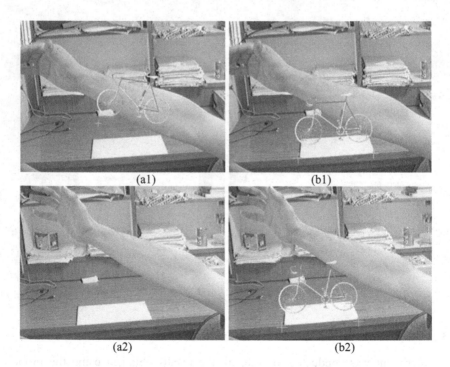

(a1)   (b1)

(a2)   (b2)

Fig. 6. Comparison with the authors' previous method [4]

this paper, it is closely related to the proposed method that currently limits its applications in the areas where the positions of the camera changed significantly. Two other possible solutions can be considered:

1. *Incremental estimation of the projective matrices*. This estimation will be based on the information of the previous frame. A major problem is the error accumulation that will lead to severe drifts and failure after a while.

2. *Estimation based on more keyframes*. More keyframes can be used which can be gathered from different viewpoints to estimate the projective matrix. However, more matching processes will be required between the current video frame and each of these keyframes. Thus, more computation time will be required and the speed will be slowed down depending on the number of the keyframes used.

6 Conclusions

In this paper, a robust point transferring algorithm is proposed based on a new nonlinear optimization model. There are two major contributions of the proposed method. Firstly, a simple and more accurate nonlinear optimization model is proposed, thus making the results more accurate. Secondly, a robust estimation is used to transfer any specified points. The initialization procedure is simple, as the points that will be used for augmentation are only required to be specified in one reference image. The transferred points can be used for registration and annotation even when the scenes are largely occluded or in the presence of moving objects.

References

1. Kato H. and Billinghurst M., "Marker Tracking and HMD Calibration for a Video-based Augmented Reality Conferencing System", *Proceedings of the 2nd IEEE and ACM International Workshop on Augmented Reality,* 1999, CA, USA, 85–94.
2. Shi J.B. and Tomasi C., "Good Features to Track", *Proceedings of the IEEE Conference on Computer Vision and Pattern Recognition*, 1994, Washington, USA, 593–600.
3. Li J., Laganiere R. and Roth G., "Online Estimation of Trifocal Tensor for Augmented Live Video", *Proceedings of the IEEE and ACM International Symposium on Mixed and Augmented Reality*, 2004, VA, USA, 182-190.
4. Yuan M.L., Ong S.K. and Nee A.Y.C., "Registration Using Natural features for Augmented Reality Systems", *IEEE Transactions on Visualization and Computer Graphics*, 12(4), 2006, 569-580.
5. Gordon I. and Lowe D.G., "Scene Modeling, Recognition and Tracking with Invariant Image Features", *Proceedings of the IEEE International Symposium on Mixed and Augmented Reality*, 2004, DC, USA, 110-119.
6. Vacchetti L., Lepetit V. and Fua P., "Stable Real-time 3D Tracking Using Online and Offline Information", *IEEE Transactions on Pattern Analysis and Machine Intelligence*, 26(10), 2004, 1385-1391.
7. Comport A., Marchand É., Pressigout M. and Chaumette F., "Real-time Markerless Tracking for Augmented Reality: the Virtual Visual Servoing Framework", *IEEE Transaction on Visualization and Computer Graphics*, 12(4), 2006, 615-628.

8. Lowe D.G., "Distinctive Image Features from Scale-invariant keypoints", *International Journal of Computer Vision*, 60(2), 2004, 91-110
9. Chia K.W., Cheok A.D. and Prince S.J.D., "Online 6 DOF Augmented Reality Registration from Natural Features", *Proceedings of the IEEE and ACM International Symposium on Mixed and Augmented Reality*, 2002, Darmstadt, Germany, 305-313
10. Yuan M.L., Ong S.K. and Nee A.Y.C., "A Generalised Registration Method for Augmented Reality Systems", *Computers & Graphics*, 29(6), 2005, 980-997.
11. Harris C. and Stephens M., "A Combined Corner and Edge Detector", *Proceedings of 4th Alvey Vision Conference*, Manchester, UK, 1988, 189-192.
12. Xiao J.J. and Shah M., "Two-Frame Wide Baseline Matching", *Proceedings of the IEEE International Conference on Computer Vision*, 2003, FL, USA, 603-609.
13. Zhang Z., "Determining the Epipolar Geometry and its Uncertainty: A Review", *International Journal of Computer Vision*, 279(2), 1998, 161-198.
14. Ferrari V., Tuytelaars T. and Gool L.V., "Markerless Augmented Reality with a Real-time Affine Region Tracker", *Proceedings of the IEEE and ACM International Symposium on Augmented Reality*, 2001, NY, USA, 87–96.

Accurate 3D Facial Synthesis for Plastic Surgery Simulation

Lei Wu[1], Houqiang Li[1], Nenghai Yu[1], and Mingjing Li[2]

[1] University of Science and Technology of China,
Hefei 230027, Anhui, China
wulei@mail.ustc.edu.cn, {lihq, ynh}@ustc.edu.cn
[2] Microsoft Research Asia, No. 49, Zhichun Road, Beijing 100080, China
mjli@microsoft.com

Abstract. 3D facial synthesis has been an intensive research topic in both image processing and computer graphics. So far common facial synthesizing methods were either statistic model based or laser range scanner (LRS) based. However, these methods could only provide approximate models. In this paper, we present a Magnetic Resonance Image (MRI) based 3D facial synthesizing approach, which can build accurate virtual faces for plastic surgery. This approach provides an database free modeling process so that the precision will not be limited by the face database. During modeling, we combine Sobel filter with snake algorithm to extract the 3D facial surface from noised MRI and build Bezier facial model, which facilitates the local geometric control. Furthermore, the proposed photo mapping algorithm help add realistic texture to the model. It avoids the complex and time-consuming texture fitting process while achieves satisfying result.

Keywords: 3D reconstruction, 3D face, texture mapping, plastic surgery.

1 Introduction

With the spurt of plastic surgeries in recent years, multimedia assisted post-surgery appearance design and prediction (PADP) has become imperative for surgery evaluation, since unsatisfying surgical outcome has caused great anxiety for both surgeons and patients. A critical technique for PADP is accurate 3D facial synthesis, which has been studied for over twenty years. Initially, parametric surface was used for facial animation [11]. However, due to the sparse sampling of real face, the model was not accurate enough for PADP. In 1988, a Finite Element Method (FEM) was proposed by X. Q. Deng to deal with the deformable model of skin [4]. This model was good at stress and strain analysis, but it was not clear how to control the model's shape. Thereafter, various techniques came out for the geometric face modeling [3, 5, 15, 16]. Unfortunately, none of them provided any easy geometric control method. Later, Blanz and Vetter proposed a morphable model [1] to reconstruct 3D face from one or several photos. This method used a large face database to predict the modeling parameters. However, the model's precision depends on the similarity between patients' faces and sample faces in the database. So it was unstable for PADP neither.

T.-J. Cham et al. (Eds.): MMM 2007, LNCS 4352, Part II, pp. 269–278, 2007.

In 1996, Koch and Gross [6] stated the use of FEM in simulating facial surgeries. Their method could calculate facial deformation under certain forces caused by the surgery, but it could not provide a convenient way to design the shape. Burgert and Salb [2] designed a surgical auxiliary system, which could help transforming an unsymmetrical face to a symmetric one. In 2002, Koch et al [7] summarized the framework for facial surgery simulation. However, the use of FEM model without parametric mesh made their geometric control process time-consuming and difficult to apply. Recently, Takácsa and Pieperb [14] presented a novel facial modeling method by synthesizing facial photos and Magnetic Resonance Images (MRI). They added texture to the model by a complex texture fitting method, and still did not provide an easy geometric control method.

In this paper, a new multi-model method is proposed for accurate 3D facial synthesis and easy geometric control by combining the 3D volume model with parametric surface model. Face database is not required in the modeling process. We manage to extract 3D facial data directly from noised Magnetic Resonance Images (MRI) of patient's head. Using snake algorithm, smooth facial contours are accurately obtained from MRI. Based on these contours, we build the Bezier mesh model, by which we can reshape the 3D face using a few control points. Besides, we propose an accurate photo mapping algorithm that can map the whole photo to the model directly. To achieve this goal, we only need to mark three pairs of corresponding points on both 2D photo and 3D face model manually. Complex and time-consuming texture fitting process [9] is no longer needed. The robustness is tested by both facial deformation and various photos of different individuals. These improvements and proposed methods greatly help perform the PADP.

The rest of the paper is organized as follows: Section 2 expatiates on the 3D model construction process; Section 3 elaborates on the fast and accurate photo mapping method; Section 4 compares the facial model with the real face and shows the designed result; Section 5 concludes the paper and describes future work.

2   3D Facial Model Reconstruction

In this section, we will describe how to build a 3D facial model from MRI. First, we extract facial contours in each MRI and sample these contours. Then we use these samples to calculate Bezier control points by which we can generate the Bezier mesh. In the final step, adjacent Bezier patches engendered from these control points are combined together to form the facial surface model.

2.1   Facial Contour Extraction from MRI

MRI records the 3D shape and inner tissue density of the patient's head. Our object is to reconstruct an accurate 3D facial surface model for PADP. First we have to extract the facial contours from MRI. Because of the scanning noise, the facial contours in MRI may not be smooth. Common edge detection methods fail to extract glossy contours from MRI, which will affect the accuracy of the final facial model. In this paper, we use snake algorithm to perform the extraction. There are two advantages of applying snake to our problem: the external energy defined in this algorithm makes the curve stick intimately to the facial contour; the inner energy guarantees the smoothness of the extraction. In addition, considering the similarity between adjacent facial contours, the extracted contour in one MRI can be used as the initial snake curve for the next MRI. In this paper, Gradient Vector Flow (GVF) snake algorithm [8, 18] is used, in which the snake energy is defined as follows:

$$\varepsilon = \iint \mu(u_x^2 + u_y^2 + v_x^2 + v_y^2) + |\nabla f|^2 |V - \nabla f|^2 \, dxdy \tag{1}$$

$$f(x,y) = -E_{ext}(x,y) \tag{2}$$

$$E_{ext}(x,y) = G_\sigma(x,y) * I(x.y) \tag{3}$$

ε is snake energy; f symbolizes edge map; $E_{ext}(x,y)$ stands for the external energy; $I(x,y)$ represents the grey level of MRI and $V(x,y) = (u(x,y), v(x,y))$ denotes the GVF field; u_x, u_y, v_x, v_y refer to the derivatives of V in x and y directions.

To reduce the influence of the irrelevant energy inside the facial contour, we enhance the facial contours by filtering $E_{ext}(x,y)$ with Sobel operator.

$$E'_{ext}(x,y) = |S_x(x,y) * E_{ext}(x,y) + S_y(x,y) * E_{ext}(x,y)| \tag{4}$$

$S_x(x,y)$, $S_y(x,y)$ represents the Sobel operator in x and y directions. We use $E'_{ext}(x,y)$ as the external energy for GVF snake. Using Sobel operator, GVF snake curve is effectively prevented from shrinking into the inner brain area. Fig. 1 gives you an idea of the contour extraction results. After the contour extraction, we sample the contours at the same interval that MRI are scanned, to get a regular sample matrix.

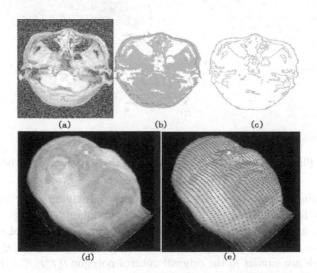

(a)   (b)   (c)

(d)   (e)

Fig. 1. Process of extract facial data from MRI

Fig. 1 (a) is one of the MRI; (b) is contour extracted by original GVF snake algorithm; (c) is extracted with Sobel combined GVF Snake Method (SSM); (d) is 3D MR volume model; (e) is the regular contour sample matrix. Comparing (c) with (b) we can see SSM has prevented snake curve from shrinking into the brain area.

2.2 Facial Mesh Generation

After facial contour extraction, we set about to generate the Bezier facial surface model. The model can be represented as a mesh of combination of Bezier patches. Every individual Bezier patch has $m \times n$ Bezier control points generated from facial contour samples. These control points determine the patch's shape by Eq. (5). Using Bezier facial mesh we can design the facial model by only adjusting a few control points. This improvement facilitates surgical design process.

$$S(u,v) = \sum_{i=0}^{m} \sum_{j=0}^{n} P_{ij} B_{im}(u) B_{jn}(v) , u, v \in [0,1] \tag{5}$$

$S(u,v)$ represents a Bezier patch, in which $B_{im}(u), B_{jn}(v)$ stand for Bernstein harmonic functions. m and n are the orders of the patch. $P_{ij}(i=1,2\cdots m, j=1,2\cdots n)$ represent Bezier control points, which fix the patch's shape. In this paper, we provide a method to calculate the control points from sample points. This method is in fact the inverse iteration of De Casteljau's algorithm. In order to explain our idea, we will first overview the De Casteljau's algorithm, which is used to compute the surface points from control points.

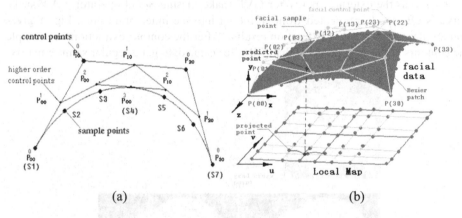

(a)   (b)

Fig. 2. (a) Illustration of De Casteljau's algorithm; (b) Illustration of the Bezier patch

Fig. 2 (a) illustrates the De Casteljau's algorithm. Imagining $P_{00}^0, P_{10}^0, P_{20}^0, P_{30}^0$ are four control points forming three line segments with midpoints $P_{00}^1, P_{10}^1, P_{20}^1$. Midpoints of Segments $P_{00}^1 P_{10}^1$ and $P_{10}^1 P_{20}^1$ are marked as P_{00}^2 and P_{10}^2. P_{00}^3 is the midpoint of segment $P_{00}^2 P_{10}^2$. This process is formulated as Eq. (6). Now we get Polygon $P_{00}^0 P_{00}^1 P_{00}^2 P_{00}^3$ and Polygon $P_{00}^3 P_{10}^2 P_{20}^1 P_{30}^0$ which are similar to the original control polygon $P_{00}^0 P_{10}^0 P_{20}^0 P_{30}^0$. The algorithm proceeds by using the newly derived polygons as the original polygon for the next iteration, in which new control polygons get closer to the samples and it stops when the deviation meets the precision need.

$$P_{ij}^k = \begin{cases} P_{ij}^0 & k=0 \\ (1-\alpha)P_{ij}^{k-1} + \alpha P_{i+1,j}^{k-1} & k>0 \end{cases} \tag{6}$$

α is a constant value and often set as $\alpha = 0.5$. P_{ij}^k is the control point P_{ij} in the kth iteration. When this algorithm proceeds along two orthogonal directions, a Bezier patch is generated. Fig. 2 (b) exemplifies the Bezier patch. P_{ij} are control points which can manipulate the patch's shape separately. Namely, we can reshape the whole patch by just moving one of these control points. This characteristic of control points greatly facilitates PADP.

In this paper, we calculate control points from facial sample points in the inverse iteration of De Casteljau's algorithm. Our algorithm is provided as follows:

Choose $nx \times ny$ samples S_{ij} ;

$\alpha = 0.5$;

For j = 1 to ny

  Set $P_{ij}^0 = S_{ij}$, $i = 0,1,\cdots, nx-1$;

  While $nx > m$

    For k = 0 to nx-1

$$P_{k+2,j}^1 = \frac{1}{\alpha} P_{k+1,j}^0 - \frac{(1-\alpha)}{\alpha} P_{kj}^0$$

$$P_{k+3,j}^1 = \frac{1}{\alpha} P_{k+2,j}^0 - \frac{(1-\alpha)}{\alpha} P_{k+1,j}^0$$

$$P_{k+2,j}^0 = P_{k+2,j}^1 ; \quad P_{k+3,j}^0 = P_{k+3,j}^1 ;$$

    End

$$P_{k,J}^0 = P_{2k,j}^0 ; \quad nx = (nx+1)/2;$$

  End

End

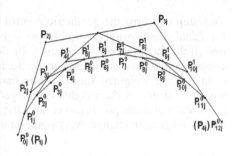

Fig. 3. Illustration of our iteration

P_{ij}^0 are original sample points, and $P_{ij}, i = 0,1\cdots, m-1; j = 0,1\cdots, n-1$ are final Bezier control points. $nx \times ny$ is the number of sample points from which $m \times n$ control points will be derived. In Fig. 3, nx, ny are set to 13 and m, n are set to 4 as an example. The iteration finishes when control points P_{ij}^0 converge to P_{ij} . As the control points P_{ij} are obtained, the Bezier patch can be represented by Eq. (5). Then we manage to mesh the facial model by combining adjacent Bezier patches together. In order to get continuous combination, the boundary points should meet certain conditions:

$$P(1,v) = Q(0,v) \tag{7}$$

$$Q_u(0,v) \times Q_v(0,v) = \alpha(v) P_u(1,v) \times P_v(1,v) \tag{8}$$

$P(u,v)$, $Q(u,v)$ stand for two adjacent Bezier patches. $P(1,v)$ and $Q(0,v)$ embody the shared boundary points. $P_u(1,v)$, $P_v(1,v)$, $Q_u(0,v)$, $Q_v(0,v)$ are the derivatives in u and v directions. Eq. (7) and (8) guarantee the boundaries are relatively smooth. From Fig. 4 (a) we can see that the Bezier facial mesh accurately attaches to the 3D MR scanning data.

(b) is the Bezier facial mesh generated from the noised scanning data. (c) is the Bezier facial mesh generated from facial samples extracted by SSM. (b) and (c) demonstrate that SSM greatly reduces the scanning noise. (d) and (e) show the result of nose deformation by changing the Bezier control points on nose.

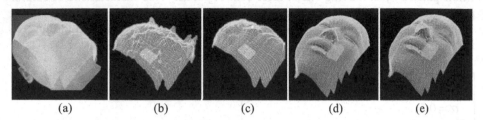

(a)   (b)   (c)   (d)   (e)

Fig. 4. (a)~(c) Bezier patches generated from extracted facial data; (d)(e) results of nose deformation

2.3 Facial Shape Deformation

This step concerns the geometric control process which is one of the key operations for facial plastic surgery in order to simulate post-surgery appearance. We plan to design the facial geometric structure by dragging a few Bezier control points. These control points are not on but near the Bezier patch. Eq. (5) indicates that Bezier patch is in fact the weighted sum of some harmonic functions with control points as the weights. If one of the weights is changed, the whole sum will change continuously. Thus, each of these points can control the whole patch's shape smoothly. In this way, we do not need to change every point on the patch to get satisfying shape.

3 Fast Photo Mapping Algorithm

In this section, we explain the convenient fast photo mapping algorithm to get more realistic surgical prediction. The traditional texture mapping algorithm needs a texture fitting process [9] in which 20 or more pairs of corresponding points are needed to match the photo to the 3D model. This process is complex and time-consuming. We propose a fast algorithm which can map the photo exactly onto the facial model in less than a second with only three pairs of corresponding points.

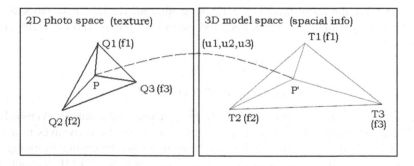

Fig. 5. Area coordinates

Based on the immutability of area coordinates, we manage to locate the facial photo pixel P, which corresponds to the 3D point P' in 3D model, and map its texture to P'. First of all, we will introduce the concept of area coordinates.

$$u_3 = \frac{S_{f_1 f_2 P}}{S_{f_1 f_2 f_3}}, u_3 = \frac{S_{P f_2 f_3}}{S_{f_1 f_2 f_3}}, u_3 = \frac{S_{f_1 P f_3}}{S_{f_1 f_2 f_3}} \tag{9}$$

$$x = \sum_{i=1}^{3} u_i x_i, \ y = \sum_{i=1}^{3} u_i y_i \tag{10}$$

f_1, f_2, f_3 (T_1, T_2, T_3 or Q_1, Q_2, Q_3) are called feature points and $\Delta f_1 f_2 f_3$ ($\Delta T_1 T_2 T_3$ or $\Delta Q_1 Q_2 Q_3$) is feature triangle. $S_{f_1 f_2 f_3}$ represents the area of the feature triangle. $S_{f_i f_j P}$ corresponds to the area of $\Delta f_i f_j P$. u_1, u_2, u_3 defined by Eq. (9) are the area coordinates of P whose orthogonal coordinates are (x, y). $x_i, y_i (i=1,2,3)$ denote the orthogonal coordinates of f_i. Eq. (10) designates the relationship between the two coordinates.

As we use three parameters u_1, u_2, u_3 to express a 2D point, the three parameters are not independent. They must meet the following equation:

$$u_1 + u_2 + u_3 = 1 \tag{11}$$

Since the two triangles' area rate is immutable after the 3D space is rotated, translated, scaled and projected into 2D space, the area coordinates of any point P in 2D photo remains the same with its corresponding point P' on the 3D facial model. Based on this idea, we define two area coordinates $\Delta Q_1 Q_2 Q_3$ and $\Delta T_1 T_2 T_3$ in 2D and 3D space separately. T_1, T_2, T_3 (or Q_1, Q_2, Q_3) represent the left pupil, the right pupil and the nose tip respectively. As shown in Fig. 6 (a) and (b). Since there are only six feature points $(T_1, T_2, T_3, Q_1, Q_2, Q_3)$, all of which are salient features, we can mark them by hand easily. The algorithm for automatic location of the facial salient features [10, 13, 17] can also be easily achieved. The whole photo mapping progress proceeds in two steps:

In Step 1, the algorithm translates the rectangular coordinates of P' in 3D model space into its area coordinates (u_1, u_2, u_3) under feature triangle $\Delta T_1 T_2 T_3$ using Eq. (10).

In Step 2, the algorithm translates the area coordinates of P' (u_1, u_2, u_3) back into rectangular coordinates (x, y) taking $\Delta Q_1 Q_2 Q_3$ as feature triangle, and maps the texture at this 2D point to its corresponding 3D point. Fig. 6 (c) shows the result of the

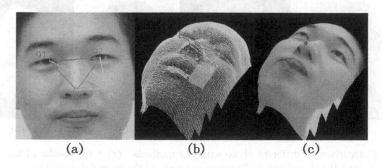

(a)   (b)   (c)

Fig. 6. Process of accurate texture mapping algorithm

Table 1. Comparison of different texture mapping methods

Method	Result	Time
Manual editing via user friendly designing software	Detailed matching	Days/weeks
Texture fitting algorithm	Detailed matching	Minutes
Our photo mapping algorithm	Detailed matching	Less than a second

accurate photo mapping algorithm. The robustness of the algorithm is tested by both large-scale geometric deformation and various photos of different people.

From Table 1, we can see that our algorithm is much faster than other texture mapping methods [9]. Fig. 7 illustrates that our photo mapping algorithm keeps the veracity as well. In the survey of 19 people, 78.9% of them think that our photo mapping results (Fig. 7 (f), (h)) are more realistic than texture fitting algorithm (Fig. 7 (b), (d)).

4   Experiment Result

We collect two patients' photos and their head MRI scan data. Each MRI dataset consists of 153 images, each of which has the resolution of 480*520 pixels. The scanning interval is 1.25mm, and each pixel covers an area of 0.8125*0.8125 mm^2. We load these data into our facial synthesis system and get the result shown in Fig. 7 (f) and (h). Since the assessment of reality is a strong subjective task, we conduct a

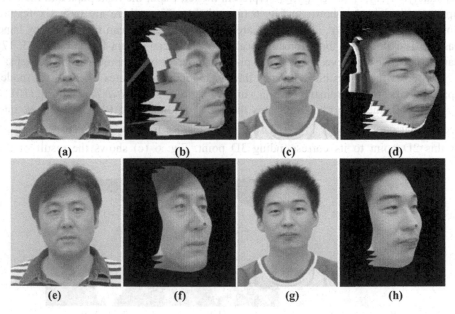

(a)	(b)	(c)	(d)
(e)	(f)	(g)	(h)

Fig. 7. Comparison of different photo mapping methods. (a) ~ (d) results of texture fitting algorithm; (e) ~ (h) photos and photo mapping results of the proposed algorithm.

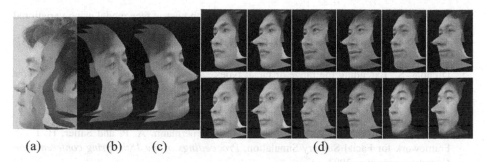

(a)   (b)   (c)   (d)

Fig. 8. Facial synthesizing results and designs of nose-lifting surgery. (a) Comparison of 3D facial model with real face; (b) original facial model and (c) the design for nose-lifting surgery. (d) Original 3D visage (left), designed visage after nose-lifting (right).

small user study by 20 participants, consisting of plastic surgeons, patients, university professors and graduate researchers, to judge the reality of the synthesized 3D facial model. In the study, two patients' virtual faces are provided to compare with their real faces, which are shown in Fig. 7 (e)~(h). 90% people including the plastic surgeons are satisfied with the accuracy and admit their relevance to plastic surgery; another 10% feel the models are tolerable but need further improvement to provide better surgical prediction. Fig. 8 exemplifies the design results of the patients' nose-lifting by manipulating the red control points on the noses. With the synthesized faces, surgeons and patients can perform PADP and evaluate the surgeons' job.

5 Conclusion

In this paper, we have presented an approach for synthesizing accurate 3D virtual faces for PADP. This approach combines spatial information from MRI and textural information from the patient's photo to build the face model. The Bezier face model enables us to design the facial geometric structure with a few control points. To make the model look more realistic, we have also presented a fast accurate photo mapping algorithm which matches the photo to the face model in less than a second. The accuracy and robustness of this algorithm are evaluated experimentally.

Our future work will comprise the following aspects: the mode of geometric control will be improved; dimensions of freedom (DOF) for geometric control will be condensed for particular surgery; automatic feature location on 3D face will be investigated. In this paper, we only evaluate the method on nose. In the future, we will investigate the possibility of applying it to other parts for more complex operations.

References

1. Blanz, V. and Vetter, T., A Morphable Model for the Synthesis of 3D Faces, SIGGRAPH99, 1999.
2. Burgert, O., Salb, T., Gockel, T., Dillmann, R., Hassfeld, S., Brief, J., Krempien, R., Walz, S. and Mu"hling, J., A system for facial reconstruction using distraction and symmetry considerations, International Congress Series, 2001.

3. DeCarlos, D., Metaxas, D. and Stone, M., An anthropometric face model using variational techniques, *Computer Graphics Proceedings SIGGRAPH*, 1998.
4. Deng, X. Q., A Finite Element Analysis of Surgery of the Human Facial Tissues, Columbia University, 1988.
5. DiPaola, S., Extending the range of facial types, *Journal of Visualization and Computer Animation*, 1991.
6. Koch, R. M., Gross, M. H. and Carls, F. R., Simulating Facial Surgery Using Finite Element Models, *SIGGRAPH96*, 1996.
7. Koch, R. M., Roth, S. H. M., Gross, M. H., Zimmermann, A. P. and Sailer, H. F., A Framework for Facial Surgery Simulation, *Proceedings of the 18th spring conference on Computer graphics,* 2002.
8. Kass, M., Witkin, A. and Terzopoulos, D., Snake: Active Contour Models, *International Journal of Computer Vision*, 1998.
9. Lee, W. S. and Nadia, M. T., From Real Faces To Virtual Faces: Problems and Solutions, *Proc. 3IA'98*, Limoges (FRANCE), pp.5-19, 1998.
10. Mahoor, M. H., Mottaleb, M. A., Facial Feature Extraction in Color Images Using Enhanced Active Shape Model, *Proceedings of the 7th International Conference on Automatic Face and Gesture Recognition,* 2006.
11. Parke, F. I. and Waters, K., Computer Facial Animation, AK Peters, 1996.
12. Phong, B.T. Illumination for computer generated images. *Communications of the ACM*, 18(6):311–317, June 1975.
13. Seo, K. H., Kim, W., Oh, C. and Lee, J. J., Face detection and facial feature extraction using color snake, *Proceedings of the 2002 IEEE International Symposium on Industrial Electronics*, IEEE Press, 2002.
14. Takácsa, B., Pieperb, S., Cebralc, J., Kissd, B., Benedekd, B. and Szijártód, G., Facial Modeling for Plastic Surgery Using Magnetic Resonance Imagery and 3D Surface Data, *Three-dimensional Image Capture and Applications*, 2004.
15. Thalmann, N. M., Minh, H., Angelis, M. and Thalmann, D., Design, transformation and animation of human faces, *Visual Computer*, 1989.
16. Todd, J. T., Leonard, S. M., Shaw, R. E. and Pittenger, J. B., The perception of human growth, Scientific American, 1980.
17. Walker, K. N., Cootes, T. F. and Taylor, C. J., Locating Salient Facial Features Using Image Invariants, *International Workshop on Automatic Face and Gesture Recognition*, 1998
18. Xu, C. Y. and Prince, J. L., Gradient Vector Flow: A New External Force for Snakes, *CVPR'97*, 1997.

Generic 3-D Modeling for Content Analysis of Court-Net Sports Sequences

Jungong Han[1], Dirk Farin[1], and Peter H.N. de With[1,2]

[1] University of Technology Eindhoven, P.O.Box 513, 5600MB Eindhoven
jg.han@tue.nl
[2] LogicaCMG, RTSE, PO Box 7089, 5605JB Eindhoven, The Netherlands

Abstract. In this paper, we present a *generic* 3-D modeling for analyzing court-net sports videos, which enables to map points in the real-world coordinates to the image coordinates. To this end, we propose a two-step algorithm to extract the feature lines and points from two perpendicular planes (ground and net plane) for determining the camera calibration parameters. In the first step, we bridge the gap between the 2-D standard court model and the image coordinate system that is described by a plane-to-plane mapping. With this mapping, it is possible to distinguish the feature lines like court lines in the ground plane. The second step is to detect the net line located in the net plane, where the line is classified as net line if it passes several tests. The feature points at well-known positions within these two planes (e.g. intersection of two lines) are utilized to calculate the camera calibration parameters. We demonstrate the performance of the proposed algorithm by evaluating it for a variety of court-net sports videos including badminton, tennis and volleyball. Results show that the algorithm is robust to partial court views or bad lighting conditions, and can be applied to various applications.

Keywords: Generic, 3-D modeling, Sports video, Content analysis.

1 Introduction

Automatic content analysis of sports video is an interesting and challenging area for computer vision, since it enables new applications, such as automatic abstracting of the most important scenes of a long sports event, virtual view generation from arbitrary view-points, or computer simulation of the sports games. For such applications, it is necessary to know the position of the important objects like player and ball in 3-D coordinate system, rather than the position in the image. For this purpose, 3-D modeling based on camera calibration has to be established from the video input to determine the coordinates mapping.

Significant research on camera modeling for sports video analysis has been performed, which can be broadly divided into two stages. Earlier publications are based on ad-hoc algorithms that were tailored to a specific sports type. In [1], the authors describe a calibration algorithm for tennis courts, using a simplified camera model that only considers the camera tilt angle, the camera distance

T.-J. Cham et al. (Eds.): MMM 2007, LNCS 4352, Part II, pp. 279–288, 2007.

from the court field, and the focal-length. In addition, the algorithm requires that the lower part of the court is non-occluded and a starting position for the searching has to be pointed manually. A different approach [2] for tennis court calibration has been proposed by Calvo *et al.*, as they apply a Hough transform on the Sobel filter output to find court lines. Assigning the lines to the court model is implemented via a set of heuristics. In this algorithm, there are several assumptions, for example, the two lines at the net are the two lines with the most votes in the Hough transform. But in most tennis videos, the net line is not marked on the court at all. A camera calibration algorithm [3] for soccer games is proposed by Yamada *et al.* This camera model includes two rotation axes, i.e., focal length and the camera position. However, the camera position is assumed to be known, which requires manual work to be carried out prior to applying the algorithm. In [4], a more robust detection of the court (for soccer videos) is introduced, but the problem is still existing, since finding calibration parameters based on court-lines requires a computationally complex initialization using an exhaustive search through the parameter space. The significant contributions in [5][6] propagate the second generation of camera modeling for sports video analysis. In [5], the authors propose a new, more generic camera calibration algorithm that can be adapted to every sports where the court consists of a sufficient number of straight lines. This configuration of court lines is able to be specified by the user and integrated into the algorithm as a court model. In [6], an improved version of [5] is presented, in which the main structure of [5] is still preserved, but most parts are replaced by more efficient algorithms in order to increase the speed to real-time processing. Generally speaking, in contrast to previous algorithms [2][4], the second generation of camera modeling [5][6] for sports analysis is fully automatic, robust against large occlusions or bad lighting, and generic to different sports, like tennis, volleyball and football. Nevertheless, it still limits to the mapping between the 3-D coordinate system and the 2-D image plane. More specifically, most existing algorithms intend to find a mapping between the image plane and a standard court plane, which is naturally a transform from one 2-D plane to another 2-D plane. The use of this modeling is unable to provide any 3-D height information of the object, which is a key parameter in some applications like virtual view generation or the case if you tend to study the trajectory of the ball in real-world.

This paper proposes a generic 3-D modeling for analysis of court-net sports video, where we contribute on two aspects. First, we exploit both the ground plane and the net plane for constructing the 3-D modeling, since they are two vertical planes that intersect in 3-D space. The court lines of the playing field and net line can be used to characterize these two planes. Second, we propose a two-step algorithm to recognize a set of features at well-known positions within these two planes. With these features, the camera calibration parameters can be found with high quality. The proposed modeling is generic in the sense that it can be adapted to every court-net sports, like badminton, tennis and volleyball, through only changing the configuration of the court and net. The approach was

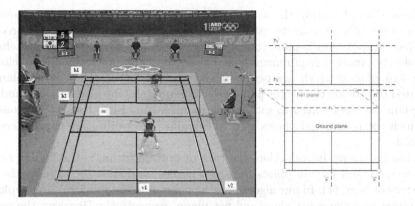

Fig. 1. The planes, lines and points are selected in the image and the correspondences in the standard model are determined. Six intersection points are used for calibration.

found to be robust against cases where large parts of the court are occluded or out of view.

The paper is organized as follows, Section 2 gives an overview of camera calibration theorem. Section 3 describes the mapping algorithm between the image and a 2-D standard court model. Section 4 presents the method for detecting the net line in the image and the approach for computing the calibration parameters. The experimental results on various court-net sports are provided in Section 5 and Section 6 concludes the paper.

2   Camera Calibration Theorem

The task of the camera calibration is to provide a geometric transformation that maps the points in the real-world coordinates to the image domain. Since the real court-net model is a 3-D scene but the displayed image is a 2-D planar, this mapping can be written as a 3×4 transformation matrix $\mathbf{M}$, transforming a point $\mathbf{p} = (x, y, z, 1)^{\top}$ in real-world coordinates to image coordinates $\mathbf{p}' = (u, v, 1)^{\top}$ by $\mathbf{p}' = \mathbf{M}\mathbf{p}$, which is equivalent to

$$
\begin{pmatrix} u \\ v \\ 1 \end{pmatrix} = \begin{pmatrix} m_{11} & m_{12} & m_{13} & m_{14} \\ m_{21} & m_{22} & m_{23} & m_{24} \\ m_{31} & m_{32} & m_{33} & m_{34} \end{pmatrix} \begin{pmatrix} x \\ y \\ z \\ 1 \end{pmatrix}.
\tag{1}
$$

Since $\mathbf{M}$ is scaling invariant, eleven free parameters have to be determined. These can be calculated from six points whose positions are known in both the 3-D coordinates and the image. Note that these six points need not be fixed, but can be selected case by case, as some points may be occluded in some views. Instead of using point features directly, we base our camera calibration algorithm on lines, since detecting the accurate position of a specific point on a court is much more difficult than to estimate the position of line segments. Moreover, the detection of lines is more robust in the sense that they are hardly occluded completely. Another requirement is that these lines and points should be selected from *two* planes, which are perpendicular to each other. The second plane is required to provide the height parameter. Fortunately, the ground plane and the net plane are very suited to satisfy this requirement. Fig. 1 shows an example in which the points and planes used to calculate the calibration parameters are marked.

From the above introduction, the task of our algorithm is the finding of the feature lines and feature points from two planes, and then to calculate the parameters of Eqn. (1). In our algorithm, the court lines and net line are employed to characterize the court plane and net plane, respectively. However, the recognition of these lines is not easy, as they have similar visual properties. To resolve this problem, we propose a two-step algorithm.

3   Court-Line Recognition Based on Mapping Between Image and Court Configuration

Since it is difficult to determine the court line only in terms of low-level features, like color and width, we use here the layout (configuration) of the court, which must be exactly equal in both the standard court model and the image. The basic approach of our algorithm is to evaluate the distance between each layout formed by different white lines and the configuration of a standard court model. The configuration with the best match is selected as the final solution. This step provides the mapping correlation between image and a 2-D standard sports court, thereby realizing the function of the court-line recognition. Since both the court and the displayed image are planar, this mapping is a homography, which can be written as a 3×3 transformation matrix $\mathbf{H}$, transforming a point $\mathbf{p} = (x, y, w)^\top$ in real-world coordinates to image coordinates $\mathbf{p}' = (x', y', w')^\top$ as $\mathbf{p}' = \mathbf{H}\mathbf{p}$. The transformation matrix $\mathbf{H}$ can be calculated from four points whose positions are both known in the court model and in the image. Here, we use the intersection points of the court lines to compute the transformation parameters.

3.1   Line-Pixel Detection

Detection of white court-line pixels is carried out in two steps. The first step of the detector imposes two conditions on a pixel in order to be classified as a court-line pixel. Its luminance should exceed a threshold σ_l, and either two pixels at a horizontal distance of $\pm\tau$ pixels or at a vertical distance of $\pm\tau$ pixels should be darker than σ_d, where $\sigma_d \ll \sigma_l$. The second condition requires that the pixel should be enclosed either horizontally or vertically by dark pixels. This prevents that white pixels in large white areas are extracted. Parameter τ equals approximately the double court-line width.

3.2 Line-Parameter Estimation

Once we have achieved the set of court-line pixels, we extract parametric equations for the lines. The process is as follows. We start with a RANSAC-like algorithm to detect the dominant line in the data set. The line parameters are further refined with a least-squares approximation and the white pixels along the line segment are removed from the data set. This process is repeated several times until no more relevant lines can be found. We subsequently explain these steps in more detail.

RANSAC is a randomized algorithm that hypothesizes a set of model parameters and evaluates the quality of the parameters. After several hypotheses have been evaluated, the best one is chosen. More specifically, we hypothesize a line by randomly selecting two court-line pixels $\mathbf{p} = (p_x, p_y)$ and $\mathbf{q} = (q_x, q_y)$. From these two points, we determine the parameters a, b for the line model

$$\begin{cases} y = a \cdot x + b & \text{if } |p_x - q_x| \geq |p_y - q_y|, \\ x = a \cdot y + b & \text{if } |p_x - q_x| < |p_y - q_y|. \end{cases} \tag{2}$$

The advantage of this line model is that it does not degenerate for vertical lines (infinite slope) and that it enables a fast approximation to calculate the distance of a point to the line. We define the approximate distance $\tilde{d}(\mathbf{g}, x', y')$ between a point (x', y') and the line $\mathbf{g}$ as

$$\tilde{d}(\mathbf{g}, x', y') = \begin{cases} |a \cdot x' + b - y'| & \text{if } |p_x - q_x| \geq |p_y - q_y|, \\ |a \cdot y' + b - x'| & \text{if } |p_x - q_x| < |p_y - q_y|. \end{cases} \tag{3}$$

For each line hypothesis, we compute a score $s(\mathbf{g})$ by

$$s(\mathbf{g}) = \sum_{(x', y') \in \mathcal{P}} \max(\tau - \tilde{d}(\mathbf{g}, x', y'), 0), \tag{4}$$

where $\mathcal{P}$ is the set of court-line pixels and τ is the line width from Section 3.1. This score effectively computes the support of a line hypothesis as the number of white pixels close to the line, weighted with their distance to the line. The score and the line parameters are stored and the process is repeated with about 25 randomly generated hypotheses. At the end, the hypothesis with the highest score is selected.

3.3 Model Fitting

The model fitting step determines correspondences between the four detected lines and the lines in the court model. Once these correspondences are known, the homography between real-world coordinates and the image coordinates can be computed. To this end, four intersection points of the lines $\mathbf{p}_i$ and $\mathbf{p}'_i$ are computed and using the four resulting projection equations $\mathbf{p}'_i = \mathbf{H}\mathbf{p}_i$, eight equations are obtained that can be stacked into an equation system to solve for the parameters of matrix $\mathbf{H}$.

Since the correspondences between the lines in the image and the model are not known *a-priori*, we iterate through configurations of two horizontal and two vertical lines in the image as well as in the model. For each configuration, we compute the parameter matrix $\mathbf{H}$ and apply some quick tests to reject impossible configurations with little computational effort. If the homography passed these tests, we compute the complete model matching error E as

$$E = \sum_{(\mathbf{p},\mathbf{q}) \in \mathcal{M}} \min(\|\hat{\mathbf{p}}', \mathbf{Hp}\|_2 + \|\hat{\mathbf{q}}', \mathbf{Hq}\|_2, e_m), \qquad (5)$$

where $\mathcal{M}$ is the collection of line-segments (defined by their two end-points $\mathbf{p}, \mathbf{q}$) in the court-model and $(\hat{\mathbf{p}}', \hat{\mathbf{q}}')$ is the closest line-segment in the image. The metric $\|\cdot, \cdot\|_2$ denotes the Euclidean distance between the two points, and the error for a line segment is bounded by a maximum value e_m. The transformation $\mathbf{H}$ that gives the minimum error E is selected as the best transformation.

4   Net-Line Detection and Camera Parameter Computation

4.1   Net-Line Detection

From Section 3.2, we have obtained many lines, which can be considered as the candidates for the net line. Detection of the net line is carried out in three steps. The first step is a simple but an important scheme that excludes the court lines from the detection, because a court line looks similar to the net line in the image. Our approach is to transform each court line of the court model to the image plane, using the matrix $\mathbf{H}$. In Fig. 2, the black lines are the court lines detected by our approach.

The second step imposes three constraints that must satisfied for a line in order to be classified as a net line. These constraints are listed below.

- **Length.** We require that the net line has sufficient length. Let us first define n'_r in the right image of Fig. 1 as the bottom reference line of the net line, because it is the projection line of the net onto the ground plane. Using the matrix $\mathbf{H}$, the line n_r, which is the corresponding bottom reference line in the observed image, can be found. Experiments resulted in the requirement that the net line must be longer than $1/3$ of the length of n_r in the image.
- **Search area.** The net line must be close enough to the reference line, depending on the sports type. If the line equation of the bottom reference line n_r is $y = k \cdot x + b$, the net line must be located within the interval $[-\sigma; +\sigma]$ around the reference line, where parameter σ controls the search area, and is changed according to the chosen sports type. For instance, in badminton video, it equals approximately half the length of the whole court field. This prevents that white lines outside the court field are extracted.
- **Slope.** The orientation of the net line should be (nearly) parallel to the reference line, since line n_r is the projection line of the net on the ground

Fig. 2. Net-line detection. Left: only one line left. Right: the case where two lines pass the constraints.

plane in the image. In other words, the net line should be selected from the lines whose slope parameter is similar as that of n_r.

Usually, there are two cases after testing of the above constraints. One case is that only one line is left, which is definitely the net line (e.g., the left picture of Fig. 2). Another possible case is that there are still two lines left, since the net is in the middle connected to the ground with a binding cable in real life (see example from the right picture of Fig. 2), so that it actually consists of two slightly different line segments. In order to address this problem, we need a net-line refinement procedure.

The net-line refinement deals with the case where two lines pass the constraints mentioned above. Here, we use a practical example to explain our solution shown in Fig. 2. Suppose that two lines pass the constraints, they intersect somewhere in the image. We denote the line that locates at the left of the intersection as l_1. Similarly, the right line part is noted as l_2. We also define the *start* and *end* point of n_r as $\mathbf{p}_s$ and $\mathbf{p}_e$. Based on geometry, it is feasible to find the projection points of $\mathbf{p}_s$ on l_1 as well as $\mathbf{p}_e$ on l_2, respectively. The final net line is the line connecting these two projection points $\mathbf{p}'_s$ and $\mathbf{p}'_e$.

4.2 Calibration Parameter Computation

In order to determine the eleven parameters of Eqn. (1), at least six correspondences between image positions and positions in the 3-D coordinates have to be found. In our approach, we select four points from the ground plane, and two points from the net plane. For the points on the ground plane, since courts usually do not have clear visual features, we use the intersections of lines for establishing four point correspondences (see Fig. 1 for an example). For the points on the net plane, there are no intersection points. Instead, we identify the reference line of the net line in both the model and image domain. Then, we select two points on the reference line and project those points onto the net line. Finally, we find the corresponding projected points in the model. In more detail, this runs as follows. Our basic idea is to find two points on the reference net line n_r in the image, i.e., $\mathbf{p}_s$ and $\mathbf{p}_e$ in the right picture of Fig. 2 (blue points). The projected points on the detected net line ($\mathbf{p}'_s$ and $\mathbf{p}'_e$, red points) are utilized to compute the calibration parameters. The coordinates of the projected points ($\mathbf{p}'_s$ and $\mathbf{p}'_e$) in the image domain can be computed. Using transform matrix $\mathbf{H}$, the corresponding point of $\mathbf{p}_s$ in the standard court model is obtained, whose x and y coordinates are the coordinates of $\mathbf{p}'_s$ in the 3-D model. The z coordinate of $\mathbf{p}'_s$ in the 3-D model equals to a standard height of the net (i.e., the height of the badminton net is 1.55 meters). When six points have been found, the calibration parameters can be determined by building an equation system based on the camera model and inserting the six-points pairs as data:

$$
\begin{pmatrix}
X_1 & Y_1 & Z_1 & 1 & 0 & 0 & 0 & 0 & -u_1X_1 & -u_1Y_1 & -u_1Z_1 \\
0 & 0 & 0 & 0 & X_1 & Y_1 & Z_1 & 1 & -v_1X_1 & -v_1Y_1 & -v_1Z_1 \\
\cdots & \cdots & \cdots & \cdots & \cdots & \cdots & & & & & \\
\cdots & \cdots & \cdots & \cdots & \cdots & \cdots & & & & & \\
X_6 & Y_6 & Z_6 & 1 & 0 & 0 & 0 & 0 & -u_6X_6 & -u_6Y_6 & -u_6Z_6 \\
0 & 0 & 0 & 0 & X_6 & Y_6 & Z_6 & 1 & -v_6X_6 & -v_6Y_6 & -v_6Z_6
\end{pmatrix}
\begin{pmatrix}
m_{11} \\
m_{12} \\
\cdots \\
\cdots \\
m_{33}
\end{pmatrix}
=
\begin{pmatrix}
u_1m_{34} \\
v_1m_{34} \\
\cdots \\
\cdots \\
u_6m_{34} \\
v_6m_{34}
\end{pmatrix}.
$$

(6)

Note that this makes use of the normalization $m_{34} = 1$, which is always true for our application.

5   Experimental Results

We have tested the presented algorithm on five video sequences (in total more than 1 hour) that were recorded from regular television broadcasts. Two of the sequences were tennis games on different court classes, two were badminton games, and one was a volleyball game. For our test set, the algorithm is able to find the courts as well as the net line very reliably if the minimum required amount of court lines (two horizontal and two vertical lines) and the net line are clearly visible in the image. Fig. 3 shows example pictures, where some difficult scenes have been selected. Table 1 shows the performance evaluation results of our algorithm. It can be seen that the calibration is correct for more than 90% of the sequences. Note that the evaluation method for our camera-calibration algorithm is to manually select some *feature* points (i.e., intersection of two lines) in the 3-D model. Theoretically, the corresponding points of those feature points in the image domain should also be intersections, which is ground truth data. We transform these feature points to the image domain using our calibration parameters, and measure them with ground truth data. The most common mis-calibration was caused in the case, where the net line is very close to one of the court lines and is mistakenly assigned to a court line.

Example application 1: semantic analysis of tennis video
Our previous work of [6] has been used by [7] to analyze the tennis videos at three different levels. At the pixel level, several key objects are segmented and indicated. At the object level, the moving objects are tracked in the 3-D domain. At the scene level, the system detects the important events in 88%

Table 1. Court-net detection and camera calibration

Type	Court-line detection	Net-line detection	Camera calibration
Badminton	98.7%	96.2%	96.2%
Tennis	96.1%	95.8%	93.2%
Volleyball	95.4%	91.8%	90.1%

Fig. 3. Detection of the court lines and net line

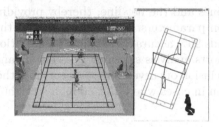

Fig. 4. Application of our 3-D modeling to player behavior analysis. Left: original image. Right: two vertical planes, where a black rectangle indicates the player's position and height. We also show the contour of the obtained bottom player based on our modeling.

of the cases, e.g., "service", using several *real world* visual features provided by the modeling. As the extension work of [6], our proposed modeling is not only capable of outputting all the functions provided by [6], but also height information. Knowing the height of the net line enables to compute the trajectory of the ball in the real-world domain. The right image of Fig. 4 shows the ball trajectory in the real world, where the ball is manually pointed in the image and transformed into the 3-D domain using our modeling.

Example application 2: player behavior analysis
Player behavior (pose) analysis is a emerging topic, because so many sports fans tend to simulate the famous players. Conventional methods in behavior analysis are based on the contour of the player detected in the image domain. For recognizing the sub-part (like arm) of the body, this contour has to be matched with a human model. But the problem here is to find the correct scaling of model to fit it with the contour of the player, because the size of the player in the image

largely depends on the distance between the player and the camera. Using our six-point modeling, this problem may be easily resolved, since the real height and width of each player can be computed, which is invariant to the distance to the camera. Fig. 4 portrays an example, in which we can see that the player who is far away from the camera is actually higher than the player close to the camera. The preliminary results of our modeling have been utilized to recognize the serving pose of the tennis player, where the accurate rate reaches 92% for the limited dataset (6 minutes tennis video).

6   Conclusions

We have presented a generic 3-D modeling technique, which is suited for content analysis of court-net sports. A main improvement as compared to [6], is that we can now establish the mapping between 2-D image and 3-D real-world coordinates, instead of a 2-D to 2-D plane mapping. Here, two major contributions are realized. First, we found the net plane and ground plane can be used for constructing 3-D modeling. Secondly, we propose a two-step algorithm to extract the court lines and the net line, thereby providing six feature points to calculate calibration parameters. The performance of the system for various court-net sports exceeds 90% accuracy on camera calibration. We also indicated its potential use in sports analysis systems. Possible enhancements of the algorithm would be the inclusion of curved line segments into the court model, which would allow calibration in cases where not enough straight lines are visible.

References

1. G. Sudhir, C. Lee and K. Jain. Automatic classification of tennis video for high-level content-based retrieval, Proc. IEEE int. workshop on content based access of image and video databases, pp. 81-90, 1998.
2. C. Calvo, A. Micarelli and E. Sangineto. Automatic annotation of tennis video sequences, Proc. DAGM-symposium, pp.540-547, Springer, 2002.
3. A. Yamada, Y. Shirai and J. Mirua. Tracking players and a ball in video image sequence and estimation camera parameters for 3-D interpretation of soccer games, Proc. 16th Int. Conf. Pattern Recognition, pp. 303-309, Aug. 2002.
4. T. Watanabe, M. Haseyama and H. Kitajima. A soccer field tracking method with wire frame model from TV images, Proc. IEEE Int. Conf. Image Proc. (ICIP), pp.1633-1636, Oct. 2004.
5. D. Farin, S. Krabbe, W. Effelsberg, P. de With. Robust Camera Calibration for Sport Videos using Court Models, in SPIE Storage and Retrieval Methods and Applications for Multimedia, vol. 5307, pp. 80-91, Jan. 2004.
6. D. Farin, J. Han, P. de With. Fast Camera Calibration for the Analysis of Sport Sequences, in IEEE Int. Conf. Multimedia Expo (ICME05), pp. 482-485, July 2005.
7. J. Han, D. Farin and P. de With. Multi-level analysis of sports video sequences, Proc. SPIE Multimedia content analysis management and retrieval, San Jose (CA), Vol. 6073, No. 607303, pp. 1-12, January 2006.

Using Camera Calibration and Radiosity on GPU for Interactive Common Illumination

Yongho Hwang, Junhwan Kim, and Hyunki Hong

Dept. of Image Eng., Graduate School of Advanced Imaging Science, Multimedia and Film,
Chung-Ang Univ., 221 Huksuk-dong, Dongjak-ku, Seoul, 156-756, Korea
hwangyh@wm.cau.ac.kr, interjh@wm.cau.ac.kr, honghk@cau.ac.kr

Abstract. Global common illumination between real and virtual objects is the process of illuminating scenes and objects with images of light from the real world. After including the virtual objects, the resulting scene should have consistent shadow configuration. This paper presents a novel algorithm that integrates synthetic objects in the real photographs by using the radiosity on graphics processing unit (GPU) and high dynamic range (HDR) radiance map. In order to reconstruct 3D illumination environment of the scene, we estimate the camera model and the extrinsic parameters from omni-directional images. The simulation results showed that our method can generate photo-realistic images.

1 Introduction

The seamless integration of synthetic objects with real photographs or video images has long been one of the central topics in computer vision and computer graphics [1~5]. For some of these applications it is important to merge the real and virtual objects using consistent illumination. However, the integration of synthetic objects in a realistic and believable way is labor intensive process and not always successful due to the enormous complexities of real-world illumination, which includes both direct and indirect illumination from complex environment.

Although many rendering tools that help in automating the synthesis process have been proposed up to now, most of them were restricted to static situations that light sources and the objects are not moved. Since various types of light sources such as spot and area lights are located from place to place in a real scene, their radiant distributions are dependent on the position of the camera to capture lights. In addition, as the performance of graphics hardware is increasing, we can capture effects that are not possible with local illumination models, such as shadows and inter-reflections in real-time [6]. The goal of this study aims at interactive common illumination, generating realistic scenes in a merged environment where illumination and shadows are consistent.

This paper presents a novel method to illuminate the computer generated objects by using the radiosity on graphics processing unit (GPU) and high dynamic range (HDR) radiance map. First, from omni-directional images we calibrate the camera parameters including one parametric camera model and motion parameters, and derive the camera response function. Secondly, we determine the scene's radiance information and generate realistic scenes with radiosity on GPU in the reconstructed 3D illumination

T.-J. Cham et al. (Eds.): MMM 2007, LNCS 4352, Part II, pp. 289–295, 2007.
© Springer-Verlag Berlin Heidelberg 2007

environment. The simulation results showed that the proposed method makes it possible to generate realistic images. It is expected that animators and lighting experts for the film industry would benefit highly from it.

The remainder of this paper is structured as follows: Sec. 2 reviews previous studies on common illumination, and the method for reconstructing 3D illumination environment of the scene is presented on Sec. 3. Sec. 4 describes the implemented radiosity on GPU algorithm and the simulation results, and the conclusion is presented in Sec. 5.

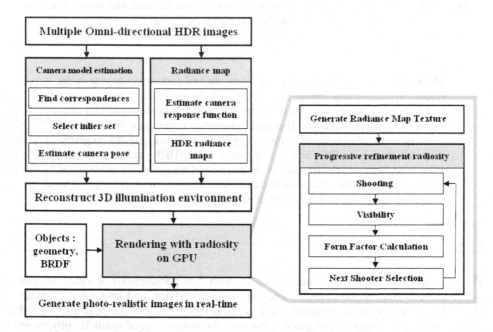

Fig. 1. Block diagram for the proposed method

2   Previous Studies

Many researches for illuminating scenes and objects with images of light from the real world have been proposed up to now. Table 1 shows previous studies may be classified according to three viewpoints: how to construct a geometric model of the scene, how to capture illumination information of the scene, and how to render the synthetic scene.

In table 1, Founier et al cannot consider illumination from outside of the input image without user's specification owing to using 2D photographs [1]. Debevec's, which is one of the most representative works, constructed light-based model by mapping reflections on a spherical mirror onto a geometric model of the scene. Therefore, a degree of realism of the rendering image depends on selecting viewpoints for observing the mirror so that the reflections on the mirror can cover the entire geometric model of the scene [2]. Sato et al simplified user's direct specification of a geometric model of the scene by using an omni-directional stereo algorithm, and

Table 1. Previous researches for common illumination

Work	Geometry	Capturing illumination	Rendering
[1]	user's specification for 3D construction of the scene	photographs	radiosity
[2]	light-based model: distant and local scene, synthetic objects	HDRI of scene reflections on a spherical mirror	RADIANCE system
[3]	omni-directional stereo algorithm	HDR omni-directional images by fish-eye lens	ray casting
[4]	user's specification	HDRI by sphere mapping	OpenGL

measured the radiance distribution. However, because of using the omni-directional stereo, it is required a prior camera calibration including positions and internal parameters, which is complex and difficult process [3]. In addition, Gibson et al proposed integration algorithms at interactive rates for augmented reality applications by using a single graphics pipeline [4].

In table 1, because previous methods for real-time scene generation were based on environment maps and shadow mapping, these have limitations of navigating objects and representing various indirect illumination effects [4, 7]. This paper addresses the issue of generating realistic scenes with radiosity on GPU in the reconstructed 3D illumination environment.

3 Reconstruction of Illumination Environment

The radiance distribution in the scene can be captured with HDR images, and the radiance information is used to calculate local or global illumination effects when including the virtual object in the real scene. However, the radiance perceived at a certain point depends on the viewing angle, on the angle of the incident light and the bi-directional reflectance distribution function (BRDF).

In this paper, omnidirectional images are used for 3D scene modeling with high resolution images, since the fisheye lens has a large field of view (FOV). At the first, we capture multiple HDR omnidirectional radiance maps at several places and estimate the omnidirectional camera model and pose parameters. And then, an illumination environment scene can be generated from radiance maps by using relative camera poses.

The camera projection model describes how 3D scene is transformed into 2D image. The light rays are emanated from the camera center and determined by a rotationally symmetric mapping function with respect to the the radius of the point and the angle between a ray and the optical axis. We derive a one-parametric non-linear model for Nikon FC-E8 fisheye converter [8].

One of the main problems is that estimating the essential matrix is sensitive to the point location errors. In order to cope with the unavoidable outliers inherent in the correspondence matches, our method is based on 9-points RANSAC that calculates the point distribution for each essential matrix. Since the essential matrix contains relative orientation and position of the camera, the inliers represent the depths of the scene points and change of the image by camera motion. By considering the point distribution, we can select effectively the inlier set that reflects the scene structure and the camera motion, so achieve more precise estimation of the essential matrix.

A standard deviation of the point density in the sub-region and that in an entire image can be used to evaluate whether the points are evenly distributed. First, 3D patches are segmented by the same solid angle in the hemi-spherical model and then they are projected onto the image plane as shown in Fig. 2.

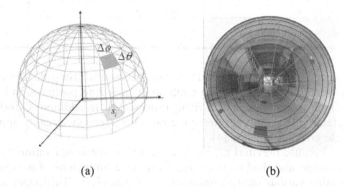

(a)   (b)

Fig. 2. Segmented sub-regions (a) Segmented 3D patch by uniform solid angle in hemi-spherical model (b) 2D projected sub-regions and inlier set (red dots)

We compute the standard deviation of two densities that represents a degree of the point distribution in each sub-region relative to the entire. The obtained information is used as a quantitative measure to select the evenly distributed point sets. In the final step, we estimate the essential matrix from the selected inlier set by minimizing the cost function that is the sum of the distance error of the inliers. In [9], considering the point distribution makes it possible to achieve relatively better performance as the iteration number increases.

After computing camera positions, we can reconstruct the scene structure and the illumination environment. Each HDR image is generated based on a set of images taken from the same viewpoint of the scene, but with a different exposure. The end result is one image containing radiance values instead of ordinary RGB values [10]. However, 3D reconstruction results of scenes were heavily affected by using a simple omnidirectional camera model. In our simulation, the result images were generated in the textured hexahedron by user's specification. The geometry reconstruction and HDR image capturing are considered as pre-processing steps.

4 Interactive Common Illumination

4.1 Progressive Radiosity on GPU

Radiosity is a widely used method for rendering based on an analysis of light reflections off diffuse surfaces. Among the numerous algorithms to implement this method, we use a technique of progressive radiosity on GPU and multiple render targets (MRTs) to accelerate components of the radiosity method [5].

The relationship between the actual radiance or radiosity and the pixel values can be known from the omnidirectional camera's response function which is estimated from HDR radiance map [10]. We treat the surfaces in the real scene as diffuse reflectors. Using multiple images from multiple viewpoints allows us to retrieve diffuse and specular reflectances for relighting of real scenes. The real scene is represented with projected textures in which the radiosity and residual energy are stored simultaneously. Given the reconstructed model of the scene, which is subdivided into patches, we can estimate the diffuse properties from the images by using the average intensity and reflectance [11].

When computing radiosity exchanges between two patches, the incoming irradiance is multiplied by the form factor and an attenuation factor, which varies from zero when the patches are mutually completely occluded, to one when the patches are entirely mutually visible. In order to test a visibility, we use a stereographic projection, which is rendered from the point of view of the shooter in a frame buffer as shown in Fig. 3. If an element is visible from the shooter, the next step is to compute the radiosity that it receives.

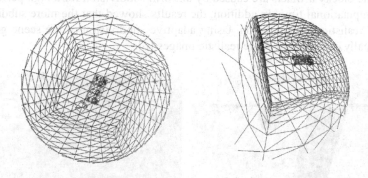

Fig. 3. Stereographic projection of scene from each shooter to test visibility

Progressive refinement techniques achieve fast convergence by always shooting from the scene element with the highest residual power. To find the next shooter, reciprocal of total radiosity value is rendered as a z-value at 1×1 pixel frame buffer, and then we use a simple z-buffer maximum algorithm. The final converged results are accurate representation of global illumination in the reconstructed environments.

4.2 Experimental Results

We have implemented the radiosity by using Cg language [12] on NVIDIA GeForce 7900 GTX with P4 2.8GHz system. In Fig. 4, a gallery scene, which contains 10,768 element texels, has been rendered. Computer-graphics objects now appeared to be illuminated by the light of the environment they are in. In our implementation, we set the resolution of 256×256 textures subdivided with 16×16 texels on each surfaces uniformly. In the simulation results, we have checked that the average computational time of the stereographic projection, form factor and the next shooter selection are

Fig. 4. Generated images by radiosity on GPU

1.2, 1.0 and 0.3 milliseconds, respectively. The frame rate of the total rendering process is over 60 fps (frames per second).

A differential rendering technique is used to generate an accurate shadow of the synthetic objects on the real scene [2]. The bleeding effect of inter-object is shown in Fig. 5. The blocky artifacts are caused by uniform subdivision for a high performance in the computational time. In addition, the results showed that the more subdivisions, the more realistic the simulation. Using adaptive subdivision of the scene geometry hierarchically can generate more realistic images [6].

Fig. 5. Detail of bleeding effects between object surfaces

5   Conclusion

We have presented a novel method to illuminate the computer generated images by using the radiosity on GPU and HDR radiance map. First, from omni-directional images we estimated the omnidirectional camera parameters. Secondly, we determined the scene's radiance information and generated realistic scenes in the reconstructed 3D illumination environment. The simulation results showed that our algorithm can generate realistic images. Future study will introduce more precise camera model of the omnidirectional camera and reconstruct accurate 3D scene geometry to cope with dynamic situations. In addition, an adaptive subdivision method will be implemented for more realistic image generation in real-time.

Acknowledgments. This research was supported by the Korea Culture and Content Agency on the 2006 CT project.

References

1. A. Fournier, A. Gunawan, and C. Romanzin,: Common illumination between real and computer generated scenes. Proc. of Graphics Interface, (1993) 254-262
2. P. Debevec,: Rendering synthetic objects into real scenes: Bridging traditional and image-based graphics with global illumination and high dynamic range photography. Proc. SIGGRAPH 98 (1998) 189-198
3. I. Sato, Y. Sato, and K. Ikeuchi,: Acquiring a radiance distribution to superimpose virtual objects onto a real scene. IEEE Trans. on Visualization and Computer Graphics, vol. 5, no. 1, (1999) 1-12
4. S. Gibson and A. Murta,: Interactive rendering with real-world illumination. Proc. of the 11th Eurographics Workshop on Rendering, (2000) 365-376
5. K. Jacobs and C. Loscos,: Classification of illumination methods for mixed reality. Computer Graphics Forum, vol. 25, no. 1, (2006) 29-51
6. G. Coombe, M. J. Harris, and A. Lastra,: Radiosity on Graphics Hardware. Proc. of Graphics Interface (2004) 161-168
7. K. Agusanto, L. Li, Z. Chuangui and N. W. Sing,: Photo-realistic rendering for augmented reality using environment illumination. IEEE/ACM International Symposium on Augmented and Mixed Reality, (2003) 208-216
8. Yongho Hwang and Hyunki Hong,: Estimation of Omnidirectional Camera Model with One Parametric Projection. Lecture Notes in Control and Information Sciences, vol.345, (2006) 827-833.
9. Yongho Hwang and Hyunki Hong,: 3D Analysis of Omnidirectional Images for Illumination Environment Reconstruction. Lecture Notes in Artificial Intelligence, vol.4259, (2006)
10. P. Debevec and J. Malik,: Recovering high dynamic range radiance maps from photographs. Proc. SIGGRAPH 97 (1997) 369-378
11. C. Loscos, G. Drettakis and L. Robert,: Interactive virtual relighting of real scenes. IEEE Trans. on Visualization and Computer Graphics, vol. 6, no. 4 (2000) 289-305
12. Willian R. Mark, R. Steven Glanville, Kurt Akeley, and Mark J. Kilgard,: Cg: A system for programming graphics hardware in a c-like language. Proc. SIGGRAPH (2003)

The Study of Detecting for IR Weak and Small Targets Based on Fractal Features

Zhang Hong[1,*], Liu Xiaolong[1], Li Junwei[2], and Zhu Zhenfu[2]

[1] Image Processing Center, BeiHang University, Beijing 100083, China
[2] The 207th Institute of the Second Academy of China
Aerospace Science Industry Corporation, Beijing 100854, China
dmrzhang@buaa.edu.cn

Abstract. In the paper, the detection of IR weak and small targets is investigated in natural background based on fractal features. One feature of multi-scale variance ratio of fractal surface is proposed according to the fact that the fractal feature of man made objects changes shaper than the natural background. The new feature stands out the artificial objects much better from natural background than what can be done by fractal dimension feature or fractal model fit error feature, thus inhibiting background clutters well. Local gray histogram statistics is applied to object detection in the images with feature of multi-scale variance ratio of fractal surface. Experimental results shows that the detecting algorithm based on such a feature can localize weak and small objects stably in a single-frame image, and is a effective algorithm.

Keywords: Weak and small; Fractal dimension; Fractal model fit error; Multi-scale variance ratio of fractal surface.

1 Introduction

In infrared tracking system, real-time and accurately are the keys to improve stabilization and accuracy in detecting weak and small targets with low signal-to-noise ratio(SNR).In general, the procedure of detecting of weak and small targets is: firstly, detecting potential targets in a frame image; Secondly, detecting and tracking in infrared image sequences using moving characteristic of targets. So detecting targets in a frame image is a key problem [1]. Many algorithms such as morphology algorithm、 adaptive filter algorithm、 Neural network algorithm, entropy difference algorithm [2-5] have been investigated since 1980s. When the gray difference between targets and background is unstable, the methods above can not detect weak and small targets in complex background accurately .So it is necessary to research a universality targets characteristic to detect targets. Many research findings revealed different fractal mode can coincidence the complex surface structure characteristics of natural objects well, but artificial objects can not, which is the foundation for us to detect artificial targets according to fractal characteristic. In general, the detecting [1]

---

[*] Corresponding author.
[1] Supported by the national key laboratory (51476010105HK0101).

T.-J. Cham et al. (Eds.): MMM 2007, LNCS 4352, Part II, pp. 296–303, 2007.

algorithms based on fractal features for IR weak and small targets use two fractal features: one is fractal dimension, which characterizes the roughness of surface, the other is fractal model fit error, which characterizes whether the real data has the spatial structure self-similarity or not . In general, the fractal dimension, which is assumed as a constant in each scale, can be calculated according to the linear estimation of logarithm value between measurement value and measurement scale at each scale. The fractal model fit error is the error that between the logarithm value between measurement value and measurement scale and their linear estimation. The theory is fit for ideal characteristic of fractal model. But for most natural background, there is only approximate fractal characteristic in corresponding scale scope, and which is often influenced by imaging error and quantization error. It is very difficult to describe natural background with fractal dimension. So the artificial objects often can not be detected accurately at natural background by the fractal dimension or the fractal model fit error [6].

In this paper, using superficial area measure of image gray surface in fractal theory ,we get a new fractal characteristic, that is, characteristic of multi-scale variance ratio of fractal surface, which not only reflects the changing speed of the surface of gray image at multi-scale, but also its rough degree. The more the surface of gray image changing and the more the surface of gray image getting rough, the larger the characteristic value of multi-scale variance ratio of fractal surface getting. Because the IR weak and small targets' surface changing rate is very big, we can get the threshold value with the histogram statistic method, then segment the characteristic image of multi-scale variance ratio of fractal surface, and finally detect the targets accurately. Experimental results showed the algorithm investigated in this paper can detect IR weak and small targets more accurately and suppress noise more effective compared with the fractal dimension or the fractal model fit error, and the amount of computation is less.

2 Characteristic of Multi-scale Variance Ratio of Fractal Surface

Most nature phenomena have statistical self-similarity in collectivity distributing. Pentland has proved that many natural surfaces are spatially isotropic fractals, and the gray images mapping from them are some kinds of fractal surface that has fractal properties [7].For the gray image surface, the fractal dimension can be estimated by the following equation:

$$A(\varepsilon) = K\varepsilon^{2-D} \tag{1}$$

Where D is fractal dimension, K is a constant, ε is a scale ,and A(ε) is the surface area of image in the scale ε, which can be calculated by blanket technique[8].

Supposing g(x,y) is gray image surface, for the scale ε (ε >=0), the upper surface $(u_\varepsilon(i,j)$ and the lower surface $b_\varepsilon(i,j)$ can be got by the following equation:

$$\begin{cases} g(i,j) = u_0(i,j) = b_0(i,j) \\ u_\varepsilon(i,j) = \max\{u_{\varepsilon-1}(i,j)+1, \max_{|(m,n)-(i,j)|\leq 1} u_{\varepsilon-1}(m,n)\} \\ b_\varepsilon(i,j) = \max\{b_{\varepsilon-1}(i,j)+1, \max_{|(m,n)-(i,j)|\leq 1} b_{\varepsilon-1}(m,n)\} \end{cases} \qquad (2)$$

Where, the (m,n) meeting the equation $|(m,n)-(i,j)| \leq 1$ is the eight neighborhood area at the point (i,j).

At the scale ε , the volume between the upper surface and the lower surface is:

$$V(\varepsilon) = \sum_{i,j} (u_\varepsilon(i,j) - b_\varepsilon(i,j)) \qquad (3)$$

Then, the estimation of the surface area is:

$$A(\varepsilon) = (V(\varepsilon) - V(\varepsilon-1))/2 \qquad (4)$$

For the constant K in equation (1), if all pixel value of image is equal, the fractal dimension D is 2, the surface measurement of image A(ε)=K ,which means K is irrelevant to ε . But for a image composted by different texture, K is not a constant, and is a function of ε . If two values $\varepsilon_1, \varepsilon_2$ are used in (1), we obtain

$$\begin{cases} A(\varepsilon_1) = K\varepsilon_1^{2-D} \\ A(\varepsilon_2) = K\varepsilon_2^{2-D} \end{cases} \qquad (5)$$

Separate K from equation (5),

$$K = \frac{A(\varepsilon_2) - A(\varepsilon_1)}{\varepsilon_2^{2-D} - \varepsilon_1^{2-D}} \quad \varepsilon_1, \ \varepsilon_2 = 1,2,\cdots,M \qquad (6)$$

Equation (6) shows that K reflects the spatial variety ratio of surface area of the gray image. In equation (6), if $\varepsilon_1, \varepsilon_2$ are known, then $A(\varepsilon_1)$ and $A(\varepsilon_2)$ are known, so K is the function of D. If D can be reduced, all the fractal characteristics are concentrated on K.

With equation (1), we can obtain:

$$\ln A(\varepsilon) = (2-D)\ln(\varepsilon) + \ln K \qquad (7)$$

The characteristic of fractal dimension or fractal model fit error is obtained by linear-fitting for $\ln A(\varepsilon)$ at each scale ε .It can be see that the characteristics mentioned above suppose the fractal dimension is a constant at each scale ε , which is accurate for ideal fractal. But there is no ideal fractal in nature. In practice application, the multi-scale approximate fractal characteristic is suitable for describing artificial objects and nature background.

If two values $\varepsilon_1, \varepsilon_2$ are used in (7), we obtain

$$\begin{cases} \ln A(\varepsilon_1) = (2-D)\ln(\varepsilon_1) + \ln K \\ \ln A(\varepsilon_2) = (2-D)\ln(\varepsilon_2) + \ln K \end{cases} \tag{8}$$
$$\tag{9}$$

Supposing $\varepsilon_1 = \varepsilon, \varepsilon_2 = \varepsilon + 1$ ($\varepsilon = 1, 2, \cdots, M$), using equation (8) and (9), we can obtain

$$K^*(\varepsilon) = \exp\left(\frac{\ln A(\varepsilon)\ln(\varepsilon+1) - \ln A(\varepsilon+1)\ln(\varepsilon)}{\ln(\varepsilon+1) - \ln(\varepsilon)} \right) \tag{10}$$

From equation (6) and (10), it can be seen that K^* not only reflects the roughness of the image gray surface along with the variation of scale, but also reflects the variety degree. In this paper, K^* is called multi-scale variance ratio of fractal surface.

In (6), we can see the faster the image gray surface changes along with the scale, the larger the K^* is. So combined with (10), we can obtain:

$$Mean(K^*(\varepsilon)) = \frac{1}{M} \sum_{\varepsilon=1}^{M} |K(\varepsilon)| \qquad \varepsilon = 1, 2, \cdots, M \tag{11}$$

Here, ε is a scale, M is the number of scale, Mean () is mean value function. Now, we can use equation (11) to enhance the image. From Fig 1(c), we can see $Mean(K^*(\varepsilon))$ enhances the image well.

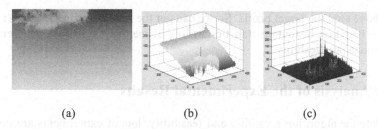

(a)   (b)   (c)

Fig. 1. Experimental results

(a) the source image;
(b) three-dimension graph of original image gray
(c) three-dimension graph of enhanced image;

3   The Algorithm of Detecting for Targets

In corresponding scale scope, the fractal characteristic of natural background keeps stable. If the scale changes little, the value of K^* is small. In spite of there is no inner characteristic in IR weak and small targets, but the fractal characteristic is instable and changes acutely along with the change of scale on the boundary of natural background and the targets. The value of K^* is large, too. So we can detect the targets by the difference of artificial targets and natural background in multi-scale fractal characteristic. Now, mapping $Mean(K^*(\varepsilon))$ ($\varepsilon = 1, 2, \cdots, M$) to image can be thought of the enhanced image. In the enhanced image, artificial targets hold the brightest part, so we can classify the targets and the background easily.

According to the size of the targets, target detecting can be classified two kinds: big target detecting and small target detecting. Big target detecting can be done in target matching and recognition, while small target detecting is the key problem in target detecting. By the character that targets hold the brightest part of the enhanced image, count the histogram Statistic of the enhanced image and accumulate the area. Beginning from the highest gray level, when the accumulated area is greater than or equal to(for the sake of high detecting ratio, generally choose greater than) the size of target, set the gray value(note as T) as the threshold value. Supposing f(x,y) is the enhanced image, the total number of pixels is M. and the pixel number of gray scale i is m_i, then the probability p_i of gray scale i is m_i / M. The threshold value t can be got:

$$t = \left\{ t \left| \sum_{i=255}^{t} p_i \geq \frac{T}{M} \right. \right\} \tag{12}$$

Transiting enhanced image to binary image using the threshold value t. That is,

$$F(i, j) = \begin{cases} 1 & f(i,j) \geq t \\ 0 & \text{otherwise} \end{cases} \tag{13}$$

Pixels above t are the target pixels. So we can get the final detecting result F(i ,j). The algorithm based on histogram statistic has lots of merits. It runs fast, segments well, and has much practicability.

4   The Analysis of the Experimental Results

To validate the algorithm's validity and feasibility, lots of experiments are done. We chose two typical IR image. The first image is 229*343, and the target contains about 6~12 pixels, as is shown in Fig 2(a). The second one is 300×300, and the target contains about 30 pixels, as is shown in Fig 3(a). For the sake of detecting precision and the demand of real-time, we choose the window with the size of 3×3 as the local processing region, and the scale range is 8.

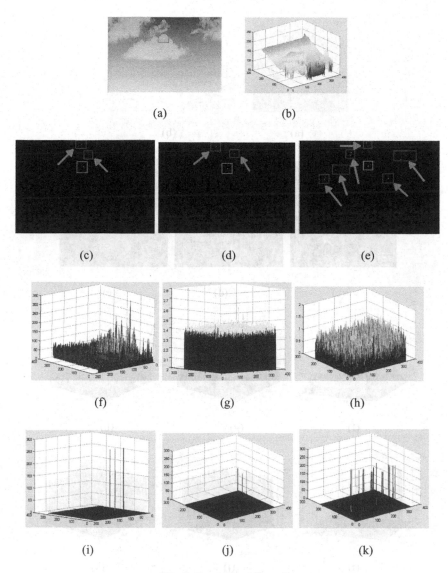

Fig. 2. Experimental results

(a).the source image; (b). the three-dimension graph of the source image gray; (c).the detecting result of our algorithm; (d). the detecting result based on the fractal dimension; (e).the detecting result based on the fractal model fit error; (f).the enhanced effect of our algorithm; (g). the enhanced effect based on the fractal dimension; (h). the enhanced effect based on the fractal model fit error; (i). the three-dimension graph of the detecting result of our algorithm; (j). the three-dimension graph of the detecting result based on the fractal dimension; (k). the three-dimension graph of the detecting result based on the fractal model fit error;

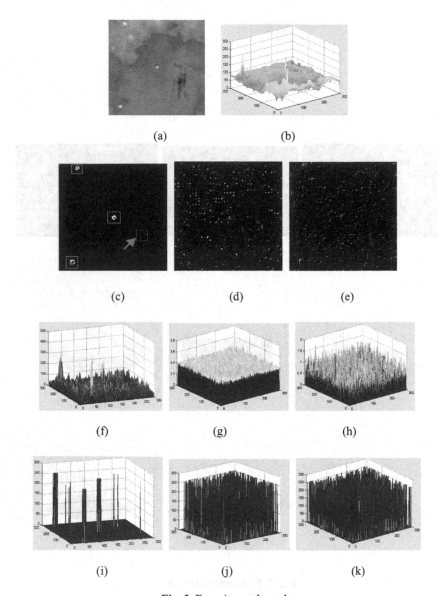

Fig. 3. Experimental results

(a).the source image; (b). the three-dimension graph of the source image gray; (c).the detecting result of our algorithm; (d). the detecting result based on the fractal dimension; (e).the detecting result based on the fractal model fit error; (f).the enhanced effect of our algorithm; (g). the enhanced effect based on the fractal dimension; (h). the enhanced effect based on the fractal model fit error; (i).the three-dimension graph of the detecting result of our algorithm; (j).the three-dimension graph of the detecting result based on the fractal dimension; (k). the three-dimension graph of the detecting result based on the fractal model fit error;

In Fig 2 and Fig 3, red panes represent the real targets, and blue diamonds indicated by red arrow are false targets. From Fig 2 and Fig 3, we can see that the fractal dimension and the fractal model fit error can also detect the small targets, but they are very sensitive to the noise. When the targets become big, they fail. And the calculation amount of algorithm based on the fractal dimension and the fractal model fit error is large. The algorithm based on characteristic of multi-scale variance ratio of fractal surface is effective when the target becomes big from very little (in a certainly scope), and is insensitive to the noise. The detecting result contains few false targets, and the calculation amount is small. So it is a very practical and effective detecting algorithm for IR weak and small targets.

5 Conclusions

The paper deduces a new fractal characteristic-- multi-scale variance ratio of fractal surface using the surface area measure of the gray surface of the image in fractal theory. In multi-scale, this characteristic can not only reflects the changing speed of the gray surface of image at multi-scale, but also its rough degree. The faster the gray surface of image changes, the larger the multi-scale variance ratio of fractal surface is. Because the changing ratio of the superficial area of the gray surface of the IR weak and small target is large, we can get the threshold value by the method of histogram statistic, segment the image of the multi-scale variance ratio of fractal surface, and finally detect the targets well. Experimental results indicate that, compared with traditional fractal dimension and fractal model fit error methods, the proposed multi-scale variance ratio of fractal surface has better effect when standing out the target's fractal characteristic, obvious better ability of resisting noise interference, and less calculation amount. In a word, it is a very practical and effective weak and small targets detecting algorithm.

References

1. WEI Ying. : A target detection method based on a new multi-scale fractal feature [J]. Journal of Northeastern University (Natural Science), Vol.26,2005.11 : 1062~1065
2. L.Yang, J.Yang and K.Yang.: Adaptive detection for infrared small target under sea-sky complex background. Electronics Letters,19th August 2004 Vol.40 No.17.
3. Spyros Panagopoulos and John J.Soraghan. : Small-target detection in sea clutter. IEEE Transactions on geosciences and remote sensing,Vol.42,NO.7,July 2004:1355~1361
4. G.-D.Wang,Ch.-Y.Chen and X.-B Shen. :Facet-based infrared small target detection method. Electronics Letters,27th October 2005,Vol.41,N0.22
5. Jian-Nan Chi,Ping Fu,Dong-Shu Wang,Xin-He Xu. : A detection method of infrared image small target based on order morphology transformation and image entropy difference. Proceedings of the Fourth International Conference on Machine Learning and Cybernetics, Guangzhou, 18-21 August 2005:5111~5116.
6. LI Jun-wei. : Study on the target detection algorithm based on fractal [J]. Infrared and Laser Engineering, Vol.32No.5, 2003.10 : 468~471
7. PENTLAND A.: Fractal based description of natural scenes [J]. IEEE Trans on PAMI, 1984 ,6(6) : 661 - 674.
8. Zhang Kun-hua, Wang Jingrq and Zhang QLhcng,. : Image Edge Detecting Method Based on Fractal Feature. Opto-Electmic Engineering, vol. 28, no. 6, pp. 52-55, 2001.

Visual Features Extraction Through Spatiotemporal Slice Analysis*

Xuefeng Pan[1,2], Jintao Li[1], Shan Ba[3], Yongdong Zhang[1], and Sheng Tang[1]

[1] Institute of Computing Technology, Chinese Academy of Sciences,
Beijing 100080, China
{xfpan,jtli,zhyd,ts}@ict.ac.cn
[2] Graduate School of Chinese Academy of Sciences,
Beijing 100080, China
[3] School of Science, Beijing Institutes of Technology,
Beijing 100081, China

Abstract. In this paper we propose a novel feature extracting method based on spatiotemporal slice analyzing. To date, video features are focused on the character of every single video frame. With our method, the video content is no longer represented with every single frame. The temporal variation of visual information is taken as an important feature of video in our method. We examined this kind of feature with experiments in this paper. The experiment results show that the proposed feature is effective and robust for variant video content and format.

Keywords: feature extraction, spatiotemporal slice, DCT, similarity measuring.

1 Introduction

In the past decade, the content-based video processing has found applications in many fields such as video indexing, video retrieval, video annotation and video search. Various features such as color, shape, texture, and motion have been used for representing the video content. Nevertheless, the performance of existing methodology for representing visual information is far from satisfactory. The gap between low-level features and the high-level semantics presented in video data makes it difficult to map the features to semantic concepts. Traditional methodologies emanating from textual and image information processing are being challenged.

So far most existing video features are focused on the character of every single video frame. This kind of processing pattern ignores the temporal information of video and is inefficient. The temporal variation of visual information is an important feature of video which makes video differ from static picture. However, this feature has not been intensively discussed in prior works.

In this paper, we explore a temporal visual feature based on spatiotemporal slice and examine its effectiveness by experiments. Our approach is based on the frequency

---

* This work was supported by Beijing Science and Technology Planning Program of China (D0106008040291), and the Key Project of International Science and Technology Cooperation (2005DFA11060).

T.-J. Cham et al. (Eds.): MMM 2007, LNCS 4352, Part II, pp. 304–313, 2007.

domain analyzing of spatiotemporal slice. Spatiotemporal slice is a set of two–dimensional (2-D) images extracted along the time dimension of an image sequence. It gathers the variation in time dimension of video content in one static picture. Previous works on temporal slice include visual motion model, epipolar plane image analysis, surveillance monitoring, periodicity analysis, video partitioning, motion characterization and segmentation as mentioned in [1]. Ngo did lots of work in video content analyzing by temporal slices analysis: using color, texture and statistical information to detect camera cut, wipe and dissolve for video partitioning [2]; using 2D structure tensor histogram to analyze the camera and object motions [3]; incorporating motion and color features to cluster and retrieval video shots [1].

Unlike the existing works, we focus our attention on the utilization of frequency domain features extracted from spatiotemporal slices for video shots classification and video copy detection. The proposed approaches are mainly devoted to extract the temporal features of video using spatiotemporal slice analysis. We use a simple method to get the spatiotemporal slice from a video. By analyzing the frequency domain information we can get the temporal variation represented in the slice. Because temporal variation in video is a prominent feature to human visual perception it can be taken as a feature to represent the video content.

Instead of analyzing video content from one frame to another, our approach analysis all frames of a given period of time as a whole. This is the major difference between our method and conventional approaches. The thesis of our method is "taking the variation of video clip as an important feature," the variation feature of video represented by spatiotemporal slice is used to analysis the video content.

The rest of this paper is organized as follows. Section 2 introduces the concept of spatiotemporal slice. Section 3 proposes an algorithm to extract the feature of spatiotemporal in frequency domain. The application of the feature proposed is given in Section 4. Section 5 concludes our proposed works.

2   The Concept of Spatiotemporal Slice

We introduce the concept of temporal slice by giving an example and some definitions. Spatiotemporal slice is a collection of scans in the same position of every frame which indicates the coherency of the video as shown in Figure 1.

That is, a slice is a finite plane in the 3-D spatiotemporal image volume at a given position with a given orientation [4]. Denote f_i as an $M \times N$ image which is the i_{th}

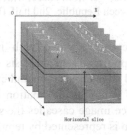

Fig. 1. Get a horizontal slice from a sequence

frame of a frame sequence, we can get the horizontal slice h_i and the vertical slice v_i as below:

$$h_i = \sum_{x=1}^{M} \sum_{y=\frac{N}{2}-w}^{\frac{N}{2}+w} \alpha_y f_i(x,y) \quad \text{and} \quad \sum_{y=\frac{N}{2}-w}^{\frac{N}{2}+w} \alpha_y = 1 \tag{1}$$

$$v_i = \sum_{y=1}^{N} \sum_{x=\frac{M}{2}-w}^{\frac{M}{2}+w} \alpha_x f_i(x,y) \quad \text{and} \quad \sum_{x=\frac{M}{2}-w}^{\frac{M}{2}+w} \alpha_x = 1 \tag{2}$$

Where w controls the width of the slice, and α controls the weight of the pixel line. When $w=0$, $\alpha=1$, the slice is just the middle row or column of f_i. When $w \neq 0$, the slice is compromised by rows or columns rounding the middle one with different α. By cascading slices over time, we acquire a 2D image H formed by horizontal slices and a 2D image V formed by vertical slices. We can get other kinds of slice by pointing the position in frame where to generate slice.

In this paper we focus our attention on the temporal coherency of video clips. For convenience, we only use the row at the middle of frame to cascade horizontal temporal slice using by setting $w=0$, $\alpha=1$ in (1):

$$h_i = \sum_{x=1}^{M} f_i(x, \tfrac{N}{2}) \tag{3}$$

Figure 2 shows two spatiotemporal slices we get from a soccer video clip and a movie clip using (3):

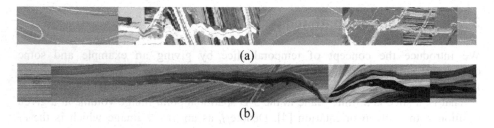

(a)

(b)

Fig. 2. Parts of spatiotemporal slice get from soccer video clip using (3). (a) 2004 European Championship, Netherlands vs. Czech Republic, 2nd half. (b) Movie: Chorists.

Spatiotemporal slice represents a video with image dimension and temporal dimension. It gives us an opportunity to analysis contents in video with context coherency. Ngo uses temporal slice to partition and cluster video shots in [1], [2]. We believe that the coherency of temporal information is an important feature of video clip. Because the temporal slice image cascades the slice from every frame over time the temporal variation of video is represented by temporal slice naturally.

3   Extract Feature of Spatiotemporal Slice in Frequency Domain

In this part we introduce our method to extract feature of spatiotemporal slice in frequency domain. From a video clip which has W frames we can generate a $W \times H$ horizontal slice (H is the height of frame). With this $W \times H$ horizontal slice, we change the size of slice to make its height equal to N using linear interpolation. Then we convert the slice to gray image and segment the gray slice into $N \times N$ blocks. By analyzing the frequency domain features of these blocks we can generate the variation information of video clip in every N frames.

In this paper, we choose the discrete cosine transform (DCT) on the 2D image date to analysis the blocks in frequency domain. We use the absolute value of DCT coefficients to form a gray image. The value of every pixel is clamped to 0 and 255. This kind of images shows the feature of slice blocks in frequency domain.

An example of analyzing temporal slices blocks is described as follows:

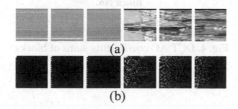
(a)

(b)

Fig. 3. An example of spatiotemporal slice blocks DCT. (a)Blocks segmented from slice, N =32. (b) Corresponding DCT images of blocks in (a), N =32.

From Fig. 3(b), we can classify blocks in 3(a) into two catalogs easily. The first three blocks in 3(a) is much smoother than other three block in 3(a). This implies that the frames sequence represented by first three slice blocks in 3(a) have less variation in temporal dimension than the frames sequence represented by other blocks in 3(a). Correspondingly, the first three blocks in 3(b) obviously have less bright pixels than other three blocks in 3(b). The sum of DCT AC coefficients above a preset threshold of first three slice blocks in 3(a) has smaller value than that of other blocks in 3(a). This is reflected in 3(b) clearly. So we believe the DCT AC coefficients can reflect the intensity of visual variation over time.

After getting the DCT image of all blocks, we calculate the sum of DCT AC coefficients above a preset threshold value for every block. Then we represent the sum of every block in a feature vector for the whole video.

We use the DCT AC coefficients sum as the feature of every slice block. And the whole video can be represented with the vector of all the sums. This vector can be visualized with a curve as show in Figure 4. We denote this feature curve as spatiotemporal Slice DCT Curve (SDCTC). This kind of feature is useful in video content analysis because it reflects the visual variation over time. In next section, we will introduce some of its applications.

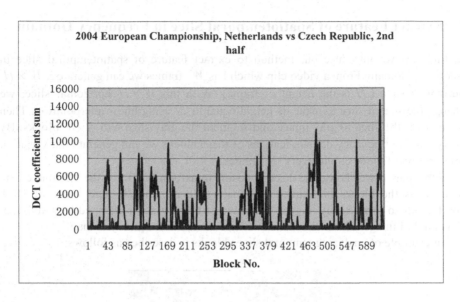

Fig. 4. DCT AC coefficients sums of blocks

4   Applications

In this section we introduce two applications of the SDCTC. One is view classification in soccer video; the other is video copy detection.

4.1   View Classification in Soccer Video

In this subsection, we propose an algorithm to classify views in soccer video based on the temporal slice through frequency domain analysis.

In the literature, semantic analysis of soccer video generally involves use of shot type classification. But most of previous work in soccer video view classification is mainly based on analyzing color information in each frame. In this paper, we introduce a new method through spatiotemporal slice analysis.

Most of previous work is focus on analyzing color information in each frame to classify shots into different views. A common way is to use a predefined range of hue value to detect field region as mentioned in [5]. Other methods use statistical models such as GMM [6], [7] or distance metrics in different color space [8] to get the dominant color model. Then playfield can be segmented with mathematical morphology or other image segmentation technique such as region growing [7]. All these statistic methods use frames as sample to get the model. But how to choose appropriate samples is seldom discussed. Besides this, the training of model take considerable efforts and one model will not fit all kind of playfield. That is we may be obliged to train a model for every other soccer video.

In this paper, we present an algorithm for analyzing the view types in soccer video by temporal slice features mentioned above. The method we propose is simple, unsupervised and robust to noise of the video. We analyz the temporal slice of the video in frequency domain and classify the shots into long view or mid-close view using simple rules. Because this method need not choose sample to train the model, it can be used in different soccer videos without change.

Based on observation, we find that the smooth parts of slice presenting the long view in the soccer video well. So we map blocks of slice to long view or mid-close view using the DCT analysis results naturally. By calculating the harmonic means of SDCTC, we get the gate value to classify the blocks of slice into smooth ones and unsmooth ones.

An example is given in Figure 5. With the gate value, we can tell the smooth parts from the unsmooth parts. Figure 5 is a classify result in which the smooth parts are tagged with blue while the unsmooth parts are tagged with green.

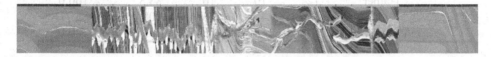

Fig. 5. Result of classifying the blocks

Figure 6 gives the frames from the corresponding parts of video. Our algorithm differs from the previous methods in that it no longer classifies views only depending on single frame information. So it is robust to noises in soccer video.

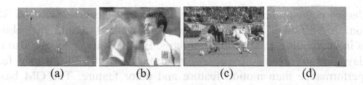

(a)   (b)   (c)   (d)

Fig. 6. View classification based on slice DCT analysis: (a), (d) are from the blue tagged parts, long view; (b), (c) are from the green tagged parts, not long view

In order to examine the effectiveness of our method, we choose 5 different matches from 2002 World Cup, 2004 European Championship, 2005 UEFA Champions League, English Premier League, Italian Series A. For each match, we select 20 continuous shots randomly.

The method proposed is used to classifies these shots. We use a simple rule to determine the view type of a shot: if 50% of the blocks in each shot are long, we take the shot as a long one. In the experiments we use the same algorithm and no gate value are resettled. Classification results of the shots are in Table 1.

Furthermore, we compute the recall and precision rates of results. We define the recall as the ratio of correct detected shots to the truth and the precision as the ratio of correct detected shots to all detected shots. We compute recall and precision rates for each kind of matches. The experiment results show our method is effective for all these 5 kinds of soccer match regardless the playfield color variation.

Table 1. Result of View Classification

Match	View Type	Truth	Detect	Correct	Recall (%)	Prec. (%)
W. C.	Long	8	9	8	100.0	88.9
	Other	12	11	11	91.7	100.0
E. C.	Long	6	6	6	100.0	100.0
	Other	14	14	14	100.0	100.0
UEFA C. L.	Long	7	8	7	100.0	87.5
	Other	13	12	12	92.3	100.0
E. P. L.	Long	7	9	7	100.0	77.8
	Other	13	11	11	84.6	100.0
I. S. A.	Long	8	10	8	100.0	80
	Other	12	10	10	83.3	100.0
TOTAL	Long	36	42	36	100.0	85.7
	Other	64	58	58	90.6	100.0

Then we calculate the recall and precision rate for all selected shots. The recall ratio and the precise ratio are also sound. The results show our method is effective for shots classification in soccer video. The spatiotemporal (frequent domain) feature performs well in representing the visual information of video.

4.2 Video Copy Detection

We introduce a new similarity metric for video copy detection based on SDCTC in this section. An efficient video copy detection method should be robust to the distortions in digitization and encoding process. Besides this, it should also cope well with display format conversions [9]. As mentioned in [10], the ordinal feature has superior performance than motion feature and color feature. The OM based video copy detection has been study in [11-13]. But the number of partitions is critical because discriminability of system will be weakened as the number of partitions is reduced as pointed out in [9].

Since video is a process that evolves with time, we believe that this kind of feature can be used for video copy detection. In this paper we use SDCTC similarity to

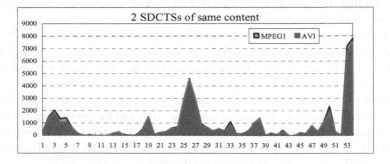

Fig. 7. The SDCTC of two clips with the same content: The differences between the two SDCTC (MPEG1 and AVI)

measure the similarity of video clips. Because SDCTC does not rely on one by one image visual features, it is robust to the change in single frame. The SDCTCs of two video clips with the same content but in different formats (MPEG1 and AVI) are showed in Figure 7. It can be noticed that the two SDCTCs are similar though there are some small differences.

Besides this, SDCTC is very compact. For every block there is one integer. If the block size is set as 32, we can use less than 3000 integers to present about one-hour video content.

Let $C_X = (X_1, X_2, \cdots, X_L)$ and $C_Y = (Y_1, Y_2, \cdots, Y_L)$ denote the SDCTC of two video clips with the same duration. L is the block number of the spatiotemporal slice. Video Feature Curve Similarity (VFCS) of the two clips is defined by

$$VFCS(C_X, C_Y) = 1 - \frac{\sum_{i=1}^{L} d(X_i - Y_i)}{\sum_{i=1}^{L} (X_i + Y_i)} \tag{4}$$

Where $d(\cdot)$ is the distance metric defined on the VFCS (in this paper we use L_1 distance).

Let $C_Q = (Q_1, Q_2, \cdots, Q_m)$ and $C_T = (T_1, T_2, \cdots, T_n)$ $(m \le n)$ denote the SDCTC of the query clip Q and the target clip T. We use VFCS to locate the Q in T. The matching process is as the following steps.

(1) Shift C_Q along C_T from the beginning of C_T, and compute VFCS at every step. Let $C_T^i = (Y_i, Y_{i+1}, \cdots, Y_{i+m-1})$ denote some part of C_T has the same block num as C_Q starting at block i, where $i \le n - m + 1$

(2) The local maximums of the $VFCS(C_Q, C_T^i)$ $(i = 0, \cdots, n - m + 1)$ values which above a certain threshold are taken as matches.

We use some video clips to show the distinguishing capability of the features. We divide a video into 24 segments. Then use each segment as the query clip to search the same content on the original video.

Table 2. Uniqueness test

Similarity	Mean	Stdev.
S_{same}	0.982201	0.026535
S_{diff}	0.264375	0.064546

Note: *Mean* is the average value of the similarity; Standard Deviation. *Stdev.* is the standard deviation of the similarity.

In the experiment, all query segments are correctly located in the original video, and no false alarm exists. We give the similarity (S_{same}) between the query clips and the located clips having the same content, and the similarity (S_{diff}) between the query clips and other clips having different content in Table 2.

These results show that the correlation between clips with the same content is much larger than the clips with different content using our similarity measure methods. So this kind of correlation is quite stable.

We present another experiment focusing on robustness. A video clip segmented from a soccer video is used in this experiment. The original video is compressed in MPEG1. We compress the segmented clip in different formats, resolutions. Especially, we reformat the clip to make it with 'pillar-box' as shown in Figure 8. Then we measure the similarity of every reformatted clip and original one using (4).

Fig. 8. Reformatted clip with 'pillar-box'

The original format is 352×288 in MPEG1. We reformat the clip in AVI with the resolution 352×288 and 320×180; in MPEG1 with the resolution 320×180; in MPEG1 and AVI with 'pillar-box'. The similarity of every clip and the original one using (4) is shown in Table 3.

Table 3. Robustness test

Reformatted clip	Similarity
352×288 in AVI	0.963846
320×180 in AVI	0.932875
320×180 in MPEG1	0.856289
320×180 in AVI with 'pillar box'	0.777337
320×240 in MPEG1 with 'pillar box'	0.805518

From Table 3 we can see the similarity of clips with the same content is much higher than the similarity of clips with different content shown in Table 1. Our method is robust to the change in compress format and resolution. Besides this, the method can also deal with format conversions to different aspect ratio (16:9) even with pillar-box.

5 Conclusion

In this paper, we have developed a novel feature extraction scheme for video content representation. We proposed a visual feature that based on analyzing temporal variation in frequent domain using slice DCT. Since video is a process that evolves with time, the temporal feature for video clips can present the video content well. The proposed feature is robust to the format, resolution variation in transcoding process.

Especially, the proposed algorithm can also deal with conversion to different aspect ratio even with pillar-box. Besides this, the proposed feature is compact to represent the video content. The experiments show the feature proposed is effective and robust.

References

1. Chong-Wah Ngo, Ting-Chuen Pong, Hong-Jiang Zhang: On Clustering and Retrieval of Video Shots through Temporal Slices Analysis, IEEE Transactions on Multimedia, Vol. 4, No. 4, December 2002, Page(s):446-458
2. Chong-Wah Ngo, Ting-Chuen Pong, and Roland T. Chin: Video Partitioning by Temporal Slice Coherency, IEEE Transactions on Circuits and Systems for Video Technology, Vol. 11, No. 8, August 2001, Page(s):941-953
3. Chong-Wah Ngo, Ting-Chuen Pong, and Roland T. Chin: IEEE IP, Motion Analysis and Segmentation through Spatio-temporal Slices Processing, IEEE Transactions on Image Processing, Vol. 12, No. 3, March 2003, Page(s):341-355
4. Peng. S. L, Medioni. G, Interpretation of image sequences by spatio-temporal analysis, Workshop on Visual Motion, March 1989. Page(s):344 - 351
5. O. Utsumi, K. Miura, I. Ide, S. Sakai, and H. Tanaka, An object detection method for describing soccer games from video. ICME2002, Aug 2002, Page(s):45–48.
6. Mark Barnard, Jean-Marc Odobez, Robust Playfield Segmentation using MAP Adaptation, Proceedings of the 17th International Conference on Pattern Recognition (ICPR'04)
7. Shuqiang Jiang, Qixiang Ye, Wen Gao, Tiejun Huang, A New Method to Segment Playfield and Its Applications in Match Analysis in Sports Video, ACM MM'04, October 10–16, 2004, New York, New York, USA
8. A. Ekin, and A. Murat Tekalp, Robust dominant color region detection and color-based applications for sports video, International Conference on Image Processing 2003
9. Changick Kim, Bhaskaran Vasudev: Spatiotemporal Sequence Matching for Efficient Video Copy Detection, IEEE Transactions on Circuits and Systems for Video Technology, Vol. 15, No. 1, January 2005, Page(s):127-132
10. Arun Hampapur, Ki-Ho Hyun, Ruud Bolle: Comparison of Sequence Matching Techniques for Video Copy Detection. Proc. Storage and Retrieval for Media Databases, Jan. 2002, Page(s): 194-201
11. Rakesh Mohan: Video Sequence Matching. Proc. Int. Conf. Audio, Speech and Signal Processing (ICASSP), Vol. 6, Jan. 1998, Page(s): 3697-3700.
12. Changick Kim, Bhaskaran Vasudev: Spatiotemporal Sequence Matching for Efficient Video Copy Detection, IEEE Transactions on Circuits and Systems for Video Technology, Vol. 15, No. 1, January 2005, Page(s):127-132
13. Xian-Sheng Hua, Xian Chen, Hong-Jiung Zhnng: Robust Video Signature Based on Ordinal Measure, International Conference on Image Processing (2004). Page(s):685-688

High Quality Color Interpolation for Color Filter Array with Low Complexity*

Kwon Lee and Chulhee Lee

Dept. Electrical and Electronic Eng., Yonsei Univ.,
134 Shinchon-Dong, Seodaumoon-Ku, 120-749 Seoul, Korea
chulhee@yonsei.ac.kr

Abstract. In this paper, we propose fast color interpolation methods for color filter array (CFA). The proposed methods exploit correlations among the three color components. It has been reported that the quality of color interpolation can be significantly improved by utilizing correlation among color components. However, the complexity of such methods may increase significantly compared to those methods which separately interpolate each color component. On the other hand, the major application of CFA is portable imaging devices such as digital cameras or mobile phones. For portable devices, power consumption is an important issue. In this paper, we propose high quality color interpolation methods with reduced complexity. Experimental results show that the proposed methods provide noticeable improvements without significantly increasing the system complexity.

1 Introduction

Digital image sensors have been widely used in various image devices which include digital cameras, camcorders and mobile phones. For a practical purpose, instead of using three color sensors for the corresponding color channels, many digital imaging systems use a single-chip sensor to reduce cost and size. In the single-chip image sensor, color images are encoded by a color filter array (CFA) and subsequent color interpolation produces full-color images from sampled color images. Fig. 1 shows the Bayer color filter array pattern, which is widely used in digital image sensors due to its excellent color signal sensitivity and good color restoration. In Fig. 1, each color filter provides red, green, and blue signals and the resulting sampled RGB images need to be interpolated using an interpolation algorithm.

Researchers have proposed numerous interpolation methods for color interpolation due to its importance [2-9]. Among various interpolation methods, the linear interpolation method has been frequently used for many applications due to an acceptable SNR (signal-to-noise ratio) and a fast processing time. However, this linear interpolation method tends to blur edges by averaging the surrounding pixels to interpolate a missing pixel.

* This research was supported by the MIC (Ministry of Information and Communication), Korea, under the ITRC (Information Technology Research Center) support program supervised by the IITA (Institute of Information Technology Assessment) (IITA-2005-(C1090-0502-0027)).

T.-J. Cham et al. (Eds.): MMM 2007, LNCS 4352, Part II, pp. 314–322, 2007.
© Springer-Verlag Berlin Heidelberg 2007

Hamilton *et al.* proposed a linear interpolation method with an adaptive strategy. They applied an edge detection algorithm and proposed to interpolate along the edge rather than across the edge [2]. Kimmel proposed an edge weighted interpolation algorithm and then applied inverse diffusion to the whole image as an enhancement filter [8]. Efforts have been also made to exploit correlations between color components to produce better images. Sakamote *et al.* proposed a linear interpolation method exploiting color correlations, where red and blue pixels are used to produce the effective estimate of correlation for missing green pixels [10]. Although interpolation methods which use correlations between RGB channels provide noticeably better performance, the complexity of such methods also increases significantly. In particular, the method proposed by Chang *et al.* provides good performance [9]. However, its complexity far exceeds those of other interpolation methods. On the other hand, the major application of CFA is portable imaging devices which include digital cameras and mobile phones, and power consumption is an important problem for such potable devices. In other words, although high quality color reproduction is an important issue, it needs to be done with minimum complexity. In order to address these issues, we propose high quality color interpolation methods with reduced complexity.

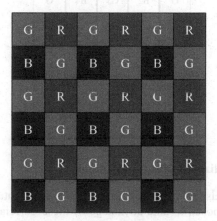

Fig. 1. Bayer CFA patterns

This paper is organized as follows. In Section 2 presents previous interpolation methods. In Section 3 introduces modified interpolation methods. The experimental results are presented in Section 4. Section 5 provides the conclusion.

2 Color Interpolation for Color Filter Array

In this section, we briefly review a few existing interpolation methods for color filter array. First, we discuss a bilinear interpolation method which separately performs interpolation for each color channel. The bilinear interpolation method is also used in the proposed methods. Then, we review interpolation methods which utilize color correlation to produce improved color reproduction.

2.1 Bilinear Interpolation

The bilinear interpolation method has been widely used in image processing due to its simplicity and low complexity. In the bilinear interpolation method, the value of a missing pixel is computed from nearest pixels (Fig. 2). For example, green and blue pixels at the center can be computed as follows:

$$G7 = \frac{G3 + G6 + G8 + G11}{4}$$

$$B7 = \frac{B2 + B4 + B10 + B12}{4}$$

However, bilinear interpolation tends to produce blurred edges. The bilinear interpolation ignores edge information and it does not take advantage of color correlations.

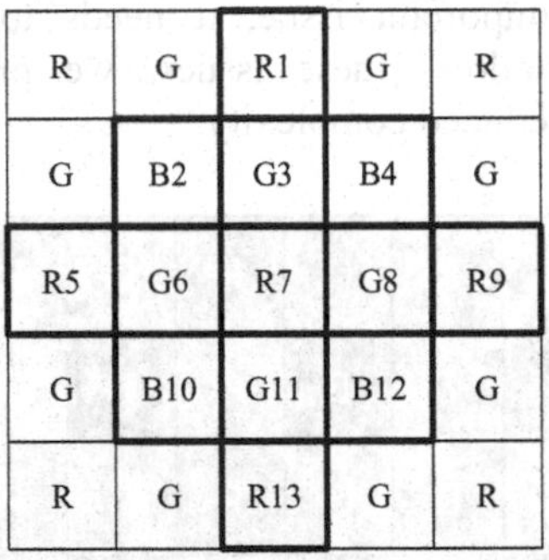

R	G	R1	G	R
G	B2	G3	B4	G
R5	G6	R7	G8	R9
G	B10	G11	B12	G
R	G	R13	G	R

Fig. 2. Reference Bayer CFA pattern

2.2 Interpolation Utilizing Color Correlations [6]

Typically, RGB channels have high correlations. In order to interpolate missing colors of CFA, Pei *et al.* proposed to take advantage of these correlations among the RGB channels [6]. In particular, Kr is defined as green minus red and Kb as green minus blue:

$$Kr = G - R \tag{1}$$

$$Kb = G - B.$$

For most images, the contrasts of Kr and Kb are flat over small regions. Thus, to interpolate missing values, we can use color information. Instead of performing interpolation in a single color channel domain, we simply transform the operation into Kr and Kb domains. This model reduces interpolation errors and improves image quality. Compared with other color difference models, the complexity of this model is lower since multiplication and division are not required. To implement the proposed model, we only use add and shift operations.

In Fig. 2, in order to estimate the missing green value at the center (R7), the four Kr values around the R7 pixel ($Kr3$, $Kr6$, $Kr8$, and $Kr11$) are calculated.

Since the red values around R7 are not available, one must interpolate the missing red values to compute Kr s. For instance, we may interpolate the missing pixel values using bilinear interpolation. In other words, $Kr3$ and $Kr6$ are obtained as follows:

$$Kr3 = G3 - R3 = G3 - \frac{1}{2}(R1 + R7)$$

$$Kr6 = G6 - R6 = G6 - \frac{1}{2}(R5 + R7).$$

Then, the missing green value is computed as follows:

$$G7 = R7 + \frac{1}{4}(Kr3 + Kr6 + Kr8 + Kr11).$$

The G value at a B pixel can be obtained by performing interpolation in the Kb domain. In practice, it can be implemented as follows:

$$G7 = R7 + \frac{1}{4}\left[G3 - \frac{1}{2}(R7 + R1) + G6 - \frac{1}{2}(R7 + R5) \right.$$

$$\left. + G8 - \frac{1}{2}(R7 + R9) + G11 - \frac{1}{2}(R7 + R13) \right]$$

$$= \frac{1}{2}R7 + \frac{1}{4}(G3 + G6 + G8 + G11) - \frac{1}{8}(R1 + R5 + R9 + R13).$$

Once the green value is computed, it is used to compute the missing red and blue values as follows:

$$R3 = G3 - \frac{1}{2}(Kr1 + Kr7) \qquad (2)$$

$$B7 = G7 - \frac{1}{4}(Kb2 + Kb4 + Kb10 + Kb12). \qquad (3)$$

Since we already computed green values at the R and B pixels, we can easily calculate the Kr and Kb values.

2.3 Color Interpolation with Weighted Color Differences [9]

However, the method described in the previous section may produce distortions for edge areas since Kr and Kb are obtained by an averaging operation. In other words, its performance is bounded by the inherent limitation of bilinear interpolation. In order to address this problem, Chang et al. proposed to use weighted color differences and iteration [9]. For example, the color difference value Kx at R7 in Fig. 2 is calculated as follows:

$$K_X = \frac{\dfrac{Kr6}{1+\alpha6} + \dfrac{Kr8}{1+\alpha8} + \dfrac{Kr3}{1+\alpha3} + \dfrac{Kr11}{1+\alpha11}}{\dfrac{1}{1+\alpha6} + \dfrac{1}{1+\alpha8} + \dfrac{1}{1+\alpha3} + \dfrac{1}{1+\alpha11}} \qquad (4)$$

where Kr is defined in (1). In (4), α s are weights along the four adjacent directions and calculated as follows:

$$\alpha6 = |R7 - R5| + |G6 - G8|$$
$$\alpha8 = |R7 - R9| + |G8 - G6|$$
$$\alpha3 = |R7 - R1| + |G3 - G11|$$
$$\alpha11 = |R7 - R13| + |G11 - G3|$$

Then, the missing green value is computed as follows:

$$G = R + K_X.$$

Next, the red and blue values are calculated using the estimated green value. After all missing colors are interpolated, the identical procedure is repeated using the estimated color pixels to further improve color interpolation. It is reported that repeating the procedure noticeably improve the picture quality. Although this method provides very good performance, the method requires a large number of operations, including multiplication and absolute operations, which may not be desirable in portable devices where power consumption is critical.

3 Proposed Interpolation Methods for CFA

3.1 High Quality Color Interpolation with Low Complexity (HQCILC)

Although the interpolation method [6] provides good image quality with low complexity, it fails to take a full advantage of color correlation. In order to calculate color difference constants Kr and Kb, missing red and blue values are computed using bilinear interpolation. Consequently, the method inherits the drawbacks of bilinear interpolation and its performance improvement would be limited. The color interpolation method proposed by Chang et al. addresses this problem by using weighted sums and repeating the interpolation procedure [9]. However, its complexity increases drastically. Since CFAs are mainly used in potable devices where power consumption is an important problem, low complexity is a critical issue.

In order to provide high quality images without increasing complexity significantly, we propose a color interpolation method which efficiently uses correlations between three colors. The proposed method first uses the procedure proposed by Pei et al. [6], which fills all missing colors. For instance, the missing green pixel is computed as follows:

$$G7 = R7 + \frac{1}{4}(Kr3 + Kr6 + Kr8 + Kr11)$$
$$= R7 + \frac{1}{4}(G3 - R3 + G6 - R6$$
$$+ G8 - R8 + G11 - R11)$$

where missing red and blues pixels are initially interpolated using bilinear interpolation. In the proposed method, we repeat the same procedure with the newly estimated values. Since all missing RBG pixels are estimated, the estimated values would be better than the initial estimated values which are interpolated using bilinear interpolation. Fig. 3 illustrates the proposed interpolation method. First, Kr s and Kb s are computed using estimated pixels obtained by bilinear interpolation. Then, green pixels are computed using Kr s and Kb s. Once all missing green pixels are estimated, red and blue pixels which were interpolated by using bilinear interpolation are computed again using the estimated green pixels using (2) and (3). Finally, the same procedure is repeated with newly interpolated pixels. This procedure may be repeated more than one time. Experiments show that repeating the procedure twice produced the best results. Thus, in the proposed method, the procedure is repeated twice.

3.2 Fast Hybrid Color Difference Interpolation (FHCDI)

We also propose another fast hybrid interpolation method using a weighted color difference method [9] and ECI method [6]. Although the weighted color difference method outperforms others, its complexity is very high. On the other hand, the ECI method has very low complexity. By taking the advantages of each method, we propose a fast hybrid color difference method.

The initial interpolation is identical as that of the weighted color difference method. In the iteration interpolation, instead of using a weighted color difference method, we use the ECI method to refine RBG color interpolation. This method reduces complexity and provides improved performance compared to the weighted color difference method.

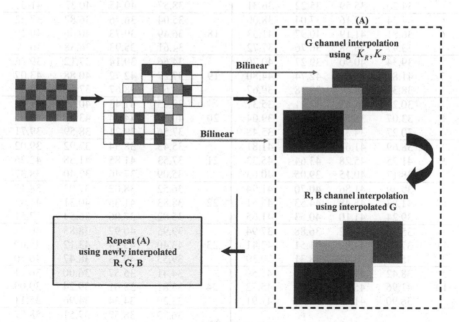

Fig. 3. Block diagram of the proposed HQCILC interpolation method

4 Experimental Results

Experiments were conducted in order to evaluate the performance of the proposed methods. We compare the proposed methods with two existing demosaicking

Table 1. PSNRs comparison : PSNR result(in dB) of the red, green and blue planes are listed in the 1st, 2nd and 3th rows of each image

Image	Pei[6]	Chang [9]	HQCILC	FHCDI	Image	Pei[6]	Chang [9]	HQCILC	FHCDI
	33.13	36.57	35.86	37.37		31.29	33.88	35.38	35.12
1	35.54	40.46	39.98	40.99	13	32.59	36.85	38.09	37.50
	33.23	36.75	36.45	37.99		30.91	33.04	34.37	34.17
	36.40	37.46	35.71	36.93		33.94	35.35	33.25	34.67
2	40.65	43.38	40.88	43.06	14	37.67	40.22	38.06	40.09
	38.07	40.35	38.26	40.43		34.36	35.10	33.95	35.54
	39.69	41.21	39.59	41.13		36.20	37.93	36.40	37.71
3	42.76	45.55	43.12	45.52	15	39.91	42.43	41.10	42.67
	38.75	39.69	38.58	40.50		37.60	39.23	38.84	40.23
	37.25	38.13	36.51	37.67		37.23	40.12	39.85	41.02
4	41.57	43.02	41.89	43.26	16	39.89	44.02	43.43	44.32
	40.16	40.94	40.78	42.00		36.81	39.29	39.11	40.29
	34.54	36.66	35.65	36.75		39.28	41.84	41.53	42.35
5	36.59	40.45	39.41	40.83	17	40.53	44.36	44.30	44.65
	34.20	35.59	35.22	36.31		38.57	40.45	40.32	41.01
	34.24	37.16	37.04	38.00		35.04	36.76	36.87	37.22
6	36.81	41.19	40.97	41.53	18	36.49	39.73	40.06	40.20
	33.97	36.58	36.76	37.72		34.61	35.93	36.38	36.72
	39.34	40.90	39.27	40.70		34.66	39.14	37.12	39.76
7	41.89	44.69	42.74	44.80	19	37.27	42.72	40.88	43.07
	38.34	39.47	38.18	39.67		34.57	38.67	37.10	39.48
	30.27	34.43	32.91	35.31		38.75	41.43	40.41	41.75
8	33.07	38.56	37.01	39.04	20	40.59	44.54	43.58	44.83
	30.27	34.31	33.17	35.48		37.56	39.21	38.59	39.71
	38.69	41.64	40.09	41.81		35.43	38.34	37.92	39.02
9	41.25	45.28	43.64	45.33	21	37.53	41.85	41.58	42.26
	38.17	40.15	39.05	40.63		35.09	37.46	37.40	38.37
	39.49	41.86	40.70	41.94		36.52	38.02	37.03	38.17
10	41.83	45.48	44.53	45.61	22	38.83	41.35	40.31	41.42
	39.24	41.10	40.53	41.65		35.82	37.06	36.54	37.51
	35.25	37.72	36.88	37.94		39.95	40.97	38.83	40.33
11	37.99	41.99	41.51	42.41	23	43.40	45.14	43.12	45.09
	35.87	38.42	38.31	39.39		39.53	40.38	38.47	40.10
	38.42	41.43	39.49	41.59		34.41	35.57	36.00	36.11
12	41.96	45.52	43.99	45.72	24	35.81	38.61	39.24	39.09
	38.90	41.30	40.40	41.91		33.29	34.34	34.96	35.11
						36.23	38.52	37.51	38.77
					Ave rage	38.85	42.39	41.39	42.64
						36.16	38.12	37.57	38.83

methods: the method proposed by Pei *et al.* [6], and the method proposed by Chang *et al.* [9]. In this paper, 24 test images are used in [9].

Table 1 shows the PSNR comparison of the 24 images. The method proposed by Chang *et al.* outperforms the method proposed by Pei *et al.* The proposed HQCILC method (high quality color interpolation with low complexity) shows inferior performance compared to the method proposed by Chang *et al.*, though its performance is better than that of the method proposed by Pei *et al.* On the other hand, the proposed FHCDI method (fast hybrid color difference interpolation) shows the best performance.

Table 2 shows the complexity comparison of the four methods. As can be seen in Table 2, the method proposed by Chang *et al.* requires the largest number of operations which include multiplications while the method proposed by Pei *et al.* requires the smallest number of operations. Although the proposed HQCILC method requires a larger number of operations than the method proposed by Pei *et al.*, the

Table 2. Complexity comparison : the number shows a number of times that performing each operation to obtain a green pixel

	Pei [6]	Chang [9]	HQCILC	FHCDI
Add	8	62	24	39
Shift	3	4	5	5
Absolute		16		8
Multiplication		18		9

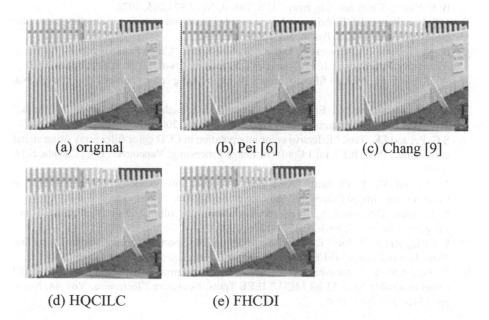

(a) original   (b) Pei [6]   (c) Chang [9]

(d) HQCILC   (e) FHCDI

Fig. 4. Cropped regions of 19th image: (a) Original image, and interpolation result of (b) Pei's method (c) Chang's method (d) proposed HQCILC method (e) proposed FHCDI method

number of operations is much smaller compared to the method proposed by Chang *et al.* On the other hand, the proposed HQCILC method provides noticeable improvement compared to the method proposed by Pei *et al.* Furthermore, the proposed FHCDI method requires a smaller number of operations compared to the method by Chang *et al.* while it provides the best performance.

Fig. 4 show cropped images obtained by the four interpolation methods. In Fig. 4b, some interpolation artifacts are observed. The other three results are very similar. Since the performance of three methods (Fig. 4b, 4c, 4d) are very similar in PSNR and perceptual evaluation, the complexity may become an important issues.

5 Conclusions

In this paper we propose two high quality color interpolation methods with low complexity. The proposed methods utilize color correlations. The initial interpolation is performed using bilinear interpolation and subsequent interpolation is performed by utilizing color correlation to fill all missing color pixels. Then, the procedure is repeated using the newly estimated pixels to improve performance. Experimental results show that the proposed methods provide high quality interpolation results without significantly increasing complexity.

References

1. B. E. Bayer, "Color imaging array," U.S. Patent, No. 3,971,065, 1976.
2. J. F. Hamilton and J. E. Adams, "Adaptive color plane interpolation in single sensor color electronic camera," U.S. Patent, No. 5,629,734, 1997.
3. B. K. Gunturk, Y. Altunbasak, and R. M. Mersereau, "Color Plane Interpolation Using Alternating Projections," IEEE Trans. Image Processing, vol. 11, no.9, September 2002.
4. W. T. Freeman, "Median filter for reconstructing missing color samples," U.S. Patent, No. 4,724,395, 1998.
5. R. Ramamanth and W. E. Snyder, "Demosaicking methods for Bayer Color arrays," Journal of Electronic Imaging, vol. 11, pp306-315, July, 2002.
6. S.C. Pei and I.K. Tam, "Effective color interpolation in CCD color filter array using signal correlation," Proc. IEEE Int'l Conf. On Image Processing, Vancouver, B.C. Canada, Sept. 2000.
7. X. Li and M. T. Orchard, "New Edge Directed Interpolation," IEEE International Conference on Image Processing, Vancouver, Sept. 2000.
8. R. Kimmel, "Demosaicking: Image reconstruction from color CCD samples," IEEE Trans. Image Process, vol. 7, no.3, pp.1221-1228, 1999.
9. L. Chang and Y. P. Tan, "Effective use of Spatial and Spectral Correlations for Cole Filter Array Demosaicking," IEEE Trans. Consumer Electronics, vol. 50, no. 1, Feb. 2004.
10. T. Sakamoto, C. Nakanishi, and T. Hasse, "Software pixel interpolation for digital still cameras suitable for a 32-bit MCU," IEEE Trans. Consumer Electronics, Vol. 44, No. 4, pp. 1342-1352, Nov. 1998.

A Two-Level Matching Scheme for Speedy and Accurate Palmprint Identification

Fang Li, Maylor K.H. Leung, and Xiaozhou Yu

School of Computer Engineering, Nanyang Technological University, Singapore 639798
asfli@ntu.edu.sg

Abstract. Although palmprint based authentication approaches have shown promising results recently, efforts are still required to achieve higher performance with low time complexity for their use in real-life high security applications. Based on these requirements, the concept of two level matching scheme using line matching in Hough space and Curve segment Hausdorff Distance (CsHD) are explored and developed for speedy and accurate palmprint identification in this paper. This method combines the advantages of both local and global feature approaches, which is able to not only absorb the variance of palmprints by transforming the palmprint pattern into a new domain, but also overcome the problem of high computation complexity when the database size increases. The system employs low-resolution palmprint images captured by normal digital camera and achieves higher identification accuracy with lower time complexity.

Keywords: line, curve, palmprint, Hough space, Hausdorff distance.

1 Introduction

Biometrics has been an emerging field of research in the recent years and is devoted to identification of individuals using physical traits. As unauthorized users are not able to display the same unique physical properties to have a positive authentication, reliability will be ensured [1]. Among all the biometric features, palmprint is well-known for several advantages such as stable line features, low-resolution imaging, low-cost capturing device, and user friendly interface [2]. Although palmprint based authentication approaches have shown promising results recently, efforts are still required to achieve higher performance with low time complexity for their use in real-life high security applications. To achieve the desired accuracy and efficiency, the proposed system explored and developed a two-level matching scheme using line matching in Hough space and Curve segment Hausdorff Distance (CsHD) [3].

A palmprint image contains various features, including geometrical features, principal lines, ridges, minutiae points, singular points and texture [4]. Lines and texture are the most clearly observable features in low-resolution (such as 100 dpi) palmprint images. Principal lines and wrinkles, called line features, are more appealing than the palm texture for human vision. This observation motivates us to develop a matching scheme for the palm lines.

T.-J. Cham et al. (Eds.): MMM 2007, LNCS 4352, Part II, pp. 323–332, 2007.

However, the traditional exhaustive line matching methods are very time consuming. The line matching process was applied to all of the template sets to search for the best matching. With the increasing of the database size, it becomes inapplicable. A two-level matching system is proposed to take advantage of the simplicity of global feature and accuracy of local feature. A global feature with low computation complexity is used to select a small set of similar candidates at a coarse level for further matching. This work proposes a line matching method in Hough space, which extracts global line layout of the whole palmprint for coarse-level filtering. The Hough Transform (HT) is a powerful technique for line detection [5]. Its main advantage is that it is relatively unaffected by noise or gaps in lines. In case a slightly broken line is caused by a partial occlusion in one image but not in the other, two corresponding peaks will still be formed and matched after transforming these lines to Hough space. If we convert all the lines in image space to points in parametric (ρ, θ) space, the line matching problem in the image space can be converted into a point-matching problem in Hough space [6].

The local information extracted from position and orientation of individual line is used for further fine-level matching. A new scheme - Curve segment Hausdorff Distance (CsHD) [3], which measures the dissimilarity between two sets of curve segments, is proposed to screen further and generate the best matches. The name curve segment Hausdorff distance derives from the well-known shape measurement method Hausdorff Distance (HD). It is a distance defined between two sets of points. Unlike most shape comparison methods that build a one-to-one correspondence between a model and a test image, HD can be calculated without explicit point correspondence. Huttenlocher[7] studied the possibility of comparing images in terms of Hausdorff distance, where Hausdorff distance is viewed as a function of the translation of a model with respect to an image. Their test results show that Hausdorff distance transform is powerful for shape comparison, more tolerant of perturbations in the locations of pixel points. Instead of matching 2 sets of points using HD, we propose the novel idea to generalize HD to match 2 sets of higher level primitives such as curves with the following additional characteristics besides HD's advantage of that no explicit correspondence is required between images so as to simplify the matching process [8]:

1. Points on one curve must match to points on another curve.
2. Line orientation difference is taken into consideration to compute the dissimilarity between 2 lines.

The proposed CsHD works on the line segments extracted from the palm images and organizes them in a more proper way by regrouping the consecutive line segments into a curve segment. Then the distances between two lines, between two curves and between two images are constructed systematically.

The system employs low-resolution palmprint images captured by normal digital camera. This method combines the advantages of both global and local feature approaches, which is able to not only absorb the variance of palmprints by transforming the palmprint pattern into a new domain, but also overcome the problem of having complex computation when the database size increases Experiments had been conducted on a palmprint database collected by Hong Kong Polytechnic

University. 99% identification rate has been achieved with much reduced running time. There are not many published works in this area and therefore this is an interesting and challenging research topic.

The rest of this paper is organized as follows: Section 2 introduces the structure of the proposed two-level palmprint identification system. Line matching in Hough space [6] and CsHD are discussed in details in Section 3. Section 4 presents the results for identification. Finally, the conclusion and future work are highlighted in Section 5.

2 System Overview

Fig. 1 shows the block diagram of the proposed two-level palmprint matching system. In the preprocessing module, processes such as line detection, image thresholding, thinning, contour extraction, and polygonal approximation are applied to extract Line Edge Map (LEM) [11] from a palm.

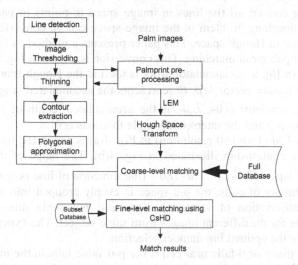

Fig. 1. Block diagram of proposed hierarchical palmprint matching system

LEM is then transformed to Hough space to extract the global pattern of the palmprint. At the same time, the line segments set is stored as local information for further fine-matching. Section 3 presents the details of these two stages.

3 Proposed Two-Level Matching Scheme

In order to combine the advantage of simplicity of global features and accuracy of local features, two level matching approach is proposed to match between the input images and the templates from the database: coarse-level matching and fine-level matching. A line matching method in Hough space is proposed to facilitate the fast selection of a small set of similar candidates from the database at coarse level for further processing. A new scheme - Curve segment Hausdorff Distance (CsHD) [3], which measures the dissimilarity between two sets of curve segments, is proposed to screen further and generate the best matches.

3.1 The First Stage: Coarse-Level Matching

This section presents a line matching method in Hough space for palmprint matching at coarse level. The global pattern of line orientation and distance to origin is introduced to define the global palmprint features.

3.1.1 Hough Space Transform

Most papers related to HT deal with the detection of straight lines from a binary image [5]. In Hough transform process, lines in image space are transformed into peak points in the parameter space, i.e., Hough space [6]. As for our research, after pre-processing, the whole palmprint image is approximated using straight line segments. If we convert all the lines in image space to points in parametric (ρ, θ) space, the line matching problem in the image space can be converted into a point-matching problem in Hough space. This paper presents a method of line matching in Hough space for palmprint matching. This conversion is shown in Fig.4. As suggested by Duda and Hart [6], a accumulator array is used as the Hough space for the lines. Two dimension feature vector $L(\rho, \theta)$ represents the accumulated length of the lines. The value in accumulator cells, $L_{\rho\theta}$, is the accumulated length of the lines whose distance to origin is ρ and the intersection angle to x-axis is θ.

The sample LEM (160x160 resolution) in Fig. 4(a) is converted into the ρ-θ plane according to the relationship illustrated in Fig. 4(b). The range of the accumulator array is $-160\sqrt{2} \leq \rho \leq 160\sqrt{2}$, $0° \leq \theta < 180°$ (the direction of line is ignored). In order to reduce the number of cells, the ρ-θ space is evenly grouped into 16x9 cells. It is based on the observation of variance of position and angle due to illumination condition change for the different images from same subject. The experimental results in Fig. 5 approve the optimal bin number selection.

It is possible that ρ or θ falls near cell if the ρ-θ value falls in the margin. This can be tackled by growing a window with (ρ, θ) as center. Instead of updating one cell, we update all the cells within the window by ratio of the area. Different window sizes (η x cell width)x(η x cell height) according to different ratio η were selected and experimented. The accuracy was measured in similarity based queries by "Bull's Eye Percentage Score" (BEP) [9]. BEP is defined for each query as the percentage of correct matches with respect to the query's class that appear within 2C top retrieved results, where C denotes the size of the considered query class. The results are illustrated in Fig. 2. η=0.5 got the highest accuracy; therefore, window size is defined as (half of cell width)x(half of cell height) in this research. Instead of updating one cell, we update all the cells within the window by ratio of the area. One example is given in Fig. 3. Line A's ρ-θ value falls in the margin. A window is growing as shown in Fig. 3 and 2/9's area, 1/9's area, 4/9's area, and 2/9's area belongs to C1,

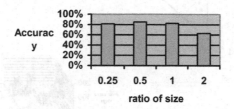

Fig. 2. Accuracy test with respect to different window size for marginal lines

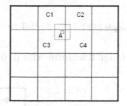

Fig. 3. Marginal line handling

C2, C3, C4 respectively. Assume the length of line A is 9. The accumulated length of the four cells increase by 2, 1 4, 2 respectively.

Feature vector $L(\rho, \theta)$ is thus simplified to 16x9 integers to represent the global pattern of the palmprint, which is 162B only for a 108KB image. The conversion result is shown in Fig. 4c and 4d in numeric way and 3D view respectively. The sample accumulator cell under circle in Fig. 4(c) shows the accumulated length for all the lines with $\rho=15$ and $\theta=5$ is 69. It is shown that the line-matching problem in image space can become a point-matching problem in parametric (ρ-θ) space.

3.1.2 Distance of Global Line Structure

Instead of matching intervals in image space, peaks in Hough space which represent lines in the image space are matched. Hence, by converting these line segments to ($\rho-\theta$) space, the positions and orientations of principal lines and wrinkles can be easily described using a feature vector $L(\rho,\theta)$. The distance of global structures between Model image m and Test image t, $i.e.$, the coarse-level distance between two images is calculated as follows:

$$dist(global) = \sum_{\rho \in [1,16], \, \theta \in [1,9]} (L_{m_{\rho\theta}} - L_{t_{\rho\theta}})^2 \tag{1}$$

The time complexity for matching one pair is $o(pq)$. p the maximum bin number of ρ-dimension and q is the maximum bin number of θ-dimension. Since p and q are normally fairly small (in this research, p and q are 16 and 9 respectively), the matching process is very efficient.

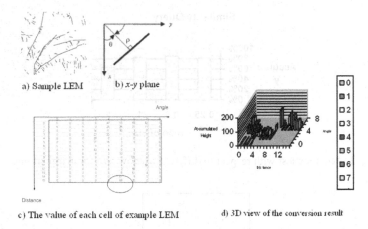

a) Sample LEM   b) x-y plane

c) The value of each cell of example LEM   d) 3D view of the conversion result

Fig. 4. Hough transform with ρ- θ plane

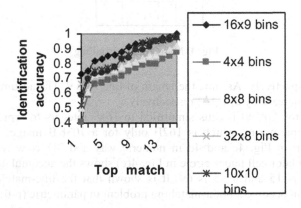

Fig. 5. Identification accuracy of Coarse-matching: Effect of different bin numbers

3.1.3 Result of Coarse-Level Matching

Because HT works by accumulating a large number of votes, it is relatively insensitive to small vote fluctuation caused by noise and occlusion. Take the curve in Fig. 4 as example, even under poor segmentation and all the line segments are broken, it will not affect the final result significantly. This scheme can achieve 73% accuracy for top 1 match and 100% accuracy for top 15 matches, as shown in Fig. 5. We have tried different bin numbers for ρ-θ space. 16x9 bins is the optimal choice.

3.2 The Second Stage: Fine-Level Matching

After coarse-level matching, only 73% of the input images can be matched to genuine if only first match is considered. A careful examination of failed examples reveals that the palmprint images with similar principal lines can be impostors if only global and principal line information is considered. However, if we also look into the local information of each line, such as position and orientation information, we can distinguish the impostor from genuine.

3.2.1 Hausdorff Distance

Hausdorff distance (HD) is one of the commonly used measures for shape matching and has been widely investigated [7][10]. It is a distance defined between two sets of points. Unlike most shape comparison methods that build a one-to-one correspondence between a model and a test image, HD can be calculated without explicit point correspondence. Hausdorff Distance (HD) is the "maximum distance of a set to the nearest point in the other set" as

$$h(A,B) = \max_{a \in A} \min_{b \in B} \| a - b \| \qquad (2)$$

where a and b are points of sets A and B respectively, where is any norm, e.g. Euclidean distance. It should be noted that Hausdorff Distance is oriented (we could say asymmetric as well). A more general definition of Hausdorff Distance would be:

$$H(A,B) = \max(h(A,B), h(B,A)) \qquad (3)$$

which defines the Hausdorff Distance between A and B, while eq.2 computes Hausdorff Distance from A to B (also called directed Hausdorff Distance). HD is one of the commonly used methods in image processing and matching applications. It measures two images' dissimilarity without explicit point correspondence.

3.2.2 Line Segment Hausdorff Distance (LHD)

The original HD is a distance defined between two sets of points [7]. LHD [8][11] extends the concept to two sets of line segments. Applying the concept on the line edge map (LEM) [8] of an image, each line set captures the complete feature vector set of one image. Hence, we can measure two images' dissimilarity based on line features using LHD. It has been adopted in a number of applications, such as logo recognition [11].

3.2.3 Curve Segment Hausdorff Distance (CsHD)

Line features on palmprint include both curves and straight lines. Since a curve can be interpreted as a consecutive run of connected lines, a curve segment Hausdorff distance (CsHD) [3] can be implemented on top of LHD. Not like some palmprint identification and verification systems [10], location of endpoints of each principal line is not essential for the proposed curve segment Hausdorff distance (CsHD). It makes uses of structural and spatial information and is robust to noise, occlusion and broken lines. The usage of high level primitives (lines and curves) has conceptually provided more and better distinctive capability for recognition which will be proven later in our experiment. The novel technique has been applied on line and curve segments generated from palmprints under different situation with encouraging results that supports the concept experimentally. Moreover, the proposed technique is simple in concept, efficient and easy to implement. Future work can employ the technique on more application areas and further enhance its recognition accuracy.

The proposed CsHD can be seen as a hybrid of template and syntactic matching approaches. The curve segment collection (LEM) of an image object is treated as a template which captures the inherent structural relationships of curves. At the same time, a curve is a consecutive run of connected line segments, and can be described/matched using string attribute grammar. The relationships between curve segments can be modelled using graph. In our previous research, we simplified the modelling using attribute grammar [3].

4 Experiment Results

A series of experiments were carried out using a palmprint database from Biometric Research Centre, The Hong Kong Polytechnic University. Palmprint images from 100 individuals (6 images for each person) [12]. The images were collected using a special palmprint capture device. The subjects mainly consisted of volunteers from the students and staffs at the Hong Kong Polytechnic University with a wide range of age distribution and different genders.

4.1 Identification

An identification system examines whether the user is one of enrolled candidates [26]. In our experiment, 3 images are randomly chosen from one person as the model images and the rest three are used as test images for identification. Thus, a palmprint database of 100 classes was created. During the experiments, the LEM feature of each image was extracted and two-level matching was used. The matching result and comparisons are tabulated in Table 1. An average recognition rate 95%, 95%, and 98% were achieved by the technique proposed in [13], [14] and [2] respectively. The experiment results demonstrate that the two-level matching method has achieved the highest accuracy.

4.2 Speed

The matching algorithm is implemented with Microsoft VC++ and works on a NEC (CPU 3GHZ, RAM 1GB) personal computer with Windows XP. The execution time

Table 1. Comparison of different palmprint identification methods

		Duta et al. [13]	You et al. [14]	Zhang & Zhang[2]	Two-level matching (proposed)
Database size	Subject	3	100	50	100
	Image	30	200	200	600
Feature		Feature points	Texture and feature points	Wavelet Signatures	Lines feature
Matching criteria		Euclidian distance	Global texture energy + point Hausdorff distance	Euclidian distance	Line matching in Hough space + Curve Segment Hausdorff distance
Recognition rate		95%	95%	98%	99%
Search Method		sequential	hierarchical	sequential	two-level

for the preprocessing, feature extraction, coarse level matching, fine level matching are 408ms, 61ms, 9.8x10-5ms, and 2.1 ms. For identification, if the database contains images for 100 persons, and each person registers three palmprint images, the total identification time of our proposed two level matching scheme is about 500.5294ms (408+61+9.8x10-5x300+2.1x15) while the traditional sequential approach requires 1099ms (408+61+2.1x300). It shows the efficiency of our two-level matching system compared to sequential method. Moreover, the efficiency will be more obvious when database is large.

5   Conclusion and Future Works

This paper describes two-level matching in the proposed palmprint recognition system. When the numbers of input and model images are large, the price for brute force matching between the input and model images is high. To cut down CPU time, instead of linearly searching all models in database, a coarse-matching module is proposed to select a moderate number of candidate models for fine-matching. In this study, simple and easily computed shape features are designed to index all the models and generate a moderate number of likely models with respect to an input. A line-based Hough Transform method is proposed to extract global features for coarse-level filtering in this system. Since the majority samples have been filtered out by the coarse-level filtering, the execution speed of fine-level identification has been significantly increased. The novelty of this research also lies in identifying principal lines using watershed segmentation algorithm. The local neighbourhood information of principal lines is first time used as a means to measure similarity. It works by first extracting consistent and structurally unique local neighbourhood information from inputs or models, and then voting on the optimal matches. It performs speedy interpretation of input images and retrieval of structurally similar models from large database according to the input. The local information extracted from position and orientation of individual line is used for further fine-level identification. Curve Segment Hausdorff Distance (CsHD) algorithm is applied for local line matching.

Instead of matching 2 sets of points using HD, we propose the novel idea to generalize HD to match 2 sets of higher level primitives such as curves. A novel distance computation between 2 curves is first derived. Based on this new distance, a novel scheme CsHD without explicit feature correspondence can be implemented to compute a distance measure between 2 sets of curves. It is tolerant to missing lines or gaps on curves.

This two-level matching method not only overcomes the problem of time consuming in palmprint identification system, but also achieves high accuracy. The experiment results prove the usefulness of this algorithm.

We still have much work to be done in the future to improve this method.

- To solve the skewing problem in palmprint matching.
- To consider more local information to enhance the accuracy further.
- To employ the technique on more application areas.

References

1. Z. Riha and V. Matyas, "Biometric authentication systems", FI MU Report Series, FIMU-RS-2000-08, November 2000.
2. L. Zhang, and D. Zhang, "Characterication of palmprint by wavelet signatures via directional context modeling", IEEE Transactions on Systems, Man. And Cybernetics-Part B: Cybernetics, vol. 34, no.3, pp. 1335-1347, 2004
3. Y.X. Zhou, and M.K.H. Leung, "Shape Recognition using Curve Segment Hausdorff Distance", Proceedings of the 18th International Conference on Pattern Recognition (ICPR06).
4. D. Zhang, W. K. Kong, J. You, and M. Wong, "Online palmprint identification", IEEE Transactions on Pattern Analysis and Machine Intelligence, vol. 25, no. 9, pp. 1041-1050, 2003.
5. F.H. Cheng, W.H. Hsu, and M.Y., Chen, "Recognition of handwritten Chinese characters by modified Hough Transform techniques", IEEE Transactions on Pattern Analysis and Machine Intelligence, vol. 11, no. 4, pp. 901-916, 1989.
6. Z.N., Li, "Stereo correspondence based on line matching in Hough space using Dynamic Programming", IEEE Transactions on System. Man. and Cybernetics, vol. 24, no. 1, pp. 144-152, 1994.
7. D.P. Huttenlocher, G.A. Klandeman, and W.J. Rucklidge, "Comparing images using the Hausdorff distance", IEEE Transactions on Pattern Analysis and Machine Intelligence, vol. 15, no. 9, pp. 850-863, 1993.
8. Y.S. Gao, and M.K.H. Leung, "Face recognition using line edge map", IEEE Transactions on Pattern Analysis and Machine Intelligence, vol. 24, no. 6, pp. 764-779, 2002.
9. B.S. Manjunath, Introduction to MPE-7:multimedia content description interface: Wiley, 2002.
10. X.L. Yi, and O.I. Camps, "Line-Based recognition using a multidimentional Hausdorff Distance", IEEE Transactions on Pattern Analysis and Machine Intelligence, vol. 21, no. 9, pp. 901-916, 1999.
11. J.Y. Chen, M.K.H. Leung, and Y.S. Gao, "Noisy logo recognition using line segment Hausdorff Distance". Pattern Recognition, vol. 36, pp. 943-955, 2003.
12. Palmprint database from Biometric Research Center, The Hong Kong Polytechnic University. Available: http://www4.comp.polyu.edu.hk/~biometrics/
13. N. Duta, A.K. Jain, "Matching of palmprints", Pattern Recognition Letters, 23:477-485, 2002.
14. J. You, W.K. K, D. Zhang, and K.H. Cheung, "On hierarchical palmprint coding with multiple features for personal identification in large databases", IEEE Transactions on Circuits and Systems for Video Technology, vol. 14, no. 2, pp. 234-243, 2004.

Improving Quality of Live Streaming Service over P2P Networks with User Behavior Model

Yun Tang[1], Lifeng Sun[2], Jian-Guang Luo[1],
Shi-Qiang Yang[2], and Yuzhuo Zhong[2]

[1] Tsinghua University, Beijing 100084, P.R. China
{tangyun98,luojg03}@mails.tsinghua.edu.cn
[2] {sunlf,yangshq,zyz-dcs}@mail.tsinghua.edu.cn

Abstract. In this paper, we mainly investigate how to improve the streaming quality of service over Peer-to-Peer (P2P) networks with the benefit of practical service traces. Considering that the QoS of P2P live streaming is generally affected by high dynamics in peer community, we abstract the online duration model of end users and then exploit this characteristic to improve the stability and encourage contribution in P2P networks, which in turn facilitates the quality of streaming.

The first effort involves the online information when constructing video delivery tree and hence achieves less playback disruption. The other algorithm takes the online duration into account when selecting neighbor peers for data exchange and advocates more mutual cooperation between peers. The experiment results show that the proposed schemes could respectively achieve higher stability and better delivery quality.

1 Introduction

It is quite interesting and challenging to streaming live media contents to a large number of end users. In absence of network infra structure support, application layer multicast or overlay multicast was proposed to provide group communications with the ease of deployment [1 4]. They generally explored the peer-to-peer (P2P) technique to effectively explored the cooperative paradigm among numerous end users. The core concept in P2P is that each peer, also interchangeably called node or user, plays the role of both client and server at the same time. With each participant contributing individual computation, storage and bandwidth resources into collective pool, the overall system performance is hence amplified to hundreds or even thousands times. After the first practical work in this field, DONet/CoolStreaming[5], several commercial P2P live streaming systems have been successfully deployed to date [6-8]. Our experiences have demonstrated that P2P won its popularity to support a large user group[8].

However, most of overlay construction protocols involved significant management overheads to accommodate high dynamics in peer community. In face of the fact that the streaming quality and system reliability is essentially affected by the churn, that is, peers could join and leave the system independently and continuously, we mainly investigate how to improve QoS of P2P live streaming

T.-J. Cham et al. (Eds.): MMM 2007, LNCS 4352, Part II, pp. 333–342, 2007.
© Springer-Verlag Berlin Heidelberg 2007

in this paper. With the aid of practical service traces from deployed P2P live streaming system [8] and a popular client/server (C/S) based content provider, we abstract the online duration model of end users and further exploit this model to propose two schemes, aiming to facilitate the quality of streaming service between peer-pair. Our study goes beyond exiting work in following two aspects.

1) Characterizing online duration model of end users. We make statistical analysis to service logs from P2P system with concurrent online users more than **200,000** for broadcasting Spring Festival Evening show in Jan. 2006 over global Internet and about **8 million** service traces from C/S system in CCTV-News[1]. We characterize online duration model through a comparative study and validate the statistically positive correlation between elapsed online duration and expected remaining online time.

2) Improving QoS of P2P live streaming with the aid of online duration. We propose two schemes from different perspectives to improve the quality of streaming service with respect to different understandings to QoS. The first effort involves the online duration information when constructing video delivery tree. The key idea is to offer the peers which have longer elapsed online duration and larger upload capacity positions close to the source, resulting in less playback disruption. The other algorithm takes the online duration into account when selecting neighbor peers for data exchange and advocates more mutual cooperation between peers. The experiment results show that the proposed schemes could respectively achieve higher stability and better delivery quality.

The balance of this paper is organized as follows. Sec.2 presents the statistic analysis to service traces and online duration model. Then we propose the Low Disruption Tree Construction algorithm and Incentive-based Differentiated Service mechanism in Sec.3 and Sec.4 respectively. Some experiment results are also provided. Sec. 5 ends this paper.

2   Online Duration Model of End Users

As known, the high churn of peers substantially poses great challenge on comfortable playback quality in streaming applications. In this section, we hence abstract the online duration model of end users for further improvement. The comparative study between P2P and C/S not only sheds lights into the model itself, but also validate the statistically positive correlation between elapsed online duration and expected remaining online time.

2.1   Statistical Analysis to Service Traces

In previous work, we have designed, implemented and deployed a practical P2P live video broadcasting system over global Internet [8]. As a scalable and cost-effective alternative to C/S approach, it was adopted by CCTV to live broadcast

---

[1] CCTV: China Central Television Station, http://www.cctv.com

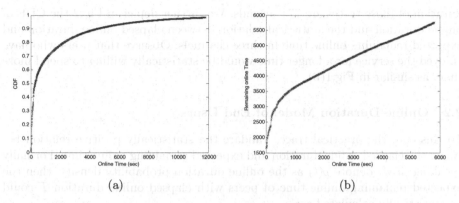

(a)   (b)

Fig. 1. Analysis to online duration of practical service logs: (a)CDF of online duration; (b)Relation between elapsed online duration and expected remaining online time

Spring Festival Evening show at Feb. 2005 and Jan. 2006. In the second deployment, more than 1,800,000 users from about 70 countries subscribed the service and the maximum concurrent users reached its peak about 200,000 at Jan. 28th, 2006.

Here we depict the cumulative distribution function (CDF) of online duration and relation between elapsed online duration and expected remaining online time in Fig.1. It is obvious that in Fig.1(b) peers who had stayed longer also would be expected to spend more time. To further validate this statistically positive relation, we make the same analysis to service traces from C/S systems. Since *end users have little knowledge on whether the service is provided via C/S or P2P technique*, we aim to figure out the similar observations through this comparative study.

We studied 8,314,245 million traces of CCTV-News program between Oct. 2004 and Jan. 2005 from centralized streaming servers. The average online

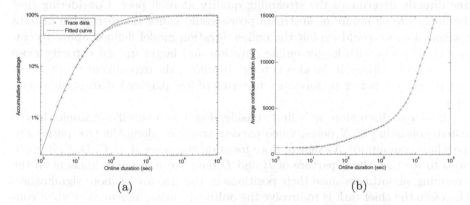

(a)   (b)

Fig. 2. Analysis to online duration of practical service traces:(a)CDF of online duration; (b)Relation between elapsed online duration and expected remaining online time

duration of those traces are 772 seconds. We further depict in Fig.2 the CDF of online duration and the statistical relation between elapsed online duration and expected remaining online time in three channels. Observe that users who have enjoyed the service for a longer time would be statistically willing to spend more time, as similar in Fig.1(b).

2.2 Online Duration Model of End Users

To this end, the practical traces validate the statistically positive relation between the elapsed online duration and expected remaining online time. Formally speaking, if we denote $p(t)$ as the online duration probability density, then the expected remaining online time of peers with elapsed online duration T could be statistically calculated as:

$$E(t - T|t \geq T) = \frac{\int_T^\infty (t - T)p(t)dt}{\int_T^\infty p(t)dt} \tag{1}$$

According to the analysis in above subsection, we have following online duration model of end users:

$$E(t - T|t \geq T) \propto T \tag{2}$$

While the model of online duration seems quite intuitive, it is in essence important when we recognize that it reflects the stability of peers. In the next two sections, we will exploit this model to improve the QoS of P2P live streaming in two distinct arenas.

3 Exploiting Online Duration for Streaming Stability

Most of previous overlay construction protocols adopt video delivery tree to disseminate media contents to end users. Obviously, the stability of this delivery tree directly determines the streaming quality at each peer. Considering that the departure or failure of upstream peers would cause the disruption of data transmission, we could exploit the online duration model defined above to employ those peers with longer online duration and larger upload capacity close to the source. Although the idea is rough intuitive, the experiment results show that it achieves better performance in terms of low playback disruption at end users.

For sake of discussion, let's first consider Fig.3 as a specific example. In the system consisting of N peers, video packets transmit along the tree paths into the whole community. As shown, if we focus on the peers A, B, C, D, E, it is obvious to see that the departure of B and D have more negative impacts on the streaming smoothness since their positions in the tree are of more significance. Therefore the chief task is to involve the online duration information when constructing the video delivery tree so as to avoid frequent departure of peers at more important positions, or at least in a large probability.

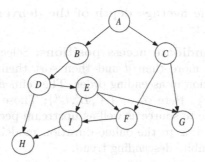

Fig. 3. A case of video delivery tree

Now we begin to describe the tree construction scheme with elapsed online duration of each peer. Due to page limitation, here we only explain the join process of a peer and it is quite easy to recall this process if refinement or maintenance is required. In the scope of this paper, we reasonably assume a centralized authority has the complete information about the service capacity and online duration of all peers to highlight the effectiveness of the online duration model. The distributed algorithm will be studied as future work. As shown in Fig.4, peers A to E have composed a 5-peer tree. The 2-tuple at each peer indicates the upload capacity in terms of downstream serving peers and elapsed online duration, respectively. We denote the upload capacity of peer A as $cap(A)$ and its online duration as $dur(A)$. $(5, 600)$ means $cap(A) = 5$ while $dur(A) = 600$.

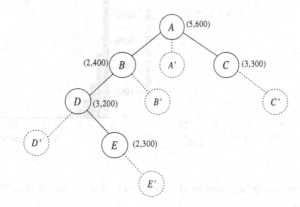

Fig. 4. Tree construction with candidate access positions

For a new peer F with $cap(F) = 3$,we term its available join positions in the current tree as the candidate access positions ϕ_F, i.e. $\phi_F = \{A', B', C', D', E'\}$, presented as the dotted circles in Fig.4. Then F chooses the position to join the video delivery tree according to following steps:

Step 1: Calculate the average depth of the delivery tree. In Fig.4, the average depth is $\bar{d} = 1.4$;

Step 2: Sort the candidate access positions. Select the positions in ϕ_F whose depths are not more than $\bar{d}$ and then sort them with respect to the ancestors' online duration in ascending order. The refined candidate access positions is denoted as ϕ'_F. Here $\phi'_F = \{A', B', C'\}$; Those two steps are to find available positions close to source as well as upstream peers with larger elapsed online duration; According to the online duration model, the stability of each position in ϕ'_F also exhibits descending trend.

Step 3: Calculate the impacts after joining the tree. Calculate the ratio r of the number of peers whose service capacity are more than that of F to total number of peers in delivery tree after F's join. In Fig.4, $r \approx 0.143$; The purpose of this ratio is to help determine the final access position.

Step 4: Calculate the possible access position in ϕ'_F. Multiply the ratio r with the residual upload capacity in ϕ'_F as p. Then we have $p = 0.143 \times [cap(A') + cap(B') + cap(C')] = 1$.

Step 5: Choose the final access position. According to ϕ'_F and p, select the access position to join. Since in the exemplary tree, $p = 1 < cap(A') = 3$, F will join at A'. Note that if there are more than one peer in ϕ'_F with same conditions, then randomly select one as the access position for F.

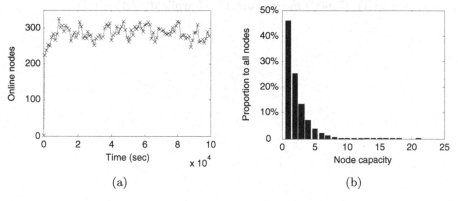

(a)   (b)

Fig. 5. Experiment setup:(a)Number of online peers during simulation;(b)Distribution of upload capacity

The main advantage of introducing online duration into tree construction is to keep the peers at higher positions as stable as possible. It should be stressed that we also consider the upload capacity of peers in this scheme. To verify this point of view, we compare it with (1)Random-select: randomly select access positions in the tree;(2)Min-depth: select the access position with minimum depth in the tree; (3)Max-online: select the access position with maximum online duration. We conduct 10-round simulation experiments with about 350 peers in each round. The user arrival pattern follows Poisson process ($\lambda = 1$), while the upload capacity and the number of online nodes during simulation are shown in Fig.5.

The experiment results are averaged through 10 rounds and depicted in Fig.6. For ease of discussion, we adopt the metric "accumulative interrupt time" to evaluate the performance of the proposed scheme ,Random, Min-depth and Max-online. Any change of upstream peers will result in an interruption aggregation. Observe that the proposed scheme exhibits best performance as compared to others since it considered both the online duration and upload capacity into the video delivery tree construction.

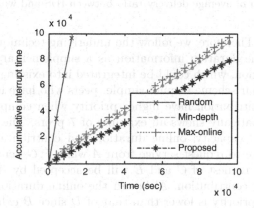

Fig. 6. The performance of proposed scheme in terms of playback interruption

4   Exploiting Online Duration for Cooperation Incentive

In addition to improve the stability of streaming service, the online duration model of end users in Eq.(2) could also be used to facilitate the mutual cooperation between peer-pair. In this section, we present how to exploit the statistically positive relation between elapsed online duration and expected remaining online time to study incentive mechanism in P2P live streaming.

Along with the popularity of P2P networks in large-scale applications over Internet, the non-cooperative *"freeriders"* [9,10] emerged as one critical problem that determined the future success of such applications. Since a peer acts as both a client and a server, it benefits from the system and shares the cost with other peers. A rational peer will come to a conclusion that the best strategy is to consume as much as possible without any individual contribution, which in turn undermines the global system performance.

Considering that both freeriding and online duration belong to user behaviors, we intuitively take the advantage of the latter to defeat the former. A rich literature of previous works fought a battle at the front of incentive study, including credit-based, reputation-based and game theoretic approaches [11-15]. Most of them generally evaluated the contribution of each peer and provide differentiated

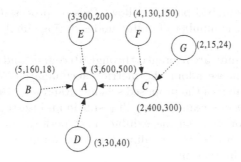

Fig. 7. Comparison of average delivery ratio between IDS and without incentive

service accordingly. Therefore, we follow the underlying technique and highlight the use of the online duration information as a supplementary component in contribution evaluation, which could be integrated into existing schemes.

The key idea in our scheme is quite simple: peers who have larger online duration and more contribution have higher priority when competing streaming service. Fig.7 schematically shows an example of 7 peers. The 3-tuple at each peer denotes upload capacity, online duration and contribution, respectively. B, C, D, E would like to request service from A while F, G demands video segments from C. The request of C and E will be accepted by A owing to their online duration and contribution. Although the online duration of B is larger than that of D, its priority is lower than that of D since B exhibits freeriding-like behaviors in terms of low contribution and long online duration. Formally speaking, we denote the priority of peer P as I_P, then I_P could be calculated as

$$
I_P = \begin{cases} \frac{\gamma C_P}{dur(P)}, \frac{C_P}{dur(P)} < \delta; \\ \gamma C_P + dur(P), \frac{C_P}{dur(P)} \geq \delta; \end{cases} \tag{3}
$$

where C_P denotes contribution of P which could be calculated as similar in [14], γ is the normalized factors and δ is system-specific and configurable threshold. With this online duration based differentiated service, peers with high priority are rewarded with good upstream peers and obtain better quality in return, while peers with low priority would like to contribute more to enhance their priority. As compared to gossip-based neighborship management protocol in [5,8], this scheme will bring more stable neighborship between peers and individual contribution, as evidenced by following experiments. It should be pointed out that here we reasonably assume a trusted third party exists to aggregate, compute and feedback the priorities of peers. It is quite interesting to study the distributed algorithms in ongoing work.

To verify the proposed scheme, we conduct experiments over the Planetlab. In total, we utlized about 350 machines as peers in our simulation and simulates streaming rate as 30 packtes per second. The user arrival pattern follows Poisson process ($\lambda = 1$), while the upload capacity is the same as that in Fig.5(a). The experiment results are averaged through 10 rounds.

In Fig.8, we evaluate the performance of proposed scheme in terms of streaming quality and communication overhead. Fig.8(a) depicts the average delivery ratio, which is calculated as the ratio of packets that arrive before the playback deadline to the total packets, and indicates that with proposed scheme the average delivery ratio is lower than that without incentive mechanism. It is becasue rational peers are encouraged to make more contribution and the online duration based priority results in better stability of the overlay. Fig.8(b) measures both data and control messages induced by proposed scheme in KB and graph the percentage overhead of each peer(for ease of exposition, we depict them at every 5 peers). We observe that most peers experience an overhead of around 1%. Overall, the modest overhead is about 0.87%.

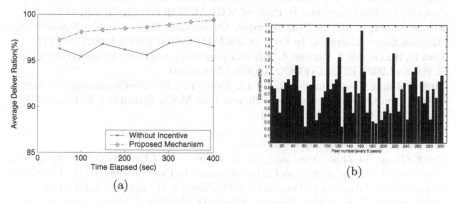

Fig. 8. Performance of proposed scheme:(a)Comparison of average delivery ratio between proposed scheme and without incentive; (B)Percentage overhead of each peer (every 5 peers)

5 Conclusion and Future Work

In this paper, we mainly discuss two distinct approaches to exploit the online duration model of end users to either improve the stability of video delivery tree or encourage the mutual cooperation in peer community. The first scheme involves the online information when constructing video delivery tree and the other scheme takes the online duration into account when selecting neighbor peers for data exchange. The simulation experiments demonstrate that both schemes achieves better QoS in P2P live streaming. We believer that the efforts in this paper shed lights in the area of characterizing user behavior profile to improve P2P system performance properties.

Future research could proceed along several arenas. One is to extend this paper to distributed implementation. It is also interesting to study how to aggregate the online duration information reliably without central authority.

Acknowledgement

The authors gracefully thank the anonymous reviewers for their comments. This work is supported by the National Natural Science Foundation of China under Grant No.60432030 and No.60503063, National Basic Research Program (973) of China under Grant No.973 2006CB303103.

References

1. Yang-hua Chu, Sanjay G. Rao, Hui Zhang: A Case for End System Multicast", In Proc. of 2000 ACM SIGMETRICS (2000) 1-12.
2. Miguel Castro, Peter Druschel, et al: SplitStream: High-Bandwidth Multicast in Cooperative Environments. In Proc. of 2003 ACM SOSP (2003) 298-313.
3. Suman Banerjee, Bobby Bhattacharjee, Christopher Kommareddy: Scalable Application Layer Multicast. In Proc. of 2002 ACM SIGCOMM (2002) 205-217.
4. Tran D, Hua K, Do T. Zigzag: An efficient peer-to-peer scheme for media streaming. In Proc. of 2003 IEEE INFOCOM (2003) 1283-1293.
5. Xinyan Zhang, Jiangchuan Liu, Bo Li, Yum, Y.-S.P.: CoolStreaming/DONet: A Data-Driven Overlay Network for Efficient Live Media Streaming. In Proc. of 2005 IEEE INFOCOM (2005) 2102-2111.
6. PPLive, http://www.pplive.com.
7. PPStream, http://www.ppstream.com.
8. Meng Zhang, Li Zhao, Yun Tang, et al: Large-Scale Live Media Streaming over Peer-to-Peer Networks through Global Internet. In Proc of 2005 ACM Multimedia Workshop on Advances in Peer-to-Peer Multimedia Streaming (2005) 21-28.
9. Stefan Saroiu, P. Krishna Gummadi, Steven D. Gribble: A Measurement Study of Peer-to-Peer File Sharing Systems. In Proc. of 2002 SPIE Multimedia Computing and Networking (2002)
10. Adar E., Huberman B.A.: Free Riding on Gnutella. First Monday 5, 10. 2000.
11. Philippe Golle, Kevin Leyton-Brown, Ilya Mironov: Incentive for Sharing in Peer-to-Peer Networks. In Proc. of 2001 ACM Electronic Commerce (2001) 264-267.
12. Weihong Wang, Baochun Li: To Play or to Control: A Game-based Control-theoretic Approach to P2P Incentive Engineering. In Proc. of 2003 IEEE International Workshop on Quality of Service (2003) 174-194.
13. Bram Cohen: Incentives Build Robustness in BitTorrent. Online, available at http://www2.sims.berkeley.edu/research/conferences/p2pecon/papers/s4-cohen.pdf
14. Ahsan Habib, John Chuang: Incentive Mechanism for Peer-to-Peer Media Streaming. In Proc of 2004 IEEE International Workshop on Quality of Service (2004) 171-180.
15. Guang Tan, Stephen A. Jarvis: A Payment-based Incentive and Service Differentiation Mechanism for P2P Streaming Broadcast. In Proc. of 2006 IEEE International Workshop on Quality of Service (2006) 41-50.

Coopetitive Multimedia Surveillance

Vivek K. Singh, Pradeep K. Atrey, and Mohan S. Kankanhalli

School of Computing, National University of Singapore,
Singapore
{vivekkum, pradeepk, mohan}@comp.nus.edu.sg

Abstract. 'Coopetitive' interaction strategy has been shown to give better results than similar strategies like 'only cooperation', 'only competition' etc [7]. However, this has been studied only in the context of visual sensors and for handling non-simultaneous events. In this paper, we study this 'coopetitive' strategy from a multimedia surveillance system perspective, wherein the system needs to utilize multiple heterogeneous sensors and also handle multiple simultaneous events. Applying such an interaction strategy to multimedia surveillance systems is challenging because heterogeneous sensors have different capabilities for performing different sub-tasks as well as dissimilar response times. We adopt a merit-cum-availability based approach to allocate various sub-tasks to the competing sensors which eventually cooperate to achieve the specified system goal. Also, a 'coopetition' based strategy is adopted for effectively utilizing the information coming asynchronously from different data sources. Multiple simultaneous events (e.g. multiple intrusions) are handled by adopting a predictive strategy which estimates the exit time for each intruder and then uses this information for enhanced scheduling. The results obtained for two sets of surveillance experiments conducted with two active cameras and a motion sensor grid are promising.

1 Introduction

Recently a fair amount of interest has been generated on devising effective interaction and feedback mechanisms for multisensor surveillance[7,3,1]. For example, Singh and Atrey [7] propose the use of 'coopetitive' interaction approach for sensor interaction. Coopetition is a process in which the sensors compete as well as cooperate with each other to perform the designated task in the best possible manner. Intuitively, the process is similar to that of two partners in the card game of 'bridge' trying to outbid each other (compete), even though they are doing so for the benefit of the team (cooperate) in a bigger context. Such an interaction mechanism helps in improving the system performance by employing the best sensor for each (sub) task and also makes available the remaining sensors for undertaking other tasks if required.

While the above mentioned coopetitive strategy promises to be an effective interaction approach it has so far been studied for interaction between cameras alone. Similarly, other sensor interaction works like [3,1] have also focused on interaction mechanisms between cameras only.

T.-J. Cham et al. (Eds.): MMM 2007, LNCS 4352, Part II, pp. 343–352, 2007.

On the other hand, effective surveillance often requires multi-modal information which is obtained from more than one type of sensors. Hence, while adopting the salient features of coopetitive interaction as described in [7], in this paper we tackle the problems from a heterogeneous sensor perspective. Our key contributions are :

1. Applying the 'coopetitive' interaction strategy to multimedia surveillance systems wherein multiple heterogenous sensors are employed which may have different functional capabilities as well as dissimilar response times.
2. Enhancing the system capability to handle multiple simultaneous events e.g. handling multiple simultaneous intruders in monitored space.

In heterogeneous sensor environments each sensor has a different capability for handling the different sub-tasks i.e. divisible components of the system goal. While some sensors may be able to accomplish multiple types of sub-tasks, others may be able to do only one such type of sub-task. We adopt a suitability-cum-availability strategy for appropriately allocating the various sub-tasks to each of these sensors. Firstly, for each sub-task, a list of suitable sensors is made. Sensors are then allocated from this suitability list based on their availability.

Also, dissimilar sensors may have different response times. For example in a typical surveillance setup, a camera could be working at 4 frames/sec but a motion sensor may be providing information 6 times per second. Thus, to effectively utilize the information arriving asynchronously from such disparate sources, we adopt a 'coopetition' based strategy. The sensors 'compete' to provide information about newer events of interest. However, only the genuinely 'new' information is accepted by the system and the rest is termed as recurrent. Thus only the 'winning' sensor is allowed to trigger responses required for handling newer events of interest.

Handling multiple events which lead to concurrent sub-tasks is also a non-trivial issue as the system must decide an order for handling them such that the global output is maximized. To resolve this issue we employ a predictive strategy which allows us to estimate the deadlines for completing each sub-task beyond which they can not be completed satisfactorily. For example, in a multi-intruder scenario, the system evaluates the estimated time of exit for each intruder and then checks if the currently focused intruder shall still remain in monitored area even if it focuses on a newer intruder first. This additional information opens the doors to various predictive scheduling strategies which can in turn help to maximize the system performance.

To measure the effectiveness of our proposed approach we conduct experiments using two cameras and a grid of motion-sensors. However, it may be worth noting that we currently connect all the sensors to a central computer which acts as central coordinator/controller. Thus, we presently circumvent many complexities of distributed decision making like network delay, coordination cost etc. which are beyond the scope of the current work.

We define the system goal for the experiments as obtaining atleast three high resolution frontal facial images of any intruder entering the monitored premises. Hence the two major sub-tasks are localizing the intruder and focusing on him (for obtaining his facial images). The motion sensor grid provides the localization information about the intruder while the cameras can provide both localization information as well as the facial data. The requirements for effective sub-task allocation among dissimilar sensors as well as the need to handle multiple simultaneous intrusion events makes these surveillance scenarios quite challenging.

Garcia et al in [3] described coordination and conflict resolution between cameras. Collins group [1] has done some pioneering work in multi-camera cooperation strategies. However, both of these works do not employ the use of competition which is we advocate as an integral part of coordination together with cooperation. Also, they deal only with cameras while we we want to be able to handle heterogenous sensors. We have earlier described 'coopetitive' interaction strategy with a homogeneous sensor (cameras) perspective in [7]. However, in that work we do not handle the issues posed by dissimilarity between sensors and also do not handle multiple simultaneous events e.g. multiple intrusions which we do in this work.

Doran et al [2] have described different types of cooperation from an artificial agent perspective. Murphy et al [6] illustrate cooperation between heterogeneous robots based on 'emotions'. Hu et al [4], discuss the relationships between local behaviors of agents and global performance of multi-agent systems. While these works provide insights into different types of cooperation from an agent perspective they do not discuss the practical issues which are faced in implementation of such interactive strategies across heterogeneous sensors. Lam et al [5] have described a predictive method for scheduling tasks on panning cameras. Their intention is to schedule resource intensive tasks at a time when the system load is least. While their idea of scheduling is interesting, this work does not deal with the either the interaction strategy or the practical issues of of heterogeneous sensing. Hence, we realize that there are no existing works which tackle the problem of effective interaction between multiple sensors while also considering the issues posed by their heterogeneousness.

The outline of the remainder of this paper is as follows. Section 2 describes how we tackle the issues of appropriate sub-task allocation, asynchronous data utilization and multiple simultaneous events handling. Section 3 describes the experimental results obtained for the surveillance experiments. The conclusions and possible future works have been discussed in Section 4.

2   Proposed Work

2.1   Coopetitive Framework for Heterogeneous Sensors

The generic algorithm for 'coopetitive' interaction strategy is shown in figure 1. Upon arrival of each new surveillance object S_Obj (i.e the object or the person under observation), the system divides the overall goal into sub-tasks. These sub-tasks are allocated to the available sensors based on a suitability-cum-availability strategy. Initially, the sensors 'compete' to be allocated the various sub-tasks and later 'cooperate' with each-other to better perform the respective allocated sub-tasks. The roles i.e. sub-task allocation can be swapped if environment changes or it is realized that the current sub-task allocation is no longer appropriate.

A key point to note is that 'coopetition' does not specify any particular type of sensor, measure of merit or even type of scenario. For example, this work describes 'coopetition' between two cameras and motion sensor grid but nothing restricts us from using audio sensors, pressure sensors etc. which may be suitable for some other scenario. Similarly, the measure of merit can also be chosen based on the system task. For example in tracking-like applications, resolution of facial images obtained, body blob size, physical proximity to the sensor, and camera resolution/quality all form reasonable measures of merit for handling competition between sensors for task allocation. Lastly, 'coopetition' does not restrict itself to any particular type of application. It is equally relevant to multiple search teams operating in rescue effort or multiple satellites providing data about approaching tsunami/storms etc.

More details about 'coopetitive' strategy in general can be found in [7]. Here we focus on issues which are unique to heterogeneous multimedia sensor systems.

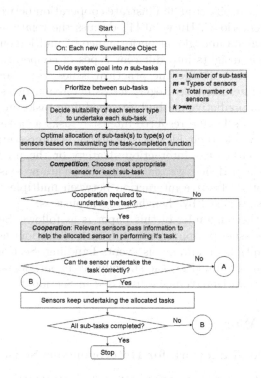

Fig. 1. Proposed 'coopetitive' strategy for heterogeneous sensor interaction

Firstly, the system needs to allocate sub-tasks to sensors based on the suitability of each type of sensor for the various sub-tasks. Let there be n different sub-tasks viz ST_1 through ST_n, each of which can be undertaken by one or more of the m different sensor types viz $SensorType_1$ through $SensorType_m$ as shown in figure 2. Each sensor type has one or more member sensors which can be represented as $Sensor_1$ through $Sensor_o$. It is possible to come up with a set $STCap_i$ for each sub-task that contains the list of all sensors which can handle the ith sub-task. We must note that at any instant, there must be atleast one sensor capable of handling each sub-task i.e. $\forall STCap_i : STCap_i \neq \emptyset$. Our approach for allocating the sensors to the various sub-tasks is as follows.

Step 1: Choose the most restrictive sub-task p which can be undertaken by the least number of sensors i.e. $STCap_p : \forall STCap_i, \cap(STCap_p) \leq \cap(STCap_i)$

Step 2: If $STCap_p$ has only one sensor as its member, Allocate it.

Step 3: If it has more than one member, Allocate from the sensor-type with the highest availability.

Step 4: Remove the allocated sub-task and the sensor from the allocation pool.

Step 5: If number of sub-tasks in pool $\neq 0$, Go to Step 1

Step 6: After all sub-tasks have been allocated the minimum one sensors, allow the 'redundant' sensors to also perform tasks per their capabilities.

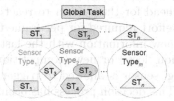

Fig. 2. Sub-tasks and their allocation

Now, let us understand this allocation in our surveillance setup which has two sub-tasks: S_Obj localization and S_Obj focusing. The S_Obj focusing can be undertaken by the two cameras while the S_Obj localization can be done by two cameras as well as the motion-sensor grid. The better suited of the two cameras is allocated the S_Obj focusing task. Thus for our experimental setup, the camera which can obtain better frontal facial images of the intruder is allocated the focusing task. Similarly, the sensor (camera or the motion-sensor grid) which provides first information about a 'new' intruder handles the localization task (further discussed in section 2.2).

2.2 Handling Asynchronous Data

In multimedia surveillance, the system may encounter asynchronous data about similar context coming from multiple sensors at different time intervals. To understand this, let us look at a scenario as shown in figure 3 in which two types of sensors are providing similar type of information. The first sensor starts giving information at $t = 0$ and continues to provide information at the interval of 10 time-units. On the other hand sensor 2 starts providing information from $t = 15$ and continues to do so every 15 time-units.

Fig. 3. Coopetition approach for using asynchronous data

In our surveillance setup a similar situation arises when motion sensor grid and cameras both compete to provide localization information for a new S_Obj. Whichever sensor provides the information about the first S_Obj for the first time clearly 'wins' the competition for the first case. For subsequent cases, the sensors could either be providing recurrent information about an already focused S_Obj or it could be the information about a genuinely new S_Obj. Finding whether the S_Obj is old or new is important for the system to react accordingly as normally the initial overhead for the system to react to a new object are significantly more than the effort required for per-frame tracking of an old object. Hence we compare each new information with the last 'winning' entry to see if it is recurrent (competition 'lost') or new (competition 'won'). Only the information from the 'winning' sensor is allowed to trigger the response process for handling a 'new' S_Obj. This decision process has been demonstrated in figure 3 with w_1, w_2 etc. representing the winning entries. The recurrent information on the other hand is simply added to the position information vector which is maintained for each individual S_Obj currently being focused and used for per-frame tracking.

2.3   Handling Multiple Simultaneous Events

A multimedia surveillance system must decide the order for undertaking the various sub-tasks. Certain sub-tasks might always be required to be undertaken before others. For example, in our scenario, localization needs to be done before the facial images can be captured. Hence the system undertakes such tasks first. However, when dealing with multiple simultaneous surveillance events, the system may encounter multiple sub-tasks which can be executed in any arbitrary order. In such situations, the system must choose the execution order so as to maximize the global output function. Such a global output function can be represented as $\sum_{i=1}^{n} w_i \times ST_i$, where w_i is the weight/importance assigned to the ith sub-task. This signifies that in case of a conflict i.e. if undertaking only one of the z remaining sub-tasks is possible, we must choose the one with the highest importance. We represent the conflicting z sub-tasks as CST_1 though CST_z and assume that they are arranged in order of their importance in a descending order. Let us represent our set of sub-tasks which can be actually be completed as $CanDo$. Hence our combined strategy for undertaking the various tasks using a 'greedy' algorithm is as follows:

$CanDo \leftarrow CST_1$

For: r= 1 to z

if (CST_r can still be completed after finishing CST_{r+1})

$CanDo \leftarrow CanDo \bigcup CST_{r+1}$

else

Do nothing;

Next r

We encounter such a conflicting scenario in our implemented scenario when multiple intruders enter the monitored space simultaneously. Using a predictive methodology the system constantly keeps track of the $ETEx$ (Expected Time of Exit) for each S_Obj. If the system realizes that intruder r is going to stay inside the monitored premises even if it 'takes time off' to focus on intruder $r+1$ first, then it would do so. Else, it would continue to focus on intruder r. The estimate on how long the intruder shall stay inside the monitored premises can be undertaken using Kalman filter approach by keeping track of position and velocity vectors of the various intruders as described in [7].

3   Experimental Results

We conduct two sets of experiments to verify the suitability of our proposed approaches. In first experiment we consider a single door enclosed environment setup like that commonly found in ATM lobbies or museum sub-sections. The system task is to obtain at least 3 frontal facial images of 200px by 200px resolution (which suffices for most face identification/expression recognition algorithms[8]) for each intruder and then continue to obtain more images if there are no other intruders. The setup consists of two active cameras, one placed directly above the entrance and the other directly above the principal artifact e.g. ATM machine. Essentially, the setup is similar to that described in [7] but now we also have an additional motion-sensor grid covering the entire premises to provide additional localization information.

In this experiment, we compare the performance of 'only cooperation', 'only competition', 'coopetition without MPC' and 'Coopetition with MPC' approaches for heterogeneous sensors and also see how they relate to the results obtained using only cameras [7]. In 'only cooperation' interaction approach sensors try to help each other in better performing their sub-tasks e.g. by passing S_Obj localization information. However there is no differentiation between sensors based on their worthiness and inappropriate sensors may also be passed information and allocated critical roles e.g. face capturing sub-task may be allocated to the camera in opposite direction with the face.In 'only competition' approach, the sensors do not help other sensors in performing their sub-tasks. So, in this case the cameras need to perform both S_Obj localization and focusing on their own. In 'coopetition' based approach the sensors help each other, but do so only if the other sensor is worthy of performing the allocated sub-task. Relating to our setup, the S_Obj location is transferred only to the appropriate camera(s) which use this information to focus on the S_Obj and obtain facial images better. In 'coopetition with

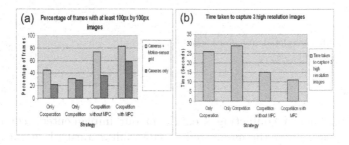

Fig. 4. Comparison of interaction strategies

MPC' approach the sensors have the additional advantage of using a predictive methodology to order and perform their sub-tasks.

For this experiment, the volunteer intruders were asked to enter the monitored premises for a one minute duration and intentionally avoid getting their facial images captured by the cameras. Twenty rounds of this experiment were conducted for each strategy and we compare the average data based on the percentage of frames for which atleast 100px by 100px images were obtained (figure 4a) and the time taken to capture three 200px by 200px facial images (figure 4b). Hence in all, we used data from 80 one minute rounds using two cameras each working at 768px by 576px with 4 fps for obtaining these results.

The presented figure 4a also shows the image capturing results obtained for similar setup with cameras alone [7]. We notice consistent increase in face capturing capability with the addition of motion-sensor grid. This corroborates well with the additional localization information available from motion-sensor grid which is faster (no need to continuously pan) and more robust (non-frontal face situations can also be handled). We notice that the 'coopetitive with MPC' strategy significantly outperforms the other strategies for heterogeneous sensors too and is able to obtain appropriate facial images for 82% of frames.

Figure 4b shows that the average time taken to obtain three 200px by 200px frontal facial images is also the least (11 sec) for 'coopetitive with MPC' approach. This is due to appropriate allocation of sensors to the sub-tasks, ability to obtain localization information from other sensors and performing forward state estimation for intruder's trajectory. As one each of these features is not present in 'only cooperation', 'only competition' and 'coopetitive(without MPC)' approaches respectively, the 'coopetitive with MPC' approach works better.

Being convinced about the superiority of 'coopetitive' interaction approach over 'only competition' and 'only cooperation' approaches, in the second experiment we closely compare the two variants of 'coopetition' with an aim to verify the gains obtained by using a predictive strategy for handling multiple simultaneous events. While the proposed methodology poses no limitation on the number of such simultaneous events, we use a two intruder base case scenario to demonstrate its effectiveness. We consider the scenario of a walkway leading

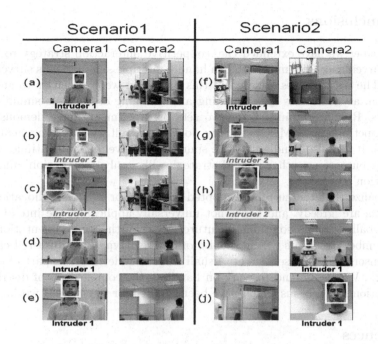

Fig. 5. Two example scenarios with multiple simultaneous events

to an important establishment e.g. control room for a nuclear plant etc. with a system goal of obtaining three high resolution(200px by 200px) frontal facial images of two intruders simultaneously walking across the walkway with differing speeds. The system uses a predictive methodology to decide which intruder shall exit the monitored walkway first and then plan the order of focusing on them as to maximize the probability of capturing appropriate images for both of them. We conducted 20 rounds of experiments and found that the 'coopetitive with MPC' approach which uses a predictive strategy was able to obtain appropriate images for both intruders 85% of times as compared to 'coopetitive without MPC' approach which could do so only 65% of times.

Two example scenarios have been shown in figure 5 with time-instances labelled (a) through (j). Scenario1 shows how the system handles two intruders simultaneously walking towards the important room (direction from camera2 towards camera1). The camera1 notices the intruder1 first(5a) but then realizes that intruder2 is going to exit much faster and it has high probability of capturing intruder1 even after completing intruder2 focusing task. Thus it focuses on intruder2(5b). After obtaining three images of intruder2(5c) it goes back to focus on intruder1(5d) and captures it's three high resolution images(5e). Scenario2 shows a similar case where intruder1 is detected first(5f) but intruder2 is focused(5g) as it is exiting faster and it's 3 facial images are obtained(5h). However, this time around intruder1 changes his direction and camera2 is required to focus on it(5i) and obtain three high resolution images(5j).

4   Conclusions

In this paper we have extended the 'coopetitive' interaction strategy to multimedia surveillance systems which can handle multiple simultaneous surveillance events. The major issues handled in this extension were of sensor to sub-task allocation, asynchronous data handling and handling of multiple simultaneous sub-tasks. Results obtained from two sets of experiments have demonstrated that 'coopetition with MPC' strategy does work well with heterogeneous systems too. It can also handle multiple simultaneous events and continues to significantly outperform other related strategies like 'only cooperation' and 'only competition'.

We realize that the currently adopted methods for sub task allocation and scheduling are 'greedy' and hence not universally applicable. We intend to explore globally optimal solutions in future work. Further experimentation with larger number of sensors which are also of different type (e.g. infra-red camera, audio sensors, pressure sensors etc.) shall also be undertaken as part of our future work. We also intend to work on handling the complexities of distributed coordination mechanisms which have been ignored for the current work.

References

1. R. Collins, A. Lipton, H. Fujiyoshi, and T. Kanade. Algorithms for cooperative multisensor surveillance. *Proceedings of the IEEE*, 89(10):1456 – 1477, 2001.
2. J. E. Doran, S. Franklin, N. R. Jennings, and T. J. Norman. On cooperation in multi-agent systems. *The Knowledge Engineering Review*, 12(3):309–314, 1997.
3. J. Garcia, J. Carbo, and J. M. Molina. Agent-based coordination of cameras. *International Journal of Computer Science and Applications*, 2(1):33–37, 2005.
4. B. Hu, J. Liu, and X. Jin. From local behaviors to global performance in a multi-agent system. In *IEEE/ACM conference on Intelligent Agent Technology*, 2004.
5. K.-Y. Lam and C. K. H. Chiu. Adaptive visual object surveillance with continuously moving panning camera. In *ACM International workshop on Video Surveillance and Sensor Networks*, pages 29–38, 2004.
6. R. R. Murphy, C. L. Lisetti, R. Tardif, L. Irish, and A. Gage. Emotion-based control of cooperating heterogeneous mobile robots. *IEEE Transactions on Robotics and Control*, 18(5):744–757, 2002.
7. V. K. Singh and P. K. Atrey. Coopetitive visual surveillance using model predictive control. In *ACM International workshop on Video Surveillance and Sensor Networks*, pages 149–158, 2005.
8. Y.-L. Tian, L. Brown, A. Hampapur, S. Pankanti, A. W. Senior, and R. M. Bolle. Adaptive visual object surveillance with continuously moving panning camera. In *IEEE workshop on performance evaluation of tracking and surveillance*, 2003.

Efficient H.264/AVC Video Encoder Where Pattern Is Used as Extra Mode for Wide Range of Video Coding*

Manoranjan Paul and Manzur Murshed

Gippsland School of IT, Monash University, Churchill Vic 3842, Australia
{Manoranjan.Paul,Manzur.Murshed}@infotech.monash.edu.au

Abstract. Pattern-based video coding representing moving regions in macroblock has very good potential for improved coding efficiency over existing standard H.264/AVC in the very low bit-rate range. However, the coding efficiency diminishes compared to H.264 with the bit rates because variable block sizes of H.264 for motion estimation and compensation are successfully selected for any bit rates using weighting between bit rate and image quality. The existing pattern-based video coding scheme could not handle this flexibility with bit rates due to its fixed size and lack of verification with other modes of H.264. In this paper we propose two large and one small pre-defined pattern sets and treat them as extra modes of H.264. We also investigate the weighting factor between bit rate and image quality compared to the existing one. The experimental results confirm the superiority of our approach compared to H.264 and other existing pattern-based video coding for not only the very low bit rate range but also wide range of bit rates.

Keywords: Video coding, pattern matching, moving regions.

1 Introduction

Recently H.264/AVC standard [6] introduced block based *motion estimation* (ME) and *motion compensation* (MC) coding system using variable-block size (from 16×16 to 4×4) to approximate the shape of the moving objects within the *Macroblock* (MB). It requires separate motion vector for each partition and the choice of partition size. The number of partition types has a significant impact on coding efficiency. Choosing larger partition sizes (16×16, 16×8, 8×16) requires relatively small number of bits for motion vectors and the type of partition at the expense of containing significant amount of bits in the motion compensated residual error in areas of high detail. On the contrary, choosing smaller partition sizes (8×4, 4×8, 4×4) may give a lower bits residual at the expense of larger number of bits for motion vectors and the type of partition. However, there would be two issues which cannot be successfully handled with this partitioning concept. First thing is that we observed that in low to mid range of bit rates most of the MBs are motion estimated and compensated using larger partitions so that variable block size concept is ineffective in this area. Second thing is

---

* This research was supported under the Australian Research Council's Discovery scheme (project number DP0666456).

T.-J. Cham et al. (Eds.): MMM 2007, LNCS 4352, Part II, pp. 353–362, 2007.
© Springer-Verlag Berlin Heidelberg 2007

that no block based standard video coding can exploit the intra-frame temporal redundancy which is static in success frames.

To address this problem, Fukuhara et al. [1] first proposed pattern based coding using four MB-partitioning patterns of 128-pixels each. ME and MC was carried out on all eight possible 128-pixel partitions of an MB and the pattern with the lowest prediction error was selected. By treating identically each MB, irrespective of its motion content, also resulted in a higher bit-rate being incurred for those MBs which contained only static background or had moving object(s), but with little static background. In such cases, the motion vectors for both partitions were almost the same and so only one could be represented.

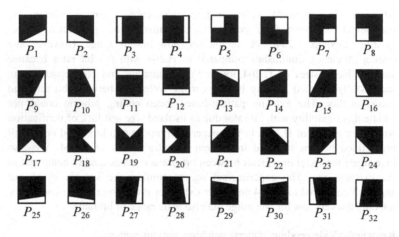

Fig. 1. The pattern codebook of 32 regular shaped, 64-pixel patterns, defined in 16×16 blocks, where the white region represents 1 (motion) and black region represents 0 (no motion)

The MPEG-4 [4] video standard first introduced the concept of content-based coding, by dividing video frames into separate segments comprising a background and one or more moving objects. But for real-time application no content-based coding algorithm is a competitor of block-based coding due to the lack of automatic object segmentation algorithm. To address the limitations of [1], Wong et al. [11] exploited the idea of partitioning the MBs via a simplified segmentation process that again avoided handling the exact shape of moving objects, so that popular MB-based motion estimation techniques could be applied. Wong et al. [11] classified each MB into three distinct categories: 1) Static MB (SMB): MBs that contain little or no motion; 2) Active MB (AMB): MBs which contain moving object(s) with little static background; and 3) Active-Region MB (RMB): MBs that contain both static background and part(s) of moving object(s). SMBs and AMBs are treated in exactly the same way as in H.26X. For RMB coding, Wong assumed that the moving parts of an object may be represented by one of the eight predefined patterns P_1–P_8 in Figure 1. An MB is classified as RMB if by using some *similarity* measure, the part of a moving object of an MB is well covered by a particular pattern. The RMB can then be coded using the 64 pixels of that pattern with the remaining 192 pixels being skipped as *static background*. Successful pattern matching can theoretically therefore have a maximum compression ratio of 4:1 for any MB. The actual achievable compression ratio will be lower due to the computing overheads for handling an additional MB type, the pattern identification numbering and pattern matching errors.

Figure 1 shows the complete 32-pattern codebook (PC), which forms the basis of the *real time pattern selection* (RTPS) algorithm [8]. The RTPS algorithm successfully introduced relevant measure together with pattern similarity measure to speed up the whole process with arbitrary size of pattern set without degrading the image quality.

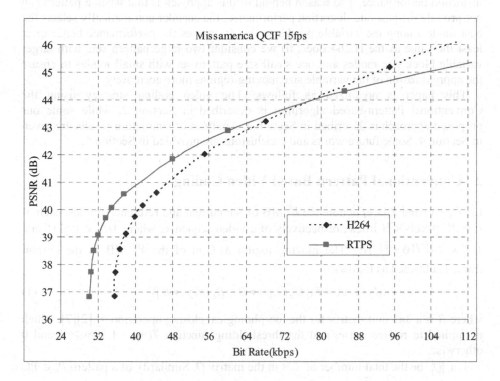

Fig. 2. Rate-Distortion curves of the H.264 and RTPS using the QCIF *Miss America* video sequence

The Figure 2 shows the comparison between the rate-distortion curves generated by the H.264 and RTPS (updated with H.264 features) algorithms using the *Miss America* video sequence. It is interesting to observe that for very low bit rate (64kbps) range the performance of the RTPS algorithm is better compared to the H.264 by around 1.0 dB. But the performance of the RTPS is diminishing with bit rates against the H.264 and once the performance is worse.

To analysis the performance of RTPS algorithm, we easily observe that the moving region covered by the best-matched pattern template provides relatively less bits with better image quality; on the contrary, uncovered moving region provides poor image quality. Since at very low bit rate, a large scale distortion is occurred, thus image distortion due to the uncovered moving region is negligible compared to the high distortion in overall image. As a result, pattern-based video coding algorithm outperforms the H.264 standard for very low bit rate range. When the target bit rate is high, the distortion in uncovered moving region is relatively high compared to overall image distortion. As a result the rate-distortion performance of pattern-based coding diminishes with bit rates compared to the H.264.

To address this problem we proposed two ways, i) we consider pattern-based coding is as a mode, i.e., selected MB will be processed using pattern, and other variable block size modes, then we will pick that mode which provides us best rate-distortion performance. The reason behind of this approach is that when a pattern can not provide the best rate-distortion performance, the encoder automatically selects the best mode among the variable blocks so that it ensures the performance better or at least the same as the H.264 does, ii) we consider two large pattern sets with larger variable block size modes and one small size pattern set with small modes to ensure the approximation of the variable size moving regions more accurately.

This paper is organized as follows. The video coding strategy using the Conventional Pattern-based algorithm is described in Section 2, while some our proposed approach is described in Section 3. Analyses of simulation results are given in Section 4. Some future works and conclusions are provided in Section 5.

2   Conventional Pattern Based Video Coding

Let $C_k(x,y)$ and $R_k(x,y)$ denote the kth MB of the current and reference frames, each of size W pixels $\times H$ lines, respectively of a video sequence, where $0 \le x, y \le 15$ and $0 \le k < W/16 \times H/16$. The moving region $M_k(x,y)$ of the kth MB in the current frame is obtained as follows:

$$M_k(x, y) = T(| C_k(x, y) \bullet B - R_k(x, y) \bullet B |) \tag{1}$$

where B is a 3×3 unit matrix for the morphological closing operation $\bullet$ [2][7], which is applied to reduce noise, and the thresholding function $T(v) = 1$ if $v > 2$ and 0 otherwise.

Let $|Q|_\ell$ be the total number of ℓ's in the matrix Q. Similarity of a pattern $P_n \in$ PC with the moving region in the kth MB can be defined efficiently [9] as

$$S_{k,n} = |M_k|_1 - |M_k \wedge P_n|_1. \tag{2}$$

Clearly, higher the similarity lower will be the value of $S_{k,n}$. Obviously all MBs are not examined using pattern. The eligible MBs are called candidate RMB (CRMB) and defined as $8 \le |M_k|_1 < T_S + PatternSize$, where T_S and $PatternSize$ are the predefined *similarity threshold* and one of $\{16,64,128\}$ respectively. The candidate CRMB is classified as an RMB and its moving region is represented by a pattern P_i such that

$$P_i = \arg \min_{\forall P_n \in PC} (S_{k,n}) | S_{k,n} < T_S) \tag{3}$$

otherwise, the CRMB is classified as an AMB. For a given PC, an image sequence is coded using the general pattern based coding (PBC). To avoid more than four 4×4 block of DCT calculations for 64 residual error values per RMB, these values are rearranged into an 8×8 block. It avoids unnecessary DCT block transmission. A similar inverse procedure is performed during the decoding.

By this conventional pattern-based coding approach, if a MB is classified as CRMB and the similarity threshold permits it to classify as a RMB, then this MB is finally classified as RMB irrespective of its rate-distortion performance compared to the other available modes. This strategy performs very well when the operational target bit rate very low. As mentioned in earlier, the moving region covered by the best-matched pattern template is motion estimated and compensated and the rest of the region is treated as *static region* which is simply copied from the reference MB in the decoder end. Since the uncovered region is three times of the pattern template covered region, successful pattern matching can theoretically therefore have a maximum compression ratio of 4:1 for RMB. It is obvious that sometimes a *tiny* portion of object may remains in so called *static region* which is considered in pattern-based video coding. This *tiny* portion of object has little influence in very low bit rate range as significant amount of image distortion is occurred due to the course quantization in overall image. However, this tiny portion of object may have significant impact when the operational bit rate is relatively high where finer quantization is used to improve the image quality. In this case rate-distortion performance of RMB may not be better than that of other modes. As a result the overall coding performance would degrade.

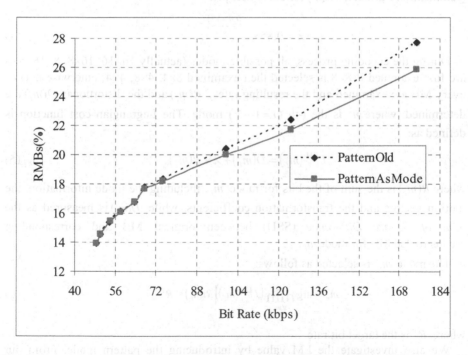

Fig. 3. Percentage of RMBs classified using conventional PBC (PatternOld) and PBC as one of H.264 modes (PatternAsMode) using a number of QCIF video sequences against bit rates

The experimental results reveal that using conventional approach of PBC, the percentage of SMB and MBs classified by larger modes (e.g., 16×16, 16×8, 8×16) decreases and RMB increases with bit rates. After a certain bit rate, when small modes are dominant modes, the increase of RMB should decrease for better rate-distortion performance. The conventional PBC could not do it because its rate-distortion performance is not compared to the other modes for final mode selection decision. Simply if we compare the rate-distortion performance of PBC with other rate-distortion performance generated by other modes and then finally we select minimum one, the overall performance will be better. The percentage of RMB using both conventional PBC (*PatternOld*) and PBC as a mode (*PatternAsMode*) is shown in Figure 3. The figure shows that within 60 to 80 kbps bit rates, the percentage of RMB using PatternAsMode is decreasing compared to the PatternOld. Later we will show that within that bit rate range, the performance of PatternAsMode is better than PatternOld.

3 Our Approach

The method of Lagrange multipliers (LM) is used to trade off between the quality of the compressed video and the bit rate generated for different modes. In this method, the LM (λ) is first calculated with an empirical formula using the selected *Quantization Parameter* (QP) for every MB [4]:

$$\lambda = 0.85 \times 2^{\frac{(QP-12)}{3}}. \tag{4}$$

During the encoding process, all possible modes (actually 16×16, 16×8, 8×16, 8×8 are first examined if 8×8 is selected then examined 8×4, 4×8, 4×4, otherwise not) of every MB are examined and the resulting rates, $R(m_i)$ and the distortions, $D(m_i)$ are determined, where m_i is the i-th ($i = 1 \cdots 7$) mode. The Lagrangian cost function is defined as:

$$J^{LM}(m_i) = D(m_i) + \lambda \times R(m_i). \tag{5}$$

where $R(m_i)$ is the sum of the bits for mode m_i, including the mode information, the motion vectors and the transformation coefficients, while $D(m_i)$ is measured as the *Sum of Square Difference* (SSD) between original MB and corresponding reconstructed MB for mode m_i.

The mode m_n is selected as follows:

$$m_n = \arg \min_{\forall m_i} \left(J^{LM}(m_i) \right) \middle| R(m_i) \le R^T \tag{6}$$

where R^T is the target bit rate.

We also investigate the LM value by introducing the pattern mode. From our experimental results (see Fig. 4) we observed that the relationships between QP and LM are almost same for H.264 and H.264 with pattern as an extra mode using *Miss*

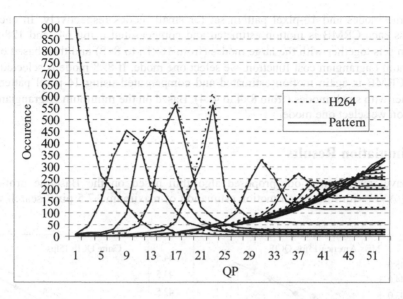

Fig. 4. Occurrence vs. macroblock QP for various Lagrange parameters (0.05 0.25 0.5 1 4 25 100 250 400 730 1000 1500 2500 4000 6000 10000). The occurrence of macroblock QP values gathered while coding first 100 frames of the *Miss America* video sequence using H.264 itself (H264) and H.264 with pattern as an extra mode (Pattern).

America sequence. Same relationship is also observed for different video sequences. Thus, we conclude that no modification is required in LM value, as the relationship between the LM and QP remains same after successfully introducing the extra pattern mode.

In our approach we proposed three sets of patterns of 128-pixel, 64-pixel, and 16-pixel. The 64-pixel 32 patterns are same as Figure 1, and other two sets are given in Figure 5. We do not claim that this choice of shapes and number of patterns in PC set is the best but simply observe that, with this arbitrary choice of PCs, our algorithm provides better performance compared to the existing algorithm. It is left for future work to determine the best PC sets.

Fig. 5. The pattern codebook of four regular shaped, 128-pixel patterns, defined in 16×16 blocks in top row and 16-pixel patterns defined in 8×8 blocks in bottom row, where the white region represents 1 (motion) and black region represents 0 (no motion)

In our approach we determine extra two and one Lagrangian cost function using bit rates and distortions generated by PBC algorithm using 64- and 128-pixle pattern sets for large modes and 16-pixel pattern set for small modes respectively. In encoded process each CRMB is motion estimated and compensated using 64- and 128-pixel pattern sets together with the large modes (from 16×16 to 8×8) and then based on the minimum Lagrangian cost function, we select one mode. If 8×8 mode is selected then each CRMB is again motion estimated and compensated using 16-pixel pattern set together with small modes (from 8×4 to 4×4). Based on the minimum Lagrangian cost function we select one mode.

4 Simulation Results

We have implemented our proposed algorithm based on the Baseline profile of H.264/AVC with full search motion estimation of maximum ±7.5 pixel search width

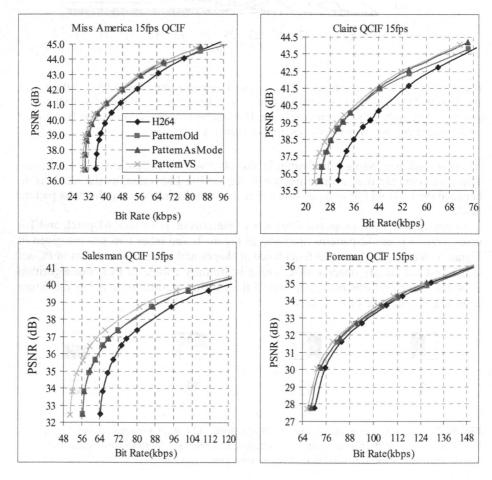

Fig. 6. Coding performance comparisons for four standard test video sequences by the H.264, conventional PBC (PatternOld), PBC as mode of H.264 (PatternAsMode), and PBC with three different pattern sets (PatternVS)

[13] for a number of standard [10] video sequences with QCIF format namely, *Foreman, Miss America, Claire, Car phone, News, Salesman, Suzie,* and *Grandma.* But for brevity we show our rate-distortion performance using the first 100 frames of four standard video sequences. In this experiment, the GOP size is fifteen and we use only *I* and *P* frames. From now on, conventional pattern-based video coding, patter-based video coding as mode, and pattern-based video coding with three variable size PC sets is termed as *PatternOld, PatternAsMode,* and *PatternVS.*

The final rate-distortion performance is demonstrated in Figure 6 for four QCIF standard video sequences with 15 *frames per second* (fps). The experimental results reveal that at a wide range of bit rates the PBC using three different pattern set and pattern as a mode outperforms both the conventional PBC and the H.264 standard. For more specific, the PBC with three different PCs performs as high as 1.5dB (for Salesman) at 100 kilo bit rates (kbps).

5 Future Works and Conclusions

Video coding using pattern templates representing moving regions in macroblock has already established its potentiality for improving coding efficiency over existing standard H.264/AVC in the very low bit-rate range. However, the coding efficiency diminishes compared to H.264 with the bit rates because variable block sizes of H.264 for motion estimation and compensation are successfully selected for any bit rates using weighting between bit rate and image quality. The existing pattern-based video coding scheme cannot handle this flexibility with bit rates due to its fixed size and lack of competition with other modes of H.264. To improve the performance in wider range of bit rates we treat pattern-based video coding as an extra mode and we also incorporate two large and one small pre-defined pattern sets in existing scheme. The experimental results confirmed that this new scheme improves as high as 1.5dB image quality compared to the H.264 standard at the same bit rates. We do not claim that this choice of pattern set is the best but there would be other combination of pattern set provides better results. We observed that, with this arbitrary choice of pattern set, our algorithm provides better performance compared to the existing algorithm. It is left for future work to determine the best pattern set.

References

[1] Fukuhara, T., K. Asai, and T. Murakami, "Very low bit-rate video coding with block partitioning and adaptive selection of two time-differential frame memories," *IEEE Trans. Circuits Syst. Video Technol.,* 7, 212–220, 1997.

[2] Gonzalez, R.C. and R. E. Woods, *Digital Image Processing,* Addison-Wesley, 1992.

[3] ISO/IEC 13818, MPEG-2 International Standard, 1995.

[4] ISO/IEC N4030, MPEG-4 International Standard, 2001.

[5] ITU-T Recommendation H.263, "Video coding for low bit-rate communication," Version 2, 1998.

[6] ITU-T Rec. H.264/ISO/IEC 14496-10 AVC. Joint Video Team (JVT) of ISO MPEG and ITU-T VCEG, JVT-G050, 2003.

[7]   Maragos, P., "Tutorial on advances in morphological image processing and analysis," *Opt. Eng.*, 26(7), 623–632, 1987.

[8]   Paul, M., M. Murshed, and L. Dooley, "A real-time pattern selection algorithm for very low bit-rate video coding using relevance and similarity metrics," *IEEE Trans. on Circuits and Systems on Video Technology*, vol. 15, no. 6, pp. 753–761, June, 2005.

[9]   Paul, M., Murshed, M. and Dooley, L., "A new efficient similarity metric generic computation strategy for pattern-based very low bit-rate video coding," Proc. of the *IEEE Int. Con. of Acoustics, Speech, and Signal Proc.* (ICASSP-04), vol. 3, pp. 165–168, May, 2004.

[10] Shi, Y.Q. and H. Sun, *Image and Video Compression for Multimedia Engineering Fundamentals, Algorithms, and Standards*, CRC Press, 1999.

[11] Wong, K.-W., K.-M. Lam, and W.-C. Siu, "An Efficient Low   Bit-Rate Video-Coding Algorithm Focusing on Moving Regions," *IEEE trans. circuits and systems for video technology*, 11(10), 1128–1134, 2001.

[12] Weigrand, T., H. Schwarz, A. Joch, and F. Kossentini, "Rate-contrained coder control and comparison of video coding standards," *IEEE Trans. on Circuits and Systems on Video Technology*, 13 (7), 688–702, 2003.

[13] Richardson, I. E. G., "H.264 and MPEG-4 video compression," *Wiley Press*, 2003.

Performance Enhancement of Error Resilient Entropy Coding on Block Based Bitstream of SPIHT

Jeong-Sig Kim and Keun-Young Lee

Image Communication Lab., School of Information and Communication Engineering,
SungKyunKwan University, 300 Chunchun-dong, Jangan-gu, Suwon, Kyunggi-do,
Republic of Korea
condor@mickey.skku.ac.kr, kylee@ece.skku.ac.kr

Abstract. Standard image and video techniques designed to provide the bitstream with some level of protection against channel errors usually add a controlled amount of redundancy. This redundancy may take the form of resynchronization makers which enable the decoder to restart the decoding process from a known state in the event of transmission errors. The Error Resilient Entropy Code(EREC) is a well known algorithm designed to reduce the added redundant information. Wavelet tree coding provides the most efficient of image compression currently available with respect to rate-distortion. This paper presents a performance enhancement of EREC on the bitstream of SPIHT, which greatly improves its ability to maintain the compressed image quality in the event of random errors. This paper demonstrates that Efficient and Robust EREC(EREREC) improves the image quality of SPIHT in the presence of channel errors. The simulation result shows that the quality of transmitted image is improved when compared to the existing EREC on SPIHT.

Keywords: DCT, Error Resilient Entropy Coding, SPIHT(Set Partitioning in Hierarchical Tree), VLC(Variable-Length Code), Wavelet Transform.

1 Introduction

In recent years, there has been some outstanding research in image and video compression over error-prone environment channels such as wireless, mobile, and internet communications. Two important problems arise in the implementation of multimedia services. The first is the limited capacity of wireless and mobile channels. To solve this problem, source coding techniques have been developed to reduce the required capacity of the signal. The second problem is that the quality of many channels can suffer from signal fading and interference, resulting in erroneous transmission. Most of the existing source coding techniques for error-free channel transmission can suffer from serious degradation if any of the compressed data is corrupted. Generally, compressed data (image or video) faces the problem that a small error in the bitstream can have a catastrophic effect on the quality of images or videos. Therefore, many error handling techniques have been

T.-J. Cham et al. (Eds.): MMM 2007, LNCS 4352, Part II, pp. 363–372, 2007.

suggested, such as layered coding[1], Forward Error Correction(FEC)[2], Automatic Repeat Request(ARQ), Error Detection, Error Concealment[3], Error-Resilient Coding[4],[5],[6] and so on.

In the previous error handling techniques, the nature of the highly compressed digital video is such that existing error detection and correction strategies such as FEC do not work well. FEC uses lots of redundancy bits. ARQ works by allowing the receiver to request portions of the transmitted data to be resent, in the event that they are corrupted or do not arrive at all. However, this technique is not adequate for multimedia broadcasting, as quite often the receiver does not have a backchannel to signal to the transmitter which parts of the multimedia have been lost. Moreover, even when it does, the retransmitted data arrives too late, because the multimedia data has already been displayed. Error-resilient coding which reduces redundancy due to channel coding, nonetheless protects against error propagation. An error-resilient coding technique for image and video transmission has been proposed which uses a bit rearrangement technique in Error Resilient Entropy Coding (EREC)[4]. The aim of the EREC algorithm is to supply an error-resilient scheme for coding the data bits generated by block based compression algorithms. The EREC algorithm has attracted considerable attention, because it allows the spatial propagation of transmission errors to be significantly improved without any sizeable overhead. The idea behind EREC is to re-group the variable-length data blocks into the fixed length slots. Consequently, the receiving end can achieve automatic resynchronization at the beginning of the slot. The EREC algorithm has been applied to DCT block based image coding, but Steven Whitehouse and Nick Kingsbury [7] also applied it to wavelet zerotree coded image data. The EREREC(Efficient and Robust EREC)[6] algorithm described in our previous work significantly improves on the EREC[4] algorithm, by considering the statistical distribution of the long and short blocks.

In this paper, we propose a new method which combines the EREREC[6] algorithm described in our previous work with the SPIHT[8] algorithm, in order to accomplish better error resilience. We use the structures of the spatial orientation tree[8], in which each tree is coded independently, and group the wavelet coefficients according to the corresponding spatial blocks. By doing so, a highly efficient source coding can be obtained in order to search for self-similarity fully in the coefficients across the different scale-levels of the wavelet transform. Then, EREC is applied to reorganize these variable-length data bits into fixed length slots for transmission over erroneous channels. At the receiving end, the start bit of each slot can be automatically determined in order to synchronize the data bits. Besides, since each tree of SPIHT is coded bit-layer by bit-layer, error propagation has less noticeable effects on bits located at low bit-layers. Therefore, we propose a new algorithm which adds the EREREC function of our previous algorithm to SPIHT. The proposed algorithm has good performance since it calculates and selects the maximum and average consecutive long/short blocks.

When our proposed algorithm is simulated, it shows that the quality of the compressed digital image is better than that afforded by the traditional EREC method on SPIHT in the events of transmission errors.

2 Set Partitioning in Hierarchical Tree (SPIHT)

Several wavelet image compression algorithms have been proposed in the literature, of which SPIHT[8] is one of the most popular. SPIHT uses a zero-tree coding scheme to code each bit plane. As shown on the left side of Fig.2, SPIHT segments each subband into 2×2 sets in the transform domain. Each cell in these 2×2 sets in the higher level relates to a 2×2 set in the lower level in a descendant direction. In each tree, if one node is insignificant with respect to a given threshold, all of its offspring will most probably be insignificant with respect to the same threshold. This is a well known self-similarity property in insignificant across different wavelet frequency scale levels.

The main algorithm partitions the wavelet decomposed image into significant and insignificant partitions based on the following function;

$$S_n(T) = \begin{cases} 1, & max_{(i,j) \in T} \{|C_{i,j}|\} \geq 2^n \\ 0, & otherwise \end{cases} \tag{1}$$

where $S_n(T)$ is the significance of a set of co-ordinates, T, and $C_{i,j}$ is the value of the coefficient value at co-ordinate i, j. There are two passes in the algorithm - the sorting pass and refinement pass. The sorting pass is performed on the list of insignificant sets (LIS), the list of insignificant pixels (LIP) and the list of significant pixels(LSP). The LIP and LSP consist of nodes containing single pixels, while the LIS contains nodes having descendants. The maximum number of bits required to represent the largest coefficients in the spatial orientation tree, n_{max}, is obtained as follows ;

$$n_{max} = \lfloor \log_2 (max_{(i,j)} \{|C_{i,j}|\}) \rfloor \tag{2}$$

During the sorting pass, those co-ordinates of the pixels which remain in the LIP are tested for significance by using eq.(1). The result, $S_n(T)$, is sent to the output. Those co-ordinates which are significant will be transferred to the LSP, as well as their sign bit to the output. Those sets in the LIS which consists of nodes with descendants will also have their significance tested. Those that are found to be significant will be removed and partitioned into subsets. Those subsets with a single coefficient which are found to be significant will be added the LSP, or if they are insignificant, they will be added to the LIP.

During the refinement pass, the nth most significant bit of the coefficients in the LSP is sent to the output. Then, the value of n is decreased by 1, and the sorting and refinement passes are repeated. This continues until either the desired rate is reached or $n = 0$, and all the nodes in the LSP send all their bits to the output. The latter case will result in almost perfect reconstruction, as all of the coefficients are processed completely. Moreover, the bit rate can be controlled precisely in the SPIHT, because the output is produced in the form of single bits and the algorithm can be terminated at any time.

3   Error Resilient Entropy Coding (EREC)

EREC[4] was originally proposed to handle the sequential transmission of variable-length coded DCT data blocks over noisy channels. In the case of DCT based block image coding schemes such as JPEG, H.263 etc., the length of the coded binary bits in one block is generally different from those of the other blocks. If these variable-length blocks are multiplexed sequentially for transmission, channel errors may corrupt the boundary information between the blocks and, hence, result in catastrophic decoding of the image. The key idea behind the EREC is the re-organization of the variable-length data blocks into fixed slots with negligibly increased data size.

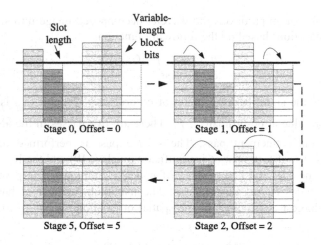

Fig. 1. Original EREC

As shown in Fig.1, the data in the blocks is allocated to the corresponding slots, starting from the beginning of each block. Blocks that are larger than the slot size are truncated and the remaining data are put into other slots having available space according to a predefined offset sequence. Therefore, at the receiving end, the start of each block can be automatically determined as the start of each fixed length slot. In the absence of channel errors, the decoder can follow the same algorithm to recover all variable-length blocks using the same offset sequence. When channel errors occur, error propagation in EREC decoding will more likely affect the data close to the end of each block than that close to the beginning of each block. This characteristic fits well with the wavelet tree embedded coding we used.

In our scheme, coefficients are encoded from the highest bit-layer(lowest frequency band) to the lowest bit-layer(highest frequency band). Therefore, the importance of the coded data generally decreases along the bitstream from the beginning to the end. In the case of noisy channels, error propagation will more likely affect the lower bit-layers, which results in less distortion energy.

4 Proposed Algorithms

4.1 Composing Wavelet Coefficients of SPIHT

After the hierarchical wavelet decomposition, there is a direct relationship between the wavelet coefficients and corresponding image content. Coefficients corresponding to the same orientation components of the image at different decomposition levels are grouped into a wavelet tree structure. This wavelet tree is rooted in the lowest frequency subband and, out of each 2×2 root node, one node has no descendent and every other coefficient has four offspring in the higher frequency subband of the same orientation, thus forming trees. The set of four coefficients at the lowest frequency band and their descendents (if any) represent the wavelet transform of the $2^{n+1}\times2^{n+1}$ square block of the image, where n is the number of the decomposition levels. The left-hand side of Fig.2 shows the spatial orientation wavelet tree structure[8] formed by the self-similarity property and the right-hand side of Fig.2 is its equivalent square block image content when all coefficients in the wavelet tree are grouped. These data are the frequency component for a specific image area with the same block size at the corresponding position.

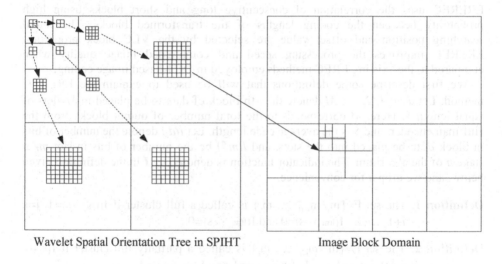

Wavelet Spatial Orientation Tree in SPIHT   Image Block Domain

Fig. 2. Wavelet Tree in SPIHT and its equivalent image content

After the coefficient regrouping, one tree corresponds solely to one image block. For each wavelet tree, the SPIHT is employed to encode it independently. By doing so, multiple wavelet tree coding can be considered as the re-organization of the single SPIHT coded bitstream into multiple variable-length segments, and each variable-length segment corresponds to a single wavelet tree and, thus, a single spatial block in the original image.

Accordingly, this scheme can also be regarded as a block based coding method. And EREC can be applied to re-organize these multiple variable-length parts in order

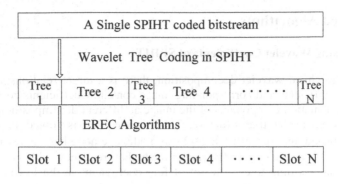

Fig. 3. Wavelet coding in SPIHT and EREC

to obtain an error resilient coding. Fig.3 shows the basic idea behind the wavelet tree coding in SPIHT and EREC[9].

4.2 Efficient and Robust EREC (EREREC)

EREREC uses the correlation of consecutive long and short blocks using high probability between the coding lengths of the transformed blocks. The initial searching position and offset value are selected by the VLC block properties. EREREC improves the processing speed and compressed image quality when compared to the existing EREC methods employed in DCT based image coding.

We first describe some definitions that will be used to explain the EREREC method. Let d_i, $i=1, 2, ..., M$ denote the i-th block of data to be placed in M slots of equal length S. Here, M corresponds to the total number of output blocks from the Huffman encoder, and S is the average code length. Let $l(d_i)$ denote the number of bits in block d_i to be placed into the slots, and $l(m_i^n)$ be the number of bits in slot m_i at stage n of the algorithm. The indicator function is denoted by I in the definition given below, and we drop n for convenience.

Definition 1. The set $F=\{m_i, m_{i+1}, ..., m_k\}$ is called a full cluster if $I_{\{l(m_j) \geq S\}}=1$, $j=i$, $i+1, ..., k$, $I_{\{l(m_{i-1}) < S\}}=0$ and $I_{\{l(m_{k+1}) < S\}}=0$.

Definition 2. The set $E=\{m_i, m_{i+1}, ..., m_k\}$ is called a partially full cluster if $I_{\{l(m_j) < S\}}=0$, $j=i, i+1, ..., k$, $I_{\{l(m_{i-1}) \geq S\}}=1$ and $I_{\{l(m_{k+1}) \geq S\}}=1$.

Therefore, the probability of block d_i finding a partially full slot m_j is high for $j>i+1$ when $l(d_i) \geq S$, since those output blocks whose length exceeds S are more likely to be followed by similar blocks. Similarly, those blocks whose size is less than the average length of a slot will precede blocks of a similar nature. That is, the clustering of blocks is highly correlated with the VLC block length. So, a block has to cross the full cluster and reach the partially full cluster in the consecutive stages to be placed in a slot. If $F_1, F_2, ..., F_r$ and $E_1, E_2, ..., E_s$ denote the r full clusters and the s partially full clusters, respectively, then the average length of each cluster is given by

$$L_f = \left\lceil \frac{1}{r}[C(F_1) + C(F_2), ..., C(F_r)] \right\rceil \tag{3}$$

$$L_e = \left\lceil \frac{1}{s}[C(E_1) + C(E_2), ..., C(E_s)] \right\rceil \tag{4}$$

where C denotes the cardinality of a set and $\lceil \cdot \rceil$ is the ceiling function. On average, a block crosses $\lceil (L_f + L_e)/2 \rceil$ slots to find a free slot. This suggests should speed up the packing of the data bits into the slots. Therefore, the searching step size (SP) is given below

$$SP = \left\lceil \frac{L_f + L_e}{2} \right\rceil \tag{5}$$

Since spatially neighboring blocks have similar properties, there is a chance to reduce the slot searching time. This property can reduce the searching step, which involves searching for empty slots and filling the unfilled bits in these slots with the extra bits from the remaining large slots, so that, in the proposed method, the extra bits from the large slots are placed in nearby slots. We calculate the maximum number of consecutive long blocks (L_l) and short blocks (L_s), rather than the average slot length (S). Then, we find the start position (P_{max}) of L_l consecutive long blocks and the start position (P_{min}) of L_s consecutive short blocks, using eqs. (6) and (7), respectively.

$$P_{max} = \arg\ max_p \left(\sum_{i=p}^{p+L_l} l(d_i) \right) \tag{6}$$

$$P_{min} = \arg\ min_p \left(\sum_{i=p}^{p+L_s} l(d_i) \right) \tag{7}$$

By using these values, the initial position ($P_{initial}$) is given by eq.(8)

$$P_{initial} = (P_{min} - P_{max} + M)\ \bmod\ M \tag{8}$$

where M is the total number of blocks. $P_{initial}$ means the spatial distance between the consecutive long blocks with the summation of maximum block bits and the consecutive short blocks with the summation of minimum block bits, so the chance that the large slots can find small slots can be maximized with this offset value. Therefore, we suggest that the initial position be used as the initial offset value (Φ_1), and we use it to calculate the offset sequence values of the consecutive stages.

Once the SP is decided by eq.(5), the offset sequence values are calculated by eq.(9)

$$\Phi_{k+1} = \begin{cases} (\Phi_1 + k \cdot SP)\ \bmod\ M\ , & k = odd \\ (\Phi_1 - k \cdot SP)\ \bmod\ M\ , & k = even \end{cases} \tag{9}$$

where $k=1, 2, 3, ...$, and the '+' and '−' symbols refer to the forward and backward searching directions, respectively. Φ_{k+1} is the number of searching iterations. We must examine eq.(9) carefully. Since the offset value increases as SP, if we chose some SP, all offset values are not searched in any case (i.e, the offset value can have the same value as the previous offset after some iterations). Therefore, we find the necessary condition to avoid offset repetition. If a prime factor of the SP is $\{1, x_1, x_2, ..., x_m\}$ and a prime factor set of the total slot is $\{1, y_1, y_2, ..., y_n\}$, then offset repetition can be decided as follows.

If any value of x_i ($i = 1, 2,..., m$) does not match y_j ($j = 1, 2, ..., n$) except 1, then all of the offset sequence values can be selected once by eq.(9). On the other hand, the values of the offset sequence cannot be selected once only if the above condition is violated. In that case, we adjust the SP value to assure that the necessary condition can be satisfied. The detailed operations are shown below,

Detail-1: When the same factors exist between the prime factors of the SP value and the prime factors of the total slot, with the exception of a prime factor of 1, eq.(9) cannot search all of the offset values and, hence, repetition occurs.

Detail-2: The value of SP increases one by one until the necessary condition is found. Then, new offset sequence values are decided by using the value of the new SP in eq.(9).

In the above explanation, the SP value can be incremented or decremented. Since the probability of finding an empty slot is higher with a large offset value, due to the spatial correlation of the neighboring blocks, we increment the SP value. ERERERC changes the initial offset more adaptively than the existing EREC methods and depends on the characteristics of the image blocks.

5 Simulation Results

We simulated the 512×512 8bits/pixel Lena image which is transformed to 4 decomposition levels by the wavelet transform. In this case, 1024 wavelet trees are constructed, as referred to in the figure and equation of section 4.1. Then, the ERERERC algorithm is applied to these trees. In the decoding process of the algorithm, it is necessary for the proposed method to find the end of each block in the absence of channel errors. In our experiment, we obtain self-termination by utilizing the value of the stop-layer for the encoding and decoding of each wavelet tree.

Fig.4 shows the BER versus PSNR at 0.54bpp and table 1 describes the numerical values of Fig.4. The proposed algorithm produces an image quality which is about 0.3~1.5dB higher than that afforded by the existing algorithm against random errors.

Table 2 shows the processing iteration number and bpp of EREC and the proposed ERERERC algorithm on SPIHT. The proposed method requires less iterations than the existing method, because it considers the statistical distribution of the long and short blocks. After the block data have been collected, the decoder can reconstruct the image. Therefore, the iteration number influences both the encoding and decoding time. Suppose one slot has errors and the decoder tries to recollect the dispersed data bits. Since the slot has errors, every block which searches for its data in that slot is also marked as an error block, because it does not know whether that slot has its data. Therefore, the iteration number also influences the quality of the reconstructed image.

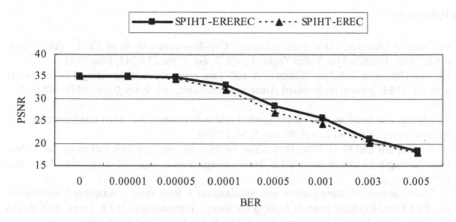

Fig. 4. BER vs. PSNR at 0.54bpp

Table 1. BER vs. PSNR at 0.54bpp

BER	Number of Errors	SPIHT-EREC	SPIHT-EREREC
0	0	35.0236	35.0236
1×10^{-5}	1	35.02	35.023
5×10^{-5}	7	34.4765	34.8464
1×10^{-4}	14	31.9144	33.077
5×10^{-4}	71	26.7541	28.3095
1×10^{-3}	142	24.4461	25.7786
3×10^{-3}	427	20.2019	21.0166
5×10^{-3}	712	17.9454	18.4202

Table 2. Iteration number for EREC processing speed

bpp	PSNR	SPIHT-EREC	SPIHT-EREREC
0.99	38.4577	1023	932
0.54	35.0236	1018	349
0.33	31.7939	939	282

6 Conclusion

In this paper, we investigated the integration of SPIHT and EREREC for robust image transmission. After hierarchical wavelet decomposition, the spatial orientation tree is used to group the wavelet coefficients corresponding to the same image content block and to reorganize the variable length coded bitstreams into fixed length slots. The experimental results show that the proposed method is more error resilient and less complex than the existing EREC method.

References

1. Mohammad Ghanbari and Vassilis Seferidis : Cell-loss concealment in ATM video codecs, IEEE Trans. Circuits Syst. Video Technol., vol. 3, no. 3, pp. 238-247, June 1993.
2. Hiroshi Ohta and Tokuhiro Kitami : A cell loss recovery method using FEC in ATM network, IEEE Journal on Selected Areas in Communi., vol. 9, no. 9, pp. 1471-1483, Dec. 1991.
3. Yao Wang and Qin-Fan Zhu : Error control and concealment for video communication: A Review, Proc. Of the IEEE, vol. 86, no. 5, May 1998.
4. D. W. Redmill and N. G. Kingsbury : The EREC: An error resilient technique for coding variable-length blocks of data, IEEE Trans. Image Processing, vol. 5, pp. 565-574, Apr. 1996.
5. R. Chandramouli, N. Ranganathan and Shivaraman J. Ramadoss, : Adaptive Quantization and Fast Error-Resilient Entropy Coding for Image Transmission, IEEE Trans. on Circuits and Systems for Video Technology, Vol. 8, No. 4, pp. 411-421, August 1998.
6. Jeong-Sig Kim, Ju-Do Kim and Keun-Young Lee : The Efficient and Robust Error Resilient Entropy Coding of Compressed Image for Wireless Communications, IEICE Transactions on Fundamentals of Electronics, Communications and Computer Sciences, vol. E88-A, no. 6, June 2005.
7. Steven Whitehouse and Nick Kingsbury : The Error Resilient Entropy Code Applied to Zerotree Coded Image Data, 1999 IEEE 3rd Workshop on Multimedia Signal Processing 13-15, pp. 425-430, Sept. 1999.
8. Amir Said and William A. Pearlman : A New, Fast, and Efficient Image Codec Based on Set Partitioning in Hierarchical Trees, IEEE Transactions on Circuits and Systems for Video Technology, vol. 6, no. 3, pp.243-250, June 1996.
9. Lei Cao and Chang Wen Chen : Robust Image Transmission Based on Wavelet Tree Coding and EREC, International Conference on Image Processing 2001, Proceedings 2001, Vol. 3, pp. 222-225, Oct. 2001.

FIDP: A Novel Architecture for Lifting-Based 2D DWT in JPEG2000

Bao-Feng Li and Yong Dou

National Lab for Parallel and Distributed Processing, NUDT
Changsha, Hunan Province, P.R. China
{lbf, yongdou}@nudt.edu.cn

Abstract. In this paper, we propose a deeply parallel architecture called Fragment-based Interleaving Dual Pipelines(FIDP) which can exploit all parallelisms in Lifting-based 2D DWT algorithm. FIDP adopts a fragment-based samples consumption policy and consists of two row processors and two column processors. These processors are organized as interleaving dual pipelines to operate effectively. FIDP takes $N^2/4+N/2+1$ cycles to finish a N×N 2D DWT while requires only 5N+2 buffer.

1 Introduction

JPEG2000 [1] accepts discrete wavelet transform (DWT) instead of discrete cosine transform (DCT) as the transform algorithm because DWT supports higher performance than DCT. Researches [2] show that DWT consumes a considerable portion(> 25%) in JPEG2000 coding stream. So the performance of DWT has been a key problem for real-time systems. In this case, it's best to implement DWT with a dedicated hardware. Lifting-based DWT [3] has low computational and memory requirements and is adopted in most implementations.

In this paper we analyze the computational features of 2D DWT algorithm and propose a parallel architecture called Fragment-based Interleaving Dual Pipelines (FIDP). FIDP consists of two row processors(RPs) and two column processors(CPs). The RPs and CPs consume image samples in fragment-based order. And the operations on them are organized as two interleaving pipelines. The results show that FIDP has achieved a higher performance(with a speedup 2 over the current fastest design) while maintaining moderate memory requirements. More specifically, the contributions of our work are:

- A new fragment-based samples consumption policy is proposed. This policy can reduce the memory requirement and increase the performance.
- The operations on FIDP is organized as two interleaving pipelines based on the characteristics of the lifting-based 2D DWT algorithm. FIDP has achieved a higher performance(with a speedup 2) by fully exploiting the parallelisms in the algorithm. At the same time, an efficient data reuse policy is adopted to avoid ultra increase of memory requirement.
- An efficient memory system is presented to provide sufficient data for so many processors.

T.-J. Cham et al. (Eds.): MMM 2007, LNCS 4352, Part II, pp. 373–382, 2007.

2 Fragment-Based Samples Consumption Policy

Two filters are recommended in JPEG2000 - 5/3 and 9/7 filter. We take 5/3 filter as an example in this paper. However our work is not limited to this. It can be easily extended to 9/7 filter and multi-level DWT. Moreover, we also make some assumptions: the input image is stored in matrix A, and the size is N×N.

2.1 Parallelism Analysis for Lifting-Based 2D DWT

Typical 5/3 filter with boundary extension [4] can be described with equations:

$$Y_{2i+1} = \begin{cases} X_{2i+1} - (X_{2i} + X_{2i+2})/2 & 0 \le i < N/2-1 \\ X_{2i+1} - X_{2i} & i = N/2-1 \end{cases}$$

$$Y_{2i} = \begin{cases} X_{2i} + (Y_{2i-1} + Y_{2i+1} + 2)/4 & 0 < i < N/2-1 \\ X_{2i} + (Y_{2i+1} + 1)/2 & i = 0 \end{cases}$$

For 2D DWT, above transform is firstly applied to every row, and then to every column. There are three kinds of parallelisms in 2D DWT algorithm: 1. transforms on different rows; 2. transforms on different columns; 3. transforms on rows and transforms on columns. No data dependency exists in the 1st and 2nd cases while a RAW dependency occurs in the 3rd case.

Many architectures [5, 6, 7, 8] have been proposed for lifting-based 2D DWT. However, these architectures did not exploit the three parallelisms fully. So they failed to achieve a higher performance. In our design, we try to exploit all the three parallelisms to maximize the performance.

2.2 The Proposed Fragment-Based Samples Consumption Policy

According to the order that samples are consumed, we can divide existing architectures into two categories. The first is the **line-based** architecture [6, 7, 8]. In line-based architecture, image samples are read and processed line by line. The RP may start computing as soon as one line samples are ready, instead of whole image. But the delay from RP's starting to CP's starting is long. The second is the **Z-scan** architecture [5]. In Z-scan architecture, image samples are read and processed out of order. Transform on one row is broken to perform another transform on another row. In other words, row transform consumes samples in row-fashion and produces results in column-fashion. So CP can start earlier than that in line-based. However, it's obvious that the memory organization is more complex. Though CP can start earlier, it has to be paused periodically because RP can not produce enough samples in time. Moreover, the performance loss caused by pause is much greater than the gain brought by earlier start.

Our design adopts an improved line-based policy called **fragment-based samples consumption policy**. Because starting a row transform does not need all samples in one row, operations on foregoing samples can parallel with reading of forthcoming samples. The fragment-based policy breaks input image into fragments according to the computing requirement. Every fragment includes necessary samples which RP/CP requires in one computation. Hence the processers

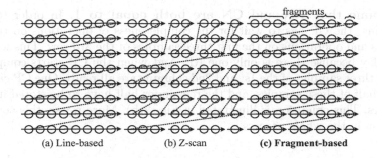

(a) Line-based   (b) Z-scan   (c) Fragment-based

Fig. 1. Difference between fragment-based policy and the other two

start earlier, communication is hidden, and performance is improved. Fig. 1 shows the difference between fragment-based policy and the other two.

3   The Interleaving Dual Pipelines Architecture

Our parallel interleaving dual pipelines architecture consists of two RPs and two CPs. The RPs operate on different rows, and the CPs operate on different columns. The operations on the architecture are organized as interleaving dual pipelines based on the fragment-based samples consumption policy.

3.1   Discussion of Possible Architectures

Theoretically, since transforms on different rows/columns have no data dependency, more RPs bring better performance. However, when we look deep inside the 2D DWT algorithm, we find several characteristics:

1) Each RP consumes two new samples and produces two results which belong to two columns in each operation except the start or end of one row.

2) Current computations use the data produced by the foregoing computations in process of transforming one row/column.

3) RPs produce results in row-fashion while CPs consume samples in column-fashion. And CPs use the results produced by RPs.

Based on these characteristics, we give a brief analysis as follows where RN and CN represents the number of RPs and CPs respectively:

1) Assume that RN and CN are both greater than 2. There are two cases to be considered. **a)** If all RPs begin computing at the same time, they will produce 2×RN results which belong to two different columns in every operation. Therefore, only 2 CPs can start since the 1st and 2nd characteristics mentioned above. The remainder (CN-2) CPs leave unused. And the rest of results produced by RN RPs have to be stored in extra memory. So some CPs are wasted, and extra memories are required. Fig. 2(a) illustrates this condition. **b)** If the RPs do not start simultaneously, some RPs are also wasted. Besides above, to control so many processors is a great difficulty.

2) Assume that RN and CN are both equal to 1. In order to start computing, the CP has to wait for the completeness of operations on the first two rows and operations on the first three samples of the 3rd row. This will take N+1 delay because there is only one RP. And when the CP starts computing, the first three samples of the 1st and 2nd columns are all ready. One CP can only process half of these samples, and the remainder half have to be stored in extra memories. This condition is illustrated in Fig. 2(b). More worse, this condition will go on in the whole process.

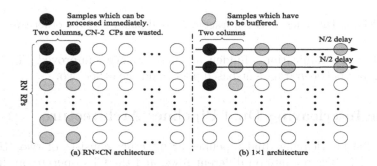

Fig. 2. Analysis of possible architectures

3) Assume that RN and CN are both equal to 2. The delay that CPs start after RPs is N/2+1 because there are two RPs. Moreover, the samples produced by RPs which belong to two different columns can be processed simultaneously. Consequently the memory requirement is reduced, as illustrated in Fig. 3.

From above, there are two RPs and two CPs in our design.

3.2 The System Architecture

The system consists of two RPs, two CPs, a buffer memory(BM) used to buffer results between RPs and CPs, and a main memory(MM) which provides the RPs with original image samples, as illustrated in Fig. 4(a). Initially input image is stored in external memory(EM). It is read into main memory row-by-row. The RPs perform row transforms and write results to the BM. Once sufficient samples have been produced, the CPs start column transforms. The results from CPs are written back to the MM, and then MM switches these data out to EM for next-level decomposition or coding. The RPs operate on different rows to exploit the 1st parallelism. The CPs are set for the 2nd parallelism. And separate RPs and CPs are set for the 3rd parallelism.

The RPs and CPs are organized as interleaving dual pipelines to process the image effectively. Operations on previous rows and the reading of next rows from external memory are processed parallelly.

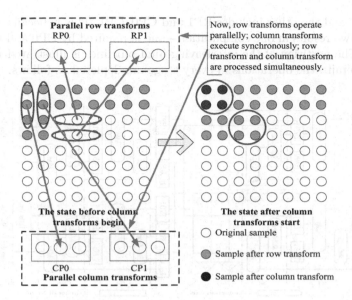

Fig. 3. The optimal architecture

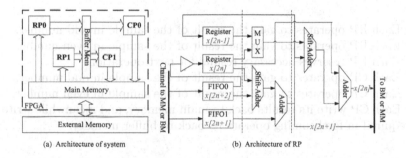

(a) Architecture of system   (b) Architecture of RP

Fig. 4. Architectures of system and RP

3.3 Row/Column Processor

RP and CP are the same with computations. They have the same architecture illustrated in Fig. 4(b). Each RP/CP includes two shift-adders, two adders, two register and two input FIFOs. The shift-adders and adders together perform computations. The registers are used to hold necessary values for subsequent computations. The input FIFOs are employed to receive and buffer samples sent by MM(for RP) or BM(for CP). Each RP/CP is pipelined according to the lifting steps. All RPs and CPs together compose the interleaving dual pipelines.

3.4 Interleaving Dual Pipelines

According to the data dependency and dataflow of 2D DWT algorithm, we organize the RPs and CPs as interleaving dual pipelines - one includes RP0 and

CP0/CP1, and the other includes RP1 and CP0/CP1. This is because each RP produces two results in one computation - one is required by CP0 and the other by CP1. The partition of the interleaving dual pipelines is illustrated in Fig. 5. In more details, the operations in every stage are depicted as follows.

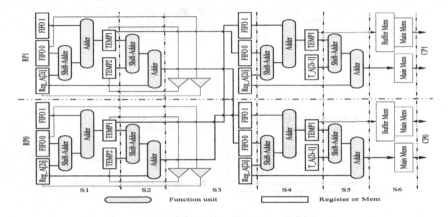

Fig. 5. The interleaving dual pipelines

S1: Each RP operates to gain the result of the sample in odd number.
S2: Each RP operates to gain the result of the sample in even number.
S3: Each RP reserves necessary results for next operation.
S4: Each CP operates to gain the result of the sample in odd number.
S5: Each CP operates to gain the result of the sample in even number.
S6: Each CP write its results back to main memory, and meanwhile write the data required in forthcoming operations back to buffer memory.

3.5 Memory Organization

The memory system includes main memory module and buffer memory module.

1) Main memory module
The functions of the main memory include sending samples to RPs and receiving results from CPs. It consists of two banks and the control logic. Each bank has a separate read port and a write port, as illustrated in Fig. 6(a).

Each bank holds the odd rows or even rows. The width of the read port is twice that of one sample because every computation of RPs needs two new samples. The width of the write port is also twice that of one sample since the two CP produce two results in every cycle. EM sends data into the MM through write ports. When RPs are operating on the foregoing samples, EM can send the forthcoming data into the MM.

The capacity of the MM is 4N, and each bank is 2N to store two rows samples. We take the process of bank 0 for an example. Initially the 1st row is read into bank 0. When one of RPs (assume RP0) is operating on the 1st row, the 3rd row is read in and placed in the remainder N. When RP0 finished operations on the 1st row, it can immediately start operations on the 3rd row. Meanwhile the 5th row will be read in and occupy the space which holds the 1st row before. This process is repeated until all the odd rows are processed.

2) Buffer memory module

The function of buffer memory is to buffer results between RPs and CPs. It consists of three banks, two registers and the control logic. Each bank has a separate read port and a write port, as Fig. 6(b) depicted.

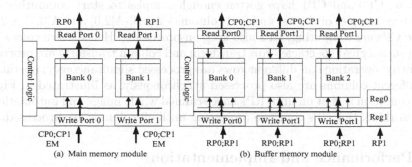

Fig. 6. The memory organization

The three banks hold the latest results produced by RPs respectively because these results belong to three rows. Each bank has the size N. Because the computations of RPs are the same with that of CPs, the width of the read ports and the write ports is also the same.

There are four results produced when both CPs compute once. These results are written back to MM. Only two of them can release the space occupied in BM. The rest two have to be reserved in BM for forthcoming operations. The two registers are used to temporarily store the results produced by RP1. When the spaces released by CPs are available, they are moved to the spaces. For instance, the 1st row produced by RP0 is stored in bank 0 and the 2nd row produced by RP1 in bank 1. And then the two results of the 3rd row produced by RP0 are stored in bank 2. Meanwhile, the two results of the 4th row produced by RP1 in one computation are stored in the two registers firstly, and then moved to the space released by CPs. So we reduce the memory requirement from 4N to 3N+2.

3.6   Parallel Execution Example

In following, we explain how FIDP works through an example. We assume that the input image size is 8×8 and stored in the array - A[0:7,0:7].

MM sends the first three samples of the 1st and 2nd rows (A[0,0]-A[0,2] and A[1,0]-A[1,2]) to RP0 and RP1 respectively. RP0 begins computing when it has received the first three samples of the 1st rows. When finished, it sends the results to corresponding CPs (new A[0,0] to CP0 and new A[0,1] to CP1) and retains the new A[0,1] and A[0,2] for next computing. At the same time, RP1 does the same thing on samples of the 2nd row.

MM continues to send A[0,3] A[0,4] to RP0 and A[1,3] A[1,4] to RP1. RP0 performs computing on the received samples. When finished, it sends new A[0,2] to CP0 and new A[0,3] to CP1. It also reserves necessary values needed by next computing. RP1 does the same thing. This process is repeated until all samples of the first two rows are processed.

RP0 and RP1 continue to process the samples of next two rows (3rd and 4th). At the time when RP0 finished operation on the first three samples of the 3rd row, CP0 and CP1 have gotten enough samples to start computing (the first three samples of the 1st and 2nd columns - A[0,0]-A[2,0] and A[0,1]-A[2,1]). While CPs are computing, RPs also keep on processing. Hence there comes into being such a great spectacle - row transform and column transform are processed parallelly; operations on different rows are processed simultaneously; operations on different columns are also processed synchronously, as illustrated in Fig. 3. This condition is kept on until RPs have scanned whole image and automatically stop working. But CPs continue processing until all columns are processed.

4   Performance and Implementation

1) Performance analysis: Each RP/CP takes $N/2$ cycles to transform one row. Since there are two RPs and two CPs in FIDP, every processor will process $N/2$ rows/columns in a $N \times N$ 2D DWT. Total time every processor consumes is $N^2/4$. Moreover, the delay between row transform and column transform is $N/2+1$. So the total time required to finish a $N \times N$ 2D DWT is $N^2/4+N/2+1$.

2) Memory requirement analysis: researchers generally take the capacity of the buffer memory between RP and CP to estimate the memory requirement of all kinds of 2D DWT architectures. So the memory requirement of FIDP is the sum of the capacity of the BM($3N+2$) plus the capacity which is used to reserve data for forthcoming computations in CPs($2N$) - $5N+2$.

3) FPGA-based implementation: we developed a Verilog HDL model for FIDP. The memories are simulated as arrays. The datapath is 16 bits wide. The design is simulated with ModelSim V5.5e. The result matches that of the C code exactly. Furthermore, we have synthesized RP module, CP module and whole datapath unit in Altera Quartus II V4.1 considering the Stratix II FPGA family. The estimated operation frequency of whole datapath unit is 145.54MHz. The results of synthesis are listed in Table 1.

Table 1. Results of Implementation for 5/3 filter

	RP Module	CP Module	2×2 array
Size(ALUTs)	243	996	1316
Registers	128	481	466
f_{max}(MHz)	173.55	139.02	145.54

5   Comparison with Other Related Works

We compare our design with several latest presented works [5, 6, 7, 8] in execution time, memory requirement and operation frequency. Table 2 lists the results of the comparison. The columns show the performance, memory requirement, frequency of operation, architecture and design type respectively. In the architecture column, 'P' represents Processor, 'R' represents RP, and 'C' represents CP. The number follow them is the number of corresponding unit. For example, 'R1C1' denotes that there are one RP and one CP in the design.

Table 2. Comparison with related works

Design	Performance	Mem Requirement	Frequency	Architecture	Design Type
1 [6]	N^2	$3N^2/4$	300	P1	ASIC
2 [5]	$3N^2/4+6$	N	100	R1C1	ASIC
3 [7]	$N^2/2+2N+L_s$	4N	200	R2C2	ASIC
4 [8]	$N^2/2+L_s$	5N	67	R1C1	FPGA
FIDP	$\mathbf{N^2/4+N/2+1}$	**5N+2**	**145**	**R2C2**	**FPGA**

Among the five designs, only design [5] adopted Z-scan samples consumption policy, the others are all line-based or the improvement. In design [6], there is only one processor to be used for row transform firstly and then column transform. It does not exploit any parallelisms. So it has the worst performance and the greatest memory requirement. Design [5] is Z-scan architecture which has one RP and one CP. For the reasons we described in Section 2, it has an unsatisfied performance, but its memory requirement is good. It only exploits the 3rd parallelism. In design [7], there are two RPs and two CPs like FIDP. But the two RPs cooperates on the same row - one is used for odd samples and the other for even samples. The operations on the two CPs are the same. As a result, design [7] only take advantage of the 3rd parallelism. Design [8] is implemented on FPGA. It consists of one RP and one CP, so it has the same problem occurs in design [5, 7]. Its performance is $N^2/2+L_s$ where L_s is the system latency. Its estimated frequency is 67MHz compared to our 145MHz.

Only FIDP has exploited three parallelisms of 2D DWT to achieve the highest performance(with a speedup 2 over current fastest design [7, 8]). And also an efficient data reuse policy and efficient memory organization are adopted to reduce memory requirement. The comparison shows that FIDP has the best performance and moderate memory requirements.

6   Conclusions

Existing architectures proposed for 2D DWT have not fully exploited the parallelisms in the algorithm. In this paper, a Fragment-based Interleaving Dual Pipelines(FIDP) architecture is proposed to take advantage of all parallelisms effectively. FIDP takes a new fragment-based samples consumption policy. And the operations on FIDP are organized as interleaving dual pipelines. For a N×N 2D DWT, FIDP takes only $N^2/4+N/2+1$ cycles while maintains $5N+2$ memory requirements. We also develop a FPGA-based implementation for FIDP. The estimated frequency of operation is 145.54MHz.

Acknowledgements

Our work is supported by the National Science Foundation of China under contract # 90307001 and #60633050.

References

1. *JPEG2000 Committee Draft*. Available: http://www.jpeg.org/jpeg2000/CDs15444.html.
2. C.J. Lian. Analysis and architecture design of block-coding engine for ebcot in jpeg2000. *IEEE Transactions on Circuits and Systems for Video Technology*, vol.13, no.3, pp.219-230, 2003.
3. W. Sweldens. The lifting scheme: A construction of second-generation wavelets. *SIAM Journal of Mathematical Analysis*, vol.29, pp.511-546, 1997.
4. K.C.B. Tan. An embedded extension algorithm for the lifting based discrete wavelet transform in jpeg2000. *ICASSP*, vol.4, pp.3513-3516, 2002.
5. J.S. Chiang. Vlsi architecture of low memory and high speed 2-d lifting-based discrete wavelet transform for jpeg2000 applications. *IEEE International Symposium on Circuits and Systems 2005*, vol.5, pp.4554-4557, 2005.
6. K. Zhu. An efficient VLSI implementation of DWT for JPEG2000. *IEEE International Conference on Neural Networks & Signal Processing*, pp.990-993, 2003.
7. K. Andra. A vlsi architecture for lifting-based forward and inverse wavelet transform. *IEEE Transactions on Signal Processing*, vol.50, no.4, pp.966-977, 2002.
8. S. Barua. An efficient architecture for lifting-based two-dimensional discrete wavelet transforms. *Integration, the VLSI Journal*, vol.38, pp.341-352, 2005.

Analysis of Monotonic Responsive Functions for Congestion Control

C. Chen[1], Z.G. Li[2], and Y.C. Soh[1]

[1] Centre for Modeling and Control of Complex Systems, Nanyang Technological University
50 Nanyang Avenue, Singapore 639798
{pg03167863, eycsoh}@ntu.edu.sg
[2] Media Division, Institute for Infocomm Research
21 Heng Mui Keng Terrace, Singapore 119613
ezgli@i2r.a-star.edu.sg

Abstract. The convergence of response functions of memoryless window-based congestion control protocols is analyzed in this paper. All the control schemes (or response functions) is classified into 4 types according to the monotony of their response functions. Sufficient conditions are established for the convergence of Type 1 scheme, which includes most of the existing protocols such as additive-increase multiplicative-decrease (AIMD), generalized AIMD, binomial congestion control (BCC), Choose Your Response Function (CYRF) and so on. Type 4 scheme is not convergent while Type 2 and Type 3 schemes are conditional convergent, and their convergent conditions are derived. Furthermore, the proposed scheme can be made TCP-friendly and TCP-compatible. The proposed scheme can also be used to design multimedia friendly congestion control protocols. Thus the proposed result is very useful for extending the network service to different applications.

1 Introduction

TCP congestion control and avoidance mechanisms have been studied for decades. The additive-increase multiplicative-decrease (AIMD) scheme is the most successful congestion control algorithm, and has been widely deployed in Internet. Jain et al. [1][2] have proved that the AIMD scheme converges to fairness and efficiency under synchronous feedback. The scheme can guarantee the users, who are sharing a bottle-neck link, an equal share of bandwidth while making full use of the available bandwidth. Such a scheme can guarantee fairness and efficiency without any explicit exchanging of information. This is arguably the main reason for the success of TCP.

Recently, many new applications have been deployed over the Internet that includes voice over IP, video conference, video streaming, audio streaming, mission-critical financial data, etc. These applications have different requirements on transport protocol and TCP may not be suitable for these applications [3][4]. For example, for the video streaming application, one requires a smooth transmission rate and cannot tolerate the half-decrease procedure of AIMD and the minimum throughput should be greater than a threshold [5]. These cannot be guaranteed by TCP. Thus there is a need to design new congestion control algorithms to satisfy the demands of these applications.

T.-J. Cham et al. (Eds.): MMM 2007, LNCS 4352, Part II, pp. 383–392, 2007.

To address this problem, we consider the convergence of schemes named monotonic response function (MRF) with the form [5]

$$\text{I:} \quad x_s(k+1) \leftarrow x_s(k) + w_s f\left(\frac{x_s(k)}{w_s}\right), \tag{1}$$

$$\text{D:} \quad x_s(k+1) \leftarrow x_s(k) - w_s g\left(\frac{x_s(k)}{w_s}\right) \tag{2}$$

by a simple fairness index [6]

$$F = \sum_{s=1}^{n} \frac{x_s^2}{w_s^2} - \frac{1}{n}\left(\sum_{s=1}^{n} \frac{x_s}{w_s}\right)^2, \tag{3}$$

where w_s is the weighting factor of flow s.

It is required that $f(x) > 0$, $x \geq g(x) > 0$. This is to guarantee that the I policy always increases the window size and D policy decreases the window size while bounded away from 0 (i.e. there is no negative window size after a D policy). $f(x)$ and $g(x)$ are monotonic functions, and it is required that at least one of $f(x)$ and $g(x)$ is strictly monotonic. Another condition is 1-responsiveness, i.e. $g(x) > f(x)$, thus each D policy will cover the effect of the I policy.

All the congestion control schemes is classified into 4 types according to the monotony of their response functions. The main result is that the Type 1 scheme, where $f(x)$ is a monotonic non-increasing function and $g(x)$ a monotonic nondecreasing function, converges to fairness and efficiency. The convergent conditions of Types 2, 3 and 4 schemes are also studied. Our results include the CYRF and extend 1-CYRF schemes [7]. The proposed scheme can be used to design multimedia friendly congestion control protocols, and these can be helpful when extending the network service for different applications.

The rest of this paper is organized as follow. Preliminary knowledge is provided in Section 2. We classify the control schemes in Section 3. Section 4 contain the convergence results of the 4 types of schemes. Experimental results are presented in Section 5. Finally, several concluding remarks are given in Section 6.

2   Preliminary Knowledge

2.1   Network Model

Similar to [7,5], we only consider the classical memoryless model of source adaptation, and allow only binary feedback, either through packet loss or an ECN-like indication.

Normally, a synchronous feedback assumption is imposed on the network [7,2], i.e., it is assumed that all the flows in the network get the same feedback and get the feedback simultaneously. The feedback is binary and limited to a single bit indicating whether the network is overloaded, i.e. a (1), or if the bandwidth is not fully utilized, i.e. a (0). When an ACK is received and the feedback is 1, the next window size is computed by the policy D. If the feedback is 0, the policy I is used to calculate the next window size.

The capacity of network is treated as a constant. Hence when the sum of window sizes exceeds the constant, an overloaded signal will be sent out.

Besides the feedback signal, it is also assumed that the responsive functions have the following three features:

1. *1-Responsiveness*

   Let Δ_I and Δ_D be the increase and the decrease in window size resulting from a single application of I and D, respectively. A flow is said to be 1-responsive if

   $$|\Delta_I| \leq |\Delta_D|. \tag{4}$$

   In other words, the decrease in window size from a single application of D must at least wipe out the previous increase resulting from the last application of I.

   It can be easily shown that AIMD, GAIMD, BCC, LOG and SIGMOID are 1-responsive [7][8][9]. Thus, in the rest of this paper, unless otherwise stated, the protocols are supposed to be 1-responsive.

2. *Smoothness and Efficiency*

   Smoothness is an important property when video, audio or speech is transmitted over the network [3]. Same as in [7], a window increase (decrease) policy is said to be smooth if the window size increase (decrease) from a single I/D policy is at least an order of magnitude smaller than the current window size, i.e. $|\Delta x| \ll x$.

   Meanwhile, the policies are required to move the total bottleneck link utilization closer to the link capacity. This can be achieved by the principle of negative feedback [2], i.e., each flow increases its window size when the bottle link is underutilized and decreases its window size when it is overloaded.

3. *TCP-Friendly and TCP-Compatibility*

   To guarantee the display quality of video at the receiver side, smooth source adaptation schemes are being widely studied [3]. This type of source adaptation schemes are also required to be TCP-friendly. In this section, necessary and sufficient conditions are provided for a 1-responsiveness function with a smooth increase policy to be TCP-friendly. 1-responsiveness is required since the analysis is highly related to the procedure in steady state.

   Theorem 1. *[5] A smooth 1-responsive flow is TCP-friendly in the steady state if and only if*

   $$\frac{(1 + \dot{f}(\frac{x}{w}))g(\frac{x}{w})}{f(\frac{x}{w})} \propto \frac{x}{w}. \tag{5}$$

   Theorem 2. *[5] A smooth 1-responsive flow is TCP-compatible in the steady state if and only if*

   $$f(\frac{x}{w}) = \frac{3(1 + \dot{f}(\frac{x}{w}))g(\frac{x}{w})}{2\frac{x}{w} - (1 + \dot{f}(\frac{x}{w}))^m g(\frac{x}{w})}. \tag{6}$$

3   Classification of Schemes

We first classify the response functions, i.e. $f(x)$ and $g(x)$, given in equations (1) and (2), according to their monotony under the assumptions that $f(x)$ and $g(x)$ are monotonic functions. The monotony of I/D is divided into the following groups:

- $Group I_1$: $f(x) > 0$ and it is a nonincreasing function.
- $Group I_2$: $f(x) > 0$ and it is an increasing function.
- $Group D_1$: $x \geq g(x) > 0$ and it is a nondecreasing function.
- $Group D_2$: $x \geq g(x) > 0$ and it is a decreasing function.

Table 1. The classification of response functions

$D \downarrow \backslash I \rightarrow$	$GroupI_1$	$GroupI_2$
$GroupD_1$	Type 1	Type 3
$GroupD_2$	Type 2	Type 4

The schemes are then classified into 4 types according to the groups that I and D belong to. They are defined as in Table 1.

Remark 1. For simplicity of classification of Type 1 functions in Table 1, we have included cases where both $f(x)$ and $g(x)$ are not strictly monotonic. However in subsequent analysis, it is required at least one of $f(x)$ and $g(x)$ is strictly monotonic. Thus, the actual Type 1 functions must satisfy the additional condition that at least one of $f(x)$ and $g(x)$ is strictly monotonic.

4   Convergence of Response Functions

It can be shown from (3) that

$$F = \sum_{1 \le i,j \le n, i \ne j} (\frac{x_i}{w_i} - \frac{x_j}{w_j})^2.$$

Clearly, F has the following features:

1. $F \ge 0, \forall x_1, \cdots, x_n$.
2. $F = 0$ when $\frac{x_1}{w_1} = \cdots = \frac{x_n}{w_n}$.

Thus, the fairness index is a kind of Lyapunov function [6].

There are two kinds of method to show the convergence, one is that Lyapunov function is always non-increasing along the whole switching sequence [5], and the other is that Lyapunov function is non-increasing along a sub-sequence of the whole switching sequence [6]. The former will be applied to illustrate the convergence of Type 1 Response Functions, and the latter one will be used to derive the sufficient conditions for the convergence of Types 2 and 3 Response Functions.

4.1   Convergence of Type 1 Response Functions

We shall first provide the following two results on the convergence to fairness (3) [5].

Theorem 3. *(n-flow Fairness Condition) n flows with window sizes $x_i(1 \le i \le n)$, sharing a bottleneck link, will eventually converge to a fair allocation of bottleneck link bandwidth if*

$$\sum_{1 \le i,j \le n, i \ne j} (\frac{x_j}{w_j} - \frac{x_i}{w_i})(\frac{\Delta x_j}{w_j} - \frac{\Delta x_i}{w_i}) \le 0 \qquad (7)$$

is satisfied after each application of policy D or I, and at least one of the two policies ensures a strict inequality condition.

Theorem 4. *Type* 1 *response functions converges to fairness for* $n(> 2)$ *flows.*

Clearly, AIMD, GAIMD, BBC, LOG and SIGMOID are special cases of Type 1 response functions.

4.2   Convergence of Type 4 Response Function

It is easy to see that none of the policies of Type 4 response function satisfies the requirement of Theorem 3, thus the Type 4 Response Function is not convergent.

4.3   Convergence of Types 2 and 3 Response Functions

We now consider the convergence of Types 2 and 3 response functions. Note that it is difficult to analyze such schemes since one of the policies will reduce the fairness. Thus the 1-responsive property is assumed. Under the assumption, the policies will be run with an order $DII \cdots DII \cdots$. The interval between two D's is treated as an *epoch*. Thus if at the end of each epoch, the fairness increases in comparison with that at the beginning of the epoch, the system will approach fairness eventually. We shall study the procedure and derive the convergent conditions of Types 2 and 3 response functions.

For convergence of types 2 and 3 response functions, both $f(x)$ and $g(x)$ are assume to be strictly monotonic. Otherwise, they are not convergent.

In this section, we shall analyze a procedure which contains two users. Suppose that two users start from an arbitrary position $[x_2(0), x_1(0)]$, $(\frac{x_2(0)}{w_2} > \frac{x_1(0)}{w_1})$. If after a series of D/I policies, the fairness index approaches 0, i.e. the window sizes of the two users approach to be the same, then the corresponding response function is convergent.

F-E Transformation. We consider the convergence via the following transformation:

$$\mathbf{f} = \frac{x_1}{w_1} - \frac{x_2}{w_2}, \tag{8}$$

$$\mathbf{e} = x_1 + x_2. \tag{9}$$

The two transformations are linear independent and thus the system's adjustment policies can be written as:

$$[\mathbf{f}(k+1), \mathbf{e}(k+1)] = [\mathbf{f}(k), \mathbf{e}(k)] + [\Delta_f^{\mathbf{f}}(k), \Delta_f^{\mathbf{e}}(k)], \tag{10}$$

$$[\mathbf{f}(k+1), \mathbf{e}(k+1)] = [\mathbf{f}(k), \mathbf{e}(k)] + [\Delta_g^{\mathbf{f}}(k), \Delta_g^{\mathbf{e}}(k)] \tag{11}$$

where $[\Delta_f^{\mathbf{f}}(k), \Delta_f^{\mathbf{e}}(k)]$ and $[\Delta_g^{\mathbf{f}}(k), \Delta_g^{\mathbf{e}}(k)]$ are given as

$$[\Delta_f^{\mathbf{f}}(k), \Delta_f^{\mathbf{e}}(k)] = [f(\frac{x_1(k)}{w_1}) - f(\frac{x_2(k)}{w_2}), w_1 f(\frac{x_1(k)}{w_1}) + w_2 f(\frac{x_2(k)}{w_2})], \tag{12}$$

$$[\Delta_g^{\mathbf{f}}(k), \Delta_g^{\mathbf{e}}(k)] = -[g(\frac{x_1(k)}{w_1}) - g(\frac{x_2(k)}{w_2}), w_1 g(\frac{x_1(k)}{w_1}) + w_2 g(\frac{x_2(k)}{w_2})]. \tag{13}$$

The following propositions can be derived easily.

Proposition 1. *The system approach fairness when **f** approach 0.*

Proposition 2. *The D policy is run when **e** is bigger than a constant.*

Recall that the window increase or decrease policy is smooth, i.e. $|\Delta x| \ll x$. Suppose that the increase policy of a smooth protocol is successively applied two times: $x(k + 1) = x(k) + \Delta x(k)$, $x(k + 2) = x(k + 1) + \Delta x(k + 1)$. Since $|\Delta x(k)| \ll x(k)$ and $|\Delta x(k + 1)| \ll x(k + 1)$, we can write $x(k + 2) \approx x(k) + 2\Delta x(k)$ or in general $x(k + m) \approx x(k) + m\Delta(x(k))$, i.e. $\Delta(x(k + m)) \approx m\Delta(x(k))$ after m successive applications of I. Specifically, in the **f-e** system we have the following lemma.

Lemma 1. *After m successive applications of smooth I, we obtain $\Delta_f^f(k + m) \approx m\Delta_f^f(k)$ and $\Delta_f^e(k + m) \approx m\Delta_f^e(k)$.*

Convergent Conditions. We shall now derive the convergent condition for Type 2 responsive functions. Because of the 1-responsiveness property, the procedure of an epoch should be $DI \cdots ID$. We then have

$$[\mathbf{f}(k + 1), \mathbf{e}(k + 1)] = [\mathbf{f}(k), \mathbf{e}(k)] + [\Delta_g^f(k), \Delta_g^e(k)], \tag{14}$$

and according to Lemma 1, we get

$$[\mathbf{f}(k + m), \mathbf{e}(k + m)] \approx [\mathbf{f}(k + 1), \mathbf{e}(k + 1)] + [m\Delta_f^f(k), m\Delta_f^e(k)].$$

Since in the current epoch, D is the first and the last action, according to proposition 2 and smoothness of the response functions, we have $m\Delta_f^e(k) \approx -\Delta_g^e(k)$. Thus

$$m = \frac{-\Delta_g^e(k)}{\Delta_f^e(k)}.$$

To guarantee the system approaches fairness after each epoch, it requires that $m\Delta_f^f(k) > -\Delta_g^f(k)$.

Thus we have the following theorem:

Theorem 5. *For a Type 2 response function, if it satisfies*

$$\frac{-\Delta_g^e(k)}{\Delta_f^e(k)} > \frac{-\Delta_g^f(k)}{\Delta_f^f(k)}, \tag{15}$$

where Δ is as defined in equations (12) and (13), then the response function approaches fairness by epoch.

By a similar procedure we derive the convergent condition for Type 3 response functions:

Theorem 6. *For a Type 3 response function, if it satisfies*

$$\frac{-\Delta_g^e(k)}{\Delta_f^e(k)} < \frac{-\Delta_g^f(k)}{\Delta_f^f(k)}, \tag{16}$$

where Δ is as defined in equations (12) and (13), then the response function approaches fairness by epoch.

Remark 2. Since $F = \mathbf{f}^2$, condition (15) implies that F is non-increasing in each epoch, i.e. a sub-sequence of switching sequence.

Remark 3. Inequality (15) (or (16)) is equivalent to

$$\sum_{1 \leq i,j \leq 2, i \neq j} (\frac{x_j}{w_j} - \frac{x_i}{w_i})(\frac{\Delta_g^e(k)}{\Delta_f^e(k)}(f(\frac{x_i(k)}{w_i}) - f(\frac{x_j(k)}{w_j})))$$

$$\leq \sum_{1 \leq i,j \leq 2, i \neq j} (\frac{x_j}{w_j} - \frac{x_i}{w_i})(g(\frac{x_j(k)}{w_j}) - g(\frac{x_i(k)}{w_i})). \tag{17}$$

5   Experimental Results

The normal schemes such as AIMD, GAIMD, BCC (IIAD, SQRT) and LOG are type 1 and hence their convergent result are well understood. In this section, we will study the responsive function given as

$$f(x) = \frac{\alpha}{x^k \log(x)}, \tag{18}$$

$$g(x) = \frac{\beta x^l}{\log(x)}. \tag{19}$$

We name the scheme R-LOG (for Reverse-LOG). Two cases are studied with (k, l) set as $(0, 1)$ and $(1, 0)$ as examples of types 1 and 2 responsive functions, respectively.

We implement the proposed scheme in ns-2 simulator by replacing the responsive function of TCP-Reno, thus it inherits other mechanisms such as slow-start and timeout. In our experiments, the standard "dumbbell" topology is used: a single bottle-neck link with RED queue. Several TCP-reno flows run as the background traffic. All the flows start at random time.

5.1   Convergence

Since R-LOG$(0, 1)$ belongs to Type 1, it is convergent. To that prove R-LOG$(1, 0)$ is also convergent, we obtain

$$[\Delta_f^f(k), \Delta_f^e(k)] = [\frac{\sqrt{2}\alpha}{2}(\frac{1}{x_1 \log(x_1)} - \frac{1}{x_2 \log(x_2)}), \frac{\sqrt{2}\alpha}{2}(\frac{1}{x_1 \log(x_1)} + \frac{1}{x_2 \log(x_2)}))],$$

$$[\Delta_g^f(k), \Delta_g^e(k)] = [\frac{-\sqrt{2}\beta}{2}(\frac{1}{\log(x_1)} - \frac{1}{\log(x_2)}), \frac{-\sqrt{2}\beta}{2}(\frac{1}{\log(x_1)} + \frac{1}{\log(x_2)})].$$

It follows that

$$\frac{-\Delta_g^e(k)}{\Delta_f^e(k)} = \frac{x_1 x_2 \log(x_1 x_2)}{\log(x_1^{x_1} x_2^{x_2})} = m, \quad \frac{-\Delta_g^f(k)}{\Delta_f^f(k)} = \frac{x_1 x_2 \log(x_2/x_1)}{\log(x_2^{x_2}/x_1^{x_1})} = m'$$

$$m - m' = \frac{x_1 x_2}{\log(x_1^{x_1} x_2^{x_2}) \log(x_2^{x_2}/x_1^{x_1})} (2 \log(x_1) \log(x_2))(x_2 - x_1) > 0.$$

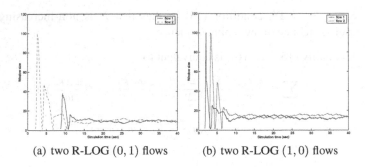

(a) two R-LOG $(0, 1)$ flows   (b) two R-LOG $(1, 0)$ flows

Fig. 1. The Convergence

Thus the condition of Theorem 5 is satisfied, and so R-Log $(1, 0)$ is also convergent. Figures 1(a) and 1(b) show the window sizes of two flows running over a bottle-neck link of the two algorithms, respectively. We can see that the two flows share the link equally and thus it is convergent.

5.2   Comparison with TCP-Reno

In this section, we will study the features of R-LOG when competing with TCP-Reno traffic. Figure 2 shows the window sizes of the competing TCP-Reno and R-LOG. It can be observed that R-LOG$(1, 0)$ has more fluctuations than R-LOG$(0, 1)$ but both have a much smoother window size variation than the TCP-Reno scheme. This is an important advantage since many applications, such as multimedia, prefer smooth traffic.

TCP-Friendly. Here, we only show the proof for R-LOG$(0, 1)$. Similar result can be easily derived for R-LOG$(1, 0)$.

TCP-friendly requires that the throughput of a scheme is inversely proportional to the the square root of the dropping rate. According to the condition for a 1-responsiveness scheme given above, we have

$$\dot{f}(x) = -\frac{\alpha}{x \log^2(x)}.$$

Hence

$$\frac{(1 + \dot{f}(x))g(x)}{f(x)} = \frac{(1 + \frac{\alpha}{x \log^2(x)})\frac{\beta x}{\log(x)}}{\frac{\alpha}{\log(x)}} \approx \frac{\beta}{\alpha}x \propto x.$$

R-LOG is TCP-friendly. This can be seen in Figure 3(a), which shows the dropping rate and the throughput of a TCP-reno and R-LOG scheme under the same environment.

TCP-Compatibility. In this subsection, we will illustrate the choices of α and β to get TCP-compatibility. From equation (6), we have for R-LOG $(0, 1)$

$$\frac{\alpha}{\log(x)} = \frac{3(1 + \dot{f}(x))g(x)}{2x - (1 + \dot{f}(x))^m g(x)} = \frac{3(1 + \frac{\alpha}{x \log^2(x)})\frac{\beta x}{\log(x)}}{2x - (1 + \frac{\alpha}{x \log^2(x)})^m \frac{\beta x}{\log(x)}}$$

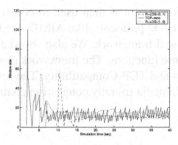

Fig. 2. The window sizes of a TCP-reno and R-LOG scheme

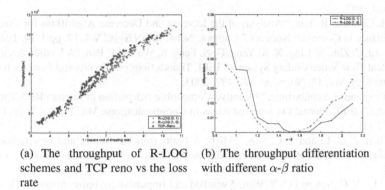

(a) The throughput of R-LOG schemes and TCP reno vs the loss rate

(b) The throughput differentiation with different α-β ratio

Fig. 3. TCP-friendly and TCP-compatibility

$$\frac{\alpha}{\beta} = \frac{3}{2} \frac{1}{\frac{1}{1+\frac{\alpha}{x \log^2(x)}} - \frac{1}{\beta(1+\frac{\alpha}{x \log^2(x)})^{m-1}} \frac{1}{2 \log(x)}}$$

i.e. when $\alpha/\beta \approx 3/2$, the scheme is TCP-Compatible and similar result can be derived for R-LOG $(1, 0)$.

Figure 3(b) shows the *normalized throughput differentiation* with different α-β ratio. The normalized throughput differentiation is defined as

$$d = (\frac{2(T_1 - T_2)}{T_1 + T_2})^2,$$

where T_1 and T_2 are the throughputs of the 2 flows. We can see that the difference of the two flows is the smallest at about $\alpha/\beta = 3/2$. This verifies our theoretical results.

6   Conclusion

In this paper, we have analyzed the convergence of monotonic response functions for congestion control. All the response functions have been classified into 4 types according to the monotony of their response functions. We derived a sufficient condition for the Type 1 response functions and it is then used to construct the desirable increase-decrease policies. Many existing protocols, like AIMD, GAIMD and BCC can be constructed by using the proposed framework. We also showed the convergent conditions for the Types 2 and 3 response functions. The framework also includes a simple method to provide TCP-friendliness and TCP-Compatibility. The results are verified via a case study where a possible multimedia friendly congestion control protocol is designed.

References

1. R. Jain, K. Ramakrishnan and D. Chiu, "Congestion Avoidance in Computer Networks with a Connectionless Network Layer," Tech. Rep. DEC-TR-506, Digital Equipment Corporation, August 1987.
2. D. M. Chiu and R. Jain, "Analysis of the Increase and Decrease Algorithms for Congestion Avoidance in Computer Network," Comput. Netw. ISDN Syst., Vol. 17, pp.1-14, 1989.
3. Z. G. Li, C. Zhu, N. Ling, X. K. Yang, G. N. Feng, S. Wu and F. Pan, "A Unified Architecture for Real Time Video Coding Systems," IEEE Transactions on Circuits and Systems for Video Technology, Vol. 13, No. 6, pp. 472-487, 2003.
4. X. Wang and H. Schulxrinne, "Incentive-Compatible Adaptation of Internet Real-Time Multimedia," IEEE Journal On Selected Areas In Communications, Vol. 23, No. 2, pp.417-436, Feb. 2005.
5. C. Chen, Z. G. Li and Y. C. Soh, "MRF: A Framework for Source and Destination Based Bandwidth Differentiation Service," IEEE/ACM Trans. on Networking, Vol. 15, No. 4, Aug. 2007.
6. Z. G. Li, Y. C. Soh and C. Y. Wen, Switched and Impulsive Systems: Analysis, Design and Application, *Springer-Verlag*. 2005.
7. N. R. Sastry and S. S. Lam, "CYRF: A Theory of Window-Based Unicast Congestion Control," IEEE/ACM Trans. on Networking, Vol. 13, No. 2, pp. 330-342, Dec. 2005.
8. Y. R. Yang and S. S. Lam, "General AIMD Congestion Control," In *IEEE Int. Conf. Network Protocols*, Osaka, Japan, Nov. 2000, pp.187-198.
9. D. Bansal and H. Balakrishnan, "Binomial Congestion Control Algorithms," In *Proc. IEEE INFOCOMM*, Anchorage, AL, April. 2001, pp.631-640.
10. "The Network Simulator - NS-2." [Online]. Available: http://www.isi.edu/nsnam/ns/

A Computational Estimate of the Physical Effort in Human Poses

Yinpeng Chen, Hari Sundaram, and Jodi James

Arts, Media and Engineering Program, Arizona State University, Tempe, AZ, 85281
{yinpeng.chen,hari.sundaram,jodi.james}@asu.edu

Abstract. This paper deals with the problem of estimating the effort required to maintain a static pose by human beings. The problem is important in developing dance summarization and rehabilitation applications. We estimate the human pose effort using two kinds of body constraints – skeletal constraints and gravitational constraints. The extracted features are combined together using SVM regression to estimate the pose effort. We tested our algorithm on 55 dance poses with different annotated efforts with excellent results. Our user studies additionally validate our approach.

1 Instruction

This paper deals with the problem of estimating physical effort for a static human pose using SVM regression. The problem is important in both effective pose classification and dance summarization applications. Human beings routinely are able to distinguish between *human poses that appear to be very similar* by referring to their own physical experience. For example, both pairs of poses in Fig. 1, appear to be very similar (modulo rotation). However it is trivial for human beings to see that the second pose in Fig. 1(a)-(b) is very challenging to do for most people. We conjecture

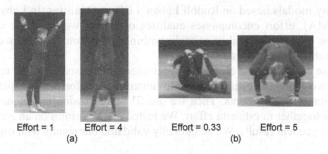

| Effort = 1 | Effort = 4 | Effort = 0.33 | Effort = 5 |
| (a) | | (b) | |

Fig. 1. Two pose pairs with similar appearance and different physical effort

that human beings pay *greater attention* to the poses with greater physical effort, as they are reminded of the difficulty of doing the pose. Note also that the *perception* of effort differs from the *subjective experience* of physical effort. Hence it is extremely

T.-J. Cham et al. (Eds.): MMM 2007, LNCS 4352, Part II, pp. 393–404, 2007.

important to develop ground truth effort estimates using the domain expertise of a trained Laban Movement Analysis expert (one of the authors).

The analysis of physical effort is playing an important role in several emerging multimedia applications – (a) online dance pedagogy and (b) biofeedback for rehabilitation.

online dance pedagogy: With high speed communication networks being available more widely, online dance pedagogy is beginning to complement traditional in-person dance training. Traditional review of dance materials (through video), is linear, and time consuming. Mechanisms that automatically summarize *key movement phrases* and present it in video form would thus be exceedingly useful. Effort based video summarization offers a an effective mechanism to communicate key ideas to the dance students.

biofeedback for rehabilitation: We have been working on developing an experiential media system [2] that integrates task dependent physical therapy and cognitive stimuli within an interactive, multimodal environment. Integrating estimates of physical effort would allow us a much richer understanding of patient rehabilitation.

Fig. 2. Left: multimodal dance, right: multimodal rehabilitation of stroke patients

Pose classification is a traditional computer vision problem [1,3]. However the focus there is appearance based matching or matching in an object based representational space. However, the classification does *not* take into account the physical experience of doing the pose, thus potentially misclassifying poses with different physical effort that appear to be similar. Other related works [6,8] deal with motion quality modals based on Rudolf Laban's Effort Qualities. In Laban Movement Analysis (LMA), effort encompasses qualities of space, weight, time and flow and represents the expressive quality of style within the dynamics of human movement rather than static human poses.

We propose a human pose effort estimation algorithm based on SVM regression. We first extract two kinds of features related to human pose effort: (a) physical constraints and (b) gravitational constraints. Then we use SVM regression techniques to combine these features together to estimate effort. We tested our algorithm on an annotated dance pose set with excellent results. We additionally validated our results with user studies.

2 Pose Representation by 3D Markers

In this section, we discuss the marker based representation of 3D human pose. Each pose consists of 35 labeled 3D marker coordinates captured from a marker-based motion capture system.

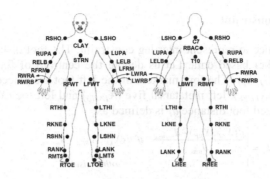

Fig. 3. Positions and labels of 35 markers

A calibrated 3D capture system provides labeled data, specifying the location on the body for each marker. Fig. 3 shows positions and labels of 35 markers. Let us denote the labeled 3D marker coordinates of a pose as $X_i=(x_i,y_i,z_i)^T$, $i=1,...,N$ where N is the number of markers (N=35). In this paper, we also use the marker label as subscript.

3   Features from Physical Constraints

Physical constraints include muscle and skeleton structure which are not related with gravity (e.g. human's torso can not lean backward easily and the two legs can not be split easily). We observe that the physical limitations mainly focus on the joints between limbs. The joint constraint can be represented by the relationship between two connected limbs. We also observe that arm movements in comparison to leg movements have a wider range of motion due to the greater mobility of the shoulder joint. Hence, in this paper, we ignore the physical limitations of shoulder joints and focus on the hip joints. We have used a simple model where the torso and thigh are related through a hip joint.

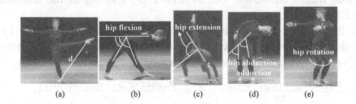

Fig. 4. Five physical constraints. (a) foot distance, (b) hip flexion, (c) hip extension, (d) hip abduction/adduction, and (e) hip rotation.

We use a simple feature, foot distance, to represent inter-leg relationship and four joint angles (1 hip *flexion*, 2 hip *extension*, 3 hip *abduction/adduction* and 4 hip *rotation*) to represent torso-leg relationship. The foot distance and four hip joint angles are shown in Fig. 4. Note that we use torso as the reference when we discuss torso-leg relationship.

3.1 Inter-Leg Constraint

We use foot distance to represent inter-leg constraint. The foot distance can be easily estimated by marker based data. Let us denote the centroid of four markers on the left/right foot as X_{LF}/X_{RF}. The four markers of the left foot are placed on the left ankle (X_{LANK}), left heel (X_{LHEE}), left metatarsal five (X_{LMTS}) and left toe (X_{LTOE}) (see Fig. 3). Thus, the normalized foot distance d_F is defined as:

$$d_F = \begin{cases} \dfrac{d(X_{LF}, X_{RF}) - d_{normal}}{d_{max}} & \text{if } d(X_{LF}, X_{RF}) > d_{normal} \\ 0 & \text{otherwise} \end{cases} \tag{1}$$

where $d(\cdot)$ is L_2 distance metric, d_{normal} is the foot distance when a person stands naturally, and d_{max} is the maximum possible foot distance for the person which equals the sum of lengths of two legs. If foot distance is less than d_{normal}, there is no inter-leg effort ($d_F = 0$). However the overall pose may have other efforts due to other body constraints.

3.2 Torso-Leg Constraints

There are three degrees of freedom (DOFs) in left/right hip joint – (a) *flexion/extension*, (b) *abduction/adduction* and (c) *rotation*. We use three joint angles to represent these three DOFs. The three joint angles between two limbs can be obtained by using three non-co-linear positioned markers on each limb. We selected three markers (X_{C7}, X_{T10}, X_{RBAC}) on the torso, three markers (X_{LBWT}, X_{LTHI}, X_{LKNE}) on the left thigh and three markers (X_{RBWT}, X_{RTHI}, X_{RKNE}) on the right thigh to compute left/right hip joint angles. The details for computing joint angles are found in [4]. We select natural standing pose as the reference whose left/right hip joint angles are zero.

Let us denote θ_{LEF} and θ_{REF} as the left and right hip *flexion/extension* (ref. Fig. 4 (b), (c)). The relationship between torso and left leg (or right leg) is said to be flexion if θ_{LEF} (or θ_{REF}) is positive, else it is extension. Let θ_{LAA} and θ_{RAA} be the left and right hip *abduction/adduction* (ref. Fig. 4 (d)). A positive value means abduction and negative value means adduction. Let us denote θ_{LR} and θ_{RR} as the left and right hip rotation (ref. Fig. 4 (e)).

The hip flexion and hip extension have to be measured separately because hip flexion require less efforts than the extension due to the presence of pelvis-vertebrate joint. The overall hip flexion θ_F and hip extension θ_E can be computed by:

$$\theta_F = \frac{\theta_{LEF} \cdot u(\theta_{LEF}) + \theta_{REF} \cdot u(\theta_{REF})}{2\pi}, \quad \theta_E = \frac{-\theta_{LEF} \cdot u(-\theta_{LEF}) - \theta_{REF} \cdot u(-\theta_{REF})}{2\pi}, \tag{2}$$

where θ_{LEF} and θ_{REF} are left and right hip flexion/extension angles, $u(\cdot)$ is standard step function.

In contrast to hip flexion and extension, we do not distinguish hip abduction and hip adduction and consider them equivalently. This is because hip extension needs more effort than hip flexion whereas the effort difference between hip abduction and hip adduction is small. Hence, the hip abduction/adduction θ_A is defined as follows:

$$\theta_A = \frac{|\theta_{LAA}| + |\theta_{RAA}|}{2\pi}, \tag{3}$$

where θ_{LAA} and θ_{RAA} are left and right hip abduction/adduction angles.

In similar manner to hip abduction/adduction, we combine the left and right hip rotation together to compute the hip rotation as follows:

$$\theta_R = \frac{|\theta_{LR}| + |\theta_{RR}|}{\pi}, \tag{4}$$

where θ_{LR} and θ_{RR} are left and right hip rotation angles. We consider clockwise and anticlockwise rotations equivalently.

4 Features from Gravitational Constraints

In this section, we shall discuss features from gravitational constraints. Gravitational constraints comprise two factors: *limb torque* and *supporting-limb effort*. *First*, we introduce gravity torque of each limb that is related to the effort of the corresponding joint. For instance, the larger the arm gravity torque, the more effort needed to be put on the shoulder. *Second*, we discuss the effort on supporting limbs. Supporting effort of a limb is inversely proportional to supporting power of the limb. For instance, since the hip and the torso have more supporting power than the legs, a sitting pose needs less supporting effort than a standing pose.

4.1 Limb Gravity Torque

In this section, we shall discuss gravity torque computation of three kinds of limbs – *arm*, *leg* and *torso* (see Fig. 5). We compute the limb gravity torque only if the

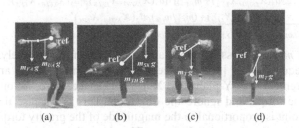

(a)   (b)   (c)   (d)

Fig. 5. Limb gravity torque. (a) arm torque, (b) leg torque, (c) torso torque with respect to hip, (d) torso torque with respect to shoulder.

limb is *not* the supporting limb. This is because limbs in contact with the ground experience a torque due to the normal reaction. This has an effect of canceling the torque of gravity on the limb. Hence effort to support the limb is reduced. Therefore, to determine the total effort required to counter-balance gravitational torque, we need to first determine supporting limbs.

Determining Supporting Limbs

Since we know the label information of markers (ref. Section 2), we can easily determine which limbs are the supporting limbs and obtain the supporting-limb vector. We first classify 35 markers into 10 groups – (1) left hand, (2) right hand, (3) left arm, (4) right arm, (5) left foot, (6) right foot, (7) left leg, (8) right leg, (9) torso and (10) hip. Then, we construct the supporting-limb vector:

$$f_{sf} = [s_{LH}, s_{RH}, s_{LA}, s_{RA}, s_{LF}, s_{RF}, s_{LL}, s_{RL}, s_T, s_H]^T ,$$
(5)

where s_{LH}, s_{RH}, s_{LA}, s_{RA}, s_{LF}, s_{RF}, s_{LL}, s_{RL}, s_T and s_H, are supporting indicator of left hand, right hand, left arm, right arm, left foot, right foot, left leg, right leg, torso and hip respectively. If any element of f_{sf} is positive, it implies that the corresponding limb is the supporting limb and zero implies a non-supporting limb. Computing this vector is a straightforward procedure based on the relationship of the markers to the ground. Each indicator except left and right foot (s_{LF}, s_{RF}) equals 1 if at least one marker on the corresponding limb is close to the ground (Z coordinate is less than threshold ε), otherwise equals 0. s_{LF} or s_{RF} equals 1 if more than two markers on the left/right foot are close to the ground, equals 0.5 if one or two left/right foot markers are close to the ground, otherwise equals 0. We shall show how to compute torque for non-supporting limbs in the rest of this section.

Arm / Leg Gravity Torque

We consider the arm as comprising two solid objects (forearm and upper arm) connected by the elbow joint (ref. Fig. 5 (a)). Arm torque can be easily estimated by using marker positions. Let us denote the left shoulder marker as X_{LSHO}, left elbow marker as X_{LELB}, the centroid of 4 left forearm markers (X_{LELB}, X_{LFRM}, X_{LWRA} and X_{LWRB} in Fig. 3) as X_{LFA}, the centroid of 3 left upper arm markers (X_{LSHO}, X_{LUPA} and X_{LELB}) as X_{LUA}. The left arm gravity torque T_{LA} is:

$$T_{LA} = \frac{m_{UA} \cdot g \cdot d_2(X_{LSHO}, X_{LUA}) + m_{FA} \cdot g \cdot d_2(X_{LSHO}, X_{LFA})}{m_{UA} \cdot g \cdot d_3(X_{LSHO}, X_{LUA}) + m_{FA} \cdot g \cdot [d_3(X_{LSHO}, X_{LELB}) + d_3(X_{LELB}, X_{LFA})]}$$
$$= \frac{d_2(X_{LSHO}, X_{LUA}) + (m_{FA}/m_{UA}) \cdot d_2(X_{LSHO}, X_{LFA})}{d_3(X_{LSHO}, X_{LUA}) + (m_{FA}/m_{UA}) \cdot [d_3(X_{LSHO}, X_{LELB}) + d_3(X_{LELB}, X_{LFA})]} ,$$
(6)

where m_{UA} and m_{FA} are mass of upper arm and forearm respectively, we know the ratio m_{FA}/m_{UA} equals 0.723 [5], g is acceleration of gravity, $d_2(\bullet)$ and $d_3(\bullet)$ are L_2 distance measurement in X-Y plane and X-Y-Z 3D space. Here, we only consider the magnitude of the torque and ignore the direction. This is because the effort on the corresponding joint is proportional to the magnitude of the gravity torque.

The torque in (6) is a normalized torque. The denominator is the maximum torque for arm which equals the torque when the arm is horizontally stretched. In a similar manner, we can also obtain right arm gravity torque T_{RA}. Hence, the overall arm gravity torque is defined as the scalar sum of the two arm torques:

$$T_A = u(s_{LH} + s_{LA}) \cdot T_{LA} + u(s_{RH} + s_{RA}) \cdot T_{RA} ,$$
(7)

where T_{LA} and T_{RA} are left and right arm gravity torque respectively, s_{LH}, s_{LA}, s_{RH}, and s_{RA} are supporting indicators of left hand, left arm, right hand and right arm respectively, $u(\cdot)$ is standard step function. If $s_{LH} + s_{LA} > 0$ which means left arm is supporting limb, left arm torque T_{LA} should be incorporated in effort computation. In the similar manner, we can determine if right arm torque T_{RA} should be considered.

In a similar manner to arm gravity torque computation (ref. equation(6) and (7)), we can compute the left leg gravity torque T_{LL} and right leg gravity torque T_{RL} and overall leg gravity torque T_L (ref. Fig. 5(b)).

Torso Gravity Torque

Computing torso gravity torque (T_T) differs with computing arm or leg torque. If the torso is lying on the floor or if the supporting limbs include both arm and leg, the torso torque equals zero $(T_T=0)$. If the body is supported only using the arms (ref. Fig. 5 (d)), the torso torque is with respect to the shoulder $(T_T = T_{T\text{-}SHO})$. If the body is supported only using legs or the hip (ref. Fig. 5 (c)), the torso torque is with respect to the hip $(T_T = T_{T\text{-}HIP})$. The torso torque with respect to shoulder $(T_{T\text{-}SHO})$ and the torso torque with respect to hip $(T_{T\text{-}HIP})$ can be computed as follows:

$$T_{T\text{-}SHO} = \frac{d_2(X_{SH},X_T)}{d_3(X_{SH},X_T)}, \quad T_{T\text{-}HIP} = \frac{d_2(X_W,X_T)}{d_3(X_W,X_T)}, \tag{8}$$

where X_W is centroid of four waist markers, X_{SH} is centroid of 2 shoulder markers, X_T is the centroid of 5 torso markers.

4.2 Supporting-Limb Effort

We now present an algorithm to compute supporting-limb effort. Intuitively, the human puts effort on the limbs in contact with the ground (supporting limbs) to support the body. This effort is related with the supporting limb power. The supporting limbs with large supporting power will decrease the amount of effort required holding the pose. Therefore, we estimate supporting-limb effort by combining the estimation of all supporting limb power.

Using supporting-limb vector (equation (5)), we can estimate the power of supporting limbs heuristically. The left arm supporting power p_{LA} is computed by:

$$p_{LA} = \begin{cases} s_{LH} \cdot \alpha_{A1}(1+\sin|\theta_{LE} - \frac{\pi}{2}|) & \text{if } s_{LA} = 0 \\ \alpha_{A2} & \text{if } s_{LA} \neq 0 \end{cases}, \tag{9}$$

where s_{LH} and s_{LA} are supporting indicators of left hand and left arm respectively, θ_{LE} is left elbow angle and α_{A1} and α_{A2} are two constant weights $(\alpha_{A1} > \alpha_{A2})$. We consider the supporting using the whole arm and hand supporting separately, since hand supporting has more power than laying the whole arm on the ground. If the left arm lies on the ground $(s_{LA} \neq 0)$, the supporting power is a constant α_{A2}, otherwise the supporting power of the left arm is related with s_{LH} and θ_{LE}. If s_{LH} equals 1 which means that the left hand is in contact with the ground, as the elbow angle θ_{LE} comes close to 90 degrees, the supporting power of the left arm decreases. We can obtain the right arm supporting power p_{RA} in the similar manner.

We can also compute the leg supporting power p_{LL} in the similar manner:

$$p_{LL} = \begin{cases} s_{LF} \cdot \alpha_{L1}(1+\sin|\theta_{LK} - \frac{\pi}{2}|) & \text{if } s_{LL} = 0 \\ \alpha_{L2} & \text{if } s_{LL} \neq 0 \end{cases}, \tag{10}$$

where s_{LF} and s_{LL} are supporting indicators of left foot and left leg respectively, θ_{LK} is left knee angle and α_{L1} and α_{L2} are two constant weights ($\alpha_{L1} > \alpha_{L2}$). We can obtain the right leg supporting power p_{RL} in the similar manner.

The torso support power p_T and hip support power p_H are defined as:

$$p_T = s_T \cdot \alpha_T, \quad p_H = s_H \cdot \alpha_H, \tag{11}$$

where s_T and s_H are supporting indicators corresponding to torso and hip respectively and α_T and α_H are two constant weights. The values of α_{A1}, α_{A2}, α_{L1}, α_{L2}, α_T and α_H are determined by heuristic intuition that torso and hip have more power than legs and legs have more power than arms. Hence we heuristically set $[\alpha_{A1}, \alpha_{A2}, \alpha_{L1}, \alpha_{L2}, \alpha_T, \alpha_H]^T = [0.03, 0.02, 0.25, 0.2, 0.9, 1]^T$.

We postulate that the supporting limb power is additive. Hence, the overall supporting limb power p of a pose is the summation of power of all supporting limbs:

$$p = p_{LA} + p_{RA} + p_{LL} + p_{RL} + p_T + p_H . \tag{12}$$

The supporting limb effort is inversely proportional to the overall supporting limb power p. However, if the overall supporting power of the pose is large enough, the supporting limb effort difference between two poses is very small. Hence, we compute a thresholded supporting effort E_s as follows:

$$E_s = (1 - \frac{p}{\beta}) \cdot u(\beta - p), \tag{13}$$

where p is the overall supporting limb power, β is a predefined threshold and $u(\cdot)$ is standard step function. If p is larger than β, the overall supporting limb effort is zero.

5   Effort Estimation Using SVM Regression

Combining the five physical limitations, three limb torques and supporting-limb effort, we can construct a feature vector for every pose:

$$F = [d_F^\gamma, \theta_F^\gamma, \theta_E^\gamma, \theta_A^\gamma, \theta_R^\gamma, T_A^\gamma, T_L^\gamma, T_T^\gamma, E_s^\gamma]^T, \tag{14}$$

where d_F, θ_F, θ_E, θ_A, θ_R, T_A, T_L, T_T and E_s are foot distance, hip flexion, hip extension, hip abduction/adduction, hip rotation, arm gravity torque, leg gravity torque, torso gravity torque and supporting limb effort respectively, γ is a constant. It is easy to know that as feature (e.g. foot distance) increases, the effort required increases non-linearly. Hence, γ should be larger than 1. In the experiment, we select $\gamma = 1.5$.

In order to estimate the effort by using all extracted features, we use SVM regression [7] to combine all features together. In training phrase, each training pose is represented by a feature vector F (eq(14)) and an annotated effort value which is considered as the ground truth G. The goal of SVM regression is to find a function $g(F)$ that has at most ε deviation from the ground truth G for all the training data, and at the same time is as flat as possible. The function g takes the form:

$$g(F) = K(w, F) + b \text{ with } w \in \Omega, b \in R, \tag{15}$$

where Ω denotes the space of the pose effort feature vector, $K(\cdot, \cdot)$ denotes a kernel operator (e.g. linear, polynomial or rbf (radial basis function)). Flatness in the case of

(15) means that one seeks a small $\|w\|$. The appropriate w and b can be obtained by solving a standard optimization problem [7]. In testing phrase, effort estimation includes two steps: (a) extract feature vector F (eq. (14)) and (b) estimate effort use SVM regression model obtained in training phrase by:

$$E = g(F) = K(w, F) + b \ , \tag{16}$$

where w and b are the solution of SVM regression on the training dataset.

6 Experiments

We test our human effort estimation algorithm on a dance pose dataset which includes 55 annotated poses. Each pose is annotated with an effort value from zero to five by one of the authors who is an expert in dance and kinesiology. Zero means no effort and five means maximum effort for human to hold a pose. She made these annotations when she held these poses by herself. These annotations are made by her real experience rather than through visual impression of the poses (e.g. through watching video of the poses). These 55 poses include 6 levels (0-5), 5 poses for each level (different poses that have the same effort) and 5 variation poses between consecutive levels. This is a fine grained estimation of physical effort by an expert.

In our experiments, we select one pose as testing data and other 54 poses as training dataset and compute leave-one-out cross validation to evaluate our algorithm. With 54 training poses, we can train a SVM regression model and apply it on the testing pose to estimate the effort. We repeat this process until every pose is selected as testing data and its effort estimation value is obtained. Hence, we can compute the difference between estimation value and ground truth to evaluate our algorithm.

6.1 Evaluation

Let us denote the effort ground truth of 55 poses as G_i, $i=1,...,55$, and the effort estimation results obtained by using our algorithm as E_i, $i=1,...55$. Hence, the estimation error is defined as the mean square root error:

$$err = \sqrt{\frac{1}{55} \sum_{i=1}^{55} (E_i - G_i)^2} \ . \tag{17}$$

In this paper, we use the estimation error to evaluate our algorithm, the smaller the error is, the better performance our algorithm has.

6.2 Experiment Results

In our experiments, we try 3 kernels in SVM regression – (a) linear kernel, (b) polynomial kernel and (c) rbf kernel. For each kernel, we adjusted maximum acceptable deviation ε, trade-off constant C and kernel parameter (e.g. the degree of polynomial kernel or the gamma of rbf kernel) to minimize the estimation error. We observe that polynomial kernel is better than both the linear kernel and rbf kernel in our experiments. Using the polynomial kernel, the estimation error is minimized when

$\varepsilon=10^{-7}$, $C=27$ and polynomial power = 2. The mean absolute deviation from ground truth is 0.204. The standard deviation (eq.(17)) is 0.295.

Fig. 6 shows eleven dance poses in increasing order of effort. For each pose, we show the effort ground truth (G) and our estimation result (E). It is easy to observe that our estimation efforts are very close to the ground truth value.

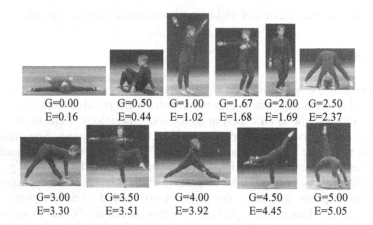

| G=0.00 | G=0.50 | G=1.00 | G=1.67 | G=2.00 | G=2.50 |
| E=0.16 | E=0.44 | E=1.02 | E=1.68 | E=1.69 | E=2.37 |

| G=3.00 | G=3.50 | G=4.00 | G=4.50 | G=5.00 |
| E=3.30 | E=3.51 | E=3.92 | E=4.45 | E=5.05 |

Fig. 6. Effort estimations for 11 dance poses. G is ground truth effort and E is our estimation results.

Fig. 7 plots the ground truth and our estimation efforts for all 55 poses. We can see that estimation efforts are close to the ground truth values for most poses. The maximum deviation larger than the ground truth is $d_1=0.627$ and the maximum deviation less than the ground truth is $d_2=0.873$.

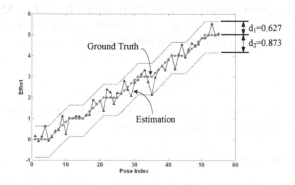

Fig. 7. Comparisons between ground truth and effort estimation for 55 poses

6.3 User Studies

We conducted user studies to determine the relationship between our computational pose effort measure and human perception of the physical experience. A group of 11 subjects with different backgrounds were presented with 50 pairs of pose images that were randomly selected from the 55 annotated poses. They were then asked to determine if the first pose A (on the left) needs more effort than the pose B (on the right). To enable this, we presented the users with seven statements – "pose A needs much more effort than pose B", "… more effort…" etc. The user could only mark one statement to be true. Then we mapped an integer from -3 to 3 to each test pair as *perceptual effort difference* (PED) between two poses. Positive integer means the first pose needs more effort than the second pose and vice versa. Large absolute values of the PED imply greater perceptual effort differences between the poses.

We classified the 550 shape pairs in the user studies into 7 classes based on the PED assigned by users and computed the average *estimate effort difference* (EED) for each class using Eq.(16) (shown in Fig. 8 (a)). The figure shows that our computational effort measure (using EED) is highly correlated with the perception of the effort difference. Fig. 8 (b) shows sensitivity curve. The region above the curve is the differentiable region – i.e. with probability greater than 97%, for poses whose *estimate effort differences* (EED) lie in that region are differentiable by the user. The difference threshold is small for poses with small effort.

The user studies indicate two clear results (a) our estimation of physical effort is correlated with human perception and physical experience, (b) the sensitivity to the effort difference is proportional to the effort of the pose that has larger effort – i.e. *user always compare the pose which has smaller effort with the pose which has larger effort*. Intuitively this means that people can use small pose effort differences to distinguish amongst poses with small effort, and require large differences in effort to tell apart poses with significant effort. As part of our future work, we plan to use effort based techniques to summarize human dance movement.

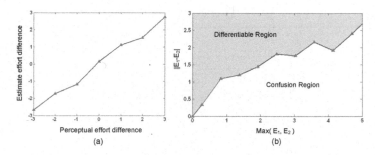

(a) Perceptual effort difference

(b) Max(E_1, E_2)

Fig. 8. Relationship between perceptual effort and our computational effort estimation. (a) EED-PED curve, (b) sensitivity curve showing the differentiable region (dark) and the region of confusion (light). Two poses with pose effort difference in this dark region can be differentiated with high probability.

7 Conclusion

In this paper, we have presented a human pose effort estimation algorithm based on SVM regression. There are two key innovations (a) Using both skeletal constraints and gravity constraints to estimate human pose efforts, (b) Using SVM regression algorithm to combine features for effort estimation. We evaluated our framework on 55 annotated dance poses. Our experimental results are excellent with mean square root error 0.295. In the future, we are planning to incorporate our pose effort framework into pose recognition algorithms. We also planning to incorporate pose effort into dance summarization applications.

References

[1] S. BELONGIE, J. MALIK and J. PUZICHA (2002). *Shape matching and object recognition using shape contexts.* IEEE Transactions on Pattern Analysis and Machine Intelligence **24**(24): 509-522.

[2] Y. CHEN, H. HUANG, W. XU, et al. (2006). *The Design Of A Real-Time, Multimodal Biofeedback System For Stroke Patient Rehabilitation,* SIG ACM Multimedia, Santa Barbara, CA, Oct. 2006.

[3] D. FORSYTH and J. PONCE (2003). Computer vision : a modern approach. Englewood Cliffs, N.J., Prentice Hall: xxv, 693.

[4] H. HUANG and Y. CHEN (2005). *Marker Setup and Parameter computation for biofeedback system.* AME Program, Arizona State University, AME-TR-2005-20, 2005.

[5] K. KAHOL, P. TRIPATHI and S. PANCHANATHAN (2003). *Gesture segmentation in complex motion sequences,* ICIP 2003, Barcelona, Spain, Sept 14-17, 2003.

[6] R. LABAN (1971). The Mastery of Movement. Boston, Plays.

[7] A. J. SMOLA and B. SCHOLKOPF (2004). *A tutorial on support vector regression.* Statistics and Computing **14**: 199-222.

[8] L. ZHAO and N. I. BADLER (2005). *Acquiring and validating motion qualities from live limb gestures.* Graphical Models **67**(1): 1-16.

A Matching-Based Approach for Human Motion Analysis

Weilun Lao[1], Jungong Han[1], and Peter H.N. de With[1,2]

[1]Eindhoven University of Technology
P.O. Box 513, 5600MB Eindhoven
The Netherlands
[2]LogicaCMG Netherlands
P.O. Box 7089, 5600JB Eindhoven
The Netherlands
{w.lao, jg.han, P.H.N.de.With}@tue.nl

Abstract. This paper presents a novel approach to implement estimation and recognition of human motion from uncalibrated monocular video sequences. As it is difficult to find a good motion description for humans, we propose a matching scheme based on a *local descriptor* and a *global descriptor*, to detect individual body parts and analyze the shape of the whole body as well. In a frame-by-frame process, both descriptors are combined to implement the matching of the motion pattern and the body orientation. Moreover, we have added a novel spatial-temporal cost factor in the matching scheme which aims at increasing the temporal consistency and reliability of the description. We tested the algorithms on the CMU MoBo database with promising results. The method achieves the motion-type recognition and body-orientation classification at the accuracy of 95% and 98%, respectively. The system can be utilized for an effective human-motion analysis from a monocular video.

1 Introduction

Human beings can estimate and recognize human motions with high accuracy and robustness. To simulate this capability, efforts have been taken using various algorithms [1,2] with encouraging results. Successful estimation of the pose and motion type of people would allow the semantic analysis of human activities in video sequences. This process is very important and useful in various applications such as surveillance, human computer interaction, virtual reality and content-based video database query and retrieval.

Some research has been done to address the problem of effective human-motion analysis from uncalibrated monocular video sequence. There are two different approaches: appearance-based and body-part-based methods. Appearance-based approaches make use of the configuration of the whole body instead of specific body parts. In literature [3], specific static and stride parameters are used to perform motion recognition. Hidden Markov Models (HMM) can be used to perform the task of gait-based identification when the appearance of different shapes is

T.-J. Cham et al. (Eds.): MMM 2007, LNCS 4352, Part II, pp. 405–414, 2007.
© Springer-Verlag Berlin Heidelberg 2007

learned as an initial distribution [4]. The appearance-based approaches can simplify the estimation and collection of training data since detailed labeling of the body components is not required. However, appearance-based techniques are significantly affected by the body postures and the camera viewpoint. For example, they cannot effectively distinguish the sequence captured from the front and the back of the person as their appearances are very similar to each other.

For the body-part-based approaches [5,6,7], different body parts (face, torso, the limbs, etc.) are located for detecting the person, using different features. The geometric configuration of each body part is modeled prior to performing the pose estimation of the whole human body. In other words, the estimation of the body-part positions can be used to interpret a person's pose and activity. These component-based approaches extract some elements of the body which guide the whole-body tracker. Then, a human activity can be represented as a collection of body parts moving in a specific pattern. However, the highly accurate detection of body parts remains a challenging problem due to the variances of pose and clothing.

The core of our method is a technique for matching an object in a data set, which is measured by investigating the similarity of body components and the silhouette. In this paper, we use a novel representation for the body parts and body shape, referred to as *local descriptor* and *global descriptor*, in order to facilitate the motion analysis in a robust way. Having a query frame, the combination of body parts and the body appearance is an effective aid for searching of the corresponding labeled frame in the data set. This combination guarantees a successful match, even if the detected contour of foreground objects is not precisely known. After this, the human-motion analysis related to a specific query sequence can be obtained. Furthermore, although not discussed explicitly in this paper, our scheme can successfully infer the pose, sometimes even when partial self-occlusion occurs. This improvement is important for potential applications like surveillance, when both the motion type and the specific orientation are required.

To solve the challenging problem of accurately analyzing human motion from uncalibrated video sequences, our contributions lie in two aspects. First, we propose a novel matching scheme to implement motion recognition, based on a weighted linear combination of local and global descriptors for a detected person. The properties of the query frame can be obtained after its labeled matching frame in the data set is retrieved. The other advantage involved is that we have employed a simple but effective spatial-temporal matching scheme. It can discriminate cyclic motions when spatial features are not sufficient. As a whole, our approach captures the human motion and analyzes its activity classification, which are essential for object/scene analysis and behavior modeling of deformable objects. Such scene analysis at the semantic level can be explored for specific applications, such as surveillance, tennis sports analysis and 3D gaming.

The structure of this paper is as follows. We briefly introduce every step involved in the algorithms in Section 2. Section 3 introduces our proposed matching functions. Local and global descriptors and spatial-temporal matching approaches are explained in detail. Promising experimental results are presented in Section 4. Finally, Section 5 dicusses conclusions and future work.

2   Algorithm Overview

The top-down block diagram of our proposed algorithm is depicted in Figure 1, which contains four different steps. First, at the pre-processing step, each image covering an individual body is segmented to extract the blob representing foreground objects. The detected blobs are refined to produce a human silhouette afterwards. Second, at the modeling step, we implement the body-part detection, referred to as a set of local descriptors. For the shape-based analysis, we define a global descriptor. In our scheme, the similarity of different shapes plays an important role. Both the local descriptors and global descriptor are combined to implement a matching scheme. Every input frame is tested to find its corresponding human-motion image in the prerecorded data set. Then, a spatial-temporal cost function is proposed to distinguish different motion patterns of cyclic motion. Next, the outcome of modeling module is fed into the semantics module for further analysis. It can implement motion classification associated with the data set. The above techniques can be applied to a specific application. For example, the geometry/motion information of the reconstructed 3-D model is essential for tennis-sports performance analysis. The players and coaches can benefit from the video-based performance analysis to improve their training. The technical details involved at all the steps are described in the following section.

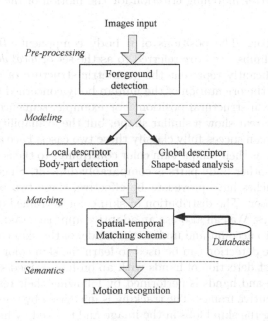

Fig. 1. The block diagram of our proposed algorithm

3   Matching Function for Body-Motion Estimation

3.1   Foreground Object Detection

As the first step, the foreground objects are detected employing background subtraction. This general approach can be used to segment moving objects in a scene assuming that the camera is stationary and the lighting condition is fixed. First, we store the image of the background $I_{bg}(x, y)$, as a reference image, without the foreground object. Then, given an original image $I_{ori}(x, y)$ from a particular sequence, feature detection of moving objects is performed within that image, but is restricted to areas where $||I_{ori}(x, y) - I_{bg}(x, y)|| > \delta$. Parameter δ is an adaptively chosen difference threshold. During experiments, we have found usually distorted and split blobs, which are still corresponding to the same person. To improve the blob segmentation, we perform a few iterations of morphological operations. Moreover, shadows cast on the background can be erroneously labeled as foreground. The shadow-removing approach of [8] is used in our scheme. The false segmentation caused by shadows can be minimized by computing differences in a color space that is less sensitive to intensity changes.

3.2   Local Descriptor and Global Descriptor

After the human silhouette is available, we propose a new hierarchical approach to describe the human motion. We design several local descriptors for relevant human body parts and a global descriptor for the body shape. This representation enables a better matching criterion for the motion of the complete human body.

Local Descriptor. The positions of n body components $B = (b^1, b^2, ...b^n)$ (like face, torso, limbs, etc.) are referred to as the set of *local descriptors*. These descriptors significantly represent the geometric structure of a particular person. Afterwards, the orientation of the human body concerned can be estimated based on its known structural position. For example, sequences captured from the front and the rear show a similar shape, but the availability and location of the person's face can successfully classify these two cases. Face and hands can be reliably detected, as their unique skin color contributes to the accurate detection. The detection of other body parts is comparably difficult. Since the color-based detection approaches have proved to be effective, these two body components are currently chosen. The distribution of skin color is trained off-line on a large database of images. We can also use an adaptive approach taking different lighting conditions into account and update the model of the skin color continuously. Additionally, face detection can be used to learn the skin color and obtain more precise and robust detection of hands with an on-line trained skin model. Next, tracking the face and hands is performed by following their respective detected blobs over consecutive frames. The tracking is initialized by the size and position of the blobs using the skin blobs in the image and tracked by finding the nearest blob in the next frame. During occlusion with two hands (when crossing each other), left and right hand share the same blob until they split again. During occlusion with the body, the last detected position of a hand blob is maintained until a new blob re-appears close to this position and is assigned to the lost hand. For each frame in the sequence, the detected positions of the face and hands are represented as the normalized coordinates in the bounding box fitting to the detected human silhouette. If the face/hands are not detected, their coordinates are set to zero. Finally, for every frame l, we denote the position of the detected body component j as b_l^j. In our current work, $j \in \{1, 2, 3\}$, as only the face and two hands are the detection targets. Evidently, more body components can be incorporated in the scheme.

Global Descriptor. In addition to the detection of body components, we develop a shape-based *global descriptor*, based on the feature of shape contexts (SCs) [9]. This feature proves to be an effective tool for analyzing a particular shape. SCs are based on representing a shape by a set of sample points from the internal and external contours of an object, which are found by an edge detector (e.g. Canny detector). Suppose the shape of a detected body is represented as a set of n points $S_p = \{p_1, p_2, ..., p_n\}$, sampled from the internal and external contours of the shape. We use bins that are uniform in log-polar space, making the descriptor more sensitive to positions of sample points with smaller radius than to sample points farther away. For each point p_i on the shape, we compute a histogram h_i of the relative coordinates of all the remaining $n - 1$ points in S_p (these remaining points are in the set S_r, hence S_r excludes p_i). Taking p_i as the center point, we divide the space around p_i in a log-polar scale and define histogram bins on this grid accordingly. Then we count the number of points from S_r that are enclosed in each bin[9]. The number of points in each bin is the outcome of the function histogram $h_i(k)$, where k denotes the bin number. The histogram $h_i(k)$ is called the *shape context* of the point p_i. Similarly, we can calculate the shape context of every point q_i on the query shape with a set of points $S_q = \{q_1, q_2, ..., q_n\}$. Based on the shape contexts for all the points p_i and q_i, we can measure the similarity between the shape S_p and the shape S_q. Let $d(S_p, S_q) = \sum_i d(p_i, q_i)$ denote the distance between these two shapes, then this distance can be calculated by

$$d(S_p, S_q) = \sum_{i=1}^{n} d(p_i, q_i) = \frac{1}{2} \sum_{i=1}^{n} \sum_{k=1}^{K} \frac{[h_i(k) - h_i'(k)]^2}{h_i(k) + h_i'(k)} , \qquad (1)$$

where n represents the number of sampled points on the shape, $h_i(k)$ and $h_i'(k)$ denote the K-bin normalized histogram of p_i and q_i, respectively. The above concept allows us to formulate our matching of a test (query) frame to a reference frame. In essence, the proposed global descriptor intends to investigate the similarity between the shape of a given person and its matching shape in the data set. It embeds both the external contour and internal contour of the shape and attempts to derive more information about the shape description.

3.3   Matching Using Local and Global Descriptors

After the local descriptor and global descriptor for a detected person in the frame are available, we combine them to produce a distance metric as shown in Equation (2) for matching. The estimation based on this metric aims at finding the optimal match between the query frame and its corresponding frame in the data set. The distance for matching one image to another is defined as a sum of two terms. The first term measures the relative spatial similarity in the detected body structure, and the second one measures the shape similarity in the two frames. Given a query frame l, now we can find its matching frame m in the data set for which the following function is minimal, hence

$$\arg\min_m w_{local} * \left(\sum_{j=1}^{ncom} w_j \|b_l^j - b_m^j\|^2 \right) + w_{global} * d(S_l, S_m) , \qquad (2)$$

where w_{local} and w_{global} are the weighting parameters for local descriptor and global descriptor, respectively. Parameter $d(S_l, S_m)$ represents the distance between the shape S_l and S_m, $ncom$ denotes the number of body components for detection, w_j is the scalar weighting factor for different detected body parts and $\|b_l^j - b_m^j\|^2$ denotes the distance of those body parts between two frames. From Equations (1)-(2), we are able to find the matching frame m. Then the key properties (motion type, orientation, etc.) of the query frame l are estimated from the labeled reference frame m. To improve the analysis accuracy, a temporal consistency can be enforced. For example, if more than half of the frames in a test sequence belongs to a particular motion type T, the whole sequence is labeled accordingly.

3.4   Spatial-temporal Matching for Cyclic Motion

In some classification cases, e.g. to distinguish a walking person carrying a subject from a normal walking person, only the spatial information is sufficient for classification. The combination of both local and global descriptors of a shape is applicable in such case. However, when the temporal information is essential, an elegantly designed spatial-temporal matching scheme is necessary. For example, to distinguish fast walking from slow walking, the temporal consistency should be considered. For this reason, we propose an approach that exploits motion dynamics and yet enforces temporal consistency.

Figure 2 shows the connectivity of different nodes, where each node represents a frame in a reference video sequence including a cyclic human motion. Suppose a cycle of motion (like walking) in the data set is composed of N frames in a reference set $F = (F_1, F_2, ..., F_N)$. We define in advance a so-called state-transition cost $C_{a,b}$, where a and b represent the (time-)index of the frames stored in the data set F (for simplicity, we have left out the frames F in the subscript to obtain a simplified notation and to avoid double subscripts). The value of $C_{a,b}$ depends on a distance metric between the ath frame and the bth frame. We propose to use a simple cost function, like the difference between the index numbers, hence $C_{a,b} = b - a$ for $b \geq a$ and $C_{a,b} = 0$ for $b < a$. In the data set F, it should be noted that the Nth frame is followed by the first frame of the second cycle of the cyclic motion. Given a particular test sequence F' with N' frames, the matching is performed as explained in Section 3.2 on a frame-by-frame basis. After the matching, we obtain a set of shape-matching indexes $I = (I_1, I_2, ..., I_{N'})$ for every test frame F'_a with $1 \leq a \leq N'$, which is exactly the corresponding index of the frame in the data set F. For example, if the first test frame F'_1 is matched with the reference frame F_5, we obtain $I_1 = 5$.

Let us now distinguish between various motion patterns by computing the most probable class (e.g. motion type) for the test sequence. This class can be found by calculating the total path cost in the test sequence

$$C_{N'} = \sum_{l=2}^{N'} C_{I_{l-1}, I_l} \,, \tag{3}$$

where C_{I_{l-1}, I_l} indicates the path cost from the test frame F'_{l-1} to F'_l. In this way, the total cost $C_{N'}$ is used to classify different motion types.

Let us illustrate this classification with an example. Suppose we have a reference sequence of a motion cycle containing 30 frames for a slowly walking person. Given a test sequence with 10 frames which can be matched to the reference frame in the index order $\{5, 8, 11, ..., 28, 1, 4\}$, the path cost C_{10} can be calculated by $C_{10} = C_{5,8} + C_{8,11} + ... + C_{28,1} + C_{1,4}$. Since all frame index differences are 3, the result of this example gives $C_{N'} = 30$. Finally, with this result, we estimate the motion type (fast or slow walking) of the test sequence F' by comparing it to the cost for the reference sequences.

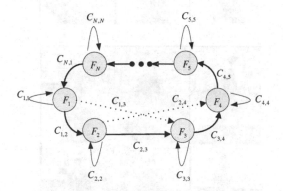

Fig. 2. Computation path for the classification of a cyclic motion

4   Experimental Results

We have tested the presented algorithms on the CMU MoBo database. This database contains a number of video sequences, which contain various subjects performing different types of motion on a treadmill. For each subject, the

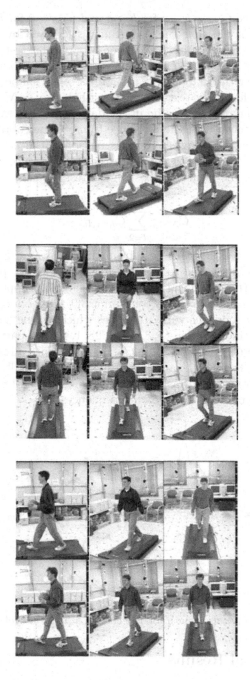

Fig. 3. Examples of the retrieved images after the matching

database provides six sets of video sequences collected by six stationary cameras from different viewpoints. In our experiment, we selected the sequences of one subject (number 04006), each sequence being 30 frames (frames numbered 400-429) in length. For the data set, we selected from the aforementioned preselected sequences, the sequences with three types of motion (slow walk, fast walk, walking with a ball). For each motion type, five different sequences were used, covering five different viewpoints (vr03_7, vr05_7, vr07_7, vr13_7 and vr17_7). Thus, 15 sequences were contained in the data set. For testing, three other subjects (numbers 04022/04037/04068) were chosen to provide 60 test sequences. Every test sequence is 1 second long, recorded at 30 frames/s.

Using the techniques described in Section 3, we processed the sequences to evaluate our proposed method. First, the face and hands are detected and the shape context of the human silhouette is calculated for every frame in the data set to provide reference data. Afterwards, we input the test sequences to the system and implement the matching function driven by both local and global descriptors. After every frame is matched to a corresponding one in the data set, the type of the motion and body orientation can be labeled accordingly. Some examples of the matching frames are shown in Figure 3. The 1st, 3rd and 5th rows of images are from test sequences. The 2nd, 4th and 6th rows of images are from the data set. Moreover, the motion-type and orientation classification results are summarized in Table 1. It shows that we achieve the activity classification and body-orientation classification at the accuracy of 96% and 98%, respectively. These results indicate that our proposed approach is reasonably accurate.

Table 1. Recognition results on the CMU database

Motion type	Number of sequences	Motion recognition errors	Body-orientation recognition errors
Fast walk	20	2	0
Slow walk	20	1	0
Ball	20	0	1
Total	60	3	1

5   Conclusions and Future Work

This paper has presented a matching-based approach for the human motion analysis from a monocular video. The whole process detects the human motion, classifies the motion types and detects the body orientation. We have introduced a novel matching scheme to implement motion recognition based on a combination of local and global descriptors for detecting a moving human body. The local descriptors refer to body parts where we basically use the hands and the face. We applied a simple skin-color detection and prior knowledge about most likely positions to identify the hands and the face. The global descriptor is based on sample points along the contour of the human body. We have adopted the concept of shape contexts to derive histograms where sample points occur in the image. The histograms are used for matching a query sequence with the human motion in a data set. We have defined a matching function that is based on the accumulated Euclidean distances of the body parts and the global difference between the shape histograms of the global descriptor.

We have also defined a spatial-temporal matching function to distinguish query motion cycles in human motion and match those to already stored sequences in a data set. We have shown that a simple cost function based on the differences between time indexes of video frames within a sequence can be used to distinguish motion patterns. Our approach was evaluated and showed a good effectiveness, as it implements the activity classification and orientation classification at the accuracy of 96% and 98%, respectively, in the CMU MoBo database.

We are currently working on a faster matching method, as well as the collecting and labeling more training sets with a large variety of poses and activities. The presented work should finally lead to the object/scene analysis and behavior modeling of deformable objects.

References

1. Moeslund, T.B., Granum, E.: A Survey of Computer Vision-Based Human Motion Capture. Computer Vision and Image Understanding, Vol. 81 (2001) 231–268
2. Wang, L., Hu, W., Tan, T.: Recent Development in Human Motion Analysis, Pattern Recognition, Vol. 36 (2003) 585–601
3. Bobick, A. and Johnson, A.: Gait Recognition Using Static Activity-Specific Parameters, Proc. Conf. Computer Vision and Pattern Recognition, Vol. 1 (2001) 423–430
4. Wang, L., Ning, H., Hu, W. and Tan, T.: Gait Recognition Based on Procrustes Shape Analysis, Proc. *IEEE* Conf. Image Processing, Vol. 3 (2002) 24–28
5. Haritaoglu, I., Harwood, D. and Davis, L.: W4: Real-Time Surveillance of People and Their Activities, *IEEE* Trans. Pattern Analysis and Machine Intelligence, Vol. 22, No. 8 (2000) 809–830
6. Ioffe, S. and Forsyth, D.A.: Probabilistic Methods for Finding People, Int'l J. Computer Vision, Vol. 43, No. 1 (2001) 45–68
7. Lee, M.W. and Malik, J.: A Model-Based Approach for Estimating Human 3D Poses in Static Images, *IEEE* Trans. Pattern Analysis and Machine Intelligence, Vol. 28, No. 6 (2006) 905–916
8. McKenna, S.J., Jabri, S., Duric, Z. and Wechsler, H.: Tracking Interacting People, Proc. *IEEE* Conf. Automatic Face and Gesture recognition (2000) 348–353
9. Belongie, S., Malik, J. and Puzicha, J.: Shape Matching and Object Recognition Using Shape Contexts, *IEEE* Trans. Pattern Analysis and Machine Intelligence, Vol. 24, No. 24 (2002) 509–522
10. Shi, J., Gross, R.: The CMU Motion of Body (MoBo) Database, Technical Report CMU-RI-TR-01-18, Robotics Institute, Carnegie Mellon University (2001)

Face Recognition Using Kernel Uncorrelated Discriminant Analysis

Licheng Jiao, Rui Hu, Weida Zhou, and Yi Gao

Institute of Intelligent Information Processing
And National Key Laboratory for Radar Signal Processing
Xidian University, Xi'an 710071, China
lchjiao@mail.xidian.edu.cn

Abstract. Feature extraction is one of the most important problems in face recognition task. In this paper, we use kernel uncorrelated discriminant analysis to extract the optimal discriminant features for face recognition. The method also solves the so-called "Small Sample Size" (SSS) problem, which exists in most Face Recognition tasks. Experimental results on the Yale face database and AT&T face database show the effectiveness of this method.

1 Introduction

Face recognition is an active research area in the field of computer pattern recognition. The research work on face recognition is composed of three main problems: segmentation, feature extraction, and recognition. Compared to other pattern recognition problems, face recognition is much more difficult, because there are always various changes in face images such as view point, illumination, facial expression conditions and so on. So extracting efficient features of face images becomes very important to face recognition systems.

Principal component analysis (PCA) and linear discriminant analysis (LDA) are two of the most commonly used methods for feature extraction, which can effectively reduce the number of features. The idea of PCA is to generate a set of orthogonal vectors by maximizing the variance overall the samples, while linear discriminant analysis seeks to find the direction which maximizes between-class scatter and minimizes the within-class scatter. Foley and Sammon [1] proposed optimal discriminant vectors. Uncorrelated linear discriminant analysis (ULDA) first proposed by Jin et al. [2] is proved to be more powerful than that of Foley-Sammon optimal discriminant vectors. Ye et al. [3] presented an efficient algorithm to compute the optimal discriminant vectors of ULDA and at the same time addressed the SSS problem of ULDA. Recently, Liang and Shi [5] generalized the ULDA approach for extracting nonlinear features via the kernel trick and proposed the kernel uncorrelated discriminant analysis (KUDA). However this method can not solves the so-called "small sample size" (SSS) problem, which exists in most Face Recognition tasks. In this paper, we use the Kernel Uncorrelated Discriminant Analysis solved by Generalized Singular Value Decomposition (KUDA/GSVD), which can be used regardless the singularity of the scatter matrixes [7], to extract the features for face

T.-J. Cham et al. (Eds.): MMM 2007, LNCS 4352, Part II, pp. 415–422, 2006.

recognition tasks. The method has been tested in terms of classification, on the AT&T face database and the YALE face database. Experimental results show the effectiveness of this method.

The remainder of this paper is organized as following: We briefly recall uncorrelated discriminant vectors and kernel discriminant vectors in section 2. Kernel Uncorrelated Discriminant Analysis using Generalized Singular Value Decomposition (KUDA/GSVD) are stated in section 3. The effectiveness of KUDA/GSVD for face recognition is shown by YALE face database and AT&T face database in section 4. And some concluding remarks are given in the last section.

2 Kernel Uncorrelated Discriminant Vector

Uncorrelated linear discriminant analysis (ULDA) [2] [3] [4] was proposed for feature extraction. The feature vectors transformed by ULDA were shown to be statistically uncorrelated, which is a desirable property for many applications. ULDA aims to find the optimal discriminant vectors that are S_t-orthogonal (Two vectors x and y are S_t-orthogonal means that $x^T S_t y = 0$).

For convenience, Table 1 lists the important notations used in the following parts of this paper.

Table 1. Notations

Notations	Descriptions
N	Number of data
n	Dimension of the original data
c	Number of the classes
N_l	Number of data in the lth class
G	Transformation matrix
S_b	Between-class scatter matrix
S_w	Within-class scatter matrix
S_t	Total-class scatter matrix

Recently some nonlinear extension of ULDA based on kernel function (KUDA) has been proposed, Liang and Shi [5] has proposed a kernel uncorrelated discriminant analysis method using eigenvalue decomposition method. According to Liang and Shi, the optimal discriminant vectors of KUDA can be generated as follows: Let S_b^F, S_w^F, and S_t^F represent the between-class scatter matrix, the within-class scatter matrix, and total-class scatter matrix respectively, after projecting the features into a new feature space F, the Fisher criterion in F is $J(\omega) = \omega^T S_b^F \omega / \omega^T S_w^F \omega$. The first discriminant vector ω_1 is the eigenvector that maximizing the criterion $J(\omega)$. The

$(r+1)$th optimal discriminant vector ω_{r+1} is the eigenvector that maximizing the criterion $J(\omega)$ under the statistically uncorrelated constraints: $x^T S_t y = 0 (i = 1, \cdots, r)$. By using kernel trick the Fisher criterion in F can be written as $J(\alpha) = \alpha^T S_b^F \alpha / \alpha^T S_w^F \alpha$, where $S_b^F = KWK$, $S_w^F = K(I_N - W)K$, $S_t^F = KK$, K is an $N \times N$ kernel matrix, I_N is the $N \times N$ identity matrix, and $W = diag(w_1, \cdots w_i, \cdots, w_c)$, c is the number of categories, w_i is a $N_l \times N_l$ matrix with all terms equal to $1/N_l$. Assume that $\alpha_1, \cdots, \alpha_r$ are obtained, then the $(r+1)$th pseudodiscriminant vector, denoted by α_{r+1}, is the eigenvector corresponding to the largest eigenvalue of the eigenequation $PS_b^F \alpha = \lambda S_w^F \alpha$, where $P = I_N - S_t^F D^T (DS_t^F (S_w^F)^{-1} S_t^F D^T)^{-1} DS_t^F (S_w^F)^{-1}$, $D = [\alpha_1, \cdots, \alpha_r]^T$.

3 Kernel Uncorrelated Discriminant Analysis Using Generalized Singular Value Decomposition

During the last section, Liang and Shi [5] provide an efficient way to compute optimal discriminant vectors for KUDA. However, this method is not available when S_w^F or S_t^F is singular namely the "Small Sample Size" (SSS) problem, which exists in most face recognition tasks. In Zheng's paper [6], a subspace based method is presented to solve the singularity problem. In this paper, we use the Kernel Uncorrelated Discriminant Analysis solved by Generalized Singular Value Decomposition (KUDA/GSVD), which can be used regardless the singularity of the scatter matrixes [7], to extract the features for face recognition tasks.

According to Ye [3] we can draw the following conclusion that features from Eq. (1) are linear uncorrelated

$$G = \arg \max_{G \in R^{p \times t} : G^T S_t^F G = I_t} (trace(G^T S_w^F G)^{-1} G^T S_b^F G) \qquad (1)$$

since $\mathbf{S}_t^F = \mathbf{S}_w^F + \mathbf{S}_b^F$, the problem above is equivalent to

$$G = \arg \max_{G \in R^{p \times t} : G^T S_t^F G = I_t} (trace(G^T S_t^F G)^{-1} G^T S_b^F G) \qquad (2)$$

where $S_b^F = KWK$, $S_w^F = K(I_N - W)K$, K is an $N \times N$ kernel matrix, I_N is the $N \times N$ identity matrix, and W is a $N \times N$ matrix, $W = diag(w_1, \cdots w_i, \cdots, w_c)$, w_i is a $N_l \times N_l$ matrix with all terms equal to $1/N_l$, so W can be decomposed into $W = ww^T$. In this case,

$$S_b^F = K w w^T K = K_b (K_b)^T$$
$$S_w^F = K(I-W)(K(I-W))^T = K_w (K_w)^T \qquad (3)$$
$$S_t^F = K_t K_t$$

Let the SVD of K_t be in the following:

$$K_t = U \Sigma V^T \qquad (4)$$

where K_t is defined in Eq. (3), U and V are orthogonal, $\Sigma = \begin{pmatrix} \Sigma_t^2 & 0 \\ 0 & 0 \end{pmatrix}$, $\Sigma_t \in R^{t \times t}$ is

diagonal, and $t = rank(S_t^F)$.

As in Ye [3] there are two lemmas, to compute the optimization problem in equation (2). Here we extend those lemmas into the following forms, which can be used in KUDA/GSVD.

For S_b^F, S_w^F and S_t^F, there exists a nonsingular matrix $X \in R^{N \times N}$ such that:

$$X^T S_b^F X = X^T H_b H_b^T X = D_1 = diag(\alpha_1^2, \cdots, \alpha_t^2, 0, \cdots 0)$$
$$X^T S_w^F X = X^T H_w H_w^T X = D_2 = diag(\beta_1^2, \cdots, \beta_t^2, 0, \cdots 0)$$

where $1 \ge \alpha_1 \ge \cdots \ge \alpha_q > 0 = \alpha_{q+1} = \cdots \alpha_t, 0 \le \beta_1 \le \cdots \le \beta_t \le 1$,

$D_1 + D_2 = \begin{pmatrix} I_t & 0 \\ 0 & 0 \end{pmatrix}$, $q = rank(S_b^F)$, H_b and H_w are defined in Eq.(3),

and $X = U \begin{pmatrix} \Sigma_t^{-1} & 0 \\ 0 & I \end{pmatrix}$ (Σ_t^{-1} is defined in Eq. (4)).

Define a trace optimal problem as follows:

$$G = \arg \max_{G^T G = I_l} trace((G^T W G)^{-1} G^T B G),$$

where $W = diag(w_1, \cdots, w_u) \in R^{u \times u}$ is a diagonal matrix with

$0 < w_1 \le \cdots \le w_u$, and $B = diag(b_1, \cdots, b_u) \in R^{u \times u}$ is also diagonal

with $b_1 \ge \cdots \ge b_q > 0 = b_{q+1} = \cdots = b_u$, i.e. $rank(B) = q$. Then $G^* = \begin{pmatrix} I_q \\ 0 \end{pmatrix}$ solves

the optimization problem with $l = q$.

From the description above, the main result is stated in the following, as in reference [3]:

Let the matrix X be defined as in Lemma 1 and let $q = rank(S_t^F)$. Then

$$G^* = X \begin{pmatrix} I_q \\ 0 \end{pmatrix}$$ solves the optimal problem in Eq. (2) with $l = q$.

From the analysis above, the main steps of Kernel Uncorrelated Discriminant Analysis using Generalized Singular Value Description (KUDA/SVD) can be summarized in the following.

Algorithm: KUDA/GSVD

Input: input data matrix $X = [x_1, \cdots, x_N] \in R^{n \times N}$ with c

       classes and a kernel function K

Output: Optimal discriminant vectors $\{ \phi_i \}$

    1. Compute H_b, H_w and H_t as in Eq. (3)

    2. Compute GSVD on the matrix pair $\{ H_b^T, H_w^T \}$ to obtain the matrix X, as in Lemma 1.

    3. $q = rank(H_b)$

    4. $\phi_i \leftarrow X_i (i = 1, \cdots, q)$

Fig. 1. procedure of the KUDA/GSVD algorithm

4 Experimental Results

4.1 Experiments with AT&T Face Database [8]

The AT&T data set consists of 400 faces images, taken at the Olivetti Research Laboratory in Cambridge, UK, in which there are 40 subjects and each has 10

Fig. 2. Samples of face images in the AT&T face database

variations conditions under homogeneous background, with each containing 10 different images taken at different time, with vary in pose and scale, and the lighting varying slightly. Each image in the database is of size 112×92. Figure 2 shows images of two subjects in AT&T face database. To reduce the computational complexity, each face image was downsampled to 23×28 pixels.

To evaluate the performance of the KUDA/GSVD method, we test KUDA/GSVD on the AT&T face database. The experiment is similar to that done by Yang [9]. The leave-one-out errors for different method are summarized in Table II. We can see that our method obtains the best performance on this data set.

Table 2. Performance on AT&T face data sets

Method	Reduced Space	Misclassification Rate(%)
Eigenface	40	2.50 (10/400)
Fisherface	39	1.50 (6/400)
ICA	80	6.25 (25/400)
SVM, d=4	N/A	3.00 (12/400)
LLE # neighbor=70	70	2.25 (9/400)
ISOMAP, ε =10	30	1.75 (7/400)
Kernel Eigenface, d=2	40	2.50 (10/400)
Kenel Eigenface, d=3	40	2.00 (8/400)
Kenel Fisherface (P)	39	1.25 (5/400)
Kenel Fisherface (G)	39	1.25 (5/400)
KUDA	39	1.0 (4/400)

For further evaluate the performance of the method we also do experiment on how the "Correct Rate" varies with different number of features. In this experiment we use Gaussian kernel for KUDA method. We use K-Nearest- Neighbors (KNN) for classification. The results can be seen in Figure 3.

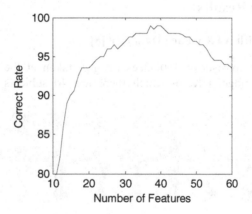

Fig. 3. Plot of correct rate with varying number of features

4.2 Experiments with YALE Face Database [10]

The YALE face database contains 165 face images, in which there are 11 images per subject, one per different facial expression or configuration: center-light, with glasses, happy, left-light, without glasses, normal, right-light, sad, sleepy, surprised, and wink. Figure 4 shows images of two subjects in YALE face database. For computational efficiency, each image was downsampled to 29×41 pixels.

To evaluate the performance of the KUDA/GSVD method, we test KUDA/GSVD on the YALE face database. The experiment is similar to that done by Yang [9]. The

Fig. 4. Samples of face images in the YALE face database

leave-one-out errors for different method are summarized in Table III. We can see that our method obtains the best performance on this data set.

Table 3. Performance on YALE face data sets

Method	Reduced Space	Misclassification Rate(%)
Eigenface	30	28.48 (47/165)
Fisherface	14	8.48 (14/165)
ICA	100	28.48 (47/165)
SVM, d=3	N/A	18.18 (30/165)
LLE # neighbor=10	30	26.06 (43/165)
ISOMAP, ε =20	60	27.27 (45/165)
Kernel Eigenface, d=2	80	27.27 (45/165)
Kenel Eigenface, d=3	60	24.24 (40/165)
Kenel Fisherface (P)	14	6.67 (11/165)
Kenel Fisherface (G)	14	6.06 (10/165)
KUDA	14	2.42 (4/165)

And we also do experiment on how the "Correct Rate" varies with different number of features. In this experiment we use Gaussian kernel for KUDA method. We use K-Nearest- Neighbors (KNN) for classification. The results can be seen in Figure 5.

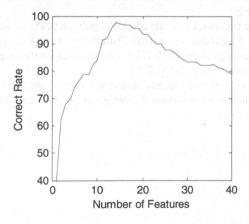

Fig. 5. Plot of correct rate with varying number of features

From Figure 4 and Figure 5 we can see that when the number of features equals to C-1(C is the number of categories) the curves of Correct Rate reach the highest point. After that the curves becomes to decline with increasing number of features, which also testify the Fukunag [11] dimension theorem.

5 Concluding Remarks

In this paper, we use the Kernel Uncorrelated Discriminant Analysis solved by Generalized Singular Value Decomposition named KUDA/GSVD, to extract the features for face recognition tasks. The KUDA/GSVD method also solves the so-called "Small Sample Size" (SSS) problem, which exists in most Face Recognition tasks. Experimental results on the Yale face database and ORL face database show the effectiveness of this method.

Reference

1. W. Zheng, L. Zhao and C. Zou, "Foley-Sammon optimal discriminant vectors using kernel approach", IEEE Transactions on Neural Networks, vol. 16, NO.1, pp. 1-9, Jan. 2005
2. Z. Jin, J. Yang, Z. Tang,and Z. Hu, "A theorem on the uncorrelated optimal discriminant vectors", Pattern Recognition, vol. 34, pp. 2041-2047, 2001
3. J. Ye, R. Janardan, Q. Li, and H. Park, "Feature Extraction via Generalized Uncorrelated Linear Discriminant Analysis", In Proceedings of the 21st Internation Conference on Machine Learning, Banff, Canda, 2004
4. Z. Jin, J. Yang, Z. Hu, and Z. Lou, "Face Recognition Based on the Uncorrelated Discriminant Transformation", Pattern Recognition, vol. 34, pp. 1405-1416, 2000
5. Z. Liang, P. Shi, "Uncorrelated Discriminant Vectors using a kernel method", Pattern Recognition, vol. 38, pp. 307-310, 2005
6. W. Zheng,, "A Note on Kernel Uncorrelated Discriminant Analysis", Pattern Recognition, vol. 38, pp. 2185-2187, 2005
7. C. Park, and H. Park, "Nonlinear Discriminant Analysis Using Kernel Functions and the Generalized Singular Value Decomposition", SIAM Journal on Matrix Analysis and Applications, to appear
8. ORL Face Database ftp://plucky.cs.yale.edu/CVC/pub/images/yalefaces
9. M. Yang, "Kernel Eigenfaces vs. Kernal Fisherfaces: Face Recognition Using Kernel Methods", In Proceedings of the Fifth IEEE International Conference on Automatic Face and Gesture Recognition, pp. 215-220, 2002
10. YALE Face Database http://cvc.yale.edu/projects/yalefaces/yalefaces.html
11. K.Fukunaga, Introduction to Statistical Pattern Recognition, Academic Press, New York, 1990

Recognition of SAR Occluded Targets Using SVM

Yi Gao, Rui Hu, Licheng Jiao, Weida Zhou, and Xiangrong Zhang

Institute of Intelligence Information Processing
and National Key Lab for Radar Signal Processing
Xidian University, Xi'an, 710071, China
potatogao@hotmail.com

Abstract. A novel method for automatic occluded targets recognition in SAR images is proposed in this paper. Different SAR occluded targets are simulated based on actual vehicles from the MSTAR database, and are recognized using SVM classifier by grouping recognition based on the targets azimuth angles. It is shown that the proposed method outperforms the typical methods in accuracy at high occlusion, and robustness to occlusion with experiments considering accuracy and confusion matrix.

1 Introduction

SAR automatic target recognition (ATR) has become an active research area in recent years [15]-[17], and many methods have been proposed for the recognition of non-occluded targets in SAR images. However, it happens frequently that targets such as tanks, canons, and vehicles are hidden or partially hidden (occluded) [16]. Therefore, it is significant to study the recognition system for occluded targets in SAR images.

Most of the available SAR target recognition methods tend to use global features, such as shape, principal axis, and outline, which are optimized for non-occluded targets. Among them, template matching is a typical method, in which, the global features are used. It is not appropriate for the recognition of the occluded targets because the object outline and principal axis are changed by occlusion [18]. Furthermore, SVM [19], [20] has been successfully used for SAR ATR [6], but it has not been applied for SAR occluded targets recognition. Bhanu [1]-[4] develops a model-based ATR system based on invariant local features of the targets. The accuracy of his approach to SAR occluded targets is nearly 100% when the percent occlusion is not so high (less than 70%). But it decreases sharply to only about 50% when dealing with targets at high percent occlusion (70%-90%).

An effective recognition approach for occluded targets in SAR images is proposed in this paper. After the SAR occluded targets were rationally simulated, with good generalization, SVM is used here to improve the accuracy of the SAR occluded target recognition. Experimental results show little difference in accuracy between our presented approach and that of paper [2] at low percent occlusion, while the accuracy of our approach is above 90% at high percent occlusion.

T.-J. Cham et al. (Eds.): MMM 2007, LNCS 4352, Part II, pp. 423–432, 2007.

2 SAR Occluded Targets Recognition

2.1 Occluded Targets in SAR Image

Peaks are important features for SAR ATR and are widely used in it. They are denoted as local maxima in both range and cross-range of SAR images. Unlike optical images, a typical SAR image shows the structure of target by a wealth of peaks corresponding to scattering centers in nature and has no obvious lines or edges within the boundary of the target. Therefore, SAR images of the same target taken at different azimuth angles show great differences, which makes recognition much more difficult. It must be pointed that the number of peaks of different targets are different, and this also happens to the same target at different azimuths.

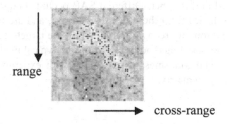

range

cross-range

Fig. 1. Peaks in SAR image (dots in the bright region)

At present, there are no real SAR data with occluded targets available to the public. However, the research of this problem is necessary. Therefore, a reasonable simulating method of the occluded targets is given first.

2.2 Simulation and Recognition of SAR Occluded Targets

The target recognition approach proposed in this paper was designed especially for occluded targets in SAR images, which consisted of a training procedure and a test procedure. Fig. 2 gives the block-diagram of the whole recognition procedure.

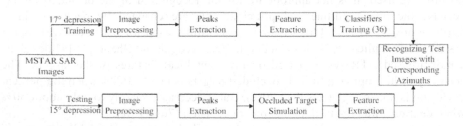

Fig. 2. Flow chart of the SAR occluded target recognition system

2.2.1 Image Preprocessing

Speckle noise exists in raw SAR images, which may disturb the process of extracting peaks. So we first reduce the speckle noise in SAR images. Then the segmentation of target ROI is implemented to obtain the real peaks of the target. In the dataset we adopt, the targets are all located in the center of the images. Therefore, the center area is used to partition the target from the image, which eliminates the disturbance of background. The image preprocessing procedure can induce to the following steps:

Step1	Reduce speckle noise by median filter.
Step2	Normalize the pixel values of the images to [0, 1].
Step3	Threshold the pixel values of the image at certain threshold value.
Step4	Dilate the image to fill small gaps between regions, and then erode to have one large ROI and little regions.
Step5	Discard the small regions with a size filter.
Step6	Dilate the image to reinforce some bright points on the edge of the target.
Step7	The values of the original image hold in the region that are nonzero, the other is set to 0, and then the 54×54 subimage in the center is cropped as the ROI of the original image.

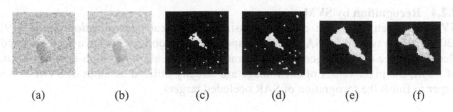

(a)   (b)   (c)   (d)   (e)   (f)

Fig. 3. Results after processing of each step in 2.2.1. (a) original image, (b) denoised image, (c) segmented, (d) dilated & eroded, (e) size filtered, (f) ROI.

In *step 4* and *step 6* of image preprocessing, the extent of dilating and eroding should be carefully controlled in order to make the original target exactly covered. Similar steps of image preprocessing were adopted in paper [2], [9].

2.2.2 Peaks Extraction

Peaks were detected in raster scan order in ROI of the original image obtained in section 2.2.1. For each pixel, if its value is not less than the maximal value of its local 8-neighbor, it will be labeled as peak. Fig. 1 shows a SAR image with its peaks. It should be noticed that the same number of peaks in different images is used in paper [1], [2], [3], and [4], but the number of peaks can be different in this paper.

2.2.3 Simulation of Target Occlusion

The method we simulate the target occlusion is similar to the method presented in paper [2]. At first, the peaks encountered in order in the range direction are removed after the number of peaks to be removed was computed. Then the same number of pixels with random magnitudes were added at random locations within the occlusion area. Then we obtained the simulated SAR occlusion targets with size 54×54.

It should be noticed that, when simulating occlusion, the different directions we choose from 4 perpendicular directions (cross-range, opposite cross-range, up range

426   Y. Gao et al.

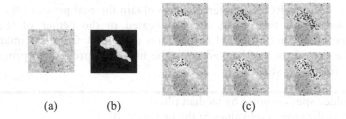

(a)   (b)   (c)

Fig. 4. (a) MSTAR sample image, (b) ROI, and (c) occluded targets under different percent occlusion (30%, 60%, and 90% from left to right). The upper 3 images in (c) are used in *Exp. 1*, while the lower 3 images are used in *Exp. 2* in section 3.

and down range) only make little difference in accuracy theoretically since there are enough images for each target in MSTAR with their azimuths evenly distributed between 0° and 360°. We choose range direction for removing peaks in this paper. Fig. 4 shows a sample of SAR image.

2.2.4 Recognition by SVM
SVM has been shown an efficient classifier with great generalization ability [19], [20]. It also was used for SAR ATR in paper [6], and good results have been obtained. Because of the excellent generalization and processing ability to high-dimension data of SVM, the pixel values of each image are directly utilized as input of SVM in this paper to finish the recognition of SAR occluded targets.

3 Experimental Results and Analysis

3.1 Database

The database used in this paper is from MSTAR public database [7], [8]. Targets in the database include: BMP2 Armored Personnel Carrier (APC), BTR70 APC, T72 Main Battle Tank, whose details are given in Table 1. SAR target samples of the 3 classes at 15° depression with different azimuth are shown in Fig. 5.

Table 1. Details of MSTAR Database used in this paper

Targets	Training Set (17° depression) Serial Number	Number	Training Set (15° depression) Serial Number	Number
BMP2	sn-9563 (#1)	233	sn-9563 (#1)	195
	sn-9566 (#2)	232	sn-9566 (#2)	196
	sn-c21 (#3)	233	sn-c21 (#3)	196
BTR70	sn-c71	233	sn-c71	196
T72	sn-132 (#1)	232	sn-132 (#1)	196
	sn-812 (#2)	231	sn-812 (#2)	195
	(sn-s7)[1] (#3)	(228)	sn-s7 (#3)	191

[1] Training set of T72 sn-s7 is not used for training in this paper.

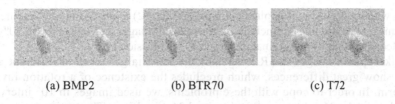

(a) BMP2   (b) BTR70   (c) T72

Fig. 5. SAR images samples of MSTAR database at 15° depression

3.2 Experimental Results

In our experiments, the span of the random magnitudes needs to be discussed when adding random pixels. We simulated the occlusion in two cases: in *Exp.1*, the magnitudes are evenly distributed in [0, 1]; in *Exp.2*, the span is [0.8, 1]. Then in *Exp.1*, the value is completely random, in which case the number of bright points in the region of target will decrease, and the target will be heavily disturbed. In *Exp.2*, the pixels added are all "bright points", which keeps the number of target peaks constant, so that the disturbance is less than *Exp.1*.

We use target images at 17° depression to train classifier and evaluate the performance of the classifier by recognizing target images at 15° depression with certain percent of occlusion. We make two different settings in each experiment due to the difference of training set: (1) single training set is used, which means only original

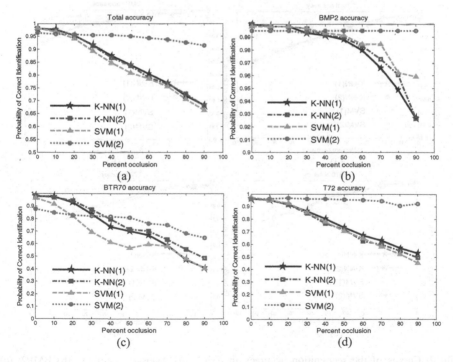

(a)

(b)

(c)

(d)

Fig. 6. Curves of the recognition accuracy in *Exp.1*. (a) Average accuracy. (b) BMP2. (c) BTR70. (d) T72. Where (1) uses single training set, (2) uses multiple training sets.

images without occlusion is applied to train classifier; (2) multiple training sets are used, which means the training set includes non-occluded images and images with 10%-90% simulated occlusion using original images at 17° depression as well.

Unlike optical images, SAR images of the same target taken at different aspect angles show great differences, which precludes the existence of a rotation invariant transform. In order to cope with these problems, we used images in 10° intervals in azimuth to make 36 groups and then trained 36 classifiers. The testing images were recognized by corresponding classifier according to their azimuths.

Linear SVM was used as classifier compared to KNN in this paper. C in SVM is chosen by 10-fold cross-validation.

Exp.1   The number of peaks decreases
Fig. 6 gives the curves of average accuracy and the recognition accuracy of 3 targets separately with the occlusion percent. Table 2 lists the accuracies of 3 targets separately and of the whole testing set. We also give the confusion matrices of the targets at 20 and 70 percent occlusion in Table 3.

Exp.2   The number of peaks holds
Fig. 7 gives the curves of average accuracy and the recognition accuracy of 3 targets separately with the occlusion percent. Table 4 lists the accuracies of 3 targets separately and the average accuracy. The confusion matrices of the targets at 20 and 70 percent occlusion are given in Table 5.

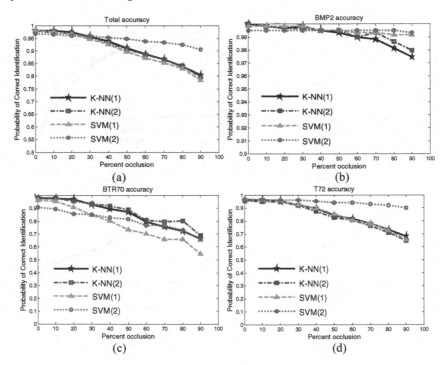

Fig. 7. Curves of the recognition accuracy in *Exp.2*. (a) Average accuracy. (b) BMP2. (c) BTR70. (d) T72. Where (1) uses single training set, (2) uses multiple training sets.

Table 2. Recognition accuracies in *Exp.1*

Classifier	Testing set Occlusion	(1) Single training set				(2) Multiple training sets			
		BMP2	BTR	T72	Average	BMP2	BTR	T72	Average
KNN	0	100%	98.0%	96.1%	98.02%	100%	98.5%	96.1%	98.10%
	10%	99.8%	97.5%	95.4%	97.58%	99.8%	96.9%	95.4%	97.51%
	20%	99.8%	92.9%	91.6%	95.31%	99.8%	94.4%	91.4%	95.46%
	30%	99.3%	83.7%	86.4%	91.58%	99.7%	87.2%	84.5%	91.43%
	40%	99.2%	73.5%	80.2%	87.40%	99.2%	79.6%	76.5%	86.67%
	50%	98.8%	69.9%	73.4%	83.81%	99.0%	71.4%	72.0%	83.52%
	60%	98.0%	66.8%	67.2%	80.37%	98.3%	69.9%	62.5%	78.97%
	70%	96.6%	58.7%	63.1%	76.85%	97.3%	63.3%	60.0%	76.48%
	80%	94.9%	47.5%	57.0%	71.94%	96.1%	55.6%	54.8%	72.67%
	90%	92.7%	40.8%	52.9%	68.28%	92.7%	48.5%	49.7%	67.99%
SVM	0	99.8%	96.4%	97.3%	98.24%	99.5%	87.8%	96.1%	96.34%
	10%	99.8%	91.8%	95.4%	96.78%	99.5%	84.7%	96.1%	95.90%
	20%	99.8%	82.1%	92.6%	94.21%	99.5%	82.7%	96.6%	95.82%
	30%	99.7%	69.4%	85.4%	89.23%	99.3%	82.1%	96.2%	95.53%
	40%	99.3%	61.2%	78.0%	84.76%	99.5%	81.6%	96.2%	95.53%
	50%	99.2%	56.6%	70.6%	80.88%	99.5%	80.6%	95.5%	95.09%
	60%	98.5%	59.7%	64.8%	78.53%	99.5%	76.0%	95.2%	94.29%
	70%	98.5%	58.2%	58.1%	75.46%	99.5%	75.0%	94.3%	93.77%
	80%	96.3%	48.0%	52.2%	70.55%	99.5%	68.4%	90.6%	92.60%
	90%	95.9%	40.3%	45.2%	66.30%	99.5%	64.8%	92.4%	91.50%

Table 3. Recognition confusion matrices in *Exp.1*. (a) for 20% occluded targets, (b) for 70%.

20% Occluded Testing targets		(1) Single training set			(2) Multiple training sets		
		BMP2	BTR70	T72	BMP2	BTR70	T72
KNN	BMP2	586	0	1	586	0	1
	BTR70	11	182	3	9	185	2
	T72	49	0	533	50	0	532
SVM	BMP2	586	0	1	584	0	3
	BTR70	29	161	6	22	162	12
	T72	43	0	539	20	0	562

(a)

70% Occluded Testing targets		(1) Single training set			(2) Multiple training sets		
		BMP2	BTR70	T72	BMP2	BTR70	T72
KNN	BMP2	567	12	8	571	10	6
	BTR70	67	115	14	67	124	5
	T72	193	22	367	216	17	349
SVM	BMP2	578	3	6	584	0	3
	BTR70	78	114	4	33	147	16
	T72	230	14	338	33	0	549

(b)

Table 4. Recognition accuracies in *Exp.2*

Classifier	Testing set Occlusion	(1) Single training set				(2) Multiple training sets			
		BMP2	BTR	T72	Average	BMP2	BTR	T72	Average
KNN	0	100%	97.96%	96.05%	98.02%	100%	98.47%	95.53%	97.88%
	10%	99.83%	97.45%	96.39%	98.02%	99.83%	97.96%	94.85%	97.44%
	20%	99.66%	96.94%	95.53%	97.51%	99.66%	95.41%	94.67%	96.92%
	30%	99.83%	92.86%	92.44%	95.68%	99.66%	93.37%	92.10%	95.53%
	40%	99.49%	89.29%	89.69%	93.85%	99.49%	91.84%	87.46%	93.26%
	50%	99.32%	87.24%	84.36%	91.21%	99.49%	88.78%	82.47%	90.70%
	60%	98.98%	79.59%	81.62%	88.79%	98.98%	80.61%	80.58%	88.50%
	70%	98.81%	75.51%	78.01%	86.59%	99.32%	79.59%	76.12%	86.59%
	80%	98.13%	72.45%	73.37%	83.88%	98.64%	80.10%	70.96%	84.18%
	90%	97.44%	66.33%	68.04%	80.44%	97.96%	68.88%	64.78%	79.63%
SVM	0	99.83%	96.43%	97.25%	98.24%	99.49%	90.82%	96.39%	96.92%
	10%	99.83%	95.41%	96.05%	97.58%	99.49%	89.29%	96.22%	96.63%
	20%	99.83%	90.82%	95.53%	96.70%	99.49%	85.71%	96.05%	96.04%
	30%	99.83%	84.69%	92.78%	94.65%	99.49%	85.20%	96.22%	96.04%
	40%	99.49%	80.10%	89.86%	92.60%	99.49%	82.65%	95.36%	95.31%
	50%	99.49%	73.47%	85.40%	89.74%	99.49%	81.63%	94.50%	94.80%
	60%	99.32%	70.41%	80.58%	87.18%	99.49%	76.53%	93.99%	93.85%
	70%	99.32%	65.82%	77.84%	85.35%	99.49%	76.53%	92.96%	93.41%
	80%	99.15%	65.82%	72.85%	83.15%	99.49%	72.96%	92.10%	92.53%
	90%	99.15%	54.59%	65.46%	78.39%	99.32%	65.82%	90.03%	90.55%

Table 5. Recognition confusion matrices in *Exp.2*. (a) for 20% occluded targets, (b) for 70%.

20% Occluded Testing targets		(1) Single training set			(2) Multiple training sets		
		BMP2	BTR70	T72	BMP2	BTR70	T72
KNN	BMP2	585	0	2	585	0	2
	BTR70	5	190	1	6	187	3
	T72	26	0	556	30	1	551
SVM	BMP2	586	0	1	584	0	3
	BTR70	15	178	3	18	168	10
	T72	26	0	556	23	0	559

(a)

70% Occluded Testing targets		(1) Single training set			(2) Multiple training sets		
		BMP2	BTR70	T72	BMP2	BTR70	T72
KNN	BMP2	580	1	6	583	1	3
	BTR70	44	148	4	37	156	3
	T72	119	9	454	129	10	443
SVM	BMP2	583	0	4	584	0	3
	BTR70	65	129	2	35	150	11
	T72	126	3	453	41	0	541

(b)

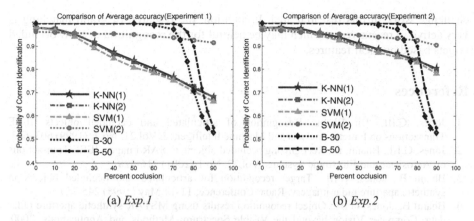

Fig. 8. Comparison of average accuracy in *Exp.1* and *Exp.2* with the results of [2], where (1) uses single training set, (2) uses multiple training sets

Fig. 8 gives the comparison of average accuracy in *Exp.1* and *Exp.2* with the results of paper [2], where B-30 and B-50 stand for the results in [2] using 30 and 50 scatters separately.

From Fig. 6 (a) and Fig. 7 (a), it can be concluded that the proposed method can be successfully used for recognition of SAR occluded targets, especially effective for highly occluded targets.

Fig. 6 and Fig. 7 also indicate that both of the average accuracies of SVM (2) in *Exp.1* and *Exp.2* is above 90% when the targets are 90% occluded, which show excellent performance of SVM. There is little difference between KNN (1) and KNN (2), while accuracy of SVM (2) does not decrease so much as the increase of percent occlusion, which shows good generalization of SVM over KNN.

As we can see in Fig. 8, accuracy of [2] is nearly 1 at low occlusion, a little higher than those of our method, but they are sharply dropped to about 50% at 70%-80% occlusion, while the accuracy of our method is above 90% using SVM (2), and about 70% to 80% using KNN and SVM (1), which is much higher than that of [2]. The results reveal excellent performance and robustness of our method at high occlusion.

Separate comparison of (b)-(d) in Fig. 6 and Fig. 7 shows that occlusion makes different influence on different targets. The order of influences on 3 targets by occlusion is: BMP2>T72>BTR70.

4   Conclusions

An effective recognition approach for occluded targets in SAR images is proposed in this paper. The performance of the recognition method was evaluated on three targets from MSTAR database in terms of accuracy and confusion matrix. Experimental results show that the method can get high recognition accuracy at low and especially at high percent occlusion. The results also indicate the robustness to occlusion and good generalization of the proposed approach.

The image pixel values were used as features directly in this paper. The extraction of other discrimination features which can well describe SAR occluded images is a challenge work in this research area. In addition, the research of graph matching is very active in recent years, which may be helpful for the recognition of SAR occluded targets based on local features.

References

1. Jones, G.III., Bir Bhanu: Recognition of articulated and occluded objects. IEEE Transactions on Pattern Analysis and Machine Intelligence, Vol.21, No.7, (1999) 603–613
2. Jones, G.III., Bhanu, B.: Recognizing occluded objects in SAR images. IEEE Transactions on Aerospace and Electronic Systems, Vol.37, No,1 (2001) 316-328
3. Bhanu B., Jones, G.III.: Target recognition for articulated and occluded objects in synthetic aperture radar imagery. Radar Conference, 11-14 May (1998) 245-250
4. Bhanu B., Jones, G.III.: Object recognition results using MSTAR synthetic aperture radar data. Computer Vision beyond the Visible Spectrum: Methods and Applications, 2000. Proceedings, IEEE Workshop on 16 June (2000) 55-62
5. Yang, Y.N., Qiu Y.X., Lu C.: Automatic Target Classification — Experiments on the MSTAR SAR Images, SNPD/SAWN 2005, (2005) 2-7
6. Zhao, Q., Principe, J.C.: Support vector machines for SAR automatic target recognition. IEEE Transactions on Aerospace and Electronic Systems, Vol.37, No.2, (2001) 643-654
7. Keydel Eric, R. Shung, Wu Lee, T. Moore: MSTAR Extended Operating Conditions, A Tutorial. SPIE, Vol.2757, (1996) 228-242
8. T. D. Ross, S.W. Worrell, et al: Standard SAR ATR evaluation experiments using the MSTAR public release data set. SPIE Proceedings: Algorithms for Synthetic Aperture Radar Imagery V, Vol.3370, (1998) 566-573
9. Zhang, C.: Research on Automatic Target Recognition in High Resolution SAR Images. PhD Thesis, National University of Defense Technology, (Oct,2003)(in Chinese)
10. Han, P.: SAR Automatic Target Recognition and Related Techniques. PhD Thesis, Tianjin University, (Jan,2004) (in Chinese)
11. Bian, Z.Q., Zhang, X.G.: Pattern Recognition (second edition). Tsinghua University Press, (2000) (in Chinese)
12. Richard O. Duda, Peter E. Hart, David G. Stork: Pattern Classification (Second Edition). John Wiley & Sons, Inc., (2001) (in Chinese)
13. Gao, G., Ji, K.F., Kuang, G.Y, Li, D.R.: Targets Peak Feature Extraction From High-Resolution SAR Image. Signal Processing, Vol.25, No.1, (2005) 232-235 (in Chinese)
14. Guo, G.R, et al: Electromagnetic Feature Extraction and Target Recognition [M], National University of Defense Technology Press, (1996) (in Chinese)
15. Kuang, G.Y., Ji, K.F., Su, Y., Yu, W.X: A Survey of Researches on SAR ATR. Jurnal of Image and Graphics, Vol.8 (A), No.10, (2003) 1,115-1,120 (in Chinese)
16. B. Bhanu, D. Dudgeon, E. Zelnio, A. Rosenfeld, D. Casasent, and I. Reed: Introduction to the Special Issue on Automatic Target Detection and Recognition. IEEE Trans. Image Processing, Vol. 6, No. 1, (1997) 1-6
17. D. Dudgeon, R. Lacoss: An overview of automatic target recognition. The Lincoln Laboratory Journal, Vol.6, No.1, (1993) 3-9
18. Yi, J.H., B. Bhanu, and Li, M.: Target Indexing in SAR Images Using Scattering Centers and the Hausdorff Distance. Pattern Recognition Letters, Vol. 17, (1996) 1,191-1,198
19. Vapnik, V.N.: The Nature of Statistical Learning Theory. New York: Springer-Verlag, (1995)
20. Platt, J.: Fast training of support vector machines using sequential minimal optimization. In B. Schlkopf, C. J. C. Burges, and A. J. Smola, editors: Advances in Kernel Methods-Support Vector Learning, Cambridge, MA: MIT Press, (1999) 185-208.

Discovery of Image Versions in Large Collections

Jun Jie Foo, Ranjan Sinha, and Justin Zobel

School of Computer Science & IT
RMIT University, Melbourne, Australia, 3001
{jufoo,rsinha,jz}@cs.rmit.edu.au

Abstract. Image collections may contain multiple copies, versions, and fragments of the same image. Storage or retrieval of such duplicates and near-duplicates may be unnecessary and, in the context of collections derived from the web, their presence may represent infringements of copyright. However, identifying image versions is a challenging problem, as they can be subject to a wide range of digital alterations, and is potentially costly as the number of image pairs to be considered is quadratic in collection size. In this paper, we propose a method for finding the pairs of near-duplicates based on manipulation of an image index. Our approach is an adaptation of a robust object recognition technique and a near-duplicate document detection algorithm to this application domain. We show that this method requires only moderate computing resources, and is highly effective at identifying pairs of near-duplicates.

1 Introduction

Many digital images found on resources such as the web are copies or variants of each other. Identification of these near-duplicate images is a challenging problem, as two versions are rarely identical. They may differ in filename, format, and size; simply saving an image may lead to bitwise differences due to the variations in the coding standards in different software. Some common modifications include conversion to greyscale, change in color balance and contrast, rescaling, rotating, cropping, and filtering. These are instances where the near-duplicates — which we term *co-derivative* — are derived from the same digital image source, and are sometimes known as identical near-duplicates [8]. Non-identical near-duplicates — which are of interest in media tracking and filtering [8,23] — are images that share the same scenes or objects. In this work, we do not address non-identical near-duplicates due to their subjectivity in interpretation.

Although the detection of copied digital images has been extensively researched in the field of digital watermarking [6,9,11,12], such methods are ill-suited for retrieval applications [16,19]. Similarly, content-based retrieval [22] techniques are unsuitable, as they are designed to identify images with similar traits and have limited effectiveness for this task [3,17,20].

For the task of retrieval of near-duplicate images in response to a query, Ke et al. [14] have demonstrated near-perfect accuracy using PCA-SIFT local descriptors. Lu and Hsu [16] demonstrated an effective method of image hashing for retrieval of near-duplicate images. However, little prior work concerns

T.-J. Cham et al. (Eds.): MMM 2007, LNCS 4352, Part II, pp. 433–442, 2007.
© Springer-Verlag Berlin Heidelberg 2007

sifting a collection to find all near-duplicate pairs. The RIME [3] system was designed to address this issue using a cluster-based approach. However, the severity of the image alterations is limited. Recently, Zhang and Chang [23] propose a framework that identifies near-duplicate images using machine learning by graph matching. They present an application of this detection for topic and semantic association, wherein they observe average effectiveness on a small collection of images; efficiency and scalability remains an issue.

In this work, we propose a new method for automatically identifying the co-derivative images in a large collection, based on analysis of the index generated by an existing robust object-recognition technique. The rationale is that co-derivative images (or their sub-parts) should share identical objects that are unlikely to be matched in unrelated images. As such, using such an approach enables us to identify candidate near-duplicate pairs, which we can then process in more detail to verify whether they are indeed co-derivative.

To avoid the inefficiency inherent in quadratic-cost comparison of every pair of images, we apply the concept of *discovery* [1] that is used to identify near-duplicate documents to show that it can be adapted for images. We explore an approach that exploits the PCA-SIFT local descriptors [14] indexed using locality-sensitive hashing [5], which have been shown to be highly effective for near-duplicate image retrieval. With this approach, co-derivatives are likely to have features with similar hash values; processing the hash table provides an efficient mechanism for identifying candidate pairs.

Using collections of 10,000 to 40,000 images, we show that even severely altered co-derivative images can be efficiently identified using our approach. For mild alterations, including moderate cropping and alterations to properties such as hue and intensity, both accuracy and completeness typically exceed 80%, while computational costs remain reasonable.

2   Co-derivative Detection and the Discovery Problem

Zhang and Chang [23] and Jaimes et al. [8] have broadly categorized duplicate images into three main categories by the type of changes, namely scene, camera, and image. Image changes describe digital editing operations such as cropping, filtering, and color, contrast, or resolution alteration. It is these changes that we define to lead to images being *co-derived*, since they are derived from the same digital source; we investigate the discovery of such images in this paper.

The problem of automatic identification of pairs of co-derivative images can be conceptualized using a *relationship graph* [1], where each node represents a unique image; the presence of an edge between two nodes reflects a co-derivative relationship between the images. This discovery process of the relationships in a given collection is a challenging task due to the quadratic number of potential edges (image pairs) for a collection of images [23].

In this paper, we borrow concepts from near-duplicate document detection [1,2,21]. Text documents are parsed into representative units of words or characters; these units can be indexed in an *inverted file* [24], where each entry contains

Fig. 1. An example of a co-derivative image; the lines depict the matching PCA-SIFT local descriptor matches

the postings list of documents (IDs) in which this particular unit occurs, along with any auxiliary information. Co-derivative document detection algorithms exploit the postings list to generate the relationship graph; the principal differences between the algorithms in the literature lies in unit selection heuristics [1].

Broder et al. [2] propose counting the number of possible document pairings (edges) in each postings list to identify the number of co-occurring units in any two documents. Although this method is effective, it is costly, as the number of unique edges that can be generated is quadratic to the length of the postings list. Shivakumar and Garcia-Molina [21] address the scalability issues with a filter-and-refine scheme, based on hash-based probabilistic counting. The key idea is to set an upper-bound on the number of unique edges by *coarse* counting in the first-pass — using a hash table — to discard edges that do not have sufficient co-occurring units. This method is efficient, that is, given a hash table of sufficient size the number of identified edges can be dramatically reduced [1,21]. Our approach is to adapt such methods to the image domain, using, instead of postings, *distinctive interest points* [13] and *locality sensitive hashing* [5].

Distinctive interest points. Images can be characterized by local or global features, such as color, shape, texture, or salient points [22]. Local image features such as interest points have been shown to be robust for applications of object recognition and image matching [18]. Intuitively, co-derivative images should share identical objects; thus robust object recognition techniques are well-suited for this application domain. We use the SIFT [15] interest point detector and the PCA-SIFT local descriptors, as they have been demonstrated to be effective for query-based co-derivative image retrieval [4,14]; for convenience, we refer to them as a *PCA-SIFT feature*. An illustration that it works well is shown in Figure 1. In this pair of images, the dashed lines connect corresponding (automatically detected) PCA-SIFT features; as can be seen, the matching is accurate.

To generate local descriptors, PCA-SIFT uses the same information as the original SIFT descriptor, that is, location, scale, and dominant orientations. Ke et al. [13,14] have empirically determined that $n = 36$ feature spaces for the local descriptor performs well for object detection, and, specifically, for near-duplicate image retrieval; wherein any two PCA-SIFT local descriptors are deemed similar (a match) within an Euclidean distance (L_2-norm) of $3,000$. Hence, we use the same setting in this work, where the only difference lies in similarity assessment of PCA-SIFT local descriptors, which we describe later.

The number of PCA-SIFT local descriptors is dictated by that of the key-points which SIFT detects, typically ranging from hundreds to thousands per image (depending on image complexity). To recognize two objects with reasonable reliability, a minimum match of 5 local descriptors has been empirically observed to work [13]. To index such a considerable number of PCA-SIFT local descriptors for a large image collection is costly, but fortunately, the number of keypoints that SIFT generates can be significantly reduced by varying the threshold value in the second stage, which has been demonstrated to significantly improve efficiency with only slight loss in accuracy [4]. Here, we use the original approach,[1] as our emphasis is on effectiveness.

Locality sensitive hashing. Given units that can be extracted from images and used to assess co-derivation, we need a method of indexing these units so that features from co-derived images are gathered together. Such clustering should allow efficient determination of the relationship graph. In this paper, we make use of the locality sensitive hashing (LSH) structure used to index the PCA-SIFT features for approximate nearest-neighbor search [5,7].

All points sharing identical hash values (collisions) within a given hash table are estimated, by the Manhattan distance (L_1-norm embedded in the Hamming space), to be closer to each other than those that do not. Thus, the search space of an approximate nearest-neighbor match is greatly reduced to those that share identical hash values. Hence, the greater the number of hash-collisions between points from two images, the higher the probability that they are co-derivatives due to increased PCA-SIFT feature matches; whereby a feature match is approximated by a hash-collision in L_1-norm instead of an L_2-distance of 3,000.

An additional L_2-norm verification can be used to discard false positive matches under the L_1, but has been observed to have limited impact on effectiveness [5]. Moreover, any additional verification is costly in our application as we aim to identify all instances of co-derivatives. In this work, we assume similarity of two PCA-SIFT features by a hash-collision in the L_1-norm.

3   Deriving the Co-derivative Relationship Graph

To generate the relationship graph of an image collection we apply a refine-and-filter scheme. As a first-pass pruning strategy, we use hash-based probabilistic counting (explained below) to quickly discard pairs of images that are not near-duplicates, after which the pruned collection is further processed so that false positives are discarded. Hash-based probabilistic counting is suited to this domain because of the character of the PCA-SIFT features. The post-indexing phase of PCA-SIFT features of an image are mapped to a series of hash-keys across l LSH hash tables, such that two features sharing identical hash-keys are, with high confidence, close to each other in a d-dimensional space. Each hash-key

---

[1] An average of around 1,600 descriptors are extracted per image on our collection.

can be treated as a unit, akin to words in text, and thus an image is transformed into a series of representative units that can be stored in a postings list; each entry consists of a list of images that contains PCA-SIFT features that share identical hash-keys.

As in the approach of Shivakumar and Garcia-Molina [21] for relationship graph generation, all possible image pairs (edges) in every postings list are hashed to an array A of m counters using a universal hash function h. For an edge of two nodes id_1 and id_2 that share co-occurring entries (units) in the postings list, $A[h(id_1, id_2)]$ is incremented, where id denotes the image ID; this is essentially a hash-counter. Due to hash collisions, this hash-counter can occasionally generate spurious edges, whereby edges with no co-occurring features share identical hash locations with the ones that do, resulting in a large number of false positive matches. Typically, this occurs with high probability due to incommensurate hash-counters, but, given that we are only concerned with values lower than or equal to a threshold T, the number of hash-counters can be increased by using bytes, or smaller multiples of bits, rather than words; thus the rate of hash collisions can be reduced without impact on memory usage.

As the number of matching units (PCA-SIFT features) between two co-derivative images ranges from tens to thousands, we apply thresholding to discard edges that do not have sufficient matches. Furthermore, we expect to find some image pairs that share identical objects, but are neither co-derivatives nor near-duplicates (pictures of flags, for example). Hence, we experimentally increment this parameter to find an optimal threshold for identifying all co-derivative images, while omitting as many false matches as possible.

To minimize the number of spurious edges, we accumulate the matching features between two images using exact counting, that is, we keep an integer counter for every unique edge using a static structure with no possibility of collision. As such, each counter reflects the actual number of PCA-SIFT feature matches between two images; we use the same threshold value as in the pruning strategy to discard edges without this minimum number of matching features.

4   Evaluation Methodology

For our image collection, we use three image data sets of crawled images from the SPIRIT collection [10]. To enable a meaningful evaluation, we generate a seed collection of 5,000 co-derivative images by using 100 randomly selected individual images from the same collection, each of which is then digitally transformed using 50 different alterations. Hence, each of the 50 images has a co-derivative relationship to each of the other 49 images, with a resultant 122,500 manually generated edges; each of the three image data sets — $C_1, C_2, and C_3$ — is populated with the seed collection, and randomly gathered images from the SPIRIT collection to aggregated sizes of 10,000, 20,000, and 40,000, respectively.

The list of alterations is similar to that of Ke et al. [14]:

1. **format change**: format change from .jpg to .gif (1 alteration)
2. **colorise**: each of the red, green, and blue channels are tinted by 10% (3)

3. `contrast`: increase and decrease contrast (2)
4. `severe contrast`: increase and decrease contrast 3× of original image (2)
5. `crop`: crop 95%, 90%, 80%, and 70% of image, preserve centre region (4)
6. `severe crop`: crop 60%, 50%, and 10% of image, preserve centre region (3)
7. `despeckle`: apply "despeckle" operation of ImageMagick (1)
8. `border`: a frame size 10% of image is added using random colors (4)
9. `rotate`: rotate image (by 90°, 180°, and 270°) about its centre (3)
10. `scale-up`: increase scale by 2×, 4×, and 8× (3)
11. `scale-down`: decrease scale by 2×, 4×, and 8× (3)
12. `saturation`: alter saturation by 70%, 80%, 90%, 110%, and 120% (5)
13. `intensity`: alter intensity level by 80%, 90%, 110%, 120% (4)
14. `severe intensity`: alter intensity level by 50% and 150% (2)
15. `rotate+crop`: rotate image (by 90°, 180°, and 270°), crop 50% in centre region (3)
16. `rotate+scale`: rotate image (by 90°, 180°, and 270°), decrease scale 4x (3)
17. `shear`: apply affine warp on both x and y axes using 5°, and 15° (4)

The number in parentheses is the number of instances for each alteration type.[2]

Making an arbitrary distinction based on our experience with using these techniques for image search, we separate the image alterations according to whether matches are *easy* or *hard* to detect. All alterations in categories 4, 6, 14, 15, 16, and 17 are hard, as are the 8× scalings in categories 10 and 11; all other alterations are (relatively!) easy.

As all three of our collections represent real-world images, we do not expect to find many instances of transformations as severe as those of our seeded images. Thus the seeded images are essential for evaluating the effectiveness of our approach on identifying severely altered co-derivatives; moreover, they also serve as a good testbed for testing the limits of various threshold values (denoted by T_n) to derive an optimal setting for identifying co-derivatives.

For all three collections, images are converted into greyscale[3] and resized to 512 pixels in the longer edge. Experiments used a two-processor Xeon 3 GHz machine with 4 GB of main memory running Linux 2.4. The effectiveness of our approach can be evaluated by assessing the relationship graph. An ideal human-evaluated relationship graph of the entire image collection, otherwise known as a *reference graph* [1], provides a benchmark for measuring a co-derivative detection algorithm. We use the evaluation metrics of *coverage* and *density* [1], which are similar to recall and precision in information retrieval. The coverage of a computer-generated relationship graph is the completeness relative to the reference graph; the density is the proportion of edges that are correct.

In practice, generation of a complete reference graph is implausibly difficult. However, given that we have a pre-generated reference graph with the use of a seed collection, we can evaluate the coverage of a relationship graph using the ratio of pre-determined edges that are identified in the reference graph. True

---

[2] All alterations are created using ImageMagick, http://www.imagemagick.com
[3] The PCA-SIFT features are extracted from greyscale images and hence are inherently robust against color changes.

Table 1. Estimated coverage (%), average precision (%), and number of identified edges of the co-derivative relationship graph generated using collections C_1, C_2, and C_3; seven threshold values ranging from T_4 to T_{256} are used

	T_4	T_8	T_{16}	T_{32}	T_{64}	T_{128}	T_{256}
Collection C_1							
Coverage	93.5	91.3	88.5	84.3	77.5	68.2	54.9
Average precision	22.0	55.7	83.3	92.1	93.2	91.7	89.4
No. of edges	2,754,583	579,428	187,167	123,536	102,678	86,762	68,286
Run-time (mins)	6.5	5.1	6.7	5.1	4.7	6.0	5.1
Collection C_2							
Coverage	93.6	91.4	88.6	84.6	78.0	68.9	55.9
Average precision	18.8	51.4	80.9	91.3	93.0	91.6	89.4
No. of edges	6,660,498	1,211,766	304,877	155,629	114,054	91,522	70,892
Run-time (mins)	12.4	9.3	8.5	8.4	8.3	8.2	8.1
Collection C_3							
Coverage	93.6	91.5	88.8	84.7	78.2	69.2	56.4
Average precision	16.8	48.8	79.4	90.8	92.9	91.5	89.4
No. of edges	15,559,155	2,499,650	551,458	226,994	137,399	99,132	73,528
Run-time (mins)	28.3	18.2	16.0	15.6	15.6	15.5	15.3

density of a relationship graph cannot be appropriately evaluated without a complete reference graph of the entire collection; thus, to estimate density, we can select edges from the computer-generated graph to determine if co-derivative relationships exist between connecting nodes, a labour-intensive process. For a less resource intensive evaluation, we also evaluate the average precision of the computer-generated relationship graph — the ratio of co-derivative edges to the total identified edges in that graph for each image used in coverage estimation.

5   Results

We experiment with seven threshold values (T) from 4 to 256 — doubling progressively — for each collection. Images are a match if the number of shared features exceeds the threshold. As shown in Table 1, using our algorithm, the seeded co-derivative images are detected with high overall effectiveness for all collections. As anticipated, coverage favors low threshold values whereas precision favors higher thresholds. A small number of feature matches between two images is insufficient to discard non co-derivatives pairs, due to spurious edges that are generated by images that share similar or identical objects. Evaluation time does not rise drastically with collection size, suggesting, in this preliminary implementation, that this approach should scale to much larger collections.

A threshold of 16 or 32 leads to large gains in precision, and reductions in evaluation time, without great loss of coverage. Thus the number of shared

Table 2. Estimated coverage and average precision (%) of the co-derivative relationship graph generated using collections C_1, C_2, and C_3; hard and easy alterations are evaluated separately thresholding from T_4 to T_{256}

			T_4	T_8	T_{16}	T_{32}	T_{64}	T_{128}	T_{256}
Collection C_1	Easy	Coverage	97.1	95.9	94.4	91.8	87.4	80.6	68.5
		Average precision	18.0	53.6	86.0	96.7	98.5	98.5	97.8
	Hard	Coverage	87.1	83.0	78.0	70.9	59.9	46.3	30.7
		Average precision	29.2	59.5	78.6	83.9	83.9	79.4	74.4
Collection C_2	Easy	Coverage	97.1	96.0	94.5	92.0	87.7	81.1	69.4
		Average precision	14.9	48.7	83.2	95.9	98.2	98.4	97.8
	Hard	Coverage	87.2	83.2	78.3	71.4	60.6	47.2	31.9
		Average precision	25.7	56.1	76.7	83.3	83.7	79.4	74.4
Collection C_3	Easy	Coverage	97.1	96.0	94.5	92.1	87.9	81.3	69.8
		Average precision	13.0	45.8	81.6	95.3	98.1	98.4	97.9
	Hard	Coverage	87.4	83.4	78.5	71.7	61.0	47.6	32.4
		Average precision	23.6	54.0	75.7	82.9	83.6	79.3	74.5

features between some co-derivative images (after severe alterations) occasionally does not rise above the noise level; indeed, operations such as severe cropping, shearing, or scaling may make images appear unrelated even to humans. To explore this further, we separately measured coverage and precision for easy and hard alterations, as shown in Table 2. As can be seen, much of the difficulty is due to the hard alterations. For the easy alterations, coverage and precision uniformly remain above 80% and 95%, respectively, from threshold 16 up to 128. Note too that collection size has little impact on the accuracy of the method.

Also shown in Table 1 is the number of identified co-derivative edges for each threshold value. We observe a considerable reduction in the identified edges — for all three collections — while the threshold value is increased. The observed coverage, relative to the number of identified edges, indicates that our approach is indeed effective for narrowing the search space for the candidate edges. Table 1 further shows that the number of identified co-derivative edges — for all threshold values — follows a linear trend as the collection size grows, even though the growth of the number of total edges is quadratic. This indicates that the growth of an index structure should also grow linearly, which makes this a scalable approach for moderate-sized image collections.

For our final experiment, estimation of the density of our generated relationship graph, we manually sample 100 identified edges that do not exist in the reference graph on collection C_3 — our largest available collection. Because we are concerned with only co-derivative images and not near-duplicates, a random sampling of edges from the set of identified edges is inappropriate as PCA-SIFT features are likely to identify all instances of near-duplicates; hence, a random sampling can result in no matches found by our definition. For a more meaningful evaluation, we first rank the edges by their number of matching features, and sample using the top 10% of the identified edges. We conjecture that co-derivative pairs should have more matching features between them than non co-derivative pairs; hence a simple ranking is appropriate to quantify the differences. The estimated density is observed to be 96%, but we believe this to be an overestimate due to a reasonable number of exact duplicates that may have been crawled from different sources. Nevertheless, this experiment demonstrates that, in addition to the seeded co-derivative images, other unseeded instances are also identified with high effectiveness.

6   Conclusions

We have proposed a new method for automatic identification of the pairs of co-derivative images in a large collection. We have demonstrated that near-duplicate text document detection techniques can be effectively adapted for images indexed using PCA-SIFT local descriptors and locality sensitive hashing. Our findings here corroborate our hypothesis, that co-derivative images can be automatically and effectively identified using a refine-and-filter scheme: a first-pass strategy identifies all images that share identical objects so that a smaller image set can be further processed for co-derivative pairs. Accuracy is high, especially for less severe image alterations, and the computational costs are moderate. That is, our method provides effective discovery of duplicates and near-duplicates, and thus is a practical approach to collection management and protection of copyright.

References

1. Y. Bernstein and J. Zobel. A scalable system for identifying co-derivative documents. In *Proc. SPIRE Int. Conf. on String Processing and Information Retrieval*, pages 55–67, October 2004.
2. A. Z. Broder, S. C. Glassman, M. S. Manasse, and G. Zweig. Syntactic clustering of the web. *Computer Networks*, 29(8-13):1157–1166, 1997.
3. E. Chang, J. Z. Wang, and G. Wiederhold. RIME: A replicated image detector for the world-wide web. In *Proc. SPIE Int. Conf. on Multimedia Storage and Archiving Systems III*, 1998.
4. J. J. Foo and R. Sinha. Pruning SIFT for scalable near-duplicate image matching. In *Proc. ADC Australasian Database Conference*, Feb 2007.
5. A. Gionis, P. Indyk, and R. Motwani. Similarity search in high dimensions via hashing. In *Proc. VLDB Int. Conf. on Very Large Data Bases*, pages 518–529, Edinburgh, Scotland, UK, September 1999. Morgan Kaufmann.
6. F. Hartung and M. Kutter. Multimedia watermarking techniques. *Proceedings IEEE (USA)*, 87(7):1079–1107, 1999.
7. P. Indyk and R. Motwani. Approximate nearest neighbors: Towards removing the curse of dimensionality. In *Proc. STOC Int. Conf. on Theory of Computing*, pages 604–613, Dallas, Texas, USA, May 1998. ACM Press.
8. A. Jaimes, S.-F. Chang, and A. C. Loui. Duplicate detection in consumer photography and news video. In *Proc. MM Int. Conf. on Multimedia*, pages 423–424, 2002.

9. N. F. Johnson, Z. Duric, and S. Jajodia. On "Fingerprinting" images for recognition. In *Proc. MIS Int. Workshop on Multimedia Information Systems*, pages 4–11, Indian Wells, California, October 1999.

10. H. Joho and M. Sanderson. The spirit collection: an overview of a large web collection. *SIGIR Forum*, 38(2):57–61, 2004.

11. X. Kang, J. Huang, and Y. Q. Shi. An image watermarking algorithm robust to geometric distortion. In *Proc. IWDW Int. Workshop on Digital Watermarking*, pages 212–223, Seoul, Korea, November 2002. Springer.

12. X. Kang, J. Huang, Y. Q. Shi, and Y. Lin. A DWT-DFT composite watermarking scheme robust to both affine transform and JPEG compression. *IEEE Trans. Circuits and Systems for Video Technology*, 13(8):776–786, 2003.

13. Y. Ke and R. Sukthankar. PCA-sift: A more distinctive representation for local image descriptors. In *Proc. CVPR Int. Conf. on Computer Vision and Pattern Recognition*, pages 506–513, Washington, DC, USA, June–July 2004. IEEE Computer Society.

14. Y. Ke, R. Sukthankar, and L. Huston. An efficient parts-based near-duplicate and sub-image retrieval system. In *Proc. MM Int. Conf. on Multimedia*, pages 869–876, New York, NY, USA, October 2004. ACM Press.

15. D. G. Lowe. Distinctive image features from scale-invariant keypoints. *Int. Journal of Computer Vision*, 60(2):91–110, 2004.

16. C.-S. Lu and C.-Y. Hsu. Geometric distortion-resilient image hashing scheme and its applications on copy detection and authentication. *Multimedia Systems*, 11(2):159–173, 2005.

17. J. Luo and M. A. Nascimento. Content based sub-image retrieval via hierarchical tree matching. In *Proc. MMDB Int. Workshop on Multimedia Databases*, pages 63–69, November 2003.

18. K. Mikolajczyk and C. Schmid. Scale and affine invariant interest point detectors. *Int. Journal of Computer Vision*, 60(1):63–86, 2004.

19. A. Qamra, Y. Meng, and E. Y. Chang. Enhanced perceptual distance functions and indexing for image replica recognition. *IEEE Trans. Pattern Analysis and Machine Intelligence*, 27(3):379–391, 2005.

20. N. Sebe, M. S. Lew, and D. P. Huijsmans. Multi-scale sub-image search. In *Proc. MM Int. Conf. on Multimedia*, pages 79–82, Orlando, FL, USA, October–November 1999. ACM Press.

21. N. Shivakumar and H. Garcia-Molina. Finding near-replicas of documents and servers on the web. In *Proc. WebDB Int. Workshop on World Wide Web and Databases*, pages 204–212, March 1998.

22. A. W. M. Smeulders, M. Worring, S. Santini, A. Gupta, and R. Jain. Content-based image retrieval at the end of the early years. *IEEE Trans on Pattern Analysis and Machine Intelligence*, 22(12):1349–1380, December 2000.

23. D. Zhang and S.-F. Chang. Detecting image near-duplicate by stochastic attributed relational graph matching with learning. In *Proc. MM Int. Conf. on Multimedia*, pages 877–884, October 2004.

24. J. Zobel and A. Moffat. Inverted files for text search engines. *ACM Computing Surveys*, June 2006.

User-Friendly Image Sharing in Multimedia Database Using Polynomials with Different Primes

Ching-Nung Yang[1], Kun-Hsuan Yu[1], and Rastislav Lukac[2]

[1] Department of Computer Science and Information Engineering
National Dong Hwa University, Taiwan
cnyang@mail.ndhu.edu.tw
[2] Department of Electrical and Computer Engineering
University of Toronto, Canada
lukacr@dsp.utoronto.ca

Abstract. Recently, Thien and Lin proposed a user-friendly (k, n)-threshold scheme which employs Lagrange interpolation to produce shadow images representing a shrunken version of the original image. In this paper, we introduce a new framework which uses more $(k-1)$-degree polynomials with different primes to enhance the functionality of the user-friendly (k, n)-threshold framework and obtain more effective performance for large k. Since the proposed framework significantly reduces reconstruction errors compared to the previously published user-friendly schemes, it is suitable for modern visual communication applications where features, such as distributed trust, secure transmission and storage, fault tolerance, and high-quality image reconstruction are required.

1 Introduction

In the so-called (k, n) secret sharing framework [1], where $k \le n$, the content of a secret message is divided into n shadows or shares in the way that requires at least k shares for the message reconstruction. As proposed in [2]-[6], the framework can produce both meaningful and meaningless shares, depending on the application constraints and user's requirements. For example, Thien and Lin used $(k-1)$-degree polynomials to secure the confidentiality of the shares during transmission over public multimedia networks by encrypting the secret image into noise-like shadow images with size $1/k$ times that of the original image [2]. Since encryption functionality can complicate share identification and management, e.g. in private networks, the same authors proposed in [3] to share user-friendly shadow images. The term "user-friendly" means that shadow images are a shrunken version of the original image and have insufficient quality to recover the input image for practical use in high-end applications by expanding the shadow image directly. However, using k or more arbitrary shadows in the reconstruction process results in the restored high-quality image. By looking like a portrait [3], shadow images have limited spatial resolution and quality which, however, should not affect performance of image reconstruction if the threshold constraint, suggesting the presence of at least k shadow images for reconstruction, is satisfied.

T.-J. Cham et al. (Eds.): MMM 2007, LNCS 4352, Part II, pp. 443–452, 2007.

To manage the shadow images and avoid using the wrong shadows for reconstruction, Thien-Lin scheme is the first scheme to address the management problem using this user-friendly shadow images. This paper introduces a new user-friendly image sharing framework that substantially outperforms the scheme of [3] in terms of the image quality, while holding the same shadow features. Moreover, it will be shown that the user-friendly scheme proposed by Thien and Lin introduces processing errors and that this is not the case when the proposed refined concept is employed.

2 Previous Works

2.1 Thien-Lin Image Sharing Scheme

The (k, n)-threshold scheme in [2] produces n noise-like shares by dividing the original image into τ non-overlapping k-pixel blocks, each of which is represented in the equivalent share representation as follows:

$$S_j(r) = (P_{jk} + P_{jk+1}r + P_{jk+2}r^2 + ... + P_{jk+k-1}r^{k-1}) \bmod p \qquad (1)$$

where $S_j(r)$ represents the shadow pixel associated with the jth block and rth shadow image, for $0 \le j \le \tau-1$ and $1 \le r \le n$. The value of $S_j(r)$ is generated using the original pixel values P_{jk}, P_{jk+1}, ..., P_{jk+k-1} included in the jth block. To enforce the confidentiality of $S_j(r)$ as well as its suitability for most image coders, the prime number $p = 251$ was recommended. By this setting, $S_j(r)$ is constrained between 0 and 250, i.e. within the conventional 8-bit gray-scale or color component representation.

Similarly to the above scheme, the user-friendly image sharing solution presented in [3] produces shadows with size $1/k$ times that of the original image. However, after k-pixel blocks are identified in the original image, the solution in [3] classifies them as smooth (for $\left|P_{max} - \tilde{P}_{n-1}\right| \le 8$) and coarse (for $\left|P_{max} - \tilde{P}_{n-1}\right| > 8$) blocks. The classification criterion is defined via $\left|P_{max} - \tilde{P}_{n-1}\right| = Max\{P_{n+i} - \tilde{P}_{n-1} : i \in [0, k-1]\}$, where $\{P_n, P_{n+1}, ..., P_{n+k-1}\}$ denotes a k-pixel block and $\tilde{P}_{n-1}$ is the last pixel in the previous coded block, for $n = jk$.

For smooth blocks, the pixel differences $a_i = P_{n+i} - \tilde{P}_{n-1} + 8$, for $i \in [0, k-1]$, are used as the input to $S_j(r) = ((a_0 + a_1 r + a_2 r^2 + ... + a_{k-1} r^{k-1}) \bmod p)$ with the prime number $p = 17$ denoting the upper constraint. Assuming for the sake of simplicity that $S_r = S_j(r)$, the jth pixel value in the rth shadow image is expressed as $\hat{P}_{r,j} = \tilde{P}_{n-1} + S_r - 8$.

Since in coarse blocks $\left|P_{max} - \tilde{P}_{n-1}\right|$ may far exceeds 17, the pixel differences should be expressed as $a_i = \left[\dfrac{P_{n+i}}{17}\right]$ where [ ] denotes the rounding function. Note that $\left[\dfrac{255}{17}\right]$ is equal to 15 keeping $p = 17$ suitable for coding. If $P_{base} < \tilde{P}_{n-1}$, then the shadow pixel is given by $\hat{P}_{r,j} = P_{\text{base}} - S_r$, otherwise $\hat{P}_{r,j} = P_{\text{base}} + S_r$ where P_{base} is a multiple of 17 and very close to P_{max}.

In the decoding phase, comparing the pixel value in the shadow image via $\left| \hat{P}_{r,j} - \tilde{P}_{n-1} \right| \leq 8$ (or > 8) differentiates the type of blocks. By reversing the encoding, the smooth blocks can be reliably recovered whereas the coarse blocks are usually recovered with distortion due to the original structural content (edges and fine details). The interested reader can find the additional information on the issue in [3]. Repeating the procedure for all shadow pixels restores the secret image with processing errors, as shown below.

2.2 Thien-Lin's User-Friendly Scheme Analysis

Decoding smooth blocks produces $P_{n+i} = \tilde{P}_{n-1} + a_i - 8$ where a_i is determined using k or more shadows through Lagrange interpolation. Since $a_i \in [0, 16]$ the value of $(a_i - 8) \in [-8, 8]$. Thus, using $\tilde{P}_{n-1} \in [0, 7]$ and [248, 255] during coding respectively results in the recovered values $P_{n-i} \in [-8, -1]$ and [256, 263] which are out of the conventional 8-bit image representation. This suggests that the scheme of [3] may introduce errors in smooth image areas.

For the coarse blocks, if $P_{\text{max}} \in [239, 255]$ and $P_{\text{max}} \geq \tilde{P}_{n-1}$ then $P_{\text{base}} = \lceil P_{\text{max}} / 17 \rceil \times 17 = 255$. As opposed to this case, if $P_{\text{max}} \in [0, 16]$ and $P_{\text{max}} < \tilde{P}_{n-1}$ then $P_{\text{base}} = \lfloor P_{\text{max}} / 17 \rfloor \times 17 = 0$. Both cases, i.e. $P_{\text{base}} = 255$ and $P_{\text{base}} = 0$, result in shadow pixels $\hat{P}_{r,j} > 255$ and $\hat{P}_{r,j} < 0$, respectively. Since the scheme produces incorrect S_r the quantization values of a coarse block are not correctly recovered, thus producing processing errors in edge areas.

Although produced errors can result in the introduction of serious visual impairments in the reconstructed image, the drawbacks of the scheme in [3] are not obvious or known due to the fact that the test images used in [3], such as 512×512 images Lena, Jet and Baboon, do not contain many areas with critical (close to 0 or 255) pixel's values. The number of error blocks and error rates corresponding to the popular (k, n)-threshold schemes, the achieved errors are very small. For instance, the use of $(2, n)$ scheme on the image Lena corresponds to 3 error blocks of total 131072(=512×512/2) blocks, resulting in the error rate 0.0023%(=3/131072). Even better results, namely no processing errors, were achieved for the Jet image, whereas the maximum error rate equal to 0.202% was obtained for the $(8, n)$ scheme applied to the Baboon image (the detail error blacks and error rates, please see the full version). However, testing the considered threshold configurations on the image Lena with numbers, which is a well-known image available from USC-SIPI database, fully reveals the drawbacks of the scheme presented in [3], many numbers difficult to recognize or removed altogether, (please see the full version). To overcome the problem, we suggest that the pixel values should be modified every time when errors may occur. Namely, smooth blocks with $\tilde{P}_{n-1} \in [0, 7]$ and [248, 255] should be processed using $\tilde{P}_{n-1} = 8$ and $\tilde{P}_{n-1} = 247$, respectively. For the coarse block, the pixel values $P_{n+i} \in [0, 16]$ and $[239, 255]$ should be replaced by $P_{n+i} = 17$ and $P_{n+i} = 238$, respectively. Our approach, hereafter referred to as 'corrected' Thien-Lin's scheme, produces better visual quality and significantly outperforms conventional Thien-Lin's scheme, as the corresponding PSNR increased from 15.17 dB to 34.66 dB.

3 The Proposed Framework

We now introduce a unique (k, n) user-friendly image sharing framework based on multi polynomials. To present the concept, we first describe the construction of a basic $(2, n)$ scheme and then introduce its enhanced version which can overcome the lack of structural information in shadow images. Extensions to higher-order $(k > 2)$ threshold configurations will be proposed, as well.

3.1 A Basic (2, n)-Scheme

The proposed framework starts the encoding process by choosing a set of 2^k prime numbers. Thus, $(2, n)$-threshold configurations operate using four prime numbers $\{p_0, p_1, p_2, p_3\}$ constrained by $p_0 < p_1 < p_2 < p_3$ and $p_3 \leq 251$. Note that the different primes will result in the different performance and that the optimal selection of prime numbers will be discussed later in this paper. After the prime numbers are selected, the procedure continues by dividing the original image into non-overlapping k-pixel blocks ($k = 2$ in our case), which are processed from right-and-bottom to left-and-up. In each two-pixel block, the least significant bits (LSBs) are modified as (00), (01), (10), or (11) to respectively indicate the prime number p_0, p_1, p_2, or p_3 used in encoding the next block.

Assuming that (P_n, P_{n+1}) and (P_{n-2}, P_{n-1}) represent the current and previous two-pixel blocks and that the values (P_0^i, P_1^i) corresponding to the initial block are set to zero, LSBs in the previous block can be determined as follows:

$$\begin{cases} (00) \text{ for } |P_{max} - P_{n-1}| \leq (p_0 - 1)/2, \\ (01) \text{ for } (p_0 - 1)/2 < |P_{max} - P_{n-1}| \leq (p_1 - 1)/2, \\ (10) \text{ for } (p_1 - 1)/2 < |P_{max} - P_{n-1}| \leq (p_2 - 1)/2, \\ (11) \text{ for } (p_2 - 1)/2 < |P_{max} - P_{n-1}| \leq 250, \end{cases} \tag{2}$$

where $P_{max} \in \{P_n, P_{n+1}\}$ denotes the pixel value in the current block with the largest difference from the last pixel P_{n-1} in the previous block and $|P_{max} - P_{n-1}|$ is given by

$$|P_{max} - P_{n-1}| = Max\{|P_n - P_{n-1}|, |P_{n+1} - P_{n-1}|\}. \tag{3}$$

Using the prime number $p_3 = 251$ we can only process $|P_{max} - P_{n-1}| \in [-125, 125]$. However, $|P_{max} - P_{n-1}|$ can be any number from -255 to 255. Therefore, we also use the second LSB level (i.e. 7th bit) of the pixel in the previous block to extend the range from $[-125, 125]$ to $[-250, 250]$. Thus, the pixel difference can be expressed as $((R-125)\times 2 + x)$ with R denoting the value recovered from the polynomial with $p_3 = 251$ and x indicating the 7th bit of the pixel in the previous block. For example, the utilization of $R = 5$ and $x = 1$ results in the pixel difference equal to -239. The remaining values, i.e. $[-255, -251]$ and $[251, 255]$, can be easily managed by modifying the original image via histogram straitening to the intensity range $[0, 250]$. To extend the range from $[-125, 125]$ to $[-250, 250]$ we also use the 7th bit for the polynomial associated with p_3. Since altering the 7th bit for the determined p_i may produce blocks with values out of the desired range, we possibly need to add ± 2 or ± 4 to the altered values to preserve the completeness of two LSB levels. Repeating the above procedure creates the preprocessed image. Because the procedure alters only LSB entries to indicate p_0, p_1 and p_2 or two LSB levels to indicate p_3, the original and preprocessed images are visually identical.

Determining the prime number for the current block from the previous block in the preprocessed image allows to calculate:

$$\begin{cases} f_0 = P_n - P_{n-1} + (p_i - 1)/2 \\ f_1 = P_{n+1} - P_{n-1} + (p_i - 1)/2 \end{cases} \text{for } i = 0,1,2 \tag{4-1}$$

$$\begin{cases} f_0 = \lfloor (P_n - P_{n-1})/2 \rfloor + (p_i - 1)/2 \\ f_1 = \lfloor (P_{n+1} - P_{n-1})/2 \rfloor + (p_i - 1)/2 \end{cases} \text{for } i = 3 \tag{4-2}$$

which are shared, in the way similar to Eq. (1), by mod p_i, $i \in [0, 3]$, as $(1, S_1)$, $(2, S_2)$, ..., (n, S_n) to produce shadow pixels using the following polynomial:

$$S_j(r) = ((f_0 + f_1 r) \bmod p_i), \tag{5}$$

where f_0 and f_1 are defined in Eq.(4), for $i = 0, 1, 2$ and 3.

The process generates shadow pixels $\hat{P}_{r,j}$ associated with the rth shadow image and the jth block in the original image. The value of $\hat{P}_{r,j}$ is equal to $S_r \bmod p_i$ and is close to the average value of the pixels in the block. For example, if $S_r \bmod 17$ is equal to 4 for the j-th block with the pixel value (122, 128), then $\hat{P}_{r,j} = 123$ since the average pixel 125 (=(122+128)/2) is closest to 123 in the set of numbers (..., 106, 123, 140, ...) which correspond to the remainder 4 in the mod 17 operation. Thus, the $\hat{P}_{r,j}$ value contains the information about S_r and the gray level of the block.

The decoding process starts by determining the prime number from the initial shadow pixels and producing S_r from $\hat{P}_{r,j}$. Then, applying Lagrange polynomial recovers (f_0, f_1) which can restore the corresponding (P_n, P_{n+1}) through Eq. (4-1) and (4-2). Each recovered block (P_n, P_{n+1}) is used to determine the prime number for the subsequent block. Repeating the decoding procedure for each spatial location in shadow images restores the pre-processed image.

Fig. 1 shows the results obtained using a (2, 4) scheme with $\{p_0, p_1, p_2, p_3\} = \{17, 61, 131, 251\}$. The scheme encodes a 512×512 image shown in Fig. 1(a) into four 512×256 shadows, with examples shown in Figs. 2(c) and (d). Note that the scheme

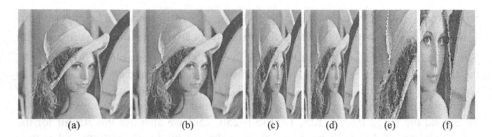

(a)   (b)   (c)   (d)   (e)   (f)

Fig. 1. Results of the proposed (2, 4) basic solution with {p0, p1, p2, p3}={17, 61, 131, 251} using the image Lena: (a) 512×512 original image; (b) restored image with PSNR 50.53 dB obtained using two 256×512 shadow images shown in (c)-(d); (e)-(f) enlarged parts of the image shown in (d)

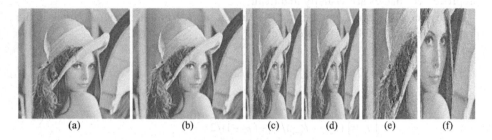

(a)   (b)   (c)   (d)   (e)   (f)

Fig. 2. Results of the proposed (2, 4) enhanced solution with {p0, p1, p2, p3}={17, 61, 67, 131} using the image Lena:(a) 512×512 original image; (b) restored image with PSNR 48.88 dB obtained using two 256×512 shadow images shown in (c)-(d); (e)-(f) enlarged parts of the image shown in (d)

can restore high-quality image from any two of four generated shadow images. Fig. 1(b) shows the image restored using the shadow images shown in Figs. 2(c) and (d). The PSNR of the restored image is 50.53 dB which is a significant improvement of corrected Thien-Lin's method with PSNR equal to 37.91 dB. However, visual inspection of cropped image areas shown in Figs. 1(e) and (f) reveals that our basic solution spoils some edges and fine details in shadow images due to the large prime number in the modular function and resulting large differences. We now introduce an enhanced solution which prevents from edge fluctuations in shadow images at the expense of a little lower quality of the recovered image.

3.2 An Enhanced (2, *n*) Scheme

From extensive experimentation and detailed analysis of generated results we found that the edge problems should be attributed to the prime numbers p_2 and p_3. Therefore, we further reduce the quantization step size for p_2 and p_3 by dividing $|P_n - P_{n-1}|$ and $|P_{n+1} - P_{n-1}|$ by 2 and 4, respectively. Moreover, we constrain the prime numbers as $p_0 < p_1 < p_2 < p_3$ and $p_3 = 131$, where (131×2) is near and no less than 255 to process $|P_n - P_{n-1}|$ and $|P_{n+1} - P_{n-1}|$ up to 255. If the actual encoding operation is guided by p_3, then the second (i.e. 7th bit) and third (i.e. 6th bit) LSB levels of the previous block should be accordingly modified to represent the remainder of modulo 4. Similarly, the use of p_2 in the actual encoding operation requires the alteration of the second LSB level to represent the remainder of modulo 2. Furthermore, to match new design characteristics, we replace Eq. (2) with its enhanced version:

$$\begin{cases} (00) \text{ for } |P_{max} - P_{n-1}| \le (p_0-1)/2, \\ (01) \text{ for } (p_0-1)/2 < |P_{max} - P_{n-1}| \le (p_1-1)/2, \\ (10) \text{ for } (p_1-1)/2 < |P_{max} - P_{n-1}| \le (p_2-1), \\ (11) \text{ for } (p_2-1) < |P_{max} - P_{n-1}| \le 255. \end{cases} \tag{6}$$

Similarly to our basic $(2, n)$ scheme, we now use the 7th bit for the polynomial with p_2 to extend the range from $[-(P_2-1)/2, +(P_2-1)/2]$ to $[-(P_2-1), +(P_2-1)]$ and 6th and 7th bits for the polynomial with p_3 to extend the range from $[-65, +65]$ to $[-255, +255]$. This suggests that ±2, ±4 or ±8 may be employed to preserve the completeness of the three LSB levels. Finally, the last change compared to our basic solution lies in the replacement of Eq. (4) with the following formulas:

$$\begin{cases} f_0 = P_n - P_{n-1} + (p_i-1)/2 \\ f_1 = P_{n+1} - P_{n-1} + (p_i-1)/2 \end{cases} \text{ for } i = 0,1 \tag{7-1}$$

$$\begin{cases} f_0 = \lfloor (P_n - P_{n-1})/2 \rfloor + (p_i-1)/2 \\ f_1 = \lfloor (P_{n+1} - P_{n-1})/2 \rfloor + (p_i-1)/2 \end{cases} \text{ for } i = 2 \tag{7-2}$$

$$\begin{cases} f_0 = \lfloor (P_n - P_{n-1})/4 \rfloor + (p_i-1)/2 \\ f_1 = \lfloor (P_{n+1} - P_{n-1})/4 \rfloor + (p_i-1)/2 \end{cases} \text{ for } i = 3. \tag{7-3}$$

Fig. 2 shows the results obtained using the enhanced (2, 4) scheme with $\{p_0, p_1, p_2, p_3\} = \{17, 61, 67, 131\}$. Comparisons of Fig. 1b and Fig.2b can hardly reveal that the restored image obtained using the enhanced solution has slightly lower quality than the image restored using our basic solution, but the actual PSNR reduced from 50.53 dB to 48.88 dB which is still significantly larger than 37.91 dB corresponding to corrected Thien-Lin's scheme. On the other hand, Figs. 2(e) and (f) clearly show that the proposed enhanced solution preserves edges and fine details, thus outperforming our basic solution in terms of the shadow image quality.

3.3 A General (k, n) Scheme (please see the full version)

3.4 Selection of Prime Numbers for (k, n) Schemes (please see the full version)

3.5 Theoretical Estimation of PSNRs

In this subsection, we will analytically estimate PSNR of the images produced using a (k, n) image sharing scheme with $\{p_0, p_1, p_2, p_3\}$. Assuming that N_i determines the number of pixels processed by the prime p_i, the total number of pixels in the original image can be expressed as $N = (N_0 + N_1 + N_2 + N_3)$. The mean square error in our basic solution is, in average, 1/2 for $\{p_0, p_1, p_2\}$ and 7/2 for p_3 since the process modifies LSB (for $p_0, p_1,$ and p_2) or two LSB levels (for p_3) of the original pixels. Thus, the restored image PSNR can be estimated via

$$\text{PSNR}_{est} = 10 \times \log_{10} \left(255^2 \bigg/ \left(\frac{N_0 + N_1 + N_2}{N} \times \frac{2}{k} \times \frac{1}{2} + \frac{N_3}{N} \times \frac{2}{k} \times \frac{7}{2} \right) \right) \tag{8-1}$$

where the term $2/k$ is due to the utilization of two LSB levels in each k-pixel block to indicate the prime number. Using the same approach for our enhanced solution provides the following expression:

$$\text{PSNR}_{est} = 10 \times \log_{10} \left(255^2 \bigg/ \left(\frac{N_0 + N_1}{N} \times \frac{2}{k} \times \frac{1}{2} + \frac{N_2}{N} \times \frac{2}{k} \times \frac{7}{2} + \frac{N_3}{N} \times \frac{2}{k} \times \frac{35}{2} \right) \right) \tag{8-2}$$

Note that Eq. (8-1) and (8-2) correspond to the restored images. To introduce similar expressions for shadow images, we have to first calculate the average mean square error for p_i. Assuming that $v \in [0, p_i - 1]$ is the shared value corresponding to some block in the original image and the average value of the pixels in this block is denoted as $m \in [0, 255]$ which is uniformly distributed with probability $f(m)dm$, the generated shadow pixel value will be a multiple of v near to m. Due to the quantization operations used in the proposed framework, the mean square error $\overline{e^2}$ is defined as:

$$\overline{e^2} = \sum_{v \in [0, p_i - 1]} \left[\int_{v}^{v + p_i / 2} f(m)(m-v)^2 \, dm + \int_{(v+p_i)-p_i/2}^{(v+p_i)+p_i/2} f(m)(m-(v+p_i))^2 \, dm \right.$$

$$\left. + \dots + \int_{(\lfloor 255/p_i \rfloor \times p_i) - p_i/2}^{(\lfloor 255/p_i \rfloor \times p_i)} f(m)(m - (\lfloor 255/p_i \rfloor \times p_i))^2 \, dm \right]. \tag{9}$$

Since $f(m)$ can be considered as a constant f in the integration interval, the above expression can be rewritten as:

$$\overline{e^2} = \sum_{v \in [0, p_i - 1]} f \times \left(\int_{-p_i/2}^{p_i/2} m^2 \, dm \right) = \sum_{v \in [0, p_i - 1]} f \times \left(p_i^3 / 12 \right)$$

$$= \left(p_i^2 / 12 \right) \times \left(\sum_{v \in [0, p_i - 1]} (f \times p_i) \right) = \left(p_i^2 / 12 \right), \tag{10}$$

where $\left(\sum_{v \in [0, p_i - 1]} (f \times p_i) \right)$ denotes the overall probability for the averaged pixel values in

the image block, and hence the sum is equal to 1 and the average mean square error is given by $\left(p_i^2 / 12 \right)$. Thus, the shadow image PSNR can be estimated as follows:

$$10 \times \log_{10} \left(255^2 \bigg/ \sum_{i \in [0,3]} (N_i / N) \times (p_i^2 / 12) \right) \tag{11}$$

4   Experimental Results

To determine the performance of the proposed user-friendly image sharing framework, a number of test gray-scale images have been utilized. Examples such as

Table 1. Comparisons of the proposed solutions with Thien-Lin's method

Secret image / (k, n) scheme	PSNR of the recovered image (dB)			Average PSNR of expanded shadows (dB)			Improved gain	
	[3]	Method 1	Method 2	[3]	Method 1	Method 2	Δ_1	Δ_2
Lena / $(2, n)$	37.37 $(37.91^{\#1})$	50.53 $(50.68^{\#2})$	48.88 $(48.06^{\#2})$	24.80 $(24.78^{\#1})$	23.32 $(23.45^{\#3})$	26.52 $(26.29^{\#3})$	12.62	10.97
Lena / $(4, n)$	36.12 $(36.29^{\#1})$	52.56 $(52.87^{\#2})$	49.80 $(48.53^{\#2})$	20.74 $(20.74^{\#1})$	20.69 $(20.41^{\#3})$	23.52 $(24.20^{\#3})$	16.27	13.51
Lena / $(8, n)$	34.35 $(34.66^{\#1})$	54.23 $(54.64^{\#2})$	50.36 $(48.96^{\#2})$	17.61 $(17.61^{\#1})$	17.20 $(17.75^{\#3})$	20.79 $(22.26^{\#3})$	19.57	15.70
Jet / $(2, n)$	39.19 $(39.19^{\#1})$	49.76 $(50.47^{\#2})$	47.88 $(47.61^{\#2})$	25.65 $(25.65^{\#1})$	23.14 $(23.51^{\#3})$	27.14 $(27.00^{\#3})$	10.57	8.69
Jet / $(4, n)$	37.81 $(37.81^{\#1})$	51.88 $(52.67^{\#2})$	49.00 $(48.41^{\#2})$	21.17 $(21.17^{\#1})$	20.72 $(20.77^{\#3})$	23.66 $(23.20^{\#3})$	14.07	11.19
Jet / $(8, n)$	36.11 $(36.11^{\#1})$	53.82 $(54.68^{\#2})$	49.89 $(49.40^{\#2})$	17.84 $(17.84^{\#1})$	17.76 $(18.56^{\#3})$	21.10 $(24.97^{\#3})$	17.71	13.78
Baboon / $(2, n)$	34.75 $(34.77^{\#1})$	49.17 $(49.68^{\#2})$	45.22 $(44.56^{\#2})$	20.55 $(20.57^{\#1})$	18.52 $(19.01^{\#3})$	22.53 $(22.96^{\#3})$	14.40	10.45
Baboon / $(4, n)$	33.28 $(34.1^{\#1})$	50.20 $(51.38^{\#2})$	45.67 $(45.14^{\#2})$	17.07 $(17.07^{\#1})$	16.82 $(16.76^{\#3})$	19.71 $(21.43^{\#3})$	16.10	11.57
Baboon / $(8, n)$	33.02 $(33.85^{\#1})$	51.91 $(52.97^{\#2})$	46.42 $(46.21^{\#2})$	14.53 $(14.53^{\#1})$	14.75 $(15.00^{\#3})$	17.86 $(20.15^{\#3})$	18.33	12.57
Lena with numbers/ $(2, n)$	15.17 $(34.66^{\#1})$	49.38 $(48.98^{\#2})$	45.60 $(44.10^{\#2})$	18.06 $(18.16^{\#1})$	17.13 $(19.33^{\#3})$	19.28 $(23.71^{\#3})$	14.72	10.94
Lena with numbers/ $(4, n)$	14.42 $(36.39^{\#1})$	51.18 $(50.83^{\#2})$	45.91 $(45.01^{\#2})$	14.14 $(14.06^{\#1})$	14.73 $(17.04^{\#3})$	16.90 $(21.79^{\#3})$	14.79	9.52
Lena with numbers/ $(8, n)$	13.99 $(35.22^{\#1})$	52.81 $(52.55^{\#2})$	47.23 $(46.12^{\#2})$	12.25 $(12.37^{\#1})$	12.72 $(15.12^{\#3})$	15.62 $(20.20^{\#3})$	17.59	12.01

Method 1: The proposed *basic* solution with $\{p_0, p_1, p_2, p_3\}$={17, 61, 131, 251}
Method 2: The proposed *enhanced* solution with $\{p_0, p_1, p_2, p_3\}$={17, 61, 67, 131}
#1: Corrected Thien-Lin method
#2: Estimated PSNR of the recovered image: Eq. (8)
#3: Estimated PSNR of the shadow image: Eq. (11)
Δ_1: Improved gain = PSNR of Method 1 − PSNR of corrected Thien-Lin method)
Δ_2: Improved gain = PSNR of Method 2 − PSNR of corrected Thien-Lin method)

the 512×512 image Lena, Jet and Boboon are used to emulate the application scenario. Note that these test images vary in the statistics and the complexity of the structural content (edges and fine details), thus suggesting their suitability to evaluate the robustness of our framework. Table 1 allows for comparisons of the proposed basic and enhanced solutions against Thien-Lin's scheme. To facilitate the comparisons, various (k, n) schemes with k=2, 4 and 8 are used in this work. Note that in addition to the achieved PSNR values, we also list the entries corresponding to corrected Thien-Lin method as well as PSNR estimates obtained using the formulas proposed in Eq. (8) and Eq. (11). As it can be seen, the estimated values are very close to the actual PSNR, thus proving the correctness of our derivations. Moreover, the proposed frameworks holds excellent trade-off between shadow and restored image quality and that clearly outperforms Thien-Lin's method. Comparing improvement gains reported in Table 1 indicates that the benefits resulting from the use of our framework instead of Thien-Lin's scheme increase for large k due to more frequent occurrence of coarse blocks. For example, the percentage of coarse blocks in the image Lena is 37.95%, 57.06% and 75.20% for $(2, n)$, $(4, n)$ and $(8, n)$ schemes, respectively. Since Thien-Lin's scheme introduces most errors in edge areas where the proposed framework still enforces perfect reconstruction due to the employed refined processing concepts, the differences in performance become more obvious. This behavior is confirmed also analytically by theoretical PSNR which increases with k.

5 Conclusion

A new user-friendly (k, n) image sharing framework was introduced. The proposed framework uses different prime numbers and refined processing concepts to produce user-friendly shadow images with quality reasonable for practical applications and allow for reconstruction of visually pleasing restored images for high-end applications. A number of practical solutions were introduced and their performance was evaluated, both experimentally and analytically using the proposed tools. Experimental results showed that our framework is robust, produces excellent results for various (k, n)-threshold configurations, and clearly outperforms the previous solutions.

References

1. Shamir, A.: How to share a secret. Communications of the association for computing machinery. (1979) 612-613.
2. Thien, C.C. and Lin, J.C.: Secret image sharing. Computer & Graphics, Vol. 26, no. 5. (2002) 765-770
3. Thien, C.C. and Lin, J.C.: An image-sharing method with user-friendly shadow images. IEEE Transactions on Circuits and Systems for Video Technology, Vol. 13, no. 12. (2003) 1161-1169
4. Lin, C.C. and Tsai, W.H.: Secret image sharing with steganography and authentication. Journal of Systems & Software, Vol. 73, no. 3. (2004) 405-414
5. Feng, J.B., Wu, H.C., Tsai, C.S., and Chu, Y.P.: A new multi-secret images sharing scheme using Lagrange's interpolation. Journal of Systems & Software, Vol. 76, no. 3. (2005) 327-339
6. Chang, C.C. and Hwang, R.J.: Sharing secret images using shadow codebooks. Information Sciences, Vol. 111, no. 1-4. (1998) 335-34

Accelerating Non-photorealistic Video Effects Using Compressed Domain Processing

Wen-Hung Liao

Department of Computer Science, National Chengchi University,
Taipei, Taiwan
whliao@cs.nccu.edu.tw

Abstract. Recently, various non-photorealistic rendering (NPR) techniques have been developed for computers to generate images of different artistic styles automatically. Due to the complexity of the algorithms, however, most NPR methods are limited to the processing of still images. It is the objective of this paper to extend and improve existing NPR techniques to enable near real-time processing of video. The enhancement will be achieved by compressed domain processing. By exploiting the relationship among I, P, and B frames, different strategies can be developed to increase the efficiency of the NPR algorithm. Experimental results have demonstrated the efficacy of the proposed methods and validated the near real-time creation of NPR video effects.

Keywords: Non-photorealistic rendering, compressed domain processing, MPEG standards.

1 Introduction

In computer graphics, photorealistic rendering techniques are aimed at generating artificial images of simulated environments that look "just like the real world." Conversely, non-photorealistic rendering (NPR) can be defined as any technique that produces images in a style other than realism. Recently, NPR has been become practical on personal computers thanks to rapid advances in hardware technology. Commercial software packages that can convert images into different artistic styles are abundant. Common examples of NPR effects include water color, oil paint and charcoal. However, current solutions are limited to the processing of still images due to the complexities of the NPR algorithms. Attempts to extend the creation of NPR effects to video have been made only recently [1][2], and most of the proposed methods are concerned about the realistic synthesis of artistic styles. That is, most algorithms are aimed at extending the methods designed for images to arrive at a consistently looking video. Speed is an issue of lower priority, since the computation is usually carried out off-line.

With the prevalence of low-cost recording devices, digital video acquisition and analysis is no longer beyond the reach of average users. Whereas fidelity may be of primary concern in commercial-grade film creation, in certain desktop applications, interactivity may be a more significant requirement. For example, we have developed an interactive multimedia software named 'DDPlayCam'[3] that combines face

T.-J. Cham et al. (Eds.): MMM 2007, LNCS 4352, Part II, pp. 453–460, 2007.
© Springer-Verlag Berlin Heidelberg 2007

detection with special effects to create amusing scenes in real-time. At present, the maximum resolution is limited to 320x240 to ensure a smooth operation. We have traded spatial resolution for higher frame rates since we believe an application with low latency can retain the user's interest and promote its usability. Application of NPR effects is restricted for the same reason. It is therefore the main objective of this paper to explore methods to speed up the creation of NPR video to make the interactive multimedia more versatile.

An intuitive approach to generate NPR video is to apply the NPR algorithm for images frame by frame and combine the individual pictures to form a dynamic scene. Not only is such a method inefficient, it also suffers from temporal incoherence where random flickering may appear in the output video. In [1], the 'paint over' technique was introduced to reduce the flickering. Optical flow was also taken into account to warp the brush stroke between frames. Since both improvements were achieved by exploiting temporal relationship, it is reasonable to expect that similar results can be obtained by undertaking the NPR generation problem in the compressed domain. Moreover, boost in performance can be realized as NPR effects will be applied to certain frames in a sequence and then propagated accordingly.

The rest of this paper is organized as follows. In Section 2 we review the MPEG standard and outline possible directions for manipulating the video in the compressed domain. Section 3 formulates the strategy for compressed domain processing. A generic method to create oil-paint effect is utilized to demonstrate the process. We then present some experimental results, along with discussions on the improvements in processing speed. A brief conclusion and outlook for future improvements are given in Section 4.

2 Compressed Domain Processing

With the standardization of video formats such as MPEG-1, 2 and 4, much of the multimedia content available nowadays is in compressed format already. Compressed domain features can be extracted directly from the data stream without conversion. They haven been used for video segmentation and object detection [4]. However, there is no previous work on enhancing NPR performance using compressed domain processing.

In MPEG-1 and 2 video, the compressed data encode the frequency domain coefficients as well as motion vectors. Every linear operator in the spatial domain has an equivalent in the frequency domain. Manipulating the compressed DCT coefficients can only yield linear operations. As such, no significant NPR effects can be created in this manner. To illustrate, Fig.1 depicts a high-pass filtered image where the computation is carried out purely in the DCT domain. It has a 'mosaicing' effect. Applying low-pass or band-pass filters, however, does not yield any interesting 'style'. As a result, our subsequent discussion will be centered at the utilization of motion vector information to speed up the NPR generation.

MPEG standards exploit temporal redundancy to reduce the data required to code the image sequences. Three types of frames: I, P and B have been defined. Only I frames need to be coded independently. P frame is computed from the previously coded I- or P-frame by prediction based on motion compensation. B-frames can be recovered using bi-directional motion compensation. A typical MPEG frame sequence depicting the relationship among I-,P- and B-frames is given in Fig. 2.

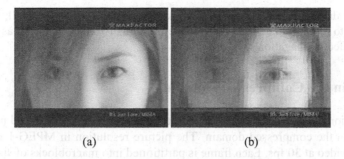

(a)   (b)

Fig. 1. (a) original frame (b) Butterworth high-pass filtered

Potential speed enhancement arises from the readily available motion vectors in successive frames. In Fig. 2, each group of pictures (GOP) contains nine frames. The proposed compressed-domain NPR algorithm works as follows: We will first apply still image NPR effect to the I-frame. We then propagate results obtained in I-frame to other frames in the group using motion compensation. This will reduce the flickering since inter-frame motion has been considered. In addition, because full-frame computation has to be done only once, the proposed method will be computationally efficient. Of course, we also need to consider the situation when predictive coding fails. This happens when the prediction error exceeds a certain threshold. In this case, the macroblock itself has to be encoded, and NPR on this portion needs to be performed independently.

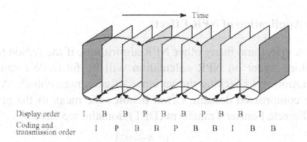

➤ Time

Display order   I   B   B   P   B   B   P   B   B   I
Coding and
transmission order   I   P   B   B   P   B   B   I   B   B

Fig. 2. MPEG sequence

To summarize, there are four important issues we need to take into account in compressed domain processing:

1. Manipulating DCT coefficients of the macroblocks of I-frame is straightforward. However, most NPR operations are non-linear in nature. They can be performed only in the spatial domain. Very limited NPR effects can be created by changing the DCT coefficients.
2. The routine process is to decompress I-frame and apply NPR in the spatial domain. Effects in other frames of the same GOP can be produced by propagation
3. If the content of successive frames changes drastically, motion compensation will not work well. We may have to apply NPR to P- or B-frames since propagation from I-frame can not compensate for the discontinuity.

4. If the difference between the I-frames of successive GOPs is small, there is no
   need to re-apply the NPR. NPR of the previous I-frame will serve as the source
   for effect propagation.

3 NPR in the Compressed Domain

In this section, we will use MPEG-1 video to illustrate NPR creation and propagation
processes in the compressed domain. The picture resolution in MPEG-1 is 352x240
for NTSC video at 30 fps. Each frame is partitioned into macroblocks of size 8x8. We
will employ a generic histogram-based algorithm outlined in Fig. 3 to create oil-paint
effect. Notice that this algorithm is chosen mainly due to its simplicity so that we can
focus on the framework of compressed-domain analysis instead of the details of a
particular NPR creation process.

```
For y= 1: height
    For x=1:width
        find most frequent value M in (x,y)'s
n*n neighborhood
            oil_paint_image(x,y)= M;
```

Fig. 3. Algorithm used to generate oil-paint effect

3.1 Selective Application of NPR Effects

For the oil-paint effect and many other NPR algorithms, if the region to be processed
is uniform, efforts spent on NPR calculation will be futile. We can prevent these
redundant operations by checking the variance of each macroblock. And the test can
be done in the compressed domain. Let m denotes the mean of the pixel values in a
block. In the Discrete Fourier Transform (DFT) domain, we have:

$$m = F(0,0) = \frac{1}{MN} \sum_{x=0}^{N-1} \sum_{y-0}^{M-1} f(x,y) \tag{1}$$

where F is the DFT of f. The variance can be computed according to:

$$
\begin{aligned}
\sum_{x=0}^{N-1} \sum_{y=0}^{M-1} [f(x,y)-m]^2 &= \sum_{x=0}^{N-1} \sum_{y=0}^{M-1} f^2(x,y) - 2m \sum_{x=0}^{N-1} \sum_{y=0}^{M-1} f(x,y) + \sum_{x=0}^{N-1} \sum_{y=0}^{M-1} m^2 \\
&= \sum_{u=0}^{N-1} \sum_{v=0}^{M-1} F^2(u,v) - 2MNm^2 + MNm^2 \\
&= \sum_{u=0}^{N-1} \sum_{v=0}^{M-1} F^2(u,v) - MNm^2 \\
&= \sum_{u=0}^{N-1} \sum_{v=0}^{M-1} F^2(u,v) - F^2(0,0)
\end{aligned}
\tag{2}
$$

In other words, the variance is the sum of the squares of the AC coefficients in the compressed domain. Even though Equation (2) is derived using DFT definition, the same conclusion holds in the DCT domain as the basis functions in DCT are orthonormal and Parseval's theorem is valid. Therefore, we can use the rule shown in Fig. 4 to check if NPR computation needs to be performed in a particular block:

```
Variance =sum of all AC² in the macro block
if( Variance < threshold )
    ApplyNPR(macro block)
else
    macro block = macro block of source image
```

Fig. 4. Applying NPR selectively

The macroblock in MPEG-1 is of size 8x8. The corresponding DCT coefficients are stored in a zigzag manner. We can regard it as a 1D array. The first element is DC. The others (2-64) are AC coefficients. In the actual implementation, we use Y-channel (in YUV system) information to compute the variance.

Fig. 5 depicts an image before and after applying the oil-paint effect. Figs. 6 and 7 demonstrate the results of selective NPR by setting the threshold to 100 and 1000, respectively. For this particular type of effect, no remarkable visible differences can

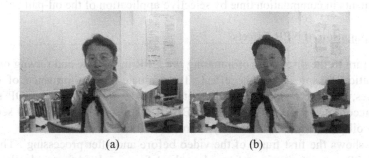

(a)   (b)

Fig. 5. (a) original image (b) with oil-paint effect

(a)   (b)

Fig. 6. (a) sum of AC² in green blocks < 100 (b) applying oil-paint effect selectively

(a)   (b)

Fig. 7. (a) sum of AC² in green blocks < 1000 (b) applying oil-paint effect selectively

Table 1. Performance enhancement by selective NPR application

Threshold	0	100	200	1000
Time (sec)	1.09	0.875	0.719	0.65
% of blocks not processed	0%	21.5%	34.5%	45%
Speedup	0%	20%	33%	40%

be detected if the slowly-varying blocks are not processed. Table 1 summarizes the improvements in computation time by selective application of the oil-paint effect.

3.2 Propagation of NPR Effects

We now turn to the discussion of initiating the NPR in I-frame and relying on motion compensation to spread out the effect. To evaluate the performance of different approaches, we use a video segment containing 419 frames with a GOP structure defined according to: IBBPBBPBBPBBPBB. It takes approximately 400 seconds to apply the oil-paint algorithm frame-by-frame. The frame rate is 1.05.

Fig. 8 shows the first frame of the video before and after processing[1]. The spatial domain NPR computation is performed on the I-frame only. Afterwards, the result is converted back to the compressed domain. P- and B-frames are reconstructed using the normal decoding process. The total computation is drastically reduced. It requires only 28.4 seconds to process the video, a speedup of approximately 15, corresponding to the size of the GOP group. In addition, flickering has been reduced significantly compared to the frame-by-frame approach.

Propagation from I-frame does not always work, however. For example, if significant changes occur between consecutive frames, as depicted in Fig. 9, the effect in Fig. 9(a) will not show up in Fig. 9(b). Under such circumstances, we will have to recover the P- and B-frames and apply the NPR accordingly, as demonstrated in Fig. 10. Again, the condition can be checked in the compressed domain since:

---

[1] The video is available for download at: http://140.119.164.91/liang/NPR.htm

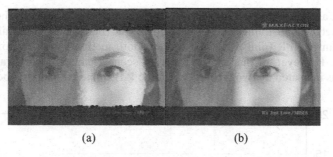

(a)   (b)

Fig. 8. (a) original video (b) I-frame oil-paint effect

$$\|f - g\|^2 = \|F - G\|^2 \qquad (3)$$

where f, g are spatial domain and F, G are frequency domain representations, respectively. If we set the difference threshold to be 60% (i.e., 60% of the pixels have changed values), the computation time is increased to 56.5 sec, or 7.7 fps.

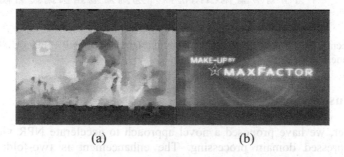

(a)   (b)

Fig. 9. (a) (b) Consecutive frames with abrupt changes in video content

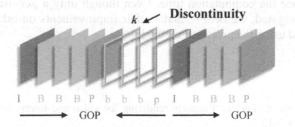

Fig. 10. b and p frames will require independent NPR

Finally, to investigate the effect of I-frame propagation, we define the percentage difference between two color images I_1 and I_2 as:

$$\% \, Diff \; = \; 100 \; x \frac{\left|I_1(R)\text{-}I_2(R)\right| + \left|I_1(G)\text{-}I_2(G)\right| + \left|I_1(B)\text{-}I_2(B)\right|}{I_1(R) + I_1(G) + I_1(B)} \qquad (4)$$

where R, G, and B refer to the individual color channels. Fig. 11 shows the percentage difference between all-frames and I-frame only NPR (black) as well as all-frames and selective frames NPR (pink). In most frames, both methods give approximately the same result. However, at places where abrupt scene changes occur (frame 255 and frame 417 as indicated by two arrows), selective P,B frame NPR does a better job.

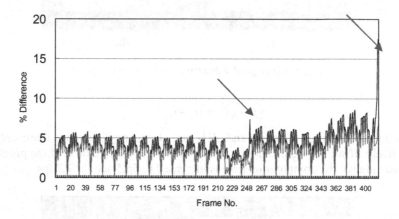

Fig. 11. Percentage difference between all frames and I-frame only NPR (black), all frames and selective frames NPR (pink)

4 Conclusions

In this paper, we have proposed a novel approach to accelerate NPR video effects using compressed domain processing. The enhancement is two-fold: flickering reduction and speedup. We have used MPEG-1 video to demonstrate the NPR generation and propagation process. We have also developed a selective NPR scheme to further reduce the computation time. Even though only a generic NPR algorithm has been investigated, we believe that similar improvements on other types of NPR can be obtained using the proposed methodology.

References

[1] A. Hertzmann, K. Perlin, "Painterly rendering for video and interaction", Proceedings of NPAR 2000: 7-12.
[2] J. Wang, Y. Xu, H. Shum, M. F. Cohen , "Video Tooning", ACM Trans. on Graphics (Proc. of SIGGAPH 2004), Vol. 23, No. 3, p.574-583, 2004.
[3] DDPlayCam: http://www.ddplaycam.tv
[4] Wang, H., Divakaran, A., Vetro, A., Chang, S.F., Sun, H., "Survey of compressed-domain features used in audio-visual indexing and analysis", Journal of Visual Communication and Image Representation(14), No. 2, June 2003, pp. 150-183.

A Color Image Hiding Scheme Based on SMVQ and Modulo Operator

Chi-Shiang Chan[1] and Chin-Chen Chang[2]

[1] Department of Computer Science and Information Engineering
National Chung Cheng University, Chiayi, Taiwan, 621, R.O.C.
[2] Department of Information Engineering and Computer Science,
Feng Chia University, Taichung, Taiwan, 40724, R.O.C.

Abstract. In this paper, we shall propose an image-hiding scheme to embed color secret images into their compression codes. The color host image is compressed by using the CSMVQ algorithm. Meanwhile, the color secret image is embedded during the production of the compression code. To get this job done, we must have the power to partition the state palette to sub-state palettes quickly and temporarily. In our new method, we sort the different colors in the palette to gather similar colors. In addition, there is a modulo operator we use to partition the state palette dynamically. This way, the secret data can be embedded into the compression code after the state palette is partitioned. According to our experimental results, the image quality of both the color host image with the secret data embedded in and the reconstructed color secret image is good when our proposed method is used.

Keywords: Data hiding, image hiding, image differencing, color palette.

1 Introduction

Vector Quantization (VQ) [4, 6] was introduced as an image compression scheme. To improve the compression rate of the VQ method, many researches have been done and the results proposed and discussed. For example, Side Match Vector Quantization (SMVQ) [5] is one of them. On the basis of the SMVQ method, Chang and Chen built their method, called the variable-rate SMVQ with a block classifier (CSMVQ) method, to further improve the chance of finding a similar element for the original block. The main concept of CSMVQ is to produce a state codebook temporarily for a block. Therefore, CSMVQ needs only few bits to recode the index of the state codebook.

Since VQ is an important image compression technique, many researchers have been on their journey in quest of an ideal secret data protection method that combines the concept of data hiding and the VQ method [2, 3, 8]. Basically, a VQ-based image-hiding technique partitions a codebook into several smaller codebooks, and then partitioned smaller codebooks will be used to indicate the values of the secret data. For example, we assume that a codebook is to be partitioned into two smaller codebooks. The simplest way to partition a codebook is as follows. For a codeword, we find its closest codeword in the codebook. Then, one of this pair of closest codewords is assigned to the first smaller codebook, while the other one of the pair is assigned to the

T.-J. Cham et al. (Eds.): MMM 2007, LNCS 4352, Part II, pp. 461–470, 2007.

second smaller codebook. Then, these two codewords are marked as processed. After all the pairs of closest codewords are done with this assigning procedure, the two smaller codebooks are ready. Then, in the embedding procedure, if the value of a secret bit is 0, then the first smaller codebook is searched for the closest codeword to the block in the host image; otherwise, when the secret bit value is 1, then the second smaller codebook is searched for the closest codeword to the block in the host image.

This way, we keep track of exactly which smaller codebook each codeword belongs to. And in the extracting phase, we can decide the values of the secret bits through the indices of the codewords. According to the description above, the most important thing here is that both the encoding and decoding ends must have the partitioned codebooks in hand beforehand. Besides, once the codebook has been partitioned, the elements in partitioned codebooks cannot be changed.

In this paper, we shall propose our new method of combining data hiding with image compression that hides a color secret image into the compression code. In order to improve the compression rate, the color host image will be encoded by CSMVQ. The color secret image will be embedded into the compression code during the encoding process. The embedding of the secret data will be done in a similar way to VQ-based secret data hiding. The major difference here, however, is that the existing methods partition the codebook beforehand, but because the state palette is produced temporarily, we must have way to partition the state palette dynamically. In our method, we sort the colors in the palette to gather similar colors. Besides, we use a modulo operator to partition the state palette dynamically. In this paper, we shall refer to this partitioned state palette as the sub-state palette. The secret data can be embedded into the compression code by means of searching the colors in the sub-state palette. Besides, the secret data can be extracted according to the number that indicates the specific sub-state palette.

2 Related Work

In order to further improve the compression rate of VQ, Kim [5] proposed his SMVQ method. The idea of SMVQ is that the current block can be predicted by referencing its neighboring blocks. In their method, there are two kinds of blocks in the image: seed blocks and residual blocks. The seed blocks are the blocks encoded and decoded by using the original VQ method, while the residual blocks rely on a predictive method to get encoded and decoded. The details of SMVQ are as follows.

At the encoding end, an original image is divided into non-overlapping blocks. The blocks in the first row and first column are set as seed blocks. On the other hand, the other blocks, called residual blocks, are reconstructed by using a predictive method. Fig. 1 below shows the way the residual blocks are predicted.

As Fig. 1 indicates, suppose we have four blocks here and the size of each block is four by four. We assume that the current block we want to reconstruct is the block X, and its neighbors, namely block U and block L, have been reconstructed with all the pixel values in them already known. Now, we want to use the pixel values in U and L to reconstruct block X. Since neighboring blocks tend to be alike, we take it that the

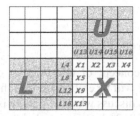

$$(X1, X2, X3, X4, X5, ?, ?, ?, X9, ?, ?, ?, X13, ?, ?, ?)$$

Fig. 1. The way to predict the residual blocks

pixels in block X will probably be highly similar to the pixels in blocks U and L. The value of pixel $X1$ may be close to the values of pixels $L4$ and $U13$, so we take $(U4+U13)/2$ as its predicted value. The rest of the pixel values in the first row and first column of block X are set as their nearest pixel values in blocks U and L. That is, we set the pixel value $X2$ as $U14$, $X3$ as $U15$, and so on. After that, we can get some predicted pixels in block X.   In Fig. 1, the vector ($X1$, $X2$, $X3$, $X4$, $X5$, ?, ?, ?,$X9$, ?, ?, ?, $X13$, ?, ?, ?) is obtained by filling in the predicted pixels. The symbol "?" means it does not matter what the value is in the position. We only compare the positions that have predicted values with the codewords in the codebook. Finally, we can find a closest codeword.

For the closed codeword, we calculate the mean square error between it and the original block. If the mean square error is larger than a predetermined threshold, then the codeword found is unacceptable. This block must be set as a seed block. That means this block has to be encoded by using the VQ method. Otherwise, the codeword found is accepted, and we set this block as a residual block. At the decoding end, we can follow this way and find such acceptable codewords, for which we do not need to record the indices. It goes without saying that we need one additional bit for each block to record the type of block, as either seed block or residual block. Then, at last, the compression code can be obtained by using SMVQ.

Based on the concept of SMVQ, Chang and Chen [1] have also offered a method called variable-rate SMVQ with a block classifier (CSMVQ) to improve the chance of getting an acceptable codeword for a block. Among the many components their method consists of, the most important part is the concept of state codebook. In the original SMVQ method, the only one closest codeword is found for a block to estimate the mean square error. However, Chang and Chen's method finds as many as sixteen closest codewords according to the predicted pixels to form a state codebook for a block. Then, the closest codeword in the state codebook can be picked out according to the original block. If the mean square error between a found codeword and the original block is unacceptable, we set it as a seed block. Otherwise, only four bits are needed to record the index because the total number of codewords in the state codebook is sixteen. Because the method produces a state codebook with sixteen codewords, there is a higher probability for the original block to get an acceptable codeword.

3   The Proposed Method

3.1   The Embedding Procedure

In this section, we apply the concept of CSMVQ to encode a color host image. Meanwhile, a color secret image will be embedded into the color host image.

Before going any further, let's discuss what the palette is all about. For a given color secret image in RGB color model, 24 bits are needed to represent a color pixel. That means the total number of possible colors for each color pixel in RGB color model is 2^{24}. Although there can be so many possible colors, the human eye cannot in fact distinguish some of them from each other. In light of this human perceptual limit, the color quantization process can be applied so as to save the storage without changing the color so much as to appear odd. In the color quantization process, finding a set of representative colors to stand for all possible colors is a practical way of simplification. Here, the set of representative colors is called a palette. Generally, a palette consists of 256 colors. For each color pixel, only eight bits (one pixel) are needed to determine its index. The palette concept is quite similar to the codebook concept except that the elements in a palette have three dimensions (three pixels), while the elements in a codebook have sixteen dimensions if the size of the block is four by four.

When the palette is obtained, a color image can be quantized by using the palette. That is, a closest color pixel in the palette can be found for each color pixel in the RGB color model. Then, the original color pixel can be replaced by the found color pixel in the palette. To keep track of the color, all we need here is to store the index. After recording the indices for all the color pixels, we can get a paletted image, which is also called an indexed-color image. According to the indices, a color image can be reconstructed at last.

Note that, for each color pixel, 8 bits are needed to record an index because there are 256 colors in a palette. In order to save even more storage space, we apply CSMVQ to compress a color image. Meanwhile, we want to embed a color secret image when the compression process is being performed. Besides, to achieve our goal, the color pixels in the palette have to be sorted. In our experiments, two kinds of sorting algorithms are employed to sort the palette. The first one is the principal component analysis technique [7], and the second algorithm sorts the colors in the palette according to the luminance value [9]. Therefore, the more similar these color pixels are, the closer their indices are. This will help us in embedding the color secret image into the CSMVQ compression code.

In the embedding procedure, the color secret image is processed differently from the color host image. For a color secret image, we transform it into a paletted image according to the sorted palette so as to reduce the storage cost. On the other hand, for a color host image, CSMVQ is applied: First of all, we define the pixels called seed pixels. For seed pixels, we search the closest colors in the palette and record their indices with eight bits. In our proposed method, the color pixels on the first row and first column of the host image are taken as the seed pixels first.

The rest of the pixels may be either seed pixels or residual pixels depending on the quality of the reconstructed color pixel values. In Fig. 2, we assume that the current color pixel to be reconstructed is P_C. Then, the values of the pixels on top of it and to the left of it, namely P_U and P_L, must be known.

For most ordinary images, there is a good chance that the color of a pixel will turn out to be approximately the same as its neighbor. Therefore, the predicted value of P_C is derived by following Formula (1).

$$(R_C, G_C, B_C) = ((R_U+R_L)/2, (G_U+G_L)/2, (B_U+B_L)/2)$$ (1)

For the predicted color pixel, we search the sorted palette to find the most similar color pixel. Assume that the index of the most similar color pixel is i, and the size of the state palette is S. Then, we range the state palette from $i- (S/2-1)$ to $i+ (S/2)$. For example, in Fig 3, if the size of the state palette is 8, then the range of the state palette is from i-3 to i+4. Note that the range of corresponding indices in the state palette is from 0 to S-1.

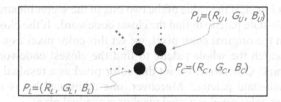

Fig. 2. SMVQ with a state codebook

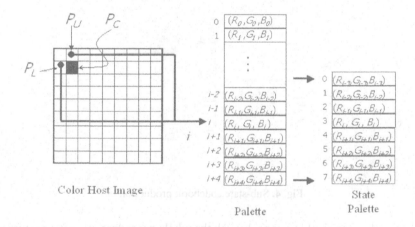

Fig. 3. State codebook production

Now, we have produced the state palette for P_C according to P_U and P_L. In the next step of CSMVQ, the most similar color pixel in state palette is found and its index recorded. However, in our proposed method, there is still one important step away; that is, the secret paletted image has to be embedded in the host color image. The following are the details to show how the state palette helps in our new method in embedding a secret paletted image into a host color image.

Here, the secret paletted image can be seen as a sequence of bit stream. Now, we want to break the state palette down into sub-state palettes. First of all, we must decide how many sub-state palettes we need. The number of sub-state palettes depends on the number of secret bits that can be embedded into a color pixel. That is, assume that the total number of sub-state palettes is N. Then, we can tell which sub-state palette a codeword belongs to by following the formula below:

$$P = i \bmod N, \tag{2}$$

where i stands for the index value in the state codebook, and P is the index number of the sub-state codebook that index i belongs to.

For example, if we want to partition a state codebook into four sub-state palettes, then according to Formula (2), the first sub-state palette consists of indices 0 and 4; the second sub-state palette consists of indices 1 and 5, and so on. After the partitioning of the sub-state palettes, we search them to find the color pixel that is closest to the original color pixel, that is, P_C in Fig. 3.

For instance, in Fig. 4, if the value of the two bits in the secret bit stream is 3, then we search the third sub-state palette to find the closet codeword. If the closest color pixel is still far away from the original color pixel, we set this color pixel as a seed pixel. This means we must search the whole palette to find the closest codeword and record its index with eight bits. Otherwise, we set this color pixel as a residual pixel and record its index in the sub-state palette. Moreover, one additional bit is needed to record whether the current color pixel is a seed pixel or a residual pixel.

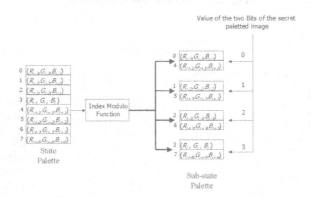

Fig. 4. Sub-state codebook production

When each color pixel has gone through the whole procedure, we get a compression code for the color host image. Moreover, the secret paletted image has now already been embedded into the compression code.

3.2 The Extraction Procedure

If the current color pixel is a seed pixel, we can reconstruct this color pixel by way of its index on the palette. On the other hand, if the current color pixel is a residual pixel, we use the same procedure as in the embedding procedure to produce the state palette. Assume that the index is i. Then, we can get the color pixel through the index i and the state palette. Moreover, the pattern value of secret bits can be calculated by the modulo formula as shown below.

$$B = (i \bmod N), \tag{3}$$

where the symbol B stands for the pattern value of secret bits. Again, the symbol N represents the total number of sub-state palettes. The flowchart of the extraction procedure is shown in Fig. 5.

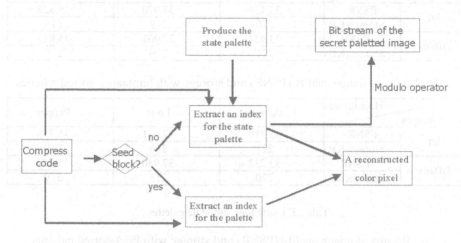

Fig. 5. The flowchart of the extraction procedure

4   Experimental Results

In our experiments, we picked out four color images as test images. The color images, "Baboon," "Lena" and "Pepper," were taken as color host images. The size of the color host images was 512×512. The other two images, called "Tiffany" and "Jet," worked as color secret images. The size of the color secret images was 128×128. To begin with, the color quantization process was executed to transform the color secret images into their corresponding paletted images.

Here, the way to sort the color pixels in the palette plays a very important role. In our procedure, the state palette is obtained by putting together continuous indices. This way, the sorting algorithm puts similar color pixels as close as possible, so that we have the biggest chance to put a suitable color pixel in the state palette. In order to show the influence different sorting algorithms have on the image quality and storage space, in our experiment, the palette was sorted by the PCA sorting technique [7] and by the luminance value [9].

Table 1 shows the results of partitioning the state palette into two sub-state palettes according to Formula (2). This means each color pixel in the color host image can hold only one secret bit at most. To show how they compare, Table 2 shows the partitioning of the state palette into four sub-state palettes, where each color pixel in the color host image can hold two secret bits. In the tables, the *PSNR* values came from the original color host images and decoded color host images. In addition, the tables also show the storage space taken up by the compression code.

Table 1. Using two sub-state palettes

(a) Results of image quality (PSNR) and storage with PCA-sorted palettes

Secret images	Host images	Baboon	Lena	Pepper
Jet	PSNR	33.436	37.970	35.828
	Storage(KB)	220	219	218
Tiffany	PSNR	33.427	37.961	35.827
	Storage(KB)	221	220	219

(b) Results of image quality (PSNR) and storage with luminance-sorted palettes

Secret images	Host images	Baboon	Lena	Pepper
Jet	PSNR	33.210	37.931	35.758
	Storage(KB)	221	216	219
Tiffany	PSNR	33.232	37.930	35.754
	Storage(KB)	220	215	219

Table 2. Using four sub-state palettes

(a) Results of image quality (PSNR) and storage with PCA-sorted palettes

Secret images	Host images	Baboon	Lena	Pepper
Jet	PSNR	34.072	38.047	35.795
	Storage(KB)	250	232	243
Tiffany	PSNR	34.087	38.055	35.797
	Storage(KB)	252	237	247

(b) Results of image quality (PSNR) and storage with luminance-sorted palettes

Secret images	Host images	Baboon	Lena	Pepper
Jet	PSNR	33.895	38.055	35.451
	Storage(KB)	251	236	247
Tiffany	PSNR	34.110	38.035	35.477
	Storage(KB)	255	235	244

According to the tables, the color host images with PCA-sorted palettes have high PSNR values and do not occupy much storage space in most cases. This means the color host images have better quality. The storage space needed by PCA-sorted palettes is smaller than that needed by luminance-sorted palettes. In the tables, it is shown that PCA-sorted palettes would be a good choice. Another difference between Table 1 and Table 2 is that the storage needed in Tables 2 is larger than that in Table 1. The reason is that the results in Table 2 came from partitioning the palette into four sub-state palettes. However, the cost to pay for this is that the probability of finding a suitable color in one sub-state palette became lower. On the contrary, in our procedure, the whole palette is searched to find the closest color and have its index recorded with eight bits. As a result, the storage needs rise up in the most cases, which pays off because the quality of the color host images turned out to be better than that in Table 1.

In Fig. 6, there are decoded color host images by different methods. In Fig. 7, we show the reconstructed color secret images processed by the sorted palette. In addition, the paletted images obtained by using the PCA-sorted palette and the luminance-sorted palette are both shown in Fig. 7.

(a) The result with two sub-state palettes by PCA-sorting

(b) The result with two sub-state palettes by luminance -sorting

(c) The result with four sub-state palettes by PCA-sorting

(d) The result with four sub-state palettes by luminance -sorting

Fig. 6. The decoding results

(a) Reconstructed color secret image

(b) A paletted secret image by using PCA-sorted palette

(c) A paletted secret image by using luminance-sorted palette

(d) Reconstructed color secret image

(e) A paletted secret image by using PCA-sorted palette

(f) A paletted secret image by using luminance-sorted palette

Fig. 7. The resultant paletted secret images and their corresponding color secret images by using PCA-sorted palette

According to the experimental results above, by using our mew method, we can obtain both good decoded color host image quality and good reconstructed color secret image quality.

5 Conclusions

In this paper, we have proposed a novel method to hide a color secret image into the compression code. In the first step, color quantization is performed on the color secret image to reduce the storage cost. The result here is a paletted image. Second, the color host image will go through CSMVQ. In order to hide the secret paletted image into the compression code, we partition the palette into sub-state palettes quickly and temporarily.

We sort the color pixels in the palette to gather the similar color pixels. Moreover, we use the modulo operator to partition the state codebook dynamically. As a result, the secret data can be embedded into the compression code through searching the color pixels in the sub-state palette. Besides, the secret data can be extracted according to the modulo of the index values. Experimental results show that the proposed method can successfully embed the color secret image into a color host image. Good color stego-image quality can be obtained, and the quality of the reconstructed color secret image is also very good.

References

[1] R. F. Chang and W. T. Chen, "Image Coding Using Variable-Rate Side-Match Finite-State Vector Quantization, " *IEEE Transactions on Image Processing*, vol. 2, 1993, pp. 104-108.

[2] K. L. Chung, C. H. Shen and L. C. Chang, "A Novel SVD- and VQ-based Image Hiding Scheme," *Pattern Recognition Letters*, vol. 22, no. 9, July. 2001, pp. 1051-1058.

[3] W. C. Du and W. J. Hsu, "Adaptive Data Hiding Based on VQ Compressed Processing," *IEE Proceedings-Vision, Image and Signal Processing*, vol. 150, no. 4, 2003, pp. 233-238.

[4] R. M. Gray, "Vector Quantization," *IEEE ASSP Magazine*, 1984, pp. 4-29.

[5] T. Kim, "Side Match and Overlap Match Vector Quantizers for Images," *IEEE Transactions on Image Processing*, vol. 1, 1992, pp. 170-185.

[6] Y. Linde, A. Buzo and R. M. Gray, "An Algorithm for Vector Quantizer Design," *IEEE Transactions on Communications*, vol. 28, Sep. 1980, pp. 84-95.

[7] R. C. T. Lee, Y. H. Chin and S. C. Chang, "Application of Principal Component Analysis to Multikey Searching," *IEEE Transactions on Software Engineering*, vol. SE-2, no. 3, Sep. 1976, pp185-193.

[8] Minho and K. Hyoungdo, "A Digital Image Watermarking Scheme on Vector Quantization, " *IEICE Trans. Inf. & Syst.*, vol. E85-D, no. 6, 2002, pp. 1054-1056.

[9] D. H. Pritchard, "U. S. Color Television Fundamentals – a Review," *IEEE Transactions on Consumer Electronics*, vol. CE-23, no. 4, 1977, pp. 467-478.

Computer Interface to Use Eye and Mouse Movement

Eun Yi Kim[1], Se Hyun Park[2], and Bum-Joo Shin[3,*]

[1] Department of Internet and Multimedia Engineering, Konkuk Univ., Korea
eykim@konkuk.ac.kr
[2] School of Computer and Communication, Daegu Univ., Korea
sehyun@daegu.ac.kr
[3] Department of Bio-Systems, Pusan National Univ., Korea
Tel.: +82-55-350-5417; Fax: +82-55-350-5440
bjshin@pusan.ac.kr

Abstract. In this paper, an interface using eye and mouse for the handicapped people is proposed. The eye regions are localized using neural network (NN)-based texture classifier that discriminates the facial region into eye class and non-eye class, and then are tracked using mean-shift procedure. The mouse region is detected based on edge information and then tracked using template matching. To assess the validity of the proposed system, it was applied to the interface system and was tested on a group of 25 users. The results show that our system has the accuracy of 99%.

1 Introduction

During the last decades, considerable interest has been shown in video-based interfaces that use human gestures to convey information or to control devices and applications [1, 2]. Users can create gestures by a static hand or body pose, or by a physical motion, including eye blinks or head movements. Among these, facial features movements, such as a gaze direction, eye blinks, and mouth opening/closing, have a high communicative value that allows for the extraction of human intention or orders. Moreover these interfaces can support the people who can not use the keyboard or mouse due to severe disabilities, Due to these, such an interface has gained many attractions, so far many systems have been developed [3-6].

In this paper, we develop the PC-based HCI system using multiple facial features such as mouth and eye, then the major advantage of our system is to provide accurate features tracking and to express user's various intentions. It receives and displays a live video of the user sitting in front of the computer. The user moves the mouse pointer by moving his (her) eyes, and clicks icons and menus by opening and closing his (her) mouth.

To evaluate the proposed method, the system is used as the interface of web browser to convey the user's command via his (her) eye and mouth movements. The proposed system is tested on 25 peoples, then the results shows that our system has the accuracy of 99% and confirms that our system is robust to the time-varying illumination and less sensitive to the specula reflection of eyeglasses. Also, the results

---

* Corresponding author.

T.-J. Cham et al. (Eds.): MMM 2007, LNCS 4352, Part II, pp. 471–478, 2007.

show that it can be efficiently and effectively used as the interface to provide a user-friendly and convenient communication device.

This paper is structured as follows. We describe face detection in section 2, eye detection in section 3 and mouth detection in Section 4. And then section 5 describes facial features tracking in section 5. Based on the tracking results, mouse operations implemented in section 6. Section 7 contains results of using this system, and then section 8 concludes with general observations.

2   System Overview

The overall process of the system is shown in Fig. 1. In our system, the facial region is first obtained using skin-color model and connected-component analysis. Thereafter the eye regions are localized using NN-based texture classifier that discriminates the facial region into eye class and non-eye class, and then mouth regions localized using edge detector. Once the eye and mouth regions are localized, they are continuously and correctly tracking by mean-shift algorithm and template matching, respectively. This enables us to accurately detect user's facial feature regions even if they put on the glasses in the cluttered background. Once facial feature regions are detected in the first frame, the respective features are continuously tracked by a mean-shift and template matching. Based on the tracking results, mouse operations such as movement or click are implemented.

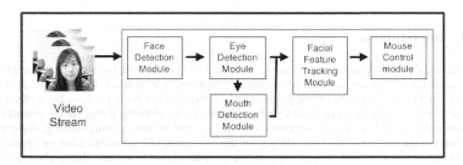

Fig. 1. The overall configuration of the system

3   Face Detection Module

Detecting pixels with a skin-color offers a reliable method for detecting face part. In this work, the skin color is represented in the chromatic color space, where it can be represented by 2D Gaussian distribution, $G(m, \Sigma^2)$, which is described in our previous work [7].

Once the skin-color model is created, the most straightforward way to locate the face is to match the skin-color model with the input image to identify facial regions. As such, each pixel in the original image is converted into chromatic color space, and then compared with the distribution of the skin-color model. By thresholding the matched results, we obtain a binary image. For the binary image, the connected-component analysis is performed to remove the noise and small region. The generated connected-components (CC) are filtered by their attributes, such as size, area, and location. Then the facial regions are obtained by selecting the largest components with skin-colors.

4 Eye Detection Module

We assume that the eye has a different texture from the facial region and is detectable. For this, we use an MLP to automatically discriminate between eye regions and non-eye ones in various environments. The input layer of the network has 57 nodes, the hidden layer has 33 nodes, and the output layer has 1 node. Adjacent layers are fully connected. Fig. 2 describes the architecture of the MLP-based texture classifier.

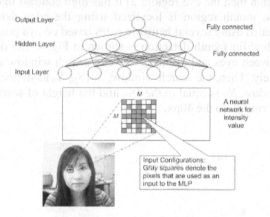

Fig. 2. The architecture of the MLP-based texture classifier

The input of a network is the gray-level values of the raw pixels within a small window, which is described by the shaded pixels from the input window in Fig. 2. After training, the neural network outputs the real value between 0 and 1 for eye and non-eye respectively. If a pixel has a larger value than the given threshold value, it is considered as an eye; otherwise it is labeled as non-eye.

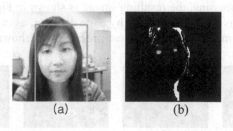

Fig. 3. An example of eye detection. (a) the classified image by the neural network, (b) the detected eye region after post-processing.

Fig. 3 shows the classification result using the neural network. In Fig. 3(a), the pixels to be classified as eyes are marked as blue. We can see that all of the eyes are labeled correctly, but there are some misclassified regions as eye. To eliminate false alarms, we use the CCs result posterior to the texture classification. Then, we used the heuristics using features of CCs such as area and geometric alignment. Using these two heuristics, the classified images are filtered, then the resulting image is shown in Fig. 3(b). In Fig. 3(b), the extracted eye region is filled green for the better viewing.

5 Mouth Detection Module

In this section, we try to detect mouth region. To reduce the complexity of mouth detection, it is detected based on the position of eye regions. Then two following properties are used: 1) it has place within distance between two eye positions, and in the lower facial region than the eye region; 2) it has high contrast in comparison with surroundings. Thus, mouth region is localized using the edge detector within the search region estimated using several heuristic rules based on eye position.

The search window for mouth detection is shown in Fig. 4. Let denote D_H and D_V be the distance between eyes and distance between search window and the center of two eyes, respectively. Then, the search window, $S=(S_H, S_W)$ is defined as follows: the width of search window, S_W is equal to the D_H, and the height of search window, S_H is experimentally determined to the 40px.

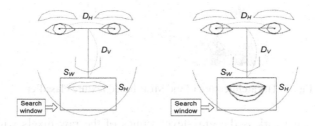

Fig. 4. Search window to detect mouth region

The detection result within estimated region includes narrow edges and noises. For discrimination of these noises, we use CCs result posterior to the facial boundary. Through this post-processing, the resulting image is shown in Fig. 5. Facial boundary was detected as well as real mouth region by edge detector, as can be seen in Fig. 5(a) – 5(c). Then the final mouth region after post-processing is shown in Figs. 5(b) - 6(d).

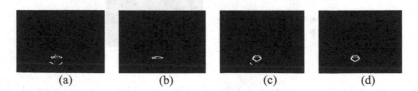

(a)   (b)   (c)   (d)

Fig. 5. An example of mouth detection

6 Facial Features Tracking Module

6.1 Mean-Shift Based Eye Tracking

To track the detected eyes, a mean shift algorithm is used, which finds the object by seeking the mode of the object score distribution [9]. In the present work, the color distribution of detected pupil, $P_m(g_s) = -(2\pi\sigma)^{-1/2}\exp\{(g_s-\mu)^2\sigma^1\}$, where the μ and σ are set to 40 and 4 respectively. The distribution is used as the object score distribution at site s, which represents the probability of belonging to an eye.

A mean shift algorithm is a nonparametric technique that climbs the gradient of a probability distribution to find the nearest dominant mode. The algorithm iteratively shifts the center of the search window to the weighted mean until the difference between the means of successive iterations is less than a threshold. The search window is moved in the direction of the object by shifting the center of the window to the weighted mean.

The weighted mean, i.e. the search window center at iteration $n+1$, m_{n+1} is computed using the following equation,

$$m_{n+1} = \sum_{s \in W} P_m(g_s) \cdot s \bigg/ \sum_{s \in W} P_m(g_s) \tag{1}$$

The search window size for a mean shift algorithm is generally determined according to the object size, which is efficient when tracking an object with only a small motion. However, in many cases, objects have a large motion and low frame rate, which means the objects end up outside the search window. Therefore, a search window that is smaller than the object motion will fail to track the object. Accordingly, in this paper, the size of the search window of the mean shift algorithm is adaptively determined in direct proportion to the motion of the object as follows:

$$W_{width}^{(t)} = \max\left(\alpha\left(\left|m_x^{(t-1)} - m_x^{(t-2)}\right| - B_{width}\right), 0\right) + \beta B_{width}$$

$$W_{height}^{(t)} = \max\left(\alpha\left(\left|m_x^{(t-1)} - m_x^{(t-2)}\right| - B_{height}\right), 0\right) + \beta B_{height} \quad (t>2) \tag{2}$$

where α and β are constant and t is the frame index. This adaptation of the window size allows for accurate tracking of highly active objects.

6.2 Template Matching Based Mouth Tracking

When the mouse is detected in the first frame, it is used as a template to determine the position of the mouse in the next frame [10]. Using this template, the tracking module searches user's mouse in a search window, where is centered at the position of the feature in the previous frame. The template is iteratively shifted within this search window and compared with the underlying sub-images.

The result of the comparison of a template and a sub-image is represented by a matching score. The matching score between a component and a template is calculated using Hamming distance. The Hamming distance between two binary strings is defined as the number of digits in which they differ. We calculate the matching score for all templates and pick the templates with the best matching score.

Fig. 6 shows the results of the facial features tracking, where the facial features are drawn out white for the better viewing. As can be seen in Fig. 6, the facial features are accurately tracking.

Fig. 6. Tracking result of facial features

7 Mouse Control Module

The computer translates the user's eye movements into the mouse movements by processing the images received from the PC camera. Then the processing of a video sequence is performed by the proposed facial features tracking system. The system determines the center of eyes in the first frame as the initial coordinates of mouse, and then computes it automatically in subsequent frames. The coordinates of mouth region and eye regions in each frame are sent to the operating system through Window functions. Mouse point is moved according to eye movement. If a user opens one's mouth, we consider that a user intends to click menus or icons on the corresponding screen region.

8 Experimental Results

To assess the effectiveness of the proposed method, the interface system was tested on 25-users through web browsers. Each user was given an introduction to how the system worked and then allowed to practice moving the cursor for five minutes. The five-minute practice period was perceived as sufficient training time by the users. In the web browser, each user was asked to click the item (ex. Icon, menu, etc.) thirty

Table 1. Processing time

Stage	Time (*ms*)
Face Detection	60
Eye Detection	110
Mouth Detection	47
Tracking	62
Average Time	78

times with the mouse using eyes and mouth movement. For each test, the user's time to click the item was recorded.

Table 1 shows the time taken to detect the face and facial features, and track them. In the system, the detections of facial features and face are once executed for the initial frame and only tracking is executed for the subsequent frame. Therefore, the average time to process a frame is about 78 *ms*, and then our system process more than 12 frames/sec.

Table 2. Test result

	Click	Non-Clicked
When the user intends to click the menu	747 (99%)	3 (1%)
Otherwise	0 (0%)	750 (100%)

Table 2 presents the accuracy to be taken to click the item in the web browser. We can see that the system is mostly operated the mouse operation correctly.

Table 3. Timing comparison between Eye Mouse [4] and proposed method.

Method	Measure	Time/sec
Eye Mouse [4]	Mean	0.66s
	Deviation	0.02s
Proposed method	Mean	0.49s
	Deviation	0.06s

Table 3 presents the average time to be taken to click the item in the web browser, when playing with Eye Mouse [4] and the proposed method. The latter is about 1.5-times faster than the former and can reduce tiredness and inconvenience.

Consequently, the proposed system can supply a user-friendly and convenient access to a computer in real-time operation. Since it does not need any additional hardware except a general PC and an inexpensive PC camera, the proposed system is very efficient to realize many applications using real-time interactive information between users and computer systems.

9   Conclusions

In this paper, we implemented the welfare interface using multiple facial features detection and tracking as PC-based HCI system. The proposed system has worked very well in a test database and cluttered environments. It is tested with 25 numbers of people, and then the result shows that our system has the accuracy of 99% and is robust to the time-varying illumination and less sensitive to the specula reflection of eyeglasses. And the experiment with proposed interface showed that it has a potential to be used as generalized user interface in many applications, i.e., game systems and home entertainments.

Acknowledgments. This work was supported by Korea Research Foundation Grant (R-04-2003-00010187-0).

References

1. Sharma, R., Pavlovic, V.I., Huang, T.S.: Toward multimodal human-computer interface. Proceedings of the IEEE , volume 86 , pp. 853 – 869 (1998)
2. Scassellati, Brian.: Eye finding via face detection for a foveated, active vision system. American Association for Artificial Intelligence. (1998)
3. Anthony Hornof, Anna Cavender, and Rob Hoselton.: EyeDraw: A System for Drawing Pictures with Eye Movements. ACM SIGACCESS Accessibility and Computing, Issue 77-78 (2003)
4. Eun Yi Kim, Sin Kuk Kang.: Eye Tracking using Neural Network and Mean-shift. LNCS, volume 3982, pp. 1200-1209 (2006)
5. Michael J. Lyons.: Facial Gesture Interfaces for Expression and Communication. IEEE International Conference on Systems, Man, Cybernetics, volume 1, pp. 598-603. (2004)
6. Yang Jie, Yin DaQuan, Wan WeiNa, Xu XiaoXia, Wan Hui.: Real-time detecting system of the driver's fatigue. ICCE International Conference on Consumer Electronics, 2006 Digest of Technical Papers. pp. 233 - 234 (2006)
7. Schiele, Bernet., Waibel, Alex.: Gaze Tracking Based on Face-Color. School of Computer Science. Carnegie Mello University (1995)
8. Chan a. d. c., Englehart K., Hudgins B., and Lovely D. F.: Hidden markov model classification of myoeletric signals in speech. IEEE Engineering in Medicine and Biology Magazine, volume 21, no. 4, pp. 143-146 (2002)
9. D. Comaniciu, V. Ramesh, and P. Meer.: Kernel-Based Object Tracking. IEEE Trans. Pattern Analysis and Machine Intelligence, volume 25, no. 5, pp. 564-577 (2003)
10. C.F. Olson.: Maximum-Likelihood Template Matching. Proc. IEEE Conf. Computer Vision and Pattern Recognition, volume 2, pp. 52-57 (2000)

Advanced Agent-Delegated Route Optimization Protocol for Efficient Multimedia Services at Low-Battery Devices

Ilsun You and Jiyoung Lim

Department of Information Science, Korean Bible University,
205 Sanggye7-Dong, Nowon-Gu, Seoul, 139-791, South Korea
{isyou, jylim}@bible.ac.kr

Abstract. The appreciation of various mobile multimedia services causes a paradigm shift in the Internet. Since the introduction of the route optimization in the Mobile IPv6, various approaches are proposed to solve the problem such as the handover latency and the excessive signaling message exchanges and enhance security. In spite of this improvement they are not enough for the low-battery mobile devices to service the audio and video streaming seamlessly because of the handover time and the computation of the mobile node. We propose an advanced agent-delegated route optimization protocol for seamless multimedia services at low-battery mobile devices.

1 Introduction

A paradigm shift is underway in the Internet. Along with a growing appreciation of the Internet as a communication platform for business, academia and entertainment, services raise the desire for anytime, anywhere network access. This development is driven by new, real-time and multimedia applications such as audio and video streaming, IP telephony or video conferencing, which are of particular convenience when ubiquitously accessible.

The Internet Engineering Task Force develops Mobile IPv6 [1] to enable operation of traditional transport-layer protocols and applications in the mobile node (MN). Mobile IPv6 allows the MN to be addressed by two IP addresses. A static home address (HoA) serves as the identifier for transport-layer protocols and applications. A care-of address (CoA) is used for the purpose of routing and is reconfigured by roaming the MN.

Mobile IPv6 provides the route optimization that enables data packets to be directly relayed between the MN and its correspondent node (CN) to minimize the packet overhead and the propagation latency. The route optimization is protected through a 'return-routability (RR) procedure'. It is based on the following two observations: First, a reachability check at the HoA authenticates a registering MN. Second, a reachability check at the CoA prevents redirection-based flooding attacks and so authorizes a MN to claim that CoA [2]. The standard route optimization is limited by the capabilities of the RR procedure. First, the RR procedure does not protect against an impersonator on the path between the MN's home agent (HA) and the CN.

T.-J. Cham et al. (Eds.): MMM 2007, LNCS 4352, Part II, pp. 479–486, 2007.

This is not conceivable under the higher security needs. Second, the RR procedure consumes a significant of the overall handover latency. Since the route optimization was originally developed with intent to improve support for interactive real-time applications, those applications doubtless suffer from prolonged handover latency.

In order to improve security and inefficiency problems caused by the RR procedure, the Optimized Mobile IPv6 (OMIPv6) series have been researched and drafted into the network working group in IETF [3-9]. They are composed of the initial phase and the subsequent movement phase. In the initial phase, the MN and the CN use their own public key method to establish a strong long-term key, which enables the CN to trust the MN's HoA. The subsequent movement phase employs such strong key to optimize successive binding updates without repeating the RR procedure. The OMIPv6 protocol [3] which is based on the purpose-built keys (PBK) [4] lets the MN and the CN execute only binding update without the HoA and CoA tests during the subsequent movement phase. Thus it does not allow the CN to verify the MN's CoA causing the protocols to be vulnerable to redirection-based flooding attacks. To combat this problem the OMIPv6-CGA protocol [5] adopting Aura's cryptographic generated address (CGA) [6] to enhance its security adds the CoA test to its subsequent movement phase. However it requires one additional round-trip time (RTT) for data transmission according to the CoA test. The OMIPv6-CGA-CBA protocol [7] applies the early binding update and credit-based authorization (CBA) [8] to optimize the CoA test. While it optimizes the latency, it does not decrease the amount of the signaling messages according to the MN's mobility. Thus it is not suitable for mobile devices since the wireless channel requires the more energy than that of the computation. The CoA test delegation protocol [9] is proposed to reduce the energy loss by delegating the CoA test to the network infrastructure. It suffers from the latency according to the CoA test while it relieves the MN from exchanging a considerable amount of signaling messages with the CNs.

For mobile devices our proposed protocol is a low energy consumed protocol that delegates the MN's access router to process the CoA test, which reduces the signaling message exchanges and the consumed power. Also for seamless multimedia service our proposed protocol performs the early binding update by adopting the CBA.

This paper is structured as follows. Chapter 2 describes the motivation and our proposed scheme. Chapter 3 analyzes it focusing on the handover latency and signaling message exchanges. Finally, this paper concludes in chapter 4.

2 Proposed Protocol

The OMIPv6 series use their own public key methods to allow the CN to have the strong assurance about the correctness of the MN's HoA. This makes it possible for the HoA test to be eliminated from the subsequent movement phase. The MN and the CN need to perform only the CoA test before exchanging the BU and BA messages. However, the CoA test results in one RTT delay, which is the main factor of the handover latency at the subsequent movement phase. Thus the OMIPv6 series have tried to optimize the CoA test for the handover latency. This section analyzes the CoA test approaches used in the OMIPv6 series, and propose a new agent-delegated route optimization protocol.

2.1 Notation

- | denotes the concatenation.
- Kbmperm denotes the strong long-term key established between the MN and the CN during the initial phase.
- ESN denotes an Extended Sequence Number.
- MH-Data1 denotes the content of the Mobility Header where the authenticator in the Binding Authorization Data option is zeroed.
- MH-Data2 denotes the content of the Mobility Header excluding the Authenticator in the Binding Authorization Data option.
- K_{CN} denotes the CN's secret key
- CNI denotes a CoA nonce index, HNI denotes a HoA nonce index.

2.2 Motivation

The OMIPv6 series use the strong long-term key, Kbmperm established during the initial phase to optimize subsequent binding updates without repeating the RR test. In the case of the OMIPv6 protocol, the MN and the CN exchange only their BU and BA messages. Though such an optimization guarantees the maximum efficiency, it does not allow the CN to verify the MN's CoA, causing the protocols to be vulnerable to redirection-based flooding attacks.

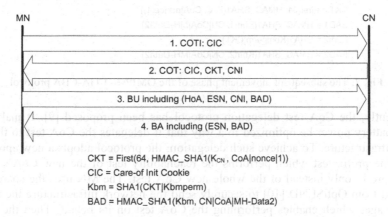

MN   CN

1. COTI: CIC

2. COT: CIC, CKT, CNI

3. BU including (HoA, ESN, CNI, BAD)

4. BA including (ESN, BAD)

CKT = First(64, HMAC_SHA1(K_{CN}, CoA|nonce|1))
CIC = Care-of Init Cookie
Kbm = SHA1(CKT|Kbmperm)
BAD = HMAC_SHA1(Kbm, CN|CoA|MH-Data2)

Fig. 1. The subsequent movement phase of the OMIPv6- CGA protocol

The OMIPv6-CGA protocol solves the problem in a way that the CN and the MN perform the CoA test before exchanging their BU and BA messages. As shown in Fig. 1, the MN should wait for the COT message to compute Kbm because the key is derived from CKT. This incurs one additional RTT overhead. To avoid such an overhead, the OMIPv6-CGA-CBA protocol adopts CBA, which parallelizes the CoA test with regular communication, while defending against redirection-based flooding attacks. Fig. 2 depicts the subsequent movement phase of the OMIPv6-CGA-CBA protocol. In the phase, the MN and the CN start the transmission of data packets while verifying the MN's new CoA. This makes the OMIPv6-CGA-CBA protocol optimize the latency caused by the CoA test. But, when compared to that of the OMIPv6-CGA protocol, the protocol does not decrease the amount of the MN's mobility signaling messages. Thus, the MN should still dedicate its battery power to exchange such messages with its CNs. In particular, since the wireless channel needs the more energy than that of the computation, the MN communicating with multiple CNs needs to consume the significant amount of its available energy when it moves fast.

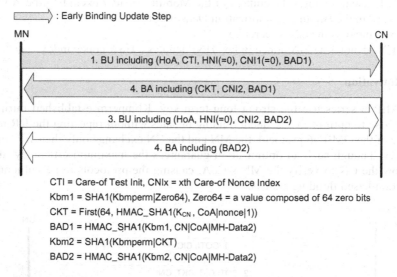

Fig. 2. The subsequent movement phase of the OMIPv6- CGA-CBA protocol

Recently, the CoA test delegation protocol has been proposed [9]. It makes the MN's battery power be optimized in a way that it delegates the CoA test to the network infrastructure. To achieve such delegation, the protocol adopts a new approach, called the prefix test which performs the reachability test of the new CoA's 64-bit subnet prefix only instead of the whole new CoA test. The MN uses the shared key obtained from OptiSEND [10] to securely send the network infrastructure the mobility package, which enables performing the CoA test on its behalf. Then the MN's access router (AR) in its behalf performs the prefix test by exchanging the prefix test init (PreTI) and prefix test messages (PreT) messages with its CNs. Though the protocol relieves the MN from exchanging a considerable amount of signaling messages, it suffers from the latency incurred by the CoA test because the MN should derive Kbm from the prefix keygen token (PKT) included in the PreT message. Thus, the CoA test delegation protocol needs to improve such latency when it is applied to the multimedia streaming service. This paper uses CBA to improve this protocol while optimizing the CoA test overhead.

2.3   The Proposed Advanced Agent-Delegated Route Optimization Protocol

In this section, we improve the CoA test delegation protocol with CBA. Our proposed protocol lets the MN execute the early binding update firstly, then allowing the AR to perform the complete binding update on behalf of the MN. This makes it possible for this protocol to achieve the same handover latency as the OMIPv6-CGA-CBA protocol in addition to minimizing the MN's energy. Fig. 3 illustrates the proposed protocol, which is divided into three steps as follows: the delegation step, the early binding update step and the complete binding update step.

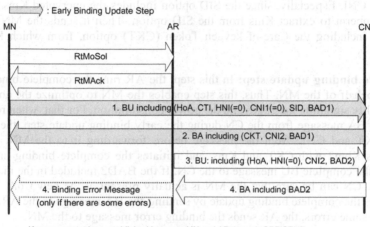

Fig. 3. The proposed protocol

Preliminaries: It is assumed that the MN and its new access router (AR) share a secret key Kma through the OptiSEND protocol [10]. If it is not available, the MN can use its own public key to share Kma with the AR during the delegation protocol. In this case, the MN needs to perform one more public key operation. The MN and the CN are supposed to establish a strong long-term key, Kbmperm during the initial phase of the OMIPv6 series. That is, this protocol can be applied as the subsequent movement phase for OMIPv6-like protocols.

Delegation step: This step is the same as that of the CoA test delegation protocol. The MN delegates the complete binding update to its new AR. The MN sends the AR the router mobility solicitation (RtMoSol) message including its mobility package which is necessary for the CoA test. The RtMoSol message can be used to manage the MN's mobility package stored in the AR. When receiving the RtMoSol message, the selected AR replies with the router mobility acknowledgment (RtMAck) message. These messages are authenticated through the key, Kma. For detail information, please refer to [9].

Early binding update step: In this step, the CoA test is performed in parallel with the data transmission from and to the MN's new CoA. Especially, CBA is used to prevent the misuse of unverified CoAs. To indicate the early binding update, the BU message should include the Care-of Test Init (CTI) option, the SID option, zero HNI and zero CNI. Especially, since the SID option includes the encrypted Kms, the CN uses Kbmperm to extract Kms from the SID option. Then it sends the MN the BA message including the Care-of keygen Token (CKT) option, from which Kbm2 is derived.

Complete binding update step: In this step, the AR runs the complete binding up-date on behalf of the MN. Thus, this step enables the MN to optimize the amount of the mobility signaling messages and the power consumption. For that, when receiving the early BA message from the CN during the early binding update step, the AR ex-tracts CKT and CNI2 from the message before forwarding it to the MN. Then, it computes Kbm2 with CKT and Kms, and initiates the complete binding update by sending the complete BU message to the CN. If the BAD2 included in the message is valid, the CN can be sure that the MN is actually present at the new CoA. The CN concludes the complete binding update by sending the BA message to the AR. Only if there are some errors, the AR sends the binding error message to the MN.

3   Analysis

This chapter analyzes the proposed protocol in terms of the handover latency, the battery power consumption and the security.

Handover Latency: The handover latencies of the proposed protocol and others can be derived as Table 1. As shown in Table 1, our proposed protocol achieves the same handover latency as the OMIPv6 protocol, which performs only the binding update without any address tests.

Battery power consumption: The MN's battery power consumption depends on its mobility signaling messages and computational operations. The proposed protocol needs the MN to consume its power for the delegation protocol as shown in Table 2, which summaries the handover latencies and the MN's battery power consumptions of the proposed protocol and the others' subsequent movement phases. However, such power consumption is much less than those of the OMIPv6-CGA and OMIPv6-CGA-CBA protocols because the message exchanges are occurred locally and once each handover.

Security: In the subsequent movement phase, one of the most critical attacks is the redirection-based flooding attack, which the legitimate MN launches maliciously. In spite of the best method to prevent this attack, the strict CoA test results in the considerable delay during the subsequent movement phase. Thus, there is a trade-off between efficiency and security. In order to optimize such trade-off, our protocol uses the prefix test with CBA. Because the prefix test validates the subnet prefix of the MN's foreign network, it can provide almost same security as the CoA test.

Table 1. Handover latencies of our proposed protocol and others

Protocol	Lsend (RTT)	Lrecv (RTT)
RR	M×N×Max(RTTcot, RTThot) = 2MN	M×N×(Max(RTTcot,RTThot)+RTTbu) = 3MN
OMIPv6	0	M×N×RTTbu = MN
OMIPv6-CGA	M×N× RTTcot = MN	M×N×(RTTcot + RTTbu) = 2MN
OMIPv6-CGA-CBA	0	M×N×RTTbu = MN
Ours	0	(Max(RTTreg, N×RTTbu))×M = MN

* N: the number of the MN's CNs, M: the number of handovers
RTTcot: the RTT for the CoA test (=1RTT), RTThot: the RTT for the HoA test (=2RTT)
RTTbu: the RTT for exchanging the BU and BA messages (=1RTT),
RTTreg: the RTT for the delegation step (<1RTT)
Lsend: the latency until the MN starts to send data packets
Lrecv: the latency until the MN starts to receive data packets

Table 2. Comparison of the OMIPv6 series and ours

Protocol	Handover Latency		MN's Battery Power Consumption	
	Lsend (RTT)	Lrecv (RTT)	Additional Signaling Messages	Computation Overhead
(1)	2MN	3MN	(HoTI+HoT+CoTI+CoT)×M×N	0
(2)	0	MN	0	0
(3)	MN	2MN	(COTI+COT)×M×N	0
(4)	0	MN	(BU+BA)×M×N	2×HMAC×M×N
(5)	0	MN	(RtMoSol+RtMAck)×M	2×HMAC×M×N

* (1) The RR Protocol, (2) The OMIPv6 Protocol, (3) The OMIPv6-CGA Protocol,
(4) The OMIPv6-CGA-CBA Protocol, (5) The Proposed Protocol

The above analysis shows that the proposed protocol can optimize both the handover latency and power consumption while keeping the same security level as other protocols.

4 Conclusions

In this paper, we analyzed the various CoA test approaches used by the OMIPv6 series to combat the redirection-based flooding attacks. They are not suitable for the MN with the low battery since they have an amount of computation for the security. When multimedia services are provided at roaming mobile devices, the seamless handover is a very important factor. The existing approaches should wait to transmit data packets after moving to another area.

We proposed the agent-delegated route optimization protocol which delegates the AR to perform the CoA test for the security and adopts the early binding update for the fast handover latency. Our protocol has the same amount of the MN's data transmission waiting time as that of the OMIPv6-CGA-CBA protocol, the dominant candidate for the standard OMIPv6 protocol, after moving the MN while its energy consumption is lower than those of the OMIPv6-CGA and OMIPv6-CGA-CBA protocols. So our proposed protocol is suitable for ubiquitous multimedia MIPv6 environments in terms of the seamless handover and the energy consumption.

References

1. D. Johnson, C. Perkins and J. Arkko, "Mobility Support in IPv6," IETF RFC 3775, June 2004.
2. Arkko J., Aura T., Montenegro G., Nikander P., Nordmark E., "Mobile IP Version 6 Route Optimization Security Design Background," IETF RFC 4225 , Dec. 2005.
3. W. Haddad, F. Dupont, L. Madour, S. Krishnan and S. Park, "Optimizing Mobile IPv6 (OMIPv6)," IETF Internet Draft, draft-haddad-mipv6-omipv6-01.txt, Feb. 2004 (Work in progress).
4. S. Bradner, A. Mankin and J. Schiller, "A Framework for Purpose-Built Keys (PBK)," IETF Internet Draft, draft-bradner-pbk-frame-06.txt, Oct. 2003 (Work in progress).
5. W. Haddad, L. Madour, J. Arkko and F. Dupont. "Applying Cryptographically Generated Addresses to Optimize MIPv6 (CGA-OMIPv6)," IETF Internet Draft, draft-haddad-mip6-cga-omipv6-04, May 2005 (Work in progress).
6. T. Aura, "Cryptographically Generated Addresses (CGA)," IETF RFC 3972, March 2005.
7. J. Arkko, C. Vogt and W. Haddad, "Applying Cryptographically Generated Addresses and Credit-Based Authorization to Mobile IPv6," IETF Internet Draft, draft-arkko-mipshop-cga-cba-04.txt, June 2006 (Work in progress).
8. W. Haddad, S. Krishnan and F. Dupont, "Mobility Signaling Delegation in OptiSEND," IETF Internet Draft, draft-haddad-mipshop-mobisig-del-01.txt, June 2006, (Work in progress).
9. C. Vogt and et. el., "Early Binding Updates for Mobile IPv6," IEEE Wireless Communications and Networking Conference, no. 1, pp.1440-1445, March 2005.
10. W. Haddad, S. Krishnan, and J. Choi, "Secure Neighbor Discovery (SEND) Optimization and Adapation for Mobility: The OptiSEND Protocol", IETF Internet Draft, draft-haddad-mipshop-optisend-01.txt, March 2006 (Work in progress).

A Study on Key Distribution and ID Registration in the AAA System for Ubiquitous Multimedia Environments*

Seo-Il Kang[1], Deok-Gyu Lee[2], and Im-Yeong Lee[1]

[1] Division of Computer Soonchunhyang University, #646,Eupnae-ri, Shinchang-myun, Asan-si, coogchungnam-Do, 336-745, Republic of Korea
{kop98, imylee}@sch.ac.kr
[2] Electronics and Telecommunications Research Institute, #161 Gajeong-Dong, Yuseong-gu, Daejeon, 305-700, Korea
deokgyulee@etri.re.kr

Abstract. Media environment has been rapidly changed these days. Internet provides multimedia environment and has become a part of our everyday life as a new advertisement media. Authentication methods typically involve an authentication server in the home network from the authentication server of the external network, and then the external network is notified with the authentication result in the home authentication server. This paper discusses and proposes a key distribution protocol that ca be used when the user moves the external network and to ensure secure communication with the external authentication server. As the proposed technology does not receive the reissue of authentication from the home authentication server in case moving between the external authentications servers, authentication server overload can be reduced and the home network can be made to issue the key using the registered password.

Keywords: Multimedia service, Authentication, ID registration, key distribution.

1 Introduction

As information technology further develops, many kinds of network-based multimedia services are being made available for public use. Users register their information on the multimedia service server and are able to avail of the services after making their payment. In such a process, the user can get authorization permission in using the resources or multimedia services, or can get access to the multimedia service server through an authentication process in which the multimedia service server duly authenticates the users. Further, the accounting process will be required according to multimedia service time or resources. Therefore, authentication, authorization, and accounting (AAA) is widely being implemented in public services because it can integrate and provide these processes. In this paper, hence, the authentication service in accordance with node movement is placed in the external

---

* This research was supported by MIC(Ministry of Information and communication), Korea, under the ITRC(Information Technology Research Center) support program supervised by the IITA (Institute of Information Technology Assessment).

T.-J. Cham et al. (Eds.): MMM 2007, LNCS 4352, Part II, pp. 487–493, 2007.

authentication server to ensure efficient authentication, while a key is simultaneously produced for secure communications with the external authentication server. The proposed method requires the establishment of a secure communication channel in the external authentication server, and the key will be shared between the mobile node and external authentication server. This paper proposes the security requirement in Chapter 2, studies the existing research on AAA in Chapter 3, describes the proposed method in Chapter 4, analyzes the proposed method with the security requirement in Chapter 5, and finally describes the conclusion and suggests the direction for future studies in Chapter 6.

2   Security Requirement

Among the services that use authentication, authorization, and accounting (AAA), the most important is the authentication service. Authentication, before proceeding with authorization and accounting, ensures that only duly registered users are allowed to access the offered multimedia service. Authorization is to be given and entrusted through the authentication, which is also implemented to give the user access rights, use of multimedia service, etc. To provide authentication, AAA should have an authentication protocol. At this point, the standard AAA document describes various technologies that can be applied, from ordinary passwords to one-time passwords (OTP). This plan ensures that the symmetric key is defined, obtained by the authentication server and the user. In the key distribution for the communication or service thereafter, the home authentication server should be the main server to generate the key used in the external network, and the terminal user can receive the generated key that can be used in the external network through the key generation factor transmitted from the authentication server. The following security requirements, therefore, are suggested.

. Only the rightful user can check the message.
. The transmitted message should not be copied, cancelled or forged halfway, and the user shall report any event of copying, cancellation, or forgery.
. The rightful user should immediately verify his/her identification to the rightful server.
. Any third party should not be able to use the message by stealth that the rightful user sends.
. Any third party should not be able to pose as the rightful user
. Any third party should not be able to pose as the rightful authentication server.
. The user should verify the key identified to the one external network.

The above security requirements prevent any third party in posing as the rightful user and in illegally obtaining the information through the traffic analysis of the message. In addition, the key should be shared on the secure communication and the authenticated user should obtain the authority of access to the service. Key distribution requires verification that the individual in the communication uses the equivalent key. In order to share the same key, verification can be used through the encryption. Moreover, although there are other security requirements for AAA, this paper's main discussion is on the authentication and key distribution.

3 Research Trends

This paper also studies research trends on AAA key distribution. Authenticating with AAA is performed through the extensible authentication protocol (EAP), which basically utilizes the ID and password method, bio-metric technology, and OTP technology. This chapter discusses the method of applying the authentication technology and key distribution.

3.1 AAA System of Multimedia Service

Users use various media service in Ubiquitous Environments. It is important that we authentication the user to use various media service. AAA system offers the Authentication of users. The service can be requested in the outside and inside network. Therefore the authentication must be provided in the outside and inside network. We expand AAA system and must offer a user authentication of an outside network. Therefore we can offer a multimedia service to the user. A service environment of the user can forecast a mobile environment. Because to be provided the service as move in a Ubiquitous Environments. We find out about AAA system which is provided therefore with a mobile environment and market service.

3.2 AAA Area Registration Under the Mobile Environment

This method suggests the simplification of the process for authentication of hands-off and mobile terminal node generated from the frequent movement of mobile terminals in the AAA structure under a mobile IP environment. The mobile terminal node should be re-authenticated from the AAA server in the home network for the local movement and the vulnerability of generating or receiving the transmission of new session key required in the authentication between agents should be solved. The use of authentication extension message (AEM), which can process the authentication in the AAA structure, can solve this problem. The composition of this message includes the verification value and algorithm that can authenticate from the early authentication server. Its advantage is that it does not require the FA setup by providing this kind of message. The mobile node supports the authentication service and fast hands-off by using the hash value and algorithm in this method after receiving the AEM authentication expansion message for home registration. This method can maintain the terminal message after receiving the message and get authentication by providing the algorithm and authentication value to the external network. This method, however, does not give access yet to the home authentication server with the notification of self-authentication to the external server for the terminal. In this case, the authentication server of all areas should reply to AEM without requesting the early authentication of the terminal that has the AEM message. Although the authentication process is simple, maintaining each AEM message requires a lot of overhead, and all servers and the home server should communicate at least more than once without knowing where to access.

4 Proposed Method

The proposed method stores the authentication message in the authentication server of the external network after accessing the home authentication server and receiving the authentication through the other network by the user who uses the mobile node. When the mobile node accesses the authentication server of another network, the existing external authentication server near the mobile device provides the authenticated information, reducing the home network's overhead. Also, sharing the secure key between the external authentication server and mobile terminal should be established in order to make a secure communication as it provides the authenticated information through the external authentication network. As shown in Fig. 1, the mobile node gets the authentication of the home network by accessing the external network A, then receives the authentication by sending the authentication message to external network A when the mobile node accesses external network B. It is not necessary to get the authentication by accessing the authentication server of the home network and to maintain the connection of authentication with the external network for all terminals, which are registered in all home networks to reduce the overhead.

4.1 System Coefficient

In this proposed method, the following system coefficients are used.

. MN: Mobile node
. $AAAL_A$, $AAAL_B$: external network authentication server A and B
. AAAH: Home authentication server
. KS: The symmetric key that the mobile node and home authentication server confidentially share
. R*: The random number generated in the pseudo random number (*: each mobile node, home authentication server, external network)
. ID*: * represents the individual and becomes each individual's ID for identification
. Pk_*: the public key of *   . Sk _*: the private key of *
. h( ): Secure one-way function

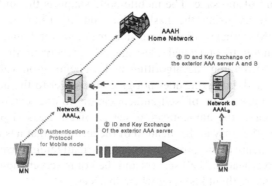

Fig. 1. Entire proposed method

. PIN: the personal identification code and becomes the password registered by the user.
. S_i: I is corresponding to the index number and S_i is registered to home authentication server and mobile node in advance.
. Sig*: The signature of the individual corresponding to *
. E*[ ]: message m from the encryption key of *

4.2 Proposed Protocol

4.2.1 Authentication Protocol for Mobile Node

In the proposed protocol, the ID_{MN}, PIN and S_i of the user are stored in the authentication server of the home network with the symmetric key secretly shared.

Step 1. To get the service by accessing the external network with the mobile node for the user, the following data is transmitted.

$$ID_{MN}, E_{KS}[h(ID_{MN}\|S_i),i]$$

Step 2. The external authentication server cannot decode the ID and message so that the following message is transmitted to the authentication server of the home network. It is encrypted with the public key of the home authentication server and transmitted with the private key of the external authentication server by signing his/her own ID and the hash of random number.

$$E_{P\_AAAH}[ID_{MN}, E_{KS}[h(ID_{MN}\|S_i),i], R_{AAAL_A}]$$

$$Sig_{S\_AAAL_A}[ID_{AAAL_A}, h(R_{AAAL_A}))]$$

Step 3. The authentication server of the home network verifies the signature of the message transmitted from the authentication server of home network and mobile ID by decoding it with the secret key, then finds the S_i value of i with the symmetric key and verifies the value by connecting with ID_{MN} and hashing the value.

$$h(ID_{MN}\|S_i) \underset{=}{?} h'(ID_{MN}\|S_i) \quad h(R_{AAAL_A}) \underset{=}{?} h'(R_{AAAL_A})$$

4.2.2 ID and Key Exchange of the External AAA Server

Step 1. The home authentication server gets the rightful value during the verification process, generates the following message, and transmits a single message to the external authentication network. Another message is transmitted to the user with the mobile terminal.

$$E_{KS}[\alpha, ID_{MN2}], E_{P\_AAAL_A}[Sig_{S\_AAAH}(h(R_{AAAL_A})), g^\alpha (\bmod n)]$$

Step 2. The external authentication server generates and provides the temporary ID for the user while simultaneously generates the session key for using with the mobile node.

$$ID_{MN2} = ID_{MN} \oplus R_{AAAL_A}, \quad SK_{AAAL_A,MN} = g^{\alpha\alpha_{AAAL_A}} \bmod n$$

$$E_{SK\_AAAL_A,MN}[ID_{MN2}, R2_{AAAL_A}]$$

Step 3. The mobile node establishes the session key by using the data transmitted from the home network server and generates the same ID by decoding the encrypted message and includes the message that was communicated with external network.

$$SK_{AAAL_A, MN} = g^{\alpha x_{AAAL_A}} \bmod n, E_{SK\_AAAL_A, MN}[ID_{MN}, ID_{MN2}, R2_{AAAL_A}]$$

4.2.3   ID and Key Exchange of the External AAA Servers A and B

Step 1. The mobile node makes the transmission after getting the authentication from network A and gets the authentication of network A for the service when belonging to network B. It sends the following message to network B.

$$E_{P\_AAAL_B}[ID_{MN2} \| R_{MN} \| E_{SK\_AAAL_A, MN}[ID_{MN2} \| R2_{AAAL_A}], h(R_{MN})]$$

Step 2. Network B sends the following data to network A through the following operation.

$$ID_{MN2}, R_{MN}, E_{AAAL_A}[E_{SK\_AAAL_A, MN}[ID_{MN2} \| R2_{AAAL_A}]]$$

Step 3. Network A authenticates the user's mobile node with the transmitted data from network B and sends the authenticated information to network B through the signature of network A.

$$E_{P\_AAAL_B}[Sig_{S\_AAAL_A}[ID_{MN2}]]$$

Step 4. Network B generates the ID by using the one previously transmitted from the user and then generates the session key.

$$ID_{MN3} = ID_{MN2} \oplus R_{MN}, \quad SK_{AAAL_B, MN} = g^{x_{AAAL_B}R_{MN}} \bmod n$$

$$E_{SK\_AAAL_B, MN}[ID_{MN3}, R_{AAAL_B}]$$

Step 5. The user verifies the transmitted information from network B by taking the public key from network B and generating the session key and ID with the selected random number.

5   Analysis of the Proposed Method

The proposed protocol is analyzed in terms of its authentication and key distribution strengths in accordance with the requirements mentioned in Chapter 2.

. Only the rightful individual should be able to verify the message. The message is encrypted and transmitted using the symmetric key that the early home authentication server and the terminal share in secret, and the protocol ensures confidentiality by using the public key in the message for the external network. The message is provided in the proposed method by using the value of ID and signature so as to verify the rightful generation of message.

. The transmitted message should not be copied, cancelled or forged midway, and should be recognized in case of copying, cancellation or forgery. To identify the copy, cancellation and forgery in the proposed method, each message includes two kinds of content. The signature value is provided by hashing the content included in the encrypted message in case of receiving the message and transmitting it to the other individual.

. Any third party should not be able to use the message. The early authenticated message has the OTP concept in Si to prevent retransmission. Moreover, the early generated random value is used in case of retransmitting the other value, the used random value is stored in each server, and it requests to generate and transmit the message again when the same random value is sent. Then, the message made of the same random value cannot be retransmitted.

6 Conclusion

The proposed method receives the authentication from the home authentication server through the temporary external network using the mobile terminal for the service provided to the user. To ensure the security of the multimedia service, information is encrypted using the session key. And then, credibility of the data is ensured with the signature. When the external network has the registration information of the user, the other external network gets the multimedia service of nearby external network without receiving it from the home network server. This results to the decrease of overhead and simultaneously establishes the key for the security of communication with the external network or multimedia service. With the establishment of this session key, the security of each communication is ensured.

The requirement of authentication will increase with the increase of registration for the mobile terminal hereafter, and the authentication server in the home network will produce large overhead in providing the authentication while simultaneously requiring key management for the terminal. Therefore, further research should be performed on the key management for the mobile terminal and in the external network.

Reference

1. F. Johansson, "Mobile IPv4 extension for carrying network access identifiers," 2004 June.
2. I. Artur Hecker, Houda Labiod, Ahmed Serhrouchnei "Authentis: thorough incremental authentication models to secure interconnected Wi-Fi WLANs," ASWN2002
3. S. Patel, "Weaknesses of North American wireless authentication protocol," IEEE Wireless Communications, vol. 4, no. 3, June 1997.
4. Qiang Tang, J.Mitchell, "On the security of some password-based key agreement schemes," Cryptology ePrint Archive, 2005.
5. Yu Chen, Terrance Boult, "Dynamic home agent reassignment in mobile IP," IEEE-WCNC02, 2002.
6. "AAA authorization application examples," RFC 2905
7. "AAA Authorization Framework," RFC 2904
8. "Remote Authentication dial In User Service(RADIUS)," RFC 2865
9. IEEE Standard 802.1X-2001. IEEE Standard for Local and metroplitan area networks-Port-Based Network Access Control. June, 2001

A Distributed Broadcast Algorithm for Wireless Mobile Ad Hoc Networks

Li Layuan, Zheng Feng, Li Chunlin, and Sun Qiang

School of Computer Science, Wuhan University of Technology, Wuhan, 430063, P.R. China
jwtu@public.wh.hb.cn

Abstract. In Wireless mobile ad hoc networks, many unicast and multicast protocols depend on broadcast mechanism to finish control and route establishment functionality. In a straightforward broadcast by flooding, each node will retransmit a message to all it neighbors until the message has been propagated to the entire network. So it will become very inefficient and will be easy to result the broadcast storm problem. Thus an efficient broadcast algorithm should be used to less the broadcast storm caused by broadcast. Due to the dynamic nature of ad hoc networks, global information of the network is difficult to obtain, so the algorithm should be distributed. In this paper, a distributed heuristic-based algorithm is presented. The algorithm is based on joint distance-counter threshold scheme. It runs in a distributed manner by each node in the network without needing any global information. Each node in an ad hoc network hears the message from its neighbors and decides whether to retransmit or not according to the signal strength and the number of the receiving messages. By using the JDCT algorithm, it's easy to find the nodes that consist of the vertices of the hexagonal lattice to cover the whole networks. The algorithm is very simple and it is easy to operate and has a good performance in mobile wireless communication environments. A comparison among several existing algorithms is conducted. Simulation results show that the new algorithm is efficient and robust.

Keywords: Ad Hoc networks; broadcast algorithm; wireless networks; broadcast storm.

1 Introduction

A mobile ad hoc network is a self-organizing network without any existing fixed communication infrastructure support. Because of its independence of a fixed infrastructure and its instant deployment and easy reconfiguration capabilities, the ad hoc wireless networking technology shows great potential and importance in many situations, such as in military and disaster-relief applications.

However, in a single channel ad hoc network, all the nodes communicate over a unique common radio frequency, and when a node transmit a message all its neighbors will "hearing" the message in the same time. There may be also more than one node starting to transmit message to a node at the same time, consequently cause a packet collision. Moreover, as all the nodes are always in movement, each node's broadcast

T.-J. Cham et al. (Eds.): MMM 2007, LNCS 4352, Part II, pp. 494–501, 2007.

radius and power supply are limited, and there is no infrastructure or centralized management in ad hoc networks, a mobile host may not be able to communicate directly with other hosts in a single-hop fashion. So the specialized routing algorithms for data in such a network, in contrast with the conventional fixed or cell networks, is extremely difficult and must be redesigned completely.

In mobile ad hoc networks, the research of routing is still at the beginning and some routing protocols have been put forward [1-6]. Most of these protocols depend on a broadcast mechanism [6]. In flooding, each node that receives a message retransmits that message to all it neighbors until the message has been propagated to the entire network. Despite its poor scalability and inefficient bandwidth usage [7-9], flooding is very useful because it can achieve maximal coverage, distance preservation, and redundancy. Without any reliance on knowledge about the network topology, flooding performance does not degrade with increased node mobility.

2 Notations and Assumptions

In general, an ad hoc network can be mapped to a unit disk graph $G(t)=(V, E)$, where V is the set of nodes and E is the set of logical edges where two nodes are connected if their geographical distance is within a given transmission range r. Considering the effect of the mobile nodes, $G(t)$ is a time-relevant function.

The symbols and definitions used in this paper are defined as follows:

Definition 1: The distance $d(x, y)$ between two nodes x and y in $G(t)$ is defined the distance between x and y within their transmission ranger, $d(x, y) \leq r$.

Definition 2: $c(x)$ denotes the number of received messages in node x during broadcast.

Definition 3: D_{Th} denotes a distance threshold, where $0 \leq D_{Th} < r$.

Definition 4: C_{Th} denotes a counter threshold, where $C_{Th} \geq 0$.

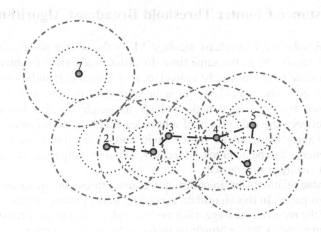

Fig. 1. An ad hoc network

Definition 5: $N(x)$ is a set of neighbors of node x, where for each neighbor y, $d(x,y) \leq r$. For example, in Fig.1, the neighbors of node 1 consist of node 2, 3 and they can represent as $N(1) = \{2,3\}$.

Definition 6: $I(x)$ is a subset of $N(x)$, $I(x) \subseteq N(x)$ where for each of its member y, $y \in I(x)$ and $d(x,y) \leq D_{Th}$. In Fig. 2, $I(1) = \{3\}$.

Definition 7: $E(x)$ is a subset of $N(x)$, $E(x) \subseteq N(x)$ where for each of its member y, $y \in E(x)$ and $D_{Th} < d(x,y) \leq r$. For instance, in Fig. 2, $E(1) = \{2\}$.

Definition 8: $Rt(S)$ is a set of nodes that retransmit the message from source node S, where

$$Rt(S) = \left\{ x \mid x \in \left\{ \{E(x_1) \cap E(x_2) \cap \cdots E(x_k)\} \cup \{x \notin \{E(x_1) \cap E(x_2) \cap \cdots E(x_k)\}, c(x) < C_{Th}\} \right\} \right\}$$
$$x_1, x_2, \cdots, x_k \in N(x)$$

Definition 9: R is defined as the coverage ratio of a broadcast algorithm during broadcast, the number of mobile nodes receiving the broadcast message divided by the total number of mobile nodes in an ad hoc network.

The following assumptions are made in our system model.

1) Mobile nodes in an ad hoc network share a single common channel, and a message transmitted by a node reaches all its neighbors in the same time.

2) The maximum transmitting radius of each node in the network is the same.

3) There are no unidirectional links, and each link between a pair of nodes is a perfect bi-directional link.

4) The broadcast messages do not require an explicit acknowledgement to confirm the reception.

5) Each node retransmits the message only once.

3   Joint Distance-Counter Threshold Broadcast Algorithm

When a transmission of a broadcast message M by the source node occurred, all its neighbors will receive M in the same time. In order to alleviate the broadcast storm problem [6], a node has to assess the redundancy of a broadcast and decide whether to rebroadcast or not. The redundancy of a broadcast associates with the additional coverage caused by the source node and all its neighbors. [6] has revealed the relationship between the redundancy of a broadcast and the additional coverage. The further the distance between the source node and its neighbors is, and the larger additional coverage can be acquired. Moreover, the more neighbors of a node are, the less additional coverage is acquired.

Based on these relationships, joint distance-counter threshold broadcast algorithm is proposed in this paper. In this algorithm, according to the distance of its neighbors and the number of the received message, each node decides whether to retransmitting M or not. First, when a node x send a broadcast message M, all its neighbors will hear M and compute $d(x,y)$ according the receiving signal strength. If $d(x, y_i) > D_{Th}$, $y_i \in N(x)$ then wait for a short time which is determined by a distance and counter relevant function. The delaying helps to avoid many nodes to transmit all at once. If node y_i hasn't received any messages during this short delay, it will transmit M at once. Otherwise; it will compute the distance from the sending node again. If $d(x, y_i) \leq D_{Th}$, $y_i \in N(x)$ then depend on the number of the received message in node y_i to decide whether to retransmitting M or not. And if $c(y_i) < C_{Th}$, node y_i will wait a short delay and if there is not any other messages heard in this period, it will transmit M immediately. If $d(x, y_i) \geq D_{Th}$, then wait for a short time again.

A comparison with the distance-based algorithm, the counter-based algorithm, and the JDCT Algorithm will be given through an example in Fig.2. First, some assumptions are given as follows,

1) The sequence of retransmission is decided by its distance to the source node. The further the distance is, the earlier a node may retransmit M. For example, in Fig.2, $d(S,1) > d(S,7) > d(S,3) > d(S,5) > d(S,4) > d(S,6) > d(S,2)$, the sequence of retransmission is 1-7-3-5-4-6-2.

2) There are no collisions and contentions during broadcast, and $C_{Th}=3$.

In Fig.1, node S is a source node which broadcast a message M, node 1-7 are neighbors of S which will receive M all at once. Form aforementioned definitions, we can get,

$N(S) = \{1, 2, 3, 4, 5, 6, 7\}, E(S) = \{1, 3, 4, 5, 7\}, I(S) = \{2, 6\}$.

$N(1) = E(1) = \{2,6,7,S\}, I(1) = \Phi$.

$N(2) = \{1,3,4,6,S\}, E(2) = \{1,3,6\}, I(2) = \{4, S\}$.

$N(3) = E(3) = \{2,4,5,S\}, I(3) = \Phi$.

$N(4) = \{2,3,S\}, E(4) = \{3,S\}, I(4) = \{2\}$.

$N(5) = E(5) = \{3,6,7,S\}, I(4) = \Phi$.

$N(6) = \{1,2,5,7,S\}, E(6) = \{1,2,5\}, I(4) = \{7,S\}$.

$N(7) = \{1,5,6,S\}, E(7) = \{1,5,S\}, I(7) = \{6\}$

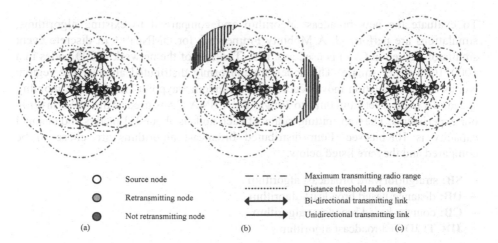

○ Source node	— ·· — Maximum transmitting radio range
◐ Retransmitting node	········ Distance threshold radio range
● Not retransmitting node	←→ Bi-directional transmitting link
	→ Unidirectional transmitting link

(a)   (b)   (c)

Fig. 2. Comparison for redundant to broadcast among (a) distance-based algorithm, (b) counter-based algorithm, and (c) JDCT algorithm

According to [6], the retransmitting node set of distance-based algorithm (Fig.2. a), $Rt_{DB}(s)$ and counter-based algorithm (Fig.2. b), $Rt_{CB}(s)$ is,

$$Rt_{DB}(S) = \{1,2,3,4,5,6,7\} .$$

$$Rt_{CB}(S) = \{1,2,3,7\} .$$

The sum of transmitted M in distance-based algorithm and counter-based algorithm is 34 times and 25 times. In Fig.2 b, the shaded region is the uncovered area caused by using counter-based algorithm. The results match the analysis in [6], which shows that the distance-based algorithm provides a better reachable but worse saved broadcast and more latency time than the counter-based algorithm does.

In Fig.2 c, each node uses the JDCT algorithm to decide whether to retransmit or not. The nodes decide as follows,

S1: Node 1 is the furthest node among the neighbor nodes of the source S, so node 1 retransmits M first.

S2: As $N(1) = E(1) = \{2,6,7,S\}, I(1) = \Phi, c(6) = c(2) = 2, d(S,3) > d(1,7)$, node 3 retransmits M.

S3: As $N(3) = E(3) = \{2,4,5,S\}, I(3) = \Phi, c(2) = 3, d(S,7) > d(3,4), d(3,5)$, node 7 retransmits M, node 2 quits retransmitting M.

S4: As $N(7) = \{1,5,6,S\}, E(7) = \{1,5,S\}, I(7) = \{6\}$, $c(6) = 3$, from definition 8, the retransmit- ing node set $Rt_{JDCT}(S) = \{1,3,4,5,7\}$. The sum of transmitted M is 28 times.

So, in Fig.2, the JDCT algorithm can get the same reachable as distance-based algorithm at the cost of 1 additional retransmitting node and 3 additional transmitted M than counter-based algorithm.

4 Simulation Results

To evaluate the new broadcast algorithm and compare it to existing algorithms, simulations are performed. A Mobility Framework for OMNeT++ (a discrete event simulator written in C++) is used as a tool. The size of the network is 100 nodes in a 1000*1000 meter square. The nodes are uniformly distributed all over the region. Nodes in the simulation move according to "random waypoint" model. The mobility speed of a node is set from 0m/s to 30m/s. The CSMA/CA is used as the MAC layer in our experiments. The transmitting radius of each node is about 231 meters and channel capacity is 10Kbits/sec. Four distributed broadcast algorithms are chose to be compared and they are listed below.

- **SB:** straightforward broadcast algorithm
- **DB:** distance-based broadcast algorithm
- **CB:** counter-based broadcast algorithm
- **JDCT:** JDCT broadcast algorithm

The performance measures of interest are:

- **Average latency:** defined as the interval between its arrival and the moment when either all nodes have received it or no node can rebroadcast it further.
- **Ratio of Saved Rebroadcast (RSR):** The total number of nodes not delivered broadcast packets is divided by the total number of nodes receiving the broadcast message.
- **Ratio of Collision (RC):** The total number of collision is divided by the total number of packets supposed to be delivered during broadcast.
- **Total Number of Contention (TNC):** the total number of contention during broadcast.
- **Total Number of Received Messages (TNRM):** the total number of received messages is the sum of the number of messages heard by each node during broadcast.

The first set of experimental results (Fig.3) demonstrates average RSR versus distance threshold using distance-based algorithm and JDCT algorithm with $R=1$. The result shows that JDCT algorithm obtains higher SRS than the distance-based algorithm. When $D_{Th} \approx 0.9r = 210$meters, the RSR of both distance-based algorithm and JDCT algorithm get their maximum value of SRS, about 52% in JDCT and 28% in DB. This is understandable, because with the increase in threshold value, number of retransmitting nodes decrease. When $D_{Th} > 0.9r$, the distance-based algorithm can't cover the whole network in our simulation scenarios, however, the JDCT can cover the whole network. When $0.87r < D_{Th} \leq r$, the JDCT can find nodes to consist of the vertices of the hexagonal lattice. Thus a high RSR value can be acquired. As the threshold value increases, there are not enough nodes to be found by DB to cover the whole network. However, although nodes selected by the distance threshold are not enough to consist of the vertices of the hexagonal lattice, as the counter threshold is used, the JDCT can also keep a full coverage to the network.

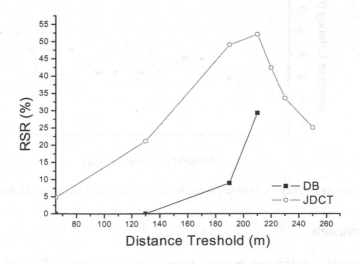

Fig. 3. Distance threshold D_{Th} vs. RSR ($R=1$)

In Fig.4-5, the results are gotten with the parameters of $R=1$, $D_{Th}=0.9r$, $C_{Th}=3$. Fig.4 shows the ratio of saved rebroadcast using different algorithms with varying node speeds (from 0 to 30m/sec). The average latency of different broadcast algorithms with varying node speeds is reported in Fig.5.

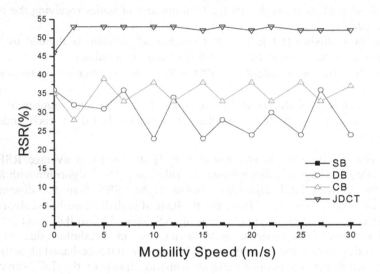

Fig. 4. Ratio of saved rebroadcast vs. mobility speed

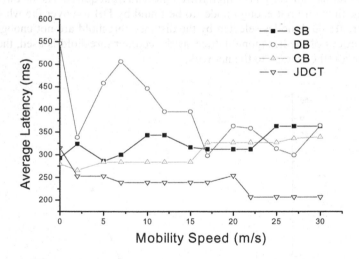

Fig. 5. Average Latency vs. Mobility speed Ratio of Saved Rebroadcast vs. Mobility speed

5   Conclusion

In this paper, a distributed heuristic-based algorithm named JDCT algorithm is presented. The algorithm is based on joint distance and counter threshold scheme. It runs in a distributed manner by each node in the network without needing any global information. The experiments have demonstrated the efficiency of proposed broadcast algorithm. The broadcast storm problem is alleviated by significant reduction in the number of rebroadcast nodes, contention and collision in the network. Its efficiency and robustness in mobile networks make it a good choice for mobile ad hoc networks. Our future work includes a performance evaluation of the JDCT broadcast algorithm in realistic simulation environments with packet collision and node mobility. In addition, we will embed our JDCT algorithm to some routing protocols such as AODV protocol to investigate its efficiency in ad hoc networks.

Acknowledgment

This work is proudly supported in part by the Grand Research Problem of the National Natural Science Foundation of China under Grant No. 90304018, 60672137 and Key Project of Wuhan.

References

1. Li Layuan, Li Chunlin. A QoS multicast routing protocol for dynamic group topology. Information Science, 2005,169(1-2): 113-130.
2. Li Layuan,Li Chunlin. A routing protocol for dynamic and large computer networks with clustering topology. Computer Communications, 2000, Elsevier, UK, 23(2): 171-176.
3. Sung-Ju Lee, William Su, Mario Gerla. Ad hoc Wireless Multicast with Mobility Prediction. IEEE ICCCN'99, Boston, MA, Oct. 1999.
4. Li Layuan, Li Chunlin. "A distributed QoS-aware multicast routing protocol." Acta Informatica, Springer, Germany, 2003, 40 (3): 221-233.
5. J. Cartigny and D. Simplot. Border Node Retransmission Based Probabilistic Broadcast Protocols in Ad-Hoc Networks. In Proc. 36th International Hawaii International Conference on System Sciences (HICSS'03), Hawaii, USA. 2003.
6. Y.-C. Tseng, S.-Y. Ni, Y.-S. Chen, and J.-P. Sheu. The Broadcast Storm Problem in a Mobile Ad Hoc Network. Wireless Networks, 2002, 5 (8): 153-167.
7. J. Broch et al. A performance comparison of multi-hop wireless ad hoc network routing protocols. Proc. ACM MOBICOM, 1998.
8. R. Dube, C. D. Rais, K.-Y. Wang, and S. K. Tripathi. Signal stability based adaptive routing (SSA) for ad hoc mobile networks. Technical Report CS-TR-3646, University of Maryland, College Park, Aug. 1996.ï
9. Li Layuan and Li Chunlin. The QoS routing algorithm for ATM networks. Computer Communications, No.3-4,Vol.24,2001,pp.416-421.

Dynamic MAP Selection Scheme in HMIPv6 Network⋆

Wonsik Chung and SuKyoung Lee

Dept. Computer Science Yonsei University, Seoul, Korea
{wschung,sklee}@cs.yonsei.ac.kr

Abstract. In hierarchical mobile IPv6 networks, when an inter-domain handover occurs, mobile nodes suffer from excessive signaling traffic and long handover latency. Further, the selection of MAP and its load status critically affect the overall system performance. Therefore, we propose a dynamic MAP selection scheme that seeks to distribute load among MAPs as well as reduces inter-domain handovers. Performance is evaluated from not only an analytic model of average signaling cost but also a simulation. The analytical and simulation results show that our proposed scheme improves load distributedness and reduces inter-domain handovers and signaling cost compared to another existing approach.

1 Introduction

Hierarchical Mobile IPv6(HMIPv6) [1] was designed to reduce long handover time and excessive signaling traffic associated with MIPv6 by employing a hierarchy of Mobile Anchor Points(MAPs). However, even in HMIPv6 networks, Mobile Nodes(MNs) still suffer from the long handover latency, especially when they move across MAP-administrated domains due to their high mobility. Thus, Internet Engineering Task Force(IETF) HMIPv6 [1] suggests to select the furthest MAP, in order to avoid frequent inter-domain handovers. The furthest MAP, however, can be a bottleneck as the site grows since the corresponding MAP suffers from the overload due to the increased data traffic to be tunneled as well as Binding Update(BU) signaling. Besides, most MNs select the furthest MAP with the distance-based selection algorithm, so that the overload condition becomes even more severe. To mitigate the bottleneck problem, multiple MAPs are proposed to be configured into the form of a multi-level hierarchy in the same site [2]-[4]. Within a hierarchy of MAPs, some efforts have been made towards selecting an appropriate MAP for MNs according to the moving speed of MN [3],[4]. However, it is not addressed how to resolve the bottleneck when a MAP is overloaded. Besides, in [4], the velocity range is fixed for each MAP.

In this paper, we propose a dynamic MAP selection scheme that distributes the load as well as reduces inter-domain handovers by selecting a MAP which supports the MN's velocity as mentioned in [1] and [4]. Moreover, the velocity

---

⋆ This work was supported by grant No.R01-2006-000-10614-0 from the Basic Research Program of the Korea Science & Engineering Foundation.

T.-J. Cham et al. (Eds.): MMM 2007, LNCS 4352, Part II, pp. 502–509, 2007.

range of MAP is dynamically updated depending on the velocities of MNs which are currently serviced by the MAP.

Further, we develop an analytical model of the average signaling cost for inter-domain handover to investigate the performance of another existing approach with its basis on the IETF HMIPv6 as well as our scheme. It is shown via simulation and numerical results that the proposed dynamic MAP selection scheme can significantly reduce the number of inter-domain handovers and the average signaling cost and distribute load better compared to the IETF HMIPv6 based approach.

In the rest of the paper, we describe our dynamic MAP selection scheme in Section 2 and then investigate the signaling cost for inter-domain handover in Section 3. In Section 4, the performance of the proposed scheme is evaluated through simulations. Section 5 concludes the paper.

2   Dynamic MAP Selection Scheme

Our proposed MAP selection scheme that is called Load and Velocity based MAP (LV-MAP) in this study, facilitates inter-operability between AR and its associated MAPs by signaling information exchanged between them. Based on the information, each AR contains a MAP cache which stores the load status at its associated MAPs and the information related to the velocity of MNs which are currently serviced by the MAPs to decide an optimal MAP on behalf of MNs.

2.1   Proposed MAP Selection Algorithm

In a HMIPv6 network, MAPs are organized as a tree structure with height n where each MAP m_i supports MNs the velocity of which ranges from $v_{i,min}$ to $v_{i,max}$. Let m_{i_p} represent the parent of MAP m_i. Similarly, among the children of MAP m_i, let m_{i_c} be the one with which an MN whose velocity is $v_{i,min}$ is able to associate provided that $v_{i,min}$ is less than the velocity of MN which enters a HMIPv6 network. Otherwise, m_{i_c} denotes a child MAP with which a new MN can associate. Note that an MN is capable of associating only with a MAP that is a parent of the corresponding AR.

Now, we present our LV-MAP algorithm. Let v_u be the velocity for MN u. For MN u which enters a HMIPv6 network, the corresponding AR selects a MAP, m_k $(1 \leq k \leq n)$ among its associated MAPs, the velocity range of which includes v_u or is nearest to v_u if v_u does not belong to the range of any MAP.

We define the maximum load at a MAP as the maximum number of sessions from MNs that the MAP can process. Let ρ_i and $\rho_{i,max}$ be the current load at the ith MAP and the maximum sustainable load the ith MAP can handle. Then, for selected MAP m_k, if $\rho_k < \rho_{k,max}$, then the MN u registers with the MAP m_k. Otherwise, if the selected MAP, m_k is overloaded, then one of the following operations is performed according to where the MAP, m_k is located in the tree. Note that the following operations are considered by the associated AR.

– m_k is the root.

1) $\rho_{k_c} < \rho_{k_c,max}$: If $v_u < v_{k,min}$, the MN u registers with MAP m_{k_c}. Otherwise, among the MNs associated with the MAP m_k, one with the slowest moving speed is re-associated with m_{k_c} while the MN u registers with m_k.

2) $\rho_{k_c} = \rho_{k_c,max}$: The MN u registers with its Correspondent Node (CN) and Home Agent (HA).

– m_k is a leaf node.

1) $\rho_{k_p} < \rho_{k_p,max}$: Between the MN u and the MN whose speed is $v_{k,max}$, the MNs with higher and lower speeds are associated with m_{k_p} and m_k.

2) $\rho_{k_p} = \rho_{k_p,max}$: The MN u registers with its CN and HA.

– m_k is an internal node.

If both m_{k_p} and m_{k_c} are not yet overloaded, the less overloaded one is selected and the same action is taken as that when m_k is a leaf or the root MAP. Otherwise, if all the neighboring MAPs are overloaded, the MN u registers with its CN and HA.

2.2   Inter-domain Handover Process

To further reduce long handover delay incurred for inter-domain handover, our proposed scheme operates based on the extension of the basic hybrid scheme of HMIPv6 and FMIPv6 [5]. For LV-MAP scheme, the detailed signaling procedure for inter-domain handover is illustrated in Fig. 1(a). The signaling procedure works in the same way as in F-HMIPv6 [5] except that new MAP(nMAP) should update the MAP cache maintained in its associated ARs by sending MAP options defined in [1].

When an MN moves out of the current domain, the old MAP does not need to update the change of its load status and velocity range since the corresponding ARs can update their cache entry for the MAP when a new MN registers with the MAP or the cache entry is expired, as a format of soft state de-registration.

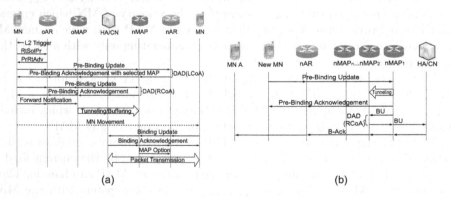

(a)   (b)

Fig. 1. Signaling for (a)inter-domain process for LV-MAP and (b)re-association

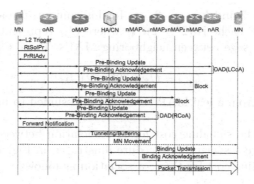

Fig. 2. Signaling for inter-domain handover process for DMAP

When the selected MAP is found to be overloaded, an MN currently serviced by the MAP may be re-associated with one of the neighboring MAPs, as explained in section 2.1. Fig. 1(b) shows the signaling for re-associating MN A currently serviced by nMAP$_1$ with nMAP$_2$. First, nMAP$_1$ forms a temporary tunnel to nMAP$_2$ and starts tunneling the packets destined for the MN A. Then, nMAP$_1$ registers with nMAP$_2$ on behalf of the MN A by sending BU, as in HMIPv6. On receipt of the BU from nMAP$_1$, nMAP$_2$ obtains a Regional CoA (RCoA) and then sends a BU to the MN A's HA to register the new RCoA.

For comparison purpose, we introduce another MAP selection algorithm based on [1], that is called Distance-based MAP (DMAP) selection in this study. In DMAP, an MN always attempts to register with the MAP at the highest level. In case that the MAP is overloaded, it should probe the MAP at the next highest level. This probing process is repeated downward the MAP tree till a non-overloaded MAP is met. When all the MAPs in the domain are found to be overloaded, the normal MIPv6 procedure is performed. Fig. 2 shows the signaling procedures for DMAP when an inter-domain handover occurs.

3   Signaling Cost for Inter-domain Handover

In our analysis of the signaling cost for inter-domain handover, for simplicity, suppose that we have MAPs organized as a binary tree structure with height n.

We denote by C_{A-B} the average cost of exchanging a message between nodes A and B. Then, let C_f represent the total signaling cost for inter-domain handover in F-HMIPv6. On the basis of the signaling procedure in [5], the total cost is calculated as follows:

$$C_f = 7C_{MN-oAR} + 5C_{oAR-oMAP} + 4C_{oMAP-nMAP}$$
$$+ 4C_{nMAP-nAR} + 2C_{MN-nAR} + 2C_{nMAP-HA/CN} \tag{1}$$

Let $C_{p,s}$ be the signaling cost for LV-MAP scheme when an MN registers with a MAP on the sth level. Then, the new status information of the MAP should be sent through the links from the MAP to its associated ARs, where the number of the links is $2^k - 2$ and $k = n + 2 - s$. In this context, the additional cost for updating the MAP cache is $(2^k - 2)C_M$ where C_M represents a signaling cost for exchanging message between neighboring MAPs. Then, $C_{p,s}$ is expressed as follows:

$$C_{p,s} = C_f + (2^k - 2)C_M \qquad (2)$$

where C_{MAP-AR} from a leaf MAP to an AR is assumed to have the same cost as C_M.

Let C_r denote the signaling cost for re-association between an existing MN and a MAP. The re-association procedure illustrated in Fig. 1(b) enables us to evaluate the signaling cost for the re-association as follows:

$$C_r = 3C_M + 2C_{MAP-HA/CN} + C_{nMAP-nAR} + C_{MN-nAR} \qquad (3)$$

where C_f already includes the signaling costs for the new MN.

Let p_b and $C_p^{(i)}$ be the average session blocking probability for MN at a MAP and a signaling cost for inter-domain handover in case that a MAP at the ith level is selected, respectively. Then, supposing that the deployed hierarchical MAP structure has at least three levels, the inter-domain handover signaling cost for LV-MAP is as follows:

$$C_p^{(i)} = (1 - p_b)C_{p,i} + \frac{1}{2}p_b(1 - p_b)(C_{p,i+1} + \frac{1}{2}C_r) \qquad (4)$$
$$+ \frac{1}{2}p_b(1 - p_b)(C_{p,i-1} + \frac{1}{2}C_r) + p_b^3 C_{MIPv6}, \quad \text{for } 1 < i < n$$

$$C_p^{(n)} = (1 - p_b)C_{p,n} + p_b(1 - p_b)(C_{p,n-1} + \frac{1}{2}C_r) + p_b^2 C_{MIPv6} \qquad (5)$$

$$C_p^{(1)} = (1 - p_b)C_{p,1} + p_b(1 - p_b)(C_{p,2} + \frac{1}{2}C_r) + p_b^2 C_{MIPv6} \qquad (6)$$

where $C_{MIPv6} = 2C_{MN-oAR} + 2C_{MN-nAR} + 2C_{nAR-nMAP} + 2C_{nMAP-HA}$ denotes the signaling cost for registering with HA in case that an MN is blocked from a MAP hierarchy. In our analysis, we assume that the velocities of MNs are uniformly distributed over all levels in the hierarchy of MAPs. It is also assumed that when the selected MAP, m_k suffers from overload, either a newly arrived MN or one of the MNs serviced by the selected MAP registers with the least overloaded one with equal probability. The least overloaded MAP is selected between m_{k_c} and m_{k_p} with equal probability as well. Then, the average signaling cost for inter-domain handover in LV-MAP scheme is given by

$$C_{LV} = \frac{1}{n}C_p^{(1)} + \frac{1}{n}C_p^{(n)} + \sum_{k=2}^{n-1} \frac{1}{n}C_p^{(k)}. \qquad (7)$$

For DMAP scheme, based on the signaling presented in Fig. 2, the average signaling cost for inter-domain handover is expressed as follows:

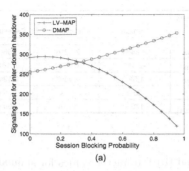

Parameter	Value
C_{MN-oAR} , C_{MN-nAR}	5
$C_{oAR-oMAP}$, $C_{nAR-nMAP}$	10
$C_{nMAP-HA/CN}$	30
$C_{oMAP-nMAP}$	15
C_M	10

(a)   (b)

Fig. 3. (a)Comparison of inter-domain handover signaling costs for LV-MAP and DMAP, and (b)Parameter values for numerical results

$$C_{DMAP} = (1 - p_b)\{C_f + p_b(C_f + C_{MAP}) + \cdots + p_b^{n-1}(C_f + (n-1)C_{MAP})\}$$
$$+ p_b^n\{(C_f - C_{MN-oAR} - C_{oAR-oMAP}) + (n-1)C_{MAP}\} \tag{8}$$

where C_{MAP} is given by $C_{MAP} = 2C_{MN-oAR} + 2C_{oAR-oMAP} + 2C_{oMAP-nMAP}$ as the signaling cost for probing a MAP. The parameter values assumed for numerical examples are shown in Fig. 3(b), which are obtained from [6].

Fig. 3(a) plots the signaling cost versus the session blocking probability for DMAP and LV-MAP schemes when an inter-domain handover occurs. From this figure, we observe that LV-MAP requires higher signaling cost than DMAP when the session blocking probability is low since it has to update MAP cache for each handover while DMAP only needs to register with HA/CN. Interestingly, as the session blocking probability increases, the signaling cost for LV-MAP decreases, contrary to DMAP. This is because under LV-MAP, the MAP cache update cost is not induced for blocked sessions while under DMAP, all arriving sessions attempt to register with the root MAP first even at high load.

4   Performance Evaluation Via Simulation

We evaluate the performance of our proposed LV-MAP scheme via simulation results, comparing with DMAP scheme in terms of total number of inter-domain handovers, signaling cost for inter-domain handover, and load distributedness. The network topology used in the simulation is shown in Fig. 4(a). Each AR in the figure provides a circular topology with radius of 500 m and the maximum number of MNs each MAP can serve is 10. During the simulation, each MN can generate at most one session, the duration of which has an exponential distribution with a mean of 180 s. A session arrival process follows a poisson distribution with various mean values ranging from 0.2 to 1.

For mobility of MNs, we use the Smooth Random Mobility model [7]. The mobility characteristics of MNs are classified into three classes with the same ratio: vehicle, bicycle, and pedestrian as done in [3]. Each class has a maximum speed, v_{max}, and initial velocity of MN is chosen from the two preferred speed

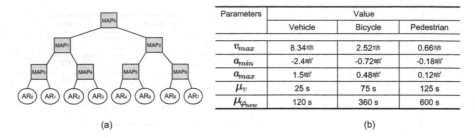

(a)

Parameters	Value		
	Vehicle	Bicycle	Pedestrian
v_{max}	8.34 m/s	2.52 m/s	0.66 m/s
a_{min}	-2.4 m/s²	-0.72 m/s²	-0.18 m/s²
a_{max}	1.5 m/s²	0.48 m/s²	0.12 m/s²
μ_v	25 s	75 s	125 s
$\mu_{\varphi_{new}}$	120 s	360 s	600 s

(b)

Fig. 4. (a)Simulation network topology, and (b) Parameter values for simulation

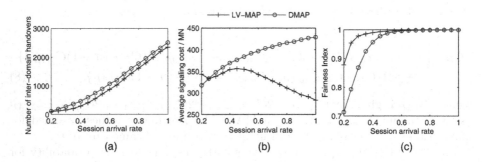

(a)   (b)   (c)

Fig. 5. Simulation Results

values, $\frac{3}{5}v_{max}$, v_{max}, and the uniform distribution of range $[0, v_{max}]$ with probabilities of 0.2, 0.5, and 0.3, respectively. The MN's target speed is updated at a time interval which follows an exponential distribution with a mean of μ_v s. Whenever a new target speed is decided, the MN accelerates or decelerates until the target speed is reached or a new target speed is decided again. The MN selects a random acceleration/deceleration value from $[a_{min}, a_{max}]$. It also decides whether or to change its movement direction or to keep it with probabilities of $\frac{1}{6}$ and $\frac{5}{6}$, respectively, at a time interval with an exponential distribution the mean of which is $\mu_{\varphi_{new}}$ s. The parameter values for simulation, which are obtained from [3] and [7], are given in Fig. 4(b).

Fig. 5(a) shows the total number of inter-domain handovers versus session arrival rate during the simulation time. We observe that our proposed scheme reduces around 12% of inter-domain handovers over DMAP in average. This is due to the fact that LV-MAP considers the MN's velocity.

The average signaling overhead per MN is plotted in Fig. 5(b). As expected from the numerical result in Fig. 3(a), we observe from Fig. 5(b) that the average signaling overhead for LV-MAP starts to decrease after the session arrival rate reaches around 0.5 while the signaling overhead for DMAP scheme increases with the increase of session arrival rate. Thus, we know that under LV-MAP, the signaling cost for inter-domain handover is less than that under DMAP when the hierarchy of MAPs is overloaded, as we intended for LV-MAP scheme.

To investigate the load distributedness, we use the fairness index of loads observed at all the levels in the MAP hierarchy. In Fig. 5(c), we plot the fairness index value versus session arrival rate. This figure shows that the fairness index value for LV-MAP is maintained at higher level than DMAP for all values of session arrival rate. Thus, we know that LV-MAP performs better in distributing the load, than DMAP scheme. On the other hand, we observe that at high session arrival rate (higher than 0.8), the two schemes are getting similar fairness index value because the load of all the MAPs approaches full capacity.

5 Conclusion

In this paper, we propose a dynamic MAP selection algorithm, LV-MAP(Load and Velocity based MAP) for HMIPv6 networks. The proposed scheme selects an optimal MAP based on MN's mobility. Further, LV-MAP scheme distributes load among MAPs.

The simulation and numerical results indicate that LV-MAP provides better performance than DMAP which is based on the IETF HMIPv6, in terms of the frequency of inter-domain handovers, the average signaling cost for inter-domain handover, and the load distributedness, especially for overloaded network.

References

1. H. Soliman, C. Castelluccia, K. El Malki, and L. Bellier. :Hierarchical Mobile IPv6 Mobility Management (HMIPv6). RFC 4140. (August 2005)
2. S. Pack, M. Nam, and Y. Choi. :A Study on Optimal Hierarchy in Multi-Level Hierarchical Mobile IPv6 Networks. IEEE GLOBECOM. (2004)
3. K. Kawano, K. Kinoshita, and K. Murakami :Multilevel Hierarchical Mobility Management Scheme in Complicated Structured Networks. IEEE LCN. (2004)
4. E. Natalizio, A. Scicchitano and S. Marano. :Mobility Anchor Point Selection Based on User Mobility in HMIPv6 Integrated with Fast Handover Mechanism. IEEE WCNC. (2005)
5. J.M. Jang, D.H. Kwon, and Y.J. Suh. :An Efficient Handoff Mechanism with Reduced Latency in Hierarchical Mobile IPv6. LNCS, Vol. 3090 (2004) 184-194
6. W. Ma and Y. Fang. :Dynamic Hierarchical Mobility Management Strategy for Mobile IP Networks. IEEE JSAC, Vol. 22(4), (2004) 664-676.
7. C. Bettstetter:Smooth is better than sharp: Random Mobility Model for Simulation of Wireless Networks. ACM MSWiM. (2001)

A New Fingerprinting Codes for Multimedia Contents

Jin-Heung Lee[1], Tea-Hun Lim[2], Keon-Woo Kim[3], and Sang-Uk Shin[1]

[1] Department of Information Security Graduate School, Pukyong National University,
599-1 Deayeon 3-Dong, Nam-Gu, Busan, Korea
[2] Interdisciplinary Program of Mechatronics, Pukyong National University
[3] Electronics and Telecommunications Research Institute, 161 Gajeong-Dong,
Yuseong-Gu, Daejeon, Korea
jinhung@hanmail.net, lth1553@hanmail.net, wootopian@etri.re.kr,
shinsu@pknu.ac.kr

Abstract. Digital fingerprinting is a technology for enforcing digital rights policies where by unique labels, known as digital fingerprints, are inserted into content prior to distribution. As we use it, we can trace illegal users. These fingerprints are typically embedded into the content using watermarking techniques that are designed to be robust to a variety of attacks. Also, it must secure against collusion attack that some colluders remove and alter their fingerprints. In this paper, we propose easily fingerprint generation technique by using *trace* of primitive polynomial. The proposed scheme can generate codes more easily and have more buyers than existing schemes. Our scheme is secure against collusion attack with two colluders. And we proposed a new watermarking algorithm that embeds and extracts securely by using MPSK(M-ary Phase Shift Keying) technology. The proposed watermarking algorithm has *semi-robustness*. Therefore it is effective in conspirator detection.

Keywords: Digital Fingerprinting, Watermarking for Fingerprinting Code, Trace, Copyrights Protection.

1 Introduction

In reference [1], digital watermarking is the enabling technology to prove of ownership on copyrighted material, detect the originator of illegally made copies, monitor the usage of the copyrighted multimedia data and analyze the spread spectrum of the data over networks and servers. Content provider selling the piece of contents(e.g. image) embeds a mark in the copies. There are two basic kinds of mark: fingerprints and watermarks. A watermark is a message that allows ownership of the marked content to be proven, where as a fingerprint allows buyer identification.

Fingerprinting is a technique for copyright protection. In [2,3], fingerprints are embedded in contents to identify different copies. Thus every user's copy is made unique, while still being close to the original. This ensures that an illegal copy stands out. Distribution of different copies to valid users will facilitate

T.-J. Cham et al. (Eds.): MMM 2007, LNCS 4352, Part II, pp. 510–519, 2007.

identifying the illegal users. The problem of fingerprinting can be divided into sub-problems, which can be addressed individually: the problem of embedding and the problem of coding.

Collusion attacks are not an issue for watermarking, but should be considered in the case of fingerprinting scheme [4]. In a collusion attack, a group of dishonest buyers compares their copies in order to locate differences between them and tries to fabricate a new content whose mark is either no longer recoverable or does not allow identification of any of the colluders.

In reference [5], Dittmann presents a technology for combining a collusion secure fingerprinting scheme based on finite geometries and a watermarking mechanism with special marking points for digital images. This method can extract colluders when 2 people among 3 people collude. Also, he proposed d-detecting code which can detect all colluders when colluder is d person based on finite projective space. But this method has many problems if the number of buyers increases because of projective plane composition.

Trappe and Wu proposed ACC(Anti-Collusion Code [6]) for multimedia data using BIBD(Balanced Incomplete Block Design). And, they proposed algorithm that can detect colluders using this fingerprinting code. ACC are designed to be resistant to averaging, and able to exactly identify groups of colluders. A problem of this code is that the required code length increases according to the number of buyers. So it is difficult to apply it to Internet environments. Also, because the form of the code is simple, it has problem that is predicted easily by attacker.

In this paper, we propose new fingerprinting code generation method, and design the watermarking algorithm that is applied to the proposed. The proposed fingerprinting scheme uses *trace* of primitive polynomial. The proposed scheme can generate codes more easily and have more buyer than the existing schemes. Also, we propose the watermarking algorithm with *semi-robustness* property that embeds and extracts securely by using MPSK(M-ary Phase Shift Keying) technology.

This paper is organized as following. In session 2 we described related work. We present a new fingerprinting code that is resistant to collusion attack and applicable watermarking algorithm to fingerprinting code in session 3 and 4. And we examine safety by experimental estimation about proposal method. Finally, session 5 is conclusion.

2   Related Works

A survey of fingerprinting code techniques is presented in [7]. The first on fingerprinting in the presence of collusions is [8], where a fingerprinting scheme is presented where the number of copies an opponent must obtain in order to erase the fingerprints is specified. An important paper in the area of collusion secure fingerprinting is [9].

2.1   2-Detecting Fingerprinting Scheme

Dittmann et al[5]. described a fingerprint as a collection of marking positions that are either marked with '1' or not marked, being equivalent to '0'. The idea is to construct fingerprint codewords that intersect with other fingerprint codewords in unique ways. Assuming that the unique intersection point cannot be changed, as in the marking assumption, it will determine all of the colluders.

The concept of unique intersections has a nice geometric interpretation. For fingerprinting codes that can detect at most two colluders, the codewords that make up Γ can be represented by the edges on the triangle. The projective space PG(2,2) of dimension 2 (i.e. it is a plane) and order 2 has 7 points and 7 lines(the circle through the points 2, 4 and 6 counting as a line). Any two users have a unique intersection point being a vertex of the triangle. Even if the users remove the detectable marks, the intersection will remain intact, revealing the identities of the two colluders.

Definition 1. *A codebook is a set* $\Gamma = \{\gamma^1, \gamma^2, \cdots, \gamma^M\} \subseteq \sum^l := \{s_1 s_2 \cdots s_l \mid s_i \in M\}$ *of M codewords of length l, over some finite alphabet* $\sum$. *Any subset* $\Gamma' \subset \Gamma$ *is also a valid codebook. Also,* γ^i *can be written as* $\gamma^i = \gamma_1^i \gamma_2^i \cdots \gamma_l^i$.

Customer 1 buys a copy of the document with fingerprint 1(line including point 1,2,3), and customer 2 gets a copy with fingerprint 2(line including point 1,5,6). They compare their documents to generate a pirate copy. The two documents differ at the marking positions 2, 3, 5 and 6. In the worst case, they can unmark all those points. However, they can not detect marking position 1 if a "good" watermarking scheme has been used. If they sell the pirated copy, it will eventually fall into the hands of the copyright owner. The copyright owner will then start the pirate tracing algorithm and detect point 1 and from this point the two pirate customers 1 and 2.

2.2   Anti-collusion Fingerprinting Codes

The idea of using the unique intersection of codes to determine colluders is also used by Trappe et al. in [6] and [10]. Instead of taking a geometric approach, Γ is designed using the BIBD(Balanced Incomplete Block Design) from combinatorial design theory. The drawback of the BIBD codes is that they are only resilient to the AND operator, which is not always an effective model of collusion.

Definition 2. *A* (v, k, λ)-*BIBD is a pair* (X, A), *where A is a collection of k-element subsets(blocks) of a v-element set X, such that each pair of elements of X occur together in exactly λ blocks.*

A (v, k, λ)-BIBD has $b = \lambda(v^2 - v)/(k^2 - k)$ blocks. Corresponding to a block design is the $v \times b$ incidence matrix $M = (m_{ij})$ defined by

$$m_{ij} = \begin{cases} 1 \text{ if the } i\text{th element belongs to the } j\text{th block} \\ 0 \text{ otherwise} \end{cases}$$

If we assign the codewords as the bit-complement of the column vectors of M then we have a $(k-1)$-resilient ACC. For the example of existing fingerprinting code, the initial ACC are available two colluders detections. The columns of the following matrix $C = \{0010111, 0101101, 0111010, 1001011, 1011100, 1100110, 1110001\}$ represent the code vectors of an ACC built from a (7,3,1)-BIBD.

This code requires 7 bits for seven users and provides 2-resiliency since any two column vectors share a unique pair of 1 bit. Each column vector c of C is mapped to $\{\pm 1\}$. The code modulated watermark is then $w = \sum_{i=1}^{v}(f(c_i))u_i$. When two watermarks are averaged, the locations where the corresponding AND-ACC agree and have a value of 1 identify the colluding users.

$$w_1 = -u_1 - u_2 + u_3 - u_4 + u_5 + u_6 + u_7$$
$$w_2 = -u_1 + u_2 - u_3 + u_4 + u_5 - u_6 + u_7$$

For example, the w_1 w_2 shown above represent the watermarks for the first two columns of the above (7,3,1) code, when they used the antipodal form and changed '0' to '-1'. The average $(w_1 + w_2)/2$ has coefficient vector $(-1,0,0,0,1,0,1)$. The fact that a '1' occurs in the fifth and seventh location uniquely identifies users 1 and 2 as the colluders.

3   A New Fingerprinting Code

3.1   Our Concept

The both schemes described above fundamentally 2-resistant fingerprinting schemes. But, these schemes have very difficult to create projective space and BIBD matrix. Therefore, if the number of users who have fingerprinting code increases, it may be impossible to find projective space and BIBD matrix. As a result, it is hard to apply in system environment that have many and unspecified users. In this paper, we propose the scheme that can solve these problems and create code easily.

Pirates can try collusion attack from shared contents. Our concept to detect this uses peculiar position of fingerprinting code. This is similar to concept of ACC algorithm of reference [6]. But, we do not use particular matrix just as it is. We compute *trace* by primitive polynomial. And then, we create fingerprinting code from cyclic matrix of *trace*. This method has a characteristic that can create easily many codes.

3.2   *Trace* of Primitive Polynomial

Usually digital fingerprinting code must satisfy following properties. First, it must detect exactly legal user and user who distribute illegally, and be able to perform efficiently copyright protection system. Also, fingerprinting code should be difficult to delete and alter by those who have incomplete information for fingerprinting code. Finally, it must be able to divide the pirate in small part of contents distributed unlawfully. The proposal fingerprinting code is efficient and resistant to collusion attack using *trace* of primitive polynomial.

Let $F = GF(p)$ and $K = GF(p^n)$, where p is prime. Then by Theorem 1, we may view F as a subfield of K. If α is an element of K, its *trace relative* to the subfield F is defined as follows,

$$Tr_K^F(\alpha) = \alpha + \alpha^p + \alpha^{p^2} + \cdots + \alpha^{p^{n-1}}.$$

Theorem 1. *([11])   For every divisor d of n, $GF(p^n)$ contains exactly one subfield isomorphic to $GF(p^d)$; and $GF(p^n)$ has no other subfields .*

For example, let $K = GF(2^4)$, $F = GF(2)$. We define K via the irreducible polynomial $f(x) = x^4 + x^3 + x^2 + x + 1 = \Phi_5(x)$, where $\Phi_d(x)$ is dth cyclotomic polynomial. Letting α denote the element $x \bmod f(x)$, (alternatively α is a root of the equation $f(x) = 0$ in K) we know that every element $\beta \in k$ can be expressed uniquely as $\beta = \beta_0 + \beta_1\alpha + \beta_2\alpha^2 + \beta_3\alpha^3$. Then by $Tr(\alpha + \beta) = Tr(\alpha) + Tr(\beta)$ and $Tr(\lambda\alpha) = \lambda Tr(\alpha)$, we have

$$Tr(\beta) = \beta_0 Tr(1) + \beta_1 Tr(\alpha) + \beta_2 Tr(\alpha^2) + \beta_3 Tr(\alpha^3).$$

Thus in order to compute $Tr(\beta)$ for any β it is sufficient to compute $Tr(1)$, $Tr(\alpha)$, $Tr(\alpha^2)$, and $Tr(\alpha^3)$. Clearly $Tr(1) = 1+1+1+1 = 0$. Now $Tr(\alpha) = \alpha + \alpha^2 + \alpha^4 + \alpha^8$; this could be computed in a straightforward manner in $GF(16)$. But notice that if $f(x) = (x-\alpha)(x-\alpha^2)(x-\alpha^4)(x-\alpha^8) = x^4 + c_1 x^3 + c_2 x^2 + c_3 x + c_4$ is the minimal polynomial of α, then $Tr(\alpha) = c_1$. Next we have $Tr(\alpha^2) = Tr(\alpha) = 1$. Finally note that since $f(x) \mid \Phi_5(x)$, $\alpha^5 = 1$ and so $\alpha^3 = \alpha^8$, i.e. α^3 is conjugate to α, and so $Tr(\alpha^3) = Tr(\alpha) = 1$. Summarizing, we have shown without any calculation that

$$Tr(1) = 0, Tr(\alpha) = Tr(\alpha^2) = Tr(\alpha^3) = 1.$$

And so, if $\beta = (\beta_0\beta_1\beta_2\beta_3) = \beta_0 + \beta_1\alpha + \beta_2\alpha^2 + \beta_3\alpha^3$, $Tr(\beta) = \beta_1 + \beta_2 + \beta_3 = \beta(0111)$. The next theorem gives the relationship between all these *traces*.

Theorem 2. $Tr_F^K(\alpha) = Tr_F^E(Tr_E^K(\alpha))$

We continue to assume that $F \subseteq E \subseteq K$ are finite fields with $F \cong GF(p)$, $K \cong GF(p^n)$ and let $\alpha \in K$. We saw in example that in one particular case the *trace* of α could be determined from the coefficients of the minimal polynomial of α. In the next theorem, we will see that $Tr_F^K(\alpha)$ can always be expressed in terms of the coefficients of the minimal polynomials of α. Thus let

$$\alpha, \alpha^p, \alpha^{p^2}, \cdots, \alpha^{p^{d-1}} \quad (d \mid n)$$

be the conjugates of α(with respect to the subfield F). Then the minimal polynomial of α is, by definition,

$$(x - \alpha)(x - \alpha^p) \cdots (x - \alpha^{p^{d-1}}) = x^d + c_1 x^{d-1} + \cdots + c_d$$

where the coefficients $c_1, c_2, \cdots, c_d$ can in principle be determined by multiplying out the d factors on the left. Let $K = GF(2^3)$, $F = GF(2)$, with defining polynomial $f(x) = x^3 + x + 1$. Using above-mentioned numerical formulas, we constructed $Tr(\alpha^i)$.

3.3   A New Fingerprinting Code

We construct collusion-secure fingerprinting code as following using $Tr(\alpha^i)$. We first create $2^m - 1 \times 2^m - 1$ periodic sequence M by using $Tr(\alpha^i)$. Here, m denotes maximum degree of primitive polynomial.

$$
M = \begin{pmatrix}
Tr(\alpha^0) & Tr(\alpha^1) & Tr(\alpha^2) & Tr(\alpha^{2^m-1}) \\
Tr(\alpha^1) & Tr(\alpha^2) & Tr(\alpha^3) & Tr(\alpha^0) \\
& \vdots & \cdots & \\
Tr(\alpha^{2^m-1}) & Tr(\alpha^0) & Tr(\alpha^1) & Tr(\alpha^{2^m-2})
\end{pmatrix}
$$

We describe the set M_i containing k codewords. Define M_i as the set of rows of matrix M such that M_i contains k codewords each of length $2^m - 1$. We show that all the rows of M are independent about position of bit. The fingerprinting codes are constructed by using the above set M containing k codewords. If there are N buyers, each buyer j is assigned a different M_i.

The following M is created by using primitive polynomial $f(x) = x^3 + x + 1$. *Trace* that is created by given polynomial $f(x)$ is same with $\{1001011\}$. At the next time, we compose vector $\{0010111, 0101110, 1011100, 0111001, 1110010, 1100101\}$ being shifted *trace*. This can be used to row vectors of M, and it becomes user's fingerprinting codes. This code requires 7 bits for 7 users and provides 2-resiliency since any two vectors share a unique pair of '1' bits. Each bit of row vector M_i is mapped to $\{\pm 1\}$. If two colluders take an average row vector, we can confirm collusive users from the fact that the colluded vector has value of 1 on equal position of M. For example, if we assign the first row and the second row of M to user1 and user2 respectively, it is as following that

$$
w_1 = s_1 - s_2 - s_3 + s_4 - s_5 + s_6 + s_7
$$
$$
w_2 = -s_1 - s_2 + s_3 - s_4 + s_5 + s_6 + u_7
$$

where s is othogonal signal about each position bits. We assume, when a sequence of fingerprinting code is colluded, that the detected binary sequence is the logical AND of the fingerprinting codes M_i. Copies made illegally by two colluders have $(0,-1,0,0,0,1,1)$ vector. To have '1' at the same time on sixth and seventh position of this vector is no one but user1 and user2. Therefore, we can confirm that colluders made copies illegally are user1 and user2 by this uniquely identifies.

If use $f(x) = x^3 + x + 1$ with above example, code length of M has result such as Trappe's (7,3,1)-BIBD. But, $(v, k, \lambda)-$BIBD's do not necessarily exist for an arbitrary choice of v, and k. Therefore, Trapper's scheme has many problems when the number of users is increasing. On the other hand, because the proposed matrix M creates *trace* by using primitive polynomials, we can generate fingerprinting code for many users. If user increases, a proposed technique selects dth primitive polynomials only, and makes new M.

New fingerprinting code about each buyer creates with row vector of M. When selecting any two codes among whole code, selected fingerprinting codes has equal bits value at position of $2^m/4$. Therefore, we can detect two colluders who attempt collusion attack by using bit position uniquely identifies user1 and user2.

4   Watermarking Algorithm for Fingerprinting Code

Watermarking technology that uses spread spectrum embeds watermark information in contents as spreads it using PN(pseudo-noise) sequence that is used much in existent digital communication. We can encrypt easily watermark information taking advantage of spread spectrum. And, inserted signal is diffused in frequency domain. So, it can not be perceptible and can detect simply[12,13].

We propose algorithm that embeds and detects fingerprinting information by spread spectrum using PN sequence. Fingerprinting information that is inserted by PN sequence can regard as noise such as white noise in contents. As fingerprinting information is embedded, it is embedded and changed in frequency domain. So it maximizes optical effect as it keeps characteristic of PN sequence. Also, for effective detection of collusion attack, it has *semi-robustness* unlike existent watermarking algorithms. We define *semi-robustness* characteristic as following: if a bits of codeword is changed by collusion attack, it decreases signal, otherwise it doesn't decrease signal. Because equal codeword bits detect exactly original signal by characteristic of robustness, the proposed algorithm can search for colluders by vector value of this codeword.

4.1   Embedding Algorithm

PSK(Phase Shift Keying) is technology of communications that offers various transmission speed to use phase difference of signal. QPSK that extends concept of PSK or Binary PSK is used much in radio communication. While BPSK divides two signals of only 1 and 0, QPSK divides 4 digital signals. Therefore it is technology that can transmit data of 2 times within same time because it can transmit 2 bit digital signal of $\{00, 01, 10, 11\}$.

MPSK includes BPSK and QPSK, and it has level of N signal. For example, if send signal that become quantization in 16 steps at once, it must alter multilevel signaling that has at least 16 signals angular. In this case, one carrier signal is divided 16 different phase, and can create 16-PSK. When it is $N = 2$ in MPSK, it becomes BPSK because it uses two kind of signal, and when it is $N = 4$, it becomes QPSK. We propose a new watermarking algorithm applying MPSK mode about watermark sequence. The watermark w is given by the following;

$$w = \begin{cases} s_{128 \cdot i + j}, & 0 \leq j \leq 127 \ (if \ m_i = 1) \\ s_{128 \cdot i - j}, & 0 \leq j \leq 127 \ (if \ m_i = 0) \end{cases}$$

Where m_i and s denotes fingerprinting information and PN-sequence to be embedded respectively. Each user embeds PN-sequence changed by each fingerprinting code m_i in contents as watermark information.

4.2   Detection Algorithm of Fingerprinting Code

Fingerprints extraction is consisted of two steps. First, we detect the embedded watermark sequence s'. And, extract fingerprinting code using detected sequence and correlation of PN-sequence. Cross correlation is to calculate phase difference using the extracted watermark and PN-sequence information. That is.

$$Corr_{[n,k]}[n] = \frac{1}{K} \sum_k s'_{[128 \cdot n + k]} \cdot s_{[128 \cdot n + k]}, \ 0 \leq k \leq 127$$

where n is length of inserted fingerprinting code. And the more length of fingerprinting code is long, the more phase is changed. So it secures that it has to take length of PN-sequence long for security.

4.3   Test Result

We inserted fingerprinting code to six grayscale 256×256 pixel images (Lena, Baboon, Fishingboat, Opera, Pentagon, Airplane) using the proposed algorithm. And, we extracted fingerprinting information after we do compression and collusion attack to inserted image. PSNR of images to be fingerprinting is not able to recognize difference visually by fixing watermark strength to keep more than 38dB. We generated fingerprinting codes by using primitive polynomial $f(x) = x^3 + x + 1$, and inserted each generated codeword to different buyer's copies. Fingerprinting code is consisted of each row vector of matrix M created by trace and this code has one bit for synchronization. Generated fingerprinting code is as following;

$$User1 : (0, 1, 0, 1, 1, 1, 0)$$
$$User2 : (1, 0, 1, 1, 1, 0, 0)$$

Next code shows instance of fingerprinting code that is allocated to user-1 and user-2. Average vector (0,0,0,1,1,0,-1) represents code that detects from new contents that are made after user 1 and user 2 average their each contents. We can detect two colluders who have the fifth and sixth bits '1' at the same time from average code vector.

Figure 1 shows the result that detects fingerprinting code from image which is colluded by two users. In figure 1, correlation coefficients of watermark that is detected from colluded image are more than 0.3. Also, correlation of position vector that designates colluder keeps correlation more than 0.9. We selected codewords that have '1' on the same position with average vector (0,0,0,1,1,0,-1). Namely, we can find that colluders are users who are allocated vector of (0,1,0,1,1,1,0) and (1,0,1,1,1,0,0) among codeword.

Usually, image on Internet is used loss-compressed image of JPEG, GIF etc. Therefore, fingerprinted image must not delete and alter inserted code by loss-compression. We performed average attack and mosaic attack for fingerprinting code is embedded. Figure 2 shows detected result of fingerprints after we performed JPEG and collusion attack.

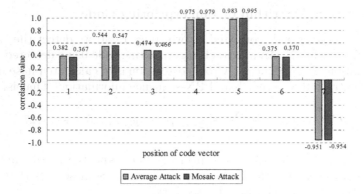

Fig. 1. Correlation detection for images that collusion attack is done by two colluders

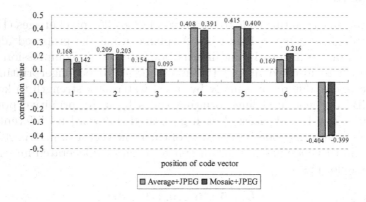

Fig. 2. Correlation detection for images that performed JPEG and collusion attack

5 Conclusion

In this paper, we proposed new collusion-secure fingerprinting code and proposed MPSK watermarking algorithm for inserting generated fingerprinting codes. The proposed fingerprinting code was available to detect colluders to collusion attack such as average attack and mosaic attack by two colluders. And, MPSK watermarking algorithm confirmed efficient watermarking algorithm for fingerprinting code because that has *semi-robustness* characteristic.

We resolved the problem of the code length in existing algorithms by using periodic matrix of *trace*. The proposed code is very short, and can generate code easily. And, we presented watermarking algorithm that is suitable to the proposed fingerprinting code. Through our study, it is possible to embody tracing system and content distribution system. The proposed fingerprinting code considered only two colluders among many copies. Future work will resolve further colluders problems and it has to study watermarking algorithm that is robust to various image processing.

Acknowledgement. This research was supported by the Program for the Training of Graduate Students in Regional Innovation which was conducted by the Ministry of Commerce Industry and Energy of the Korean Government.

References

1. M. Swanson, M. Kobayashi, A. Tewfik, "Multimedia Data Embedding and Water-marking Technologies," Proc. of IEEE, Vol. 86, No. 6, pp.1064-1087, June. 1998.
2. B.Pfitzmann and M.Schunter, "Asymmetric Fingerprinting", EUROCRYPT'96, LNCS 1070, pp.84-95, 1996.
3. D.Kirovski, H.S.Malvar, and Y.Yacobi, "Multimedia Content Screening Using a Dual Watermrking and Fingerprinting System", ACM Mutimedia, 2002.
4. V. Wahadaniah, Y.L. Guan, and H.C. Chua, "A New Collusion Attack and Its Performance Evaluation", Proceedings of IWDW, pp.88-103, 2002.
5. J.Dittmann, A.Behr, M.Stabenau, P.Schmitt, J. Schwenk and J.Ueberberg, "Combining Digital Watermarks and Collusion Secure Fingerprints for Digital Image", SPIE J. Electron. Image, Vol. 9, pp.456-467, 2000.
6. W.Trappe, M.Wu, J.Wang, and K.J.Ray Liu, "Anti-collusion Fingerprinting for Multimedia", IEEE Transction on Signal Processing, Vol. 51, N0. 4, pp.1069-1087, 2003.
7. Borko Furht and Darko Kirovski, Multimedia Securrity Handbook, CRC Press, 2005.
8. G. R. Blakley, C. Meadows, G. B. Purdy, "Fingerprinting Long Forgiving Messages", CRYPTO'85, pp.180-189, 1985.
9. D. Boneh , J. Shaw, "Collusion Secure Fingerprinting for Digital Data", IEEE Transaction on Information Theory, Vol IT-44, pp. 1897-1905, 1998.
10. Min Wu, W. Trappe, Z. Jane Wang, and K. J. Ray Liu, "Collusion-Resistant Fingerprinting for Multimedia", IEEE Signal Processing Magazine, pp.15-27, 2004.
11. Robert J. MacEliecs, Finite Fields for Computer Scientists and Engineers, Kluwer, 1986.
12. L. Boney, A. H. Tewfik and K. N. Hamdy, "Digital Watermarks for Audio Signals", IEEE Proceedings of Multimedia, pp. 473-480, 1996.
13. I. J. Cox, J. Kilian, T. Leighton and T. Shnmoon, "A Secure, Robust Watermark for Multimedia", Proc. Workshop on Information Hiding, 1996.

Content and Location Addressable Overlay Network for Wireless Multimedia Communication*

Wu Huafeng[1,2]

[1] Shanghai Maritime University
Shanghai, 200135, China
[2] Department of Computer Science and Engineering, Fudan University
Shanghai, 200433, China
wuhuafeng@fudan.edu.cn

Abstract. With the rapid development of wireless multimedia communication and Peer-to-Peer overlay network, it is envisioned that building a content and location addressable overlay network for wireless multimedia communication is promising. In this paper, based on a special structure, Geographically Hierarchical Index (GHI), we propose an efficient algorithm, Content and Location Addressable overlay Network (CLAN) algorithm, which makes p2p multimedia communication over MANETs applicable and efficient, satisfying three goals: efficiency, scalability and adaptability to node movement.

Keywords: wireless multimedia communication; peer-to-peer; MANET; distributed computing.

1 Introduction

With more and more gadgets such as file viewer, MP4 player and DVD player being equipped on wireless communication devices via technologies such as Wi-Fi, Bluetooth, mobile ad hoc network (MANET), which is characterized as multi-hop wireless communications between mobile devices[1], comes to play a great role. MANET enables more and more multimedia applications such as sharing and exchange of documents, pictures, music, and movies on mobile devices which can spontaneously self-organize into a communication structure without any fixed infrastructure. To enable efficient communication among nodes in the network, most of the recent research efforts in MANET focus on the lower layers, such as link layer, network layer and transport layer, but not the application layer. However current Peer-to-peer (P2P) systems mostly work on wired networks. It is envisioned that building a content and location addressable p2p overlay network over MANET for wireless multimedia communication is promising, tapping the synergetic potential hidden in these two decentralized and self organizing networks, P2P systems and MANETs.

* This paper was supported by the Special Science and Research Funds of the Shanghai Municipal Education Commission for the Selection and Cultivation of Young Faculty.

T.-J. Cham et al. (Eds.): MMM 2007, LNCS 4352, Part II, pp. 520–527, 2007.
© Springer-Verlag Berlin Heidelberg 2007

To build a p2p overlay network over MANET for wireless multimedia communication, several unique challenges exist. Similar to P2P systems over internet, to enable effective data exchange in mobile P2P multimedia communication over MANET, the key is to devise search mechanisms to find and retrieve a data object of interest in MANET. In this paper, we propose an efficient algorithm, CLAN: a Content and Location Addressable overlay Network algorithm for P2P multimedia communication over MANET, that enables efficient P2P information search and retrieval over MANETs. Firstly we introduce a Geographically Hierarchical Index (GHI) structure, after that, we construct the CLAN algorithm. Lastly, through NS2 simulation, we demonstrate that CLAN is feasible over MANET and can work better than other existing p2p protocol, such as flood and CAN.

The remaining part of this paper is organized as follows. After introducing the system scenario and motivations behind our proposal in Section 2, we present CAR in Section 3, which includes the GHI structure design and CLAN construction. Algorithm simulation and evaluation is presented in Section 4. We compare our proposal with related works, in Section 5. Section 6 concludes the paper.

2 Scenario and Motivation

The nodes of MANET are mobile, and self-organize to provide and use services, guaranteeing wireless communication to end-users. Each node in MANET has limited radio range and we assume that all nodes have the same radio range. A node can communicate with other nodes within its radio range directly or the ones out of its radio range indirectly through multi-hop relay. Any node may join or leave the network, resulting in dynamic relationship changes. In addition, nodes may move, resulting in dynamic topology changes.

We assume that each node knows its own position as well as its immediate neighbors' position through GPS devices. And we assume that the positioning devices have enough accuracy for this application. Thus we can use the existing geographical routing protocol as our basic routing protocol for the wireless network.

We setup such a MANET scenario, with N nodes, each with a unique nodeID, uniformly distributed in a squared region Z. And each node also provides certain number of sharable data objects. We assume that each data object is associated with a well known single-attribute key. Then CLAN will search for a data according to its key value, firstly the request node send a request to the index node, which will further find the resource node and inform it of the required data, then the resource node will directly send the required data to the request node. Besides its' such basic functionality, our motivation and goals mainly lie in following three sides:

Scalability, CLAN should be scalable in terms of network size as well as the amount of sharable multimedia information stored in the network.

Efficiency, due to the scarce resources, it is desirable that a node can find a nearby source node without traveling much further than the source node itself.

Adaptability to node mobility, index nodes must be intelligently selected so that the index structure can adapt to node movement without incurring extra overhead.

3 CLAN Design

3.1 Introduction of GHI

To overcome the drawbacks of directly utilizing a standard DHT in a P2P protocol over MANET, mainly due to its flat id space, we impose a Geographically Hierarchical Index (GHI) structure over the id space to divide it into a hierarchy of zones, rather than a flat of zones (we have proposed it in another paper, p2p multimedia sharing over MANET, which would be included in Springer-LNCS proceedings). Opposite with the DHT, we strictly map the GHI to the physical geographical coordinate system, which are usually prescribed by latitude and longitude. At any point in time, the entire coordinate space is statically, hierarchically partitioned along with the geographical coordinate. And in our GHI, we introduce a hash function H which takes the key value of a data object and the geographical boundary of a square as inputs, and generates an output that is a geographical coordinate bounded by the specified boundary. Then the entire region is partitioned into 4 equal-sized squares while each of these squares is partitioned further into 4 smaller children squares, and so on. This process goes round and round till the side length of the smallest zone (we here define it as the unit zone), L, is less than $r/\sqrt{2}$, where r represents the radio range so that any two nodes in a unit zone can communicate directly with each other, i.e., they are within each other's radio range. We define the squares from the highest grade, namely the entire region, to the lowest grade with increasing number of digits, and within the same grade with increasing numeric value clockwise from the up-left quarter zone. The total times of the partition for the entire region is denoted as partition depth, m. Fig.1 gives an example of 4-grade, namely $m = 4$, GHI structure.

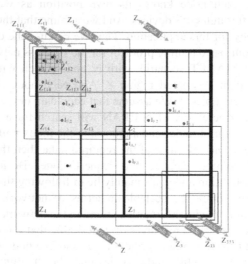

Fig. 1. GHI structure

3.2 CLAN Construction

Nodes Join, Leave and Move

Join. As described in section 3.1, the whole network is associated with a hash function H. So when a node joins the network, it publishes the index information of its locally stored data objects to the network as follows. For each of its locally stored data objects, it first calculates a set of hashed geographical coordinates using the geographical boundaries associated with each grade of the zones that it resides in and the key of the data object as inputs. Then it publishes the index information for the data object to these unit zones where the hash point falls into. But what if there is no nodes residing in these zones, which we here define it as *vacuum zone*? To deal with such issue, we prescribe that the zone which is closest to the hashed geographical coordinates and not a vacuum zone should bear the corresponding responsibilities, storing the index information published by the source nodes.

Leave. When a node leaves the network gracefully, it firstly withdraws all the objects it is currently publishing, and then transfers the index information to those nodes within the same zone. Once it the only one node in the unit zone, then it should transfer them into the nearest unit zone.

Move. When a node is moving, it continually checks its own position to detect whether it is still within the same unit zone or it has moves out of it. If it is still within the same unit zone, then no action is needed. Once a node moves out of its previous grid cell, it becomes one of the index nodes for those data objects that have hashed coordinates mapped to the new unit zone that it moves into and is no longer an index node for those data objects having hashed coordinates mapped to its previous grid cell. Therefore, it deletes its old index information and obtains the index information from any node in its current unit zone. In addition, a node needs to republish the index information for its data objects when it moves out of a grade-i square and enters a new grade-i square within the range of the new grade-$(i-1)$ zone, parent zone.

Data Search

The purpose of the P2P system over MANET is to share *data* of interest among the nodes. Each particular data is stored on one or more nodes in the network, each called an *owner* of the data. So data search is a basic function of the CLAN algorithm, and the basic search service operation in such a P2P system is then to locate an owner of an object for an arbitrary node in the MANET.

When a node issues a search request, it includes the key associated with the requested data object, its nodeID and current GPS position. The search process mainly includes the following steps:

1. Checking its' own local data store. If a result is found, the search terminates and then step 3 is followed. Otherwise, turn to next step;

2. Invoking data lookup by sending the request to an index node, the first index node within its' own unit zone, namely its lowest grade zone (i.e., grade-i where i is the maximum grade of GHI). If an entry for the requested key is there, then the search terminates. Otherwise, the request is then forwarded to the index node at next higher grade zone, namely the parent zone. The process is repeated until either the index entry for the requested key is found or the top grade of GHI is reached without finding an index entry for the requested key. For the former case, the data search

terminates and turns to step 3. For the latter case, the search fails and a failure message is returned back to the requester node.

3. The index node for the requested data send a *transfer request*, which includes the key associated with the requested data object, requester node's nodeID and its' GPS position, to the source node which holds the data requested. According to GHI principles, data search always terminates at the unit zone where the source node resides in, thus the transfer request can reach the source node by only one hop with routing relieved.

Data Auto Retrieval

Since the node ID and location of the requester node is included in the request message, data retrieval can be done automatically from the source node to the requester node if the requester node stays in its original unit zone, and the position-based routing algorithm can be adopted [3]. Considering node mobility, there are two possible cases. The first case is that a node moves but still within its original unit zone. In this case, nothing is special for the normal retrieval. Another case is that the requester moves out of its original unit zone when the reply message reaches its original grid cell, then a traditional routing algorithm is adopted.

The term *auto* makes data retrieval in our algorithm different with and better than other algorithms in traditional P2P system. Because once the requested data is addressed then a transfer request is created by the index node and sent to the source node which will immediately transfer the requested data to the requester node. But in the traditional P2P system algorithm, the requester node must firstly retrieve the address of source node from the index node and then send a transfer request to the source node to retrieve the requested data. Thus the data auto retrieval can save one route and correspondingly the waiting time for the first arrival of requested data. Fig.2 shows a typical example of CLAN operation.

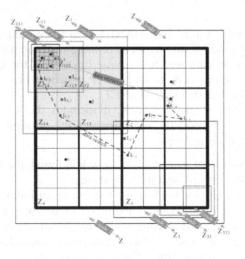

Fig. 2. CLAN Algorithm Example

4 Algorithm Simulation and Evaluation

4.1 Network Setup

In our NS-2 simulation, we prescribe that each node has a radio range 300 meter. Thus the side length of the unit zone is set to 200 meter. The network sizes are 64, 256, 1024, and 4096. The default network size is set to 1024 if unspecified otherwise. The hierarchy depth m is set to 4, and thus the side length of the whole region equals $200*2^{(4-1)}$, 1600 meter, and there are totally 64 unit zones. The nodes are initially randomly placed in the whole region. That means if the network size is 64, then there is only one node per unit zone (200*200 square region), and if 256 then 4 per unit zone, the rest may be deduced by analogy. The nodes mobility is characterized by the random waypoint model[5] with a maximum velocity ranging from 0m/s to 20m/s. The pause time is set to 0 second.

Each node holds 10 data objects. A node issues random searches into the network while the average time interval between two searches issued by a node is 20 seconds. The simulation time is 600 seconds. The results shown in following sections are averaged over 10 trials for each set of the simulation.

4.2 Evaluation

The effect of network size is firstly simulated, the results are shown as fig. 3, indicating the change of average number of messages while the number of nodes involved in the network is increased from 64 to 4096. Fig. 3 demonstrates the average number of messages with relation to the network size, comparing CLAN with CAN and flood. Obviously the performance of both CLAN and CAN is much better than that of flood, and CLAN also has advantage over CAN.

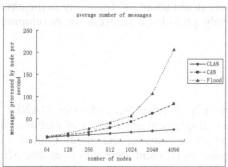
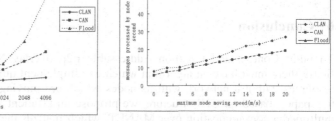

Fig. 3. Effect of network size

Fig. 4. Effect of node's mobility on message number

Then hereafter we consider the effect of node mobility, mainly on the average number of messages. The simulation results are shown as fig. 4, which indicates a almost linear relationship between the average number of messages and the node's moving speed. It indicates that the average number of messages influenced by node mobility is the least for flood, and then CLAN and most for CAN. However even the node's moving speed reached the maximum set value 20 m/s, the average number of messages of CLAN is still far less than that of Flood, also less than that of CAN. The simulation results verify the CLAN's adaptability to node mobility. The NS-2 simulation has validated these inferences, demonstrating the CLAN's feasibility, scalability and efficiency.

5 Related Work

We have proposed GHI structure, which is the basic of this algorithm, in another paper, p2p multimedia sharing over MANET, which was accepted by mmm'07 and would be included in Springer-LNCS proceedings. The first attempt of solutions which dedicate into building P2P network under mobile scenario is JXME, which try to maintain the goals of JXTA but make some amendments to make it adaptable to the mobility. However this solution only take the cell network into account, without solving the problems of applying virtual overlay network over physical network, and is thus not feasible in the MANET scenario. [6] mainly provides a more applicable cross-layer protocols stack for implementing P2P computing over MANET, to simplify the application environment for applying Pastry like protocols over MANET, but without designing an algorithm special for MANETs. Like [6], [7] also gives a kind of cross-layer protocol, embedding a query mechanism into the geographical location services, which may cause much more extra cost, due to its' need to refresh the index information corresponding to the bearing resources as the node is moving. In 7DS[8] and ORION[9], cooperative caching concept is adopted to implement P2P file sharing over MANET, but it can't predict the success rate of a query and highly depends on the search locality in the system. PROEM[12] then provides a platform for developing p2p applications over MANET, its' message is based on TCP, UDP or HTTP and presented by XML. However, it doesn't provide any mechanisms to make it adaptive to the physical topology, so we may doubt about its' feasibility in the case of large size MANET. The same, [11] mostly provides a platform for developing mobile p2p applications.

6 Conclusion

To build Content and Location Addressable p2p overlay Network over MANET, firstly there must have an algorithm which can implement quick query of multimedia resources within a network with its nodes which are moving and energy limited. In this paper, based on GHI structure, we propose an efficient algorithm to enable p2p multimedia communication over MANET, which realizes the three goals, scalability, efficiency, and adaptability to node movement. Lastly, the CLAN algorithm is simulated and validated with NS-2, showing its' feasibility and relatively better performance. To make further improvement on the efficiency on p2p multimedia communication over MANET, we would like to addresses the data dissemination issue in MANET by partitioning a multimedia file into multiple segments so that a node can acquire different segments at different times and in different locations, thus improving the data retrieval efficiency, in our future research work.

References

1. Samba Sesay, Zongkai Yang and Jianhua He, A Survey on Mobile Ad Hoc Wireless Network, Information Technology Journal 3 (2): 168-175, 2004
2. S. Verma and W. Ooi, Controlling Gossip Protocol Infection Pattern Using Adaptive Fanout. Proc. IEEE ICDCS, 2005.
3. M Mauve, J Widmer, H Hartenstein, A survey on position-based routing in mobile ad hoc networks, IEEE NETWORK, 2001
4. S Ratsanamy, P Francis, M Handley, R Karp, A Scalable Content-Addressable Network, ACM SIGCOMM Conference, 2001
5. J. Broch, D. A. Maltz, D. B. Johnson, Y.-C. Hu, and J. Jetcheva. A performance comparison of multi-hop wireless ad hoc network routing protocols. In Proceedings of MOBICOM, pages 85–97, October 1998.
6. M. Conti, E. Gregori, and G. Turi, "Towards scalable P2P computing for mobile ad hoc networks", Proc. workshop on Mobile Peer-to-Peer computing (MP2P'04), IEEE PerCom 2004 Workshops proceedings, pp. 109- 113. ...
7. G. Ding and B. Bhargava. Peer-to-peer file-sharing over mobile ad hoc networks. In Proceedings of IEEE Annual Conference on Pervasive Computing and Communications Workshops, pages 104– 109, March 2004.
8. M. Papadopouli and H. Schulzrinne. Effects of power conservation, wireless coverage and cooperation on data dissemination among mobile devices. In Proceedings of ACM Interational Symposium on Mobile Ad Hoc Networking and Computing (MobiHoc), pages 117–127, October 2001.
9. C. Lindemann and O. P.Waldhorst. A distributed search service for peer-to-peer file sharing in mobile applications. In Proceedings of International Conference on Peer-to-Peer Computing (P2P), pages 73–80, September 2002.
10. S. K. Goel, M. Singh, D. Xu, and B. Li. Efficient peer-to-peer data dissemination in mobile ad-hoc networks. In Proceedings of International Conference on Parallel Processing Workshops, pages 152– 158, August 2002.
11. G. Kortuem, J. Schneider, D. Preuitt, T. G. C. Thompson, S. Fickas, and Z. Segall. When peer-to-peer comes face-to-face: Collaborative peer-to-peer computing in mobile ad hoc networks. In Proceedings of Peer-to-Peer Computing (P2P), pages 75–93, August 2001.
12. G. Kortuem, J. Schneider. An Application Platform for Mobile Ad-hoc Networks. In Proceedings of the Workshop on Application Models and Programming Tools for Ubiquitous Computing (UBICOMP 2001). Atlanta, Georgia, 2001

A Centralized-Abstraction and Replicated-View Architecture Running on Ubiquitous Networks for Collaborative Multimedia Distance Education Services

Eung Nam Ko[1], Jong Hyuk Park[2], Deok Gyu Lee[3],
Kee Chun Bang[4], and Soo Hong Kim[5]

[1] Department of Information & Communication, Baekseok University
115, Anseo-Dong, Cheonan, Chungnam, 330-704, Korea
ssken@bu.ac.kr
[2] R&D Institute, HANHWA S&C Co. Ltd.
Blg. #1, Jangyo-Dong, Jung-Gu, Seoul, 100-797, Korea
parkjonghyuk@gmail.com
[3] Electronics Telecommunications Research Institute
161, Gajeong-Dong, Yuseong-gu, Daejeon, 305-700, Korea
deokgyulee@etri.re.kr
[4] Department of Multimedia, Namseoul University
21, Maeju-ri, Sunghwan-eup, Cheonan, Chungnam, 330-707, Korea
bangkc@nsu.ac.kr
[5] Department of Computer Software Engineering, Sangmyung University
San 98-20, Anseo-Dong, Cheonan, Chungnam, 330-720, Korea
soohkim@smu.ac.kr

Abstract. The roles of application program sharing are divided into two main parts; abstraction and sharing of view generation. Application program sharing must take different from each other according to number of replicated application program and an event command. There are two different structures. Those include CACV (Centralized-Abstraction and Centralized-View) and RARV (Replicated-Abstraction and Replicated-View).In this paper, we discuss a hybrid software architecture CARV(Centralized-Abstraction and Replicated-View) which is running on ubiquitous networks for collaborative multimedia distance education services and adopting the advantage of CACV and RARV.

1 Introduction

In the distance education, the most important element is of course the contents of the education [1]. The lecture contents may be created using web pages, multimedia creation tools, real media or animations [2, 3, 4]. Another important issue is how to delivery the contents to students effectively [5]. There are two approaches to software architecture on which distributed, collaborative applications are based. Those include CACV (Centralized-Abstraction and Centralized-View) and RARV (Replicated-Abstraction and Replicated-View). This paper describes a hybrid software

T.-J. Cham et al. (Eds.): MMM 2007, LNCS 4352, Part II, pp. 528–535, 2007.

architecture that is running on situation-aware middleware for collaborative multimedia distance education system which has an object with a various information for each session and it also supports multicasting with this information. We propose an adaptive agent of error and application program sharing based on a hybrid software architecture which is adopting the advantage of CACV and RARV for situation-aware.

2 Background: RCSM

Figure 1 shows how all of RCSM's components are layered inside a device. All of RCSM's components are layered inside a device[6].

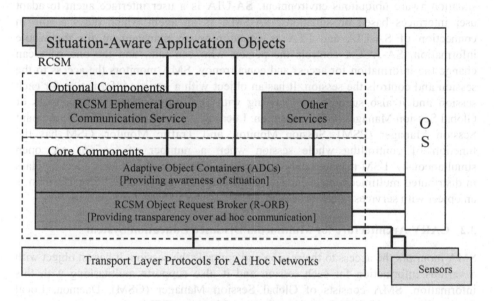

Fig. 1. RCSM's integrated components

In the Context Toolkit, a predefined context is acquired and processed in context widgets and then reported to the application through application-initiated queries and callback functions. In this Reconfigurable Context-Sensitive Middleware(RCSM), Stephen S. Yau et al.[7] proposed a new approach in designing their middleware to directly trigger the appropriate actions in an application rather than have the application itself decide which method(or action) to activate based on context. RCSM provides an Object-based framework for supporting context-sensitive applications

3 Our Approach

However, it did not include other services support in the RCSM architecture. A good example of other services in RCSM is multimedia distance education system.

3.1   Agent for Other Services in RCSM

Other services of RCSM have many agents. They consist of AMA(Application Management Agent), MCA(Media Control Agent), FTA(Fault Tolerance Agent), SA-UIA(Situation-Aware User Interface Agent), SA-SMA(Situation-Aware Session Management Agent), and SA-ACCA(Situation-Aware Access and Concurrency Control Agent). AMA consists of various subclass modules. It includes creation/deletion of shared video window and creation/deletion of shared window. MCA supports convenient applications using situation-aware ubiquitous computing. Supplied services are the creation and deletion of the service object for media use, and media share between the remote users. This agent limits the services by hardware constraint. FTA is an agent that plays a role in detecting an error and recovering it in situation-aware ubiquitous environment. SA-UIA is a user interface agent to adapt user interfaces based on situations. SA-SMA is an agent which plays a role in connection of SA-UIA and FTA as situation-aware management for the whole information. SA-ACCA controls the person who can talk, and the one who can change the information for access and concurrency. SMA monitors the access to the session and controls the session. It has an object with a various information for each session and it also supports multitasking with this information. SMA consists of Global Session Manager (GSM), Daemon, Local Session Manager (LSM), Participant Session Manager (PSM), Session Monitor, and Traffic Monitor. GSM has the function of controlling whole session when a number of sessions are open simultaneously. LSM manages only own session. For example, LSM is a lecture class in distributed multimedia environment. GSM can manage multiple LSM. Daemon is an object with services to create session.

3.2   CARV Architecture for Multimedia Distance Education System

SMA monitors the access to the session and controls the session. It has an object with a various information for each session and it also supports multitasking with this information. SMA consists of Global Session Manager (GSM), Daemon, Local Session Manager (LSM), Participant Session Manager (PSM), Session Monitor ,and Traffic Monitor. GSM has the function of controlling whole session when a number of sessions are open simultaneously. LSM manages only own session. For example, LSM is a lecture class in distributed multimedia environment. GSM can manage multiple LSM. Daemon is an object with services to create session. As shown in Figure 2 you can see the single session relationship among a FTA, GSM, LSM, PSM and the application software on LAN. Platform 1 consists of GSM, Session Monitor, and Traffic Monitor. The other platform consists of Daemon, Local Session Manager, Participant Session Manager and FTA. Each platform except platform1 has a FTA. FTA is an agent that plays a role in detecting an error and recovering it. FTA informs SMA of the results of detected errors. Also, FTA activates an error in application software automatically. It informs SMA of the result again.

   Figure 3 how is the relationship between initiator and participant of a synchronization control for multimedia distance education system. This is the local

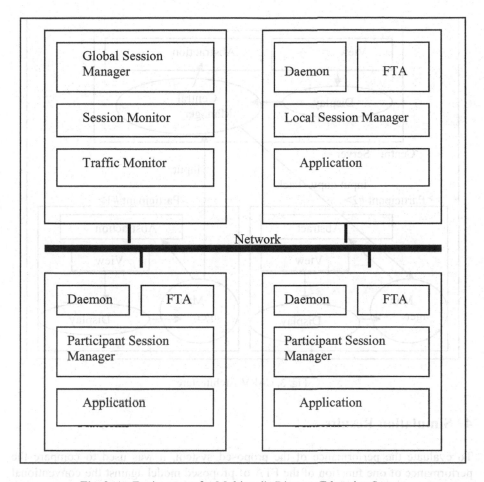

Fig. 2. An Environment for Multimedia Distance Education System

image copy of a shared object that is to be created. By showing the user the abstract of an input command beforehand, the time that is needed to confirm whether the object is managed properly can be saved. This is like FIFO, and the user is allowed to continue working with at least the minimal level of confidence. Meanwhile, a communication channel for the serialization server is allocated to the local window as an attribute and then concurrency control is in progress. This is the process in which object and command that is created for the purpose of preview is on its way to perfecting window binding on the basis of its actual attributes. This transfer guarantee concurrency and at the same time increases promptness of user interaction, and consequently becomes the solution of eliminating seam from the view. If there is an object that is registered in local window but failed to be registered in shared space due to the failure during serialization process, the user will recognize this as a slight omission and will selectively try to re-input the omitted part.

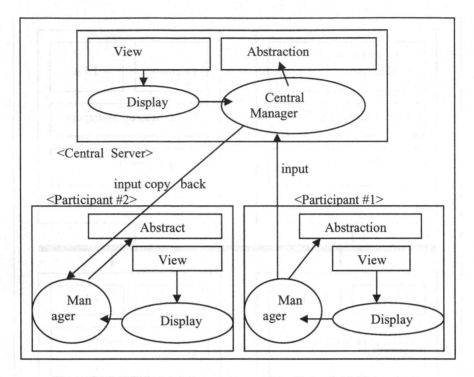

Fig. 3. CARV Architecture

4 Simulation Results

To evaluate the performance of the proposed system, it was used to compare the performance of one function of the FTA of proposed model against the conventional model by using DEVS formalism. In DEVS, a system has a time base, inputs, states, outputs based on the current states and inputs. DEVS(Discrete Event System Specification) is a formalism of being developed by Bernard P. Zeigler. The structure of atomic model is as follows [8-12].

(Simulation 1)
In the first simulation, we have considered composition component as shown in Table 1. The atomic models are EF, RA1, and ED1. The combination of atomic models makes a new coupled model. First, it receives input event, i.e., polling interval. The value is an input value in RA1. An output value is determined by the time related simulation process RA1. The output value can be an input value in ED1. An output value is determined by the time related simulation process ED1. We can observe the result value through transducer.

(Simulation 2)
In the second simulation, we have considered composition component as shown in Table 2. The atomic models are EF, RA2, and ED2. The combination of atomic

Table 1. Atomic Model and State Variable

Component	State Variable	Contents
EF(genr)	Poll_int	Polling interval
RA1	Ra_re_time App_cnt Ra_re_t_a	Response time The number of application program Accumulated response time
ED1	Tat_t_a	RAaccumulated response time

models makes a new coupled model. First, it receives input event, i.e., polling interval. The value is an input value in RA2. An output value is determined by the time related simulation process RA2. The output value can be an input value in ED2. An output value is determined by the time related simulation process ED2. We can observe the result value through transducer.

Table 2. Atomic Model and State Variable

Component	State Variable	Contents
EF (genr)	Poll_int	polling interval
RA2	Ra_re_time App_cnt Ra_re_t_a	Response time The number of application program Accumulated response time
ED2	Tat_t_a	RAaccumulated response time

We can observe the following. The application or error detected time interval is as follows. Conventional method: 2*Poll_int* App_ cnt

Proposed method: 1*Poll_int

Therefore, proposed method is more efficient than conventional method in error detected method because of App_cnt >= 1. We have compared the performance of the proposed method with conventional method.

As shown in Table 3, you can see the characteristic function of each system function for multimedia distance education [13, 14]. The roles of application program sharing are divided into two main parts; abstraction and sharing of view generation. Application program sharing must take different form each other according to number of replicated application program and an event command. There are two different structures, depending on location of processing function and place of view generation. The first is centralized architecture where only one application program exists among entire sharing agents and centralized server takes care of input processing and output. That is, the location of view generator and abstraction is the same. The second

Table 3. Comparison for Software Architecture in situation-aware environment

	Centralized	Replicated	Proposed
Set initial State	Easy	Hard	Medium
Allow Late Comer	Easy	Hard	Easy
Command Serialization	Easy	Hard	Easy
Communication Overhead	High	Low	Low
Error Detected Performance	Bad	Good	Good
Application Copy	One	More than one	More than one
Control Complexity	Low	High	High

method is replicated architecture at which application data input(event) that is generated when sharing takes place is transferred and executed. This means that only event information is separately performed [15].

5 Conclusions

RCSM provides standardized communication protocols to interoperate an application with others under dynamically changing situations. There are two approaches to software architecture on which distributed, collaborative applications are based. Those include CACV (Centralized-Abstraction and Centralized-View) and RARV (Replicated-Abstraction and Replicated-View). We propose an adaptive agent of error and application program sharing based on a hybrid software architecture which is adopting the advantage of CACV and RARV for situation-aware middleware. The roles of error and application program sharing are divided into two main parts; Abstraction and sharing of view generation. Error and application program sharing must take different from each other according to number of replicated application program and an event command. We proposed an adaptive synchronization control agent based on a hybrid software architecture which is adopting the advantage of CACV and RARV for situation-aware middleware. It described a hybrid software architecture that is running on situation-aware ubiquitous computing for a collaborative multimedia distance education system which has an object with a various information for each session and it also supports multicasting with this information. In the future work, fault-tolerance system will be generalized to be used in any environment, and we will progress the study of domino effect for distributed multimedia environment as an example of situation-aware applications.

References

[1] keongin Won, "Design Strategy of Web Contents for Intensifying Interactivity on Online Remote Education", Journal of Korean Society of Communication Design, 2001.12, Vol.04.

[2] Heinich, R.et.al, "Instructional Media and Technologies for Learning", Prentice-Hall, Inc., 1996.

[3] Yongjun Choi, Jahyo Ku, Intaek Leem, Byungdo Choi, Chonggun Kim, "A Study On Distributed Remote Lecture Contents for QoS Guarantee Streaming Service", Journal of Korea Information Processing Society", 2002, vol.9, No.4.

[4] Jaeil Kim, Sangjoon Jung, Yongjun Choi, Seongkwon Cheon, and Chonggun Kim, "Design and Implementation of Lecture Authoring Tool based on Multimedia Component", Journal of Korea Multimedia Society, 2000, Vol.3, No.5.

[5] Byungdo Choi and Chonggun Kim, "A Learning Attitude Evaluation System for Learning Concentration on Distance Education", LNCS3983, May 2006, pp.808 – 817.

[6] Saha, D.; Mukherjee, A.; "Pervasive computing: a paradigm for the 21st century", IEEE Computer, Volume: 36, Issue:3, March 2003, Page(s): 25-31.

[7] S. S. Yau, Y. Wang, D. Huang, and H. In "A Middleware Situation-Aware Contract Specification Language for Ubiquitous Computing", FTDCS 2003.

[8] Bernard P.Zeigler, Tae H. Cho, and Jerzy W. Rozenblit, A Knowledge-Based Simulation Environment for Hierarchical Flexible Manufacturing, IEEE Transaction on Systems, Man, and Cybernetics-Part A: System and Humans, Vol. 26, No. 1, January (1996), 81-90.

[9] Tae H. Cho, Bernard P.Zeigler, "Simulation of Intelligent Hierarchical Flexible Manufacturing: Batch Job Routing in Operation Overlapping" , IEEE Transaction on Systems, Man, and Cybernetics-Part A: System and Humans, Vol. 27, No. 1, January (1997), 116-126.

[10] Bernard P.Zeigler, "Object-Oriented Simulation with hierarchical, Modular Models", Academic Press, (1990).

[11] Bernard P.Zeigler, "Multifacetted Modeling and Discrete Event Simulation", Orlando, FL: Academic, (1984).

[12] Bernard P.Zeigler, "Theory of Modeling and Simulation", John Wiley, NY, USA, (1976), reissued by Krieger, Malabar, FL, USA, (1985).

[13] Eung-Nam Ko, "A Web Based Multimedia Distance Education System With An URL and Error Synchronization Function", WSEAS Transactions on Computers, Issue 4, Volume 3, October 2004, pp.1142-1146.

[14] Eung-Nam Ko, "An Access Control Mechanism Based on Situation-Aware Ubiquitous Computing for Seamless Multimedia View Sharing",LNAI 4114, August 2006, pp.1300-1305.

[15] Gil C. Park and Dae J. Hwang, "A Collaborative Multimedia Distance Education System running on DooRae", In Proceedings of International Conference on IEEE, October 1996, Beijing, China.

Asymmetric Link Dynamic Routing Algorithm for Ubiquitous Multimedia Services

Jeong-Jun Suh[1], Shan Guo Quan[1], Jeong Doo Park[1], Jong Hyuk Park[2], and Young Yong Kim[1]

[1] Department of Electrical and Electronic Engineering, Yonsei University
134 Shinchon-dong, Seodaemun-gu, Seoul, Korea
{jjun2, sgquan, dooyaa, y2k}@yonsei.ac.kr
[2] R&D Institute, HANWHA S&C Co., Ltd.
Hanwha Blg. #1, Jangyo-Dong, Jung-Gu, Seoul, Korea
hyuks00@hanwha.co.kr

Abstract. In this paper, we propose an asymmetric link dynamic routing algorithm for ubiquitous multimedia services named DRAMA (Dynamic Routing Algorithm for asymmetric link in Mobile Ad hoc networks). The proposed algorithm allows a first sink node of the unidirectional link to detect the unidirectional link and its reverse route and provide information regarding the reverse route to other sink nodes, thereby minimizing unnecessary flows and effectively using the unidirectional link. DRAMA also incooperates redirection process that actively supports a unidirectional link generated during data transmission to deal with a topology change due to the movement of node. Further, we shows the superiority of DRAMA to the existing algorithms in terms of a delay in data transmission, throughput, and transmission overhead through simulation study.

1 Introduction

In ubiquitous computing environment, it is necessary for multimedia devices to send data each other with convenience. To communicate with multimedia devices in ubiquitous computing environment, one of the communication method would be ad hoc networks. We can consider ubiquitous computing environment as movement of multimedia devices, and ad hoc networks reflect mobility of the multimedia devices. Most of ad hoc protocols [1] are designed to effectively operate over a bidirectional [6] wireless link consisting of homogeneous nodes. However, a unidirectional link [2] arises in a real situation due to various causes such as difference in transmission power among nodes, collision, and interference (or noise). Effective use of the unidirectional link reduces hop counts of path, thereby lessening time required for data transmission, delay in data transmission, and load on intermediate nodes during a relay. However, the unidirectional link increases overhead in a routing protocol designed for a bidirectional link, and discontinuity in a network may occur when the unidirectional link is not considered during path setup. Various algorithms for a unidirectional link have

T.-J. Cham et al. (Eds.): MMM 2007, LNCS 4352, Part II, pp. 536–543, 2007.
© Springer-Verlag Berlin Heidelberg 2007

been suggested but they have many defects. For instance, reverse route discovery is not performed on the assumption that a unidirectional link always has a reverse route [3], or route discovery is performed irrespective of whether a reverse route exists [4]. Second, a predetermined detour route is maintained through route discovery after a unidirectional link is detected, thereby wasting a lot of control packets such as a route request (RREQ) message and a route reply (RREP). Lastly, the existing algorithms are applicable to only a unidirectional link detected before data transmission. Therefore, it is difficult to be applied to a unidirectional link detected during data transmission.

In this paper, we propose a novel algorithm for ubiquitous multimedia services called DRAMA (Dynamic Routing Algorithm for asymmetric link in Mobile Ad hoc networks). The organization of this paper is as follows. Section 2 proposes an algorithm that detects a unidirectional link, maintains a reverse route of the unidirectional link, and solves problems due to a topology change. Section 3 compares the proposed algorithm with the existing algorithms through a simulation. Section 4 provides the conclusion of this paper.

2   DRAMA Algorithm

We suggest applying of the notion of order to the sink nodes. We denote a node that has a first unidirectional link relationship with the source node as 1st sink node. Sink node that is a 1-hop neighbor of the first sink node are referred to as second sink node. Recursively, nth sink node is defined as 1- hop neighbor of an (n-1) th sink node.

DRAMA can more effectively and actively support the unidirectional link both in the idle stage and the data transmission stage, as illustrated in Fig. 1.

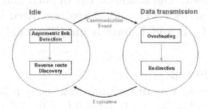

Fig. 1. Structure of DRAMA algorithm

- **Idle Stage:** Before data transmission, a first sink node detects a reverse route of the unidirectional link and provides information regarding the reverse route to other sink nodes. Therefore, it is possible to effectively use the unidirectional link without routing the reverse route.
- **Data Transmission Stage:** A topology change is immediately reflected through redirection to use a unidirectional link generated even during data transmission.

Section 2.1 explains unidirectional link discovery in the idle stage, and Section 2.2 describes use of a unidirectional link occurring during data transmission.

2.1   Unidirectional Link Discovery

(1) Detection of Unidirectional Link

During exchange of a hello message, each node compares its neighbor list with the neighbor list of a neighbor node to determine whether a unidirectional link exists. If a node is not listed in a neighbor's neighbor list, it indicates that there is a unidirectional link that uses the neighbor node as a unidirectional source node and the node as a sink node.

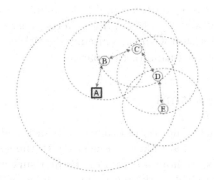

Fig. 2. Topology of unidirectional link

Referring to Fig. 2, each node compares its neighbor list with a neighbor list given from a neighbor. The neighbor list of each node is shown in Table 1. Referring to Table 1, nodes C, D, and E are not listed in the neighbor list of node A. Thus, nodes C, D and E have a unidirectional link relationship with node A.

(2) Reverse Route Setup

When a sink node detects a unidirectional link using a hello message, the sink node compares its neighbor list with a neighbor list of a unidirectional source node to determine whether a common node exists. The presence of the common node proves that the unidirectional link has a reverse route. The sink node is referred to as a first sink node. The first sink node broadcasts a *Link_info* message specifying the source node of the unidirectional link and the order of the first sink to inform the source node and other sink nodes of the reverse route.

Table 1 shows that node B, which is a common node, is listed in both the neighbor list of node C and the neighbor list of source node A of the unidirectional link, and node C is a first sink node. Node C creates a *Link_info* message and broadcasts it to neighbor nodes.

Table 1. Neighbor List of each node

	NL_A	NL_B	NL_C	NL_D	NL_E
A	**{B}**	{A,C}			
B	{B}	**{A,C}**	{A,B,D}		
C	{B}	{A,C}	**{A,B,D}**	{A,C,E}	
D	{B}		{A,B,D}	**{A,C,E}**	{A,D}
E	{B}			{A,C,E}	**{A,D}**

NL_i : NL of node i

Bold terms are NL of itself

(3) Processing of Link_info Message

• **Intermediate Node:** When an intermediate node adjacent to a source node receives the *Link_info* message, the intermediate node recognizes a reverse route of a unidirectional link and rebroadcasts the *Link_info* message to act as a relay node. In this case, priority for transmitting the *Link_info* message is given to only one node to prevent all intermediate nodes from broadcasting the *Link_info* message. Giving priority for transmitting the *Link_info* message will be described in greater detail in section 2.2.4.

• **Sink Node:** A sink node receiving the *Link_info* message updates information regarding the reverse node and compares a neighbor list of a source node with a neighbor list of each of neighbor nodes. When detecting a sink node that is a next hop neighbor having the unidirectional link relationship with the source node, the *Link_info* message is broadcasted again. In this case, information regarding the order of a sink node transmitting the *Link_info* message is included within the *Link_info* message. Each of the other sink nodes receives the *Link_info* message only when the order of the sink node transmitting this message is smaller than its order. The above process is repeated until a final sink node receives the *Link_info* message. In this way, all sink nodes having the unidirectional link relationship to the source node can recognize the reverse route.

(4) Link_info Message with Priority

Intermediate nodes or sink nodes, each transmitting the *Link_info* message to an adjacent sink node, may be present over a unidirectional link. In this case, the performance of a network deteriorates when all the nodes relay the *Link_info* message, and broadcasting flooding may occur when the *Link_info* message is transmitted using multi-hop path.

We control the problem using back-off time according to equation (1) to reduce overall overhead by minimizing unnecessary flows and allow a node with a high battery life to act as an intermediate node. That is, the existing back-off time is determined according to the battery cost of each node, thereby increasing a probability that a node with a high battery life would transmit the *Link_info* message.

$$Back\_off\ Time_{Uni} = R_i \times Back\_off() \tag{1}$$

$R_i = \frac{1}{C_i}$
R_i : battery cost at node i
C_i : node $i's$ residual battery capacity
$Back\_off() = Random() \times Slot\ time$

2.2 A Redirection Process

To actively deal with the dynamic topology change, it is required to detect and use a newly generated unidirectional link even during data transmission. Therefore, this paper proposes redirection to detect and use a unidirectional link even during data transmission.

If a high-power node moves around a node that is transmitting data, the high-power node overhears transmission of data of neighbor nodes. When transmission of data of first and last nodes is overheard, the high-power node determines them as target nodes, and broadcasts a redirect message for redirection to the target nodes. The first node receiving the redirect message determines the high-power node as a next node for subsequent data transmission. A sink node overhearing the redirect message transmits the $Link\_info$ message to use a unidirectional link.

3 Performance Evaluation and Analysis

3.1 Simulation Environment

We carry out simulation for the performance evaluation in which proposed DRAMA is applied to the AODV protocol which is a representative routing protocol. Note that DRAMA is independent of underlying routing protocols. Table 2 is the simulation setup.

In the simulation, QualNet 3.7 by Scalable Network Technologies (SNT) [7] is used as a simulator. 100 nodes are uniformly distributed in an area of 1500×1500m, low-power nodes move at a maximum speed of 10m/s, and high-power nodes move at a maximum speed of 20m/s. Also, it is assumed that the high-power nodes assume 30% of the 100 nodes, i.e., 30 high-power nodes are present in the area. The

Table 2. Simulation setup

Radio propagation	$Two\,ray\,Ground\,(1/r^4)$
MAC layer	$802.11b\,DCF\,mode$
Network layer	$AODV,\,Mobile\,IP$
Mobility model	$Random\,way-point\,model$
Traffic	$TCP,\,CBR$
Antenna	$Omni\,direction$
Protocol	$AODV$
Simulation time	$400s$

simulation is performed for 400 seconds while changing originator and target node at intervals of 100 seconds to generate 512-byte CBR traffic per second.

3.2   Performance Evaluation

In this simulation, the performance of the proposed algorithm is evaluated in terms of the following four metrics.

(1) Throughput & End-to-End Delay

Fig. 3 shows that the throughput of the proposed algorithm is the highest. This is because the existing algorithms can be applied to only unidirectional links detected before data transmission, whereas the proposed algorithm can be applied to even a unidirectional link generated due to the movement of node during data transmission.

Referring to Fig. 4, the proposed algorithm can reduce and constantly maintain an end-to-end delay through redirection, compared to the existing algorithms.

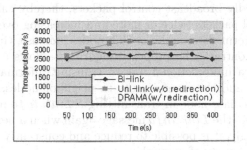

Fig. 3. Throughputs

(2) Energy Consumption

In general, a high-power node requires more energy than a low-power node, but it can be consistently supplied with sufficient power from a vehicle or a portable device. Accordingly, the amounts of battery power consumed by only low-power nodes for the respective algorithms were measured to evaluate the performances of the algorithms.

Referring to Fig. 5, DRAMA performs redirection to use an additional unidirectional link during data transmission, thereby lowering load on low-power nodes. Accordingly, the proposed algorithm requires less energy than the existing algorithms.

(3) Overhead

We compare the overheads of each algorithm with respect to the numbers of control packets required for reverse route discovery with the unidirectional link. In the simulation, we count the number of control with various number of sink nodes and relay nodes as specified in Table 3. Conventionally, a reverse route is

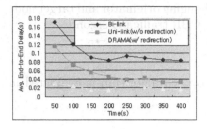
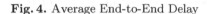
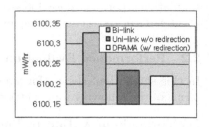

Fig. 4. Average End-to-End Delay   **Fig. 5.** Energy Consumption

predetermined through routing, that is, by transmitting an RREQ message and an RREP from a sink node of the unidirectional link to the source node [4]. Also, forward and reverse routes are separately determined during route discovery, in which a destination node receiving the RREQ message rebroadcasts it to a transmitting node [5].

Table 3 shows the result of comparison. As shown in Table 3, the existing algorithms repeatedly broadcast control packets, thereby causing transmission of the same control packets twice or more and increasing overall overhead. The more number of intermediate nodes or sink nodes increase, the more serious this problem gets. In contrast, the proposed algorithm allows a first sink node in a reverse route of a unidirectional link to transmit information regarding the unidirectional link and the reverse route to neighbor nodes, and gives priority to only one intermediate node in transmitting a *Link_info* message. Also, each sink node broadcasts the *Link_info* message again when a next-hop sink node is detected. Accordingly, it is possible to reduce and constantly maintain overhead irrespective of the density of network.

Table 3. The number of control packet

Reverse Route Routing	1 Sink		2 Sinks		3 Sinks	
	RREQ	RREP	RREQ	RREP	RREQ	RREP
3 relay	13	2	23	5	77	39
5 relay	29	3	53	8	96	44
7 relay	55	3	100	5	145	58

DRAMA	1 Sink	2 Sinks	3 Sinks
3 relay	7	18	22
5 relay	11	26	30
7 relay	15	34	38

4 Conclusions

Ad hoc networks can be one of the feasible communication networks in ubiquitous computing environment. In this paper, we propose DRAMA algorithm for ubiquitous multimedia services and analyzed its performance through simulation. Simulation reveals that the throughput of the DRAMA is at least 1.2 times greater than those of the existing algorithms and an end-to-end delay in the proposed algorithm is significantly smaller than those of the existing algorithms. In particular,

DRAMA is capable of performing reverse route discovery with a small number of control packets to minimize routing overhead, thereby making the most of a wireless link with limited resources. Moreover, the proposed algorithm reduces energy consumption of a low-power node with restricted battery power or a storage capacity, thereby increasing the lifetime of node and the connectivity of network.

Acknowledgement

This work was supported by HISP(Hybrid Intelligent Service Platform) project, funded by MOCIE(Ministry of Commerce, Industry and Energy), Korea. (10016508)

References

1. C. Perkins, E. Belding-Royer, and S. Das, Ad hoc On-Demand Distance Vector (AODV) Routing. *RFC 3561*, July 2003.
2. R. Prakash, "Unidirectional Links Prove Costly in Wireless Ad Hoc Networks," *Proceedings of the 3rd International Workshop on Discrete Algorithms and Methods for Mobile Computing and Communications*, pp. 15-22, August 1999.
3. S. Nesargi and R. Prakash, "A Tunneling Approach to Routing with Unidirectional Links in Mobile Ad-Hoc Networks," *Proceedings of the Ninth International Conference on Computer Communications and Networks*, pp. 522-527, 2000.
4. S. Agarwal, Handling Unidirectional Links in Ad Hoc Wireless Networks. *DARPA*, 2000.
5. D. Kim, C.-K. Toh, and Y. Choi, "On Supporting Link Asymmetry in Mobile Ad Hoc Networks," *IEEE GLOBECOM*, pp. 2798-2803 vol.5, 2001.
6. V. Ramasubramanian, R. Chandra, and D. Mosse, "Providing a Bidirectional Abstraction for Unidirectional Ad Hoc Networks," *IEEE INFOCOM*, pp. 1258-1267 vol.3, 2002.
7. QualNet Network Simulator, *http://www.scalable-networks.com/*

Building Detection in Augmented Reality Based Navigation System

Kisung Lee[1], Yongkwon Kim[1], Seong Ik Cho[2], and Kyungho Choi[3]

[1] Department of Information & Communication Engineering, Kongju National University,
South Korea
{klee, kyk}@kongju.ac.kr
[2] Electronics and Telecommunications Research Institute, South Korea
chosi@etri.re.kr
[3] Department of Information Engineering, Mokpo National University, South Korea
khchoi@mokpo.ac.kr

Abstract. In this paper, we propose a building detection algorithm for video based navigation system which overlays driving directions on the captured video from in-vehicle camera. We used edge segments of small size blocks within an image frame to remove background objects, trees, etc. Search range determination and edge tracing technique were also developed to determine the building area as the final step. The experiments show 88.9 % detection rate on the average and 95.9% for navigation video without trees and signs. The proposed algorithm can be also applied to point-of-interest (POI) detection for location based services (LBS) in ubiquitous computing environment.

Keywords: building detection, building recognition, telematics, augmented reality, navigation.

1 Introduction

The in-vehicle navigation service is one of the key applications among many telematics services and has been widely used so far. The conventional navigation system is based on 2D map and guides users with voice and/or arrows on the map, following the route toward the destination point. Since those navigation services provide only symbolic representation (2D map), users are often confused of their guidance especially when the road has a complex shape of intersection.

To overcome the drawback of the current navigation service, companies, research institutes, and universities have been developing next generation navigation systems which are using the real-time video captured by in-vehicle camera and overlaying their guidance over video with some graphical icons such as arrow, letter, symbol, boundary mark, etc, in order to augment the reality of their services [1-3].

One of the major features that navigation system through augmented reality (AR) can provide is POI detection from the captured navigation video. It is more important in Korea because there are many unnamed streets, which often makes the road-name-based guidance difficult in many cases. If the POIs can be identified and be marked correctly and the direction from the navigation system includes the POI's name as well, users will utilize the service more conveniently.

T.-J. Cham et al. (Eds.): MMM 2007, LNCS 4352, Part II, pp. 544–551, 2007.

Our work is the first step toward the POI detection. The algorithm detects the location of building, i.e. it determines if the specified region is building or not.

Li and Shapiro proposed building recognition algorithm for content-based image retrieval (CBIR) [4]. They used edges, classified them with many clusters based on color, direction, and so on, then analyzed inter-cluster and intra-cluster relationship to find out the building. The drawback of their algorithm is that it works if the build is big enough so it has many edges for each cluster. Another approach was published by Zhang and Kosecka [5]. Their method was aimed for location-based service (LBS) in mobile device such as camera embedded mobile phone. Since the algorithm uses many features extracted from the color image, the processing time is relatively long, in consequence, the algorithm becomes inappropriate for the AR-based navigation system requiring real-time processing.

The proposed algorithm is edge-based for fast processing time and includes detection algorithms for trees and background regions to remove other objects except buildings from the image. After removing those objects, search region for building is determined by using edge histogram in both horizontal and vertical direction, followed by edge tracing to determine the area of building within an image frame.

2   Methods

Block diagram of the proposed algorithm is shown in Fig. 1.

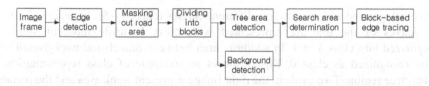

Fig. 1. Block diagram of the building recognition algorithm

After edge detection, the pre-determined mask is applied to remove vehicles and road which can cause false alarms in building detection. An image frame of the navigation video clip is divided into many small size blocks (e.g. 10x10) and slope and length of the edge segments are calculated for each block. Using those slopes, detection processes are performed for background and tree regions. After detection and removal of those detected background and tree area, search region is determined. To that end, block-based edge tracing is performed to find the building area within the search region.

2.1   Tree Area Detection

We built up a tree model that takes structure of the tree into account. A tree typically consists of stems, branches and leaves. The difference between tree and other elements (e.g. background, building, traffic signal/sign etc) is that edge segments of leaves and branches have a variety of slopes because the directions of branches and leaves are random and they are connected each other with complicated structure. The proposed algorithm utilized those properties of trees.

Fig. 2 shows pseudo-code of the tree detection algorithm proposed in this paper.

```
block(row, col);  // dimension of a block is 10x10.
for number of row
for number of col
    {   var = check_edge_slop(row, col);//slop calc.
// categorization of a block
        if  val == empty
            block(row,col) = 0;  //class 0, no edge
        else if val == varying_slope
            block(row, col) = 1; //class1,branches/leaves
        else if val == horizontal_edge
            block(row, col) = 2;  //class 2,building edge
        else if val == vertical_edge
            block(row, col) = 3;  //class3,stem/building
        else
            block(row, col) = 4;
    }
}
//inspection to detect tree area
res_inspect(col) = inspect_col(block);
//deletion of tree area
delet_tree_area(res_inspect);
```

Fig. 2. Pseudo-code of tree area detection in a block

We categorized a block into five different classes (class 0 – 5). In general, branches and leaves of the tree are represented with class 1, while most of stems are categorized into class 3 or 4. In addition, area between branch and background tends to be recognized as class 0. Fig. 3 shows an example of class representation for typical tree region. Two ovals in the right image represent trunk area and the rectangle on top means branches and leaves.

Once every block is categorized into the appropriate classes, relationship among adjacent blocks is inspected for tree detection. Column-wise searching is performed to cluster the blocks. If the class 1 blocks are connected together in vertical direction, it is labeled as leaves/branches. If the cluster consists of class 3, class 4 and limited number of class 1, it is considered as a stem or part of building.

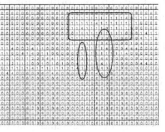

Fig. 3. Navigation image with block marks (left) and categorized blocks for tree shape (right)

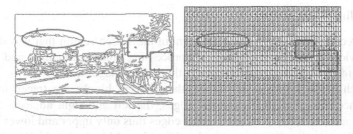

Fig. 4. Background edges in an edge image (left) and the corresponding block represent-tation(right)

Meanwhile, the building in front of trees has similar features to stems. If only several blocks are isolated in the column, they are regarded as buildings mixed with trees and discarded as noise. The boxes in Fig. 4 represent those noise blocks to be removed.

Background edges usually consist of curve lines interconnected with left and right adjacent blocks and have empty blocks (i.e. no edge, class 0) above and below. Therefore, those edges are also detected and excluded from the image frame. Circles in both left and right images of Fig. 4 are examples of the background edges.

2.2 Search Area Determination

After removal of the trees and background blocks from the road-masked edge image, the remaining area is regarded as initial search range for building detection. From that initial range, projection approach [6] of the edge segments is performed in horizontal and vertical directions to refine the search area.

Fig. 5. Search range determination based on projection data

Then, the projection data is evaluated by Eq. 1.

$$If\ p_r(i) > A\mu_r,\ then\ S(i) = 1.$$

$$Otherwise,\ S(i) = 0. \tag{1}$$

$p_r(i)$ is the projection value at index i in initial search area r. μ_r is mean of p_r and A is a coefficient for threshold. The finalized search region is chosen from minimum to maximum value of i that makes $S(i) = 1$ in both directions. Fig. 5 illustrates the refined search area (small rectangle) from the initial search region (big rectangle).

2.3 Building Recognition

Building recognition is performed only within the search region that was determined in the previous step. This can reduce the processing time significantly and makes the algorithm focus on highly possible area in the whole image frame.

For each block within search range, the adjacent blocks are traced in different tracks. Since class 2 means horizontal edges, the left and right adjacent blocks are taken into account. Class 3 means vertical edges thus only upper and lower blocks are traced while eight directions are considered for class 4 blocks in which horizontal and vertical edges are intersected).

The directions to be traced through for class 2,3 and 4, and the detected building blocks are illustrated in Fig. 6 respectively.

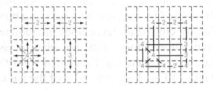

Fig. 6. Directions for block tracing in class 2, 3 and 4 (left), and an example of traced building blocks (right)

The processes described so far are image-based approach. Once the building blocks are recognized in an image frame, temporal information of the video is used to filter out the impulse errors through consecutive frames. Since the previous frame and the current one have very similar information, results of previous frames are used to estimate the building location. If the previous frames did not detect the building but apparent amount of building blocks are recognized in current frame, those blocks are regarded as false positive (FP) and will be ignored. On the contrary, when apparently-detected building blocks disappear all of a sudden in the next frame, it is considered as false negative (FN), then the algorithm change its previous decision(FN) to false positive (FP). More detailed information will be described with an example (Fig. 10) at the end of Chapter 3.

3 Experimental Results

Fig. 7 and 8 show results of the proposed algorithm. Buildings were precisely detected on both sides while small buildings near the vanishing points were not recognized since it does not have enough edge features. Small squares in Fig. 7(b) represent the detected building blocks. Note that most of the trees were excluded from the building area.

For quantitative measurement of the proposed algorithm, we collected 42 video clips captured in Dajeon City, Korea and classified those clips with four categories as follows.

1. SB: Single Building
2. MB: Multiple Buildings
3. STB: Trees + traffic signal and/or road sign + building(s)
4. ST: Trees + traffic signal and/or road sign with no building

 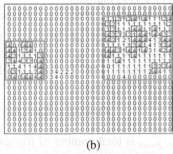

(a)   (b)

Fig. 7. Results of building recognition. (a) Initial search range(black rectangles) and tracked blocks (white circles and lines). (b) Detected buildings with class numbers.

Fig. 8. More results of building recognition

Fig. 9. Examples of SB (left rectangle) and STB (right rectangle)

If more than 50% of the building area is shown and the other portion of the area covered with trees and traffic signals and so on, the clip is classified to SB or MB, depending on the number of buildings. The left box in Fig.9 shows a typical example of SB. On the other hand, if trees, traffic signal and/or road sign cover the half of building, the image is classified into STB (right box in Fig. 9). STB is the toughest case for building detection task.

The test of the algorithm end up with the following four types of result (see below).

TP (True Positive): Building(s) in the clip and it was correctly detected.
TN (True Negative): No building in the clip, no detection.
FP (False Positive): No building(s) in the clip but tree or traffic signs were falsely recognized as building.
FN (False Negative): Building(s) in the clip, but it was not detected.

The quantitative results of the proposed algorithm show in Table 1. The number of the total frames for the experiment was 852. Among 852 frames, we collected 585 frames for MB and SB, 167 for STB, and 100 for ST respectively.

The detection rate was defined as Eq. 2

$$DetectionRate(\%) = \frac{N_{TP} + N_{TN}}{N_{total\_frame}} \times 100 \qquad (2)$$

where N_{total_frames} is total number of frames, N_{TP} is number of frames for true positive, and N_{TN} is that of true negative.

Table 1. Quantitative results of building detection

	No. of total frames	No. of TP/TN	Detection rate (%)
SB and MB	585	561	95.9
STB	167	104	62.3
ST	100	93	93.0
Total	852	758	88.9

(a)   (b)

Fig. 10. (a) Example of false positive (FP). Left rectangle was falsely detected. (b) Example of false negative (FN). Buildings on the left side were not detected.

Overall performance of the algorithm was 88.9 % of detection rate. Since STB has many tough environment where buildings are significantly overlapped by whole bunch of trees, traffic signals/signs and street lights, the detection rates of STB clips turned out to be 62.3 %. Because our target environment is suburbs, most of the building will be SB and MB types. In that case the detection rate was as high as 95.9 %. For ST clips, only TN rates were used to calculate the detection rate and 7 frames out of 100 was determined to FP's.

Fig. 10(a) shows an example of FP. The building on the right side of the image was correctly recognized while the left rectangle represents false alarm because trees there does not have many branches, mostly have strong vertical edges. Furthermore, the street lamps have 'T' shape of edges which usually appears in building area. An FN example is in Fig. 10(b). There is building on the left side of the image, but the building was not recognized. The rectangle on the left side is just searching area.

4 Conclusion

In this paper, we described a building detection algorithm for AR-based navigation systems. The proposed algorithm is edge- and block-based approach. Slopes of edge segments are calculated for each block and building was recognized by tracing adjacent blocks, followed by connecting the blocks with related classes. The algorithm also includes background and tree detection techniques.

Our results show average 88.9% of detection rate. The performance of our approach goes up to 95.9% when using SB and MB video data where more than a half of the building area was not covered with trees, traffic signs, and so on.

As a future work, we will extend the algorithm to multi-modal approach by including 2D navigation map, location information from GPS, etc to increase the detection rate. We are also thinking about the inclusion of other features to evolve the algorithm to POI detection (or building identification).

Current road masking is somewhat primitive. As a preprocessing, we will also import the existing techniques for road detection, vehicle detection, and traffic sign recognition, etc.

References

1. Z. Hu and K. Uchimura, Real-time Data Fusion on Tracking Camera Pose for Direct Visual Guidance, IEEE Intelligent Vehicles Symposium, Parma, Italy, June 14-17, 2004, pp. 842-847.
2. W. Narzt, G. Pomberger, A. Ferscha, D. Kolb, R. Muller, J. Wieghardt, H. Hortner, C. Lindinger, Pervasive Information Acquisition for Mobile AR-Navigation Systems, 5th IEEE Workshop on Mobile Computing Systems & Applications, Monterey, California, USA, October 2003, pp. 13-20.
3. http://www.bmw.co.za/products/hud/default.asp, BMW HUD website
4. Y. Li and L. G. Shapiro, Consistent line clusters for building recognition in CBIR, IEEE International Conference on Pattern Recognition (ICPR), vol 3,2002, pp. 952-956
5. W. Zhang and J. Kosecka, Localization Based on Building Recognition, IEEE Computer Society Conference on Computer Vision and Pattern Recognition (CVPR), June 2005, pp. 21-28.
6. Asako Hashizume, Shinji Ozawa, Hirohiko Yanagawa, An Approach to Detect Vacant Parking Space in a Parallel Parking Area, ITS2005, June 2005, pp. 1-5.

Local Authentication Scheme
Based on AAA in Mobile IPv6 Networks

Jong-Hyouk Lee*, Young-Ju Han, and Tai-Myoung Chung

Internet Management Technology Laboratory,
Dept. of Computer Engineering, Sungkyunkwan University,
300 Cheoncheon-dong, Jangan-gu,
Suwon-si, Gyeonggi-do, 440-746, Korea
{jhlee, yjhan, tmchung}@imtl.skku.ac.kr

Abstract. In this paper, we propose local authentication scheme to locally authorize intra-domain mobile nodes (MNs) for efficient authentication in Mobile IPv6 networks, which are based on authentication,
authorization, accounting (AAA) architecture. Frequent authentication
requests in standard AAA mechanism impose a great burden to deliver
the authentication messages between a MN and its AAA server. To solve
this problem, we propose this scheme to establish local security associations (SAs) for authentication, so the proposed scheme reduces delay
and the risk during MNs roam around a local domain. The performance
evaluation results show that the proposed scheme reduces the latency up
to 60.7% while maintaining the similar level of security to the previous
researches.

1 Introduction

Over the past several years there has been increasing the number of mobile
devices. Advances in the power of mobile devices, such as laptop computers,
personal digital assistants (PDAs), and smart phones, have opened tempting
new opportunities for a broad range of communities and laboratories. With prices
reducing and functionality increasing, it is expected that mobile devices will play
major roles in the promotion of both personal and business productivity. The
mobility implies more security threats to communications due to open mediums
in wireless networks. Thus, there is the need to develop technologies which will
jointly enable IP security and the mobility over wireless networks.

Currently, the AAA architecture for the Mobile IP relies on frequently con-
sulting the home network to authenticate the mobile user when the user roams
to a foreign network [1]. The drawback of doing so is that each time the MN
enters new foreign network, the foreign network has to send back an authentication request to the home network to be verified. This procedure causes long
handoff delays and may not be feasible for real-time applications [2,3,4]. While
the MN roams in foreign networks, a continuous exchange of confidential messages is required with the AAA server in the home network. In order to reduce

---

* Corresponding author.

T.-J. Cham et al. (Eds.): MMM 2007, LNCS 4352, Part II, pp. 552–559, 2007.
© Springer-Verlag Berlin Heidelberg 2007

the required confidential messages between the AAA server in the home network and the MN, the ticket-based scheme using an encrypted ticket that can support authentication and authorization for the MN has been proposed [5]. It reduces the delay and the risk on MN authentication in Mobile IPv6. However this scheme generates additional signaling overhead and AAA servers overhead.

In this paper, we propose local authentication scheme based on AAA architecture, which is able to securely establish a local SA for intra-domain roaming MNs. It also has low signal delay while maintaining the similar level of security to known methods. According to the performance evaluation, the proposed scheme compared to the basic AAA scheme and the ticket-based AAA scheme reduces delay up to 60.7%.

The rest of the paper is organized as follows. In section 2, we discuss targeted ticket-based scheme. Our proposed local authentication scheme is discussed in section 3. After that the performance is evaluated with previous schemes in section 4. Finally we conclude the paper in section 5.

2   Targeted Ticket-Based Scheme for Comparison

A ticket-based scheme that allows anonymous service usage in mobile application and access. This scheme can reduces the overhead when a MN requests anonymous service by utilizing the pre-encrypted ticket. In [5], the ticket granting service module of AAA server issues tickets to MNs who have been authenticated to its AAAH. Thus, the MN first requests a ticket-granting ticket from its AAAH. The ticket-granting module in the MN saves this ticket. Each time the MN requires access to a service usage, the ticket-granting module applies to the ticket granting service module of AAA server, using the ticket to authenticate itself. The authentication of MN is performed by the ticket granting service module in the AAA server and the result of authentication is forwarded to the MN. After verifying the ticket, the MN can access the service [5,6].

However, this ticket-based scheme has a few additional signaling messages when the MN requests for ticket issuing [6]. Fig. 1(a) shows exchanged additional signaling messages when the MN requests the initial registration. Four messages added are service (ticket) request message, AAA service (ticket) request message, AAA ticket issue message, and ticket issue message. The messages between the MN and the HA are based on the general Mobile IPv6 protocol, and the messages between the HA and the Home AAA server (AAAH) are based on the extended AAA protocol in Mobile IPv6 networks.

3   The Proposed Local Authentication Scheme

We propose local authentication scheme in this section. First, we present an overview of this scheme. Then, the initial registration procedure and the service request procedure are introduced.

In wireless networks, the period when a MN resides in a cell is called the cell lodging time of that MN. The period between when a call arrives at the MN and when the MN moves out the cell is called the excess life of the cell lodging time for that MN. When an intra-domain authentication request from a MN comes to the AAAH in a local network, the AAAH first checks if a local SA exists for the MN, the AAAH reuse this SA to authenticate the MN. Otherwise, the AAAH checks if the the lodging time of the MN will be greater than a threshold value. There are many methods to estimate the lodging time of a MN [7,8,9]. In our paper, we assume that the estimation result of the lodging time exists. Then, if the lodging time of the MN is greater than a threshold value, the AAAH will authenticate the MN via the basic AAA architecture and create a local SA for it. Otherwise, the AAAH simply authenticates the MN and discards the authentication request.

In Fig. 1, when the MN is on the initial registration phase in the intra-domain, the messages exchange for the authentication of the MN. In this phase, we assume that All nodes are trusted in the intra-domain and in order to make security associations between MNs and HA, the pre-shared key would be distributed in an out-of-bound manner which depends on whether the AAAH deals with the MN directly or through a registration authority. Fig. 1 shows the initial registration phase of the ticket-based scheme and the proposed scheme. As you see in Fig. 1(a), the additional messages and the processing time in the AAAH are required to issue a ticket. The ticket was made in the AAAH forwards to the MN via the HA [5]. In contrast with ticket-based scheme, the proposed scheme allows that the MN receives the authentication reply message without additional messages and processing time. In Fig. 1(b), the following steps show the proposed scheme in case of the initial registration phase for the authentication in the intra-domain. (1) Authentication Request message: When the MN requests for

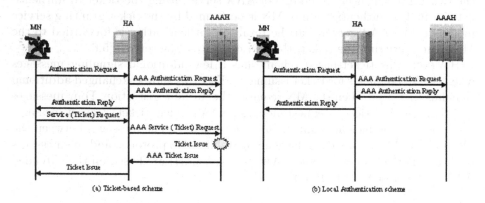

Fig. 1. Initial registration

initiating the communication, the authentication request message is sent to HA. (2) AAA Authentication Request message: Upon receiving, the authentication request message from MN is forwarded to AAAH. (3) AAA Authentication Reply message: AAAH will authorize the request and return a reply message to HA.

(4) Authentication Reply message: MN finally receives the authentication replay message from HA.

Fig. 2 shows when the MN requests to access the intra-domain network, the messages flaw for the ticket-based scheme and the proposed scheme. As you see in Fig. 2(a), ticket-based model reduces the overhead on the service request phase by using the pre-encrypted ticket. It could be done by pre-encrypted ticket system in short time. In the course of nature, the ticket-based scheme provides that ticket issuing and granting time does not take too much [5,6]. The proposed scheme does not need the ticket issuing system in the AAA server and just maintains the existing keys for authentication of the MN. As we mentioned before, if the lodging time of the MN is greater than a threshold value, the AAAH will authenticate the MN via the basic AAA architecture and create a local SA for it. Otherwise, the AAAH simply authenticates the MN and discards the authentication request. In Fig. 2(b), we describe a process for the service request phase for the authentication in the intra-domain.

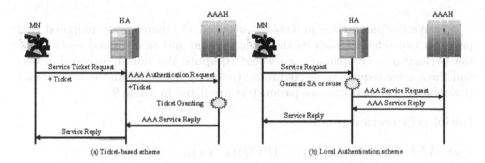

Fig. 2. Service request

(1) Service Request message: When the MN requests a service, it it required to send the service request message. (2) Local Authentication Decision: If a local SA exists for the MN, the HA authenticates the roaming MN. (3) AAA Service Request message: If a local SA does not exist, like the basic AAA model, HA needs to decrypt and encrypt them and then send the message to AAAH. (4) AAA Service Reply message: AAAH decrypts the message from HA. If the information is valid, a reply message is sent to the HA. (5) Service Reply message: MN receives reply message and decrypts and then the MN use the service.

4   Performance Evaluation

In this section, we do the performance evaluation to compare the schemes. The performance evaluation method is come from [5,6] since it is not to be denied that the performance evaluation method of [5,6] is one of the best methodology for ticket-based scheme.

4.1   Processing Time

The values for the system parameters are directly from previous works, especially from [3,6]. The time for ticket issuing and granting is obtained from [5] by considering the public key infrastructure (PKI).

Table 1. System parameters

Bit rate		Processing time	
Wire link	100 Mbps	Routers (HA,FA)	0.5 msec
Wireless link	2 Mbps	Nodes (MN)	0.5 msec
Propagation time		Ticket issuing	3.0 msec
Wire link	500 μsec	Ticket granting	3.0 msec
Wireless link	2 msec	DES	0.044 msec
Data size		MD5	0.0048 msec
Message size	256 bytes	Local-Auth Decision	6.0 msec

The system parameters in Table 1 are used to compare our proposed with previous two schemes such as the basic scheme and ticket-based scheme. For the performance comparison, we would compute the initial registration time and the service request time. According to [6], we could obtain the performance parameters. The performance parameters are listed in Table 2.

Initial registration phase

Basic AAA = $AREQ_{MN-HA} + AREQ_{HA-AAAH} + AREP_{AAAH-HA}$
$+ AREP_{HA-MN} = 9.09$ msec
Ticket-based scheme = $AREQ_{MN-HA} + AREQ_{HA-AAAH} + AREP_{AAAH-HA}$
$+ AREP_{HA-MN} + SREP_{AAAH-HA} + TI + TG = 31.15$ msec
Proposed scheme = $AREQ_{MN-HA} + AREQ_{HA-AAAH} + AREP_{AAAH-HA}$
$+ AREP_{HA-MN} = 9.09$ msec

When we compare the proposed mechanism with the ticket-based scheme, we infer that the proposed local authentication scheme has no additional signaling. Therefore, the proposed scheme minimizes the additional delay on the initial registration phase for the faster service request.

Service request phase

Basic AAA = $SREQ_{MN-HA} + SREQ_{HA-AAAH} + SREP_{AAAH-HA}$
$+ SREP_{HA-MN} = 24.09$ msec
Ticket-based scheme = $SREQ^t_{MN-HA} + SREQ^t_{HA-AAAH} + TG$
$+ SREP_{AAAH-HA} + SREP_{HA-MN} = 22.09$ msec
Proposed scheme = $SREQ_{MN-HA} + SREQ_{HA-AAAH} + SREP_{AAAH-HA}$
$+ AD + SREP_{HA-MN} = 30.09$ msec

Table 2. Performance parameters

Variables	Definitions	Values
$AREQ_{MN-HA}$	Authentication request time from MN to HA	3.52 msec
$AREQ_{HA-AAAH}$	Authentication request time from HA to AAAH	1.02 msec
$AREP_{AAAH-HA}$	Authentication reply time from AAAH to HA	1.02 msec
$AREP_{HA-MN}$	Authentication reply time from HA to MN	3.52 msec
$SREQ_{MN-HA}$	Service request time from MN to HA	8.52 msec
$SREQ^t_{MN-HA}$	Service request time from MN to HA in ticket-based	3.52 msec
$SREQ_{HA-AAAH}$	Service request time from HA to AAAH	6.02 msec
$SREQ^t_{HA-AAAH}$	Service request time from HA to AAAH in ticket-based	1.02 msec
$SREP_{AAAH-HA}$	Service reply time from AAAH to HA	6.02 msec
$SREP_{HA-MN}$	Service reply time from HA to MN	8.52 msec
$SREP^t_{AAAH-HA}$	Service reply time from AAAH to HA in ticket-based	8.52 msec
$SREP^t_{HA-MN}$	Service reply time from HA to MN in ticket-based	6.02 msec
TI	Ticket issuing time	3.00 msec
TG	Ticket granting time	3.00 msec
AD	Local authentication decision time	6.00 msec

In the service request phase, the local authentication scheme shows less performance than previous schemes, because it needs to execute the decision time of the local authentication. The ticket-based scheme shows the best performance in the service request phase, because it use the pre-encrypted ticket without additional encryptions and decryptions. However, under the ticket-based scheme it remains the case that a MN would need a new ticket for every different service. If a MN wished to access a print server, a mail server, and so on, the first instance of each access would require a new ticket and hence require the MN to increase the authentication time.

4.2 Performance Comparison

Fig. 3 shows the results of initial registration and service request delay comparison. Fig. 4(a) represents a bar graph that shows the delay comparison for initial registration and Fig. 4(b) represents service request delay comparison. As you see in Fig. 4(a), our proposed scheme shows better performance than the ticket-based scheme even though it shows the same performance the basic AAA scheme. However, if there are lots of MNs in the cell or MNs move zigzag within the overlapped area between adjacent cells, our scheme will show superior performance compared to other schemes.

Fig. 4 shows the results. Fig. 4(a), we can see that the improvement of the delay is increasing with the increase of the number of hops between the MN and its HA. At the point of the fifteenth hop, the proposed scheme costs 60.7% less than the basic AAA. Even though the ticket-based scheme shows the best performance until the fourth hop, the proposed scheme shows the better performance since at the point of the fifth hop. The benefit comes from the utilization

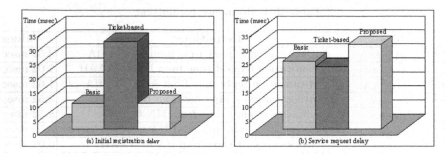

Fig. 3. Initial registration and service request delay comparison

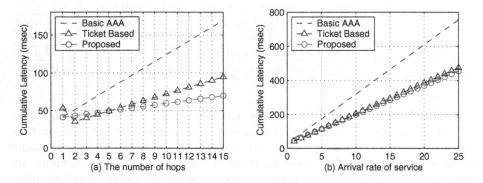

Fig. 4. Delay comparison in terms of the number of hops and service

of local authentication. Fig. 4(b), although the cost of time increases with the increase of arrival rate of service requests in all cases, the cost with proposed scheme is less than that with the basic AAA with 41.5% improvement.

5   Conclusions

In this paper, we propose local authentication scheme to locally authorize intra-domain roaming users for efficient authentication and service in Mobile IPv6 networks. By establishing a local security association, the proposed scheme becomes a promising alternative for secure and efficient authentication approach in various wireless networks. The performance comparison shows that the proposed scheme is superior to previous ones in terms of delay while maintaining the security level. Especially this proposed scheme shows the better performance in the increase of the number of hops between the MN and its HA. The proposed scheme also shows the best performance in the frequent service requests. In the future, we will describe the requirements for the efficient network management and inter-domain roaming users.

Acknowledgment

This study was supported by a grant of the Korea Health 21 R&D Project, Ministry of Health & Welfare, Republic of Korea. (02-PJ3-PG6-EV08-0001)

References

1. Jung-Muk Lim, Hyung-Jin Lim, and Tai-Myoung Chung, "Performance Evaluation of Public Key based Mechanisms for Mobile IPv4 Authentication in the AAA Environments", ICOIN 2006, January 2006.
2. Jong-Hyouk Lee, Young-Ju Han, Hyung-Jin Lim and Tai-Myung Chung, "New Binding Update Method Using GDMHA in Hierarchical Mobile IPv6", ICCSA 2005, pp. 146-155, May 2005.
3. Jong-Hyouk Lee, Byungchul Park, Hyunseung Choo and Tai-Myung Chung, "Policy Based Handoff in MIPv6 Networks", ICCSA 2005, pp. 468-477, May 2005.
4. J. Maniyeri, Z. Zhang, R. Pillai, and P. Braun, "A Linux Based Software Router Supporting QoS, Policy Based Control and Mobility", ISCC, pp. 101-107, July 2003.
5. J. Park, E. Bae, H. Pyeon, and K. Chae "A Ticket-based AAA Security Mechanism in Mobile IP Network", ICCSA 2003, pp. 210-219, May 2003.
6. Hoseong Jeon, Hyunseung Choo, and Jai-Ho Oh, "IDentification Key Based AAA Mechanism in Mobile IP Networks", ICCSA 2004, pp. 765-775, May 2004.
7. I. Chen and N. Verma. "Simulation Study of a Class of Autonomous Host-Centric Mobility Prediction Algorithms for Wireless Cellular and Ad Hoc Networks", Annual Simulation Symposium, pp. 65-72, April 2003.
8. W. Liang and W. Wang, "A Quantitative Study of Authentication and QoS in Wireless IP Networks", INFOCOM 2005, pp. 1478-1489, March 2005.
9. W. Liang and W. Wang, "A lightweight authentication protocol with local security association control in mobile networks", MILCOM 2004, pp. 225-231, October 2004.

Handover-Specific Optimization for IEEE 802.16e Sleep Mode

Jaesung Park[1], Beomjoon Kim[2,*], and Iksoon Hwang[3]

[1] Department of Internet Information Engineering, The University of Suwon,
445-743, Korea
jaesungpark@suwon.ac.kr
[2] Department of Electronic Engineering, Keimyung University, Daegu,
704-701, Korea
bkim@kmu.ac.kr
[3] System Software Department, LG-Nortel R&D Center, 431-749, Korea
iksoonhwang@lg-nortel.com

Abstract. IEEE 802.16e standard specifies sleep mode to achieve low power consumption of a mobile station (MS). Since sleep mode is defined only for the current serving base station (BS), a sleeping MS in motion performs handover even if it has no active connection. Accordingly, the power saving efficiency of sleep mode may be severely degraded in a mobile environment. In order to cover the problem, the IEEE 802.16e standard specifies a method that optimizes the sleep mode initiation process specific to handover. With the optimization, a MS that has been in sleep mode and currently performs handover is able to resume sleep mode as soon as it completes the handover process with no additional request. This paper justifies the use of the optimization by showing the simulation results that evaluate the performance gain obtained from the optimization.

1 Introduction

Recently, a project has been completed by Task Group (TG) e under IEEE 802.16 Working Group (WG) in order to support mobility of a mobile station (MS) based on the baseline standard [1] which mainly concerns a fixed subscriber station (SS). The new standard [2] provides a specification of several features related to MS's mobility such as handover, sleep mode, idle mode, and so on.

Among the features, sleep mode is one of the key features because power-efficient operation has a crucial effect on the deployment of IEEE 802.16e mobile broadband wireless access (BWA) systems under development such as Wireless Broadband (WiBro) of South Korea and Mobile WiMAX [7]. This paper discusses on a problem with sleep mode in terms of MS's mobility and introduces an optimized initiation process to cope with the problem.

---

* Correspondence to: Beomjoon Kim, Dept. Electronic Engineering, Keimyung University, 1000 Sindang-Dong, Dalseo-Gu, Daegu, 704-701, Korea. Email: bkim@kmu.ac.kr

T.-J. Cham et al. (Eds.): MMM 2007, LNCS 4352, Part II, pp. 560–567, 2007.

1.1   Problem Statement

Sleep mode has been regarded as not efficient in a mobile environment because it provides no inter-base station (BS) continuity. For example, a MS in motion, even if it is in sleep mode, has to perform the same handover procedures as other MSs with active connections. The main reason for the discontinuity is that the BS which serves a MS in sleep mode regards the MS as still active but just conservative in battery consumption. It means that the MS in sleep mode maintains a registered state with the serving BS.

In fact, the MS is highly probable to request another sleep mode initiation after handover because whether or not the MS has data to transmit or receive has nothing to do with handover. That is, the MS must be still in sleep mode unless it moves away from the current cell. However, the termination of the previous sleep mode cancels all the parameters related to the previous sleep operation. Therefore, the MS may take an unnecessary standby to examine that there is no data to transmit or receive before triggering a request message for the next sleep mode initiation. The unnecessary standby definitely degrades the performance of sleep mode in terms of power saving efficiency because the MS has to decode all the downlink frames during the standby.

1.2   The Optimized Sleep Mode Initiation

Concerning the problem, we proposed an optimized initiation process for sleep mode [8] [1] in the middle of the IEEE 802.16e standardization. The optimization proposes that when a MS that has been in sleep mode performs handover, it

- keep all the parameters related to the previous sleep mode operation
- indicate its wish to maintain sleep mode after handover by including the parameters in the message transmitted during the handover process.

Therefore, the proposed optimization facilitates a MS to resume sleep mode after handover, i.e. without waiting for a potential standby, so that the power saving efficiency of sleep mode may be maximized.

2   Sleep Mode of IEEE 802.16e

2.1   Basic Operation

Three medium access control (MAC) management messages are involved in sleep mode: sleep request message (MOB_SLP-REQ), sleep response message (MOB_SLP-RSP), and traffic indication message (MOB_TRF-IND).

Before initiating sleep mode, a MS needs to be convinced that there is no data to transmit or receive. For this purpose, a standby is usually implemented. If there is no data during the standby, sleep request message (MOB_SLP-REQ)

---

[1] The proposal was accepted in the standard as an optional feature after being harmonized with another proposal [9].

is triggered. In response to the request message, the BS transmits sleep response message (MOB_SLP-RSP). During the negotiation process, the following five parameters are determined: start-frame-number, initial-sleep window, listening window, final-sleep window base, and final-sleep exponent.

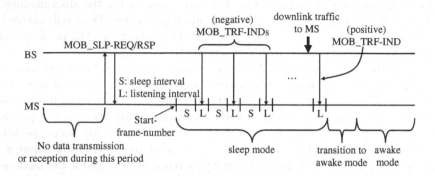

Fig. 1. Basic sleep mode operation

The basic sleep mode operation is shown in Fig. 1. If a MS receives a sleep response message that approves the transition to sleep mode, the first sleep interval begins at the start-frame-number indicated by the response message; the length of the first sleep interval is determined by the initial-sleep window and the MS may sleep during the sleep interval. After the first sleep interval, a listening interval appears in which the traffic indication message (MOB_TRF-IND) is received. By the traffic indication message, the MS is able to decide whether or not it can continue in sleep mode. If the traffic indication message indicates that there is no data to deliver (a negative indication), the next sleep interval begins.

Every time a negative indication is received, the sleep window is doubled until it becomes greater than the maximum value determined by

$$\textit{final-sleep window base} * 2^{\textit{final-sleep window exponent}}. \tag{1}$$

If downlink traffic arrives, it is notified by a positive indication at the very next listening interval. By receiving the positive indication, the MS terminates sleep mode and makes a transition to awake mode for normal operation. In this way, overall sleep mode operation repeats sleep interval and listening interval in pairs until the MS terminates sleep mode by uplink transmission or a positive indication.

2.2   Optimized Sleep Mode Initiation for Handover

Fig. 2 illustrates two cases of the sleep mode operation per handover. In the non-optimized case (Fig. 2-(a)), the MS that has performed handover transmits a sleep request message after a standby. In the optimized case (Fig. 2-(b)),

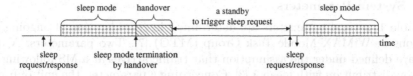

(a) non-optimized sleep mode initiation per handover

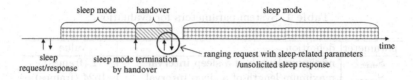

(b) optimized sleep mode initiation per handover

Fig. 2. Non-optimized vs. optimized sleep mode initiation

however, the MS begins sleep mode as soon as it receives an unsolicited sleep response message.

The optimized initiation process is accomplished by including an indication of MS's wish to continue sleep mode in the ranging request (`RNG-REQ`) message (the first arrow in the circle) that should be transmitted during handover. The indication includes several parameters related to the previous sleep mode operation at the old BS. Receiving the request message, the new BS has to transmit an unsolicited sleep response message (the second arrow in the circle) after the handover process is completed. Finally, the MS initiates sleep mode as soon as it receives the response message.

3   Evaluation Methodology

3.1   Cost Equations

Per the usage of the optimized initiation process, the cost of sleep mode is categorized by the battery consumption for:

- decoding downlink frames in listening intervals and standbys
- message transactions for handover and sleep mode initiation.

Based on the descriptions in Section 2, the cost equations of sleep mode for the optimized case (C_A) and non-optimized case (C_B) are given by

$$C_A = C_l + C_h$$
$$C_B = C_l + C_h + C_w \tag{2}$$

where C_l and C_w are the costs for downlink decoding during the listening interval and the standby and C_h is the cost for handover.

3.2   System Parameters

In Table 1, several parameters are determined in consideration of ongoing discussions in WiMAX Mobile Task Group (MTG) [7]. Two parameters, N_l and N_h, are defined under the assumption that traffic arrives at a MS following the Poisson distribution with mean λ [3]. Concerning a parameter, the unit of frames may be converted to the unit of time under the assumption that the length of a frame is 5 msec [7], and vice versa.

Table 1. System parameters for evaluation.

parameter	definition	value
S_{min}	minimum length of a sleep interval	2 (frames)
S_{max}	maximum length of a sleep interval	1024 (frames)
L	length of a listening interval	2 (frames)
t_s	length of a standby	$variable$ (frames)
λ	traffic arrival rate	$variable$
N_l	number of listening intervals during $1/\lambda$	·
N_h	number of handovers during $1/\lambda$	·
α	power cost to decode a downlink frame	1 (a unit cost)
β	power cost to perform a handover	8α
v	velocity of a MS	$variable$ (km/h)
r	radius of a cell	1 (km)

Since no information is available yet about the actual power consumption in a network interface card implemented based on [2], the ratio between the power consumed by uplink transmission and downlink decoding is assumed to be 1, referring to [5] which discusses on the power consumption of a real network interface card for IEEE 802.11 Wireless LAN. For simplicity, a unit value of cost is assigned to α which corresponds to the battery consumption for decoding a single downlink frame or transmitting a message. Considering four message transactions for ranging, capability negotiation, privacy key exchange, and registration [2], the cost for handover (β) is assumed to be eight times higher than α. As a consequence, each cost equation from (2) develops into

$$C_A = C_l + C_h = \alpha L N_l + \beta N_h$$
$$C_B = C_l + C_h + C_w = \alpha L N_l + \beta N_h + \alpha t_s N_h \tag{3}$$

3.3   Mobility Model

In order to reflect the mobility of a MS, the concept of 'cell-residence-time' is adopted. Reference [6] derives a distribution of cell-residence-time and concludes that the mean cell-residence-time is a function of MS's velocity and cell radius. Intuitively, the number of handovers between two consecutive traffic arrivals can be approximated by

$$N_h \approx \frac{1}{\lambda \cdot R} \tag{4}$$

where R denotes the mean cell-residence-time.

3.4   Simulations

By implementing the sleep mode operations and the optimized initiation process, simulations are conducted with the parameters in Table 1. A simulation runs for inter-traffic arrival time that follows the exponential distribution. During the simulations, the number of the listening intervals (N_l) and handovers (N_h) are captured and used for calculating each cost equation given by (3).

4   Simulation Results

Fig. 3 compares the total power cost of sleep mode with and without the optimized initiation process per average cell residence time. Two different values of t_s, 256 and 1024 frames, representing about 1.3 and 5 seconds, are chosen for the non-optimized case.

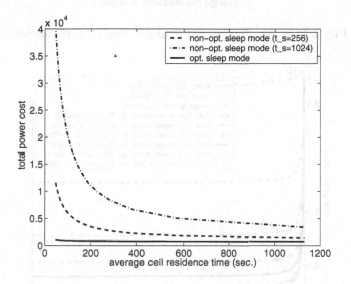

Fig. 3. Total power cost comparison between optimized and non-optimized sleep mode per cell residence time ($\lambda = 48$ calls/day)

For high mobility (a low value of cell residence time), the two non-optimized cases show very high cost. Considering the increase in the cell residence time corresponds to the decrease in N_h, it is very straightforward that the costs of the two non-optimized cases drop sharply. It can be seen that the power cost of the optimized case keeps almost constant over all the values of cell residence time. Although a small value of t_s reduces the power cost of the non-optimized sleep mode, decreasing its value is not always effective because it may cause a false sleep mode initiation.

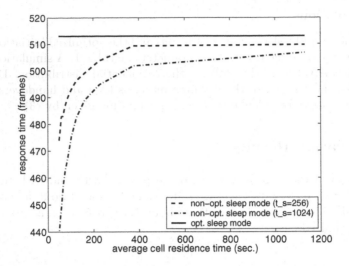

Fig. 4. Response time per cell residence time ($\lambda = 48$ calls/day)

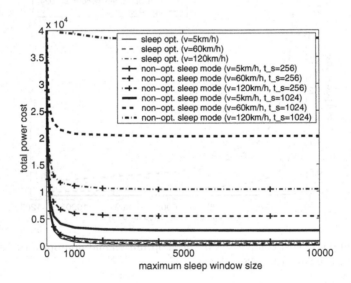

Fig. 5. Total power cost of sleep mode with and without the optimized initiation process per S_{max} ($\lambda = 48$ calls/day)

Fig. 4 shows the response time that is defined as the latency till a positive indication is delivered to a MS in sleep mode. Traffic arrivals during a standby means the zero response time. For the two non-optimized cases, traffic may arrive during a standby or before the sleep window reaches S_{max}, which corresponds to a short response time. As t_s increases, the possibility of the short response time also increases. On the other hand, the sleep window of the optimized case keeps constant once it reaches S_{max} so that its response time also keeps constant, approximately equals to a half of S_{max}.

Another simulation is conducted to figure out the effect of S_{max} on each power cost and the result is shown in Fig. 5. Increasing S_{max} may reduce the power consumption by decreasing N_l. However, the effect is not maintained over a certain value of S_{max} because a MS does not stay at a BS long enough for the sleep window to reach S_{max}. Moreover, a long sleep window corresponds to a long latency to transmit a positive indication for pending traffic.

5   Conclusions

In this paper, we have discussed on sleep mode and its optimized initiation process for handover specified in IEEE 802.16e standard. As an opposition to the common belief that sleep mode is not appropriate for mobility, this paper has attempted to justify that sleep mode can be effective even in a mobile environment by adopting the optimized initiation process. Based on the simulation results, it is convinced that the optimized initiation process offers sleep mode a considerable improvement in the power saving efficiency. Also, the optimization imposes no additional complexity because it is achieved by attaching the parameters to the message that is transmitted for handover.

References

1. IEEE Std 802.16-2004: IEEE Standard for Local and Metropolitan Area Network - Part 16: Air Interface for Fixed Broadband Wireless Access Systems. (2004)
2. IEEE Std 802.16e-2005: Part 16: Air Interface for Fixed and Mobile Broadband Wireless Access Systems - Amendment 2: Physical and Medium Access Control Layers for Combined Fixed and Mobile Operation in Licensed Bands and Corrigendum 1. (2006)
3. Y. Xiao: Energy Saving Mechanism in the IEEE 802.16e Wireless MAN. IEEE Comm. Lett. **9** (7) (2005) 595-597
4. I. F. Alkyildiz and W. Wang: A Dynamic Location Management Scheme for Next-Generation Multitier PCS Systems. IEEE Trans. Wireless Comm. **1** (1) (2002) 178-189
5. M. Stemm and R. Katz: Measuring and Reducing Energy Consumption of Network Interfaces in Hand-held Devices. IEICE Trans. Comm. **E80** (8) (1997) 1125-31
6. K. L. Yeung and S. Nanda: Optimal Mobile-Determined Micro-Macro Cell Selection. In the proceeding of IEEE PIMRC'1995 (1995) 294-299
7. The WiMAX Forum, available at http://www.wimaxforum.org/
8. B. Kim, et al.: Sleep-Window Optimization for Handover. a contribution submitted to IEEE 802.16 TGe. (2004)
   available at http://ieee802.org/16/tge/contrib/C80216e-04_435.pdf
9. V. Yanover, et al.: Sleep Mode Generic Mechanism. a contribution submitted to IEEE 802.16 TGe. (2004)
   available at http://ieee802.org/16/tge/contrib/C80216e-04_459r2.pdf

An Improvement of the Processing Delay for the G.723.1 Vocoder*

Kwang Hyoung Lee[1], So Yeon Min[2], Keun Wang Lee[3],
and Jeong Gyu Jee[4]

[1] Dept. of Internet Information, Seoil College
dreamace@seoil.ac.kr
[2] Dept. of Information & Telecommunication, Seoil College
symin@seoil.ac.kr
[3] Dept. of Multimedia Science, Chungwoon Univ.
kwlee@chungwoon.ac.kr
[4] Korea Research Foundation, Korea
jgjee@krf.or.kr

Abstract. This paper develop the complexity reduction schemes of real root method that is mainly used in the CELP (Code Excited Linear Prediction) vocoder. The real root method is that if polynomial equations have the real roots, it is able to find those and transform them into LSP (Line Spectrum Pairs). Proposed algorithm is developed by using Mel scale and is to reduce the LSP complexity That is, the searching interval is arranged by using Mel scale but not it is uniform. In experimental results, complexity of the developed algorithm is reduced about 46% in average, but the transformed LSP parameters of the proposed method were the same as those of real root method. Hence, in case of applying proposed algorithm in G.723.1 (6.3kbps MP-MLQ), the speech quality is no distortion compared to original speech quality.

1 Introduction

LPC (Linear Predictive Coding) is very powerful analysis technique and is used in many speech processing system. For speech coding and synthesis system, apart from the different analysis techniques available to obtain the LPC parameters, auto correlation, covariance, lattice, etc., the quantization of the LPC parameters is also a very important aspect of the LPC analysis, as minimization of coding capacity is the ultimate aim in these applications. The main objective of the quantization procedure is to code the LPC parameters with as few bits as possible without introducing additional spectral distortion. Whilst perfect reconstruction is not possible, subjective transparency is achievable [1~3]. Considerable amounts of work on scalar and vector LPC quantizers have already been reported in the past, but these have been predominantly directed at coding schemes operating vocoders less than 4.8kb/s. Thus these have above 9.6kb/s (APC, RELP, etc.) or at very low rate tended to be good quality but

---

* This research was supported by Seoul Future Contents Convergence (SFCC) Cluster established by Seoul Industry-Academy-Research Cooperation Project.

T.-J. Cham et al. (Eds.): MMM 2007, LNCS 4352, Part II, pp. 568–575, 2007.

high capacity schemes, e.g. 40-50 bits scalar quantization, or low capacity but only reasonable quality vector quantization schemes, e.g. 10-bit codebook vector quantization. Therefore, for medium to low bit rates, i.e. 9.6-4.8kb/s, the previously reported LPC quantization schemes are not directly applicable, hence further investigations are required.

A promising and popular method is the use of the line spectrum pairs representation of the LPC parameters. LSP is used for speech analysis in vocoders or recognizers since it has advantages of constant spectrum sensitivity, low spectrum distortion and easy linear interpolation. But the method of transforming LPC coefficients to LSP parameters is so complex that it takes much time to compute. In order to acquire LSP, the process of finding the roots of polynomial equations is implemented. The conventional methods are complex root, real root, ratio filter, Chebyshev series, and adaptive sequential LMS (Least Mean Square) methods. Among these methods, the real root method is considerably simpler than others, but nevertheless, it still suffers from its indeterministic computation time. In this paper, we propose the computation reduction scheme of real root method using the distribution of LSP parameters and the formant characteristics [2-5, 8-11]. The conventional methods are complex root, real root, ratio filter, Chebyshev series, and adaptive sequential LMS (Least Mean Square) methods. Among these methods, the real root method is considerably simpler than others, but nevertheless, it still suffers from its indeterministic computation time. In this paper, we propose the computation reduction scheme of real root method using the distribution of LSP parameters and the formant characteristics [2-5, 8-11].

2 LPC to LSP Transformation

An all-pole digital filter for speech synthesis, H(z), can be derived from linear predictive analysis, and is given by

$$H(z) = 1/A_p(z) \qquad (1)$$

where

$$A_p(z) = 1 + \sum_{k=1}^{p} \alpha_k z^{-k} \qquad (2)$$

The PARCOR system is an equivalent representation, and its digital form is as shown in Figure 1,

where

$$A_{p-1}(z) = A_p(z) + k_p B_{p-1}(z) \qquad (3)$$

$$B_p(z) = z^{-1}[B_{p-1}(z) - k_p A_{p-1}(z)] \qquad (4)$$

where

$$A_0(z) = 1 \text{ and } B_0(z) = z^{-1},$$

$$\text{and } B_p(z) = z^{-(p+1)} A_p(z) \qquad (5)$$

The PARCOR system as shown in figure 1, is stable for $|k_i| < 1$ for all i. The PARCOR synthesis process can be viewed as sound wave propagation through a lossless acoustic tube, consisting of p sections of equal length but non-uniform cross sections. The acoustic tube is open at the terminal corresponding to the lips, and each section is numbered from the lips. Mismatching between the adjacent sections p and (p+1) causes wave propagation reflection. The reflection coefficients are equal to the p_{-th} PARCOR coefficient k_p section p+1, corresponds to the glottis, is terminated by a matched impedance. The excitation signal applied to the glottis drives the acoustic tube. In PARCOR analysis, the boundary condition at the glottis is impedance matched. Now consider a pair of artificial boundary conditions where the acoustic tube is completely closed or open at the glottis [2-4].

These conditions correspond to $k_{p+1} = 1$ and $k_{p+1} = -1$, a pair of extreme values for the artificially extended PARCOR coefficients, which corresponds to perfectly lossless tubes. The value Q of each resonance becomes infinite and the spectrum of distributed energy is concentrated in several line spectra.

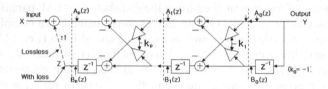

Fig. 1. PARCOR structure of LPC synthesis

The feedback conditions for $k_{p+1} = -1$ correspond to a perfect closure at the input (glottis) and for $k_{p+1} = 1$ correspond to an opening to infinite free space[5]. To derive the line spectra or line spectrum pairs(LSP), we proceed as follows, where it is assumed that the PARCOR filter is stable and the order is even. $A_p(z)$ may be decomposed into a set of two transfer functions, one having an even symmetry, and the other having an odd symmetry. This can be accomplished by taking a difference and a sum between $A_p(z)$ and its conjugate. Hence the transfer functions with $k_{p+1} = \pm 1$ are denoted by $P_{p+1}(z)$ and $Q_{p+1}(z)$:

$$\text{For } k_{p+1} = 1, \qquad P_{p+1}(z) = A_p(z) - B_p(z) \tag{6}$$

$$\text{For } k_{p+1} = -1, \qquad Q_{p+1}(z) = A_p(z) + B_p(z) \tag{7}$$

$$\Rightarrow A_p(z) = \frac{1}{2}[P_{p+1}(z) + Q_{p+1}(z)] \tag{8}$$

Substituting equation (5) into (6)

$$P_{p+1}(z) = A_p(z) + z^{-(p+1)} A_p(z^{-1}) \tag{9}$$

$$= 1 + (\alpha_1 - \alpha_p)z^{-1} + \cdots + (\alpha_p - \alpha_1)z^{-p} - z^{-(p+1)}$$

$$= z^{-(p+1)} \prod_{i=0}^{p=1} (z + a_i)$$

Similarly,

$$Q_{p+1}(z) = z^{-(p+1)} \prod_{i=0}^{p=1} (z + b_i) \tag{10}$$

As we know that two roots exits $(k_{p+1} = \pm 1)$, the order of $P_{p+1}(z)$ and $Q_{p+1}(z)$ can be reduced,

$$P'(z) = \frac{P_{p+1}(z)}{(1-z)} = A_0 z^p + A_1 z^{(p-1)} + \cdots A_p \tag{11}$$

and

$$Q'(z) = \frac{Q_{p+1}(z)}{(1+z)} = B_0 z^p + B_1 z^{(p-1)} + \cdots B_p \tag{12}$$

where

$$A_0 = 1, B_0 = 1 \tag{13}$$

$$A_k = (\alpha_k - \alpha_{p+1-k}) + A_{k-1},$$

$$B_k = (\alpha_k + \alpha_{p+1-k}) - B_{k-1} \quad \text{for } k = 1, \cdots, p$$

The LSP's are the angular of the roots of $P'(z)$ and $Q'(z)$ with $0 \le \omega_i \le \pi$ [2~4].

2.1 Real Root Method

As the coefficients of $P'(z)$ and $Q'(z)$ are symmetrical, the order of equation (11) can be reduced to p/2.

$$P'(z) = A_0 z^p + A_1 z^{(p-1)} + \cdots + A_1 z^1 + A_0 \tag{14}$$

$$= z^{p/2} [A_0(z^{p/2} + z^{-p/2}) + A_1(z^{(p/2-1)} + z^{-(p/2-1)}) + \cdots + A_{p/2}]$$

Similarly,

$$Q'(z) = B_0 z^p + B_1 z^{(p-1)} + \cdots + B_1 z^1 + B_0 \tag{15}$$

$$= z^{p/2} [B_0(z^{p/2} + z^{-p/2}) + B_1(z^{(p/2-1)} + z^{-(p/2-1)}) + \cdots + B_{p/2}]$$

As all roots are on the unit circle, we can evaluate equation (14) on the unit circle only.

$$\text{Let } z = e^\omega \text{ then } z^1 + z^{-1} = 2\cos(\omega) \tag{16}$$

$$P'(z) = 2e^{jp\omega/2}[A_0 \cos(\frac{p}{2}\omega) + A_1 \cos(\frac{p-2}{2}\omega) + \ldots + \frac{1}{2}A_{p/2}] \tag{17}$$

$$Q'(z) = 2e^{jp\omega/2}[B_0 \cos(\frac{p}{2}\omega) + B_1 \cos(\frac{p-2}{2}\omega) + \ldots + \frac{1}{2}B_{p/2}] \tag{18}$$

By making the substitution $x = \cos(\omega)$, equation (16) and (17) can be solved for x. For example, with p=10, the following is obtained.

$$P'_{10}(x) = 16A_0 x^5 + 8A_1 x^4 + (4A_2 - 20A_0)x^3 + (2A_3 - 8A_1)x^2$$

$$+ (4A_0 - 3A_2 + A_4)x + (A_1 - A_3 + 0.5A_5) \tag{19}$$

and similarly,

$$Q'_{10}(x) = 16B_0 x^5 + 8B_1 x^4 + (4B_2 - 20B_0)x^3 + (2B_3 - 8B_1)x^2$$

$$+ (4B_0 - 3B_2 + B_4)x + (B_1 - B_3 + 0.5B_5) \tag{20}$$

The LSPs are then given by

$$LSP(i) = \frac{\cos^{-1}(x_i)}{2\pi T}, \text{ for } 1 \le i \le p \tag{21}$$

2.2 The Characteristics of Mel Scale

Psychophysical studies have shown that human perception of the frequency content of sounds, either for pure tones or for speech signals, does not follow a linear scale. This study has led to the idea of defining subjective pitch of pure tones. Thus for each tone with an actual frequency, measured in Hz, a subjective pitch is measured on a scale called the 'Mel' scale. As a reference point, the pitch of a 1 kHz tone, 40dB above the perceptual hearing threshold, is defined as 1000 mels. Other subjective pitch values are obtained by adjusting the frequency of a tone such that it is half or twice the perceived pitch of a reference tone (with a known mel frequency). The unit of pitch is the Mel. Pitch in mels is plotted against frequency in equation (22). In the equation (22), frequency is plotted on a logarithmic scale and is therefore linear in musical pitch. Koenig approximates this scale by a function which is linear below 1 kHz and logarithmic above [7]. Fant gives the approximation,

$$F_{mel} = 1000 / \log 2 * \left[1 + \frac{f}{1000} \right] \tag{22}$$

3 The Fast LSP Transformation Algorithm

In the real root method, odd order LSP parameters are searched at the first time and then even order parameters are searched between odd order parameters. The searching time of odd order parameters takes up the most of transformation time because the searching is processed sequentially in the whole frequency region. But the important characteristic of LSP is that most LSP parameters are occurred in specific frequency region. And, the searching interval is uniform to acquire LSP parameter in real root method. So, to reduce the computational amount in real root method, the searching frequency interval is arranged by using mel scale but not it is uniform. In order to decrease the computational amount the characteristic of proposed algorithm is as follow. Equation (23) represents the searching interval of proposed algorithm in order to get LSP parameter. We can be known through equation (24) to (25) that the odd order in LSPs is changeable depending on the equation (23). Equation (26) and (27) represent even order in LSPs by equation (23).

$$f_{n+1} = (10^{point(n)/(1000\log2)} - 1)*1000*0.5 \quad for\ 0 \le n < 399 \tag{23}$$

where

$$f_0 = 0, \quad point(n) = index * (n+1)\ for\ 0 \le n < 399$$

$$index = F_{mel}/399, \quad F_{mel} = 1000/\log 2 * \log[1 + FS/1000], FS = 8000$$

$$Q'_n(f_n) = \left[A_0 \cos(2\pi f_n * \frac{p}{2}) + A_1 \cos(2\pi f_n * \frac{p-2}{2}) + ... + \frac{1}{2}A_{p/2} \right]$$

$$for\quad f_n : 0 \le n < 399 \tag{24}$$

4 Experimental Results

Computer simulation was performed to evaluate the proposed algorithm using a PC interfaced with the 16-bit AD/DA converter. To measure the performance of the proposed algorithms, we used the following speech data. Speech data was sampled at 8kHz and was quantized with 16bits. The data were recorded in a quiet room, with the SNR(Signal to Noise Ratio) greater than 30dB. Two steps simulation is performed in order to decrease the computation of LSP parameter by proposed algorithm. First, complexity of LPC to LSP conversion is estimated by applying the proposed algorithm from real root algorithm of CELP vocoder. Second, proposed method is applied in G.723.1 vocoder and we see how much SNR (Signal to Noise Ratio) changes in the whole performance of vocoder. LSP parameter in one of speech frames shows in figure 2 in order to compare between real root method and proposed method using the utterance 1. As showing figure 2, proposed method has the same LSP parameter value as conventional method.

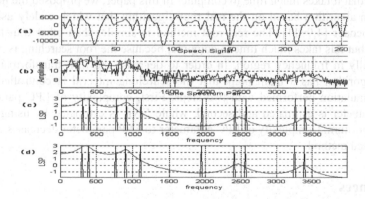

Fig. 2. The Distribution of LSP Parameters

Table 1 describes the simulation result of real root method and proposed method in the side of whole SNR of performing the G.723.1(step 2).

Table 1. The SNR of the Fast LSP Transformation Algorithm (step 2)

unit: [times/frames]		Real Root Method	Proposed Method	Decreased Ratio [%]	
Utterance 1 : 132frames	+	9057.3	5428.3	40.06	41.36
	-	6610.5	3790.5	42.66	
	*	27027.2	14148.2	47.65	48.15
	/	1648.9	846.9	48.64	
Utterance 2 : 173 frames	+	9055.8	5426.8	40.07	41.37
	-	6609.5	3789.5	42.67	
	*	27023.1	14144.1	47.66	48.16
	/	1648.6	846.6	48.65	
Utterance 3 : 142 frames	+	9056.1	5427.1	40.07	41.37
	-	6609.7	3789.7	42.66	
	*	27023.9	14144.9	47.66	48.15
	/	1648.7	846.7	48.64	
Utterance 4 : 154 frames	+	9056.5	5427.5	40.07	41.37
	-	6610.0	3790.0	42.66	
	*	27025.0	14146.1	47.66	48.15
	/	1648.8	846.8	48.64	

5 Conclusion

LSP parameter is used for speech analysis in low-bit rate speech vocoders or recognizers since it has advantages of constant spectrum sensitivity, low spectrum distortion and easy linear interpolation. But the method of transforming LPC to LSP is so complex that it takes much time to compute. In this paper, we proposed the new transformation algorithm based on the real root algorithm that which widely used in the CELP vocoder [4,9~11]. The real root method is simpler than other transformation methods but this takes much time to compute, because the root searching is processed sequentially in frequency region. In order to decrease the LSP transformation, proposed algorithm has a main point that the searching interval is controlled by mel scale. Simulation performed with two steps. First, complexity of LPC parameter to LSP parameter is estimated and second, whole SNR is estimated by using the proposed algorithm. Complexity of LPC parameter to LSP parameter decreases over 45% in proposed method.

References

1. N. Jayant and P. Noll, Digital Coding of Waveforms : Principles and Applications to Speech and Video, Signal Processing, Prentice-Hall, 1984, pp. 221-220.
2. S. Saito and K. Nakata, Fundamentals of Speech Signal, Academic Press, 1985, pp. 126-132.
3. A. M. Kondoz, Digital Speech, John Wiley & Sons Ltd, 1994, pp. 84-92.

4. M. J. Bae, Digital Speech Analysis, Dongyoung Press, 1998, pp.95-120.
5. P. Kabal and R. P. Ramachandran, The computation of line spectral frequencies using Chebyshev polynomials, IEEE Trans. on ASSP, December 1986.
6. ITU-T Recommendation G.723.1, March, 1996.
7. Thomas Parson, Voice and Speech Processing, Mac Graw Hill, pp71-73.
8. F. Soong and B. H. Juang, Line Spectrum pairs and speech data compression, Proc. of ICASSP, 1.10.1-1.10.4, 1984.
9. SoYeon MIN, MyungJin BAE, A high-speed LSF transformation algorithm for CELP vocoders, The Journal of the Acoustic Society of Korea, Vol. 20, No. 1E, March, 2001.
10. EunYoung KANG, SoYeon MIN, MyungJin BAE, A study on the reduction of LSP(Line Spectrum Pairs) transformation time using the voice characteristics, wireless2001,10, July, 2001.
11. SoYeon MIN, MyungJin BAE, A study on the frequency scaling methods using LSP parameters distribution characteristics, The Journal of the Acoustic Society of Korea, Vol. 21, No. 3, April, 2002.

Functional Architecture of Performance Measurement System Based on Grid Monitoring Architecture

Hyuncheol Kim[1,*], Seongjin Ahn[2,**], Byungyeon Park[3],
Jihyun Song[4], and Junkyun Choi[5]

[1] Dept. of Computer Science, Namseoul University,
21 Maeju-ri, Seonghwan-eup, Chonan, Korea, 330-707
hckim@nsu.ac.kr
[2] Dept. of Computer Education, Sungkyunkwan University,
53 Myungryun-Dong, Jongro-Gu, Seoul, Korea, 110-745
sjahn@comedu.skku.ac.kr
[3] Korea Institute of Science and Technology Information,
52-11, Eoeun-dong, Yuseong-gu, Daejeon, Korea, 305-806
bypark@kisti.ac.kr
[4] Dept. of Computer Engineering, Sungkyunkwan University,
300 Chunchun-Dong, Jangan-Gu, Suwon, Korea, 440-746
jhsong@songgang.skku.ac.kr
[5] School of Engineering, Information and Communications University,
119 Munjiro, Yuseong-Gu, Daejon, Korea, 350-714
jkchoi@icu.ac.kr

Abstract. With a tremendous increase of Internet users, the Internet computing environments are getting more complicated along with the network management structure in order to support diverse traffic characteristics. A successful end-to-end realization of Grid services presumes well-defined QoS measuring framework in the service provider's and customer's networks. Most traditional network performance management systems utilize a passive measuring method based on SNMP, allowing an administrator to understand only network conditions. However, it is difficult for network managing systems that are based on a passive measuring method to accurately understand the situations surrounding time-varying networks. Our objective in this paper is to describes a Grid monitoring architecture based practical measuring framework for network performance measurement. It includes concepts as well as step-by-step procedures of an active measuring method for measuring performance of any section at any time.

1 Introduction

With the advent of new computer and network technologies and the integration of various computer communication technologies, today's computing environments can

* This work was supported by grant No. R01-2004-000-10618-0 from the Basic Research Program of the Korea Science & Engineering Foundation. This work was also supported in part by MIC, Korea under the ITRC program supervised by the IITA(IITA-2005-(ITAC1090050200070001000100100)).
** Corresponding Author.

T.-J. Cham et al. (Eds.): MMM 2007, LNCS 4352, Part II, pp. 576–583, 2007.
© Springer-Verlag Berlin Heidelberg 2007

provide integrated high quality services. The network traffic has also continuously increased with remarkable growth. With the advent of various complex applications that need real-time processing and more calculations, data analysis, and cooperation systems, the development of the virtual computing technology have surpassed the system requirement of applications. This resulted the creation of Grid computing environment, where several computers or equipments linked through the Internet can be viewed as a single virtual supercomputer. In order for the Grid computing to realize a profit, it must provide generic resource sharing procedures among the regionally distributed computers[1][2].

Our objective in this paper is to describes a Grid monitoring architecture based practical measuring framework for network performance measurement[3][4]. It includes concepts as well as step-by-step procedures of an active measuring method for measuring performance of any section at any time. This paper also investigates the effects of packet loss and delay jitter on network performance[5][6].

Section 2 clarifies some key terminologies with vague and complex meanings, and also examines some previous studies on network performance measuring. Section 3 concentrates on the network model and node architecture of the proposed schemes and presents some features that provide useful information on the considered network in terms of performance improvement. Section 4 models and analyzes the proposed network performance measuring schemes. Section 5 concludes this paper by summarizing some key points made throughout and assessing the representation of analyzed results. Chapter 5 also includes concluding remarks and future research topics.

2   Related Works

2.1   Grid Monitoring System

In Global Grid Forum (GGF), there is research regarding a monitoring structure, which considers expandability, easily allowing interactions of several Grid monitoring systems upon a Grid network. A Grid monitoring structure has the purpose of making a general structure, which can accommodate specific requirements of a monitoring system, allowing easy interactions of individually different Grid monitoring systems [1][7].

The Grid Monitoring Architecture (GMA) consists of 3 elements [1][5]. The Directory Service, that supports issuing usable information, and searching. The Producer, representing the data providing part, where events are transmitted to the Consumer, and is the receiving part which requests and receives events from the Producer.

Even if management information that can be used by the Consumer and the Producer is composed as an event, information is saved in the Directory Service, and thereby is regionally dispersed, the Producer and the Consumer can still transfer information in the form of events. An event is timestamp information, which is a structure composed by specific event schemas upon performance data, and therefore event information is always transmitted directly from the Producer to the Consumer.

In a Grid environment, monitoring of a range of information occurs, and therefore the elapsed delay during the search for the required information can become

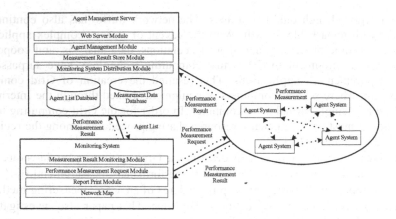

Fig. 1. System Architecture

unpredictably long. Thus, control within a clear region must be possible upon the overhead, and delay relating to collections and searches.

3 System Architecture

3.1 Total System Architecture

Fig. 1 presents the entire system structure. The system is composed of three main elements. A measuring agent management server which manages agents, saves measured performance results and agent information in the database, and serves as a web server distributing monitoring systems.

A monitoring system where performance measuring is requested to an agent, results are visually shown, and a report is output. A measurement agent system, in which substantial performance measuring occurs. The measurement agent system can individually become a client and a server to transmit and receive packets and to perform performance measurements.

The operating procedure of the performance measurement system of Fig. 1 is shown in Fig. 2. First, the agents are registered into the measurement agent management server and the network administrator or a user connects to an agent management server through the monitoring system. When connected, the receive agent lists the monitoring system and selects the transmission agent and destination agent from the management server.

When a random agent is selected, packet information is input, which is used for performance measurement and then measurement requests. The agent selected as the transmission agent accepts this request and connects with the destination agent for performance measurement. When measuring is completed, the results are transmitted to the monitoring system where a report is processed and transmitted so that it can be easily viewed by the user and the administrator[9].

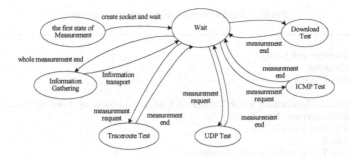

Fig. 2. Procedure of Measurement Agent System

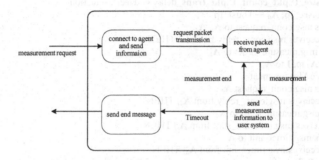

Fig. 3. Procedure of Measurement Module

3.2 Performance Measurement Algorithm

The agent receiving the performance measurement request from the management server becomes a server agent and connects to a client agent. The agents create packets, which are mutually transmitted and received, for measuring the performance of the network.

Fig. 2 presents a status diagram of the agent system. The agent stays in standby until a measurement request is received from the monitoring system, and then performs performance measurement and transmits the resulting value when it is received.

The performance measurement module of the agent system operates as presented in Fig. 3. When a measurement request arrives from the monitoring system, the corresponding agents will create a connection and receive information regarding the packets, created from the monitoring system. Using the information received, packets are created and followed by measurement.

Once the Transmission Control Protocol (TCP) connection is created between agents, A_s transmits A_d a message notification signaling that the measurement is started. A_s continues to transmit A_d data for α hours. A_d measures the amount of the data transmission at every β hours, and transmits A_s it.

After α hours, A_s transmits A_d a message notifying that the measurement will be completed. A_s transmits R to M, and M shows the download minimum value, maximum value and total average value to the user.

Table 1. Performance Measurement Algorithm

S = Agent Management Server
A_i = Agent Systems
M = Monitoring System
U = User
R = Performance Measurement Result Value(Rate, Max delay, Min delay, Loss, Variance)
T_{all} = Total Measurement Time Timer
T_{int} = Measurement Interval Timer
α = End of the T_{all}
β = End of the T_{int} ($\alpha = n\beta$, n is natural number.)
1. Performance Measurement Request
   1.1 **U.src_ip, U.dst_ip** ← User selects ip in S.agentlist_database
   1.2 **U.pkt_size, U.pkt_count, U.pkt_trans_delay** ← User's selection
   1.3. A_s ← **U.src_ip**, A_d ← **U.dst_ip**
   1.4 **M** sends msg.conn_request to A_s, A_d.
   1.5 IF (**M** receives msg.conn_reply from A_s) THEN
      M sends msg.measure_order to A_s
      M sends A_d.ip, **I** to A_s
2. Performance Measurement
   2.1 A_s sends msg.conn_request A_d
   2.2 IF (A_s receives msg.conn_reply from A_d) THEN
      A_s sends msg.measure_start to A_d
      IF (A_d receives msg.measure_start from A_s) THEN
         A_d sends msg.timer_init to A_s
         IF (A_s receives msg.timer_init from A_d) THEN
            $T_{all} = 0$, $T_{int} = 0$
         ENDIF
      ENDIF
   ENDIF
   2.3 packet ← A_s generates new packet
   2.4 FOR $T_{all} = 0$ to α DO
      A_s sends packet to A_d
      IF ($T_{int} > \beta$) THEN
         A_d calculates **R** which is value from T_{int} to β
         A_d sends **R** to A_s
         $T_{int} = 0$
      ENDIF
      $T_{int} = T_{int} + 1$
   ENDFOR
3. Measurement Result Display
   3.1 IF ($T_{all} > \alpha$) THEN
      A_s sends msg.measure_complete to A_d
      A_s sends **R** to **M**
      IF(**M** receives **R** from A_s) THEN
         M displays **R**
      ENDIF
   ENDIF

A_s creates ICMP ping packets to obtain the delay time and loss rate to reach A_d. The packet round trip time and packet loss rate are measured with packets being transmitted **U.pkt_count** times at the size of **U.pkt_size** and transmission delay time of **U.pkt_trans_dealy**. (The optimized values may depend on the network environments and applications).

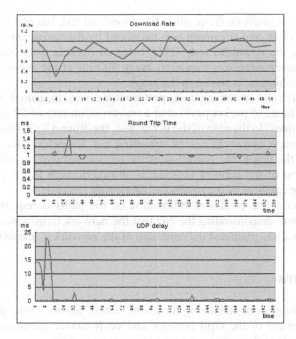

Fig. 4. Performance Measurement Results

As a final result, the current round trip delay time, current loss rate, total average round trip delay time and total loss rate are recorded.

A_s creates UDP packets to obtain the delay time and loss rate to reach A_d. Packet round trip time and packet loss rate are measured with packets being transmitted **U.pkt_count** times at the size of **U.pkt_size** and transmission delay time of **U.pkt_trans_dealy**. (The optimized values may depend on the network environments and applications).

As a final result, current delay time, current loss rate, total average round trip delay time and total loss rate are recorded. It plays the same role as the traceroute command of UNIX, tracing the path between server and client A. Client A transmits a measurement test massage to the target server. The target server receives the path measurement test message, and reports the path measurement and delays between each path to the client by running the traceroute command for the client. The final results include the IP addresses of network nodes from the target server to the client, and delay times between each node.

4   Performance Analysis

The environment for the simulation was as follows: The measurement agent management server and monitoring system run Windows XP Professional, and the measurement agent system run RedHat Linux 9.0. In addition, Microsoft Visual Studio 6.0 was used as the development software.

Fig. 4 presents a graph on the result of the download test, Internet Control Message Protocol (ICMP) test, and streaming test, measured by the two agents within the Grid network. During the download test, 32658 bytes of packets were transmitted for 10 seconds, data transmission was measured every 300 ms at the agent, and data transmission rate per unit time is shown in the graph.

For the ICMP and streaming test, performance was measured by individually transmitting 60 bytes of packet payload at a transmission rate of 50 packets/sec for a number of 200 times. In the case of the ICMP test, the Round Trip Time (RTT) values are shown in a graph, and in the case of streaming test, the delay values are expressed.

In analyzing the graph, the condition of the current network in which we can tell that the condition of the network is good, is shown through Fig. 4 presenting relatively similar appearances of the results per measuring intervals.

When more concrete condition information of the paths is required, a traceroute test was conducted, demonstrating the fact that the network transmission delay time of the entire sections was plain and the condition of the network is learned as stable.

5 Conclusions

This paper focuses on materializing a system, which allows visual confirmation of quality measurement of the Grid network and performance measurement results of individual network performances.

This system is composed of visual charts and graphs, in which every menu setup and result outputs network performance measurement, allowing even an amateur to verify the results. A user can randomly set the section to measure, packet size, packet transmission time, and packet transmission delay time, and also verify network performance through graphs and tables, comparing past measurement data with current data.

This system can therefore detect transmission delay within a network and verify the point where a bottleneck occurs Scheme performance improvement of the entire network can be achieved through monitoring information, and detouring traffic through lightly used circuits. In measuring the performance of the network circuit within a Grid system, the result can be used as a judging standard of Grid computing operation.

This results in successful Grid computing operation. However, numerous application services create actual Grid computing, and in the case of measuring the performance with identical standards, where the characteristic of traffic transmitted for each application service varies, the problem of a drop in the reliability of the measurement values could occur.

To complement such limits, research is planned for a system that operates performance measurement through the distinction of individual application services.

References

1. Jason Lee, Dan Gunter, Martin Stoufer and Brian Tierney: Monitoring data archives for Grid environments, Supercomputing, ACM/IEEE, Nov. 2002 pp. 66-66
2. I. Foster and C. Kesselman: The Grid: Blueprint for a Future Computing Infrastructure, 1999

3. Teegan, H.A.: Distributed performance monitoring using SNMP V2, Network Operations and Management Symposium, IEEE Vol. 2, Apr. 1996 pp. 616-619
4. Drake, P.: Using SNMP to manage networks, Designing Resilient Architectures, IEE Colloquium, Nov. 1991 pp 1-4
5. B. Tierney, R. AYdt, D. Gunter, W. Smith, M. Swany, V. Taylor and R. Wolski: A Grid Monitoring Architecture, GWD-I, 2002
6. L. Cottrell: Measuring and analyzing service levels: a scalable passive approach, Quality of Service, IWQoS 98 Sixth International Workshop, May 1998 pp. 3-12
7. Xipeng Xiao, Hannan, A., Bailey, B., Ni, L.M.: Tra±c engineering with MPLS in the Internet, Network, IEEE Vol. 14, Issue 2, Mar. 2000 pp. 28-33
8. Zadnik, M., Pecenka, T., Korenek, J.: Net°ow probe intended for high-speed networks, International Conference on Field Programmable Logic and Applications, Aug. 2005 pp. 695-698
9. Nakashima, T.: Experimental analysis of propagation properties implementing the path-based measurement, Advanced Information Networking and Applications, Aug. 2004 pp. 243-248

Adaptive Synchronization Scheme Using Terminal Buffering in Mobile Multimedia Networks

Gi-Sung Lee

Dept. of Computer Science Howon Univ., Korea
ygslee@sunny.howon.ac.kr

Abstract. This paper presents an adaptive synchronization scheme for compensating for the variable transmission delay and synchronizing media data through the use of terminal buffering in mobile multimedia network. The proposed scheme can meet the requirement for synchronization of media data by adjusting synchronization intervals using the maximum time delay jitter and by flexibly handling the variable queue time according to variations in delay time, and reduce media data loss time due to increase in traffic as well as data loss due to variations in delay time by using delay jitters in adjusting synchronization intervals.

1 Introduction

Over recent years, the exponential increase in the number of Internet users has accelerated the emergence of a variety of services based on mobile computing environments. Existing service structures based merely on the communication between the client and the server face difficulty in meeting users' requirements for a variety of high-speed multimedia services. However, it has become possible to overcome such limitations facing the exiting communication service structures by way of expanding the concept of the service provision system from a single system to a mobile system connected to wireless networks. In the case of such media, synchronization is becoming recognized as an important issue because, due to varying arrival time delays, the original time relation is disrupted by delays occurring on mobile communication networks or by conversion of intra-media jitters.

Mobile Terminals (MTs) have two problems in connection with live synchronization. First, the problem with mobile phones is low bandwidth. Usually, the bandwidth assigned to an MT is 1Mbps for a PDA, and 14kbps to 144kbps for a mobile phone. With hindsight, MTs have such low bandwidths that they cannot meet multimedia data's requirements for higher bandwidths. For such reasons, there is a need for an artificial synchronization functionality that enables the playout of multimedia data in a similar manner to their original time relation. If possible, this is done either through the use of application service requirements for multimedia data where time relations are disrupted, or in view-of human being's recognition limitations on data loss or delay in different kinds of media [1].

The second problem is low MT memory. The memory of a PDA that has only memory and no hard disk can be expanded up to 256MB. The memory of a mobile

T.-J. Cham et al. (Eds.): MMM 2007, LNCS 4352, Part II, pp. 584–591, 2007.

phone is much lower than this. To address these issues, a mobile terminal synchronization scheme should be in place as a means of adjusting synchronization intervals using the maximum delay jitter, and of reducing loss of data due to varying time delays, and of enabling intra- and inter-media synchronizations [2-4].

The reasons for delays lie not only in differences between the frame-generation system and the frame-playout system, but also in the fact that frames are transmitted via the mobile communication base station. When a media is transmitted remotely or during heavy network traffic, such delays are unavoidable since such multimedia use mobile communication packet networks that have low bandwidths. In addition, loss of packets due to handoff, and packet delays affect QoS significantly. It doesn't matter in the case where the frames arriving belatedly in the MT of the receiving party have regular time delays. However, in most cases, frames have irregular time delays: delay jitters between packets become larger.

This paper proposes an adaptive synchronization scheme that adjusts synchronization intervals using the maximum time delay jitter and enables intra- and inter-media synchronizations.

2 Related Work

Gayer used a method to change the transmission start-up point, to apply the filtering function and offsets to retain a normal state of a buffer [4, 7].

Gayer's method defines the transmission start-up time by transmitting roundtrip packets at the evaluation step before transferring stream media from the source. This method solved the skew problem between buffer size and media by regulating the server number that generates maximum jitters and the first transmission time of a different server. Also, this method presents an approach to keep the normal state of a buffer and thus improves the play-out rate in a distributed environment.

However, since this method is not adapted to a network state in which values of a filtering function obtained for keeping the normal state of a buffer vary with a condition, it takes a lot of time to switch to a normal state of a buffer from underflow or overflow. Since the play-out time is also not considered in a client, this method is not satisfactory to keep the normal state.

N. U. Qazi, M. Woo, and A. Grafoor, a base station serves as an interface between the wired and the wireless networks, and buffering at the base station for interfacing with the wired networks is considered to smooth inter-packet jitter delay. This method attempts only to apply synchronization to channel allocation [3].

The buffer management and the feedback scheme in which the received multimedia units are registered to the buffer at a mobile host, and their play-out time is controlled based on the middle of the buffer size, is studied in references [2, 3]. However this method can't support the required QoS level by changing a play-out time, even though the state of mobile networks is normal. D. L. Stone and K. Jeffay proposed both strategies - I-Strategy and E-Strategy [5]: the former is about whether to throw away belatedly arriving frames in accordance with the buffer strategy; and the latter is about whether to play out the belatedly arriving frames.

3 Proposed Synchronization Scheme

3.1 System Configuration

This system supports k multimedia servers, m base stations, and n mobile hosts. The base station communicates with i mobile host in the mth cell. The mobile host always has access to the multimedia servers via the base stations.

This system uses the arrival time of the subframes transferred from the multimedia server as well as delay jitter variables to enable the logical time set for playout to be displaced as much as the discontinuity tolerance time, displacing the deadline point in time of multimedia data, and changing the duration time of multimedia data frames. Such a system has the advantage of overcoming the low memory and low bandwidth of a mobile host, which is a limiting factor for mobile communication.

The multimedia server data type consists of streams that are divided into many frames based on a synchronization group, not on the same byte. Figure 1 shows the architecture of this system in which the Message Manager of the multimedia server skips the P- and B-picture according to the offset Control Function sent by the Feedback Manager of the base station during transmission. The base station stores the arrival time of subframes that arrive from each server. Multimedia data are transmitted via the Mobile Switch Center (MSC) to a Base Station (BS), and arrive in a MT.

The MT calculates the jitter compensation time of the arriving multimedia data by means of Arrive Media Processing in order to determine the relative duration time. Using Arrive Media Processing, the multimedia data determine whether the playout deadline has elapsed, and applies the maximum jitter to the duration time. The scheme proposed in this paper makes changes to the deadline time for belatedly arriving frames through the use of the maximum delay jitter, and adjusts the duration time within the time range of the synchronization interval.

3.2 Stand-By Time Adjustment Method

During the transmission of multimedia data, the low bandwidth of mobile communication networks invariably causes delays due to heavy traffic load and low mobile terminal buffer. In addition, loss of packets and packet delays due to handoff affect QoS significantly.

Fig. 2 shows the delay jitters of multimedia data, which are generated in the MT of the sending and receiving parties as a function of variations in arrival time. Such delay jitters lead to discontinuities. The objective of this multimedia synchronization policy is to play out frames without any discontinuity. The frame "a" arrives before it is played out at time "3", providing a buffer for the MT.

In the case of the I-Strategy, packets must arrive in the buffer before the point in time at which multimedia data are played out. Therefore, frames that have larger end-to-end delays than the logical time are thrown away. In the case of the E-Strategy, belatedly arriving frames are placed on stand-by in the buffer before they are played out. In this case, if a frame arrives belatedly, the delay time of all subsequent frames

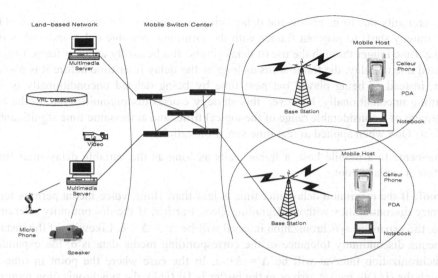

Fig. 1. System Configuration

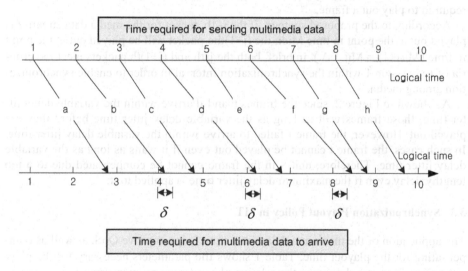

Fig. 2. Delay Jitters between the Sending Party and the MT

increases. As illustrated in Figure 2, b, d, and f are thrown away because they have arrived at the end-to-end delay time longer than the two-frame unit allowed. Thus, the I-Strategy includes three-time discontinuities when multimedia data are played out at the starting points in time 4, 6, and 8.

In the case of the E-Strategy, the frame b causes a discontinuity at the unit 4. It is placed in the buffer queue and eventually played out in the unit 5 that has a delay corresponding to three frames. Every frame that comes after the frame b causes no discontinuity due to its end-to-end delay being smaller than the three-frame unit. The E-Strategy starts to play out frames with the minimum possible delay and makes the delay time longer through the use of delay jitters. If a belatedly arriving frame is generated due to delay, the frame waits as long as the delay jitter time before it is played out, instead of being played out next time by being deleted unconditionally or by waiting unconditionally. However, this strategy causes discontinuities due to the adjustment of a considerable range of the logical time, and at the same time significantly affects QoS when applied to real-time synchronizations.

Theorem: In a mobile host, a frame waits as long as the variable delay jitter time before it is played out.

Proof: If the maximum delay jitter time is less than 10ms, voice media permits temporary discontinuities without degrading QoS. Further, if the discontinuity tolerance is δ, the expanded synchronization interval will be $\Delta' = \Delta + \delta$. Likewise, if the instantaneous discontinuity tolerance of the corresponding media data is δ, the expanded synchronization interval will be $\Delta' = \Delta + \delta$. In the case where the point in time at which the $(j+1)$th packet arrives in the buffer is Bi $(j+1)$, the synchronization requirement shall be met if Bi $(j+1)$ is smaller than, or the same as Mi $(j+1)$ which is the time required to play out a frame.

According to the proposed strategy, if the j- th packet for the media data stream I is played out at the point in time Midi, the $(j+1)$the packet will be played out at the point in time (Mi$(j+1)$ = Mij + Δ.). In brief, both the j-th and $(j+1)$th packets meet the criteria of Expression 1 within the synchronization interval in order to enable synchronization among media.

As shown in Figure 2, since the frames b and d arrive within the variable delay jitter time, those frames wait as long as the variable delay jitter time before they are played out. However, the frame f failed to arrive within the variable delay jitter time. In such cases, the frame f cannot be played out even if it waits as long as the variable delay jitter time. Therefore, unit 8 in the frame cannot be compensated due to a too lengthy delay even if the maximum delay jitter time is applied to it.

3.3 Synchronization Playout Policy in MT

The application of the maximum delay jitter time helps improve QoS, as well as compensating for the playout time. Table 1 shows the parameters necessary for the playout policy. You can determine the relative playout time by measuring media data in the smoothing buffer. Specifically, calculate the size of data that arrived within 125ms, which is the smoothing buffer delay time. P_γ refers to the playout ratio between the maximum size of data that a media can play out in the duration time, and the size of data that arrived during the smoothing buffer delay. τ_γ refers to the relative duration time required to play out arrived media.

In the case where an audio object arrives early and non-audio objects arrive belatedly in the mobile host, the jitter compensation algorithm is illustrated in Fig. 3. This algorithm applies in the case of a normal audio object.

Begin

    if $\tau_{Aa} <= \tau_b$ then

begin

    $\tau_{diff} := \tau_b - \tau_{Aa}$;

    if $\tau_{diff} <= \tau_j$ then

begin

    wait (τ_{diff}) ;

    $\tau_{\gamma-m} := \tau_{\gamma-m} + \tau_{diff}$;

end
else
begin

    wait (τ_j) ; $\tau_{\gamma-m} := \tau_{\gamma-m} + \tau_j$;

end end End.

Fig. 3. Normal Jitter compensation algorithm

The basic idea underlying this paper is to achieve inter- and intra-media synchronization through applying the maximum delay jitter time. However, in the case of exceeding 125ms, the entire duration time, despite the application of the maximum delay jitter, the overall synchronization strategy can instead be disrupted. Therefore, the maximum delay jitter should be applied in order to prevent the 125ms limit from being exceeded. The reason behind the application of the jitter compensation algorithm with a difference between the audio's relative duration time and the entire duration time is to allow the former to maintain the maximum duration time. If such a difference is smaller than 10ms, which is the maximum delay jitter, this algorithm enables the audio to wait as long as the difference, allowing for compensation of the duration time as much as the difference for non-audio media. Any difference larger than the maximum delay jitter could possibly cause great loss in audio data. Since it isn't applicable beyond the maximum delay jitter, this algorithm compensates for such differences up to the maximum delay jitter.

4 Simulation

For the purpose of this paper, experiments were performed for the proposed scheme using an IBM-compliant Pentium PC. The interfaces and algorithms were implemented using the Java development kit 1.2.2, and saved into the Microsoft MDB in petrinet.mdb files. The 1Kbyte audio data were encoded by means of the PCM encoding technique, and video frames were implemented using a resolution of 120 X 120: 24 video frames per second were encoded. In order to ensure proper packet processing, the information used for actual simulations was applied, computed using the Poisson distribution, equally to mobile networks which have 300 channels for 60 cells. One thousand GOP frames were used in performance evaluation experiments to which a maximum delay jitter time of 125ms was applied.

The following is a comparison between the proposed scheme and the existing scheme in terms of the delay jitter scheme using the maximum delay jitter time, the playout time, and loss time. Firstly, a comparative analysis between the case where an audio properly arrives in the MT, and the case where an audio improperly arrives in the MT was carried out. Experiments were conducted assuming that, if the audio properly arrives in the MT, the average delay is 100ms, and the deviation is 20ms.

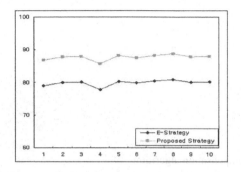 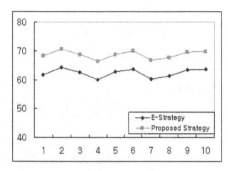

Fig. 4. Comparison of Playout Rate in the Case of Audio's Proper Arrival   **Fig. 5.** Comparison of Playout Rate in the Case of Audio's Improper Arrival

Fig. 4 shows the result of comparing the playout time between the E-Strategy and the proposed strategy in the case where an audio object arrives early. This result was obtained through conducting the experiment ten times on the playout rate of the proposed strategy when the audio object properly arrived. When the audio arrived earlier than any other media, the proposed strategy calculated the relative duration time and applied the maximum delay jitter to allow for waiting as long as the maximum delay jitter, thereby achieving an average playout rate of 87.65 compared to 79.85 achieved by the E-Strategy. Further, the proposed strategy improved the playout rate by approximately 8%.

As shown in Fig. 5, when an audio object arrived later than any other media, the E-Strategy applied the jitter compensation time algorithm to allow non-audio media to wait as long as the maximum duration time, achieving an average playout rate of 62.36 compared to 68.65 achieved by the proposed strategy. Compared to the E-Strategy, the proposed strategy showed an improved playout rate of approximately 6.3%.

5 Conclusion

This paper proposes intra- and inter-media synchronizations through the use of the smoothing buffer in a mobile terminal. Using the maximum delay jitter time of the main media (i.e., Audio), the proposed scheme was able to expand the synchronization interval in the media, and apply the maximum delay jitter time to the implementation of synchronizations among media. As a result, it synchronized the packets irregularly arriving within the expanded interval, thereby enabling optimal synchronizations without degrading QoS. It is believed this intra- and inter-media synchronization scheme is suitable for the cases of temporary increases in network load as well as in situations of unpredictable network isolations.

Acknowledgements

This work was supported by Howon University Fund, 2006.

References

1. G. Blakowski and R. Steinmetz, "A Media Synchronization Survey: Reference Model, Specification, and Case Studies," IEEE Journal on selected Areas in Communications, Vol.14, No.1, Jan. 1999.
2. R. Steinmetz, "Synchronization Properties in Multimedia Systems," IEEE Journal on selected Areas in Communications, Vol.8, No.3, Apr. 1998.
3. N. U. Qazi, M. Woo, and A. Grafoor, "A Synchronization and Communication Model for Distributed Multimedia Objects," Proc. of ACM Multimedia, 1999.
4. E. Biersack, W. Geyer, and C. Bernhardt, "Intra- and Inter-Stream Synchronization for Stored Multimedia Streams," IEEE Proc. of Multimedia '96, pp.372-381, 1996.
5. D. L. Stone, and K. Jeffay, "An Empirical Study of Delay Jitter Management Policies," Multimedia Systems/Springer-Verlag, 2004.
6. Dae-Jea Cho, Kee-Young Yoo, "The Study on Development of a Multimedia Synchronization Algorithm for Internet Based VOD Services", KIPS, Vol 8-B, No 1, Feb., 2004.
7. Gi-Sung Lee, Jeung-Gyu Jee, Sok-Pal Cho, "Buffering Management Scheme for Multimedia Synchronization in Mobile Information System," LNCS Vol. 2660, pp 545-554, 2003.

Educational Information System Using Two Phase Feature Extract in u-Learning Environment

Keun Wang Lee[1], Kwang-Hyoung Lee[2], and Jong-Cheon Park[3]

[1] Dept. of Multimedia Science, Chungwoon University, Chungnam, Korea
kwlee@chungwoon.ac.kr
[2] Dept. of Internet Information, Seoil College, Seoul, Korea
[3] School of Electrical & Computer Eng., Chungbuk National Univ., Korea

Abstract. This paper proposes an educational information system based on u-learning that supports two phase feature extract. A key frame selected by user in annotation-based retrieval takes query image of feature-based retrieval and by agent searches and displays the most similar key frame image after comparing query image with key frames in the DB through full image and center image, binary image histogram techniques which we proposed. Therefore, user can get more correct retrieval result by agent's learning through repeated retrievals about video data for the environment education of infants. From experiment, the designed and implemented system shows increase of recall rate of about 1.5% and 2.0% as precision rate 94.2% for video data scene retrieval in performance assessment.

1 Introduction

Amid recent Internet developments, rapid progress is being made in image compression technologies as well as multimedia content service technologies. As a result, the demand for information on video data is increasing, and a wide variety of video data need to be effectively managed in order to meet the vast and varying needs of different users[1]. To ensure effective management of video data, there is a need for technologies that allow for systematically classifying and integrating information on large-capacity video data. In addition, video data need to be retrieved and stored in an efficient manner to provide different users with services that meet their varying needs [2].

Studies currently being conducted on content-based video data retrieval are largely classified into the following: 1) a feature-based retrieval scheme that uses similarity by extracting features from key frames; and 2) an annotation-based retrieval scheme in which a comparative retrieval is performed on a user's annotation that has been inputted and saved for a key frame. However, both content-based video data retrieval methods have some disadvantages.

In the feature-based retrieval scheme, retrieval is performed in such as way as to extract low-level feature information (i.e., color, texture, region, and spatial color distribution) from video data [3]. In the case of the feature-based retrieval scheme that focuses on comparative retrieval through extraction of visual features from the videos themselves to calculate similarity, extracting visual features is very important. However,

T.-J. Cham et al. (Eds.): MMM 2007, LNCS 4352, Part II, pp. 592–598, 2007.

correctly extracting feature information from a lot of videos is quite difficult. In addition, matching extracted feature information to a vast amount of video data is not easy in the performance of retrieval.

In the case of the annotation-based retrieval scheme, retrieval is performed in a way that by using characters, the user attaches annotations to the semantic information of individual video data whose automatic recognition is difficult [4]. In this paper, a wireless multimedia DB system is presented that supports u-learning for environment education of infants using mobile terminals in wireless environments.

2 Related Works

QBIC (Query by Image and Video Content)[5] developed by the IBM Almaden Laboratory is a system that supports image-example-based similarity queries in addition to usersketch-based queries, and color and texture queries. Since it supports both images and video data, QBIC performs data retrieval using feature information such as shot detection, shot-to-key frame creation, and object movement.

Visual SEEK[6] developed by Columbia University is an image database system supporting color and spatial queries in which images are distinguished by features (i.e., color and histogram etc.), and additional features (i.e., image area/color, size, spatial location etc.) are used for image comparison.

Venus[7] developed by Taiwan's National Chinghwa University is used for image retrieval through establishing time and spatial relationships among objects that are displayed in each video frame through the use of metadata.

In the case where feature-based retrieval has few camera techniques or scene conversions, detecting the boundary between two shots is a very challenging task. In particular, it is very difficult to detect the boundary of scenes that make up a single story. Many existing studies have been conducted on detecting the boundary between scenes and shots using color histograms and typical colors. However, they have yet to fully support semantic-based retrieval.

3 Proposed System Architecture

The propose system consists of a video server, an agent middleware and a mobile client. The video server stores all information on video data and its metadata.

If a video data is inputted into the system, the system extracts annotation and feature information while updating its metadata in a continuous manner. The agent middleware processes users' queries coming in through the WAP gateway through the use of a query processor, and creates queries accessing the video server. It then receives responses for the queries to deal with key frame annotations and images, and sends the processed key frame images and WAP responses to the client. The mobile client accesses the agent middleware via wireless networks where mobile service-enabled terminals, its infrastructure, and a WAP gateway are in use. Fig. 1 shows the overall architecture of the proposed system.

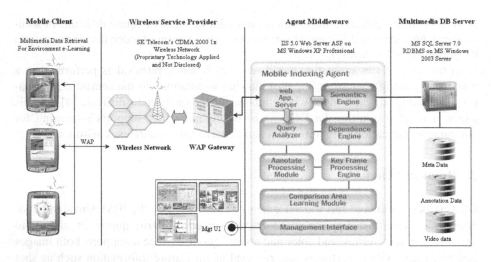

Fig. 1. The System Architecture

4   Two Phase Feature Extract

4.1   Calculation Color Distribution in Whole and Center Area

Calculate image about query image and key frame in whole & center area to calculate fast and correct color similarity of query image inputted from user and key frame abstracted in video data.

Image of n x m size abstracted from Key frame divides by center area. Because the main information is located in center area by special property of video, color distribution also should handles about center area according to special property of frame. For reflect such special property, in this thesis, we extracts feature of frame by calculates with color distribution about whole & center area.

After the query image is divided into whole & center area, all color similarity of key frames abstracted by primary comment based search and query images are calculated by R,G,B standard deviation of whole & center area. Similarity calculation procedure that use color distribution is represented in Fig. 2.

4.2   Calculation RGB Standard Deviation of Query Image

Calculate the feature of Red, Green, Blue's color distribution about whole image of Key frame like Equ. (1). Feature value which represent degree of color distribution is obtained from each RGB standard deviation about whole pixel of key frame.

$$S_{Cp} = \sqrt{\frac{\sum_{i=0}^{w}\sum_{j=0}^{h}(Cp_{|i,j|} - \overline{X_{Cp}})^2}{w \times h}} \qquad (1)$$

- Cp : Pixel Colo r(R | G | B)
- S_{Cp} : RGB Standard deviation of whole key frame image

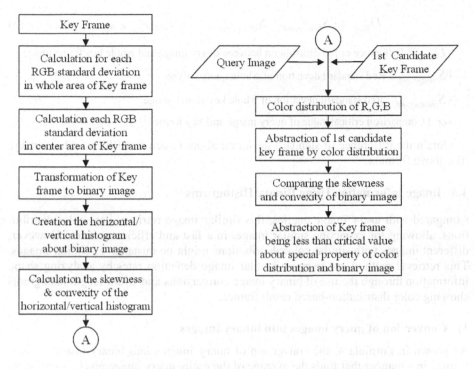

Fig. 2. Feature abstraction and similarity calculation procedure

- $Cp_{|i,j|}$: color value in I line j ranks in whole image

- $\overline{X}_{Cp}$: mean of color
- w : width of whole key frame image
- h : height of whole key frame image

For calculate color distribution in center area of key frame, calculate first about center area. Center area is the set of pixels on the first and the third quarter in whole image, independent from object position of image, image division for center area is like Equ. (2).

$$Center_{\_img} = Rect(\frac{Frame_{\_w}}{4}, \frac{Frame_{\_h}}{4}, \frac{Frame_{\_w}}{4}, \frac{Frame_{\_h}}{4} \times 3) \qquad (2)$$

The calculation of color distribution in center area follows the calculation formula of color distribution in whole area. Therefore, feature information of color distribution becomes RGB standard deviation of each whole area and each RGB standard deviation of center area.

Extracts the first similarity Key frame candidate group which the difference value of color is less than critical value by using below formula for find frame that have the most similar color distribution after comparing inputted query image to key frame stored in database. Obtain the difference of red color distribution between query image and whole key frame image like Equ. (3).

$$D_{Tred} = |\, S_{timage,red} - S_{tfframe,red} \,| \qquad (where, D_{tred} < \alpha) \tag{3}$$

- D_{Tred} : Difference of red distribution between query image and whole key frame image

- $S_{timage,red}$: Red standard deviation of whole query image

- $S_{tfframe,red}$: Red standard deviation of whole key frame image

- α : Comparison critical value of query image and key frame

Obtain the difference of standard deviation about Green and Blue of whole image like above formula.

4.3 Image Information Using Binary Histograms

Compared with users' image queries, this similar image retrieval uses color distributions, allowing for extracting similar images in a fast and efficient manner. However, different images with similar color distributions might be mistaken as similar images. This retrieval method can increase similar image detection rates by analyzing shape information through the use of binary image conversions and width-length histograms showing color distribution-based result frames.

1) Conversion of query images into binary images

As shown in Formula 4, the conversion of query images into binary images is performed in a manner that finds the average of the entire query image pixel and converts pixels whose values are below the average into black, while converting pixels whose values are above the average into white.

$$Binary_{-img}(x, y) = \begin{cases} 1, \; if \; (Frame(x, y) \geq \overline{X}) \\ 0, \; if \; otherwise \end{cases} \tag{4}$$

- $Binary_{-img}(x, y)$: Value of (x, y) pixels for binary images;

- $Frame(x, y)$: Value of (x, y) pixels for inputted frames;

- $\overline{X}$: Average of the entire pixel for inputted frames.

2) Calculation of skewness and kurtosis

A binary image displays white and black where white has a value of 1. Skewness and kurtosis can be calculated by drawing a histogram that has a frequency of the number 1 in width. The skewness of a width histogram can be calculated as in Equ. (5):

$$BF_{w\hat{a}_3} = \frac{F_{-w}}{(F_{-w} - 1)(F_{-w} - 2)} \sum_{i=1}^{F_{-w}} \frac{(H_{-wi} - \overline{X})^3}{S^3} \tag{5}$$

- $BF_{w\hat{a}_3}$: Skewness of a width histogram for binary images;

- F_{-w} : Length of the width of a binary image;

- H_{-wi} : Frequency of the ith column in the width histogram;

- S : Standard deviation of a binary image.

Formula 6 is used to calculate the skewness of a width histogram.

$$BF_{w\hat{\alpha}_4} = \frac{F_{-w}(F_{-w}-1)}{(F_{-w}-1)(F_{-w}-2)(F_{-w}-3)}\sum_{i=1}^{F_{-w}}\frac{(H_{-wi}-\overline{X})^4}{S^4} - \frac{3(F_{-w}-1)^2}{(F_{-w}-2)(F_{-w}-3)} \quad (6)$$

- $BF_{w\hat{\alpha}_4}$: Kurtosis of a width histogram for binary images;
- F_{-w} : Length of the width of a binary image;
- H_{-wi} : Frequency of the ith column in the width histogram;
- S : Standard deviation of a binary image.

5 Experiments and Evaluations

To assess the retrieval accuracy of the proposed system, user queries were performed over five hundred times. Fig. 3 shows the reproduction rate and retrieval accuracy of the proposed system.

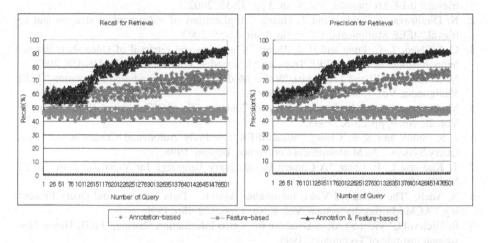

Fig. 3. The Reproduction Rate and Retrieval Accuracy of the Proposed System

As illustrated in Fig. 3, the proposed system shows high reproduction rates and retrieval accuracy. As the number of query languages increases, the retrieval accuracy of the proposed system increases because the agent learns query languages as well as it updates annotation information.

6 Conclusion

This paper proposes an infant's environment education system based on u-learning that supports two phase feature extract. In the case of the performance of annotation-based retrieval, the proposed system reduces keyword errors by the user using dependence weight values, allowing the user to make queries using more accurate and concrete keywords. In addition, in the case of feature-based retrieval, this system uses the skewness and kurtosis of a histogram as key frame image features through the use of binary image conversions. Therefore, user can get more correct retrieval result by agent's learning through repeated retrievals about video data for the environment education of infants. From experiment, the designed and implemented system shows increase of recall rate of about 1.5% and 2.0% as precision rate 94.2% for video data scene retrieval in performance assessment.

Acknowledgements

This subject is supported by Ministry of Environment as "The Eco-technopia 21 project".

References

1. N. Dimitrova, A. Zakhor, and T. Huang, "Applications of Video-content Analysis and Retrieval," IEEE Multimedia, Vol. 9 No. 3 pp. 42-55, 2002.
2. N. Dimitrova, A. Zakhor and T. Huang, "Applications of video-content analysis and retrieval," IEEE Multimedia, Vol. 9, No. 3, pp. 42-55, 2002.
3. C. W. Ngo, T. C. Pong and H. J. Zhang, "Clustering and retrieval of video shots through temporal slices analysis," IEEE Trans. on Multimedia, Vol.04, No.04, pp.446-458, 2002.
4. M. S. Kankanhalli and T. S. Chua, "Video Modeling using Strata-based Annotation," IEEE Multimedia, Vol. 7, No. 1, pp. 68-74, 2000.
5. M. Flickner, "Query by Image and Video Content : The QBIC system," IEEE Computer, Vol. 28, No. 9, pp. 23-32, 1995.
6. J. R. Smith and S. F. Chang, "VisualSEEK : A Fully Automated Content-based Image Query System," ACM Multimedia Conference, Boston, 1996.
7. T. Kuo and L. P. Chen, "A Content Based Query Language for Video Database," IEEE Multimedia, pp. 209-214, 1996.
8. S. Adali, "The Advanced Video Information System : Data Structure and Query Processing," ACM Multimedia System, Vol. 4, No. 4, pp. 172-186, 1996.
9. R. Hjelsvold, "VideoSTAR-A Database for Video Information Sharing," Ph.D. Thesis, Norwegian Institute of Technology, 1995.

Gradient Method for the Estimation of Travel Demand Using Traffic Counts on the Large Scale Network

Tae-Jun Ha[1], Seungjae Lee[2,*], Jonghyung Kim[3], and Chungwon Lee[4]

[1] Dept. of Civil Eng. Chonnam National Univ., Korea
tjha@chonnam.ac.kr
[2] Dept. of Transport. Eng, Univ. of Seoul, Korea
sjlee@uos.ac.kr
[3] Research Fellow, Incheon Development Institute, Korea
knight9@idi.re.kr
[4] Dept. of Transportation Eng, Univ. of Seoul, Korea
chungwon@uos.ac.kr

Abstract. In this study, the surveyed Trip Length Frequency Distribution (TLFD)is determined as a criterion for the reliability of evaluating the true O/D matrix. The surveyed TLFD can be used to check the similarity between the surveyed (true) Trip Length Distribution and the Trip Length Distribution of the estimated O/D matrix by the traffic counted models. When the surveyed TLFD is similar to the estimated TLFD, the reliability and correctness of the estimated O/D are high. Therefore, the objective of this paper is the development of the travel demand (O/D matrix) estimation using traffic counts on the large-scaled network. The Gradient Method is used for the model and the multi-class assignment technique is used for the equilibrium loading procedure in the model. This leads to the good guideline to the usage of the traffic count based O/D estimation in practice and gives a confidence to the transport planner. It is because the traffic counted O/D estimation models gives multiple solutions by its characteristics. In this paper we analyze the merits and demerits in each of a single-class based model and a multi-class based model in a large scale network. As a result, we have concluded that the multi-class based model has a closer value to the surveyed (true) TLFD than the TLFD of the estimated O/D matrix by the single-class based gradient method.

1 Introduction

The Origin and Destination (O-D) matrix is one of the most important elements in transportation planning process. The accuracy of the O-D matrix plays key roles in the transport planning process in order to make and evaluate various transport policies. However, due to the nature of the O-D matrix, which is the desired people's or freight's movements on urban and regional space, it is very difficult and costly to estimate the O-D matrix. Traditionally, transport planners survey the O-D movements in order to estimate the O-D matrix. Even though the cost of the O-D survey

---

* Corresponding Author.

T.-J. Cham et al. (Eds.): MMM 2007, LNCS 4352, Part II, pp. 599–605, 2007.
© Springer-Verlag Berlin Heidelberg 2007

requires high amounts of resources, the accuracy is relatively low. Even more, in the developing country, the transportation situation has changed very quickly and thus the transportation environment has been unstable. So the transportation planning should be frequently rectified according to the newly planned environment in order to capture the changed situation in the limited cost and time.

Until now, though most of the studies related to demand estimation method using traffic counts use methods based on single-class, travel demands or flows are made by mixing various classes in real networks.

In general, existing demand estimation methods based on traffic counts estimate O/D by converting a multi-class O/D matrix and traffic counts into a single-class O/D matrix and traffic counts through PCE conversion, and analyze a O/D matrix by dividing into a multi-class O/D matrix and traffic counts after multiplying an estimated O/D matrix by the fixed ratio of a single-class O/D matrix and traffic counts before PCE conversion. However, the merits of a demand estimation method based on multi-class calculate each route choice ratio about multi-class O/D, and maximize the estimation capability of multi-class by calculating each gradient, the reduction direction of objective function. Therefore, this study aims to establish a demand estimation method which considers congestion between class and class by using multi-class instead of single-class.

The main analysis direction of demand estimation methods based on traffic counts is to analyze the accuracy of estimation by using the method of error analysis. This has been conducted after comparing a basic O/D matrix with an estimated O/D matrix from a basically assumed demand in small-scaled and middle-scaled networks (see Lee and Kim, 2000). Such approaches are mainly used when we grasp the merits and demerits of models through observing the proposed models assuming true O/D matrix or true traffic counts which cannot be known in reality. However, though we are able to use such assumed network or true O/D investigating the application of models, it is nearly impossible to evaluate the reliability of estimated O/D in the case of real situations (large-scaled network). To solve these problems, we evaluated the reliability of the O/D matrix, which is estimated in a large-scaled network using TLFD (Trip Length Frequency Distribution). This is made by applying a multi-class based method which is proposed by this study to real data based on the personal trip survey of Seoul in 1996.

The result analyzed by multi-class based method has been similar to a surveyed TLFD, a true TLFD, in the TLFD analysis by zone. And, as a result of analyzing an observed traffic and an assigned traffic using chi-square method, it has been analyzed that the result of the multi-class based method has been superior to the result of the single-class based method. Therefore, the reason that the multi-class based method shows better results than the single-class based method is that the multi-class based method calculates congestion between vehicles and the rate of route choice by kinds of vehicles.

2 Related Work

Since the demand data cannot be observed directly, it must be collected by carrying out elaborate and expensive surveys, involving home or road based interviews or complicated number plate tagging schemes. By contrast, observed link volumes can be obtained easily either manually or automatically using mechanical or inductive counting devices. Thus, a considerable amount of research has been carried out to investigate the possibility of estimating or improving an origin-destination demand matrix with observed volumes on the links of the considered network. Many models have been proposed in the past such as Van Zuylen and Willumsen (1980), Van Vliet and Willumsen (1981), Nguyen (1982), Van Zuylen and Branston (1982) and Spiess (1987) among others. Most of these traditional approaches can be formulated as convex optimization problems in which the objective function corresponds to some distance function between a priori demand matrix and the resulting demand. The constraints are then used to force the assigned volumes to correspond to the observed volumes on the count post links.

Spiess(1990) proposed the gradient approach in order to estimate the O-D matrix using traffic counts. It is formulated as an optimization problem so as to minimize a measure of distance between observed and assigned volumes. The simplest function of this type is the square sum of the differences, which leads to the convex minimization problem. This is subject to the pseudo-function used to indicate the volumes resulting from an assignment of the demand matrix. The particular assignment model used must correspond to a convex optimization problem, in order for the objective function to be convex. Since the matrix estimation problem as formulated in the Spiess(1990) is highly underdetermined, it usually admits an infinite number of optimal solutions, i.e. possible demand matrices which all reflect the observed volumes equally well. In the actual planning context, we expect the resulting matrix to resemble as closely as possible the initial matrix, since it contains important structural information on the origin-destination movements. Therefore, just finding one solution to the problem in Spiess(1990) is clearly not enough. If we would have a solution algorithm which inherently finds a solution close to the starting point, we could leave the objective function as is. Fortunately, the gradient method, also called the method of steepest descent, has exactly this property that we look for. It follows always the direction of the largest yield with respect to minimizing the objective function and, thus, it also assures us not to deviate from the starting solution more than necessary. In order to implement the gradient method, we also need to provide values for the step lengths. Choosing very small values for the step length has the advantage of following more precisely the gradient path, but has the disadvantage of requiring more steps. On the other hand, when choosing too large values for the step length, the objective function can actually increase and the convergence of the algorithm would be lost. Thus, the optimal step length at a given demand can be found by solving the one-dimensional subproblem.

3   Multi-class Traffic Counts Based on Gradient Model

In this paper, the gradient model using multi class assignment is proposed. It is also formulated as an optimization problem like the single class assignment model. The objective function to be minimized is the square sum of the differences, which leads to the following convex minimization problem.

$$\min(t^m) = \frac{1}{2} \sum_{m \in M} \sum_{a \in A} (v_a^m - \bar{v}_a^m)^2$$

subject to

$$v_a^m \geq 0, \quad \forall a, m$$

$$c(\mathbf{v}^*)(\mathbf{v} - \mathbf{v}^*) \geq 0, \quad \forall \mathbf{v} \in \mathbf{V}$$

$$\sum_k f_{kw}^m = t_w^m, \quad \forall w, m$$

$$f_{kw}^m \geq 0, \quad \forall m, w, k$$

$$v_a = \sum_m \sum_w \sum_k f_{kw}^m \delta_{ak}^w, \quad \forall a$$

where,

$$\mathbf{v} = \sum_m v_a^m b_a^m$$

$$\mathbf{v}^* = \sum_m v_a^{*m} b_a^{*m}$$

$$\delta_{ka}^w = \begin{cases} 0 \text{ if } a \notin k \\ 1 \text{ if } a \in k \end{cases}$$

b_a^m : congestion weight of each class :

m : class :

t^m : matrix of each class :

v_a^m : assigned trip of class m in link a

$\bar{v}_a^m$: observed trip of class m in link a :

$c(\mathbf{v})$: cost function

4 Numerical Example

The comparison of the multi-class and the single-class gradient model has been conducted using Seoul City network, which has 1,020 zones, 6,357 nodes (including
1,020 centroids), 19,127 links (including dummy links). Using two models, we compare results based on cordonline and screenline data as well as observed traffic
counts.

The gradient method has been known that it has made the least changed base O-D
matrix. This means that the base O-D has been made in the base of the surveyed sample O-D and thus it has the surveyed TLFD information. If the base O-D has been
changed little, this means that the estimated O-D using the Gradient Method has much
information on the true people's or freight's movements. This leads to the good guideline to the usage of the traffic count based O-D estimation in practice and gives a
confidence to the transport planner. It is because the traffic counted O-D estimation
models gives multiple solutions by its characteristics.

Fig. 1. Seoul City Network

Like below Fig. 2, the surveyed TLFD is compared with each TLFD of the estimated O-D. It shows that the most similar distribution of the surveyed TLFD is from the multi class based model.

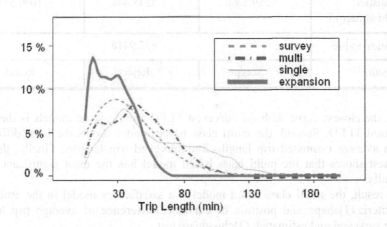

Fig. 2. Comparison of the Estimated TLFDs and the Surveyed TLFD

The calculated and the surveyed TLFD should exhibit the following two characteristics: (1) the shape and position of both curve should be relatively closed to one another when compared visually, and (2) the difference between the average trip lengths should be within 3%.

According to two criteria above, the multi class based TLFD can only be an accepted solution. Except this multi class based TLFD, the difference of average trip length between the surveyed and the estimated does not meet the mentioned criteria.

The chi-square test is implemented to test homogeneity of the result by comparison of the surveyed TLFD with the others. As you can see in the Table 2 below, statistically, the most significant TLFD is multi-class based TLFD.

Table 1. Comparison of trip lengths

	Average Travel Length (min)				Difference between average trip length (%)		
	① Survey	② Expansion	③ Single	④ Multi	Expansion (②-①/①)	Single (③-①/①)	Single (④-①/①)
Seoul	44.7	23.7	57.9	43.4	-47.0%	29.6%	-2.9%

Table 2. Comparison of the model by a Chi-Square Method

	Multi	Expansion	Single
Level of Significance	0.05		
Statistics (Chi-square)	519.2068	3245.449	1090.537
Critical value	632.9418		
Result	Accept	Reject	Reject

First, the closest curve with the surveyed TLFD among three models is the multi class based TLFD. Second, the multi class based model shows the least difference between average estimated trip lengths and surveyed trip lengths. Finally, the chi-square test shows that the multi class based model has the most significant result statistically.

As a result, the multi class based model is a satisfactory model in the aspects of three criteria:(1)shape and position of curve, (2)difference of average trip lengths between surveyed and estimated, (3)chi-square test.

5   Conclusion

In this paper the travel demand (O/D matrix) estimation model using traffic counts on the large-scaled network has been developed. The Gradient Method is used for the model and the multi-class assignment technique is used for the equilibrium loading procedure in the model. The Gradient method has been known that it has made the least changed base O/D matrix. This means that the base O/D has been made in the base of the surveyed sample O/D and thus it has the surveyed TLFD information. If the base O/D has been changed little, this means that the estimated O/D using the Gradient Method has much information on the true people's or freight's movements. This leads to the good guideline to the usage of the traffic count based O/D estimation in practice and gives a confidence to the transport planner. It is because the traffic counted O/D estimation models gives multiple solutions by its characteristics.

The surveyed TLFD is determined as a criterion for the reliability of evaluating the true O/D matrix. The surveyed TLFD can be used to check the similarity between the surveyed (true) Trip Length Distribution and the Trip Length Distribution of the estimated O/D matrix by the traffic counted models. When the surveyed TLFD is similar to the estimated TLFD, the reliability and correctness of the estimated O/D are high. Therefore, in this study, we analyzed the merits and demerits in each of a single-class based model and a multi-class based model in a large scale network. As a result, we have concluded that the multi-class based model has a closer value to the surveyed (true) TLFD than the TLFD of the estimated O/D matrix by the single-class based gradient method. Advantages of using the multiclass traffic counts based model are that the planners can estimate the O/D matrices for each class simultaneously and consider congestion effect between classes.

References

1. Nguyen, S. (1982). Estimating origin-destination matrices from observed volumes. Proceedings of the First Course on Transportation Planning Models of the International School of Transportation Planning, Amalfi, Italy, October 1982.
2. Spiess, H. (1990). A maximum likelihood model for estimating origin-destination matrices. Transpn. Res. B 21, 395-412.
3. Van Vliet, D. and Willumsen L.G. (1981). Validation of the ME2 model for estimating trip matrices from traffic counts Proceedings of The Eights International Symposium on Transportation and Traffic Theory, June 1981.
4. Van Zuylen, H.J. and Branston D.M. (1982). Consistent link flow estimation from counts. Transpn. Res. B 16, 473-476.
5. Van Zuylen, H.J. and Willumsen L.G. (1980). The most likely trip matrix estimated from traffic counts. Transpn. Res. B 14, 281-293.
6. Willumsen, L.G. (1984). Estimating time-dependent trip matrices from traffic counts. Ninth International Symposium on Transportation and Traffic Theory, VNU Science Press, 397-411.
7. Lee, S. and J. Kim(2000), Comparative study on the O/D estimation using Gradient method and Generalized Least Square method, Korea Society of Transportation

A New Distortion Correction Method for the Maps of Public Land of Korea

Dong-Hoon Jeong[1], Tae-Jun Ha[2], Byung-Guk Kim[3], and Je Jin Park[4]

[1] Senior Researcher, Korea Institute of Construction Technology, Korea
gisjeong@kict.re.kr
[2] Dept. of Civil Eng., Chonnam National University, Korea
tjha@chonnam.ac.kr
[3] Department of Geoinformatic Eng., Inha University, Korea
byungkim@Inha.ac.kr
[4] Research Associate, Korea Research Institute of Human Settlement, Korea
jjpark@krihs.re.kr

Abstract. There are about 800,000 map sheets for 36,500,000 parcels of land of Korea. They have been used for almost 100 years with the known problems of the shrinkage-expansion of the paper cadastral maps. The area of a parcel is recorded in a cadastre, and the maps are used just as a reference drawing for the location and the shape of the land. However, digitization of the maps began to reveal the problem of distortion of the map as the conflict between the areas on the cadastre and the digital maps was shown in numerical form. The distortion problem is tried to be resolved in this paper. Using the fact that original maps drawn on the plane tables in the years of 1910 to 1918 have grid lines and have been preserved well, a strategic flow was developed, which applies the refinement techniques to the digital maps with the original maps as controls. Several types of distortions and corrections were simulated, and errors between an error-free map and the distortion corrected map were evaluated. The RMS errors in the corrected digital maps were allowable, thus, the method developed in this study was applicable for the digital cadastral maps.

1 Introduction

The records for a parcel, by the laws, are the base proof of the property, whereas the maps for the parcels are just a reference to show the locations for registration, taxation, and transactions. The maps, however, are the basis for the parcel restoration.

One problem raised by the digitalization of the maps is that the area on the maps can be calculated easily because boundary points will be in coordinates, thus the discrepancies between records and maps can be exposed in public and also the statistics of the land by the records and by the maps do not coincide. The correction of the maps to compensate for the shrinkage-expansion of the map sheets has become more essential in digitalization.

A couple of algorithms to deal with the shrinkage-expansion problem on the digital maps (i.e., digitalized cadastral maps) have been presented and are being used but no satisfactory results have been obtained. One is to restore the four corner points of a

T.-J. Cham et al. (Eds.): MMM 2007, LNCS 4352, Part II, pp. 606–612, 2007.
© Springer-Verlag Berlin Heidelberg 2007

map sheet to the original dimension, and the other one is to divide a map sheet into 9 sub-regions (in 3*3 grid cells) and apply different scale factors to each sub-region. Both did not work well because of the irregularity of the distortions and the lack of the references for the scale factors for the sub-regions.

2 Proposed Methods for Shrinkage-Expansion Corrections

The Original Cadastral Maps (OCM) have been discovered in the National Record Preservation Facility. The OCM sheets were drawn by pencils on plans tables in field, and still have needle marks used in 1910~1918 for the alidade sighting. And also these OCM have fine nominal grid lines as a background.

The grid lines are in the dimensions of 30.303mm*30.303mm, which is one tenth of the Korean ancient unit of length. OCM are also distorted but the grid can be used as the references for the distortion correction as in the reseau grid plate method of photo coordinate refinement in photogrammetric works. The idea of this research is to use the grid lines of the OCM as control lines to correct the shrinkage-expansion distortion of the Digitized Cadastral Maps (DCMs). In this paper the term 'Paper Cadastral Maps (PCMs)' is used to separate the two different forms of maps. The paper cadastral maps are the ones being used today. The nodes and vertices, and lines appearing in the OCM are called the Original Nodes and Vertices (ON/OV) and the Original Lines (OL). The point where a line is bent is called a node and the point where two or more lines intersect is called a vertex. The public land in Korea has never been re-measured or re-drawn since the first surveying, that is, the OLs are still valid but, the parcels are divided or merged. The newly created nodes, vertices, and lines are called NN, NV, NL, respectively.

We do not know yet whether all the OCM exist for the 800,000 map sheets and all OCM have the grid lines. Thus, three types of correction methods are proposed: Type A - using grids on the OCM when OCM and the grid exist; Type B - using OCM when OCM exists but no grid is available; Type C - no OCM exists.

2.1 Type-A Correction

It is assumed in this Type-A correction that the OCM exists for the DCM sheet and the grid is available. The OCM's distortions are corrected by inversely applying the distortions for each and every grid cells. In this corrected OCM, the ON/OV/OL are also corrected. The nodes and vertices on the OCM are to be the reference points to correct the nodes and vertices on the DCM which is obtained by digitalization of the PCM. Table 1 shows the flow of the Type-A correction.

2.2 Type-B Correction

In Type-B correction, the assumption is that there exists the corresponding OCM for a PCM to be digitalized but grid lines do not exist or do not appear clearly. The idea is the same as in the Type-A correction, but an application of the local area grid transformation to the OCM using grid intersections is omitted. The flowchart of Type-B correction is shown in Table 2.

Table 1. Process of the Type-A Correction

Target Map	Step	Description
	1	Digitize 4 corner points, grid points and all the nodes and vertices(ON/OV)
	2	Calculate the coordinates of 4 corner points and grid points
For OCM	3	Apply 2D projective transformation to the corner points and grid points of OCM, then develop transformation equations
	4	Transform all observed points to nominal coordinate system using local area transformation (Referencing 4 corner points and grid points)
	5	Digitize 4 corner points, corresponding points to ON/OV and all other points
For DCM	6	Apply 2D projective transformation to the corner points of DCM
	7	Transform all observed points to nominal coordinate system using local area transformation (Referencing 4 corner points and ON/OV)

Table 2. Process of the Type-B Correction

Target Map	Step	Description
	1	Digitize 4 corner points and all the nodes and vertices(ON/OV)
	2	Calculate the coordinates of 4 corner points
For the OCM	3	Apply 2D projective transformation to the corner points of OCM
	4	Transform all observed points to nominal coordinate system with local area transformation (Referencing 4 corner points)
	5	Digitize 4 corner points, corresponding points to ON/OV and all other points
For the DCM	6	Apply 2D projective transformation to the corner points of DCM
	7	Transform all observed points to nominal coordinate system with use local area transformation (Referencing 4 corner points and ON/OV)

2.3 Type-C Correction

In Type-C correction, it is assumed that there is no OCM available. The only controls to be used are the four corner points of the nominal border lines. That is, the points on the DCM are transformed using 2D projective algorithm with the transformation parameters calculated by the four corner points of OCM and DCM. The Process of this type is described in Table 3.

Table 3. Process of the Type-C Correction

Target Map	Step	Description
	1	Digitize 4 corner points and all other points
For the DCM	2	Calculate the coordinates of 4 nominal corner points
	3	Transform observed points to nominal coordinate system using 2D projective transformation (Referencing 4 corner points)

3 Algorithms of the Local Area Transformation

A simple idea is adopted in the local area transformation to correct the coordinates of points. The nearer a control point is to a point, the heavier the control point's movement influence to the correction of the point. Inverse-distance-square-weighting. schema is tried, as shown in Equation 1.

$$\Delta x_a = \sum_{i=1}^{N} \left(w_i (\Delta x_i) \right) = \sum_{i=1}^{N} \frac{\dfrac{1}{(dx_i)^2}}{\displaystyle\sum_{j=1}^{N} \dfrac{1}{(dx_j)^2}} \Delta x_i$$

$$\Delta y_a = \sum_{i=1}^{N} \left(w_i (\Delta y_i) \right) = \sum_{i=1}^{N} \frac{\dfrac{1}{(dy_i)^2}}{\displaystyle\sum_{j=1}^{N} \dfrac{1}{(dy_j)^2}} \Delta y_i$$

(1)

N is the number of points used in the interpolation and d_i is the distance from the point to the ith fixed point. The sum of weight is 1. Where, Δx_a and Δy_a are the corrections for the target point ' a ' in x and y direction, respectively. dx_i and dy_i are x and y direction distance from the point ' a ' to the ith control point.

4 Simulation of the Local Area Transformation

A grid pattern is drawn using AutoCAD in the same size as the OCM(border rectangle and six cases of distortions are applied as shown in Figure 1.

The circles in Figure 1 are the control points. All the intersection points are distorted accordingly, and corrected by the local area transformation methods(inverse-distance-square weighting). The resulting coordinates of the non-control intersection points are compared to the originally generated ones. The RMS errors are tabulated in Table 4 for the six distortion cases and for the applied methods.

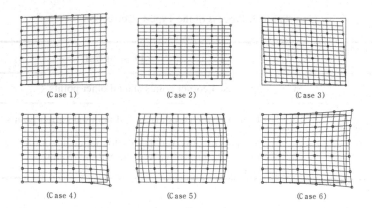

Fig. 1. Simulation of Distortions

Table 4. RMS Errors from Simulation

Distortion Case	RMSE (mm)	
	X	Y
Case 1	0.002	0.002
Case 2	0.003	0.000
Case 3	0.002	0.002
Case 4	0.281	0.264
Case 5	0.609	0.002
Case 6	0.588	0.190

From the figures in the Table 4, it can be assumed that the Inverse-distance-square-weighting is more adequate for this work than the other one. Case 2 and Case 3 would be perfectly restored by 2D projective transformation, if no random error of 0.1mm had been added. The local area transformation worked well for Case 1. For the irregular distortions as in the Cases 4, 5, and 6, the RMS errors in Y direction are about 0.2mm, which is tolerable in the cadastral works, but the RMS errors in X direction are about 0.6mm. The biggest RMS error happened on the target points along the borderline. For the borderline targets, it would be better if the targets were corrected only by the controls along the line. That is, the controls, not on the border line, adjacent to the targets made the corrections worse. Another way to deal with the points along the borderlines is needed.

5   Application of the Strategy on the Cadastral MAPS

A sample area in Taejeon-City is chosen to test the developed strategy for the distortion correction. This area is covered by four 1/600 digital cadastral maps. For the sake of evaluating the preciseness of the strategy, the OCMs for this area are generated using these DCMs (to have the true positions of the points) even though the real OCMs exist. The generated OCMs and the DCMs are distorted and random errors are added. Then the Type-A correction with the inverse-distance-square weighting method is applied.

5.1 Generation of the Distorted OCM and DCM

OCMs are preserved well under the stable temperature and humidity condition and have not been used often. Therefore, relatively small and well distributed distortions are introduced as follows:

> Map 1: case 1 distortion
> Map 2: case 2 distortion
> Map 3: case 3 distortion
> Map 4: case 5 distortion.

DCMs (digitized for the PCMs) are the ones being used for everyday public land registration and other services. Therefore, unpredictable distortions must have occurred on the maps, and thus, have to be applied for the simulation. The combined distortions in the order they are introduced to make the worst situation are as follows:

> Map 1: case 2 + case 1 + case 4 distortions
> Map 2: case 2 + case 5 distortions
> Map 3: case 4 + case 5 distortions
> Map 4: case 3 + case 1 + case 6 distortions.

5.2 Results

All the distorted points are corrected and the errors from the true positions are calculated. The RMS errors of each map are shown in Table 5.

Table 5. RMS Errors for Type-A Correction

Map	RMSE (mm)	
	X	Y
Map 1	0.090	0.095
Map 2	0.148	0.000
Map 3	0.158	0.114
Map 4	0.303	0.056

The Type-A correction produced a fairly good result, mostly within 0.2mm, a tolerable error, except in the x direction of the Map 4. This must have been caused by the ill-distribution of the control points (ON/OV) in the Map 4.

6 Conclusions

A new method was developed to deal with the distortion problem on the new digital cadastral maps. The fact that original maps drawn on the plane tables in field have been preserved well with grid lines encouraged us to apply the photo coordinate refinement technique, which are two dimensional projective transformation and local area transformation as in the reseau grid plate method. A computer program was implemented to accommodate several situations, such as, the presence or absence of the original maps and/or grid lines, and various scales and sizes of the original maps. Simulations of distortions and correction were performed on the generated grid sheets to test the local area transformation algorithm. Simulations on the cadastral maps showed fairly good results, mostly within the tolerance of 0.2mm.

It is thought, however, that the distortions in the new digital cadastral maps have to be corrected eventually and the proposed method would contribute to the accuracy of the maps.

Acknowledgement

This research was partly supported by INHA UNIVERSITY Research Grant. It was also supported by the MIC(Ministry of Information and Communication), Korea, under the ITRC(Information Technology Research Center) support program.

References

1. Charles F. Bowman : Algorithms And Data Structures An Approach In C, Oxford University Press.(1994)
2. David F. Watson : Contouring. A Guide To The Analysis And Display Of Spatial Data, Elsevier Science Inc., New York.(1992)
3. National Computerization Agency : A Building Work of Korea Comprehensive Land Information Systems, Seoul.(1994)
4. Paul R. Wolf, Charles D. Ghilani : Adjustment Computations, Statistics and Least squares in Surveying and GIS, John wiley & Sons Inc., New York.(1997)
5. Richard L. Burden, J. Douglas Faires : Numerical Analysis, Pacific Grove. Brooks/Cole Publishing Company.(1997)
6. Stephen C. Guptill And Joel L. Morrison : Elements of Spatial Data Quality, Pergamon, Oxford.(1995)
7. Tae-Seok Kang : Cadastral Surveying, Hyungseol Publishing Co., Seoul.(1994)

Establishment of Car Following Theory Based on Fuzzy-Based Sensitivity Parameters

Jaimu Won[1], Sooil Lee[2], Soobeom Lee[3], and Tae Ho Kim[4]

[1] Dept. of Urban Eng., Hanyang Univ., Seoul, Korea
drwon21@hanmail.net
[2] Dept. of Transportation Eng., University of Seoul, Seoul, Korea
sooillee@korea.com
[3] Dept. of Transportation Eng., University of Seoul, Seoul, Korea
mendota@uos.ac.kr
[4] Dept. of Urban Eng., Hanyang Univ., Seoul, Korea
traffix@hanmail.net

Abstract. Various traffic simulation programs have been developed, and the role of micro simulation increases recently, and the car following theory provides the theoretical background. However, current car following models apply the uniform driver factors regardless the characteristics of driver, vehicle and highway, then there exists a gap between the simulation result and real situation. This study is performed to derive the driver's sensitivity parameters which are even closer to the real. The fuzzy approximate reasoning can find the driver's sensitivity which varies by the traffic situation. Result shows better performance than the GM model. It means that the proposed driver's sensitivity parameters can represent the real situation better.

1 Introduction

The current studies on the car-following theory applies a uniform sensitivity parameter regardless the driver's decision making process, and it results in the gap between the result and the real situation. It is then necessary to derive the sensitivity parameters which can explain the driver's reaction under various situations. The CARSIM model applies various drivers' reaction times, but cannot verify the car-following behavior under various conditions. This paper is to overcome such the limitation of current model, and microscopic approach was made to analyze the traffic flow.

2 Fuzzy-Based Traffic Variables

2.1 Selection of Fuzzy-Based Traffic Variables

It was necessary to select the variables on traffic situation to derive the sensitivity parameters on driver's reaction. The fuzzy theory was applied because those variables are not quantitative. The processes were as following.

T.-J. Cham et al. (Eds.): MMM 2007, LNCS 4352, Part II, pp. 613–619, 2007.
© Springer-Verlag Berlin Heidelberg 2007

1) select the influencing factors to driver's reaction by preliminary survey
2) classify the perception level, and conduct 2nd survey for establishment of logical structure
3) establish the fuzzy approximate reasoning with the results of survey
4) defuzzify to quantify the result with the algorithm
5) derive defuzzified value (driver's reaction time) by the defuzzification

2.2 Establishment of Fuzzy-Based Traffic Variables

The fuzzy-based traffic condition variables were selected by two phases of survey. The first survey was on the characteristics of driver, vehicle, highway and the others.

Table 1. Contents of 1st Survey

Characteristics	Contents
Driver	gender, age, driving experience
Vehicle	make year, acceleration/deceleration ability, engine volume
Highway	# of lanes, traffic volume, geometric feature
Etc.	familiarity of roadway, time of driving, weather condition

As the result, the order of weight was weather condition, geometric feature, driving experience, familiarity of roadway and traffic volume, and the weather condition, driving experience and the traffic volumes were selected for the easiness of the application as the basic variable.

The second survey was then conducted to establish the input/output variables and the fuzzy logical relation, and presented in Table 2.

The fuzzy variables can be represented in either the continuous or discrete type, and the continuous type has the membership functions of bell or triangle shape. This

Table 2. Classification of Input/Output Variables

	Input/Output Variable		Fuzzy Term
Input Variable	Weather Condition (AP)	Visual Field is Good.	Good (GO)
		Visual Field is Fair.	Fair (ME)
		Visual Field is Bad.	Bad (BA)
	Driving Experience (EX)	Experience is Much.	Much (MA)
		Experience is in Average	Average (ME)
		Experience is Little.	Little (SM)
	Traffic Volume (VO)	Speed is Low.	Much (MA)
		Speed is Fair.	Fair (ME)
		Speed is High.	Little (SM)
Output Variable	Driver Reaction Time		Very Fast (VF)
			Fast (F)
			Average (M)
			Slow (S)
			Very Slow (VS)

study selected the triangular fuzzy variable type to represent the membership functions of the continuous fuzzy variable.

3 Car-Following Model Based on Fuzzy Traffic Variables

3.1 Establishment of Car-Following Theory by Change of Traffic Variables

In the establishment of the car-following theory corresponding to the traffic condition variables, the usable data can be acquired through the adjustment of the fuzzy approximate reasoning as following.

1) determine the membership function value of input/output variables, and the fuzzy logical relation
2) adjust the membership function of input/output variables with the survey result
3) finish the adjustment when the logical structure can explain the characteristics comparing with the observed value, otherwise adjust the fuzzy logical relation with the survey results and the observed value
4) finish the adjustment when the membership functions can explain the observed value, otherwise adjust the membership function of the input/output variable

Table 3. Determination of Input Variables

	Atmospheric Phenomena		Experience		Velocity (Valume)
Good	300~600m	Many	10~24	Many	20~50km/h
Medium	100~400m	Medium	3~15	Medium	40~80km/h
Bad	20~120m	Small	1~5	Small	70~140km/h

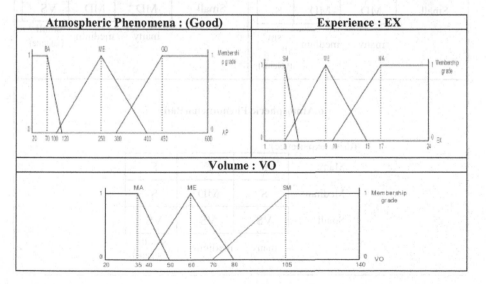

Fig. 1. Input Variables

Table 4. Determination of Output Variables

Classification	Establishment value
Very Fast	0.5sec ~ 0.8sec
Fast	0.6sec ~ 1.0sec
Medium	0.8sec ~ 1.5sec
Slow	1.2sec ~ 1.8sce
Very Slow	1.5sce ~ 2.0sec

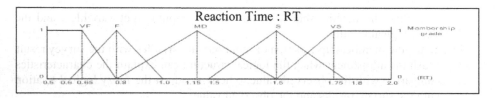

Fig. 2. Output Variables

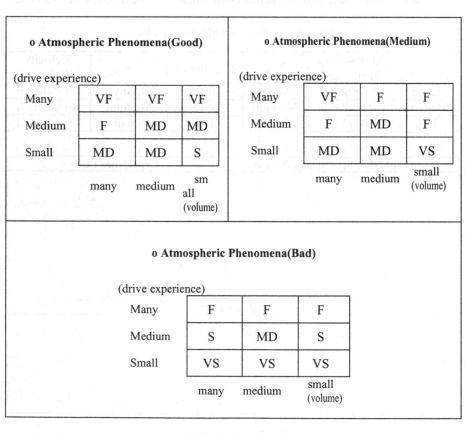

o **Atmospheric Phenomena(Good)**

(drive experience)

Many	VF	VF	VF
Medium	F	MD	MD
Small	MD	MD	S
	many	medium	small
			(volume)

o **Atmospheric Phenomena(Medium)**

(drive experience)

Many	VF	F	F
Medium	F	MD	F
Small	MD	MD	VS
	many	medium	small (volume)

o **Atmospheric Phenomena(Bad)**

(drive experience)

Many	F	F	F
Medium	S	MD	S
Small	VS	VS	VS
	many	medium	small (volume)

Fig. 3. Structure of Fuzzy Logical Relation

The result of the procedure above is shown in Table 3, Figure 1, Table 4 and Figure 2. The fuzzy logical relation is represented in Figure 3.

3.2 Establishment of Logical Relation for Fuzzy Control

The logical relation was composed in the form of "if-then"-basic concept of the fuzzy rule. This study then composed 27 (3x3x3) fuzzy rules.

(examples) Rule 1: if (AP is GO), (EX is MA) and (VO is MA) then (RT is VF)
            Rule 2: if (AP is GO), (EX is MA) and (VO is ME) then (RT is VF)
            Rule 3: if (AP is GO), (EX is MA) and (VO is SM) then (RT is VF)

4   Comparison with Current Model

The subject highway section was the uninterrupted flow facility influenced by the access roadways. On this section, the lane changing was relatively rare, and the accelerations and decelerations were frequent. The fluctuation of traffic volume was also large. The weather condition was good and the visual field was fixed to be 450m. For the traffic volume, all of three conditions were included. Three platoons were selected for each traffic conditions, and various operating types such as the constant speed, deceleration-acceleration and deceleration-constant speed- were observed.

The observed values from the field survey were compared with the results by scenario from the GM model and the proposed model. The model for scenario analysis was

$$x^{--n+1}(t+\Delta t) = a[x^{-n}(t) - x^{-n+1}(t)],$$

and the sensitivity parameter for driver in the GM model was the average value of 0.4. The sensitivity was derived by weather condition, traffic volume and driver's experience. When the traffic volume was heavy, the operating speed and acceleration rate were compared with the observed.

Table 5. Case Study (Traffic Volume: Heavy)

	Input Variable			Logical Relation	Output Variable	Sensitivity Parameter
	Traffic Volume	Weather Condition	Driving Experience		Reaction Time	
Veh. No. 2	28km/h	450m	6 yrs	Rule 4	1.15 sec	0.9
Veh. No. 3	27km/h	450m	2 yrs	Rule 7	1.50 sec	0.7

In order to quantify the performances of the models, the mean absolute percentage errors (MAPE) were measured as following

$$\text{MAPE} = \sum \frac{\left| observed - mod\ el\ result \right|}{observed} \times 100$$

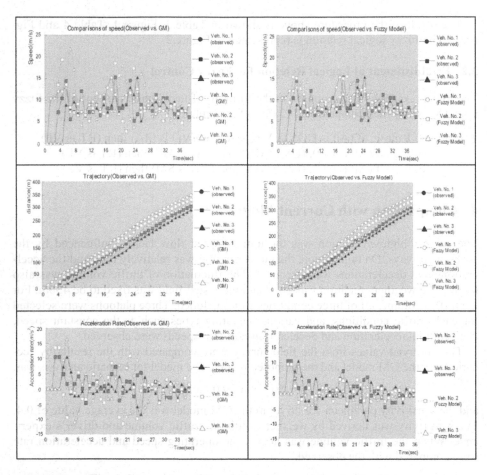

Fig. 4. Comparisons of Speed, Trajectory, and Acceleration Rate

Table 6. Result of MAPE

		Observed vs. GM Model		Observed vs. Fuzzy Model	
		Veh. No. 2	Veh. No. 3	Veh. No. 2	Veh. No. 3
Traffic Vol: Heavy	Speed	35.79%	37.21%	28.08%	26.19%
	Trajectory	14.62%	19.93%	11.98%	14.47%
Traffic Vol: Medium	Speed	37.44%	68.07%	26.82%	42.58%
	Trajectory	16.79%	22.06%	13.12%	21.89%
Traffic Vol: Low	Speed	29.31%	33.29%	19.04%	23.36%
	Trajectory	18.82%	18.89%	12.21%	9.85%

As shown in Table 6, the MAPE of the proposed fuzzy model is lower than the GM model in every aspect. It means the result from the fuzzy model is even closer to the observed value.

5 Conclusion

The sensitivity parameter of the car-following theory is essential for the traffic flow simulation model. This is dependent to various conditions, but current model has been applied an uniform value. This study provides the parameters based on the fuzzy approximate reasoning which shows better performance comparing with the other model. The extensive applications of the result may be expected in the development of traffic flow simulation model and the ITS. This paper may remain further efforts such that macroscopic approach should be conducted to overcome the limitation of microscopic approach. The extensive validation is also necessary to enhance the reliability of the observed values.

References

1. Chang, S.B., "Development of Expressway Incident Detection Model with the Artificial Neural Network", Ph.D. Dessertation, Seoul National University, 1997.
2. Son, K. B. , "Evaluation of Urban Rail Transit Route by Fuzzy Theory", M.S. Thesis, University of Seoul, 1994.
3. Korea Society of Transportation Research, "Development of Modal Choice Model with Fuzzy Approximate Reasoning", 1998.3.
4. TRB special report, "Traffic Flow Theory",1997.
5. May, A.D., "Traffic Flow Fundamentals",1990.
6. TRB special report, "Traffic Flow Theory",1975.
7. Lesort, J., "Transportation and Traffic Theory", 1996.
8. Zhang, X., and D. F. Jarret, "Stability Analysis of the Classical Car-Following Model", TRB vol 31, 1997

Development of Model for Highway Design Consistency Evaluation with Artificial Neural Network

Jeomho Lee[1] and Sooil Lee[2]

[1] Dept. of Safety Facility, Road Traffic Safety Authority, Korea
Jeomho60@hanmail.net
[2] Dept. of Transportation Eng., University of Seoul, Seoul, Korea
sooillee@korea.com

Abstract. This paper is to develop a model for evaluation of highway alignment design considering the drivers' behavior in order to enhance the highway safety. The vehicle spacing is suggested as a new evaluation index. The suggested model is based on the artificial neural network, which can explain the non-linear relationship on the highway geometric elements. The model shows better fitting comparing with the current regression models explaining only the linear relationship. It may be helpful to evaluate the safety of newly designed highway and safety improvement program for highways in-service.

1 Introduction

Current models for highway design evaluation are mainly based on the operating speed of individual vehicles, but it is required to improve the performance because the linear relationship between the speed and the geometric features on tangent segment. Most of current models are multi-linear regression models. It may cause the exclusion of independent variable which has low linearity, even though it may influence to the dependent variable. This study is to provide a new evaluation index which can consider the operating characteristics of vehicle platoon, and develop a model based on the neural network which can include the non-linear influences of geometric features.

2 Approach

The artificial neural network is applied in order to consider the non-linear relationship to the dependent variable. The artificial neural network model gets learning by experience and derives results by learning. It provides the result through the interaction between the units in the model and weight, whereas the other models generate the output with the parameters and variables. The learning process is classified into supervised and non-supervised learning by whether the intended values are given or not. In this paper, the supervised learning is suitable which can provide the vehicle spacing as the objective pattern of the neural network. The multilayered neural network is proposed considering the learning of the objective pattern. The learning is based on the multilayer structure and backpropagation algorithm which generates output as the

T.-J. Cham et al. (Eds.): MMM 2007, LNCS 4352, Part II, pp. 620–626, 2007.

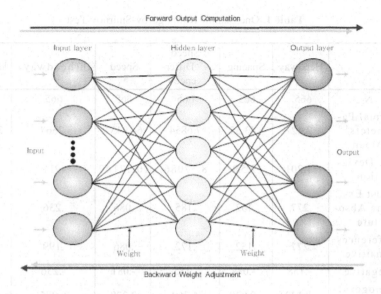

Fig. 1. Multi-Level Backpropagation Neural Network

objective pattern provides by reducing the errors of output pattern adapting the gradient descent method.

In addition, regression model is also developed with the independent variables of geometric elements and dependent variable of vehicle spacing.

3   Data Collection

One section of rural highway was selected to collect the data for the development of the model which represents the change of vehicle spacing in the platoon by the geometric features. The spacing is much influenced by the driver's characteristics, then a single unit of highway segment includes both of the tangent and the horizontal curve and a certain vehicle was observed to minimize the driver factor. The out layers in the data were eliminated with the Median Absolute Deviation (MAD) which can minimize the amount of elimination.

$$MAD = 1.4826 \text{ x } \| x_i - x_{med} \|$$
where, x_i = observed value of x,
x_{med} = median of x, and
1.4826 = correction factor to adjust MAD to be same as the standard deviation in normal distribution.

The first process was to verify the variables for which the statistical analysis for parameter is possible. When the headway was in less than six seconds, it was regarded as in a platoon and the normality was examined as following.

Table 1. One-Sample Kolmogorov-Smirnov Test

	Headway	Spacing	Speed Differ-ence	Speed	ln(headway)	ln(spacing)
N	665	665	665	665	665	665
Normal Parameters[a,b] Mean	2.42	43.55	7.6854	64.9453	.7667	3.6461
Std. Deviation	1.201	22579	8.57086	10.12142	.49115	.51158
Most Extreme Absolute	.277	.152	.185	.086	.236	.082
Differences Positive	.277	.152	.172	.086	.199	.070
Negative	-.158	-.084	-.185	-.081	-.236	-.082
Kolmogorov-Smirnov Z	7.132	2.930	4.769	2.228	6.085	1.510
Asymp. Sig.(2-tailed)	.000	.057	.000	.000	.000	.132

/*a. Test distribution is Normal, b. Calculated from data */

The hypothesis is

H_0 : The platoon represents the normal distribution, and
H_1 : The platoon represents not the normal distribution.

In a platoon, only the spacing represents the normal distribution. It is regarded to be possible to perform the parameter analysis by transforming the variable to the natural log.

4 Evaluation Model

The vehicle-to-vehicle accidents occupy more portion than the single vehicle accident, so that the design evaluation based on the individual vehicle may not be desirable. The drivers tend to keep the operating speed when they are not interrupted by the front vehicle. When the drivers follow the front vehicle, they keep the spaces from the front vehicle rather than speed. It means the vehicle spacing may be the index for the evaluation of the consistency of highway alignment considering the drivers' operating characteristics. The spacing evaluation models are separately developed for the tangent and horizontal curve segments.

4.1 Tangent Segment

The model for tangent includes the effects of geometric elements such as spacing (spacing mean; SM), vertical grade, lane width, and shoulder width as following.

$$y = 8.89 + 7.08 \ln(x) \quad (R^2=0.479)$$

where,   y = vehicle spacing (SM), and
         x = length of tangent.

According to the regression model, the fitting was 0.479 and only the length of tangent is significant.

The fitting of neural network model showed 0.702, and the most of geometric elements were to be significant.

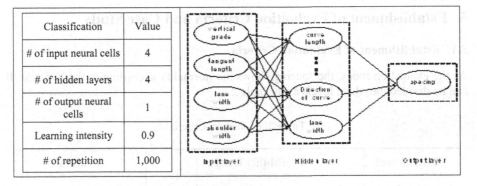

Classification	Value
# of input neural cells	4
# of hidden layers	4
# of output neural cells	1
Learning intensity	0.9
# of repetition	1,000

Fig. 2. Learning Process and Structure of Neural Network (Tangent Segment)

4.2 Horizontal Curve Segment

The model for horizontal curve segment includes the geometric elements such as spacing, vertical grade, radius, curve length, direction of curve, lane width, shoulder width, and superelevation.

In the regression model, the fitting was 0.558 and the radius was to be notably significant. On a curve segment, the drivers are influenced by both of the vertical grade and the curve radius interactively. In addition, the direction of curve could be included as the independent variable.

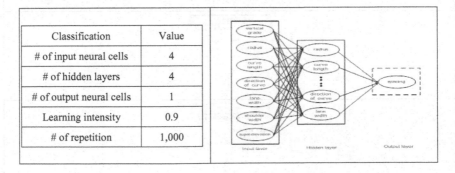

Classification	Value
# of input neural cells	4
# of hidden layers	4
# of output neural cells	1
Learning intensity	0.9
# of repetition	1,000

Fig. 3. Learning Process and Structure of Neural Network (Horizontal Curve Segment)

$$y = 17.12 + 4.82 \ln(x_1) + 0.884 x_2 - 2.275 x_3 \ (R^2 = 0.558)$$

where, y = spacing mean,
        x_1 = radius of horizontal curve,
        x_2 = vertical grade, and
        x_3 = direction of curve (0: left, 1: right).

The neural network model showed better fitting than the regression model, and the most of geometric elements were included.

5   Establishment of Evaluation Criteria and Case Study

5.1   Establishment of Evaluation Criteria

As the evaluation index, the spacing shows the normality according to the K-S test. It can be divided into three levels as in Table 2.

Table 2. Evaluation Criteria

Design Level	Probability Range	Criteria
Good	above (mean - standard deviation)	$\Delta SM \angle 4m$
Fair	(mean ± standard deviation)	$4m \leq \Delta SM \angle 12m$
poor	below (mean + standard deviation)	$12m \leq \Delta SM$

/* ΔSM : (SM for n-th segment) - (SM for (n+1)-th segment) */

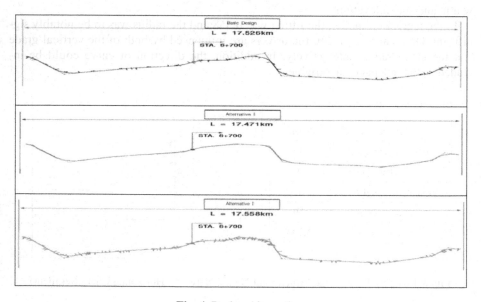

Fig. 4. Design Alternatives

5.2 Case Study

The case study was conducted with a section of four lane rural highway. There has been the basic design, and two alternatives are developed.

The result of comparison is presented for each of the alternative from the current individual vehicle based model(ΔV85) and the proposed spacing change in platoon (ΔSM) based model.

According to the results, the proposed model shows that the alternative I is the best, whereas the results from the current model cannot present the difference by the alternatives. The alternative I has was evaluated to be the best by the qualitative review by the highway safety experts.

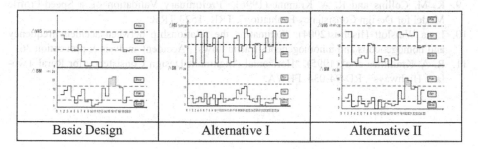

| Basic Design | Alternative I | Alternative II |

Fig. 5. Profile from Evaluation

6 Conclusion

In highway safety program, the crucial issue is the limitation in the measurement of safety performance of highway. This study focused on the development of a methodology for highway safety performance evaluation based on the alignment design consistency. It proposed the vehicle spacing in platoon as the evaluation index.

A neural network model was then developed with the data collected on a highway section. It can overcome the limitation of current model only based on the linear relationship. The proposed model can include the variables which have non-linear relationship. As the result, the proposed model shows better performance that the current one.

This paper still requires further studies on the connecting point of tangent and horizontal curve where the design inconsistency occurs easily, and three dimensional approach (both of vertical and horizontal alignments interactively) to consider the driver's operating characteristics.

References

1. Helmut T. Zwahlen(1993), Optimal Application and Placement of Roadside Reflective Devices for Curves on Two-Lane Rural Highways, FHWA/OH-94/011, Industrial and Systems Engineering of Ohio University, Ohio DOT.
2. Kataja Vogel(2003), "A comparison of headway and time to collision as safety indicators", Accident analysis & prevention 35.

3. Katja Vogel(2002), "What characterizes a "free vehicle" in an urban area?", Transpotation research part F 5.
4. R. Lamm et. al.(1998), "Recommendations for Evaluating Horizontal Design Consistency Based on Investigations in the States of the New York", TRR 1122, TRB.
5. R. Lamm et. al.(1999), Highway Design and Traffic Safety Engineering Handbook, Mcgraw-hill.
6. Sirpa Rajalin(1997), "Close-Following Drivers on two-lane highways", Accident analysis & prevention 29.
7. Bradley Efron & Robert J. Tibshirani(1993), "An Introduction to the Bootstrap", Chapman & Hall.
8. E. Hauer(1997), "Observational Before-After Studies in Road Safety": Estimating the Effect of Highway and Traffic Engineering Measures on Road Safety, Pergamon.
9. K. M. Collins and R. A. Krammes(1996), "Preliminary Validation of a Speed-Profile Model for Design Consistency Evaluation", TRR 1523,TRB.
10. Lena Winslott Hiselius(2004), "Estimating the relationship between accident frequency and homogeneous and inhomogeneous traffic flows", Accident analysis & prevention 36.
11. R. A. Krammes et al.(1995), "Horizontal Alignment Design Consistency for Rural Two-lane Highways", RD-94-034, FHWA.

Conversion Mechanism for MPEG-4 Contents Services on Web Environment

Hee-Sun Kim and Dae-Jea Cho

Division of Electronics & information Industrial Engineering, Andong National University
388 Songchon-Dong, Andong, 760-749, Korea
{hskim, djcho}@andong.ac.kr

Abstract. This paper is on the design and development of a conversion mechanism for MPEG-4 contents services on Web environment. The service was provided on Web environment first by parsing the MPEG-4 contents, then converting them to SMIL. After the two-dimensional profile of the MPEG-4 XMT and SMIL schemes was analyzed, the correlation among the nodes with the same or similar meanings was set as a rule. With the defined rule, an XSL document was created, and XMT was converted to SMIL using the converted XSL document and XSLT, which was derived from MSXML. Moreover, the two-dimensional geometric object that cannot be expressed in SMIL was authored in SVG to add SMIL media characters. Its advantage is that it services current MPEG-4 contents in various environments such as the Web or mobile environments, and it can be converted to service more playable environments if one knows the syntax definition of other scene description languages.

Keywords: MPEG-4 Contents, XMT, SMIL, Conversion Mechanism.

1 Introduction

MPEG-4 contents[1] use a scene description language called BIFS(Binary Format for Scene) to express the multimedia scene more effectively. BIFS was selected as a standard technology format for graphic data and interactive contents for DMB(Digital Multimedia Broadcasting). BIFS is a binary format and can express audio/visual objects, spatiotemporal information, and event information. It is difficult to adapt BIFS in limited environments such as the Web or mobile device, though. With a stimulated DMB service, it becomes very important to service rich interactive media in various environments, and to conduct a study that would enable MPEG-4 contents to be played on the Web and mobile environments.

This study is meaningful in the sense that already created contents in standard formats can be reused, and in the advantage of playing existing contents on a variety of environments that users already have. Therefore, this paper suggests a method of converting MPEG-4 contents to make them serviceable on Web environment.

The study on playing MPEG-4 in various environments includes XMT(eXtensible MPEG-4 Textual format)[2,3] creation and methods of converting XMT to BIFS. XMT is a textual format of MPEG-4 BIFS, and is defined to play MPEG-4 contents in various environments. XMT is an XML-based language and defines XMT-A and

T.-J. Cham et al. (Eds.): MMM 2007, LNCS 4352, Part II, pp. 627–634, 2007.

XMT-Ω. XMT-A corresponds to the BIFS structure, and is similar to X3D. XMT-Ω is a higher-level description language and is authored based on SMIL[4]. There is an authoring tool that was developed by IBM following the study on converting XMT-A to BIFS[5]. It is a two-dimensional scene authoring tool that creates XMT alpha and omega through various GUIs, which create XMT and convert XMT-A to BIFS. XMT-related studies focus on generating an audio/visual scene, such as XMT-A and XMT-Ω, converting the alpha format to the omega format, or encoding the alpha format to BIFS. As such, it does not support playback in various environments.

Therefore, this paper suggests the design and development of a conversion technology for servicing existing MPEG-4 contents that have already been developed on Web environment. Therefore, this paper deals with the design and development of a conversion method for servicing existing MPEG-4 contents on Web environment. XMT, a textual format of MPEG-4 contents, is converted to SMIL to service Web-environment-adjustable contents. With comparing the XMT node with the SMIL node, the corresponding node was directly converted, and a conversion method for the no corresponding or no supported node was suggested. Module conversion was allowed in XML-based file conversion by authoring an XSL[6] file called xmto2smil.xsl. The XSL document that was authored according to defined rules converts the XMT omega format to SMIL using the XSLT engine provided by MSXML of Microsoft Corporation.

Chapter 2 of this study describes the implementation of the SMIL MPEG-4 content conversion method for Web environment. Chapter 3 describes how an MPEG-4 converter is developed, Chapter 4 shows the development outcome, and Chapter 5 states the conclusion.

2 MPEG-4 Content's SMIL Conversion Method for Web Environment

To convert an MPEG-4 scene description to SMIL, an analysis of two documents--before and after conversion--is required. After the analysis, the correlation pattern among the nodes with the same or similar meanings is defined as a rule. With the defined rule, the XSL document is created automatically.

2.1 Conversion Method of Audio/Visual Objects

Because SMIL does not support all the media objects used in the XMT-Ω profile, the SVG file for the geographic object should be created before converting it to SMIL. It can be converted easily for image, audio, and video outputs without any additional operation except for location information conversion. The two-dimensional geometric object input requires other methods, though. It can be converted through the XSL document to create an SVG[7] file, but since Microsoft's MSXSL does not support conversion and creation of documents at the same time, it can be a problem. Therefore, the geometric object is created as an SVG file by programming this in the conversion. The created SVG file is indicated as an 'src' property in the tag of the SMIL file.

SVG is being developed as a standard for indicating vector data such as lines or polygons, with images and letters, on the Web. 2D geometric object expression of XMT in SMIL is created as SVG, with the definition as follows:

1) Rectangle Object Expression

A property that expresses a rectangle in SVG is referred to as <rect>. Properties that express <rect> are 'x' and 'y,' which indicate the starting point, and 'width' and 'height,' which indicate the length, width and height. The properties of 'width' and 'height' can be replaced by the 'size' property of the <transformation> node, a child node of XMT's <rectangle> node. S(w, h), the whole size of SVG, which expresses the rectangle object, is determined by the size of the height and width of the <outline> node, and is expressed as follows:

S(w,h)=(transformation.size[0]+outline.width, transformation.size[1] + outline.width)

'Transformation.size[0]' refers to the first vector value of the <transformation> node's 'size' property. 'Transformation.size[1]' refers to the second vector value of the <transformation> node's 'size' property. 'Outline.width' refers to the 'width' property of the <outline> node, the lower node of the <rectangle> node of XMT. The 'w' value of the whole-size S is the width of the whole media object's width, which is the sum of the <rectangle> width and the <outline> node width because the <rectangle> width increased by as much as half of the <outline> node's width towards the left and right. The height of S, or 'h', can be calculated in the same way.

2) Circle Object Expression

The <circle> node's factors are 'radius' and 'scale' in XMT. The 'radius' value shows the radius width of the shorter axis in an ellipse. Two values of the 'scale' are shown, and the longer axis's ratio is defined when the radius of the shorter axis is defined as one (1). Whereas <ellipse> is expressed as 'C(cx, cy),' the central coordinate, and R(rx, ry), the radius of the x and y axes. S(w, h), the whole size of SVG, is set with the 'width' property and the 'height' property of the <circle> node, and the 'width' property of the <outline> node influences the whole size of SVG, as follows:

S(w,h)= (2x(radius x scale[0] + outline.width), 2x(radius x scale[1] + outline.width))

3) Line Object Expression

The definition of <lines> can be drawn by defining a starting point and an ending point. If the starting point is P(x1, y1) and the ending point is Q(x2, y2), P defines the x, y coordinate value of the starting point and Q defines not only the x, y coordinate value but also the size. To express the <lines> of an XMT object, SVG uses the <polyline> node. To express the XMT object's <lines>, SVG uses the <polyline> node. <polyline> is a set of linked straight lines, and is defined by identifying the list of dots that compose straight lines. The 'point' property is expressed as follows:

Points = List of points (e.g.: point = "180, 75 209, 161")

4) Text Object Expression

The text-related nodes in XMT are <text> and <string>. The <text> node uses the 'src' property and includes character string information, which is against the media node <text> in SMIL and is a format that directly includes the character string in a tag rather than using the 'src' property. The text-related tags that are used in SMIL are

<text> and <textstream>. XMT supports both properties of 'valign' and 'halign,' but SMIL allows the use of either 'valign' or 'halign.' Therefore, the text height is limited to as high as the text height and to the use of 'halign,' and must not make differences in presentation without using 'valign.'

5) Image Expression
The image property is used in almost the same manner in XMT and SMIL. SMIL, however, requires image size information to express image location information for outputs, unlike XMT. Therefore, input image size information as a custom property.

6) Expression of Video and Audio Outputs
XMT supports H.263 and SMIL supports normal video formats such as AVI. XMT supports the AAC audio format, and SMIL supports general audio formats such as MID. The <video> node requires presentation of the location information on the display in SMIL. Therefore, video size information must be inputted as a custom property in authoring XMT.

7) Group Expression
To play the time information of various objects in a group at the same time, it was converted into the <par> node in SMIL.

2.2 Expression of Object's Location

In SMIL, a separate node is defined to express media location information. If there is no address information on the media object's location, it basically locates the center or left bottom of the display, depending on the media. Information on the size of the scene to be presented and the media object's location is expressed as the <layout> node, the <region> node, and the lower node of the <head> node.

The lower nodes of <layout> are <region> and <topLayout> in XMT and <topLayout> in SMIL, but the latter has a different meaning so it can be replaced by <root-layout> playing due to its similar role. <topLayout> in SMIL pops up a new window. If the <region> node value is not defined in XMT, information on the nodes' locations, recognized through the parsing process, should be defined in the header. One <region> should be defined with the information on the extracted regions' sizes, which should be maintained separately by node and location information in the <transformation> node. The coordinate system used in XMT and SMIL differs when it is converted. The coordinate system of XMT defines the center C(0 , 0), so the lower and left regions of point C are negative, whereas the coordinate system in SMIL defines the left top C'(0 , 0), so the value increases as the point moves towards the right and bottom.

2.3 Setting Events Between Media Objects

Events that are able to set XMT are <animate>, <animateColor>, <animateMotion>, and <set>, as with SMIL. A <set> event expresses the change of a property of an object, and includes both 'setMotion' and 'setColor.' The 'setMotion' event indicates the object's movement or change of size, and 'setColor' indicates the object. In

SMIL, the <set> event that changes the proper value is used more often than the 'setMotion' and 'setColor' events in SMIL. XMT can be replaced with event definition with geometric object event inputs that can be expressed in SML itself.

3   MPEG-4 Content Converter Supporting Web Environment

With the conversion method described in Chapter 2, a system for converting from XMT to SMIL was designed and developed. The structure of the MPEG-4 contents creator and the converter is composed of a user interface, a scene tree manager, an MPEG-4 BIFS/XMT generator, an MPEG-4 stream generator, a file converter, and a multimedia file creator. An MPEG-4 BIFS/XMT file-creating module creates two file formats--BIFS/XMT-A and XMT-Ω. To convert the generated MPEG-4 content so as to make it playable on Web environment, it must be parsed through the MPEG-4 BIFS/XMT parser to create a DOM tree. The parsed XMT DOM tree is converted into an SMIL DOM tree by the XSLT engine. The multimedia file generator creates the SMIL file.

Figure 1 shows the process of conversion coding of XMT-Ω to SMIL. An MPEG-4 BIFS/XMT file is created as an XMT DOM tree by the parser. By entering the generated XMT DOM tree and the defined XSL file for conversion, it is converted into a SMIL DOM tree by the XSLT converter. The XSL file is used or authored with the SMIL 2.0 schema as a standard and creates the conversion rule as a reference. The generated SMIL DOM tree is recorded as an XSL file and adapted to Web environment. The authored XSL file is a language that describes the method of conversion of the XMT-Ω file to SMIL. Actually, the conversion rule mentioned in Chapter 2 was authored by this file. The XSL file can be divided into two parts—the authoring SMIL's Head and Body.

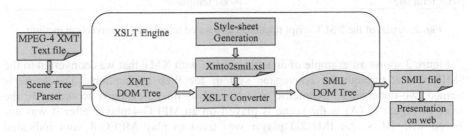

Fig. 1. The process of conversion coding of XMT-Ω to SMIL

The head part describes the focus scene's size and background color, the layout information that the authors will display, the location of the objects, the transition information, the meta information, and the switch-related processing information method, whereas the body part authors the conversion rules on the to-be-displayed object information. The authored XSL file is composed of a few templates. Conversion of objects or modules is possible by adapting the respective templates out of the root template.

4 Development Results

The MPEG-4 conversion system described in this study was developed using Visual C++ 6.0 under the MS-Windows operating system. As a parser and XSLT/Xpath processor, MSXML, which is composed of Microsoft's COM(Component Object Model), was used. Figure 2 defines the traits of the nodes that were actually convertible as part of the XSLT script document authored based on the conversion method defined in Chapter 2. It was composed as a template unit, and the authors' respective nodes in the templates and traits.

```
<xsl:template match="/">                          <!-- body -->
<xsl:apply-templates select="XMT-O">             <xsl:template match="body">
</xsl:template>                                   <body>
 <xsl:template match="XMT-O">                      <xsl:apply-templates mode="body"/>
<smil>                                            </body>
<xsl:apply-templates select="head"/>             </xsl:template>
 <xsl:apply-templates select="body"/>
</smil>                                           <xsl:template match="string" mode="region">
</xsl:template>                                    <xsl:if test="not(region) ">
                                                  <region>
<!-- head -->                                     <xsl:variable name="ty">
<xsl:template match="head">                       <xsl:value-of select=number
<head>                                            ("//XMT-O/head/topLayout/@height")/>
<xsl:apply-templates select="layout"/>           </xsl:variable>
</head>                                            <xsl:variable name="tx">
</xsl:template>                                    <xsl:value-of select=number
 <xsl:template match="layout">                     ("//XMT-O/head/topLayout/@width")/>
<layout>                                           </xsl:variable>
<xsl:apply-template select="root-layout"/>        <xsl:attribute name="id">
<xsl:for-each selelct="//XMT-O/body">             <xsl:value-of select="id"/>_region
 <xsl:if test="not(region) ">                      </xsl:attribute>
  <xsl:apply-template mode="region"/>             <xsl:attribute name="top">
 </xsl:if>                                          </xsl:attribute>
</xsl:for-each>                                     </region>
</layout>                                          </xsl:if>
</xsl:template> ...                               </xsl:template> ...
```

Fig. 2. A part of the XSLT script document generated based on the conversion method

Figure 3 shows an example of an authored file with XMT that was converted to the SMIL format through the conversion system for Web applications. The scene is formed two-dimensional geometric objects, and its image changed according to the time. In Figure 3, (A) is the scene is played on an MPEG-4 player after it was authored with BIFS. An IM1-2D player was used to play MPEG-4, and indicated changes in the scene as time passed. (B) shows the scene in which the parsed MPEG-4 content was played to create an XMT DOM tree, after which it was converted to SMIL and played with an SMIL player. RealOne player, which supports the SMIL + SVG profile, was used as the SMIL player for decoding the geometric object. Adobe SVG Viewer 3.0 was plugged into the RealOne player to view the SVG file.

XMT is composed of 10 modules and has a total of 76 nodes, whereas SMIL is composed of 10 modules and has 71 nodes. Table 1 shows the number of SMIL nodes correspond before applying converting mechanism on XMT nodes of each module and the number of SMIL nodes converted after applying it.

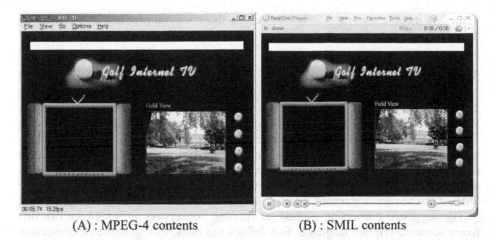

(A) : MPEG-4 contents   (B) : SMIL contents

Fig. 3. (A) is the scene is played on an MPEG-4 player after it was authored with BIFS. (B) shows the scene converted to SMIL.

Table 1. The number of convertible nodes of SMIL after applying the proposed converting mechanism

Module	(a) The number of XMT nodes (2D Profile)	(b) The number of SMIL nodes	(c) The number of convertible nodes of SMIL
M1 : Media	27	9	23
M2 : Macro	8	0	8
M3 : Structure	4	3	4
M4 : Linking	1	3	1
M5 : Transition	3	2	3
M6 : Content	4	4	4
M7 : Layout	3	5	3
M8 : Animate	8	4	8
M9 : Timing	3	4	3
M10 : Meta	2	2	2

As shown in table 1, the number of nodes differs significantly with modules M1 and M2. 'Media' module M1 differs much, however, because SMIL do not support geometric objects, and the M2 'macro' module is not used frequently so it rarely influences the node conversion authored in the 2D. The XMT node shown in (a) of table 1 indicates the rest of the nodes by module among the XMT nodes, except for the nodes for expressing 3D, and number of nodes that were converted to SMIL. The (b) is the number of SMIL nodes correspond before applying converting mechanism on XMT nodes of each module. After adapting various methods, i.e., changing names using the conversion rule or inserting them as properties, the conversion varied, as shown in (c) of table 1. It can be seen that SMIL node conversion to XMT nodes, except for the M1 module, were perfectly implemented. There were a few unconverted nodes due to the nodes for converting the XMT omega mode to the alpha mode in the M1 module, i.e., the Media module, but there was no problem in guaranteeing the converted content's semantics.

5 Conclusion

This paper suggests a conversion method for existing MPEG-4 contents services in a Web environment. The suggested conversion method converts MPEG XMT to SMIL, then provides an MPEG-4 contents service. XMT-Ω and SMIL are first compared by node, after which a conversion method for the part that does not have correspondent nodes is suggested. The XMT-Ω file is converted to SMIL by an XSMT engine and the defined XSL file for conversion. The XSL file used at that time is authored with the SMIL 2.0 schema as a standard, and designed to create conversion rules as references.

The suggested conversion method for creating conversion rules between two different scene description languages first defines the rules, then generates a conversion script according to the defined rules. It is advantageous in that it ensures the expression of existing MPEG-4 contents in various environments such as the Web or mobile environments. Moreover, to ensure as many playing environments as possible, the syntax definition of other scene description languages must be known.

References

1. ISO/IEC 14496-1:2000 MPEG-4 Systems October 2000
2. H.Kim, "An XMT Authoring System supporting Various Presentation Environments," Lecture Notes in Computer Science 3331, Springer-Verlag Heidelberg, pp.453-460, 2004.
3. ISO/IEC JTC1/SC29/WG11/N4091, Study of ISO/IEC 14496-1:2001/PDAM2:Extensible MPEG-4 Textual Format(XMT), March 2001
4. World Wide Web Consortium, Synchronized Media Integration Language (SMIL 2.0), http://www.w3.org/TR/smil20/
5. http://www.research.ibm.com/mpeg4/indexjs.htm
6. XSLT 2nd Edition, Programmer's Reference by Michael Kay
7. Scalable Vector Graphics (SVG) 1.1 Specification, W3C Recommendation, http://www.w3.org/TR/SVG11/ REC -smil, 2003

P2P Multimedia Sharing over MANET*

Wu Huafeng[1,2], Han Peng[2], Zhou Qiang[2], Yang Min[2], Sun Bing[2], and Yu Bo[2]

[1] Shanghai Maritime University
Shanghai, 200135, China
[2] Department of Computer Science and Engineering, Fudan University
Shanghai, 200433, China
{wuhuafeng,041021070,zhouqiang,m_yang,sunbing,
yubo}@fudan.edu.cn

Abstract. With the rapid development of Mobile Ad-hoc Networks (MANET) and Peer-to-Peer (P2P) computing, it is envisioned that building P2P multimedia sharing system over MANETs is promising. In this paper, we propose a geographic-information based distributed index structure, Geographically Hierarchical Index (GHI), based on which, we could design improved p2p algorithms especially for the multimedia sharing over MANET.

Keywords: multimedia sharing; peer-to-peer; MANET; distributed computing.

1 Introduction

Mobile ad hoc network (MANET), which is characterized as multi-hop wireless communications between mobile devices[1], will enable more and more multimedia applications such as sharing and exchange of documents, pictures, music, and movies on mobile devices, such as laptop, Personal Digital Assistance (PDA), etc., that can spontaneously self-organize into a communication structure without any fixed infrastructure. However most of the recent research efforts in MANET focus on the lower layers, such as link layer, network layer and transport layer, to enable efficient communication among nodes in the network. Current Peer-to-peer (P2P) systems for multimedia sharing mostly work on wired networks. In the near future, the synergetic potential hidden in these two decentralized and self organizing networks, P2P systems and MANETs, is coming into play a great role in wireless multimedia sharing.

Several unique challenges exist in potential P2P application over MANETs. Similar to P2P systems, to enable effective data exchange in mobile P2P multimedia sharing over MANET, a first step is to devise search mechanisms to find a data object of interest in MANET. However, due to the unique characteristics of MANET compared to internet based P2P systems, such as constrained transmission range, resource limits, and node mobility, simply importing DHT to MANET is not a valid solution[2] [12]. Since the standard DHT schemes treat the entire id space as a flat space, the case seeking far and neglecting what lies close can often happen when a MANET node is searching for a file, which may cause much resource waste and

---

* This paper was supported by the Special Science and Research Funds of the Shanghai Municipal Education Commission for the Selection and Cultivation of Young Faculty.

T.-J. Cham et al. (Eds.): MMM 2007, LNCS 4352, Part II, pp. 635–642, 2007.
© Springer-Verlag Berlin Heidelberg 2007

dramatically bring down the efficiency, also affecting the scalibility and. To address both of these scalability and efficiency problems, we firstly need to design a kind of index structure which can hierarchically and intellictually stroe the index information. And based on this index structure we could further design an efficient algorithm, which can work well with this structure and can deal with the node mobility, to provide a good multimedia sharing service over MANET.

In this paper, we design a kind of geographic information based hash index structure (GHI). Based on this structure, we simulate the implementation of CAN over MANET through NS2, and compare it with Flood over MANE to demonstrate the feasibility of GHI.

The remaining part of this paper is organized as follows. After introducing the system scenario and motivations behind our proposal in Section 2, we present GHI in Section 3, Algorithm simulation and evaluation is presented in Section 4. We compare our proposal with related works, in Section 5. Section 6 concludes the paper.

2 Scenario

With the term ad-hoc, we refer to the art of networking without an infrastructure. The nodes of ad-hoc network are mobile, and self-organize to provide and use services, guaranteeing wireless communication to end-users. Each node in MANET has limited radio range and we assume that all nodes have the same radio range. A node can communicate with other nodes within its radio range directly or the ones out of its radio range indirectly through multi-hop relay. Any node may join or leave the network, resulting in dynamic relationship changes. In addition, nodes may move, resulting in dynamic topology changes.

Each node is assumed to know its own position as well as its immediate neighbors' position through GPS devices or other means. Thus we can use the existing geographical routing protocol as our basic routing protocol for the wireless network.

Such a MANET scenario is setup, with N nodes, each with a unique nodeID, uniformly distributed in a squared region Z. And each node also provides certain number of sharable data objects. We assume that each data object is associated with a well known single-attribute key. Then CAN over MANET will search for a data according to its key value, firstly the request node send a request to the index node, which will further find the resource node and inform it of the required data, then the resource node will directly send the required data to the request node.

3 GHI Design

3.1 Introduction of DHT

In the standard distributed hash table (DHT), as the design of CAN[4], it centers around a virtual d-dimensional Cartesian coordinate space on a d-torus. This coordinate space is completely logical and bears no relation to any physical coordinate system. At any point in time, the entire coordinate space is dynamically partitioned among all the nodes in the system such that every node "owns" its individual, distinct zone within the overall space, namely a data object is randomly hashed to a single point in the entire space.

3.2   GHI Design

To overcome the drawbacks brought by CAN, a standard DHT, while constructed over MANET, we impose a GHI structure : *geographic based hierarchical index,* over the id space to divide it into a hierarchy of zones. Opposite with the CAN, we strictly map the GHI to the physical geographical coordinate system, which are usually prescribed by latitude and longitude. At any point in time, the entire coordinate space is statically, hierarchically partitioned along with the geographical coordinate. And in our GHI, we introduce such a hash function H which takes the key value of a data object and the geographical boundary of a square as inputs, and generates an output that is a geographical coordinate bounded by the specified boundary. And then the entire region is partitioned into 4 equal-sized squares while each of these squares is partitioned further into 4 smaller children squares, and so on. This process goes round and round till the side length of the smallest zone (we here define it as the unit zone), L, is less than $r / \sqrt{2}$, where r represents the radio range so that any two nodes in a unit zone can communicate directly with each other, i.e., they are within each other's radio range. We define the squares from the highest grade, namely the entire region, to the lowest grade with increasing number of digits, and within the same grade with increasing numeric value clockwise from the up-left quarter zone. The total times of the partition for the entire region is denoted as partition depth, m.

In GHI each data object is mapped to multiple nodes in the id space, it lies in two aspects:

> ➤ firstly one hash point per grade of zone,
> ➤ and secondly multiple index nodes within a unit zone for the same data object (i.e., all the nodes within the lowest grade unit zone where the hash point falls into will cache the index information for the same data object.) .

The first one, hierarchical hash structure, mainly improve the search efficiency, taking the advantages from locality and hierarchical index. The second one then can improve the system robustness, because there is not only one index node for an object which may incur single failure point problem.

Figure 1 gives an example of 4-grad, $m = 4$, GHI structure. The first grade, namely the entire region, denoted by Z is partitioned into four grade-2 squares Z_1, Z_2, Z_3, Z_4. Then each of these squares is partitioned into four grade-3 squares, as in Z_1: $Z_{11}, Z_{12}, Z_{13}, Z_{14}$. And then Z_{11} is further partitioned into $Z_{111}, Z_{112}, Z_{113}, Z_{114}$ and so do Z_2, Z_3, Z_4. In the figure, all the small circles, including the black one and the red one, represent the nodes. And for convenience, we prescribe as follows. Node a represent the node which has a data object with Key A, namely node a is a *Source Node* of the data object whose Key is A, likewise node b with Key B, and so on. The red circle node, as $I_{A, 4}, I_{A, 3}$, and $I_{F, 4}$ just respectively represent the grade-4 Index Node for key A, grade-3 Index Node for key A and grade-4 Index Node for key F, and so forth. Hereby the grade-i *Index Node* $I_{i, K}$ is defined as the node storing the index information for the data object whose Key is K within the entire grad-i region where the node resides.

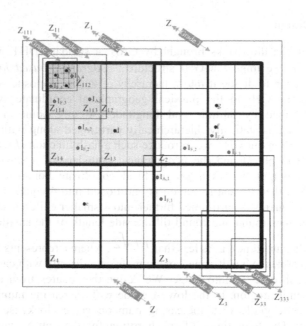

Fig. 1. GHI structure

If the grade-i (i < m) index nodes simply maintain the precise information of an object owner, i.e., its IP address, nodeID and position, for data within each of its' sub zone, it will bring such following drawbacks:

> ➢ Firstly, the higher grade index nodes will have to maintain much more index information;
> ➢ Secondly, every time a node publishes or withdraws an object, the higher level index node has to be notified and make corresponding updates.
> ➢ Thirdly, such information redundancy bring no advantages to the p2p algorithm.

Thus to overcome the above drawbacks, we only maintain precise information about individual source nodes at grade-m index nodes, as $I_{A,4}$ and $I_{F,4}$ in the figure, while higher-grade index nodes, as $I_{A,3}$, $I_{A,2}$, $I_{A,1}$, $I_{F,3}$, $I_{F,2}$ and $I_{F,1}$, maintain only coarse or aggregate information: for $i < m$, a index node of level-i stores a bool value (TRUE/FALSE) for each of its sub-zones, 4 grade-(i-1) zones, indicating whether the zone of this grade contains the object owner and if true then pointing out which sub-zone holds it.

4 Simulation

To prove the feasibility of GHI structure for P2P multimedia sharing over MANET, also to evaluate its performance, we do some simulation using NS-2. We firstly make some modification for the internet-based CAN protocol to base it on GHI structure, and then simulate it through NS-2, and lastly compare it with flood algorithm over MANET, to demonstrate its feasibility.

4.1 Network Setup

In our simulation, we prescribe that each node has a radio range 300 meter. Thus the side length of the unit zone is set to 200 meter. The network sizes are 64, 256, 1024, and 4096. The default network size is set to 1024 if unspecified otherwise. The hierarchy depth m is set to 4, and thus the side length of the whole region equals $200*2^{(4-1)}$, 1600 meter, and there are totally 64 unit zones. The nodes are initially randomly placed in the whole region. That means if the network size is 64, then there is only one node per unit zone (200*200 square region), and if 256 then 4 per unit zone, the rest may be deduced by analogy. The nodes mobility is characterized by the random waypoint model[5] with a maximum velocity ranging from 0m/s to 20m/s. The pause time is set to 0 second. Each node holds 10 data objects. A node issues random searches into the network while the average time interval between two searches issued by a node is 20 seconds. The simulation time is 600 seconds. The results shown in following sections are averaged over 10 trials for each set of the simulation.

4.2 Evaluation

In this part, we firstly measure the effect of network size on the algorithm performance, examining the algorithm's scalability. Then the effect of node mobility

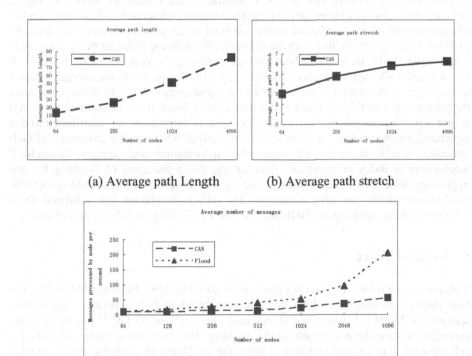

(a) Average path Length   (b) Average path stretch

(c) Average number of messages

Fig. 2. Effect of network size

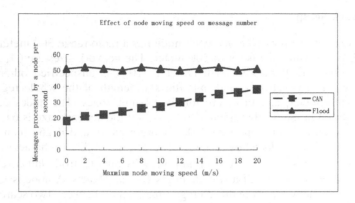

Fig. 3. Effect of node's moving speed on message number

is checked, aiming to evaluate the GHI structure's adaptability to the node mobility. Due to the absence of existing algorithm specially designed for GHI structure. We can only simulate the modified GHI-based CAN, comparing it with the flood algorithm over MANET.

The effect of network size is firstly simulated, the results are shown as fig. 2, indicating the change of average path length, average path stretch and average number of messages while the number of nodes involved in the network is increased from 64 to 4096. Fig. 2(a) shows that with the dramatically increase of nodes the average path length is gradually increased. About average path stretch, as indicated by fig. 2(b), it is not greatly affected by the network size. Fig. 2(c) demonstrates the average number of messages with relation to the network size, comparing CAN with flood. Obviously the performance of CAN is much better than that of flood. It can be claimed that CAN is not sensitive to increase of nodes, because it introduces the distributed index structure, which can bring it good scalability, and also it takes the advantage of GHI structure, which is based on geographic information and applies hierarchical mechanism in index management, thus cutting down the cases of "seeking far and neglecting what lies close at hand", and of its' design of content auto-retrievable mechanism which can save a routine. The NS-2 simulation has validated these inferences, demonstrating the GHI-based CAN's feasibility, scalability and efficiency.

5 Related Work

There are some relevant researches and studies about building P2P over MANETs. The first attempt of solutions which dedicate into building P2P network under mobile scenario is JXME[11], which try to maintain the goals of JXTA[11] but make some amendments to make it adaptable to the mobility. However this solution only take the cell network into account, without solving the problems of applying virtual overlay network over physical network, and is thus not feasible in the MANET scenario. [6] mainly provides a more applicable cross-layer protocols stack for implementing P2P computing over MANET, to simplify the application environment for applying Pastry like protocols over MANET, but without designing an algorithm special for MANETs.

Like [6], [7] also gives a kind of cross-layer protocol, embedding a query mechanism into the geographical location services, which may cause much more extra cost, due to its' need to refresh the index information corresponding to the bearing resources as the node is moving. In 7DS[8] and ORION[9], cooperative caching concept is adopted to implement P2P file sharing over MANET, but it can't predict the success rate of a query and highly depends on the search locality in the system.

6 Conclusion

With the development of MANET and internet-based P2P, it can be envisioned that the research and application of P2P multimedia sharing over MANET, which can provide mobile networked multimedia service, is promising. But limited to some of the characteristics inherent to MANET, to build P2P over MANET is simultaneously challenging. First of all, there must have an efficient index structure which can well support the mobile p2p protocol.

This paper is just trying to provide an efficient index structure, GHI, which is a geographic-information-based index structure, based on which a efficient p2p algorithm especially for MANET could be designed. Through NS-2 simulation, the efficiency and feasibility of GHI structure is demonstrated. To make further improvement on the efficiency on p2p multimedia sharing over MANET, we would like to design an efficient p2p algorithm which is based on the GHI structure and is especially for MANET.

References

1. Samba Sesay, Zongkai Yang and Jianhua He, A Survey on Mobile Ad Hoc Wireless Network, Information Technology Journal 3 (2): 168-175, 2004
2. M Li, WC Lee, Efficient Peer-to-Peer Information Sharing over Mobile Ad Hoc Networks, A Sivasubramaniam - cse.psu.edu, 2004
3. M Mauve, J Widmer, H Hartenstein, A survey on position-based routing in mobile ad hoc networks, IEEE NETWORK, 2001
4. S Ratsanamy, P Francis, M Handley, R Karp, A Scalable Content-Addressable Network, ACM SIGCOMM Conference, 2001
5. J. Broch, D. A. Maltz, D. B. Johnson, Y.-C. Hu, and J. Jetcheva. A performance comparison of multi-hop wireless ad hoc network routing protocols. In Proceedings of MOBICOM, pages 85–97, October 1998.
6. M. Conti, E. Gregori, and G. Turi, "Towards scalable P2P computing for mobile ad hoc networks", Proc. workshop on Mobile Peer-to-Peer computing (MP2P'04), IEEE PerCom 2004 Workshops proceedings, pp. 109- 113. ...
7. G. Ding and B. Bhargava. Peer-to-peer file-sharing over mobile ad hoc networks. In Proceedings of IEEE Annual Conference on Pervasive Computing and Communications Workshops, pages 104– 109, March 2004.
8. M. Papadopouli and H. Schulzrinne. Effects of power conservation, wireless coverage and cooperation on data dissemination among mobile devices. In Proceedings of ACM Interational Symposium on Mobile Ad Hoc Networking and Computing (MobiHoc), pages 117–127, October 2001.

9. C. Lindemann and O. P.Waldhorst. A distributed search service for peer-to-peer file sharing in mobile applications. In Proceedings of International Conference on Peer-to-Peer Computing (P2P), pages 73–80, September 2002.
10. S. K. Goel, M. Singh, D. Xu, and B. Li. Efficient peer-to-peer data dissemination in mobile ad-hoc networks. In Proceedings of International Conference on Parallel Processing Workshops, pages 152– 158, August 2002.
11. Akhil Arora. Carl Haywood. Kuldip Singh Pabla. "JXTA for J2METM – Extending the Reach of Wireless With JXTA Technology". White Paper, (2002)
12. M. Duigou. "JXTA v2.0 Protocols Specification". IETF Internet Draft, (2003)
13. S. Verma and W. Ooi, Controlling Gossip Protocol Infection Pattern Using Adaptive Fanout. Proc. IEEE ICDCS, 2005.
14. Ouri Wolfson Bo Xu Huabei Yin Hu Cao☐Searching Local Information in Mobile Databases (Poster) , Proc. of *the 22nd International Conference on Data Engineering*, Atlanta, GA, April 3-7, 2006.

A Hybrid MAC Protocol Based on Implicit Token and CSMA/CA for Wireless Network

Tae-Man Han[1], Dong-Won Kim[3,*], and Sang-Ha Kim[2]

[1] Robot/Telematics S/W Platform Research Team, ETRI
161 Gajeong-dong, Yuseong-gu, Daejeon, 305-350, Korea
[2] Department of Computer Science, Chungnam National University
220 Gung-dong, Yuseong-gu, Daejeon, 305-764, Korea
[3] Department of Information and Communication, Chungbuk
Provincial University, 40 Gumgu-ri, Okchon-gun, Chungbuk, 373-807, Korea
Tel.: +82-43-730-6361; Fax: +82-43-730-6369
won@ctech.ac.kr

Abstract. The proposed hybrid MAC (H-MAC) protocol characterizes distributed and asynchronous operation. It uses an implicit token for a real-time traffic and the CSMA/CA for a non-real time traffic, guaranteeing QoS. The proposed hybrid MAC protocol allocates the assured bandwidth to real time traffic and dynamically reallocates the remaining bandwidth to a non-real time data traffic.

1 Introduction

A major challenge in the MANET is to design a MAC that can handle requirements for multiple media accesses to the MANET in real time. The challenge stems from the fact that the MANET does not have a stationary and centralized coordinator such as a base station, and its topology changes frequently. Further, the MAC should satisfy the needs for QoS in real time for portability or mobility with the possibility to accommodate smaller and lighter batteries.

There are many proposals for MAC schemes to support real time applications in MANETs[1]. Conventional MACs for a WLAN usually use CSMA method, which is an asynchronous random access mechanism, because of its simple configuration and ease of implementation. IEEE802.11 [2] working group developed a MAC protocol as an international standard for the MANET as well as the infrastructured WLAN. It uses the CSMA/CA mechanism with the DCF (Distributed Coordinate Function). To avoid collisions, each node on the WLAN monitors when other nodes attempt and wait to transmit a packet. However, such a random access is not suitable for a real time and periodic traffic. To complement this, polling-based real time traffic is supported by the centralized PCF (Point Coordinator Function), which is not suitable for the MANET environment though because it does not have a centralized coordinator. Therefore, a variety of protocols have been suggested to secure the quality of real-time traffic.

---

* Corresponding Author.

T.-J. Cham et al. (Eds.): MMM 2007, LNCS 4352, Part II, pp. 643–650, 2007.
© Springer-Verlag Berlin Heidelberg 2007

A multiple access with collision avoidance/piggyback reservation (MACA/PR) [3] protocol is a combined MAC protocol of TDM (Time Division Multiplex) and CSMA/CA in a broad sense and uses a non-persistent CSMA mechanism for a datagram.   In this protocol, a node transmits a real-time traffic by referencing its reservation table and scheduling information. Therefore, the operation of the reservation table is complicated. In addition, when a new node is added to a system, the new node should learn present reservations in a listening mode for a sufficient period of time and wait until it receives a reservation table from its neighboring nodes.

Unlike a slotted mechanism, an unslotted mechanism is freed from the difficulty of synchronization. However, a slotted MAC has begun to draw an attention hence many protocols have been suggested accordingly because the provision and synchronization of a clock signal are not a problem for advanced communication systems such as a GPS (global positional system). Although a variety of slotted protocols (e.g. R-CSMA/CA[4], D-PRMA[5]) have been suggested, these protocols additionally require the GPS or a station functioning as a centralized controller.   Moreover, system synchronization is difficult, and the operation of the protocols is complicated.

Therefore, we propose a distributed and asynchronous hybrid MAC protocol guaranteeing quality of service for both real time and non-real time traffic for MANET.

The remainder of the paper is organized as follows. The proposed hybrid MAC scheme is described in Section 2. Section 3 presents performance evaluation methods and results, and some concluding remarks are given in Section 4.

2   H-MAC Protocol

The proposed H-MAC protocol characterizes distributed and asynchronous operation. It uses an implicit token for a real-time traffic and the CSMA/CA for a non-real time traffic, guaranteeing QoS.

i) DCF

One of the most important challenges in an integrated real time and non-real time network is to meet requirements for real-time traffic. To that end, we divide the frames into three priorities. The frames of different priorities have to wait different IFSs (Inter-Frame Spaces) before they are transmitted. The shortest IFS has the highest priority. The three IFSs include a distributed coordinate function IFS (DIFS), a real time IFS (RIFS), and a shortest IFS (SIFS).

Fig. 1 is a diagram illustrating the relationship between IFSs used in a distributed coordinate function of the proposed scheme. Referring to Fig. 1, the DCF uses three IFSs with different priorities. The DIFS is the longest IFS and is used by the non-real timeframes, which always have the lowest priority. The RIFS is used by a real-time reservation frame such as a RTS frame requesting the allocation and reservation of a token. The SIFS is used by immediate control frames, which always have the highest priority, such as CTS and ACK requiring immediate control. The SIFS is also used for transmitting a real-time frame packet such as a voice by a node that has already held a token. For example, the application of the CSMA/CA mechanism includes monitoring the state of a channel and transmitting a RTS after the DIFS when the channel is free for the DIFS, receiving a CTS after the SIFS, transmitting a packet after the SIFS, and generating an acknowledgement frame after the SIFS.

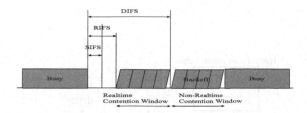

Fig. 1. Proposed DCF mechanism

ii) Node configuration and basic operation

In H-MAC, every mobile node needs to build and maintain *TRT*(Token Reservation Table), *PTC*(Passed token counter), and *TNR*(Token Number Register). The *TRT* is used by a node to participate in a voice call system by reserving a token to secure a transmission band for every frame.

The *PTC* calculates a token number passed by counting a number of *ACK [token number]* or *ACK [data]*. The *TNR* stores the token number that determines the transmission turn of a node.

Fig. 2 shows the basic operations of the node which is composed of the *TRT*, *PTC*, and *TNR*. The node monitors an event (e.g., *ACK [token number], ACK [data], CTS [token number], ACK [release token number]*) on the medium. In each case, the following operations will be happened on the components of the node.

A node that enters into the authority range of the voice call system reserves a token in the *TRT* and is given a token number corresponding to its turn for transmission. An *ACK [token number]* occurs if a real-time traffic is transmitted by other stations, and an *ACK [data]* frame occurs if a non-real time traffic is transmitted. The *PTC* of a station is updated if the station senses an *ACK [token number]* frame or an *ACK [data]* frame. Then, the updated value of the *PTC* is compared with the token number in the *TNR*. When the updated value of the *PTC* is the same as its own token number, we call this situation as token holding. At this time, the node is given a first priority to send a packet when the traffic being transmitted is terminated.

When the real time data frame or the non-real time data frame does not occur in the maximum contention window, all stations automatically increment the value of the *PTC* by one to prevent the blocking of token passing.

Each node (a voice station or a mobile terminal) participates in a voice call system on a contention basis. A procedure for a node to participate in the voice call system will now be described.

iii) Learning Phase for Participating to Voice Call System

We consider the voice call system as a concept of virtual cluster which synchronize and maintain the same *TRT*. The node which wants to participate in the voice call system observes a frame on a network for a sufficient period of time (e.g., maximum one frame period time). When the node senses the *ACK [token number]*, it requests a corresponding node to copy the *TRT* with the DIFS priority. The node can participate in the voice call system after receiving the *TRT*. If there is no activity on the medium for maximum one frame period time, the node thinks that there is nobody in the voice call system and it will create an initial *TRT*.

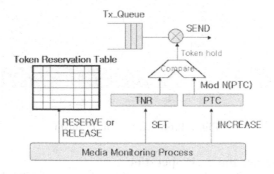

```
media_monitoring_process()
{
while(1)
    {
    if(either ACK[token number] or ACK[data] is detected)
        INCREASE the PTC;
    else if(CTS[token number] is detected)
        {
        if(I sent RTS[null])
            SET the value of token number to the TNR;
        else
            RESERVE the entry with the value of token number and
            the corresponding entry calculated by the equation like
            (N/2+token number) in the TRT;
        }
    else if (ACK[release token number] is detected)
        RELEASE the two entries reserved in the TRT;
    }
}

token_holding_procedure()
{

    Compare TNR with MOD N(PTC);
    if same, this node holds the token and can SEND a rt_PKT immediately;
    else do media_monitoring_process
}
```

Fig. 2. Node Configuration and basic operation

From this time, each node should continuously update the *TRT* while observing *CTS [token number]*, *ACK [token number]*, *ACK [data]*, or *ACK [release]* on the medium. The *PTC* increments its value by one whenever a node senses the *ACK [data]* frame. When the value of the *PTC* exceeds a predetermined value of *N*, the *PTC* is reset to one and operates like a mod N. By setting a marginal value of *N*, we can automatically provide call admission control function.

iv) Call establishment

When a medium has been blank for the RIFS period, each transmission node (being caller) transmits the *RTS [null]* frame to one of the nodes using contention method for making a call establishment. A node (being called) receiving the *RTS [null]* frame searches for an available token number in the *TRT* and notifies caller a selected token number through the *CTS [caller token number]* frame after the SIFS period. This token number included in CTS frame becomes a call identification number. Caller node stores it in the *TNR*. At the same time, a called node selects its own token number usable in a pair of caller's token number from the *TRT*. This called token number is calculated by the equation like (N/2 + caller token number) and stored in its *TNR* as its own token number.

All nodes in the voice call system, listening *CTS [caller token number]*, mark the caller's token number and the called node's token number with '*RESERVED*' in its *TRT*, thereby indicating that those numbers are allocated to and being used by a certain node in the voice call system. Contents of the *TRT* are managed in this way.

v) Voice packet transmission procedure

When all rt-nodes (e.g. voice stations) are activated, that is, participating in the voice call system, only the node which holds token can transmit packets. Holding token occurs when the value of the *TNR* equals with the value of the *PTC*.

Whenever the nodes senses *PKT/ACK [token number]* frame or the *RTS/CTS/PKT/ACK[data]* frame, the *PTC* of the nodes increases its value by one. Then, the *PTC*'s value is compared with its own token number of the *TNR*. If it is same, the node perceives that it is its turn to transmit a real-time packet because the token is being held.

The node holding the token transmits the packet in real time immediately after the SIFS period. A node receiving the packet responds through the *ACK [token number]* frame after the SIFS period. At this time, the token is passed to the next node.

When the node holding the token does not have a packet to transmit, the channel remains idle. If the channel remains idle even after the RIFS period, backlogged data stations are granted an opportunity to contend for the channel to transmit the RTS frame after the DIFS period.

vi) Data packet transmission procedure

Nrt-nodes (e.g. data stations) use the CSMA/CA mechanism. The backlogged nrt-nodes cannot transmit messages at any time. The nrt-nodes continuously observe the state of the channel and, when the channel is free during the DIFS period, sequentially go through the *RTS/CTS/PKT/ACK[data]* according to the IEEE 802.11 standard.

vii) Token circulation

When a rt-node senses the *ACK [token number]* frame that occurs when real time traffic is transmitted or the *ACK [data]* frame that occurs when non-real time traffic is transmitted, the *PTC* is updated, which leads to a token passing. When a value stored in a *PTC* plus one is the same as the value of a *TNR*, a token is deemed as being held for the next transmission.

A rt-node possesses a token and catches the token again after a token circulation period of time which is corresponding to N token passing activity time. The circulation of token is repeated. After a rt-node holds a token up to an nth time, the rt-node will obviously re-catch the voice token. Here, n is the number of allowed activated voice stations.

Token circulation time is the time taken for a rt-node to catch the token again. The token circulation time is constrained by a maximum value of a voice packet delay time and composed of n times of token holding. The n times of token holding may be either voice transmission or data transmission.

The proposed scheme monitors the token circulation to be prepared for a case where the circulation of the token is prevented, for example, when there is no traffic, or when the RTS frame collides consecutively. In other words, when no transmission occurs for a maximum contention window (CWmax), which is the longest period during which contention can occur, each node automatically adds one to the value stored in the *PTC*.

Since no traffic occurs until a node holds a token again for the next real-time transmission after transmitting a message in real time, when the node catches a token by automatically incrementing the *PTC*, it does not transmit the *PKT* frame in real time immediately after the SIFS period. Instead, the node only makes a handshake with the RTS/CTS after the RIFS period before starting its *PKT* transmission. Hence, the *PTC* of each node is refreshed.

viii) Call termination
When terminating a call, either the caller or the called may send a *'CONNECTION END'* message. A receiver of the *'CONNECTION END'* message broadcasts the *ACK [released token number]* frame to return the allocated token number to the idle state.

Automatic call admission control is performed by whether a token can be allocated or not because the number of entries in the *TRT* is limited to *N*.

We illustrate the example operations of the proposed MAC in Fig. 3.

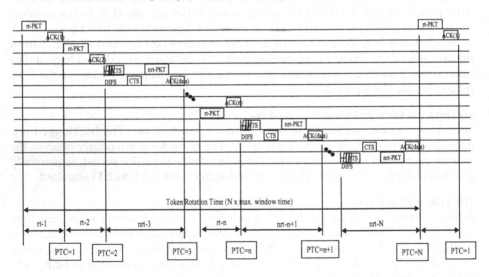

Fig. 3. Illustration of the proposed scheme operation

3   Performance Evaluation

We evaluated the performance of the proposed scheme depending on the variation of the real-time traffic load and data traffic load. The example network consists of real time stations and non-real time stations.

The number of real time stations is N_{rt} and the number of non-real time stations is N_{nrt}. The total number of the effective service slots N can be constrained by (eq.1) and it also means the number of the admitted calls by CAC function.

$$Bandwidth\_of\_Link \geq \sum_{i=1}^{N=N_{rt}+N_{nrt}} Bandwidth\_of\_Node(i) \tag{1}$$

The real time traffic should get an opportunity of transmission within a frame period. Let δ be the probability that the slot is currently available for the transmission of a packet. It represents the percentage of slots available for packet transmission per frame on the average.

$$\delta = \frac{N_{nrt}}{N_{rt} + N_{nrt}} \tag{2}$$

The state equations characterizing the operation of the hybrid channel are now written. Let $\bar{t}$ be the packet transmission window time, and P_i the probability that i packets are present in the system (in the queue on the channel) at the start of the current window time. Denote by η_K the probability that K new packets arrive to the system during the window interval $\bar{t}$. (Note that the underlying packet arrival process can be any stationary independent process.) Then

$$P_i = \sum_{K=0}^{i-1} \eta_K \{(1-\delta)P_{i-K} + \delta P_{i+1-K}\} + \eta_i (P_0 + \delta P_1). \tag{3}$$

Using the standard z-transform, one can derive the generating function

$$P(Z) = \sum_{i=0}^{\infty} P_i Z^i = (1-\delta)\sum_{K=0}^{\infty} \eta_K Z^K \sum_{i=K+1}^{\infty} P_{i-K} Z^{i-K} + \delta \sum_{i=0}^{\infty} \sum_{K=0}^{i-1} \eta_K P_{i+1-K} Z^i$$

$$+ P_0 \Omega(Z) + \delta P_1 \sum_{i=0}^{\infty} \eta_i Z^i \tag{4}$$

After mathematical manipulation we obtain

$$P(Z) = \frac{\delta P_0 (Z-1)}{Z(\delta + 1/\Omega(Z)-1)-\delta} \quad \text{where,} \quad P_0 = 1 - \frac{\Omega^{(1)}(1)}{\delta}. \tag{5}$$

Actually, $\Omega^{(1)}(1)$ means the average number of arrival packets during the mean packet transmission time. We assume the data packet arrival process is Poisson which has the mean arrival rate λ_{nrt}. The average number of packets L_{nrt} in the hybrid MAC protocol can thus be obtained as

$$L_{nrt} = \frac{\partial P(Z)}{\partial Z}\Big|_{Z=1} = \frac{\lambda_{nrt} t_{nrt}(2 - \lambda_{nrt} t_{nrt})}{2(\delta - \lambda_{nrt} t_{nrt})} \tag{6}$$

Finally, if we apply the Little's formula[6], then we get the average packet delay T_{nrt}.

$$T_{nrt} = \frac{L_{nrt}}{\lambda_{nrt}} = \frac{t_{nrt}(2 - \lambda_{nrt} t_{nrt})}{2(\delta - \lambda_{nrt} t_{nrt})} \tag{7}$$

On the other hand, the real time traffic experiences constant delay latency time T_{rt}.

$$T_{rt} = \frac{N_{rt}\bar{t}_{rt} + N_{nrt}\bar{t}_{nrt}}{2} \tag{8}$$

Fig.4 shows the analysis results. We tried to get the average packet delay time while varying N_{rt}. T_{rt} always remains constantly even if N_{rt} is changed. But T_{nrt} in case of N_{rt}=20 is shorter than the case of N_{rt}=40. It shows the effects that the bandwidth is dynamically reallocated to non-real time data traffic and the proposed method guaranties QoS for real time voice traffic.

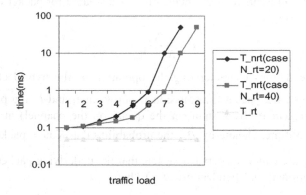

Fig. 4. Average packet delay time

4 Conclusion

This paper provides a distributed and asynchronous H-MAC protocol guaranteeing QoS for both real time and non-real time traffic on MANET. The hybrid MAC protocol allocates some bandwidth to real time traffic and the remaining bandwidth to non real time data traffic. According to an aspect of the proposed scheme, we provided a hybrid MAC protocol including the application of an implicit token passing mechanism to transmit real time traffic, and the application of the CSMA/CA mechanism to transmit non-real time traffic.

References

[1] K_C Chen, "Medium Access Control of Wireless LANs for Mobile Computing," IEEE Network, Sep 1994. pp. 50~63
[2] IEEE Standard 802.11
[3] C. R. Lin, M. Gerla, "Asynchronous Multimedia Multihop Wireless Networks," IEEE Conference Proceedings, 1997, pp. 118~125
[4] I. Joe, S. G. Batsell, "Reservation CSMA/CA for Multimedia Traffic over Mobile Ad-hoc Networks," IEEE Conference Proceedings 2000, pp. 1714~1718
[5] S. Jiang, J. Rao, D. He, X. Ling, C. C. Ko, "A Simple Distributed PRMA for MANETs," IEEE Transactions on Vehicular Technology, Vol. 51, No. 2, Mar. 2002, pp. 293~304
[6] D. Gross, Carl M. Harris, Fundamentals of Queueing Theory, John Wiley & Sons

The Vehicle Location Tracking System Using Wireless Network

Seunghyun Oh

Computer and Multimedia Department, Dongguk University,
707, seukjang-dong, Gyeongju, Gyeongbuk-do, Korea
shoh@dongguk.ac.kr

Abstract. Various intelligence styles ITS systems are developed by wireless network and development of GPS (Global Positioning System). Vehicles position track system that grasps position of vehicles by real time at control and monitoring center is a core of public transportation information system and it supplies various information that are related to the vehicles position information to user and administrator. Most existing Vehicle location tracking systems use a GPS system that is a high cost device then other things. Therefore, we designed vehicle location track system that using sensor node in which node has an inexpensive and miniaturized RF transceiver. Proposed vehicles position track system collects message that wireless ad-hoc network that is consisted of fixing sensor node that is installed along bus route and mobile sensor node that is installed to bus are happened contacting in server and manage transfer information of vehicles. Also, take advantage of bidirectional of wireless ad-hoc network it can supply bus surrounding information connected with bus position information to passenger.

Keywords: vehicle tracking, sensor node, ad-hoc network, ITS, APTS.

1 Introduction

At recent times, because wireless ad-hoc network [1] that emphasizes mobility is achieve infinite development escaping restriction of time and place, various position base services that uses mobility of wireless ad-hoc network are developed. Intelligence traffic system using wireless network can supply various information. Intelligence traffic system can classify for ATMS (Advanced Traffic Management System), ATIS (Advanced Traveler Information System), APTS (Advanced Public Transport System), CVO (Commercial Vehicle Operation) and AVHS (Advanced Vehicle and Highway System) etc. APTS includes public transportation information system, public transportation managerial system etc.., and system of various form is developed.

Vehicle position track system [2-6] that trace the position of vehicles that object of management in the public transport information system is generally use wireless LAN device or GPS device. But, it can be inappropriate that utilize GPS that expensive relatively in case of a bus that is model of public transportation. Furthermore, vehicle tracking system can only offer function that unidirectionally transmits position

T.-J. Cham et al. (Eds.): MMM 2007, LNCS 4352, Part II, pp. 651–661, 2007.

information of a bus to server when we use GPS device. In this case, there is problem that can not supply any information to passenger who rides on a bus.

In this paper, we designed vehicles position tracking system that can trace a vehicle position by real time using wireless ad-hoc network consist of sensor node that has a RF transceiver. Proposed system store and manage the vehicle position information of a bus, and is consisted of position track system server that offer lookup result of vehicles position by various interface and wireless ad-hoc network. Because a bus is move along route, selection of node location necessary to construct wireless network is easy. Vehicles position track system server receiving position information of vehicles by real time then display vehicles position on screen and create and manage log and report. Fixed sensor nodes that are installed to fixed space along bus route compose wireless ad-hoc network. Information that is collected in ad-hoc network is transmitted to sink node, and sink node communicates with server by serial interface. Sensor node that is attached to bus moves with vehicles. That is, bus node that becomes a mobile senor node communicates regularly with fixed sensor node that is installed along route.

Mobile sensor node that is installed on vehicles joins and leaves in communication distance of fixed sensor node repeatedly. When mobile node and fixed node contacts in frequency distance that communication is available message that has ID information of mobile node and ID of fixed node is created and passed to position tracking system server by real time through sink node and then vehicle position information of the detected bus is updated. Changed vehicles location Information corrects bus's position on the screen, and is stored for various log and report. Also, server transmits position based information that useful information to passenger to the mobile node in the bus. The transmitted location based information includes tourist resort name and main building which a present bus is situated.

We confirmed that proposed system can does tracking function properly that use wireless ad-hoc network by simulation and implementation of vehicles position track system server.

Composition of this paper is as following. In chapter 2, examine existing research for vehicles position track system. Chapter 3 present structures of proposed vehicles position track system and modeling the vehicles position track system. Finally, Examine results of system implementation and simulation in chapter 4 and present conclusion and the hereafter research direction in chapter 5.

2   Related Works

Existent vehicle position tracking system includes APTS's vehicles managerial system and EuroBus' vehicles allocation of vehicles control system [3, 6, 7], commercial car managerial system [2, 5]. APTS's vehicles management system informs about position and passenger of vehicles in America's advanced public transportation management system. The advanced commercial vehicle transportation system that manages freight and vehicles is offer functions to pare down distribution cost and prevention of safety accident. This system consists of freight and vehicles management system (FFMS) that manages vehicles and freight position and dangerous freight vehicles management system (HMMS) that tracking and manages vehicles that has dangerous freight, and support quick processing when safety accident occurs. EuroBus' vehicles scheduling and control system sends all information about a bus to server in the control center by transceiver that is attached to bus, and server in the control center is system that transmits position information for a bus related businessman and bus stop.

There is interface research for vehicle position information trace in intelligence traffic information system: research that examine about way to utilize wireless LAN [8], research for effective query processing method in the database that stores vehicle position information [9], study for effective tracking of moving multiple objects in the sensor network [10], and routing processing methods in the road based ad-hoc network [11]. Research [8] introduce wireless LAN in vehicles position tracking system trace a bus location of which bus has a wireless LAN card that contact to wireless LAN AP that installed along bus route. Wireless LAN provides bidirectional communication and vehicle position tracking function with proper correctness by inexpensive price, but it also has a burden in which we must construct wireless LAN AP through wired with wired infrastructure.

Research about method that process effectively query of vehicles position tracking database is proposing method to solve case that can not process all queries that user publishes because of position information that is discretely stored. For example, if store vehicle position information for some vehicles each 5 minutes, information is stored by unit 0 minutes, 5 minutes, 10 minutes, and therefore can not respond to query about 3 minutes or 1 minute's position information. This research proposing a method to respond to query about information that is not stored time information by uses past position presumes module to solve these problem.

Research about method that traces many transfer nodes in sensor network is presenting message overflow problem that happen when user transmits information to mobile sensor node. This paper explains that we can reduce quantity of messages by choose between constrained flooding that transmit in limited area and full-scale flooding that flooding to whole network according to state of vehicles.

In this paper, proposes new cost effective vehicle position tracking system that answer to all vehicle position information query using ad-hoc network of wireless sensor node. This system has advantage that can construct system with very inexpensive sensor node without complicated wired infrastructure.

3   Vehicle Position Tracking System Using Wireless Ad-Hoc Sensor Network

In this chapter, structure and function of real time vehicle position tracking system will be described. Describe about structure of server that monitoring and database role in the position tracking system, and present structure of network that is consisted of sensor node.

3.1   System Configuration and Functions

Proposed system that is consisting of vehicle position tracking system server and sensor node interface has structure such as figure 1. Vehicle position tracking system server stores and manages vehicle position information, and respond to administrator's vehicles position search query. Composition of vehicle position tracking system server is consisted of data classifier, query classification and execution control module, operation processing module and display management module, and database. Sensor node interface communicate with contacted fixed node and display the location based information that received from server on the screen. Composition of sensor node interface is server connection module, query/data transformation module, data transmit-receiver module, and display module.

The Structure of ad-hoc network that is consisted of sensor node that has RF transceiver is showed in figure 2. Fixed sensor nodes that are installed to fixed space on one whole bus route of city forms ad-hoc network, and then communicates with mobile node that is installed to bus that moves along bus route. Fixed node that succeed in communicate with mobile node make a message in which destination is sink node, and the message traverses the ad-hoc network that installed along the bus route. Server that receive message stores message and then lookup the location based information stored in the server, and server generates a location based message and transmits it to the mobile bus node.

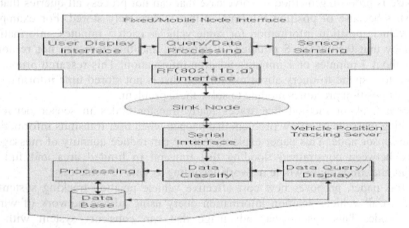

Fig. 1. An Architecture of Vehicle Position Tracking System Using Wireless Ad-hoc Sensor Network

3.2 Structure of Database

Data structure of the server can use a general commercial database based on the relational database or file system. Table 1 shows structure of used database table. Each entry of database table has following function.

- group: If sensor network divide into group, we can prevent unnecessary communication. At this time, group number means a number of groups each node belongs.
- source: The Number of the node which directly transmits a message to the sink node.
- time: Message reception time.

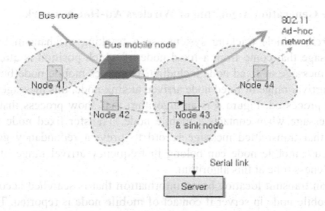

Fig. 2. An Example Architecture of Wireless Ad-hoc Network for Bus Tracking System

- origin: A number of node that makes message. Number of fixed node that contact and communicate with a moving bus
- seq_no: A message sequence number.
- hop_count: A hop number of node that flow from node that produce message in route to sink node
- bus_id: A node number of bus that offers cause of message generation, i.e. number of a bus that comes in frequency arrival range of fixed node.

Table 1. An Example of Database Table Configuration

group	source	time	origin	seq_no	hop_count	Bus_id
0x7A	0	06:15:37:46	0x1	0x1	1	1
0x7B	0x1	06:15:37:49	0x2	0x4	2	2

Vehicles position tracking information message is transmitted in TinyOS [12] message structure. Therefore, id (origin) of node that produce message is included in message, and at the same time, server can transmit suitable location base information without calculation of current bus position because the server already knows a origin node's position.

Figure 3 shows structure of packet that transmits real-time position information. In this research, we organize a database records that consists of position, send node id, hop count and additionally received time.

addr	type	group	length	source	origin	seqno	hop_cnt	Bus_ID	Padding
0	0X1	0X7A	0X1D	0	0X1	0X1	0	0X1	0X41CE08
0	0X1	0X7A	0X1D	0	0X1	0X1	0	0X1	0X41CE08
0	0X1	0X7A	0X1D	0	0X1	0X1	0	0X1	0X41CE08
0	0X1	0X7A	0X1D	0	0X1	0X1	0	0X1	0X41CE08
0	0X1	0X7A	0X1D	0X1	0X1	0X1	0X1	0X1	0X41CE08
0	0X1	0X7A	0X1D	0X2	0X1	0X1	0X2	0X1	0X41CE08
0	0X1	0X7A	0X1D	0X2	0X1	0X1	0X2	0X1	0X41CE08
0	0X1	0X7A	0X1D	0X2	0X1	0X1	0X2	0X1	0X41CE08

Fig. 3. An Example of Real-time Vehicle Position Information Packet

3.3 Message Generation Algorithm of Wireless Ad-Hoc Network

In this research, vehicle tracking system use a tracking mechanism based on the received message that come from a fixed node of which position is already known. Therefore, if message of fixed node including ID arrives mobile node(bus) that enter in frequency arrival range of fixed node arrived at sink node, this message is passed to server and is processed. Figure 4 is an algorithm that show process that fixed node generate a message when contacts a mobile node. Transfer fixed node must record and manage that transmitted message record to prevent redundancy generation of message because mobile node can belong in frequency arrival range of fixed node during suitableness time at this algorithm.

Figure 5 can transmit location based information that is searched according to the position of mobile node in server if contact of mobile node is reported. This location based information arrives in relevant fixied node along ad-hoc network, and fixed node transmits message after confirm that mobile node belongs in frequency arrival range yet. If mobile node escaped communication frequency arrival extent already, fixed node reports message delivery failure to server after discard message.

```
Algorithm FixedNode_Message_Generation()
Begin
    If (there is mobile node that enter in frequency arrival range of node)
Then
        If (contact is not repeated in threshold time) Then
            communicates with mobile node for node ID.
            creat and transmit message about contact of mobile node.
            set transmission completion flag.
        Else
            If (transmission completion flag about same mobile node is set) Then
                reset transmission completion flag.
        Sleep()
End
```

Fig. 4. Fixed Node Message Generation Algorithm

```
Algorithm FixedNode_Forward_Position_Information(Packet)
Begin
    If (target mobile node is resides in frequency arrival range yet) Then
        send a location based information packet to the mobile node
    Else
        discard Received Message.
        transmit message for transmission failure to server.
        Sleep()
End
```

Fig. 5. Fixed Node Position Information Forwarding Algorithm

4 Implementation and Experiments

To confirm function and performance of vehicle position tracking system of this research we implements system and dose simulation. Choused sensor node is a mote that has Atmega128L processor and 128KByte Flash, 2.4GHz RF transceiver chip and it run TinyOS. Maximum transmission speed is 250 Kbps. Server implementation uses Pentium processor PC, Microsoft Visual C++, and ActiveX to support Internet service.

4.1 Implementation of Vehicle Position Tracking System Server

These paragraph explains vehicle tracking functions according to message send/receive of fixed node and received message storing and query processing function about vehicle location. System implementation model is an actual bus route of one small city in Korea. This route's length is 13.8Km, and scheduled running time is 40 minutes. The vehicle is operated with 6 minute interval, and there are 20 bus stops.

Figure 6 shows tracking results on the map and the vehicle position tracking system generates change of vehicle position by communicates with fixed node that contacts mobile node. The location of vehicle can be decided by without complicated calculations because the message includes fixed node's id and contacted mobile bus node id. With a web server that connected to vehicle position tracking system server, anyone can view interested vehicle location in every time.

Figure 7 is screen that can publish a report about departure of vehicles and reaching information for administrator. All messages that received through sink node can be confirmed in this screen, and each message is classified in information about a bus, information for node, and report format.

4.2 Performance Evaluation of the Vehicle Position Tracking System Using a Simulation

The system performance evaluation is performed through simulation because we can't install sensor nodes on whole bus route. The simulation performed in ns2 [13] simulator with 802.11 [14] wireless MAC function. In the simulation, the number of bus mobile node is one and 102 connection nodes that connect bus stop nodes are used. Simulation space is set to 2300x3900M and antenna height of all nodes set to evenly by 1.5M. To save battery energy in nodes all nodes has a 256ms active time after 2secs sleep time.

Figure 8 shows a distribution of sending and receiving message of which message generated in the fixed nodes and received at sink node. Figure 8 is displaying that messages which used for valid vehicle tracking are not sufficiently sent because the time interval that routing table entry for message transmission is refresh according to vehicle's moving is widen in the AODV [15] routing protocol. But in figure 8, all transmitted messages are successfully received when AODV routing table became valid. I think that the result means that the on-demand AODV routing algorithm has a limitation to support sudden mobility in spite of advantage that AODV produces

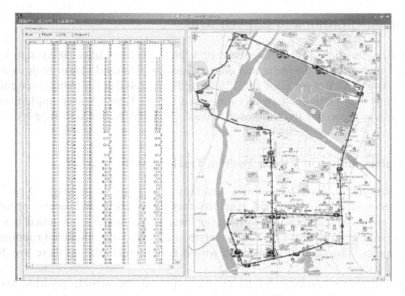

Fig. 6. A Vehicle Tracking Result and Received Message Log

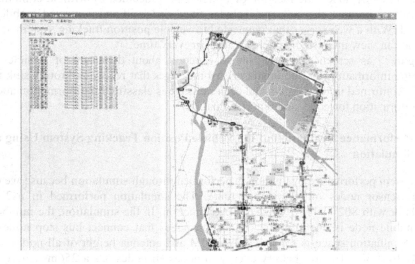

Fig. 7. A Vehicle Tracking Result and Report Message for Management

small routing message. For reference, red dot depicts a number of sent packets and small green rectangle means a received packet's number.

Figure 9 is showing the results when apply table-driven DSDV [16] routing algorithm in which routing table will be compose beforehand. When node wishes to transmit message, almost messages can transmit immediately because update message of routing table happens continuously according to transfer of mobile node. Of course, DSDV has a shortcomings of too much quantity of routing message than

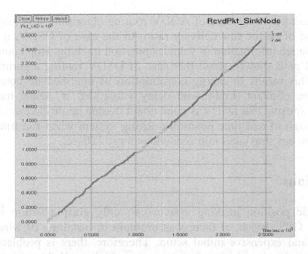

Fig. 8. AODV: Sent and Received Packet Distribution in the sink node

AODV and this is problem that must solve certainly at sensor node that have limited power supply.

Table 2 shows simulation experiment result by AODV and DSDV two routing algorithms. Delivery ratio is that ratio of received message in the sink node to

Table 2. Performance Analysis for Simulation Results

Routing Algorithm	Delivery Ratio(%)	Hop Count			End-to-end Delay(s)			Throughput(bps)		
		Avg	Min	Max	Avg	Min	Max	Avg	Min	Max
AODV	14.8	14	1	24	0.0404	0.0019	24.0	46.0	2.0	2058.9
DSDV	81.8	4	1	28	0.0272	0.0019	28.0	4459.4	1182.5	7457.8

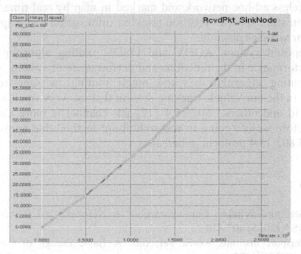

Fig. 9. DSDV: Sent and Received Packet Distribution in the sink node

transmitted message. In the case of AODV routing algorithm, it is impossible to use AODV because of its too low delivery ratio. In the case of DSDV, it is judged that DSDV pass enough information in vehicles position tracking. Hop count that means a message travel path showed result that case of DSDV routing algorithm is better in mean value. This means in energy consumption of intermediate connect node that DSDV is more efficient. End-to-end delay value that it means transfer time of message was exposing that DSDV is good about double in mean value. But, as all two values are enough in real time position tracking system when run time between the bus stop and the bus stop takes into account average 120sec.

5 Conclusions

Existent vehicle position tracking system can only grasp position information of vehicles using GPS device, or there was problem of installing of wireless LAN AP with difficult and expensive initial setup. Therefore, there is problem that can not supply necessary location base information to vehicles and there is much excessive expense or procedure to implementation being required. But, by vehicle position tracking system that propose in this research selects wireless ad-hoc network, without infrastructure construction, and can supply suitable position base information to vehicles using bidirectional data transfer facility. The Proposed system is consisted of wireless ad-hoc network that is consisted of vehicles position tracking server and sensor nodes. Our vehicles position tracking server traces a position of vehicles by tracking message that transmitted from fixed sensor node that contact moving mobile node that is installed on vehicles. Also, vehicles position tracking information stored in database, and then it can correspond to query for present and past location of target vehicle. The mobile sensor node for vehicles can receive message from server and display vehicles location based information on the connected display unit.

To implementation and experiments of this tracking system, shows a configuration model of vehicle position tracking system and simulates a system performance. The implementation system does vehicles position tracking, receiving message that happen in wireless ad-hoc network and marked in map by real time. Also, it showed that system can store vehicles position tracking information and respond by real time on question for vehicles position.

In the proposed system, AODV and DSDV routing algorithm recorded wide difference performance in the functions and performance of system. There is problem of DSDV routing algorithm has too much routing message regarding energy consumption. In the our vehicle tracking system that use very small sized data such as bus id, node id and others , 802.15.4 [17] RF channel is more suitable instead of 802.11. Therefore we are going to research about method that apply AODV routing algorithm and 802.15.4 protocol in hereafter.

References

1. William Stallings: Wireless Communications & Networks 2nd Edition, Person Prentice Hall, NJ USA (2005) 407-410
2. Korea Transport Institute, Korea Telecom: A Basic Design of Commercial Vehicle Operations(CVO) (1997)

3. Jong H. Kim: Advanced Traffic Management Systems, Communications of the Korea Information Science Society Vol.16, No.6 (1998) 5-13
4. Hyung W. Kim, sung S. Kim: An Introduction and Adaptation to Traffic Management System Using Communication Match for Goods Information Service, Korea Telecom Technical Memo, (1997)
5. Seung B. Ahn: A Service and Technology of Commercial Vehicle Operations(CVO) for Safety Improving, Korea Information Science Society Vol.16, No.6 (1998) 30-35
6. Sung Y. lee, Young R. Hong, Hyung I. Kim, Su K. Bae, Dae S. Choi: Advanced Public Transportation System, Communications of the Korea Information Science Society Vol.16, No.6 (1998) 23-29
7. Federal Transit Administration: Advanced Public Transportation Systems: The State of Art Update '96, U.S. Department of Transportation FTA-MA-26-7007-96-1, Jan. (1996)
8. Hyo S. Kang, Jai H. Kim: A Bus ITS Structure Using Wireless LAN Location Tracking Method, Korea Information Science Society Spring Conference Proceeding Vol.31, No.1(B), (2004) 502-504
9. Jun S. Oh, Yoon A. Ahn, Seung Y. Jang, Bong G. Lee, Keun H. Ryu: Desing of Vehicle Location Tracking System using Mobile Interface, Korea Information Processing Society Vol.9-D, No.6 (2002) 1071-1082
10. Sung M. Lee, Ho J. Cha: Locating Method for Multiple Mobile Nodes in Wireless Sensor Networks, Korea Computer Congress 2006, Vol.32, No.1(A) (2005)
11. So Y. Hwang, Jyoung S. Kim, Ki J. Li: Query Routing in Road-Basrd Mobile Ad-hoc Networks, Communications of the Korea Information Processing Society Vol.12-D, No.2 (2005) 259-266
12. TinyOS, http://www.tinyos.net
13. The Vint Project: The ns Manual (formerly ns Notes and Documentation), <http://www.isi.edu/nsnam/ns/doc>
14. Andy Dornan: IEEE 802.11a and 802.11g Wireless LANs, NetworkMagazine, August 05 (2003)
15. C. Perkins, E. Belding-Royer, S. Das: RFC3561: Ad hoc On-Demand Distance Vector (AODV) Routing (2003)
16. Perkins Charles E., Bhagwat Pravin: Highly Dynamic Destination-Sequenced Distance-Vector Routing (DSDV) for Mobile Computers, London England UK, SIGCOMM 94-8/94.
17. Jose A. Gutierrez, Marco Naeve, Ed Callaway, Monique Bourgeois, Vinary Mitter, Bob Heile: IEEE 802.15.4: A Developing Standard for Low-Power Low-Cost Wireless Personal Area Networks, IEEE Network September/October (2001) 12-19

A Representation of Korean Syllable Characters Defined in Hunminjeongeum

Jeongyong Byun and Seunghyun Oh

Faculty of Computer and Multimedia, Dongguk University
707 Sukjangdong, Gyeongju, Gyeongbuk-do, 780-714, Korea
{byunjy,shoh}@dongguk.ac.kr

Abstract. Korean script Hunminjeongeum (correct sounds to teach the people), called Hangul, that was distributed in 1446 can generate 39.9 billion syllabic characters by 28 basic alphabets and 5 rules. Current Hangul on computer lost scientific properties and then cannot generate all of 39.9 billion syllables because choosing syllable as a target among encoding objects of syllable, syllabic primitive, and alphabet. In this paper, we propose a coding scheme and a method of generating fonts so as to represent all syllabic characters defined in Hunminjeongeum.

Keywords: Hangul, syllabic primitives, Unicode, Jaso-type, Jamo-type, pre-composed syllable, composing font.

1 Introduction

The Hunminjeongeum (correct sounds to teach the people), called Hangul, was created in 1443 and distributed in 1446. It symbolizes 3 atomic vowels and 5 atomic consonants as fundamental tones by modeling core vocal organs, and then extends them to 28 basic alphabets that consist of vowel 11 letters and consonant 17 letters according to their loudness and wildness, and also defined 5 rules to compose syllables. They can generate 39.9 billion syllabic characters.

Hangul as phonogram has properties of phoneme writing as well as syllabic writing. Since Hangul, which has three encoding objects such as syllable, syllabic primitive (grapheme), and alphabet, chose syllable among them without considering the original principal, it lost the scientific properties on computer and therefore could not compose all of 39.9 billion syllables defined in Hunminjeongeum. The total number that can be composed by modern Hangul reaches 11,172 syllables, but current Hangul code standard for information interchange KS X 1001 represents only 2350 syllables being about 21% of possible composition. On the other hand, international character code standard KS X 1005, which imported from ISO/IEC 10646 and Unicode, represents all of modern Hangul 11172 syllables. Due to this poor expression ability of KS X 1001, Microsoft Windows privately developed Integration Hangul code which basically violates ISO 2022 and also couldn't support alphabetical order sorting.

Engineering can be perfect though science. Hangul processing is engineering to increase productivity using computer as a tool. Though perfectly examining science

T.-J. Cham et al. (Eds.): MMM 2007, LNCS 4352, Part II, pp. 662–670, 2007.
© Springer-Verlag Berlin Heidelberg 2007

for a tool and applying scientific property of Hangul for it, we can accomplish productivity and integrity of processing Hangul. On computer, now Hangul processing and presentation have much restriction at the present.

In this paper, we present a solution that can represent all syllabic characters, according to the previous mentioned principles, by developing a right encoding scheme and an optimized method of composing a full set of syllabic font in implementation level 3.

2 Related Works

Research on scientific properties of coding Hangul characters is internationally very rare except some [1,2,3,4] in Korea. Since 1987, they has been studied the scientific theories of Hunminjeongeum to resolve problems of the poor representation produced by pre-composing syllable code, that is, KS X 1001[8]. Current Hangul Jamo in Unicode [10] has been adopted as the result of the researches.

In 1992, Mark Davis had ever proposed five combining schemes that can generate 11,172 syllables. One of them is to utilize a coding scheme for spacing and non-spacing characters such as Ö and Ä. That is not suitable to the properties of Hangul. A proposal [7] on implementation level is suggested by Olle Jarnefos. Some researches [5,6] are not related to Hunminjeongeum, but related to key arrangement on keyboard of typewriter. Recently DPR Korea began to study Hunminjeongeum.[9,11]

3 Principles of Hunminjeongeum

In this chapter, structure and function of real time vehicle position tracking system will be described. Describe about structure of server that monitoring and database role in the position tracking system, and present structure of network that is consisted of sensor node.

Examine and arrange existing research [5] about Hunminjeongeum invention principle to examine closely scientific property of Hangul. First sentence of preface in the book Haerye begins with "if there exist sounds of heaven and earth nature, there exist certainly letters for sounds of heaven and earth nature that can record them." In other words, it contains intention that creates writing system that can express all sounds of heaven and earth nature. The book states that it is easy to learn because Hangul is very simple and therefore "if one is intelligent, one can learn before breakfast, and although foolish, one can learn within ten days." Chinese character that was main stream character cannot be so at all. Author of this paper analyzes properties of Hangul as follows:

- In the Jaejahae (symbolizing sounds), vowel is a modeling that sound rises from throat, passes the above of tongue, and lastly pronouced when passing between upper teeth and below teeth modeling by sky, earth, and people. Consonant modeling five importance vocal organ in person's structure of mouth by A-SE OL-SUN-CHI-WHO(ㄱ, ㄴ, ㅁ, ㅅ, ㅇ). The principle is that these sounds have accomplished creation and accomplish all sounds.

- In leading consonant, 3 basis vowels are extended to 17 according to loudness and wildness of it's sound.
- In vowel sound, basis consonant 5 letters are extended by 11 by same principles.
- In trailing consonant, [Rule 1]: end sound use again first sound. Total sum of all characters is 45 characters but leading consonant and trailing consonant are same element in shape, although phonetic value is different, 17 characters removed then become 28 characters. This is same with concept that removes equivalence relation justice of mathematics or same element of set.
- In the composing principle, it defining that leading consonant, vowel sound, and characters of trailing consonant can used by two or three characters are together or independently, and the rule is shortly defined as following.

  [Rule 2: Prolonged sound law] If attach 'ㅇ' under labial (ㅁ ㅂ ㅃ ㅍ), become lips light sound.

  [Rule 3: Book on strategy law] Extend consonant and consonant by 2 or 3 characters together.

  ✓ Leading consonant character number $|C1| = 17 + 2\Pi17 + 3\Pi17 = 5119$ characters

  ✓ Vowels character number $|V| = 11 + 2\Pi11 + 3\Pi11 = 1463$ characters

  ✓ Trailing consonant character number $|C2|$ = Consonant and equivalent = $|C1| + \{\Lambda\} = 5220$ characters

  [Rule 4: Post law] width rate vowel (. ─ ㅗ ㅜ ㅛ ㅠ) is bitter attaching under leading consonant, and length rate vowel (ㅣ ㅏ ㅓ ㅑ ㅕ) writes to leading consonant right. Trailing consonant attaches under vowel. In other words, define method to usage of pile up.

  [Rule 5: Phonetic law] Character accomplishes sound though leading consonant, vowel sound, trailing consonant gather. In other words, refer reason that why pile up character by sound word. This improves efficiency of reading better than unfasten composition like roman letters.

  ✓ Total number of character of Hunminjeongeum $|H| = C1 \times V \times C2 \cong 39,856,772,340$ (About 39,900,000,000) characters

If summarize principle of Hunminjeongeum, modeling accomplishing various kinds creation at process that sound of five vocal organs escapes out of mouth starting in throat made various voice leading consonant, vowel sound, trailing consonant 45 characters. In here, Hangul can express about 39,900,000,000 syllabic characters as great invention by 28 characters that diminish 17 characters according to equivalence relation called trailing consonant use a leading consonant with prolonged sound law, all together law, post law, production rule of sound and so on. This defines whole character set by condition presentation method for mathematics today.

4 Coding Schemes and Implementation Level

Hangul has three objects such as syllable, syllabic primitives, called Jaso, and alphabet, called Jamo. We should choose one of them so as to keep scientific properties. Then, Hangul has both properties of syllabic character and grapheme, that is, syllabic primitives. So grapheme of Hangul such as leading consonants (choseong), vowels (jungseong), and trailing consonants (jongseong) consists of a syllable and also has some information of syllabic structure. By the result, Hangul Jaso, that is, syllabic primitives, is the most suitable in three codes as the object of coding Hangul characters.

39.9 billion syllables as a full set of Hangul syllables can be composed with just 45 Jaso characters and 5 composing rules. So Hangul should be applied not in implementation level 1 but in level 3. A specialist for code, Olle Jarnefors, says that implementation level 3 is necessary for full support of **the Korean Hangul script**.

5 Code Analysis for Information Interchange

5.1 Hangul Code for Information Interchange (HCII): KS X 1001

Without scientific approach for Hangul, there are several attempts of coding Hangul characters but it turned out a trial and error and it is known that it still has some problems. Let's review the previous efforts.

HCII is enacted as first national standard in 1974 and its standard number is KS C 5601:1974. HCII is a code system for 51 Korean alphabets depending on Hangul syllabic standard officially enacted in 1933, then it is called Jamo(alphabet)-type. This follows ISO 646IRV and ISO 2022 (code extension standard) but in composing a syllable and treating it, some programmers thought that it was very inconvenient, comparing to treatment of Roman and Kana string, due to variant length of string consisting of a syllable. It wad revised to syllable-type code system with syllabic primitive information in 1982, then called KS C 5601:1982. This supports to represent a full set of 11,172 modern syllables. However this doesn't follow ISO/IEC 2022 and then it was revised to pre-composed syllable-type in 1987, and then called KS C 5601:1987, and its standard number is changed to KS X 1001:1998. This follows ISO/IEC 2022 but representation power is very poor because it is able to represent 2350 Hangul syllables and 4888 hanja (Chinese character).

Fig 1 shows the structure of control and graphic character areas of ISO 646 and ISO   2022. GL and GR as showed in Fig 1 can represent 94 graphic characters. Roman and Korean characters in two bytes code system can simultaneously represent on computer, usually by designating Roman character set to G0 and Hangul character set to G1 and calling G0 to GL and G1 to GR.

Korean Standards X 1001:1998 being pre-composed syllable-type code express by two bytes, which represent 8836 (94 x 94) characters, because graphic character area can represent maximum 94 characters. Thus this code system has very poor code spaces for 11,172 syllables, which can compose in modern Hangul, and it can also represent 2350 of 11172 syllables, that is, 21%. According to specialist's research, it is known that common syllables of about 320 cases that use in routine is lacking.

The case of Chinese characters is more serious. Since 4888 Chinese characters are supported in administration computing network system, the range of naming characters is limited into this extent. This brought a tragic result that technology controls culture. In case of word processor as another example, Haangul text editor of HanCom Inc. is high share more than MS word. The reason is because selected Korean Standards C 5601:1987 that do not support 11172 syllables. Then, as MS creates integration style code and support 11172 syllables, market was begun to

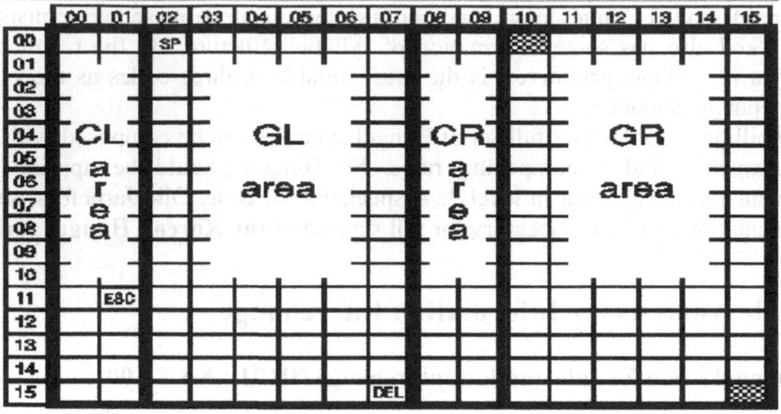

Fig. 1. Control and Graphic character Area of ISO/IEC 646

magnify. This caused a controversy that can not sort at alphabetical order, and avoided problem by changing name to International Standardization Organization 10646.

In order to solve a lot of requirements needed in Hangul character processing, I proposed Hangul Jaso-type code draft in 1992 and then badly revised draft is accepted in Seoul meeting of ISO/IEC JTC1/SC2 in June of 1992, and now called Hangul Jamo.

5.2 Chosungul Code for Information Interchange: KP X 9566

KPS 9566:1997 (KPS 9566:2000 recently announced) is north Korean character code standard for information interchange. This is naturally different to KS X 1001 because ordering of both south and north Korean alphabets is not equal each other. Especially multiple alphabet set takes different order and then the difference can not be avoided. So if both follow the scientific principles of Hunminjeongeum, the difference can be resolved through software.

5.3 International Character Code Standard: KS X 1005

KS X 1005:1995 becomes a national standard by importing ISO 10646 BMP and Unicode. This includes all characters in the world as well as three kinds of Hangul code standards, that is, Hangul Jamo (Jaso-type), Hangul Compatibility Jamo (Jamo-type), and Hangul Syllable (pre-composed syllable-type). 39.9 billion syllables as a full set defined in Hunminjeongeum can be composed using basic characters of Hangul Jamo in implementation level 3 but Unicode regulates to deal with Hangul characters in implementation level 1. Unicode and ISO/IEC 10646 BMP gave up the scientific properties of Hangul character. By treated in implementation level 3, original characteristics of Hangul should be recovered and charter 6 shows an attempt for it.

6   Generation Rule of Composing Font

Hangul is written in syllable blocks, and the bloks are composed of primitives called Jaso or Jaso code system (called Jamo in Unicode), which means a set of grapheme consisting of a syllable. There are three types of Jaso: choseong (leading consonants), jungseong (vowels), jongseong (trailing consonants). Common shorthand for the three types is C1n, hVn for horizontal type and vVn for vertical type, and C2n, for "leading consonant", "vowels", and "trailing consonants" respectively (n = 1,2,3).

Using Hangul Jaso code system, 39.9 billion syllables as a full set defined in Hunminjeongeum can be represented on computer. However, it is not easy to provide their pre-composed syllabic font sets on computer, because of heavy cost and very rare calling frequency of most fonts. Most OS now supports pre-composed syllabic font sets of 11,172 syllables of modern Hangul and phoneme font set of 240 Hangul Jamo. But most syllabic font sets are not supported and then they should be composed in implementation level three. To produce dynamic composing fonts whenever they are needed, we design their primitive fonts using FontLAB Studio 5.0 and Font Creator Professional Edition 5.0.

Here an engineering approach is tried to get high productivity in designing composing font sets. Modern Hangul has six types of syllabic block structures and Hunminjeongeum additionally has two more types to identify pronouncing order of mixed vowels of vertical type and horizontal type. Every syllabic primitive of eight block structures, that is, L, V, and T, has single character or two characters, or three

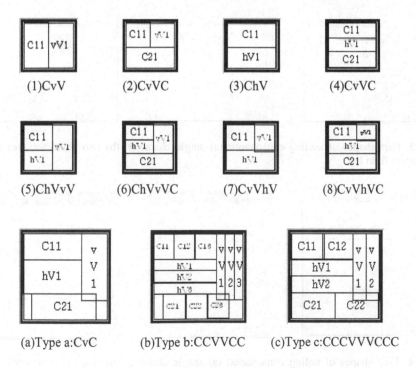

Fig. 2. Syllabic block structures: *h: horizontal, v: vertical

characters. Specially, in designing the fonts to identify pronouncing order as fig x4 we applies a graphical scheme for composed vowel strings such as " ㅏ + ㅗ + ㅜ"," ㅗ+ ㅏ + ㅜ", and "ㅗ + ㅜ + ㅏ ".

Fig. 3 shows character composition rules of combining two or three characters. According to the length of choseong primitive, one of them is selected from primitive font base, and jongseong also follows the same procedure as Fig 4.

Gen-CSFS (Generation Composing Syllabic Font Set) Algorithm

1. Extracting syllabic string between first syllabic character and last syllabic character.
2. Counting each length for L, V, and T respectively.
3. Choosing a syllabic block using each length.
4. Composing the syllabic font from primitive font base.
5. Displaying it at the position.

Jungseong, vowels, has different structure because of two shapes such as vertical type and horizontal type. According to placing rule of Hunminjeoneum, horizontal vowels are placed under leading consonants, choseong primitives, and vertical vowels are placed on right side of leading consonants. Pronouncing ordering of mixed vowels

Fig. 3. Font shapes of leading consonants; (a) single character, (b) two characters, (c) three characters from left

Fig. 4. Font shapes of tailing consonants; (a) single character (b) two characters (c) three characters from left

can be identified by each length of font shapes of vertical type and horizontal type as shown in fig.5 and fig.6.

Ordering of the same types such as fig.5(a) and fig.6(d)is determined from top to down for vertical type and from left to right for horizontal type. In case of mixed types, if a vowel is placed on the body of another vowel, the former takes precedence of the latter. For example as shown in fig.5(c), since "ㅡ" is placed on body of "ㅑ" and "ㅑ" is placed on the body of "ㅠ", the ordering is "ㅡ", "ㅑ", and "ㅠ". In case of fig.6(c), two vertical vowels are placed on a horizontal vowel, and then since two vowels have the same vertical type, ordering is from left to right and the last.

We can optimize the effort of designing a set of syllabic primitive fonts through structural analysis of 8 syllable blocks as shown in Fig. 2. Eight blocks have shape of syllabic primitives for three types respectively. Block (1) and (3) have 165 primitives, (2) and (4) have 237, (5) and (7) have 168, and (6) and (8) have 270 primitives. Then Total number reaches 840 and this requires at most 5.8% of a full set of primitives.

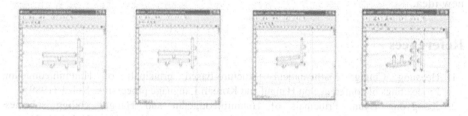

Fig. 5. Ordering of horizontal vowels for vertical type; (a) "ㅜ+ㅠ+ㅑ" (b) "ㅜ+ㅠ+ㅑ" (c)"ㅡ+ㅑ+ㅠ" (d)"ㅛ+ㅕ+ㅕ" from left

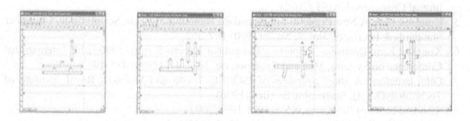

Fig. 6. Ordering of vertical vowels for horizontal type; (a)"ㅏ+ㅗ+ㅛ" (b)"ㅏ+ㅛ+ㅑ" (c)"ㅏ+ㅕ+ㅠ" (d)"ㅏ+ㅕ+ㅏ" from left

7 Conclusion Remarks

We identified scientific properties of Hangul through Hunminjeoneum and developed a suitable coding scheme and combining syllabic font sets in order to generate 39.9 billion syllabic characters defined in Hunminjeongeum.

Hunminjeongeum defined a full set of syllabic characters of Hangul with 28 basic alphabets and 5 syllabic generation rules. By the way, Hangul Jamo does not identify syllable-last characters and syllable-first characters. So if we remove Rule 1, then 28 alphabets are extended to 45 graphemes, and then if we adopt a coding scheme for the graphemes, then they can be identified. It is the most suitable code system for Hangul because its number is small set, it has properties of syllabic and phoneme, preserve scientific property, and also has expression ability for 39.9 billion syllables.

Since it is not economical to design a full set of pre-combined syllabic fonts for 39.9 billion, we support the generation programs of composing syllabic fonts. Hereby just like writing with pencil, it is possible for users to represent all syllables we want to compose on computer. This will make a restricted representation ability improve. We also developed an optimized method that can be designed in only 5.8% level of a full set.

Additionally we can solve a problem of different code system caused due to different alphabet ordering of Hangul and Chosungul. Giving coding to not multiple graphemes but basic graphemes, we can develop a sorting program. However it is not easy to writing program in case of pre-composed syllabic code system.

Further researches are needed for developing more elegant combining fonts with new idea.

References

1. Heesung Chung: Mathematical Structure-based principals of Hunminjeongeum, Proceedings of conference on Hangul and Korean Language processing, Vol. 1 (1989)
2. Jeongyong Byun: Principals of Hunminjeongeum and Hangul coding schemes, Proceedings of conference on Hangul and Korean Language processing, Vol. 3 (1991)
3. Jeongyong Byun: An Engineering of Hangul based on Principals of Hunminjeongeum, Reviews of KISS (1994)
4. Matae Ahn: Maximizing Quantification of Hangul Jamo Conjoining Method for Multi-lingual Characters, KAIST (2002)
5. Kongsok Kim: A New Proposal for a Standard Hangul (or Korean Script) Code, Computer Standards & Interfaces, Vol. 9, No. 3 (1990) 187-202
6. Kongsok Kim: Databases supporting Hangul (or Korean Script), 1990 IEEE International Conference on Systems, Man and Cyberneti cs., Nov. 4-7 (1990) 485-490
7. Olle Jarnefors: A short overview of ISO/IEC 10646 and Unicode, Royal Institute of Technology(KTH), Stockholm, Sweden (1996)
8. Standard board of RO Korea, KS X 1001:1998,2002
9. Standard board of DPR Korea, KPS 9566:1993,1997,2000
10. Unicode Standard 3.0, www.unicode.org.
11. Myeongkyu Kim: Suggestions of Improving KPS 9566, ICCKL, Shenyang in China (2004)

A Study on the Accelerator for Efficient Distribution of the Multimedia Content

Il Seok Ko

Division of Computer and Multimedia, Dongguk University, 707 Seokjang-dong,
Gyeongju-si, Gyeongsangbuk-do, 780-714 Korea
isko@dongguk.edu

Abstract. What is most important issue in web services using Multimedia Content is acceleration technique for efficient distribution of the multimedia content. Web services are based on a web-based system in which the performance of this system becomes a major factor in determining the quality of services. Thus, studies on the acceleration of the acceleration of the multimedia content are directly linked with the improvement of a web system. An improvement in the system performance can be achieved using a type of load uniformity (hereinafter called load balancing) by producing a cluster system using several server systems from a web service provider's point of view. This study investigates a method that improves the acceleration performance in a web-based service. A method that distributes loads applied to a web system itself using a dynamic load balancing method, which uses various types of information between nearby servers, was investigated from a web service provider's point of view.

Keywords: acceleration, web system, multimedia, distribution.

1 Introduction

This study attempts to perform the acceleration of the response time in web services from a web system's point of view. Thus, it is necessary to consider certain physical limitations in order to achieve the acceleration in web services. The limitation condition that should be considered in the design process of a web system can be summarized as follows.

First, it is a certain condition that exists in a physical limitation to improve the performance of a network. The physical performance of a network primarily affects the service speed in a web system. An improvement in a network should be considered with respect to technical issues and costs at the same time.

Second, it involves a certain condition that exists in a sudden increase in the system performance. A web service business periodically or non-periodically updates the performance of a web system as occasion demands. However, it is difficult to make a sudden and unexpected improvement in the system performance due to their costs.

Third, the service response time is dependent on the geographical distance between clients and servers. Although the performance of a network and system previously mentioned in the first and second conditions largely affect the service response speed,

T.-J. Cham et al. (Eds.): MMM 2007, LNCS 4352, Part II, pp. 671–677, 2007.

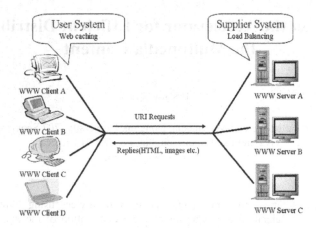

Fig. 1. Two sides to achieve the acceleration of web services

the geographical distance between clients and servers more significantly affects the service response speed.

In order to solve these limitations, approaches from a web service provider's and web service user's point of view are required as presented in Figures 1. A web-based cluster system [1,3,4,5] that uses a load balancing method from a web service provider's point of view can improve the service response speed. Also, this service response speed can be improved using a web caching [1,2,6,7] from a web service user's point of view.

An improvement method using a load distribution method presents an effective way to improve the performance rather than an improvement in the performance of an individual system itself from a web service provider system's point of view. This study configures a group using nearby servers that are geographically close to clients using a dynamic load balancing method and proposes a load balancing method that adaptively distributes users' loads to this grouped server system. The proposed technique reflects certain geographical problems and various costs that occur in several servers in order to distribute loads, which are applied to a web server. In addition, this technique can reduce costs by sharing a server and improve the processing capability of a server and response time for the overload applied in a server.

This study investigates a method that improves the acceleration performance in a web-based service. A method that distributes loads applied to a web system itself using a dynamic load balancing method, which uses various types of information between nearby servers, was investigated from a web service provider's point of view.

2 User's View: Caching

Physical performances of a network and web system itself are required to increase the performance of a web system. However, studies on certain structural approaches like a CDN (Content Delivery Network) have been actively conducted because these performance improvements require a large amount of costs [1, 2]. Also, any type of web caching significantly affects the performance of a web system. This is due to the fact that a web system can use a web system itself, extra caching server, and CDN.

A system of web caching is able to process the request of the user in an electronic commerce system and improve the performance of Internet. The performance of a web caching is dependent on an effective management in the storage scope of limited web caches. Thus, studies on replacement techniques have been largely conducted to maintain frequently used web objects in the storage scope of web caches [2,6,7]. The replacement technique for web caches reflects the characteristics of web objects. The characteristics of web system users can be summarized as follows [1,2].

- The deviation of web objects, which are referred to users, presents a large value. Thus, web caches must support variable objects effectively that are required by the user of Internet.
- Referenced web objects have a certain reference locality according to the time and region. These reference characteristics are variable with the passage of time and become major factors to decrease the performance of the existing caching technique.
- The characteristics of users, such as age, skill of Internet use, and education level, affect the reference characteristics.
- The type and characteristics of a web service affect the reference characteristics of users.
- The variability of the reference characteristics increases the deviation of object-hit ratios.
- The variability of the reference characteristics non-periodically occurred.

Changes in the variable web object reference characteristics of users in a web system decrease the performance of a web caching and become a major factor to decrease the performance of a web system. However, the characteristics of users in a web system have not been reflected in any of the existing web caching techniques. This was due to the fact that studies on the web caching techniques have been largely focused on the improvement of object-hit ratios and reduction of caching costs [2,6,7]. Thus, studies on the web caching technique that reflect the characteristics of users in a web system are required.

As previously mentioned, studies from both web service provider and web service using systems' point of view are required to improve the performance of a web system. An improvement method using a load distribution method presents an effective way to improve the performance rather than an improvement in the performance of an individual system itself from a web service provider system's point of view. This study configures a group using nearby servers that are geographically close to clients using a dynamic load balancing method and proposes a load balancing method that adaptively distributes users' loads to this grouped server system. The proposed technique reflects certain geographical problems and various costs that occur in several servers in order to distribute loads, which are applied to a web server. In addition, this technique can reduce costs by sharing a server and improve the processing capability of a server and response time for the overload applied in a server.

Moreover, studies on web caching are required from a web service using system's point of view. This study proposes a web caching technique that adaptively reflects the heterogeneity of web objects. In order to increase the efficiency of web caches, the proposed technique investigates the issue of a web caching technique as follows [1,2,6].

- The heterogeneity of web objects is closely related to the size deviation of objects. Thus, the identification of objects according to the heterogeneity makes possible to identify objects according to the size of objects.
- A web object size based algorithm, such as SIZE and LRUMIN methods, can reduce the number of cases where a large amount of small sized objects are removed by large sized objects in a storage scope. However, in the case of the reference characteristics that have a large size deviation, the performance will be decreased.
- If the object is managed according to the size of objects, the object deviation in each region can be reduced compared to that of a single object. In this case, the number of small sized objects that are produced to replace a single large sized object can be reduced due to the decrease in the size deviation.
- The reference characteristics of objects are very variable. Thus, the deviation of the heterogeneity is also variable. An adaptive caching technique is required to reflect variable reference characteristics.

The proposed web caching technique can improve the performance of a web caching technique due to the fact that it is able to adaptively reflect the reference characteristics of web objects.

3 Load Distribution

A web server group of WSG_i that consists of several web servers can be presented as a tree shape as illustrated in Figure 2. Means and functions of the node presented in the figure are as follows.

- WSG_i : Web Server Group i
- $LSGM_i$: Local Server Group Manager i
- managing load information for each LS_i in a group
- managing transmission costs according to the geographical condition between LS_{is} in a group
- task switching between LS_{is}

- LSG_j : local server group j, $1 \leq j \leq m$, m is the number of local server groups in $LSGM_i$
- LS_i : Local Server i, $1 \leq i \leq k$, k is the number of LS_s in WSG
- C_{xy} : terminal nodes (clients) of each WSG,
    - $1 \leq x \leq k$, $1 \leq y \leq n$
    - k : number of LSs in WSG
    - n : number of clients in LS

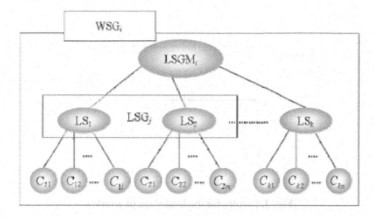

Fig. 2. Tree structure of WSG_i

As presented in Figure 2, lines that connect each node presents a network connection between servers or between servers and clients. The operation of WSG_i can be expressed as follows.

Step 1) Requesting the task of C_j for LS_i
Step 2)
- Processing tasks if LS_i can process the task of C_{xy}
- Transmitting requests to $LSGM_i$ if the load of LS_i can't process tasks
- $LSGM_i$ transmits a HTTP request by finding LS_k, which has a small load
- LS_k processes the delegated task
- Transmitting the results to LS_i
- LS_i transmits the results to C_j

3.1 Factors for the Load State of Each Server

Load states should be checked in each server to distribute loads. In order to check C_{load} that presents a load state of server, L_s and δ that present states and performance coefficients of each server, respectively, are required. Severs that are actually used in a certain system present differences in their performances. Thus, the coefficient δ is used to present these differences. Although a load state of L_s in a server presents a little high level, the load of the server, C_{load}, may presents a low level if the server has a very high performance.

Figure 3 presents certain factors that can be used to verify loads of a server.

Load verifications in each server can be performed using the CPU past history that extremely affects loads of a server, I/O past history, and wait loads of the task that is on standby in Task Queues. Thus, the load stat of L_s of a server consists of three tuples as follows.

$L_s = (\alpha, \beta, \gamma)$
L_s : load states for each server
α : average CPU past history in a time period of $(t_h - t_c)$

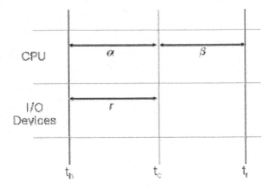

Fig. 3. Factors for the load state of a server

β : wait loads of the task that is on standby in Task Queues of a CPU in a time period of $(t_c - t_r)$

γ : I/O past history in a time period of $(t_h - t_c)$

where α and γ present the past history of CPU and I/O for a specific time period at the present time, and β presents the wait load of tasks, which will delegate a CPU, after finishing the present task.

3.2   Load Distributions of a Server According to the Prior

If a task switching is required in $LSGM_i$ based on the load state of a server, loads can be distributed by verifying the load of a local server itself using a load state adapter.

Changes in the load state of a server should be adaptively reflected in order to dynamically operate a system according to the change in the state factor of the load of a server. Figure 4 presents an adaptor that adaptively indicates the state of loads. As presented in Figure 4, states for each server can be classified as six different states, such as minimal loaded sate, lightly loaded state, mean value loaded state, lightly overloaded state, overloaded state, and maximal overloaded state according to the value of α, β, and γ that affects the load of a server.

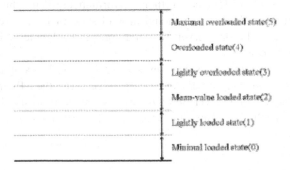

Fig. 4. Load state adaptor

Using a load state adapter, certain load states can be dynamically linked to other factors that affect the load of a server and presents the merit that the load of a local server can be managed in real-time.

In the case of the LS_i that is unable to process its own tasks, $LSGM_i$ is able to select a proper LS_i using the information of a load state adapter illustrated in Figure 3-3 based on the priority denoted as follows.

Minimal loaded sate server > lightly loaded state server > mean value loaded state server > lightly overloaded state server > overloaded state server

In addition, if all servers in a group are in an overloaded state, a task switching will not be generated and will be on standby. Also, it waits for certain loads of a server, which requested a task switching, and changes in a load state of other servers in a group.

If the load state becomes the same value for each other, a server that has a low transmission cost according to a certain geographical location for a server, which requested a task switching, is to be selected.

4 Conclusion

Web services are based on a web-based system in which the performance of this system becomes a major factor in determining the quality of services. An improvement in the system performance can be achieved using a type of load uniformity by producing a cluster system using several server systems from a web service provider's point of view. This study investigates a method that improves the acceleration performance in a web-based service. A method that distributes loads applied to a web system itself using a dynamic load balancing method, which uses various types of information between nearby servers, was investigated from a web service provider's point of view.

References

[1] Il Seok Ko, Choon Seong Leem, "An Improvement of Response Time for Electronic Commerce System," Information Systems Frontiers, vol6, no4, pp.313-323, 2004.

[2] Il Seok Ko, "ACASH: An Adaptive Web Caching method based on the Heterogeneity of Web Object and Reference Characteristics," Information Sciences, ELSEVIER SCIENCE INC., Vol.176, Issue 12., 1695-1711, 2006.6.22

[3] V. Cardellini, M. Colajanni, P. S. Yu "Dynamic Load Balancing on Web-Server Systems," IEEE Internet Computing, pp.28-39, May, 1999.

[4] Kangasharju J., Ross K. W., "A Replicated Architecture for the Domain Name System," INFOCOM 2000, Nineteenth Annual Joint Conference of the IEEE Computer and Communications Societies, vol.2, pp.660-669, 2000.

[5] Kangasharju J., Ross K. W., "A Clustering Structure for Reliable Multi-casting," Computer Communications and Networks, Proceedings, Eight International Conference, pp.378-383, 1999.

[6] Il Seok Ko, "An Adaptive Web Caching Method based on the Heterogeneity of Web Object," LNCS(ISPA2005), LNCS3758, pp.853-858, 2005.11.2

[7] S. Williams, M. Abrams, C. R. Standridge, G. Abhulla and E. A. Fox, "Removal Policies in Network Caches for World Wide Web Objects," Proc. 1996 ACM Sigcomm, pp.293-304, 1996.

A Study on Analysis of the Web-Object Reference Characteristics on the Web System

Il Seok Ko

Division of Computer and Multimedia, Dongguk University, 707 Seokjang-dong,
Gyeongju-si, Gyeongsangbuk-do, 780-714 Korea
isko@dongguk.edu

Abstract. A web caching technology is one of the major factors, which affects the performance of a web system. The existing studies related to web caching technology have been focused on an increase in object-hit ratio and a decrease in caching costs. However, a web caching technology, which analyzes and reflects the reference characteristics of the web object, is required to effectively operate a web system, because the reference characteristics of web object becomes a major factor in decreasing the performance of a web system. In this paper, we analyze the reference characteristics of web object.

Keywords: web-object reference characteristics, web system, web cache.

1 Introduction

In order to increase this web system, the physical performance of a network and the performance of a web system itself should be improved. But these are the cause of cost burden, studies on an increase in the performance through a type of structural approach, such as CDN (Content Delivery Network), have been actively conducted [1, 2, 4]. Also, web caching largely affects the performance of a web system. This is due to the fact that a web system can be widely used in various Web-based systems, such as a web system itself, different web caching servers, and CDN [2, 3, 4].

Thus, web caching can effectively deal with requirements of the user of an electronic commerce system, and improve the performance of Internet. The performance of web caching depends on the effective management of a limited storage scope of the web cache. In order to achieve this performance, studies on replacement methods to maintain the frequently used web objects in the storage scope of web cache have been largely conducted [5, 6, 7]. A replacement method for web cache should reflect the characteristics of web objects.

The referenced web object has a reference locality according to the time and region. These reference characteristics can be varied according to the passage of time, and this will be a major factor decreasing the performance of the existing caching method.

The change in the variable web object reference characteristics of the user of an electronic commerce decreases the performance of web caching, and that becomes a major factor decreasing the performance of an electronic commerce system. However, the existing web caching method fails to effectively reflect the characteristics of the user of an electronic commerce system. This is because the existing web caching

T.-J. Cham et al. (Eds.): MMM 2007, LNCS 4352, Part II, pp. 678–685, 2007.

related studies have been focused mainly on the improvement of the object-hit ratio and caching costs [2, 3, 7]. Therefore, studies in this field are required. In this paper, we analyze the reference characteristics of the web object.

2 Related Studies

1) Traditional Replacement Techniques

LRU and LFU are new methods, which apply the traditional replacement method to the field of Internet caching. In addition, SIZE and LRUMIN are based on the key. The representative methods can be summarized as follows [1, 2, 3].

① The LRU method replaces objects, which are not currently used for a long time, from the storage scope in order to configure a storage scope for new objects. This method uses the characteristics of object, which are not currently used for long time, that have the highest possibility not to reference objects in the future, and applies the locality of object reference. In addition, the LFU method primarily replaces objects, which are not frequently used, based on the frequency of references.

② The SIZE method places the largest object among the stored objects in the storage scope in order to configure a storage scope for new objects. Web cache is different to caching on hardware/file system, and is variable in the size of objects. In addition, a replacement unit of Internet cache is web objects. Thus, there exists the problem that many small-sized objects removed by a single large-sized object from the storage scope. In the case of the SIZE method, this problem can be solved replacing the largest object in the cache storage scope.

③ The LRUMIN method is a modified type of the LRU. The operation of the LRUMIN is as follows. This method sets the size of a newly introduced object as S. Then, objects, which have the size larger than S/2, will be removed using the LRU if the storage scope is not available for larger than the size of S. In this case, if there are no objects larger than S/2, objects larger than S/4 will be removed using the LRU. This method repeats these processes until the storage scope is configured to guarantee a storage scope for new objects.

2) Estimation of the reference possibility

An effective cache algorithm is used to estimate the reference possibility for the object existing in the cache, and then stores objects, which have a high possibility of referencing the near future, in the storage scope of cache. There are two leading characteristics that affect the predisposition of the reference of web objects: temporal locality and reference popularity. A replacement algorithm should be decided by reflecting on the past record of the related object for these two characteristics.

① Temporal locality

Temporal locality means that a currently referenced object has a high possibility of being referenced. From the aspect of this temporal locality, most algorithms are used just before the reference time of objects. However, the LNC-R algorithm uses the past

k_{th} reference time. This algorithm uses the LRU-K algorithm, which is a type of buffer caching method, to fit a caching method for heterogeneity objects.

② Reference popularity
The reference popularity means that an object, which has a large number of references, has a high possibility to be referenced. From the aspect of this reference popularity, certain algorithms use a number of object references. In addition to this, certain methods add an aging mechanism to protect against cache pollution.

③ Estimation of the reference possibility using a mixed method
The currently used algorithm estimates the reference possibility by considering both temporal locality and reference popularity. The LRV and MIX algorithms estimate the reference possibility by considering the prior reference time and reference numbers of objects. The past k_{th} reference time used in the LNC-R algorithm is a type of coupled method, which uses both temporal locality and reference popularity. In addition, there are some studies on the coupling method, which couples the reference popularity with the GD-SIZE algorithm based on the temporal locality. In the LUV algorithm, almost all records of the past reference are used to estimate the reference possibility of objects. The LUV algorithm is a type of generalized method of the LRFU algorithm, which is studied in buffer caching, to fit it to the characteristics of web cache.

These web caching related studies have only focused on the improvement of the performance of caching itself, and they don't reflect the probability distribution characteristics of the object reference characteristics for the user of web service system, which is the major focus of this study.

3 Analysis of Users' Reference Characteristics

3.1 Log Analysis of Characteristics of Web Object

Figure 2-4 show the results of log analysis on the characteristics of the object. Many requests were frequently made for an object of 1K-10KB like Figure 2. And request frequency rate on web object of 1k-10k was the highest like Figure 3.

These results would affect various user side characteristics such as the aging character, scholastic background, and many other factors. A concentration request about the web service includes a great deal of multimedia data, the variation of age of the user, changes in size and type of a required object. The tendency of reference differs according to this. Frequency characteristics of the user have a locality on the object-size as shown in Figure 2. Web is affected by various physical factors such as the characteristics of web service and the networks states, timing states. Therefore, object reference distribution characteristics of specific time cannot reflect total reference characteristics of web object at all. So, we must reflect request frequency of web object and size of web object in order to reflect an influence of networks effectively. Total transmission quantity can reflect reference characteristics of web object well as in Figure 4.

Total transmission quantity is the value that multiplied the request frequency by an average of requested object size. The ratio of the request frequency of an object of 1KB-10KB is the highest in the request frequency side, but the rate of an object of a 10KB-100KB is the highest in the total transmission quantity side. This means that

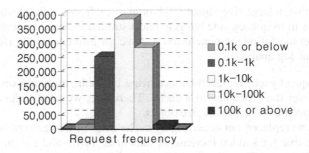

Fig. 2. Request frequency of object

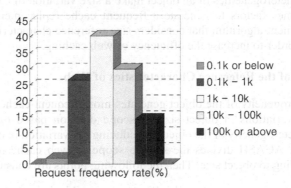

Fig. 3. Request frequency rate

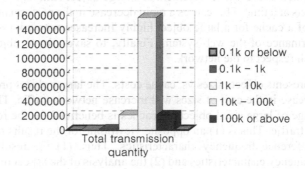

Fig. 4. Total transmission quantity

cache misses occurring in web object of 10K-100K size suddenly decreased network traffic of the system.

Analysis of the results shown in Figure 2 led us the following conclusion about the influence that reference characteristics of an object and heterogeneity of an object have on the efficiency of web cache. First, The request for a small size object (10 k or below) is frequent, and according to this, a small size object generates a frequent replacement than a large size object (10 k or above). Second, Requests for a large size object are few in frequency side but generate a sudden increase in network traffic.

We can get the following conclusion to have an influence on performance of web cache with this log analysis.

1) The frequent cache replacement occurring by cache miss of a small size object is a factor to lower the efficiency of a cache. Therefore, we must reduce the number of frequent replacements of a small size object.

2) The cache replacement occurring by cache miss of a large size object becomes a factor responsible for sudden increase of networks traffic and for the decrease in the network's efficiency. Therefore, we should reduce the replacements of a large size object.

3) Various heterogeneities of an object make a size variation of an object seriously, and this becomes factors to generate a frequent cache replacement. Therefore, the object replacement algorithm that considers size reference characteristics of an object is required in order to increase the efficiency of web caching.

3.2   Analysis of the Reference Characteristics of Web

The large heterogeneity of the object generates more frequent cache replacement and creates large variations in object size. A scope division based on object size can decrease the heterogeneity of the object by reducing the variation in object size in each divided scope. ACASH divides the storage scope of web cache into two kinds of domain according to object size. Then the following points are considered:

1) It is best to store as many web objects as possible in web cache and to save small-sized web objects in the cache with this view point.
2) As mentioned above, the replacement of a large object eliminates many small-sized web objects at a time. This causes a rapid decrease in the performance of cache. The absence of a cache for a large object highly increases network traffic and reduces the performance of the web system. Finally, to save a large object in a cache is better with respect to the network.

Figure 5 presents objects sizes vs. cache costs. The larger object presents the higher cost. An increase in the cost of sizes will increase network traffic. Thus, it is evident that the storage of large sized objects in caches is beneficial for the reduction of costs and network traffic. This is (1) an opposite viewpoint for the results of the analysis of the object reference frequency characteristics. Thus, (1) the results of the object reference frequency characteristics and (2) the analysis of the aspect of web cache costs present a trade-off for object hit ratios vs. costs.

3.3   Changes in Cache-Hit Ratio Caused by Users' References

Fig. 7 presents the change in cache-hit ratios acquired using a data smoothing method according to the change of the reference characteristics of the web object. The actual object-hit ration doesn't appear as a smoothen state as presented in Fig. 7, but it appears with undulations and outliers. It is necessary to conduct a preprocess using a certain smoothing process in order to present these data in a more smooth state as presented in Fig. 7. A smoothing process is a type of data purification that changes average data into

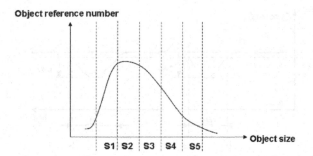

Fig. 5. Object sizes VS. object reference frequencies

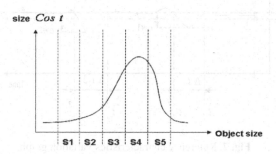

Fig. 6. Object sizes VS. cache costs

smooth data by removing non-similarity from an original set. This study applies a smoothing method with bin means, which replaces data as a mean value of bins. As described above, there are many changes in the user of an electronic commerce system due to various factors. These changes also bring changes in cache-hit ratios as illustrated in Fig. 1.

Almost all the existing studies related to the web caching have focused on the improvement of the performance of caching methods through an increase in the object-hit ratio of y-axis. However, the objective of this study is to increase the caching capability by reducing the widths of t1, t2, w1, and w2, which are generated from the results presented in Fig. 1. In order to achieve this objective, it is necessary to investigate the probability distribution characteristics of the object reference characteristics, and structural approach for a caching system rather than conduct an investigation of the caching itself, such as object-hit ratio.

As shown in Fig. 1, a rapid decrease in the object-hit ratio between t1 and t3 causes a decrease in the object-hit ratio below the mean value. In addition, a rapid increase in the object-hit ratio between t2 and t4 maintains the object-hit ratio as the mean value. These results can be caused largely by the characteristics of changes in the surfing type noted as follows.

▷ Changes in the user's preference
▷ Changes in the user's web surfing type
▷ Changes in the user: terminating the use of the existing user, starting the use of a new user

684   I.S. Ko

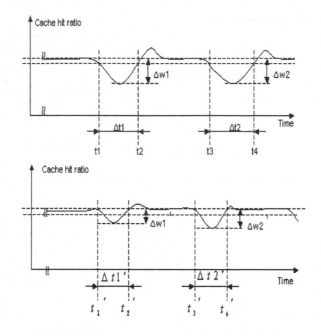

Fig. 7. Reference characteristics variation graph

In the graph, using a decrease in the width of t1 between t1 and t2, and in the width of t2 between t3 and t4, the performance of web caching can be increased. It is evident that the decrease in t1→ t1', t2→ t2', w1→ w1', and w2→ w2' increases the performance of web caching.

4 Conclusions

A web caching technology is one of the major factors, which affects the performance of a web system. The existing studies related to web caching technology have been focused on an increase in object-hit ratio and a decrease in caching costs. However, a web caching technology, which analyzes and reflects the reference characteristics of the web object, is required to effectively operate a web system, because the reference characteristics of web object becomes a major factor in decreasing the performance of a web system. In this paper, we analyze the reference characteristics of web object.

References

[1] Il Seok Ko, "Performance Improvement of Web Service System based on the Probability Distribution Characteristics," LNCS(GPC2006), LNCS3947, pp.157-164, 2006.5.3
[2] Il Seok Ko, "ACASH: An Adaptive Web Caching method based on the Heterogeneity of Web Object and Reference Characteristics," Information Sciences, ELSEVIER SCIENCE INC., Vol.176, Issue 12., 1695-1711, 2006.6.22

[3] L. Rizzo, L. Vicisano, "Replacement Polices for a Proxy Cache," IEEE/ACM Trans. Networking, vol.8, no.2, pp.158-170, 2000.

[4] H. Bahn, S. Noh, S. L. Min, and K. Koh, "Efficient Replacement of Nonuniform Objects in Web Caches," IEEE Computer, vol.35, No.6, pp.65-73, June 2002.

[5] Il Seok Ko, "An Adaptive Web Caching Method based on the Heterogeneity of Web Object," LNCS(ISPA2005), LNCS3758, pp.853-858, 2005.11.2

[6] T. Kroeger, D. Long, and J. Mogul, "Exploring the Bounds of Web Latency Reduction from Caching and Prefetching," Proc. USENIX Symp. Internet Technology and Systems (USITS 97), pp.13-22, 1997.

[7] J. Yang, W. Wang, R. Muntz, and J. Wang, "Access Driven Web Caching," UCLA Technical Report #990007, 1999.

[8] K. C. Kapur, L. R. Lamberson, *Reliability in Engineering Design*, John Wiley &Sons, 1977.

Design and Performance Analysis of the Web Caching Algorithm for Performance Improvement of the Response Speed

Yun Ji Na[1] and Il Seok Ko[2,*]

[1] Division of Internet Software Engineering, Honam University, Gwangju, Korea
yjna@honam.ac.kr
[2] Corresponding Author, Division of Computer and Multimedia, Dongguk University, 707 Seokjang-dong, Gyeongju-si, Gyeongsangbuk-do, 780-714 Korea
isko@dongguk.edu

Abstract. Until now, various web caching replacement algorithms related to this were researched. An aggravation of web object heterogeneity more frequently generates a replacement of a web object, but cannot reflect enough all kinds of characteristics of web object in these traditional replacement techniques. Especially size heterogeneity of an object has an influence on performance of a web caching seriously. Therefore, a study on web caching algorithm with size heterogeneity of an object is required.

In this study, we proposed a web object replacement algorithm with heterogeneity of a web object for performance improvement of the response speed. The algorithm is designed with a divided scope that considered size reference characteristic and reduced size heterogeneity on web object. The performance of the algorithm is analyzed with an experiment. With the experiments results, the algorithm is compared with previous replacement algorithms, and its performance is confirmed with 10%-20% elevation of object-hit ratio and an improvement of response speed.

Keywords: size variation, object heterogeneity, caching, web object.

1 Introduction

Generally we use web cache in order to improve the performance of the web base system. Cache performance depends heavily on a replacement algorithm, which dynamically select a suitable subset of objects for caching in a finite cache space. Until now LRU, LRUMIN, SIZE and various web caching replacement algorithms related to this were researched. An aggravation of web object heterogeneity more frequently generates a replacement of a web object, but cannot reflect enough all kinds of characteristics of web object in these traditional replacement techniques. Especially size heterogeneity of an object has an influence on performance of a web caching seriously. Therefore, a study on web caching algorithm with size heterogeneity of an object is required.

---

* Corresponding Author.

T.-J. Cham et al. (Eds.): MMM 2007, LNCS 4352, Part II, pp. 686–693, 2007.

In this study, we proposed a web object replacement algorithm with heterogeneity of a web object. The algorithm is designed with a divided scope that considered size reference characteristic and reduced size heterogeneity on web object. The performance of the algorithm is analyzed with an experiment. The reference characteristics of size to occur by user reference characteristics are investigated through log analysis of a web base system in the experiment. The cache scope is divided with the results of the analysis, and the replacement algorithm is tested on those divided scope. With the experiment results, the algorithm is compared with previous replacement algorithms, and its performance is confirmed with 10%-20% elevation of object-hit ratio and an improvement of response speed.

2 Related Work

Table 1 presents a comparison of various caching methods. As noted in Table 1, studies on the existing caching method have focused on the improvement of the performance of caching through an effective replacement of objects.

Table 1. Caching method

Items	Classification	Features
Traditional Method	LRU	Applicable or available for the field of Internet caching with a peculiarity of object size variability
	LRU Extensions	To prepare an affordable space for new incoming Internet objects, this procedure deletes from the latest unused objects
Based on a key	SIZE	Replace the largest objects
	LRUMIN	This method enables preventing multiple small documents from being replaced by applying the LRU only to larger objects rather than a new one in the application of LRU to Internet caching
Based on a cost	GD(Greedy Dual)-Size	This method enables deleting an object of the smallest size and the lowest transmission cost from the cache memory
	Bolot & Hoschka	This method enables selecting a deleted object using a correlative function weighted with transmission cost, object size, and the last time of request

Web-caching algorithms to relieve network congestion and access latency have proliferated in recent years. The following descriptions indicate how each algorithm selects a victim to purge from the cache.

1) LRU (least recently used): Removes the least recently referenced object first. LRU is a algorithm to replace an unused object in storage scope so that a new object gets a storage space.

2) LFU (least frequently used): Removes the least frequently referenced object first[4]. LRU and LFU have applied the traditional replacement algorithm to web caching field to have the specialty that was an object of variable size among the traditional replacement algorithms.

3) Size: Removes the largest object first. SIZE is a algorithm to replace the largest object among the objects saved in storage scope so that a new object gets a storage space. The web cache is different from traditional cache as a hardware cache and a file system cache. In web cache the unit of an exchange is a web object, and the size of an object is very variable._Therefore, in a case where the size of many objects is small, they are removed from storage scope by one object whose size is large[3]. The algorithm of SIZE improved this issue by replacing the greatest object among objects of cache storage scope for new object.

4) LRU-min: Removes the least recently referenced object whose size is larger than desired free space of size s[4]. If enough space is not freed, LRU-min sets s to $s/2$ and repeats the procedure until enough space has been freed. LRU-min is a transformation of LRU.

5) SLRU (size-adjusted LRU): $Value(i) = (1/t_{ik}) \times (1/s_i)$, where s_i is the size of object i, and t_{ik} is the number of references since the last time i was referenced[9].

Thus, web object have various characteristics. Among these, its affect much performance of web caching that is big size deflection and many object requests and diversity of object change. If we cannot reflect this characteristic properly, so that an large-sized object that use frequency is very low is saved in storage scope of a cache, it is replaced a lot of small-sized object of that a use frequency is high. Consequently the result to decrease performance of a cache is occurred in. Therefore, a study on the web-caching algorithm that reflected various characteristics of web object is required.

3 Caching Method

The number of division scope, the volume of scope to be allocated to divided scope, and the determination of size to classify an object have an important influence on the performance of web caching in this algorithm. Storage scope of the object that has an influence on web caching must be assigned in order to increase the hit ratio of cache.

The object storage scope of 10 k or above is divided into scope LARGE, and the object storage scope of 10k or less is divided into scope SMALL. Figure 1 shows the replacement algorithm that has divided cache scope.

When object requests of a client arrive, the cache administrator confirms the existence of an object in the corresponding division scope according to the size of an object. The service of the object that a client required would be provided if a cache-hit occurs. Then, the cache administrator updates the time record on when it was used so that high ranking is assigned to this object in an LRU-MIN replacement.

As was mentioned in the previous reference characteristics analysis of an object, the reference characteristics and the heterogeneity of web objects would be affected by the characteristics of web service and user's aging characteristics and user's academic background, and a timing factor. The web service that includes many different kinds of multimedia data and the object reference of a comparatively young age user increase the object reference to large size. According to this, the object reference characteristic has an extreme variation. Therefore, the size of cache scope division must be variable.

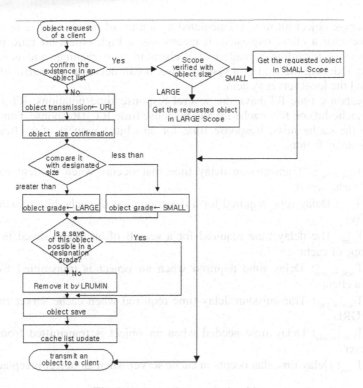

Fig. 1. cache replacement algorithm

This study experimented on the performance of a cache scope divided by 6:4 and 7:3. But the efficiency of web caching may be increased more if division scope of variable size is used according to reference characteristics of an object than by division scope of size that has been fixed.

4 Experiment

Generally, for the performance evaluation measure of the replacement algorithm, cache-hit ratio, byte-hit ratio, delay-decrease ratio, a cost-saving ratio and response time are used. In this experiment, the performance of the proposed algorithm is evaluated by comparing an average object-hit ratio and response time.

The cache-hit ratio can indicate an object-hit ratio in web caching. The average object-hit ratio can calculate an average value of an object-hit ratio on a requested object following Formula (1).

$$\text{Average object-hit ratio} = \frac{\sum_{i=1}^{n} s\_o_i \cdot n\_hit_i}{\sum_{i=1}^{n} s\_o_i \cdot n\_req_i} \times 100 \qquad \text{- Formula(1)}$$

s_oi : size of object i

n_hiti : number of hits for object i

n_reqi : number of requests for object i

An average object-hit ratio is calculated by a ratio of hit object size in size of the total object that a client requested. It means that a high object-hit ratio provides a faster response regarding a request of a client in web caching, and is capable of efficiently reducing the load of a system. Also, it can decrease the traffic of the main system and the local server system.

And response time RT have the several response time notations, RT_{ch}(Response Time of cache-hit) on the cache-hit and response time RT_{cm}(Response Time of cache miss) on the cache miss. Response time for an object request of a client has the following delay factors.

①$TDT_{client\_to\_cache}$: Transmission delay time that occurs when a client requests an object to cache server

②DDT_{cache}: Delay time required for a determination of cache-hit or cache miss of cache server

③SDT_{cache}: The delay time required for a search of an object saved in Large or Small scope of cache

④$TDT_{cache\_to\_client}$: Delay time required when an object is transmitted from cache server to a client

⑤$TDT_{cache\_to\_URL}$: Transmission delay time required when cache server requests an object to URL

⑥$TDT_{URL\_to\_cache}$: Delay time needed when an object is transmitted from URL to cache server

⑦RDT_{cache}: Delay time that occurs in cache server when an object is replaced

1) A case of cache-hit
$$RT_{ch}=TDT_{client\_to\_cache}+DDT_{cache}+SDT_{cache}+TDT_{cache\_to\_client} \text{ - Formula (2)}$$
2) A case of cache-miss
$$RT_{cm}=TDT_{client\_to\_cache}+DDT_{cache}+TDT_{cache\_to\_URL}+TDT_{URL\_to\_cache}+RDT_{cache}+TDT_{cache\_to\_client} \text{ - Formula (3)}$$

Firstly we measured object-hit ratio. The experiment method is as follows. 70% on the cache scope was assigned first to a LARGE grade, and 30% was assigned to a SMALL grade. And the experiments were conducted on object-hit performance of this algorithm and LRU, LRU-MIN, SIZE. Second, 60% on the cache scope was assigned to a LARGE grade, and 40% was assigned to a SMALL grade. Also, we experimented on the performance of these algorithms. In the figure, which showed the examination result, DIV6:4 shows 6:4 division, and DIV7:3 shows 7:3 division.

In these experiments of a hit ratio, we can get the following conclusion.

1) In the cache with small-sized capacity, the hit ratio of LRU and LRU-MIN, SIZE and the proposed algorithm were almost similar.

2) As the cache capacity grew larger, the performance of LRU and LRU-MIN, SIZE is improved. In experiment result, we can know the performance of SIZE and LRU-MIN was better than the performance of LRU.

3) And as the capacity of cache grew larger, the hit ratio performance of the proposed algorithm is more efficient than traditional replacement algorithms, and we can get 10%-15% performance enhancement.

Response time is the time required to provide the requested web object to a client. Figure 2- Figure 4 show the results of the experiment on response time. And Figure 5-Figure 6 show the gain ratio on response time.

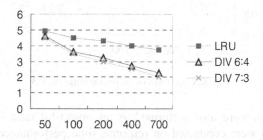

Fig. 2. Response time(sec.): compare with LRU

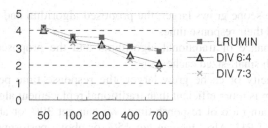

Fig. 3. Response time(sec.): compare with LRU-MIN

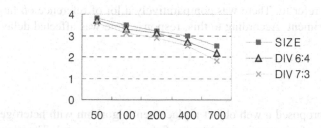

Fig. 4. Response time(sec.): compare with SIZE

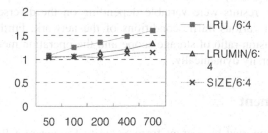

Fig. 5. Gain ratio of response time on 6:4

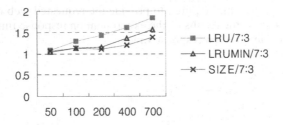

Fig. 6. Gain ratio of response time on 7:3

The experiments were also performed as an object-hit ratio in experiment one. Also, experiments were conducted on response time performance of this algorithm and LRU, LRU-MIN, SIZE. We reached the following conclusion by the experiments results of a response time.

1) As the cache scope grows larger, the proposed algorithm and LRU, LRU-MIN, SIZE all improved their response time.

2) The performance of traditional algorithms and the proposed algorithm were almost similar with small-sized cache.

3) As the capacity of cache grew larger, the response time performance of the proposed algorithm is more efficient than traditional replacement algorithms.

4) As for the gain ratio of response time, we can get 30% or above performance enhancement than LRU. Also, we can get 15% or above performance enhancement than LRUMIN and SIZE. The reason that performance enhancement of gain ratio is higher than performance enhancement of object hit ratio originated in size of the object which user refer to. There was comparatively a lot of reference on large-sized object in the experiment. According to this, response time was affected delay time of network greatly.

5   Conclusion

In this study, we proposed a web object replacement algorithm with heterogeneity of a web object for performance improvement of the response speed. The algorithm is designed with a divided scope that considered size reference characteristic and reduced size heterogeneity on web object.

The experiment results were variable depending on the diverse object reference characteristics and various traffic conditions of the network. Further researches are needed on the division-ratio of storage scope and the operation method of cache that considers this diversity dynamically.

Acknowledgement

This work was supported by a grant from Security Engineering Research Center of Ministry of Commerce, Industry and Energy.

References

[1] Il Seok Ko, "Performance Improvement of Web Service System based on the Probability Distribution Characteristics," LNCS(GPC2006), LNCS3947, pp.157-164, 2006.5.3

[2] Il Seok Ko, "ACASH: An Adaptive Web Caching method based on the Heterogeneity of Web Object and Reference Characteristics," Information Sciences, ELSEVIER SCIENCE INC., Vol.176, Issue 12., 1695-1711, 2006.6.22

[3] L. Rizzo, L. Vicisano, "Replacement Polices for a Proxy Cache," IEEE/ACM Trans. Networking, vol.8, no.2, pp.158-170, 2000.

[4] H. Bahn, S. Noh, S. L. Min, and K. Koh, "Efficient Replacement of Nonuniform Objects in Web Caches," IEEE Computer, vol.35, No.6, pp.65-73, June 2002.

[5] Il Seok Ko, "An Adaptive Web Caching Method based on the Heterogeneity of Web Object," LNCS(ISPA2005), LNCS3758, pp.853-858, 2005.11.2

[6] T. Kroeger, D. Long, and J. Mogul, "Exploring the Bounds of Web Latency Reduction from Caching and Prefetching," Proc. USENIX Symp. Internet Technology and Systems (USITS 97), pp.13-22, 1997.

[7] J. Yang, W. Wang, R. Muntz, and J. Wang, "Access Driven Web Caching," UCLA Technical Report #990007, 1999.

Induction and Implementation of Security Requirements in Each System Block

Tai-hoon Kim[1], Kouich Sakurai[2], and Sun-myung Hwang[3]

[1] Department of Information Electronics Engineering, Ewha Womans University, Korea
taihoonn@empal.com
[2] Dept. of Computer Science and Communication Engineering, Kyushu University., Japan
sakurai@csce.kyushu-u.ac.jp
[3] Department of Computer Engineering, Daejun University, Korea
sunhwang@dju.ac.kr

Abstract. When building some kinds of IT systems, security-related requirements must be considered. It is essential that not only the customer's requirements for software or systems functionality should be satisfied but also the security requirements imposed on the software or systems development should be effectively analyzed and implemented in contributing to the security objectives of customer's requirements. Though the customer's requirements must be implemented to software or systems perfectly, but these are not sufficient. The secure software or systems may be implemented by not only applying security products but also considering security requirement appended to customer's requirement. In this paper, we propose a security engineering based approach considering security when developing software or systems based on System Block Model.

1 Introduction

With the increasing reliance of society on information, the protection of that information and the systems contain that information is becoming important. In fact, many products, systems, and services are needed and used to protect information. The focus of security engineering has expanded from one primarily concerned with safeguarding classified government data to broader applications including financial transactions, contractual agreements, personal information, and the Internet. These trends have elevated the importance of security-related criteria such as ISO/IEC 21827, the Systems Security Engineering Capability Maturity Model (SSE-CMM), or ISO/IEC 15408, Common Criteria (CC) [1] [2].

In this paper, we propose a security engineering based approach considering security when developing software. And based on security block model, we propose a concept of security requirements appended to customer's requirement.

T.-J. Cham et al. (Eds.): MMM 2007, LNCS 4352, Part II, pp. 694–701, 2007.

2 System Block Model

2.1 Division of IT Systems

Implementation of any security countermeasure may require economic support. If your security countermeasures are not sufficient to prevent the threats, the existence of the countermeasures is not a real countermeasure and just considered as like waste.

First step is the division of IT systems into some parts (See Fig.1). In this paper, we divide IT systems into 4 parts. But we think this partition is not perfect one and we are now researching about that.

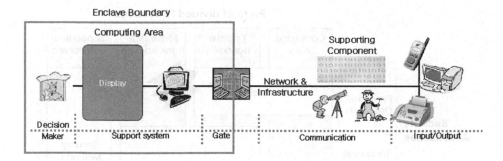

Fig. 1. Division of IT systems

Next step is construction of block matrix by using the parts of IT systems and common components we mentioned above (See the Fig. 2).

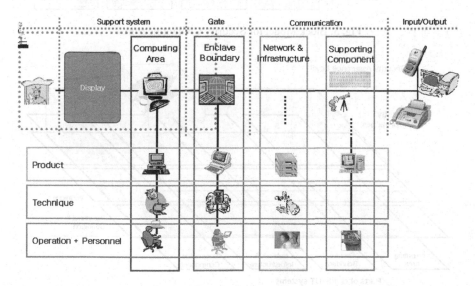

Fig. 2. Block matrix

Each cross point area of Fig.2 may be generalized and reduced into Block and matrix of Fig.3. Each Block may mean the area require security countermeasures or security method. Next step is determination of security assurance level of IT systems. Security assurance level is related to the robustness. In the concept of our Block model, all cross point area should be protected by security countermeasures.

Robustness is connected to the level or strength of security countermeasures and this idea is expressed like as Fig.4. The last step may be building security countermeasures by using Block Region.

This block matrix can be applied to information engineering and system engineering. Next is the sample can be applied to design security countermeasures for IT systems.

Parts of divided IT systems

	Computing Area	Enclave Boundary	Network & Infrastructure	Supporting Component

Security Approaches

Personnel & Operation — Security Method A

Technique

Product — Security Method B

Security Method C

Fig. 3. Block Model for Security Countermeasures

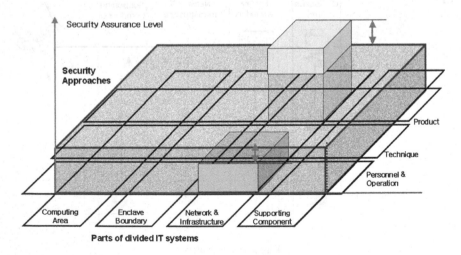

Fig. 4. Building security countermeasures by using Block Region

3 Induction and Implementation of Security

3.1 General Development Process

There are many methodologies for software or systems development, and security engineering does not mandate any specific development methodology or life cycle model. Fig.5 is used to provide a context for discussion and should not be construed as advocating a preference for one methodology (e.g. waterfall) over another (e.g. prototyping).

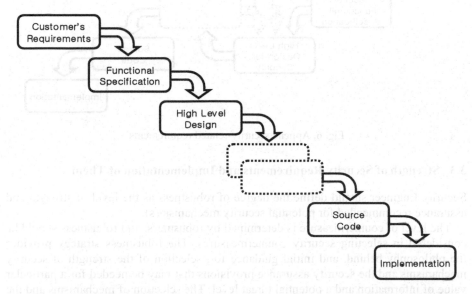

Fig. 5. The relationship between the customer's requirements and the implementation

    a) that each refinement level is a complete instantiation of the higher levels (i.e. all functions, properties, and behaviors defined at the higher level of abstraction must be demonstrably present in the lower level);

    b) that each refinement level is an accurate instantiation of the higher levels (i.e. there should be no functions, properties, and behaviors defined at the lower level of abstraction that are not required by the higher level).

3.2 Security Requirements

For the development of software, the first objective is the perfect implementation of customer's requirements. And this work may be done by very simple processes. However, if the software developed has some critical security holes, the whole network or systems that software installed and generated are very vulnerable.

    Therefore, developers or analyzers must consider some security-related factors and append a few security-related requirements to the customer's requirements. Fig.6 depicts the idea about this concept.

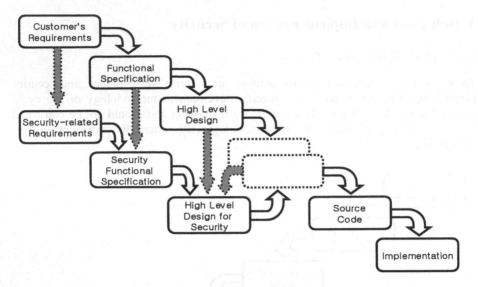

Fig. 6. Append security-related requirements

3.3   Strength of Security Requirements and Implementation of Them

Security Engineer should define the degree of robustness as the level of strength and assurance recommended for potential security mechanism(s).

The level of countermeasure is determined by robustness, and robustness should be considered in selecting security countermeasures. The robustness strategy provides the philosophy behind, and initial guidance for, selection of the strength of security mechanisms and the security assurance provisions that may be needed for a particular value of information and a potential threat level. The selection of mechanisms and the decision on the level of strength and assurance needed will be based on a Security Engineering activity that addresses the situation of a specific user, mission, and environment.

The CC will permit comparability between the results of independent security evaluations. It does so by providing a common set of requirements for the security functions of IT products and systems and for assurance measures applied to them during a security evaluation. The evaluation process establishes a level of confidence that the security functions of such products and systems and the assurance measures applied to them meet these requirements. The evaluation results may help consumers to determine whether the IT product or system is secure enough for their intended application and whether the security risks implicit in its use is tolerable.

In support of the three parts of the CC, it is anticipated that other types of documents will be published, including technical rationale material and guidance documents.

3.4   Implementation Example

For example, if the customer's requirement 'management by web' is specified, we can append some security-related requirements:

(1) Customer's requirement: We want to manage the program by web

(2) Level of robustness: By considering of assets protected and the attack potential to those assets, basic level is enough

(3) Appended requirements: Next lists are not perfect but general to all cases

(4) Grouping of security-related requirements

Requirements appended above can be classified in groups as below:

Grouping	Requirements
Identification and Authentication	-Requirements for identify mechanisms. -Requirements for authentication mechanisms. -Requirements for defining values for some number of unsuccessful authentication attempts and SF actions in cases of authentication attempt failures.
Access	-Requirements for the SF to provide the capability for SF-initiated and user initiated locking and unlocking of interactive sessions.
Cryptography	-Requirements for Cryptographic operations (Key generation and so on)
Trusted path/channels	-Requirements to establish and maintain trusted communication to or from users and the SF -Requirements for the creation of a trusted channel between the SF and other trusted IT products for the performance of security critical operations.
Auditing	- Requirements for recording the occurrence of security relevant events that take place under SF control. - Requirements for audit tools that should be available to authorized users to assist in the review of audit data.

(5) Characterizing and mapping to Security functional requirements in CC

Characterizing of requirements	Mapping to security class
- Identification - Authentication	FIA (Identification and Authentication)
- Access	FAU (Audit Review)
- Cryptographic operations	FCS (Cryptographic Support)
- Trusted path - Trusted channels	FTA (TOE access)
- Audit	FTP (Trusted path/channels)

(6) Selection of security family in the class

Security class	Mapping to security family
FIA	User authentication (FIA_UAU), User identification (FIA_UID), Authentication failures (FIA_AFL)
FAU	Security audit data generation (FAU_GEN), Security audit review (FAU_SAR), Security audit event selection (FAU_SEL), Security audit event storage (FAU_STG)
FCS	Cryptographic key management (FCS_CKM), Cryptographic operation (FCS_COP)
FTA	Limitation on multiple concurrent sessions (FTA_MCS), Session locking (FTA_SSL), TOE session establishment (FTA_TSE)
FTP	Inter-TSF trusted channel (FTP_ITC), Trusted path (FTP_TRP)

(7) Selection of security component in the family

Security family	Mapping to security component
FIA_UAU,	FIA_UAU.2 User authentication before any action, FIA_UAU.5 Multiple authentication mechanisms, FIA_UAU.7 Protected authentication feedback
FIA_UID,	FIA_UID.2 User identification before any action
FIA_AFL	FIA_AFL.1 Authentication failure handling
FAU_GEN,	FAU_GEN.1 Audit data generation, FAU_GEN.2 User identity association
FAU_SAR,	FAU_SAR.2 Restricted audit review, FAU_SAR.3 Selectable audit review
FAU_SEL,	FAU_SEL.1 Selective audit
FAU_STG	FAU_STG.1 Protected audit trail storage, FAU_STG.3 Action in case of possible audit data loss
FCS_CKM,	FCS_CKM.1 Cryptographic key generation, FCS_CKM.2 Cryptographic key distribution, FCS_CKM.3 Cryptographic key access, FCS_CKM.4 Cryptographic key destruction
FCS_COP	FCS_COP.1 Cryptographic operation
FTA_MCS,	FTA_MCS.2 Per user attribute limitation on multiple concurrent sessions
FTA_SSL,	FTA_SSL.1 TSF-initiated session locking, FTA_SSL.2 User-initiated locking
FTA_TSE	FTA_TSE.1 TOE session establishment
FTP_ITC, FTP_TRP	FTP_ITC.1 Inter-TSF trusted channel FTP_TRP.1 Trusted path

(8) Implementation of requirements to software, hardware or firmware.

4 Conclusions

In this paper, we proposed a method appending some security-related requirements to the customer's requirements by considering robustness level.

For the development of software, the first objective is the perfect implementation of customer's requirements. However, if the software developed has some critical security holes, the whole network or systems that software installed and generated may be very vulnerable.

Therefore, developers or analyzers must consider some security-related factors and append a few security-related requirements to the customer's requirements. The processes based on the refinement of the security-related requirements are considered with the processes of software implementation.

References

1. ISO. ISO/IEC 21827 Information technology – Systems Security Engineering Capability Maturity Model (SSE-CMM)
2. ISO. ISO/IEC TR 15504:1998 Information technology – Software process assessment – Part 2: A reference model for processes and process capability
3. ISO. ISO/IEC 15408:1999 Information technology - Security techniques - Evaluation criteria for IT security - Part 1: Introduction and general model
4. Tai-hoon Kim: Draft Domestic Standard-Information Systems Security Level Management, TTA, 2006

TD-CDMA Systems Using Turbo Code for Mobile Multimedia Services

Seong Chul Cho and Jin Up Kim

ETRI, Mobile Telecommunication Research Division,
161 Gajeong-dong Yuseong-gu, Daejeon, 305-350, Korea
{sccho, jukim}@etri.re.kr
http://www.etri.re.kr

Abstract. In this paper, the performance of a wireless communication system based on the TD-CDMA transmission technique is analyzed. In this paper, we present simulation results for the performance of a turbo coded TD-CDMA system with QPSK over Rayleigh fading channel model. And the system performance employing the simple averaging channel estimation is compared to the ideal case with the perfect channel estimation.

1 Introduction

IMT-2000 system can provide the voice and data services as well as mobile multimedia service up to 2Mbps with low cost. It is expected to create enormous mobile market. In addition to aforementioned services, it is very important to provide mobile Internet with low cost to mobile subscriber.

By having introduced high-speed Internet service in wireline network, Korea has made enormous progress in the IT field. However, we have not done any research work to deliver this Internet service by wireless to end-users. The Internet service shows us the asymmetric traffic pattern between uplink and downlink compared to conventional voice and video service. UTRA TDD mode is very well suited to this mobile Internet service among the IMT-2000 technologies because of the flexible assignment of time slots to either downlink or uplink [1][2]. This TDD mode has almost similar protocol structure as WCDMA mode, but shows the different modem schemes to W-CDMA. If we get this difference, we will easily develop UTRA TDD system when it is commercialized.

The third generation mobile radio system UTRA that has been specified in the 3GPP consists of two modes, FDD mode and TDD mode. The agreement recommends the use of WCDMA for UTRA FDD and TD-CDMA for UTRA TDD. TD-CDMA is based on a combination of TDMA and CDMA, whereas W-CDMA is a pure CDMA-based system [1]. We have focused our energy to develop WCDMA and cdma2000 systems. Siemens has been developed this TD-CDMA technology for a few years but we did not developed it until now. In this paper, we have evaluated the performance of the TD-CDMA for mobile Internet services

The organization of this paper is as following. Section 2 introduces the characteristics of TDD systems, and analyzes the received signal to build the receiver structure.

T.-J. Cham et al. (Eds.): MMM 2007, LNCS 4352, Part II, pp. 702–712, 2007.

In section 3, we analyze the performance of the TD-CDMA systems. Finally, our investigations are summarized and concluded in section 4.

2 TD-CDMA System

The TD-CDMA system comprises standard TDMA slotted structures where in each time slot spreading techniques are used to allow simultaneous transmission by several users. The time slots are used in the sense of a TDMA component to separate different user signals in the time domain. The TDMA frame has a duration of 10 ms and is subdivided into 15 time slots of $2560*T_c$ duration each. A time slot corresponds to 2560 chips. The physical channel signal format is presented in fig.1 [3].

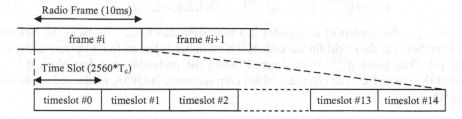

Fig. 1. Physical Channel Signal Format

Each 10 ms frame consists of 15 time slots, each allocated to either the uplink or the downlink. With such flexibility, the TDD mode can be adapted to different environments and deployment scenarios. In any configuration at least one time slot has to be allocated for the downlink and at least one time slot has to be allocated for the uplink.

A physical channel in TDD is a burst, which is transmitted in a particular timeslot within allocated radio frames. The allocation can be continuous, i.e. the time slot in every frame is allocated to the physical channel or discontinuous, i.e. the time slot in a subset of all frames is allocated only. Three types of bursts for dedicated physical channels are defined. All of them consist of two data symbol fields, a midamble and a guard period, the lengths of which are different for the individual burst types. The burst type 1 is shown in fig. 2.

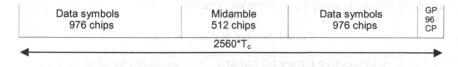

Fig. 2. Burst Structure of the Burst Type I

The duration of a burst is one time slot. Several bursts can be transmitted at the same time from one transmitter. In this case, the data parts must use different OVSF channelisation codes, but the same scrambling code. The midamble parts are either identically or differently shifted versions of a cell-specific basic midamble code [3].

The data part of the burst is spread with a combination of channelisation code and scrambling code. The channelisation code is a OVSF code, which can have a spreading factor of 1, 2, 4, 8, or 16. The data rate of the physical channel is depending on the used spreading factor of the used OVSF code. Downlink physical channels shall use spreading factor of 16. Multiple parallel physical channels can be used to support higher data rates. These parallel physical channels shall be transmitted using different channelisation codes. Operation with a single code with spreading factor 1 is possible for the downlink physical channels. The range of spreading factor that may be used for uplink physical channels shall range from 16 down to 1 [3].

The data modulation is performed to the bits from the output of the physical channel mapping procedure and combines always 2 consecutive binary bits to a complex valued data symbol. Each user burst has two data carrying parts, termed data blocks:

$$\underline{\mathbf{d}}^{(k,i)} = \left(\underline{d}_1^{(k,i)}, \underline{d}_2^{(k,i)}, ..., \underline{d}_{N_k}^{(k,i)} \right)^T, \quad i = 1,2; k = 1,...,K_{Code} \tag{1}$$

K_{Code} is the number of used codes in a time slot, max $K_{Code} = 16$. N_k is the number of symbols per data field for the code k. This number is linked to the spreading factor q_k [3]. Data block $\underline{\mathbf{d}}^{(k,1)}$ is transmitted before the midamble and data block $\underline{\mathbf{d}}^{(k,2)}$ after the midamble. The complex-valued chip sequence is QPSK modulated as shown in fig. 3.

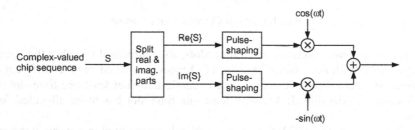

Fig. 3. Modulation of Complex Valued Chip Sequences

The data modulation is QPSK, thus the data symbols $\underline{d}_n^{(k,i)}$ are generated from two consecutive data bits from the output of the physical channel mapping procedure:

$$b_{l,n}^{(k,i)} \in \{0,1\}, \quad l = 1,2; k = 1,...,K_{Code}; n = 1,...,N_k; i = 1,2 \tag{2}$$

using the following mapping to complex symbols:

Table 1. Symbol Mapping in TDD

consecutive binary bit pattern $b_{1,n}^{(k,i)} \, b_{2,n}^{(k,i)}$	complex symbol $\underline{d}_n^{(k,i)}$
00	+j
01	+1
10	-1
11	-j

In the following fig. 4 shows the transmitter structure of the TDD system. In this Figure, the coded signals are mapped to the complex symbols for spreading and channelizing. The mapped symbols are spreaded by the orthogonal channel code which is the real value having the maximum length of 16. Then, the mapped symbols are scrambled by the encrypted code. This encrypted code is unique in each cell and it has the length of 16.

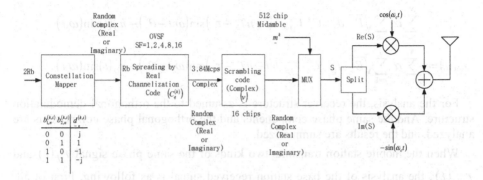

Fig. 4. Structure of Transmitter in TDD System

The following Eq. (3) shows the transmitted signal $s(t)$ from the transmitter in fig.4. The signal is composed of $s_{II}(t)$, $s_{QQ}(t)$, $s_{IQ}(t)$, and $s_{QI}(t)$.

$$s_{II}(t) = \sqrt{E_c}\, d_{I,n}^k\, C_q^k\, V_I^k\, \cos(\omega_c t)$$

$$s_{QQ}(t) = -\sqrt{E_c}\, d_{Q,n}^k\, C_q^k\, V_Q^k\, \cos(\omega_c t)$$

$$s_{IQ}(t) = -\sqrt{E_c}\, d_{I,n}^k\, C_q^k\, V_Q^k\, \sin(\omega_c t)$$

$$s_{QI}(t) = -\sqrt{E_c}\, d_{Q,n}^k\, C_q^k\, V_I^k\, \sin(\omega_c t)$$

(3)

It is assumed that a data modulator has the pulse shaping filter for a same phase signal and orthogonal phase signal. Then, based on the Eq. (3), the mobile station's transmitted signal $s(t)$ can be expressed as $s_{II}(t)$, $s_{QQ}(t)$, $s_{IQ}(t)$, and $s_{QI}(t)$.

$$s_{II}(t) = \sum_{n=1}^{q} \sqrt{E_c}\, d_{I,n}^k\, C_n^k\, V_{I,n}^k\, h(t - nT_c)\cos(\omega_c t)$$

$$s_{QQ}(t) = -\sum_{n=1}^{q} \sqrt{E_c}\, d_{Q,n}^k\, C_n^k\, V_{Q,n}^k\, h(t - nT_c)\cos(\omega_c t)$$

$$s_{IQ}(t) = -\sum_{n=1}^{q} \sqrt{E_c}\, d_{I,n}^k\, C_n^k\, V_{Q,n}^k\, h(t - nT_c)\sin(\omega_c t)$$

$$s_{QI}(t) = -\sum_{n=1}^{q} \sqrt{E_c}\, d_{Q,n}^k\, C_n^k\, V_{I,n}^k\, h(t - nT_c)\sin(\omega_c t)$$

(4)

And, after undergoing the frequency selective fading channel, the base station received signal $r(t)$ is expressed as $r_{II}(t)$, $r_{QQ}(t)$, $r_{IQ}(t)$, and $r_{QI}(t)$.

$$r_{II}(t) = \sum_{j=1}^{N_p} \alpha_j \sum_{n=1}^{q} \sqrt{E_c}\ d_{I,n}^k\ C_n^k\ V_{I,n}^k\ h(t - nT_c - \tau_j)\cos(\omega_c t - \theta_j) + n_I(t)\cos(\omega_c t)$$

$$r_{QQ}(t) = -\sum_{j=1}^{N_p} \alpha_j \sum_{n=1}^{q} \sqrt{E_c}\ d_{Q,n}^k\ C_n^k\ V_{Q,n}^k\ h(t - nT_c - \tau_j)\cos(\omega_c t - \theta_j) + n_I(t)\cos(\omega_c t)$$

$$r_{IQ}(t) = -\sum_{j=1}^{N_p} \alpha_j \sum_{n=1}^{q} \sqrt{E_c}\ d_{I,n}^k\ C_n^k\ V_{Q,n}^k\ h(t - nT_c - \tau_j)\sin(\omega_c t - \theta_j) - n_Q(t)\sin(\omega_c t) \qquad (5)$$

$$r_{QI}(t) = -\sum_{j=1}^{N_p} \alpha_j \sum_{n=1}^{q} \sqrt{E_c}\ d_{Q,n}^k\ C_n^k\ V_{I,n}^k\ h(t - nT_c - \tau_j)\sin(\omega_c t - \theta_j) - n_Q(t)\sin(\omega_c t)$$

For the analysis, the receiver structure is assumed to the orthogonal demodulation structure. And the same phase components and the orthogonal phase components are analyzed, and the results are summarized.

When the mobile station transmits two kinds of the same phase signal $r_{II}(t)$ and $r_{QQ}(t)$, the analysis of the base station received signal is as following. First of all, after passing the LPF, Sampler, and matched filter, the same phase signal can be expressed as Eq. (6), (7), (8) and (9).

$$r_{II}(t) \times \cos(\omega_c t) = \sum_{j=1}^{N_p} \alpha_j \sum_{n=1}^{q} \sqrt{E_c}\ d_{I,n}^k\ C_n^k\ V_{I,n}^k\ h(t - nT_c - \tau_j)\cos(\omega_c t - \theta_j) \times \cos(\omega_c t)$$
$$+ n_I(t)\cos(\omega_c t) \times \cos(\omega_c t)$$
$$= \sum_{j=1}^{N_p} \alpha_j \sum_{n=1}^{q} \sqrt{E_c}\ d_{I,n}^k\ C_n^k\ V_{I,n}^k\ h(t - nT_c - \tau_j)\frac{\cos(\theta_j) + \cos(2\omega_c t - \theta_j)}{2} \qquad (6)$$
$$+ n_I(t)\frac{1 + \cos(2\omega_c t)}{2}$$

$$r_{QQ}(t) \times \cos(\omega_c t) = -\sum_{j=1}^{N_p} \alpha_j \sum_{n=1}^{q} \sqrt{E_c}\ d_{Q,n}^k\ C_n^k\ V_{Q,n}^k\ h(t - nT_c - \tau_j)\cos(\omega_c t - \theta_j) \times \cos(\omega_c t)$$
$$+ n_I(t)\cos(\omega_c t) \times \cos(\omega_c t)$$
$$= -\sum_{j=1}^{N_p} \alpha_j \sum_{n=1}^{q} \sqrt{E_c}\ d_{Q,n}^k\ C_n^k\ V_{Q,n}^k\ h(t - nT_c - \tau_j)\frac{\cos(\theta_j) + \cos(2\omega_c t - \theta_j)}{2} \qquad (7)$$
$$+ n_I(t)\frac{1 + \cos(2\omega_c t)}{2}$$

$$r_{II}(t) \times \cos(\omega_c t)\Big|_{LPF} = \sum_{j=1}^{N_p} \alpha_j \sum_{n=1}^{q} \sqrt{E_c}\ d_{I,n}^k\ C_n^k\ V_{I,n}^k\ R(mT_c - nT_c - \tau_j)\frac{\cos(\theta_j)}{2}$$
$$+ \frac{n_I^*(mT_c)}{2} \qquad (8)$$

$$r_{QQ}(t) \times \cos(\omega_c t)\big|_{LPF} = -\sum_{j=1}^{N_p} \alpha_j \sum_{n=1}^{q} \sqrt{E_c} \; d_{Q,n}^k \; C_n^k \; V_{Q,n}^k \; R(mT_c - nT_c - \tau_j) \frac{\cos(\theta_j)}{2}$$
$$+ \frac{n_I^*(mT_c)}{2} \tag{9}$$

Also the orthogonal phase component signals can be expressed as Eq. (10), (11), (12), and (13).

$$r_{II}(t) \times \sin(\omega_c t) = \sum_{j=1}^{N_p} \alpha_j \sum_{n=1}^{q} \sqrt{E_c} \; d_{I,n}^k \; C_n^k \; V_{I,n}^k \; h(t - nT_c - \tau_j) \cos(\omega_c t - \theta_j) \times \sin(\omega_c t)$$
$$+ n_I(t) \cos(\omega_c t) \times \sin(\omega_c t)$$
$$= \sum_{j=1}^{N_p} \alpha_j \sum_{n=1}^{q} \sqrt{E_c} \; d_{I,n}^k \; C_n^k \; V_{I,n}^k \; h(t - nT_c - \tau_j) \frac{-\sin(-\theta_j) + \sin(2\omega_c t - \theta_j)}{2} \tag{10}$$
$$+ n_I(t) \frac{\sin(0) + \sin(2\omega_c t)}{2}$$

$$r_{QQ}(t) \times \sin(\omega_c t) = -\sum_{j=1}^{N_p} \alpha_j \sum_{n=1}^{q} \sqrt{E_c} \; d_{Q,n}^k \; C_n^k \; V_{Q,n}^k \; h(t - nT_c - \tau_j) \cos(\omega_c t - \theta_j) \times \sin(\omega_c t)$$
$$+ n_I(t) \cos(\omega_c t) \times \sin(\omega_c t)$$
$$= -\sum_{j=1}^{N_p} \alpha_j \sum_{n=1}^{q} \sqrt{E_c} \; d_{Q,n}^k \; C_n^k \; V_{Q,n}^k \; h(t - nT_c - \tau_j) \frac{-\sin(-\theta_j) + \sin(2\omega_c t - \theta_j)}{2} \tag{11}$$
$$+ n_I(t) \frac{\sin(0) + \sin(2\omega_c t)}{2}$$

$$r_{II}(t) \times \sin(\omega_c t)\big|_{LPF} = \sum_{j=1}^{N_p} \alpha_j \sum_{n=1}^{q} \sqrt{E_c} \; d_{I,n}^k \; C_n^k \; V_{I,n}^k \; R(mT_c - nT_c - \tau_j) \frac{\sin(\theta_j)}{2} \tag{12}$$

$$r_{QQ}(t) \times \sin(\omega_c t)\big|_{LPF} = -\sum_{j=1}^{N_p} \alpha_j \sum_{n=1}^{q} \sqrt{E_c} \; d_{Q,n}^k \; C_n^k \; V_{Q,n}^k \; R(mT_c - nT_c - \tau_j) \frac{\sin(\theta_j)}{2} \tag{13}$$

The demodulated data is obtained by multiplying same phase and orthogonal phase signal expressed Eq. (8), (9), (12), and (13) by same phase and orthogonal phase code, respectively. As the result, the demodulator structure of the base station can be the fig. 5.

When the mobile station transmits two kinds of orthogonal phase signal $r_{IQ}(t)$ and $r_{QI}(t)$, the analysis of the base station received signals is similar with the analysis of same phase sig0nal. Therefore, after passing the LPF, Sampler, and matched filter, the orthogonal phase signal can be expressed as Eq. (14), (15), (16) and (17).

$$r_{IQ}(t) \times \cos(\omega_c t)\big|_{LPF} = \sum_{j=1}^{N_p} \alpha_j \sum_{n=1}^{q} \sqrt{E_c} \; d_{I,n}^k \; C_n^k \; V_{Q,n}^k \; R(mT_c - nT_c - \tau_j) \frac{\sin(\theta_j)}{2} \tag{14}$$

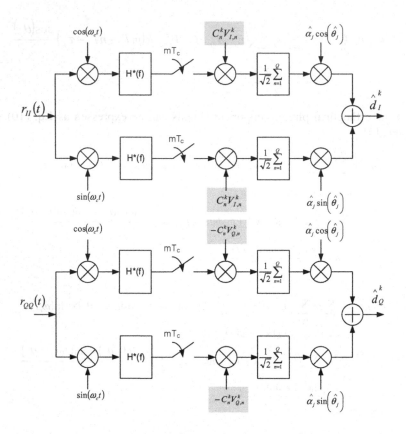

Fig. 5. Demodulator Structure for Same Phase Components

$$r_{QI}(t) \times \cos(\omega_c t)\big|_{LPF} = \sum_{j=1}^{N_p} \alpha_j \sum_{n=1}^{q} \sqrt{E_c}\ d_{Q,n}^k\ C_n^k\ V_{I,n}^k\ R(mT_c - nT_c - \tau_j) \frac{\sin(\theta_j)}{2} \qquad (15)$$

$$r_{IQ}(t) \times \sin(\omega_c t)\big|_{LPF} = -\sum_{j=1}^{N_p} \alpha_j \sum_{n=1}^{q} \sqrt{E_c}\ d_{I,n}^k\ C_n^k\ V_{Q,n}^k\ R(mT_c - nT_c - \tau_j) \frac{\cos(\theta_j)}{2} \\ - \frac{n_Q^*(mT_c)}{2} \qquad (16)$$

$$r_{QI}(t) \times \sin(\omega_c t)\big|_{LPF} = -\sum_{j=1}^{N_p} \alpha_j \sum_{n=1}^{q} \sqrt{E_c}\ d_{Q,n}^k\ C_n^k\ V_{I,n}^k\ R(mT_c - nT_c - \tau_j) \frac{\cos(\theta_j)}{2} \\ + \frac{n_Q^*(mT_c)}{2} \qquad (17)$$

The demodulated data is obtained by multiplying same phase and orthogonal phase signal expressed Eq. (14), (15), (16), and (17) by same phase and orthogonal phase code. From such analysis, same phase and orthogonal phase signals transmitted by a mobile station are expressed Eq. (8), (9), (12), and (13) and Eq. (14), (15), (16), and (17). Base on these equations, the structure of base station's demodulator is shown in fig. 6.

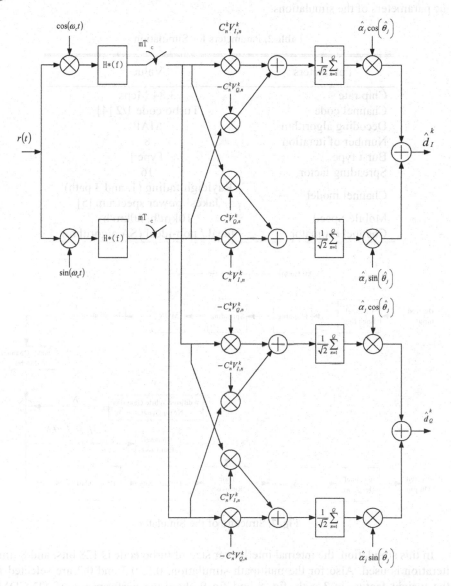

Fig. 6. Structure of Receiver in TD-CDMA System

3 Simulations

For the simulation, this paper assumes some cases. At first, 3.84Mcps TDD system is considered. And secondly, it is assumed that there is no guard interval in burst type 1. At third, the data frame is consisted of one timeslot unit having 2560 chips. Finally, it is assumed that the power control and frame synchronization is perfect. Table 2 shows the parameters of the simulations.

Table 2. Parameters for Simulation

Parameters	Value
Chip rate	3.84 Mcps
Channel code	Turbo code 1/2 [4]
Decoding algorithm	MAP
Number of iteration	8
Burst type	Type I
Spreading factor	16
Channel model	Rayleigh fading (1, and 3 path) Jakes' power spectrum [5]
Mobile Speed	10km/h, 60km/h
Channel estimator	Ideal / non-ideal (SA algorithm)

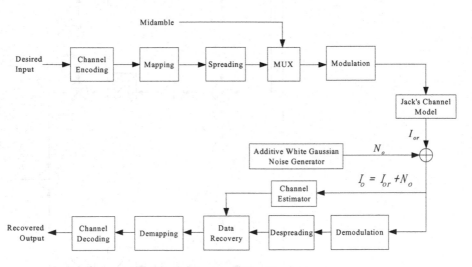

Fig. 7. Structure of the Simulator

In this simulation, the internal interleaver size of turbo code is 128 bits, and 8 times iteration is used. Also for the multipath simulation, 0.5, 0.3 and 0.2 are selected for the weight factors in 3-path. fig. 8 and fig 9 show the performance of TD-CDMA system using turbo code.

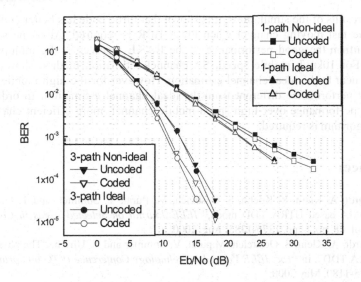

Fig. 8. BER performance at v=10km/h

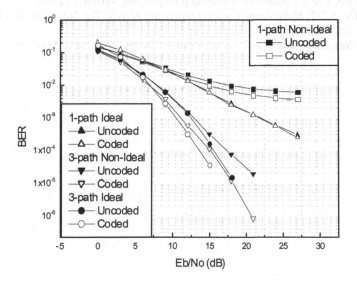

Fig. 9. BER performance at v=60km/h

4   Conclusion

In this paper, we propose and analyze a channel estimator and data demodulator structures for the TD-CDMA system, which is a TDD-based CDMA system, one of third-generation mobile communication systems. We analyze the performance of the TD-CDMA system using turbo code over mobile channel environments.

As the results of the simulations, it is shown that turbo code has better coding gains in case the fast moving channel when lower BER is required. Also, the simulation results confirm the good performance of the RAKE receiver in the multipath environment. For 10km/h mobile speed, SA channel estimation method shows the performance near to the ideal channel estimation. However for the high mobile speed, it shows the performance different from the ideal channel estimation. In order to improve the performance over high speed mobile channel, more efficient channel estimation algorithm is required.

References

1. M. Haardt, A. Klein, R. Koehn, S. Oestreich, M. Purat, V. Sommer, and T. Ulrich, "The TD-CDMA based UTRA TDD mode," *IEEE Journal on Selected Areas in Communications*, vol. 18, no. 8, pp. 1375-1385, Aug. 2000.
2. M. Haardt, A. Klein, S. Oestreich, M.purat, V. Sommer and T. Ulrich, "The physical layer of UTRA TDD", in *Proc. IEEE Vehicular Technology Conference (VTC'00 Spring)*, vol. 2, pp. 1175-1180, May 2000.
3. 3GPP TS 25.221, *Physical channels and mapping of transport channels onto physical channels (TDD)*, The 3rd Generation Partnership Project, ver. 4.0.0 Mar. 2001.
4. 3GPP TS 25.222, *Multiplexing and channel coding (TDD)*, The 3rd Generation Partnership Project, ver. 4.0.0 Mar. 2001.
5. W. C. Jakes, *Micorwave mobile communications*, Wiley-IEEE Press, May 1994.

Textual Communication in Virtual Environments for Real World Interaction

Adrian Haffegee and Vassil Alexandrov

Advanced Computing and Emerging Technologies Centre,
The School of Systems Engineering, University of Reading,
Reading, RG6 6AY, United Kingdom
sir04amh@reading.ac.uk

Abstract. Ever since man invented writing he has used text to store and distribute his thoughts. With the advent of computers and the Internet the delivery of these messages has become almost instant. Textual conversations can now be had regardless of location or distance.

Advances in computational power for 3D graphics are enabling Virtual Environments(VE) within which users can become increasingly more immersed. By opening these environments to other users such as initially through sharing these text conversations channels, we aim to extend the immersed experience into an online virtual community.

This paper examines work that brings textual communications into the VE, enabling interaction between the real and virtual worlds.

1 Introduction

The use of text within computers is huge. It formed the basis of early man/machine communications, and even in todays GUI driven interfaces it still plays an enormous role. The written word gives us the ability to store, retrieve and duplicate language; and in so doing saving countless quantities of time. In modern technology we use computerized text for communicating via email, creation of documents, control menus, status, debugging and so on. Clearly text plays an intrinsic part of the IT revolution.

Potentially two of the most familiar and widespread technologies used for instant communications in today's modern community are SMS text messages sent through the telephone networks, and Instant Messaging (IM) such as Skype or MSN messenger sent over the Internet. Indeed, recent advances are beginning to merge these areas with new devices being able to make simultaneous use of both of these services. A key factor of these technologies is their dependence on simple characters and words for delivering their content.

Virtual Reality (VR) concerns itself with human interaction to synthetic sensory experiences. A Virtual Environment (VE) can be considered as a collection of these experiences that are used to mimic a physical location, and give a user the feelings of experiencing an alternate reality [1]. The stronger these synthetic experiences are compared to the lower the user's attachment is to to the real world, can be used as a measure of immersion within the VE. Improving this

T.-J. Cham et al. (Eds.): MMM 2007, LNCS 4352, Part II, pp. 713–721, 2007.

level of immersion is one of the goals of VR technology, with systems such as the CAVE [2] being at the forefront of recent development.

Generally, VR applications tend to remain in the virtual domain, and do not contain functional real-life communication mediums. That is they have not been developed for interaction with the real world except that which is done in physically using the VR hardware. The VE can be considered as a closed system with limited boundaries. Although there are Networked Virtual Environments in which multiple dislocated users share a distributed environment [3], these can also be considered as being closed to those not actively participating within the environment.

Adopting support for basic networked textual communications such SMS text, Instant Messaging or email within the VE would instantly break the boundary between the real and virtual worlds. No longer would users have to switch away from real life when they enter the VE. This move has long ago been achieved in desktop computing, and users often have an online, interactive presence while working or playing at their computers. This has yet to happen through immersive virtual environments, and yet doing so would offer the promise of a deeper level of interactivity with the online experience. Additional advances including a true 3D user interface, the inclusion of real world video and sound, and ever increasing computational power would further improve this experience, lending toward the dream of an online enhanced reality.

This paper shows how textual communication interfaces can be created and used within a VE, and describes sample applications making use of this functionality. In the following section we will outline the uses and construction of immersive VEs. We will review existing technology that can be used for displaying 3D text within these VEs, and explore potential protocols that can be used for networking textual communications. In Section 3 we describe the work we have undertaken in bringing textual communications into VE application development. We explain the protocols chosen and outline their implementation into an existing VE development framework. Subsequently in Section 4 we will discuss sample uses of this technology, including an existing case study in which a virtual memorial has been created allowing SMS text and IM style interaction. Finally we conclude in 5, where we review the findings of this work and detail further areas of study.

2   Background and Related Work

An aim of Virtual Environment development is to create a user experience in which the participants believe in the realism of the virtual world. This does not mean they have to except the environment as reality, but rather that they believe there is a distinguishable three dimensional representation of a world that they can interact in and with. Achieving this aim is no simple task, especially when using immersive environments that actually place the user inside the virtual world. Before investigating how we would add text to such an world we first need to further familiarize ourselves with how we create and use a VE.

Development of Virtual Environments can take one of several approaches. First, any application can be developed from scratch. However this is generally unfeasible due to the size and complexity of the task which would require deep understanding of computer graphics, networking, and Human Computer Interaction. Hardware independence can be achieved by making use of graphics and control libraries such as OpenGL or CAVELib[4], or even full scene representation and control can be achieved through one of the many scenegraph library offerings[5,6]. But still combining all of the different aspects of VE creation is no easy task.

An alternative approach is to make use of one of the 3D authoring tools such as Vega Prime, Eon Realities or Virtools. Being commercial products however, these offerings are costly and have limited interoperability and extendability.

Open source frameworks are also becoming available in which developers have performed the manual work of combining external libraries with their own internal glue to create the skeletons for application development. Using these, application developers can easily construct Virtual Environments and applications. Two such frameworks are VieGen, developed here at the University of Reading (with functionality described in [7]), and inVRs[8] developed at the Johannes Kepler University in Linz. Both are currently based around the OpenSG scenegraph and enable simplified creation of networked VEs. Being open source these frameworks are easy to modify and expand and due to their commonality will share many features.

Due to the author's familiarity the research in this paper has been implemented using the VieGen framework, however it is assumed it would easily port to other OpenSG based environments (e.g. inVRs). The concepts remain regardless of any implementation used.

VieGen. has been developed as an open source Virtual Interactive Environment Generation framework. It provides a set of tools and utilities that simplify creation of VEs. Using its CAVE Scene Manager component, environments can be executed throughout the range of VR systems (CAVEs, cluster displays, powerwalls, desktops, etc). Scenes describing the desired VE can be configured through either an XML or human readable text file, allowing non-programmers to create sample applications. Scalable networking support has been provided allowing distribution of the environment and shared interaction with remote sites.

The SceneController is an optional management entity in the VieGen framework. It gives control over a hierarchy of virtual objects within the scene. As well as maintaining the position of these objects, it also uses heartbeats to control their attributes and personalities. This could involve ownership, movement and manipulation, or reaction to external stimuli (e.g. Gravity/physics, time related events, etc.). All items within a virtual environment can be treated as virtual objects. While there are a number of predefined objects such as geometric primitives, models loaded from files, 3D text or menus, new ones can be created and dynamically loaded into existing environments. Figure 1 shows existing applications that have been created using VieGen. As can be seen both these applications use the 3D text support already provided by the framework.

Fig. 1. Text within VieGen; shopper with menu (left), embedded status (right)

Until recently this text was generally only used for informational status and 3D menus. In both these cases the words would appear within the scene, and to the user they would look like blocks of text floating in the air in front of them. This text can be of various fonts, sizes and colours, all of which can be modified as required. For the menus the user selects the required option by moving their joystick-like wand to the appropriate item, at which point it would change colour allowing them to select that option.

Text in the Immersive Virtual Environment. When text is displayed on a traditional 2D display it is generally placed so the text sits on the screen facing the user. In three dimensional space more thought has to be applied as to where to place the text. This is especially true in immersive environments, and even more so when the user is able to move around the environment. To maintain a user's feeling of presence within a VE it is desirable that they do not suffer from needless distractions. If text is placed in the environment at an inappropriate position, the shifting of the user's eye focus could cause such a distraction. For this reason it is generally not ideal to locate the text directly at the display screen/wall.

With VieGen all objects can be located in the scene through different attachment points. These points can be at absolute scene positions or attached with an offset to other objects or tracked locations. Since the head and hand are often tracked these can be used as the base mounting points. This is used with the 3D menus, where when required they appear relative to the users hand position, making it easy for the user to see and select an option without an unnecessary distraction. Similarly status messages could be attached relative to the users head position, meaning the messages would follow the users gaze wherever they looked, providing a simple heads up display.

3   Technology

Choice of SMS Delivery Protocol. While directly interfacing to IM communications is achievable through the Internet, this is not the case for SMS text messaging. Since these messages originate in the telephony domain it is necessary to use a gateway to bridge these incoming Mobile Oriented (MO) services.

Many mobile data communication providers offer this functionality, with the one chosen for this research being Connection Software.

Connection Software offer various transcoding APIs for MO messages, including SMTP(email), HTTP and SOAP. Each of these can be configured for specific destinations, login usernames and passwords. The SMTP approach sends a standard email containing the SMS message and its attributes and does not require receipt acknowledgment. HTTP and SOAP are similar in that they are both text based messaging protocols for transferring information over the Internet. SOAP extends HTTP by adding an XML based communication protocol on top of the HTTP network protocol. Both of these approaches require the appropriate acknowledgment message to be returned on successful receipt of an SMS message. Since the messaging exchange is simple the SOAP approach was deemed as overkill, and the HTTP exchange method was used.

The HTTP network protocol consists of a series of text based transactions. Each transaction consists of a client sending an HTTP request to a server, and the server responding with an HTTP response. Generally the HTTP request is a GET message and is used to retrieve information (such as a Web page) from the server. However, as in this case the HTTP request can alternatively be a POST message containing information for the remote entity. Here it is information about the received SMS message. The HTTP response is used to indicate the status of the request, with is absence being indicative of the messages failure.

Once the Connection Software servers have received an incoming SMS message, they will send the HTTP POST every minute until they receive the successful HTTP response or they timeout (after a couple days of trying). They will only attempt to forward one message at a time, and will queue subsequent SMS messages until the previous ones have been successfully delivered.

The Messaging Storage and Retrieval Server. While the method above is useful in achieving guaranteed delivery of SMS messages, it is limited with additional message handling features being desired. These would include storage and retrieval of previously sent messages, or in the case of messages to be displayed to the general public, some form of content sorting and filtering.

To facilitate this extra level of service a stand alone Messaging Storage and Retrieval Server was created. This functionality was developed as a non graphical, low overhead daemon application that could be left permanently running on a host server. The daemon would constantly watch a configurable TCP port for incoming HTTP requests, either from the Connection Software servers with notification of newly received SMS messages, or from its client applications requesting status of received messages. It would store backup copies of all received messages, and whenever restarted would reload these previously stored lists. Client applications would connect to this storage daemon and could send HTTP requests to ask for a list of the SMS history and/or request to be kept informed of newly arrived messages.

By using a similar protocol to the incoming SMS HTTP POST, it was also possible to allow messages to be sent to the message server from elsewhere on the Internet. The protocol was changed slightly in that the ReplyTo and SendTo tag=value pairs referenced the sending application rather SMS sender's telephone number. By monitoring theses fields the message server was able to ascertain the original source of incoming messages and was able to handle them appropriately. In effect this new class of messages added IM style functionality, and enabled Internet connected endpoints to send textual messages for storage and display.

With the message server being able to receive and decode HTTP requests special event messages can also be sent to it, providing additional features such as clearing its stored message log, requesting updates of only particular types of messages, or turning on certain levels of filtering. This final option proved quite useful when swear words were filtered from incoming SMS texts during a public display of the technology.

VieGen Text Display Extensions. When working with textual communications it is often desirable to store the full text and only work on sections of it at a time. For instance if the text is a long email message only a small part of it may need to be displayed at once. To satisfy this requirement the TextBuffer class was developed consisting of a resizable circular buffer for holding the text. Access functions were provided for adding, removing and editing the text within the buffer. One use of this buffer might include storage for multiple incoming text messages which can be scrolled through with some of then being displayed much like a traditional IM application. Alternatively the buffer could be filled with textual output from application building or debugging, which could then be accessed much like a DOS/console display window.

Extensions to the text buffer add intelligence to the way text is displayed. This includes associating the text buffer with a predefined shape and size. As the buffer grows or shrinks the text's font is resized to always provide a good fit to this shape.

In addition to containing text for display, the textual messages could also include escape sequences for in line control of the text. These would be special sequences of characters that would only be used for altering the way the text is to be displayed. Common escape sequences could be used to modify the formatted text size, colour or font, or even for inserting special icons into the displayed stream.

4   Applications

The most obvious use of this technology is using it to receive SMS text or IM style messages directly into the VE. Generally these would be displayed in a heads up display at an attachment point relative to the users head position. This way no matter where the user moved or looked within the environment the text would still be visible, placed in front of them.

Potentially the most common use for these messages would be those for general social interactions, similar to how their non-VE counterparts are used today. Messages could be sent from user's loved ones requesting information such as what time they will be home, and these would be displayed to the user within their environment. Alternatively the messages could be related to the user's actions in the VE. These could be from other users sharing the virtual world but not physically at the same locations, and such messages could include topics such how to perform specific tasks or where to meet up. These messages could also come from outside the environment, maybe originating from a technician administering the application to remotely guide the participants.

Rather than using heads up floating text, the messages could be incorporated into items within the scene. Textual messages could be added to models of computer screens or notice boards in the environment. Multiple users could send messages to be added to these devices, and they could be used as the basis of virtual discussion lists or bulletin boards. Taking this idea a stage further leads to the case study for this paper in which a memorial has been created in virtual space which allows external interaction in the form of SMS text and IM messages.

Case Study: The Bartonwall Virtual Memorial. The Bartonwall memorial is being carried out as part of the Fusion Dead Space Project in Barton, East Oxford, UK. This project focuses on professional artists working with young people to address 'dead spaces' in their local community and improve them through creative art. The original Barton wall was created in 2004 when young people inscribed messages in wet render on a wall in memory of a friend who had recently passed away. The project will discuss and document potential changes to revamp the wall, and then make the physical changes. To highlight the project

Fig. 2. Bartonwall memorial project, showing the website(left) and the live VE(right)

and to stimulate discussion, a website[9] and a 3D virtual Bartonwall were to be created, and both of these can be seen in figure 2. Members of the community were invited to text messages of remembrance and ideas for the project, and these would be used to create the virtual wall which would be visible both on the website and during ongoing community consultations.

VieGen was chosen to enable the wall to be developed and displayed as a Virtual Environment. Its ability to run both on immersive VR systems and standalone desktop PCs meant the same application could be used for generating and updating the web page screen shots. However although it supported textual display, this were not linked to networked messaging technologies, so this new research was required.

Network Flows: A project such as this requires several computers and servers each performing different actions. As these are owned by different institutions and exist at different locations the Internet was used to connect them together. A network diagram of these components and their interactions can be found in figure 3. Text messages to be displayed can originate from either mobile phones

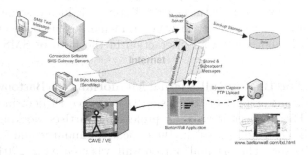

Fig. 3. The network diagram of the systems used by BartonWall

or from separate PC based applications. In the case of the SMS messages these first pass through the gateways servers belonging to Connection Software. Both of these approaches send the messages as HTTP POSTs to the Message Server for storage and forwarding as required. When the Bartonwall application starts it connects to the message server an sends an HTTP POST to request all existing stored messages. The server replies with HTTP POSTs for each of the messages and an extra one to notify that the last stored message has been sent. Upon receipt of this final message the application creates the scene, allocating the correct size and position of the text objects, and then it renders the scene. At this point the application can optionally capture a screen shot of the wall, and use this to automatically FTP the updated image to the Bartonwall website. Subsequent messages sent to the message server will result in new POSTs to the application, causing it to redraw the scene and update the website as appropriate.

5   Conclusion and Future Work

The growth in electronic textual communications has been phenomenal over recent years. It is now an accepted part of modern life, but generally is not used within Immersive Virtual Environments. Mainly this is due to these environments being seen as freestanding applications and not as multipurpose extensions for a connected lifestyle. A parallel here can be drawn with the computers of yesterday with their single tasking and limited applications. By merging the common textual communication protocols into these immersive environments it is hoped that acceptance of general purpose multi-functional VEs will start to become more commonplace.

Throughout this paper we have described a networking methodology by which textual messages could be stored and forwarded for use in a VE. We have seen how these could be displayed in an immersive environment based on the VieGen framework, and through means of an novel implementation have explored possible ways to extend on the basic heads up display.

This work has mainly focused on SMS text and a unidirectional IM style of message. Further advances could add bi-directional IM messaging which would be more in line with existing IM usage. This would require research into an optimal method for recording the text for transmission from within the immersive environment, with possible methods including voice or gesture recognition. Extending the message server to support one or more of the available IM communication protocols would greatly expand the range of potential communication partners. Support for RSS feeds, which would be decoded from incoming XML and displayed in the VE would add even more to the online experience. Indeed the list goes on, and wherever textual communications exist in the real world, there ultimately should be a demand for it from within the virtual.

References

1. Kalawsky, R.S.: The Science of Virtual Reality and Virtual Environments. Addison-Wesley, Wokingham, England (1993)
2. Cruz-Neira, C., Sandin, D.J., Defanti, T.A., Kenyon, R.V., Hart, J.C.: The CAVE: Audio visual experience automatic virtual environment. Communications of the ACM **35**(6) (1992) 64–72
3. Macedonia, M.R., Zyda, M.J.: A taxonomy for networked virtual environments. IEEE MultiMedia **4**(1) (1997) 48–56
4. VRCO website. http://www.vrco.com/ (2004)
5. Rohlf, J., Helman, J.: Iris performer: A high performance multiprocessing toolkit for real-time 3d graphics. In: SIGGRAPH, ACM Press (1994) 381–394
6. Reiners, D.: OpenSG: A Scene Graph System for Flexible and Efficient Realtime Rendering for Virtual and Augmented Reality Applications. PhD thesis, Technische Universität Darmstadt (2002)
7. Haffegee, A., Ramsamy, P., Jamieson, R., Alexandrov, V.: Creation and Control of Interactive Virtual Environments. In: International Conference on Computational Science, Springer Verlag (2006) 595–602
8. Anthes, C., Volkert, J.: inVRs - a framework for building interactive networked virtual reality systems. In: International Conference on High Performance Computing and Communications (HPCC'06), Munich, Germany, Springer (2006) 894–904
9. Allen, K.: The Bartonwall website. http://www.bartonwall.com/ (2006)

Managing Transformations and Events
in Networked Virtual Environments

Christoph Anthes, Roland Landertshamer, Helmut Bressler, and Jens Volkert

GUP, Institute of Graphics and Parallel Processing
Johannes Kepler University, Altenbergerstrasse 69, A-4040 Linz, Austria
`canthes@gup.uni-linz.ac.at`

Abstract. In the recent years a growing interest in Collaborative Virtual Environments (CVE) can be observed. Most of these systems use event-object driven architectures for consistent and clear communication inside these systems and in between them. Networked Virtual Reality (VR) applications make heavy use of position tracking data and process a vast amount of transformation matrices during their simulation steps. This observation leads to a novel approach on how communication in Networked Virtual Environments (NVEs) could take place by considering events as well as transformation data to allow for higher responsiveness within Virtual Worlds.

1 Introduction

In the area of networked VR multi-user applications like safety training, architectural walkthroughs, medical and industrial visualisations have become more and more common.

These NVEs can be designed using libraries for certain application parts, script based engines or graphical editors but still most of the available VR applications are developed fully from scratch. Common libraries for graphics display and audio output are used while the core part of the application is typically tailored to the application domain. Application parts like interaction and navigation are often redeveloped and reinvented. To overcome this problem and to provide reusable functionality our current focus of work is the inVRs (**in**teractive networked **V**irtual **R**eality system) framework, which provides expendable and configurable modules for interaction, navigation and network communication. To deal with the problem of heterogeneity of the interconnected VR systems inVRs provides an additional abstraction layer which decouples the input and output devices from the application.

Since the framework is built in a modular way, interfaces and communication mechanisms between the modules have to be designed. The communication flow between the modules and between the different instances of the NVE applications via the network has to be standardised. Event-driven systems which communicate all changes via discrete events of the VE are widely spread. Communication inside a VE engine can be typically split up into two different types of messages. This distinction of messages is based on their frequency and their

T.-J. Cham et al. (Eds.): MMM 2007, LNCS 4352, Part II, pp. 722–729, 2007.

reliability requirements. A continuous flow of messages is typically present during navigation and manipulation or animation of virtual objects. Discrete messages or events are used to change states of object inside the VE or they are needed in the network area to notify other participants of the NVE of a joining or leaving of a new user. Component based systems as described in chapter 2 do not make a distinction between these two kinds of messages. We believe that one of the most prominent problems with VR design approaches is the missing distinction between discrete events and a continuous flow of transformation data. Two managers are used to handle communication in a configurable and efficient manner. This paper will focus on these managers and give examples how they can be configured to realise concurrent object manipulation, interaction and navigation.

The following section will give an overview on the design of VEs and NVEs. Afterwards the architecture of the inVRs framework will be briefly discussed. Section 4 and 5 will describe the event manager and the transformation manager. Then an overview over the network communication will be given. To demonstrate the configurability of the transformation handling and the event handling, example communication setups will be explained. The final section concludes the paper and gives an outlook into future developments.

2   Related Work

VEs and NVEs have been researched for years in many aspects with a focus at interaction and navigation methodologies, data distribution mechanisms, factors affecting humans like presence or cybersickness.

The development VR applications is a challenging task, since all of the aspects above have to be taken into account during the design phase. An implementation from scratch is quite common using scene graphs like Inventor [1] or OpenSG [2]. Compared to low-level APIs like Direct3D or OpenGL the scene graph concept of storing the scene in a hierarchical manor using nested transformations [3] provides a more intuitive way for the user to develop graphical applications.

Combining scene graphs with animation and interaction methodologies is a common approach in component based systems. Functional and graphical nodes are considered components of the scene and can be interconnected by routing mechanisms. Inventor and VRML [4] follow this component structure. The interconnection of routes can be done with graphical editors e.g. EON Studio. Component based systems are easy to edit, if the complexity of the interconnections is low. They can be can be easily enhanced but can cause as well a high system load, since all changed attributes of the components have to be processed in the system in real time.

Other approaches to design VR applications focus on the abstraction of input and output devices like DIVERSE [5]. VRJuggler [6] not only supports various input and output devices it provides as well connections to a variety of scene graphs.

If we take a look in the field of NVEs it can be observed that in the most cases the complete state or parts of the state of the VE is replicated locally for high responsiveness. To guarantee a high consistency object-event based architectures are normally used. If a user interacts with a part of the scene an event is sent to the remote users, to lock this object. After a positive acknowledgment of this event a manipulation can be performed on the object. These conservative locking mechanisms deny truly cooperative object manipulation [7].

3   Framework Architecture

The inVRs architecture in which we embedded our transformation and event management consists of a system core module which can be enhanced by network communication, interaction, navigation and arbitrary user defined modules. To allow for device abstraction additional input and output interfaces exist.

The core module consists of two databases, one storing information about the local and the remote users - the user database - and the other storing information about the layout and interaction properties of the environment - the world database. These databases are manipulated via an event manager taking care of discrete reliable information and a transformation manager processing the continuous flow of transformation data. The input to these managers is generated by the modules for interaction, navigation and the network. Results of the processing of these managers are applied on the databases from which they are routed via the output interface on the scene graph.

3.1   Interaction and Navigation Modules

In the context of VEs navigation, travel or view-point motion control is typically considered as a part of interaction [8]. We try to distinguish navigation from classical interaction, since travel does not necessarily result in change of the VE and is not always mutual.

The interaction module is implemented as a Deterministic Finite Automaton (DFA) with the states idle, selection and manipulation. Once a state change takes place an event is generated and sent to the event manager. In the manipulation state transformation data is routed to the transformation manager. The state changes are controlled by transition functions which are implemented as interaction models. These models process the input from the input interface and are able to access data from the databases.

The navigation module combines speed, direction and orientation to a resulting transformation which is passed to the transformation manager. These three attributes are determined each by a separate model, which computes data from the input interface and can take information from the databases into account. The resulting transformation of the navigation module describes the desired position and orientation change of the user in the VE.

The models follow the strategy pattern [9]. Newly designed models can be created by inheritance using the factory pattern [9]. Therefore full flexibility and reusability for interaction and navigation is guaranteed.

4   Event Manager

The main usage of the event manager is the distribution of events inside the framework. It controls one event pipe which can be filled with events from all connected application parts or modules. The manager itself is unaware of the semantics of the events stored inside its pipe. Each event stores its source, its destination, a timestamp and event specific data. They can be used to start animations, to pick up objects, play sounds, notify participants of the NVE, that another client has joined etc.

The event manager is capable of reordering events inside its pipe based on the timestamp. Redundant events can be filtered as well. The occurrence of redundant events depends fully on the implemented communication protocol and the given network topology in the network component. If the network communication is implemented as a peer to peer topology, event reordering becomes necessary. Events can have different execution and distribution properties. They can be either executed only locally in a module connected to the event manager, they can be executed remotely on the dislocated participants system, or they can be executed locally and distributed to a remote participant of the VE via the network module.

5   Transformation Manager

The transformation manager contains an arbitrary amount of pipes. For each active transformation process one pipe is instantiated inside the manager. The pipes can be identified by a key which consists of the source of the transformation, the destination of the transformation and specific information which has to be interpreted by the destination module. Transformations are stored as set elements inside the pipes of which each contains a transformation matrix and a timestamp when it was generated. The pipe consists of several stages, which are applied at least once per frame.

At the initial application setup modifiers are registered as stages to pipes of certain keys. Each time a pipe with that key is instantiated in the transformation manager the according modifiers are attached to the pipe in the order they were registered. A modifier is able to access his transformation pipe or another transformation pipe with reading and writing permissions. Other data sources for a modifier are application parts or the user and the world database. It can take a transformation from the preceding modifier in the same pipe as input and write a transformation to his successor. A set of basic transformation modifiers which follow the strategy pattern and can be generated by following the factory pattern is directly integrated in the inVRs framework.

6   Network

The network protocol makes a clear distinction between transformations, events, and system messages. System messages are used to handle the connections between the systems. Using the inVRs framework no immediate topology is used, since the network module is fully exchangeable. One assumption for the event and transformation management is that all users are working on a fully replicated VE and use physical clocks which are synchronised via the Network Time Protocol (NTP).

If users with immersive VR systems are present in the NVE, which make use of tracking systems the tracking data is constantly streamed via UDP. Each package sent from the tracking system via the input interface represents a valid position in the physical space of the remote user. This data is used for the representation and transformation of the users avatar as well as for natural interaction.

For navigation and some types of interaction dead reckoning [10] as a predictive algorithm can be incorporated in the transformation simulator. Animation in the VE can be triggered by events and does not have to be distributed. Events for the opening and closing of transformation pipes in the transformation manager have to be transmitted in a reliable way, to guarantee a degree of consistency at the beginning and termination of an object manipulation.

7   Example Communication Setups

Standard functionality like navigation and natural interaction will be explained with the use of the managers and suggestions on how to implement concurrent object manipulation using event and transformation management are given.

7.1   Navigation

To use the transformation manager for navigation a variety of setup possibilities exist. Different navigation modes have to be selected in the navigation module to generate a transformation matrix which describes the desired transformation of the navigated object relative to the time the navigation module was called the last time. This transformation matrix acts as an input for the transformation manager. Figure 1 gives an overview on how transformations can be distributed for navigation inside the framework.

The matrices are continuously entered into a transformation pipe where several stages are process each matrix. In the first stage the transformation matrix of the last navigated position is requested from the user database and multiplied with the matrix in the pipe (*ApplyNavigationModifier*). Writing this value back on the users position would result in a simple navigation system already. The calculated value could be distributed to the remote clients, and a basic networked navigation could be provided.

To enhance the functionality and to hide latency other stages can be introduced into the transformation pipeline. Before the calculated position is updated it is distributed (*TransformationDistributionModifier*). A stage for evaluating height maps can be incorporated where the navigated position in the x,y coordinates is enhanced by a z-value retrieved from a height map (*HeightmapModifier*). Additional collision detection can be performed to check whether the resulting position is valid. If this is not the case, the previous navigated position replaces

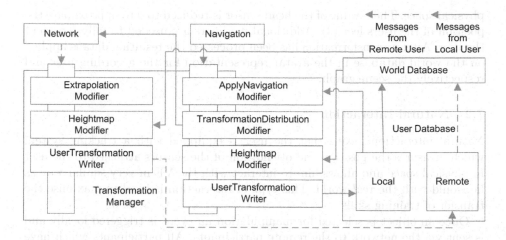

Fig. 1. Example Setup for Navigation

the actual position. If the position is valid it is finally stored in the user database, resulting in a change in the world database. For the remote clients the matrix from stage two is received.

Since the transformation manager computes a list of transformations and the average latency to the remote clients is available from the user database it is possible to apply an extrapolation based on the 1st derivation or the 2nd derivation of the position data (*ExtrapolationModifier*). On this resulting position the height and collision modifier are applied and the position is updated in the VE.

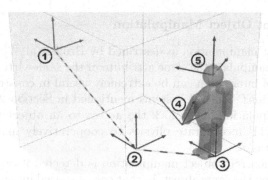

Fig. 2. Coordinate Systems of a user

To display a user equipped with a tracking system several coordinate systems are necessary as shown in Figure 2. The physically tracked area is superimposed in grey. The origin of the VE(1) is the basis for the navigated user position(2). Head (5) and hand (4) sensors are used to measure the position of the user in physical space. The z-value of the head sensor is reduced to 0 to approximate the position of the users feet (3). Additional modifiers are needed to fully represent the user. After a transformation has been processed the resulting data is applied on the world database in the avatar representation for the according user and respectively the scene graph.

7.2   Natural Interaction

Natural interaction means that the user is equipped with a tracking system which measures the position and orientation of the sensors attached to the user in physical space and allows him to interact with the VE in very similar way as he would with the real world. This type of interaction is ideal to maximise the transfer of training skills.

Once an object is selected for manipulation an event is triggered locally and is sent via the network to the remote participants. All participants which have received the manipulation event open a pipe. The event contains the information where the object was positioned in the VE, where the user picked the object (an offset to the origin of the coordinate system of the object), and a timestamp when the object was picked. With this information the VE is in a consistent state at the beginning of the manipulation. The following object transformations are generated by the interaction technique or in case of natural interaction generated by the tracking system. This information is directed into the transformation manager on which several setup possibilities come into play. Locally a *Manipulation OffestModifier* can be applied. For the remote client it can be useful to extrapolate the hand position of the remote user via the *ExtrapolationModifier* before applying a *Manipulation OffestModifier*.

7.3   Concurrent Object Manipulation

Concurrent object manipulation as described by Broll et al. [7] allows two users to concurrently manipulate the same attribute of the same virtual object in real-time. This type of interaction can be extremely useful in construction scenarios or safety applications. The VR systems mentioned in Section 2 do not support cooperative manipulation. They lock the access to an object to a single user. Froehlich et al. [11] incorporate physics to cooperatively manipulate objects during assembly tasks.

In our case concurrent object manipulation is detected if two transformation pipes are opened on the same object. In that case a special merging stage is introduced which can be implemented using Froehlich's physics approach or Broll's transformation mechanisms. The resulting transformation of the two pipes is applied on the object. Since the immediate input transformations from the local user and slightly delayed transformations from the remote user which still can be extrapolated are available it is possible to provide a relatively correct and highly responsive representation of the cooperatively manipulated object.

8 Conclusions and Future Work

The paper has introduced an alternative approach of communication inside NVEs. By having a fully replicated environment and loose consistency in combination with extrapolation and interpolation leads to relatively precise but highly responsive interaction possibilities. Example setups of the transformation and event handling have demonstrated the flexibility of the generic approach. inVRs still focuses on natural interaction which limits its application domain to NVEs rather than visualisations.

An extensive set of transformation modifiers has to be developed. The use of different extrapolation and interpolation methodologies has to be evaluated with user studies to suggest ideal setup possibilities for long distance or short distance CVEs. It would be interesting to expand the presented approach with a 3D widget system, where e.g. sliders could be handled by event and transformation management. By the use of 3D widgets it would be possible to enhance the application area into the domain of visualisations.

References

1. Strauss, P.S., Carey, R.: An object-oriented 3d graphics toolkit. Computer Graphics **26** (1992) 341–349
2. Reiners, D.: OpenSG: A Scene Graph System for Flexible and Efficient Realtime Rendering for Virtual and Augmented Reality Applications. PhD thesis, Technische Universität Darmstadt (2002)
3. Blinn, J.F.: Jim blinns corner: Nested transformations and blobby man. IEEE Computer Graphics and Applications **7** (1987) 65–69
4. Carey, R., Bell, G.: The VRML 2.0 Annotated Reference Manual. Addison-Wesley (1997)
5. Kelso, J., Arsenault, L.E., Satterfield, S.G., D.Kriz, R.: Diverse: A framework for building extensible and reconfigurable device independent virtual environments. In: IEEE Virtual Reality (VR'02). (2002) 183–190
6. Just, C.D., Bierbaum, A.D., Baker, A., Cruz-Neira, C.: Vr juggler: A framework for virtual reality development. In: 2nd Immersive Projection Technology Workshop (IPT98). (1998)
7. Broll, W.: Interacting in distributed collaborative virtual environments. In: IEEE Virtual Reality Annual International Symposium (VRAIS'95). (1995) 148–155
8. Bowman, D.A.: Interaction Techniques for Common Tasks in Immersive Virtual Environments. PhD thesis, Georgia Institute of Technology (1999)
9. Gamma, E., Helm, R., Johnson, R., Vlissides, J.: Design Patterns: Elements of Reusable Object-Oriented Software. Addison-Wesley (1995)
10. Singhal, S.K., Cheriton, D.R.: Exploring position history for efficient remote rendering in networked virtual reality. Presence: Teleoperators and Virtual Environments **4** (1995) 169–193
11. Fröhlich, B., Tramberend, H., Beers, A., Agrawala, M., Baraff, D.: Physically-based manipulation on the responsive workbench. In: IEEE Virtual Reality (VR'00). (2000) 5–12

Scalable Vector Graphics Pattern P2P-Service for Enhanced Barrier-Free Web Applications*

Kerstin Altmanninger[1] and Wolfram Wöß[2]

[1] Department of Telecooperation
Johannes Kepler University Linz, Austria
kerstin.altmanninger@jku.at
[2] Institute for Applied Knowledge Processing
Johannes Kepler University Linz, Austria
wolfram.woess@jku.at

Abstract. Most graphics used in web pages are very attractive for the eye and useful for a lot of people. However, with the extensive use of pixel graphics such as charts without additional textual description or image maps, handicapped users of web pages are encountering an ever increasing amount of barriers. Therefore, it is essential that future development on web content focuses on accommodating all kinds of disabilities. The use of Scalable Vector Graphics (SVG) provides new possibilities as well as new challenges for the accessibility of web sites. Consequently, the *Access2Graphics* implementation is embedded in a peer-to-peer (P2P) network with reusable SVG patterns for enhanced barrier-free web applications. The aim of the new architecture is to support graphic designers and web developers in making graphics accessible for as many user groups as possible.

1 Introduction

Surfing the Internet is not always as simple as a single click away. Disabled people often encounter many barriers which can be overwhelming for them. To make the "World Wide Web" (WWW) more accessible to the broader community the "Web Accessibility Initiative" (WAI) [1] works with organizations around the globe to develop strategies, guidelines and resources. Barrier-free web design offers handicapped users the ability to perceive, understand, navigate and interact in the WWW environment with as few accessibility issues as possible. Thus, it does not solely concentrate on making the web more accessible for disabled people. It also incorporates availability of web content and enhancing the web experience for as many people as possible, regardless if their disabilities are related to vision, motor, learning impairment or if someone has no disability at all. Availability problems of web content can be caused by slow network connections, limited bandwith, slow computer processing, memory, screen resolution or software agents that lack understanding on how a human perceives and interacts with a web page.

---

* This work has been partly funded by the Internet Privatstiftung Austria (IPA).

T.-J. Cham et al. (Eds.): MMM 2007, LNCS 4352, Part II, pp. 730–737, 2007.
© Springer-Verlag Berlin Heidelberg 2007

Designed to be an information portal, the web should be addressed to a broad community. That does not mean that web pages need to be designed in a non-attractive way, lacking colors and pictures. The use of style sheets, dynamically generated information and other common web design techniques leads to a more attractive web and allows at the same time the consideration of every person's specific requirements. For instance, cognitive handicapped or sometimes elderly people find that sites employing a lot of graphics are much easier to use and to understand because they support them to focus in quickly on their intended action. The fact that blind people and those with low vision cannot see graphics at all or not so clearly should not be a motivation to avoid graphics in the web. Providing an alternative text for graphics as it is proposed in the "Web Content Accessibility Guidelines" (WCAG) [2] is not always satisfactory for people with visual impairments. Physically disabled users often have problems with image maps visualized by the use of raster graphics because they are not scalable and therefore it may be difficult to select the desired object. These user groups demand a textual graphic format. The vector graphic format SVG is predestined to tackle these shortcomings. Using SVG offers a number of features to make graphics on the web more accessible than it is currently possible by using pixel graphics. Describing those features the "World Wide Web Consortium" (W3C) Note "Accessibility Features of SVG" [3] presents many techniques to benefit users with low vision, color deficit, blindness or users of assistive technologies.

Some related work has been done in this field by developing guidelines [2] [3]. Recent publications concerning access to SVG for visually impaired people focus on specialized areas, specifically extracting meta information and visualization of tactile maps [4] [5] [6]. Research on exploring SVG for visually impaired users in general is becoming more common [7]. Earlier work in this area [8] went a step further by considering every kind of disability and its relationship to graphics. Therefore the application *Access2Graphics* offers the possibility of dynamic SVG graphics generation specific to each user type. However, a basic criteria for the visualization of accessible graphics is that the designer provides textual equivalents in an appropriate way. The quality of designed graphics, in point of structuring and providing coherent textual equivalents, cannot be proven sufficiently by a toolset. To eliminate this problem as far as possible, distributed databases can offer reusable image patterns in order to be able to include them in any graphic generated by *Access2Graphics*. This approach decreases the development effort because establishing accessible and well structured graphics is a time-consuming task. Additionally, using barrier-free SVG graphics will also be possible for web developers who have no experience in designing such images.

The remainder of this paper is structured as follows. Section 2 discusses requirements of specific user groups followed by a brief introduction of the W3C SVG specification in Section 3. In Section 4 an overview of the existing *Access2Graphics* implementation is given and furthermore in Section 5 the SVG pattern P2P service is presented. Finally, Section 6 concludes the paper and gives an outlook on further research activities.

2 Requirements of Specific User Groups

People with visual disabilities, hearing impairments, physical disabilities, speech impediments or cognitive disabilities are in many cases confronted with insuperable barriers when they are working with web applications. Assistive devices like alternative keyboards or switches, braille displays and screen reading software are supporting tools to reach a higher level of access to web content, but there are still unsolved problems concerning graphics accessibility. How people with different kinds of disabilities are using the web in general is discussed in many studies [9]. When focusing on the barriers of common raster graphics, the following user groups can be identified.

Blind people need an alternative text for images postulated in the WCAG [2]. However, for blind people this description is often not sufficient. Normally graphics are composed of many different layers and therefore SVG provides text equivalents on each of these layers. In generated SVG graphs or charts it is preferable to present information in table form only. Some approaches made it possible to gain access to such graphics [4] and geographical maps [6] via a tactile display. This output device can be used in combination with textual equivalents that are accessible for blind people through voice output and braille text. In all, the amount and meaning of meta information included in graphics determines its degree of accessibility. Poor acuity (vision that is not sharp), tunnel vision (seeing only the middle of the visual field), central field loss (seeing only the edges of the visual field) or clouded vision describes the forms of *low vision*. To gain access to graphics people with low vision use screen magnifiers, screen enhancement software and screen readers. In this area user defined style sheets are growing more and more important. SVG is appropriate for high level scaling but as a drawback for people with low vision it is very difficult to gain an overview of an image that has been excessively scaled. Therefore also for users with low vision it is vital that a graphics includes as much useful textual meta information as possible. One of the most common visual disabilities are *deficiencies in color vision*, a lack of perceptual sensitivity to certain colors. To avoid problems with the definition of color graphics a textual description of the image or a user defined style sheet or graphic filter provides assistance. SVG allows graphics to include voice output. Hence, for people with *impaired hearing* acoustic information must be provided alternatively, e.g. as text. *Motorical disabilities* can affect someone using a keyboard or mouse. Static graphics have no real effect on loosing information for this user group but if graphics are interactive, problems can result. Therefore it is favorable for interactive image maps to have sufficient space between the different links. Additionally, icons themselves should be larger in size. Difficulties with reading, understanding abstract concepts, and performing mathematical calculations are examples for *cognitive disabilities*. The utilization of graphics is very important for cognitive disabled people as it can significantly improve the understanding of a web site's content. SVG may also incorporate text that needs to be as clear as possible with the simplest language appropriate. For example, charts should not contain abbreviations without additional explanation.

3   Scalable Vector Graphics

SVG, an XML-based two-dimensional graphics standard recommended by the W3C [10], can support in making graphics accessible for everybody. At its core, an SVG document is a sequence of drawing commands in plain text describing vectors that retain their resolution at any zoom factor. Furthermore, SVG allows web developers and designers to implement dynamically generated, high-quality graphics from real time data with precise structural and visual control. With this powerful technology, developers who are making use of SVG have the possibility to create a new generation of web applications based on data-driven, interactive and personalized graphics [11], currently only possible after installing the Adobe SVG plug-in. For graphics specification SVG offers a set of basic shape elements such as lines, circles, ellipses, polygons, polylines and rectangles. Additionally, it is possible to include external shapes and text in the graphics.

Fig. 1. SVG code stored in the file "SVGSmiley.svg"

The sample source code in Fig. 1 demonstrates some core features of SVG. Firstly, the standard provides a special `<g>`-tag to group elements. This feature enables a web designer to arrange graphics in layers, giving the user the opportunity to select favored layers and to view specifically requested information. Secondly, SVG provides an optional `<title>` and `<desc>` tag for each graphical layer which can be used to store meta information. However, SVG can be used in much more complex applications for generating graphs and charts resulting from database queries [12], for designing geographical maps, image maps, web sites, interactive images, or animated graphics.

While dealing with SVG-graphics, the need to define various SVG patterns came up to simplify the development of graphics. Therefore the SVG specification provides an element called `<pattern>` [10]. The idea behind this element is to offer the opportunity to predefine graphic objects which can be reused in other graphics. Patterns defined by using a `<pattern>` element are referenced by properties on an element to indicate that the given element of a graphic should be filled or stroked with it. For the approach described in this paper patterns are defined as reusable graphic objects but in a more global way for storing them in distributed databases to supply web developers with graphic fragments, e.g., symbols, logos and image fragments. In order to make reusing of SVG code possible, defined in this paper as a pattern, two possibilities arise, using the `<use>`- or `<image>`-element. The main difference between these approaches is that the `<use>` element only allows elements to be included in the canvas which were defined previously in the `<defs>` tag (e.g., `<svg>`, `<g>` or basic graphic shapes). This is in contrast to the `<image>` element which only uses patterns declared with a `<svg>` root element, referenced within the document using the `id` attribute or from a directory referencing the SVG-file.

4   Access2Graphics Application

Considering the different kinds of disabilities mentioned in Section 2, it is a fact that one and the same graphic cannot satisfy individual user requirements. Therefore the application *Access2Graphics* was implemented, which is based on user profiles and the graphics standard SVG [8]. *Access2Graphics* aims at enabling a dynamic generation of individually adapted and consequently accessible graphics applicable in any WWW environment.

Fig. 2 illustrates the workflow and generation process for context and user dependent graphics. The starting point is a user who is characterized by a profile which specifies the user's disabilities. By default the application assumes that a user has no disability and no special demands concerning the output device. If the user requests a web page containing graphics, as a result a corresponding database query is generated. At this stage the result set of the query, which is already in SVG format, considers the disability specification of the user profile. In a further step, *Access2Graphics* assembles the web page containing the user adapted images by considering both, the additional disability restrictions and the user's output device, e.g., monitor, PDA or mobile phone. Additional disability restrictions are e.g., color blindness, making it necessary to switch an image from color to black and white. *Access2Graphics* uses filters for this task. For visually impaired people, output can be processed by a Braille device. Tactile displays are not supported by the actual version of the implementation. Additionally, there is the option to obtain voice output as well.

One of the key advantages of this process is that the SVG information required for different kinds of users is stored in the database. Therefore the basic

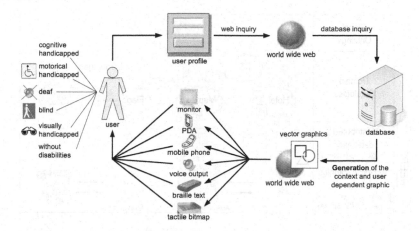

Fig. 2. Dynamic generation of context and user dependent graphics

SVG information is generated once and can then be adapted corresponding to specific demands. This is in contrast to existing solutions where the SVG information normally considers only one user demand. Of course the flexibility of *Access2Graphics* directly depends on the quality of SVG data stored in the database. Through *Access2Graphics* many types of SVG graphics can be generated, classified in charts and images which may include links to web pages or audio files. The *Access2Graphics* tool does not claim to implement each image creatable with SVG but aims on a demonstration of what is possible.

5 SVG Pattern P2P-Service Realization

With the development of *Access2Graphics* the need for sharing SVG graphics between web developers came up. Designing a graphic in an accessible way is not as easy as it seams. Basically, the definition of the structure and the provided text equivalents cannot be checked sufficiently by a toolset. To cope with this deficiency our approach provides help for graphic authors, on the one hand to shorten the design process and on the other hand to help new authors to jump into the area of designing accessible graphics in terms of offering SVG samples as guidelines.

In the upper layers of Fig. 3, ontologies are used for the semantic description [13] [14] of the underlying SVG patterns. This allows a user to navigate from a global ontology to domain ontologies in order to find a specific SVG pattern for reuse in a single *Access2Graphics* application. The advantage is that existing SVG patterns which may be spread over distributed databases can easily be found by the semantic descriptions held in the ontological hierarchy. The global ontology can be seen as a portal to the whole service and domain ontologies represent e.g., hotels, geographic maps, destinations, etc. The resulting architecture is similar to a structure of a pure P2P network (cf. Fig. 3). The existence of a central database is not given, therefore every peer provides a subset of the

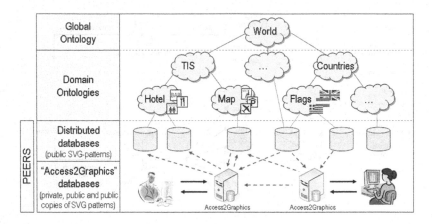

Fig. 3. SVG pattern P2P-service architecture

available SVG patterns. Different to common P2P networks, with links between nodes, we established a global ontology beyond the peers (*Access2Graphics* and distributed databases) which categorizes many different domain ontologies defined by the scope of the SVG patterns. In detail, each *Access2Graphics* user can specify public and private image patterns or can reuse public ones from other web developers. Four application scenarios are therefore possible:

1. A designer may offer some patterns for other peers by making them directly available for other *Access2Graphic* designers or
2. by uploading them on one of the distributed databases.
   In both ways the designer of the graphic patterns has to specify the ontology domains to which this graphic belongs. The mapping between the SVG patterns and the ontologies as well as the ontologies themselves are specified by OWL [15] [16].
3. The search process for public graphic patterns starts at the global ontology. Appropriate SVG patterns resulting from the previous query may either be stored in one of the distributed databases or
4. in the public area of an *Access2Graphics* application.

Besides the technical advantage of using SVG patterns also an organizational advantage is gained from public graphics patterns on distributed databases. This kind of SVG fragments could be certified as "accessible" by an authorized institution. Such a certification could consider more checks than the actual *Access2Graphics* implementation does. The entire solution significantly improves the accessibility of graphics in existing or future web applications.

6   Conclusion and Future Work

Visual, cognitive, physical and hearing impairments should not longer cause a barrier with respect to graphics that they currently do. It is a fact that pixel graphics provided without an alternative text are useless for blind people and bar charts that seem to have similar colors for different bars are difficult to distinguish by color blind people. To overcome these problems *Access2Graphics* makes images dynamically accessible for disabled web users, thus, offering a new way of exploring graphics for them by adding together pieces of former models. With the additional feature of *Access2Graphics* to offer a SVG pattern P2P-service for enhanced barrier-free web applications the gained advantage is twofold. Firstly, for web designers SVG files are reusable in the form of patterns which can also be certified as accessible. Secondly, users of web applications benefit from accessible graphics with improved structural and description quality. The underlying ontological concept offers far reaching possibilities for further developments. For example, searching for and applying public SVG patterns could be done by a semi automatic processor. Such a processor could also operate with similarities and not only with exact matchings between SVG patterns.

References

1. WAI: Web Accessibility Initiative. http://www.w3.org/WAI (2006)
2. W3C: Web Content Accessibility Guidelines 1.0, Recommendation (1999)
3. W3C: Accessibility Features of SVG, Note (2000)
4. Rotard, M., Ertl, T.: Tactile Access to Scalable Vector Graphics for People with Visual Impairment. In Proc. of the 3rd SVG Open Conference, Tokyo (2004)
5. Bulatov, V., Gardner, J.: Making Graphics Accessible. In Proc. of the 3rd SVG Open Conference, Tokyo, Japan (2004)
6. Campin, B., McCurdy, W., Brunet, L., Siekierska, E.: SVG Maps for People with Visual Impairment. In Proc. of the 2nd SVG Open Conference, Vancouver, Canada (2003)
7. Rotard, M., Otte, K., Ertl, T.: Exploring Scalable Vector Graphics for Visually Impaired Users. In: Computers Helping People with Sepcial Needs. Volume 3118., Springer (2004) 725–730
8. Altmanninger, K., Wöß, W.: Dynamically Generated Scalable Vector Graphics (SVG) for Barrier-Free Web-Applications. In: Computers Helping People with Sepcial Needs. Volume 4061., Springer (2006) 128–135
9. W3C: How People with Disabilities Use the Web, Draft (2005)
10. W3C: Scalable Vector Graphics (SVG) 1.1 Specification, Recommendation (2003)
11. Adobe Systems Incorporated: SVG. http://www.adobe.com/svg (2006)
12. González, G., Dalal, G.: Generating Graphs and Charts from Database Queries using SVG. In Proc. of the 2nd SVG Open Conference, Vancouver, Canada (2003)
13. Stuckenschmidt, H., van Hermelen, F.: Information Sharing on the Semantic Web. Springer (2005)
14. Shadbolt, N., Hall, W., Berners-Lee, T.: The Semantic Web Revisited. In Staab, S., ed.: IEEE Intelligent Systems. Volume 21. (2006) 96–101
15. W3C: OWL Web Ontology Language Overview, Recommendation (2004)
16. Mota, L., Bothelho, L.: OWL Ontology Translation for the Semantic Web. In: Semantic Computing Workshop, 14th International WWW Conference. (2005)

References

Author Index

Lecture Notes in Computer Science

For information about Vols. 1–4271

please contact your bookseller or Springer